Higher Education

and the State

in Latin America

Higher Education and the State in Latin America

Private Challenges to Public Dominance

Daniel C. Levy

The University of Chicago Press

Chicago and London

DANIEL C. LEVY is associate professor of educational administration and policy studies and of Latin American studies at the State University of New York, Albany. He is the author of *University and Government in Mexico* and, with Gabriel Székely, of *Mexico: Paradoxes of Stability and Change* and edited the forthcoming *Private Education: Studies in Choice and Public Policy.*

LC
177
.L29
L48
1986

The University of Chicago Press, Chicago 60637
The University of Chicago Press, Ltd., London

The University of Chicago Press gratefully acknowledges the contribution of the Exxon Education Foundation, whose grant has helped make publication of this volume possible.

LIBRARY OF CONGRESS CATALOGING-IN-PUBLICATION DATA
Levy, Daniel C.
  Higher education and the state in Latin America.
  Bibliography: p.
  Includes index.
  1. Higher education and state—Latin America.
2. Privatization—Latin America. I. Title.
LC177.L29L48 1986   379.81   85-21023
ISBN 0-226-47608-1

To Morris J. Levy

Contents

Contents

Tables

Abbreviations

AD   Democratic Action party (Venezuela)
AID   Agency for International Development (U.S.)
AIU   International Association of Universities
ANUIES   National Association of Universities and Institutes of Higher
          Education (Mexico)
APRA   American Revolutionary Popular Alliance party (Peru)
CAPES   Campaign for Improvement of High Level Personnel (Brazil)
CELAM   Latin American Bishops Council
CEPAL   Economic Commission for Latin America
CESGRANRIO   Center for Selection of Higher Education Candidates
          in Greater Rio de Janeiro (Brazil)
CINDA   Interuniversity Center for Andean Development
CNU   National Council of Universities (Venezuela)
CONAI   National Interuniversity Commission (Peru)
COPEI   Christian Democratic party (Venezuela)
CORFO   Chilean Development Corporation
CPU   Corporation for University Promotion
CRESALC   Regional Center for Higher Education in Latin America
          and the Caribbean
CRUP   Council of Private University Rectors (Argentina)
DAU   Department of University Affairs (Brazil)
EUDEBA   University of Buenos Aires Press (Argentina)
FCE   Federal Education Council (Brazil)
FINEP   Corporation for Financing Students and Projects (Brazil)
FLACSO   Latin American Faculty of Social Sciences
FTE   full-time teaching equivalents
FUPAC   Federation of Central American and Panamanian Universities
IASEI   Ajijic Institute on International Education (Mexico)
IBGE   Brazilian Institute of Geography and Statistics (Brazil)
ICED   International Council for Educational Development

Abbreviations

ICETEX	Colombian Overseas Technical Specialization Institute
ICFES	Colombian Institute for Higher Educational Development
IDB	Inter-American Development Bank
IIE	Institute of International Education
IMESP	Mexican Institutions of Private Higher Education
IPEA	Applied Economic-Social Research Institute (Brazil)
IPN	National Polytechnic Institute (Mexico)
ITAM	Autonomous Technical Institute of Mexico
ITESM	Monterrey Institute of Higher Technical Studies (Mexico)
IUPERJ	University Research Institute of Rio de Janeiro (Brazil)
MCE	Ministry of Education and Culture (Argentina)
MEC	Ministry of Education and Culture (Brazil)
MSJF	Mary Street Jenkins Foundation (Mexico)
OAS	Organization of American States
OECD	Organization for Economic Cooperation and Development
OPES	Higher Education Planning Office (Costa Rica)
OPSU	University Sector Planning Office (Venezuela)
PAN	National Action party (Mexico)
PDC	Christian Democratic party (Chile)
PEMEX	Mexican Petroleum Company
PIIE	Interdisciplinary Program on Education (Chile)
PRI	Institutional Revolutionary party (Mexico)
PUC	Pontifical Catholic University (Brazil)
SEP	Ministry of Education (Mexico)
SES	Socioeconomic status
SESU	Secretariat of Higher Education of MEC (Brazil)
UACA	Autonomous University of Central America (Costa Rica)
UAG	Autonomous University of Guadalajara (Mexico)
UBA	University of Buenos Aires (Argentina)
UC	Catholic University (Chile)
UCA	Catholic University of Argentina
UCH	University of Chile
UCR	University of Costa Rica
UCV	Central University of Venezuela
UDUAL	Union of Latin American Universities
UNAM	National Autonomous University of Mexico
UNE	National Union of Students (Brazil)
UNESCO	United Nations Educational, Scientific, and Cultural Organization
UP	Popular Unity (Chile)
USP	University of São Paulo (Brazil)
UTE	State Technical University (Chile)
UTSM	Santa María Technical University (Chile)

Acknowledgments

I could not have pursued this research had it not been for fortuitous affiliations with interested colleagues and supportive institutions.

A stimulating general environment was provided by Yale University's Institution for Social and Policy Studies; I thank its successive directors, Charles E. Lindblom and Richard R. Nelson. Within that institution, two research groups provided the crucial intellectual settings. First, the Higher Education Research Group offered me a unique opportunity to learn about and conduct cross-national research. While working with the group, and initially preoccupied with political relationships concerning public universities, I became aware of the striking privatization transforming Latin American higher education, rendering obsolete several dominant modes of viewing the university and its interactions with the State, private institutions, societal actors, and social classes. Simultaneously, research on comparative higher education over a broader geographical area persuaded me that the Latin American transformation was at once unusual and yet instructive in international perspective. Meanwhile, my evolving research interests were encouraged by the group's director, Burton R. Clark. He was as responsible as anyone for showing me that comparative higher education offered many attractive paths, largely untraveled, for a political scientist and Latin Americanist to explore.

Next, within the same university and policy institution I found a very different but equally congenial home at the Program for Non-Profit Organizations. Here was another unique opportunity, this time to tie my work to research on cross-sectoral comparisons involving private institutions that do not operate for profit. The program's directors, John G. Simon and Paul DiMaggio, extended every possible assistance.

At SUNY-Albany, after the field research was finished but while I was just beginning to appreciate what Yogi meant by "it ain't over till it's over," I again found a supportive environment; for this I thank, among others,

Philip G. Foster and Anthony M. Cresswell, chairs, and Robert H. Koff, dean. And throughout, the Andrew W. Mellon Foundation provided very generous financial support; I especially thank James M. Morris for the foundation's wonderfully sustained confidence.

Among those who most facilitated my field research, in diverse ways, I am indebted to Orlando Albornoz, H. Ben-Amor, Cláudio de Moura Castro, Luis Garita, Eduardo Latorre, Iván Lavados, Estuardo Marrou, and Raulino Tramontin. I also thank Manuel Araya, Patricio Arriagada, César A. Briceño, José Joaquín Brunner, Carlos Henrique Cardim, Juan Carlos Crespo, Jorge Ramón Hernández Alcerro, Alejandro Jara, Pablo Latapí, Diógenes da Cunha Lima, César Peña Vigas, and Fernando Storni. With special warmth I acknowledge the help of three good friends from doctoral student days at the University of North Carolina–Chapel Hill political science department: Patricio Chaparro, Alberto Cisneros, and Eduardo Dapieve. Naturally, but not casually, I also acknowledge with gratitude those who granted interviews. Among the scholars who read some part of the manuscript and took time to write detailed and useful comments were Eduardo Aldana Valdés, Heladio Cesar Gonçalves Atunha, José Carlos Almeida Azevedo, Alfonso Borrero, Roderic A. Camp, Burton R. Clark, Enrique D'Etigny Lyon, Paul DiMaggio, Jorge Mario García Laguardia, Roger L. Geiger, John P. Harrison, Jonathan Hartlyn, Iván Jaksić, João Batista Araujo e Oliveira, T. Noel Osborn, Luis Scherz García, Simon Schwartzman, Oscar Soria, and John H. Van de Graaff. Several of the readers and interviewees provided other valuable assistance as well.

Related talks were presented at various forums during various stages of manuscript preparation. Many were given at Yale University from 1978 to 1983. Others were given at the Lancaster International Conference on Higher Education, the CUNY Center for European Studies of the Graduate Center, the Corporación de Promoción Universitaria, the Pacific Sociological Association, the Centro de Pesquisa e Documentação de História Contemporânea do Brasil da Fundação Getúlio Vargas, the Columbia University Seminar on Latin America, the Centro de Documentación Legislativa Universitaria of UNAM, the International Sociological Association, the Latin American Studies Association, the Comparative and International Education Society, a joint CEPAL–Corporación de Promoción Universitaria conference, the UCLA Comparative Higher Education Seminar, the Ben-Gurion University Conference on Universities in Developing Areas, the SUNY Rockefeller College Policy Seminar, the Berkeley Center for Latin American Studies, the Berkeley Center for Studies in Higher Education, and the Stanford Center for Latin American Studies. I am particularly grateful to those who commented on the early presentations, when I was, I hope, still open minded.

Acknowledgments

My wife April performed a critical service by at least feigning interest in the project even when it bogged down and a more tangible service by editing passages that had the better of me. I cannot here thank all those who provided administrative or secretarial assistance, so I restrict myself to Ella Sandor, Lois Hetland, Susanna Knoble, Barbara Grubalski, Sophia Leary, and Maribel Gray. Additionally, several students helped with the library research and data analysis.

Above all, I express my boundless gratitude to my father, to whom this book is dedicated.

1 Issues and Concepts

ISSUES

Introduction and Themes

Long monopolized by public universities established as direct delegates of the State, Latin American higher education is now very much divided into two sectors—private and public. The spectacular growth of private institutions has reshaped the regional panorama, thereby helping to mold the core research concerns of this study.

The first of these concerns is whether the private-public distinction matters. Preliminary research strongly suggested that it does, so much so that the distinction might be critical to the book's most general concern—to analyze Latin American higher education systems not only in and of themselves but also in relation to the State and other "external" actors. Consequently, the private-public distinction has become the conceptual axis around which this book is organized. For each sector, the study investigates origins and growth as well as who pays, who rules, and whose interests are served. Additionally, questions of how and why are posed for issues of finance, governance, and function, again with regard to each sector.

The private-public distinction guides more than limits the study, and it should not divert attention from the most important systemic issues. After all, the two sectors together comprise the whole, and their interactions help shape it. For example, while trying to explain why private sectors have emerged and then grown disproportionally, the study emphasizes the unprecedented public growth that, for several reasons, has promoted the private surge. If the two matters were not highly interrelated, systemic rather than private-public conclusions would be more noteworthy. In reality, the matters not only can but should be explored simultaneously. Thus, had few significant private-public differences emerged, the study might still have produced important systemic answers to basic questions about Latin American higher education; that sectoral differences repeatedly prove decisive, producing contrasting as well as overlapping answers to vital political, economic, and social questions, reinforces the private-public focus. It turns out that most generalizations about Latin American higher education are more accurate when at least partially bounded by sector. It also turns out that each sector individually is best understood when seen in contrast to the other. Therefore, the ensuing study is explicitly intersectoral even though (for reasons discussed near the end of the chapter) it devotes more attention to the private than the public sector.

Private Challenges to Public Dominance

Not long ago, key questions in Latin American higher education could be addressed without sustained reference to a private-public distinction. Well into the twentieth century, Latin America allowed only marginal exceptions to public monopoly. Higher education consisted almost exclusively of public institutions authorized and subsidized by the State to act in its name. Only two of twenty nations (see table 1.1) have private sectors predating this century, and only four have private sectors predating 1940. But two more allowed private sectors in the 1940s, two more in the 1950s, and seven more in the 1960s. By the mid-1970s, eighteen of twenty nations had private sectors. In terms of enrollments, as recently as 1930 the private institutions accounted for only about 3 percent of the Latin American total and 4 percent of the "Spanish American" total (deleting Brazil).[1] By 1955, the first year for which fairly comprehensive data can be accumulated, the private sector held 14 percent of Latin America's four hundred thousand enrollments. Three-fifths of the private total were in Brazil, at once the largest and perhaps most unusual dual sector system in Latin America. Spanish America's private share was still only 7 percent. Then, between 1955 and 1975, the private share jumped from 7 to 19 percent of Spanish America's total; it jumped from 14 to 34 percent of Latin America's total.

Significantly, the private sector has managed to gain on the public sector despite unprecedented public growth. From 1970 to 1975 the public sector doubled its enrollments, as the private sector had done in each quinquennium since 1960. Of course public proportional growth is measured against a larger initial base. Total enrollments soared to near the three-and-one-half-million mark by 1975, soon increasing to more than four million, and probably nearing five million by the early 1980s. Moreover, in part because of their prestigious status and performance, many Spanish American private sectors are more important than their enrollment shares alone might indicate.

Table 1.1 provides a springboard for the entire book. It traces dual sector growth in each of twenty Latin American republics. The data are basically

2

comparable (with due caution) between 1955 and 1975; but the "latest available data," reaching into the 1980s, are drawn from myriad sources as well as from different years and should be considered separately.[2] The latest data tend to confirm that the private share has at least temporarily and roughly stabilized at a point where it accounts for about one of every three enrollments (and one of every five in Spanish America). The data also suggest that total enrollments have continued to grow rapidly, though less than in the early 1970s.

Concentrating on the period from 1955 to 1975, the breadth of privatization is impressive. Haiti and Honduras are ambiguous cases because the OAS shows some private enrollment while other sources show none. Of the eighteen other republics, only Costa Rica and Uruguay continued faithful to the tradition of State monopoly. Only Cuba, obviously based on its general revolutionary shift to full State ownership, engineered a private decline in absolute terms. Additionally, only Chile, Mexico, and Venezuela experienced private proportional declines during the 1955–75 period, and these were only 1 or 2 percent, reflecting simultaneously great private and public expansion. The private share of total enrollment grew by 5 percent or less in Bolivia and Panama, leaving ten republics (Argentina, Brazil, Colombia, Dominican Republic, Ecuador, El Salvador, Guatemala, Nicaragua, Paraguay, Peru) where the private share grew by 8 percent or more. Furthermore, Venezuela's private sector antedates our (1955) data by only two years, Costa Rica finally broke its public monopoly in 1976, and Chile took unprecedented steps toward *"destatización"* after 1973. Therefore, during an era in which keeping pace with the rapidly growing public sector would have been noteworthy indeed, private growth went beyond that. The tide toward privatization has swept most of Latin America. Each of six nations (Brazil, Colombia, Mexico, Argentina, Peru, Chile) had more than fifty thousand private enrollments by 1975, and four had more than one hundred thousand private enrollments in my latest available data.

There is much more to be said about this spectacular private growth, but that is the subject of chapter 2. For details on the data and the major problems with them, see Appendix A as well as footnote 2, chapter 1. The data in table 1.1 are used throughout the book, without making full repetitive citations to the sources and problems.

The rise of Latin America's private sector is especially noteworthy when seen in comparative perspective.[3] Most nations continue to conceive of higher education as a State responsibility properly handled through public institutions. And where, post–World War II, changes have been made in the private-public balance, most have pointed decidedly toward the public pole. Communist nations obviously do not permit private institutions to operate, with only minor exceptions. Less obvious is that most democratic West

Table 1.1 Private and Total Enrollments in Latin American Higher Education, 1955–1982

	Private Sector Foundation, Approximate Yr.	1955 # Priv. # Total	% Priv.	1960 # Priv. # Total	% Priv.	1965 # Priv. # Total	% Priv.
Argentina	1959[a]	775 151,127	1	3,848 173,935	2	20,612 246,680	8
Bolivia	1967[a]	0 10,213	0	110 12,756	1	370 16,912	2
Brazil	1940	33,364 73,575	45	42,554 96,732	44	68,194 155,781	44
Chile	1888	6,129 16,971	36	9,207 24,703	37	15,446 41,801	37
Colombia	1886	5,032 13,284	38	9,374 23,013	41	19,044 44,403	43
Costa Rica	1976	0 2,537	0	0 4,703	0	0 7,225	0
Cuba	1947	1,845 24,273	8	0 19,551	0	0 23,901	0
Dominican Republic	1962	0 3,016	0	0 4,241	0	262 5,231	5
Ecuador	1946	392 5,859	7	653 8,331	8	2,243 12,486	18
El Salvador	1965	0 1,393	0	0 2,360	0	275 3,438	8
Guatemala	1961	0 3,198	0	0 5,578	0	786 8,593	9
Haiti	—[a]	71 887	8	68 1,220	6	223 1,705	13
Honduras	—[a]	168 1,459	12	164 1,674	10	247 2,542	10
Mexico	1935	6,338 46,605	14	10,689 78,599	14	19,834 133,374	15
Nicaragua	1961	0 1,048	0	0 3,182	0	551 2,729	20
Panama	1965	0 2,298	0	0 4,030	0	232 7,247	3
Paraguay	1960	0 2,352	0	58 3,425	2	1,766 5,890	30
Peru	1917	2,348 21,029	11	4,602 40,263	11	16,513 79,259	21
Uruguay	—	0 14,550	0	0 15,320	0	0 18,507	0
Venezuela	1953	879 7,664	11	2,634 23,116	11	5,076 41,372	12
Total Latin America		57,341 403,338	14.2	83,961 546,732	15.4	171,674 859,076	20.0
Total Spanish America (without Brazil)		23,977 329,763	7.3	41,407 450,000	9.2	103,480 703,295	14.7

SOURCE: See footnote 2, chapter 1.
NOTE: See Appendix A.
   a. See footnote 2, (chapter 1) on why private enrollments are shown to precede the foundation date for the private sector.

Table 1.1 cont'd

1970 # Priv. # Total	% Priv.	1975 # Priv. # Total	% Priv.	Latest Data # Priv. # Total	% Priv.	Year
47,763	17	73,082	12	120,101	22	1982
274,634		596,736		550,556		
754	3	1,061	3	1,348	3	1978
25,595		35,364		44,946		
236,760	55	700,571	65	852,000	63	1980
430,473		1,072,548		1,345,000		
26,229	34	50,998	35	43,769	37	1980
76,979		147,049		118,978		
38,942	46	100,062	52	180,635	59	1981
85,560		192,887		306,269		
0	0	0	0	4,059	8	1981
15,729		32,928		53,915		
0	0	0	0	0	0	1980
26,342		68,882		146,240		
3,531	23	12,819	31	43,000	46	1979
15,377		41,352		93,000		
6,683	21	19,887	15	40,677	15	1980
31,824		136,695		267,000		
1,343	26	2,848	10	3,762	12	1977
5,230		28,281		30,303		
2,752	18	4,854	18	11,459	23	1980
15,284		27,675		50,890		
150	9	150	9	377	9	1978
1,607		1,607		4,186		
285	6	725	6	734	3	1981
4,744		12,086		27,843		
27,276	15	75,943	15	118,999	15	1981
188,011		506,287		785,419		
3,693	39	6,216	34	7,387	34	1977
9,385		18,282		21,449		
606	7	1,243	6	1,604	6	1977
8,159		22,581		27,820		
2,018	25	5,832	34	6,552	34	1977
8,150		17,153		19,270		
27,884		68,161	32	64,287	27	1980
128,251	22	210,071		241,861		
0		0	0	0	0	1977
27,157	0	33,664		39,392		
8,077		18,943	10	39,702	13	1981
75,105	11	194,213		307,133		
429,635		1,143,395	33.7	1,540,452	34.4	
1,453,596	29.6	3,396,341		4,481,470		
192,875		442,824	19.1	688,452	21.9	
983,123	19.6	2,323,793		3,136,470		

European systems have also been characterized as statist. Some are fully public, while others (e.g., the French) have several peripheral private institutions or just an exceptional one (e.g., Sweden's Stockholm School of Economics). The Netherlands and especially Belgium are notable for having sizeable private sectors, yet even these sectors are largely nationalized, at least in terms of State regulations and especially finance. A more significant exception, but one that has faded during this century, is found as we move from the Continent to Great Britain, and from there to most of its commonwealth and former empire. Nineteenth-century British higher education, in contrast to its Continental counterpart, was considered a private endeavor. Some private qualities persist in legal ownership, non-civil-servant employee status, and relative autonomy from the State. But British and most commonwealth universities (and certainly their technical institutions) are now generally considered public. A key indicator is the growth of State subsidization from less than 50 percent (1920) to more than 90 percent (1980) of British university income; similar transformations have occurred in nations such as Australia, Canada, Ireland, Israel, and New Zealand.[4]

Private institutions are more common in some, but not most, of the less-developed world. Areas previously under French rule have followed a statist tradition, and those under British rule can generally be grouped with their more developed commonwealth counterparts. The State is overwhelmingly responsible for higher education in Africa as well as in, though less pervasively, the Middle East. It is in Asia that one finds the principal private sectors outside the Americas. Major examples include India, Japan, the Philippines, South Korea, and Turkey. Interestingly, however, these nations tend to fall into the Brazilian pattern described in chapter 5, with private sectors usually having more quantitative but less qualitative importance (adjusted for size) than in Spanish America.[5]

Latin America's private surge contrasts sharply with a reverse trend in the United States, long spiritual home as well as international model of private higher education and limited State involvement. To color the images for emphasis, traditionally more corporatist- and statist-oriented Latin America now manages higher education in as private a way as does the United States, the latter's traditional market, pluralist, and limited State orientations notwithstanding. As recently as 1950, the U.S. private sector held half the nation's enrollments (versus roughly 10 percent in Latin America), but by 1975 the 50 percent figure had dwindled to less than 25 percent (versus 34 percent in Latin America).[6] Moreover, contrary to the picture in 1950 or decades earlier, the U.S. private sector has lost much of its "privateness," while most of Latin America's private sectors, as we shall see, are private indeed. Comparing the United States and Latin America in this way makes for an unusual political-economic juxtaposition in the relationships of private and public sectors and the State and underscores how remarkable the Latin American private surge really is. *Privatization*, therefore, can be defined not only in terms of absolute and proportional private sector growth but also in terms of the qualitative privateness that accompanies the quantitative surge.

Private-Public Policy Debates

In both the United States and Latin America, the shifting private-public balance is a matter of great policy interest and debate, but the value orientations tend to be different. The U.S. private decline is widely viewed with concern, even dismay. One may speak of a fairly broad U.S. policy consensus favoring a dual sector structure, valuing the private sector, and crediting that sector with at least a proportional share of higher education's contribution to society. Latin American opinion is much more sharply divided. By comparison, U.S. debates appear to involve rather marginal degrees of more or less privateness. Many Latin Americans, unlike all but a few U.S. counterparts, regard higher education as a responsibility of the State exclusively, allowing for delegation only to public institutions. Even among those who would not bar private sectors altogether, many are concerned that private sectors have grown inappropriately powerful and that the State has abdicated too much. Naturally, these are but generalizations and should not obscure diversity of opinion. But in higher education as in other pursuits, dominant U.S. thought has tended to give the benefit of the doubt to private actors, placing the burden of proof on those who would advocate a greater State role, while in Latin America, as in Europe, the benefits and burdens are often inverted. Many of the arguments for and against private sectors in higher education are corollaries of broader private-public debates about the proper roles of the State and of private organizations.

Classic cases for private and public sectors can be organized around four concepts: freedom, choice, equity, and effectiveness. Obviously, other values could be chosen, and the four themselves could be defined differently. All four are analyzed both in regard to the contrasting positions taken by antagonists and, where possible, the evidence sustaining or contradicting those positions. Chapter 7 provides an interpretive summary of accumulated findings. However, as an introductory note, lest individual sections along the way give a facilely favorable impression about one sector over the other, let it be clear that comparative evaluation across sectors proves to be a complex enterprise, producing complex conclusions. Consequently, positive statements about either sector should acknowledge normative considerations, qualifications to empirical tendencies, intersectoral trade-offs, limited undertakings, and the fact that apparent sectoral successes may be rooted partly in the other sector or in intersectoral dynamics. Here it will suffice merely to outline the private-public arguments in strokes broad enough to transcend but also include higher education.

First, *freedom* encompasses two major dimensions. One is institutional autonomy from external control. The other is participatory freedom, related to the latitude for constituents to express themselves without restraint from either outside or inside the institution; the higher education manifestation is academic freedom, generally referring to professors and students. Private proponents argue that freedom is greater when the State is restricted to areas unfeasible for private action. Institutional autonomy and participatory freedom are enhanced; dangers of tyranny through monopolistic control or public politicization are minimized. Opponents argue that private institutions are often unduly tied to particular groups that liberally wield power illiberally; that is, these groups broadly use power in ways that threaten both autonomy and participatory freedoms. The State, recipient of public taxes, has a proper role in providing the best services to its people and is therefore not an alien agent, as many private interests are, to the educational process.

Second, private proponents argue that private institutions are more responsive to societal *choice,* offering more diversity, adaptability, and innovation, and are less constrained by remote bureaucracy. In higher education this means choice for students ("clients"), their families, employers, donors, professors, and administrators. At a minimum, dual sectors provide more choice than one sector. Public proponents reply that private choice often perverts public purpose, that policy choices ought to be reached popularly, democratically, or consensually, and that higher education should be responsive and accountable to choice as defined in the political arena. Additionally, public proponents prefer to define choice as the ability to select among accessible alternatives, charging that their opponents emptily stress the formal liberty to choose, regardless of feasibility.

This last point about choice introduces a third debate, on *equity* or fair distribution. Some praise private institutions for reducing excessive State subsidies based on coercive payments by all, privileged and unprivileged alike, for services available only to some. Beneficiaries should pay their own way whenever possible. But critics respond that only the State can provide low costs and equal opportunity, thereby promoting equitable results and progressive social change; private institutions are generally more accessible to those who can pay or who enjoy other special advantages. Structural differentiation of the kind promoted by private alternatives allegedly tends to perpetuate class differentiation.

8

Finally, the private-public debate turns on *effectiveness*. The term can relate to efficiency—achieving maximum output for minimal input; it can also relate to a usage common in the literature on organizations—the ability to survive and garner resources. In this work *effectiveness* refers to success in carrying out selected goals. Among higher education's goals, academic quality is an obvious one; yet effectiveness also depends on fulfilling philosophical, political, social, employment, or other goals. Partisans of private institutions argue that autonomy, choice, diversity, innovation, responsiveness, and client payments, joined with the benefits of competition—including intersectoral competition—foster effectiveness. Coordination is better achieved through invisible hands, pluralism, and market mechanisms than through State mandate. Opponents reply that too much private activity leads to divisiveness and lack of coordination. A corollary stems from theories on "late development," a concept most identified with Alexander Gerschenkron:[7] while dispersed private activity may have been appropriate for the earliest developers, later developers face more structured obstacles and require more centralization of resources and more unity to achieve productive and nationally integrating results. Building strong systems, like building strong nations, requires strong States.

The private-public debate is not only a vibrant intellectual one, though it is that; it is also, at least in Latin American higher education, a policy-relevant one. Most Latin American nations have passed the point of debating whether to allow private sectors at all, but private legitimacy is fragile enough in some nations that the private-public debate is still very polarized. While policy questions now generally are matters of degree, the possible degrees vary widely. What should be the relative size of the two sectors, the private versus the State subsidization level for each, the degree of financial accountability to whom? What is the proper balance between institutional autonomy and State or other "external" control? How liberal should the State be in licensing private institutions? Should religious, business, and other private groups be allowed to function autonomous of the State? Additionally, most of the major policy issues facing the public sector itself are largely private-public issues. These include the balance of State subsidies and client payments, the degree of State control versus institutional autonomy, and the effort to serve the State and its view of societal needs versus the effort to serve society by responding to private individuals and institutions. Without indulging in the fantasy that such decisions will be significantly based on scholastic analysis of the outcomes of various private-public balances, such analysis should help to inform the debate.

Moreover, the private-public issues to be examined are relevant to higher education far beyond Latin America. This may not be obvious for single sector systems, but by the 1970s and 1980s many West European nations were seeking ways to modify the perceived problems of governing higher education through centralized structures and were voicing increased interest in shifting away from the tradition of almost total public financing. So even where the creation of private sectors is still only suggested, there is policy debate over increasing privateness within the nominally public sector, just as there is debate over how much to regulate whatever private institutions do exist. Beyond this, significant debate over the creation or official recognition of distinctly private institutional alternatives has erupted in several nations. Greece in the 1970s provides one example, though no private universities (only some commercial schools) have yet been established. In Spain, post-Franco politics have heated up private-public issues, with the Christian Democrats squaring off against leftist parties on the proper Church role. In Portugal, postdictatorial politics have sanctioned the creation of a private sector. Italy has actually made limited forays beyond its rather marginal Catholic universities; the Free International University of Social Sciences was created much as the Spanish American elite business universities analyzed in chapters 2, 4, and 6. And stirring considerable rancor, West Germany has proceeded to establish its first private university. Across the Channel, England has been wracked by debate over the creation and minimal State regulation of the University of Buckingham and other private alternatives flourishing largely because substantial tuitions were imposed on overseas students in the public institutions. As another example, New Zealand opened its first private university in 1981 amid frustrated cries that the State should intervene.

When pondering either increased privateness or actual private sector creation, West European and commonwealth nations will undoubtedly consider U.S. experience, but could also consider the experience of a region that for a long time shared its own strongly propublic cultural views and concomitant structural forms. Those West Europeans who regard private higher education as impossibly alien to their tradition might be interested to know that private higher education was widely regarded in the same way— until the late 1950s—in Argentina, one of Latin America's most Europeanized nations. Also, since nations such as Nigeria have seriously considered creating private alternatives, African scholars and policymakers might be intrigued by the profound changes wrought in a region that, as most of Africa today, handled higher education through public monopolies in its postindependence period. While no clearly applicable "lessons" can be expected, Latin American trends may be instructive, given Africa's continual expressions of dissatisfaction with dependence on European modes not designed for the less-developed world.

More obviously, the private-public debate is vibrant where two sectors already exist. This is the case in the United States; in fact, United States private-public conflict has increased since "retrenchment" has scared nearly everyone in both sectors. Finally, most of the noncommunist world, certainly including Latin America, faces related dual sector private-public decisions involving primary and secondary education.[8]

The Literature

The policy debate highlights the importance of studying a field directly involving millions of students, many thousands of professors, and large annual budgets. Indeed, higher education affects Latin America's political, economic, and social systems while it helps shape concerns from development to class to ideology. Thus one important rationale for this study is to understand major and changing phenomena; another is to investigate phenomena that have gone almost uninvestigated. In fact, the entire private or dual sector panorama in higher education has until now received little scholarly attention, especially outside the United States and perhaps Japan (see footnote 3). Similarly, comparative higher education has been a limited field, rarely explored outside the small club of industrialized democracies. Additionally, the lack of political studies on higher education, even within the United States, has been amply documented; one explanation for this lack is that U.S. political scientists have tended to see the university as an essentially "private" body, not an issue of "government."[9] That perception, shaky for the United States, would never have applied to Latin America and would in any case be a poor reason to turn away political scientists interested in more than just the formal workings of government, narrowly defined.

Still, the lacuna that this study most directly faces is the lack of work on higher education by U.S. Latin Americanists. The striking exception is student politics, which received so much attention in the 1960s that it may have contributed to the neglect of all other social science issues involving the university; the near disappearance of studies on student politics in the 1970s meant the near disappearance of U.S. studies on Latin American higher education. Of course exceptions exist, and more important, Latin Americans have written much more than U.S. Latin Americanists; some have put forth provocative interpretations, while others have written descriptive national studies. Such foci are important, and I draw widely on them throughout, but they are also inadequate. Many of the works tend to be either strictly normative, prescribing the proper role of the university in society and the importance of autonomy and university reform, or restrictively legalistic, sometimes dealing only with extinct formal structures and statutes. "Literature on the Latin American university is largely of a polemical and speculative nature, generally devoid of empirical grounding and theoretical significance."[10] So began Robert Arnove's 1967 review essay into this "still unexplored" world. Although some works have improved the situation, Arnove's assessment still holds weight. For all these reasons, therefore, it is not surprising that few U.S. Latin Americanists know much about higher education. Most could easily name a few significant works on the Church, the military, political parties, labor unions, or private enterprise, yet probably few could likewise cite works on the university.[11] Significant theoretical studies on Latin American politics, authoritarianism, corporatism, dependent development, and State-society relations have incorporated little about State-university relations. A similarly unfortunate void characterizes most broad works on given nations. In sum, as we lack major books on the Latin American university, so major books on broader subjects have generally devoted little attention to the university (other than student politics); they have had little on which to draw.

Having identified the challenges that lie directly ahead but before launching into the ensuing chapters, it is important to establish the concepts around which the findings themselves will be oriented and to tie this work to the relevant theoretical literature.

CONCEPTS
The State

The *State* has become such a fashionable term in scholarship on Latin American and comparative politics that I am tempted to grope for a substitute. Yet *State* is appropriate for this book, and an understanding of why is relevant to the major issues treated herein.

First, because this book is not about pedagogy, learning, curriculum, or, in short, the educational process per se, the term *higher education* must be linked with some concept that conveys a broad political, economic, and social orientation. *Higher Education in Latin America* would be an unsuitable title, even with a subtitle referring to private and public sectors.

Government could reasonably be substituted for *State*. Many works use the terms interchangeably; others use only one, sometimes not indicating why the unused term would be less appropriate. Notwithstanding considerable overlap between the two concepts, however, some uses are much more common to one. Each has a different center of gravity. Generally, *State* represents a larger, less transitory concept. *Government* often refers to a particular administration (e.g., Betancourt's in Venezuela, 1959–64) or even to just the top executive branch personnel, especially in parliamentary systems. Whereas *government* frequently refers to the formally political and administrative, *State* more often conjures up economic and social dimensions as well. Consequently, concepts of State and government characteris-

12

tically suggest somewhat different questions; questions associated with the State, such as those concerning "the relative autonomy of the State," tend to be closer to this study's focus. In particular, *State* more readily suggests private-public questions.[12]

There are two reasons for not using *public sector* instead of *State*. One is to reserve the term for higher education itself. Frequently cited throughout this work, *public sector* here refers to the public institutions of higher education. This usage reduces wordiness. The second reason is that *State* carries some important and appropriate connotations beyond what *public sector* generally does. Therefore, I begin but do not stop with the way some authors have equated *State* and *public sector,* for to limit the State to a conglomeration of public structures (and related personnel), juridically defined, is to treat the State statically.[13] Instead, the State is properly seen as an actor, not just an inanimate structure. Furthermore, even where the State's most distinguishing role involves the coercive preservation of order, this normally encompasses myriad legitimizing activities.[14]

Among those scholars who do see the State as an actor, some have treated it as a dependent actor—the executive arm of plural interest groups or dominant classes. Notwithstanding harsh charges to the contrary, however, few contemporary pluralist theorists or Marxists have been so extreme as to reduce the State completely to dependent status. Most pluralists have regarded the State as an actor, though often not the critical one. Most Marxists now see the State as expressing somewhat variable forms of class struggle, certainly favoring the dominant class but not necessarily acting at its precise behest.[15] A third, nonpluralist, non-Marxist tradition exists as well. Sometimes called "organic-statist," or "corporatist-authoritarian," it is based on a major independent role for the State. The tendency to associate this third ideal type with Ibero-Latin settings has been reinvigorated since the 1960s by the sustained rule of military regimes in important South American nations.[16]

Thinking of the State in a way that allows both for purposeful and independent action is not to say that the State is always capable of it, much less to deny the influence of powerful classes or interest groups upon it. In this study I see the State within a class setting, most explicitly in chapters 2 and 7 but also throughout, as I explore who rules private and public sectors and who is served by each. The relationship of class to State, like the relationship of a plurality of groups to the State, is left open for analysis. Moreover, even where a State might directly serve a dominant class, not every State institution or policy necessarily would. Rather than postulating that the State is merely a creature or even an ally of specific dominant classes or groups, I ask if public institutions are used by different interests, for

13

different purposes, than are private institutions. This is a form of inquiry into the autonomy of the State from private interests. But wherever Latin America may incline toward an organic-statist or corporatist tradition, the research question may well flow the other way: What is the nature of private interests' and institutions' autonomy from the State?

If the bounds of State influence (not to mention State concerns) are debatable and imprecise—as are the bounds of many organizations or bundles of organizations—so correspondingly must be the non-State bounds. *Private sphere* refers here to non-State. By definition, then, the State and the private sphere together comprise the sum of any society's structures and activities.[17] However, subsequent chapters refer to specific parts of the private sphere whenever appropriate, resorting to the term *private sphere* only occasionally.[18] In any event, just as the relationship between the State and the public sector is subject to investigation, so is the private sphere–private sector relationship, even though the private and public sectors are judicially and structurally parts of the private sphere and the State, respectively.

Table 1.2 indicates the four relationships concerning higher education as well as the State and the private sphere that are investigated in this study. They are as follows: the State and the private sector, the State and the public sector, the private sphere and the private sector, and the private sphere and the public sector.

In sum, the State is understood here to include the juridically public structures and personnel, lying in some variable relationship with classes, groups, and institutions, at least sometimes capable of purposeful and independent action, and generally maintaining the broad political-economic-social order through coercion and legitimacy. Such a definition should orient the study toward certain key questions and yet not presume to answer them a priori. These questions concern the strength and role of the State in comparison with the private sphere and the relationship both of the State and the private sphere to each sector of higher education.

Table 1.2 Higher Education and Its Environment

	Higher Education	
Environment	Private	Public
Private	private sector–private sphere	public sector–private sphere
Public	private sector–State	public sector–State

Private and Public

Having defined the State and, residually, the private sphere, in such a way as to explore their roles in higher education, the next task is to define private and public higher education sectors. Although the task is not as straightforward as it might initially appear, I want to avoid some of the detailed definitional analysis that might reasonably be involved.[19] Again the search is for definitions consistent with broad usage and yet specifically oriented to the major concerns of this study.

Institutions called private and public are not always behaviorally private and public, respectively. For example, private universities may receive State subsidies; public ones may receive business contributions. Abandoning dichotomies, it becomes painfully clear that private institutions are not even necessarily more private than public ones by matter of degree. So no neat empirical continuum runs between private and public poles. And ambiguity is generally greater in matters of governance and function than in matters of finance. Illustratively, considerable private-public ambiguity is found in U.S. higher education. Only in the period from after the Civil War until the mid-twentieth century did a fairly clear private-public split exist.[20] Other nations such as England and the Netherlands have notoriously elicited more confusion on private-public terminology. Fortunately for the clarity of this study and its ability to draw conclusions about privateness and publicness based largely on the research about each sector, juridical labels are closer to empirical realities of privateness and publicness in Latin American higher education.

More broadly, private-public ambiguity is by no means unique to higher education. It plagues, disillusions, or impresses analysts of many policy fields. Private-public questions are important enough to be posed continually, yet complex enough never to be resolved fully. Social science has only begun to untangle the general ambiguities discussed by Dahl and Lindblom some thirty years ago, and no wonder, for the empirical ambiguities have, if anything, increased; often frustrated but also persistent, students of public administration have felt compelled to explore "whether a meaningful and useful distinction can be made between public and private administration."[21] Organizational sociology has produced some works separating private and public and many works emphasizing crucial similarities. While much of classical liberal political-economic thought is based on the private-public distinction, "there is also a considerable body of thinking," notably but not exclusively Marxist, "which has criticized the public/private dichotomy and tried to overcome it."[22]

Awareness of private-public ambiguities has been sharpened by recent literature on corporatism. Like pluralism, corporatism generally refers to relationships between the State and society, but it has gone further in emphasizing interpenetration. A major concern in the United States is that, in Theodore Lowi's words, a delegation of State power has meant "an alienation of public domain, a gift of sovereignty to private satrapies," such that, in Grant McConnell's words, a "breaking of the boundary between public and private," the "destruction of the distinction between public and private," has resulted from private organizations encroaching on public ones.[23] Some large private companies come to make public decisions, receive direct as well as indirect subsidization, and even fall into critical dependency on the State. At the same time, many conservatives believe that the State and public organizations have encroached unduly on private organizations. In Latin America, parallel concerns also call attention to private-public interpenetration. One fear is that the State has consumed society's private organizations. Another is that the latter have penetrated the State apparatus.

All this private-public ambiguity means that we cannot rest with comparisons of nominally private and public sectors. Granted, because of the way many juridical and policy issues are posed, one important task is to contrast the nominal sectors to see what they do differently. Private and public sectors (and institutions) are here labeled according to legal nomenclature. This has the advantage of certain identification and of manageable usage; but it also, by itself, begs empirical questions and ignores empirical complexity.[24] Moreover, even when organizations are truly private at birth, their characteristics often change over time while their legal identifications rarely change. Analysts need to know how private and public these organizations really are, and in what ways. They need to compare "privateness" and "publicness." Therefore, to evaluate privatization in qualitative as well as quantitative terms, *private* and *public* can be defined in ideal-typical terms of *privateness* and *publicness*.

Three separate ideal-typical categories are used here. They deal with finance, governance, and function, each subsequently explored in discretely identified sections throughout chapters 3 through 6. Each sector is evaluated on all three categories, yielding empirical continua rather than a unidimensional continuum. There is no need to assume that private finance, for example, necessarily goes hand-in-hand with private governance. Not only do the three criteria give us a fuller view of reality but we can explore relationships among the three.[25]

Finance is the easiest criterion to define and usually the easiest to measure. An institution is private to the extent that it receives its income from sources other than the State and public to the extent that it relies on the State. The major private source is usually tuition, a term I will use to

16

subsume the basic matriculation and other fees students face. (All figures are given in U. S. dollars, unless otherwise stated.) Indirect subsidies and tax benefits can cloud the issue, but the relative straightforwardness of the financial criterion helps explain its wide use in identifying private and public. Another reason for its wide use is the implicit assumption that finance is the "input" that determines the "output" of what is ultimately done and how. This reasoning has two flaws, however. Correlations between finance and either function or governance are not always clear, and even where they are, the direction of causality should be an empirical question. Also, treating finance as input tends to overlook the fact that who pays is itself substantively important. Who is burdened—clients or the general public, rich or poor, individuals or businesses?

The governance criterion is also easy to define, but often much harder to evaluate. An institution is private to the extent that it is governed by non-State personnel and public to the extent that it is governed by the State. Again some tend to regard governance as an input determining the real output—what is done (function); again the tendency should be resisted because governance does not necessarily determine function and because governance is intrinsically important. Special attention is given to who determines policies such as resource distribution, appointment of personnel, curriculum content, and general political, economic, and social orientations. Special attention is also given to the distribution of power over these issues among students, professors, university administrators, external private interests, and the State.

Function is not only the most diffuse and difficult criterion to evaluate, it is even difficult to define. The related concept of mission might have been used, but it often carries a normative connotation, one oriented more toward goals than toward actual behavior. The university is too often philosophically defined by what it should do rather than by what it actually does.[26] Grand statements of mission often obscure the fundamental complexity, even ambiguity, of university functions. By function I mean, most simply, what the university does. Less simply, function also refers to the ramifications of what is done, especially what interests and values are served. It refers to all roles performed, including those seen as dysfunctional to certain ends. Admittedly used here as something of a catchall term for a variety of institutional attributes, function deals with such important issues as the social-class student clientele served; the human resources produced (as reflected in fields of study and in employment subsequently obtained); the values and ideologies promoted (religious, social, political); and the extent to which all the above functions are effectively promoted through academic quality, though strong reservations about the statistical indicators of quality, or indeed the meaning of quality itself, frequently lead me to fall

17

back on the diluted surrogate concept of academic prestige. Beyond all this, even where one can define and evaluate functions it is not always clear whether they are private or public functions. I indicate where private and public tendencies exist, as when graduates enter business corporations or the State bureaucracy, and do not press the issue where no clear tendencies are found. In the latter cases I analyze the different functions, regardless of private-public orientation, and identify which are performed by institutions with differing private and public financial and governance characteristics.

A final consideration relevant to how *private* and *public* are used herein concerns the nonprofit concept. Perhaps the simplest definition centers on the fact that nonprofit institutions may not distribute net earnings to their owners, but delineation of this third sector proves as difficult and blurred in practice as does the general private-public distinction. As the literature on nonprofit institutions is still slim, especially on those outside the United States, analyses of State-private balances and interactions are inappropriately limited and typically discussed in relation to industrial, agricultural, and commercial enterprises, even though much private activity occurs outside the for-profit network.[27] Critical nonprofit arenas usually include education, health, social services, and charitable and religious activities. Private education is typically nonprofit. Specifically in Latin American higher education, no nation has yet established a viable for-profit sector, at least not a legal one, and most have legally proscribed it. In sum, while the overall size and role of the State relates very much to two kinds of private organizations, the size and role of the public sector of Latin American higher education relates essentially to the nonprofit private sector. Unless otherwise indicated, therefore, *private* refers here to nonprofit private. It is used in ways specifically compatible with the emerging theoretical literature on nonprofit institutions.[28]

U.S. and European Models

This last section briefly sets Latin American higher education in comparative perspective. It sketches tiny profiles of the internationally best-known higher education forms, markedly different in privateness and publicness, that have been models for Latin America. Obviously, I can only generalize here, ignoring the complexities, variations, and exceptions found in practice; the generalizations are tendencies that appear salient when comparing U.S. and European higher education, despite some arguable degree of convergence since the 1960s.

Newly independent Latin America frequently took the French university as a model. After all, during that period France was perceived to be the world's cultural capital. Its national university seemed more relevant than multitudinous U.S. colleges to new Latin American systems that generally had only one or a few universities; centralization seemed more relevant than decentralization for societies with certain organic-statist traditions and with preoccupations for national unification. Thus, several terms with European roots—terms such as *chair, faculty,* and *licenciatura*—became part of the Latin American lexicon.[29] Similarly, I refer to primary and secondary education rather than elementary and high school education, using *schools* to denote institutions at these (non–higher education) levels.

By the middle of the twentieth century, however, U.S. models became increasingly important. The Colossus to the North was the world's first nation to move toward "mass higher education." Its universities came to be seen by many as the best and most modern, and institutional diversity increasingly characterized Latin American higher education. Furthermore, U.S. might (economic, cultural, political, and military) exerted an unrelenting force sometimes transmitted through an array of aid programs to Latin America's universities.[30] Additionally, West European universities were generally plunged into deeper crises in the late 1960s than were U.S. universities. But most of all, as we shall see throughout, Latin America's fast-growing private sector looked chiefly to U.S. models just as the public sector long looked chiefly to European models.

The Continental model—to use Burton Clark's apt label for the traditional European university—modified somewhat in recent years, is a striking approximation of some ideal-typical notions of a public university. Allowing for variation over time and locale, Continental universities form "relatively pure state systems."[31] They are created by the State (except for some ancient universities) to serve as its higher education representatives. One form is the Napoleonic university, after Napoléon's Imperial University. In fact, this form is not really a university in the conventional sense but an overarching educational structure. Instead of distinct universities, there are different professional faculties, all tied to the supervising State. By the late nineteenth century, the Napoleonic model had lost much of its force, but it had been a crucial model when much of Latin America created its first postcolonial higher education systems. Moreover, European universities remained statist even as the Napoleonic form faded. The State would generally delegate its authority to one national university or to one national university type; more than in the United States, institutional proliferation would represent replication of standardized form, not pluralist diversity.

In finance, the Continental university is almost fully sustained by the State. In governance, the State role is also crucial. Universities lack the distinct corporate identities found in the United States. Instead, the State is a powerful overarching force, while external private organizations usually play a much more limited role. The education ministry has broad authority, at least formally, regarding the distribution of subsidies, access, curriculum, and exam and degree requirements. A major goal of such tight control is to guarantee the standardization of national degrees, which are awarded by the State rather than by different universities. The major counterbalance to State authority—and a significant one—lies with the senior chaired professors, who hold considerable power over a range of pedagogical and organizational tasks and even sit on national committees that set policy. This professorial power became especially prominent with the ascendancy of the German research university late in the nineteenth century. However, the State entrusts professors with influence only after the State itself monitors appointments; moreover, chaired professors are civil servants, and their national influence is exercised largely through committees responsible to the State. Consequently, power distribution in the Continental university has been characterized as strong at the bottom or "understructure" (mostly through the chair), weak in the middle (university-wide level), and strong at the top (State).[32]

A principal function of the Continental university is to train professionals, and the basic degree is a professional one, not a general or liberal arts degree. A related function is to serve the State directly. The State bureaucracy has been the chief employer of the university's graduates. In fact, many see a State obligation (sometimes legally fixed) to employ, although the supply of graduates has periodically exceeded demand for them. But as Suleiman elaborately shows for France, the State role in elite creation is even more encompassing than its role in employing those elites, while for Goldschmidt the Continental university is "to deliberately overstate the matter . . . traditionally an enterprise of the state dedicated to the welfare of the state, and especially to the needs of the public service and the publicly acknowledged professions."[33]

No one form has dominated in the United States. Clearly, there is no U.S. counterpart to the Continental notion of a national university, the State's higher education arm. The Carnegie Commission on Higher Education has suggested a twelve-part categorization of institutions, by no means excessive, but three basic types will have to do here.[34] Again, in reality, great variation exists within the types.

Even U.S. public universities show striking differences from the Continental university; they do not come nearly as close to ideal-typical notions of publicness. Notwithstanding decades of increasing State finance, private sources (including tuition, endowments, and donations) account for roughly 20 percent of the public sector's income. The State is weaker than in the Continental model, and most of its power rests not with the national government but with fifty state governments. Conversely, external (formally beyond the institution itself) private interests, including donors, alumni,

20

and other lay groups, have often achieved influence, sometimes through participation on boards of regents or trustees. The boards generally appoint the university president—a crucial power because university-wide administration is far stronger than in Continental universities, where authority over many of the financial, planning, and some curriculum matters are left to the State. Deans usually are appointed from the administration ("above") rather than from chaired professors ("below"). Rarely do U.S. professors achieve the power of chaired professors, but power is more widely distributed among professors, including junior professors, in the U.S. departmental structure than in the Continental chair structure. Professorial power is usually greater at the academically stronger than weaker U.S. institutions. Finally, in terms of function, the U.S. public universities have not served either the professionalist or statist functions as mightily as the Continental universities have, instead performing more varied functions for both the State *and* diverse private interests.

U.S. private universities are naturally even more distinct from the Continental model. Most are financed much more by private than State funds. Important exceptions are found in research, graduate education, and student loans, in all of which the national government plays a vital role, supported by individual states. Governance is similar in many respects to that found in the public universities, but boards of trustees are likely to have greater private representation, especially by business interests, along with less representation of state officials, making state governments far less influential in general and in effect often making university administrations that much stronger. There has traditionally been little authority above these (and other) private institutions and their own trustees, except for accrediting boards (regional or professional) and, more recently, statewide coordinating boards (with variable powers according to state).

The third institutional type considered here is the liberal arts college, almost all of which are private. Liberal arts colleges are the closest offspring of the colonial and early nineteenth-century colleges, as research- and graduate-oriented universities did not appear until after the Civil War. Their funding is overwhelmingly private, even compared to the private universities. Devoted to undergraduate education, they generally lack major national government research grants and funding for graduate students. Some are well endowed, but tuition is the main source for the great majority. In governance, liberal arts colleges are tied mostly to external interests other than the State. Their trustees hire the college presidents, and most power resides in these two centers. This is especially true of the lower-quality (or liberal arts II) institutions. The higher-quality liberal arts colleges, more like the private universities, are characterized by less external (e.g., Church) influence, less paternal or authoritarian rule, and more

21

professorial influence than found in the less prestigious liberal arts colleges. Students are rarely powerful in liberal arts colleges, or in U.S. universities for that matter, except insofar as they exercise economic power in choosing their institutions. The functions of the liberal arts institutions are best defined by their enormous diversity, sometimes perpetuated through distinctive reputations based on such factors as religion, race, gender, experimental liberalism, conservative fundamentalism, and technical orientation. Most of the high-prestige liberal arts colleges are secular, while many others have a religious orientation, often posing dilemmas between particularism and the academic mainstream.

In conclusion, as I proceed to analyze in subsequent chapters the panorama of Latin America higher education, I do so in accordance with certain guiding conceptual orientations. This book is concerned with how each higher education sector relates to the State and to the private sphere. It is concerned with private institutions as nonprofit institutions that face major dilemmas generally encountered by such institutions. It is concerned not just with private and public sectors as defined by nomenclature but also with privateness and publicness as measured against ideal types relating to finance, governance, and function. It is concerned with evaluative comparisons that revolve around notions of freedom, choice, equity, and effectiveness. And the book is also concerned with the degree to which the findings relate to the principal foreign models that have influenced Latin American higher education.

Overview of Chapters

A work that moves into a relative void and nevertheless attempts to provide regional coverage clearly runs considerable risks. The dangers of generalizing about such a diverse entity as Latin America are well known. Yet the open spaces leave room for broad findings. Moreover, in higher education more than in most fields, common influences (including models) have affected many nations similarly, leading to some notably parallel norms and structures. And the use here of concepts from the social sciences, as well as a small but growing literature on nonprofit organizations, helps to identify important patterns (including three principal private-public patterns) and to infuse a degree of order into otherwise scattered and fugitive information.

However broad the study might be both in conceptual and geographical scope, several important limitations exist. As noted above, this book is not about the educational process per se. Moreover, even in terms of considerations relevant to the State and other external actors, some issues are obviously discussed less than others. A very important example is the lack of adequate attention given to certain new and specialized types of institutions that contribute to a widespread diversification in the structure of Latin American higher education. Mostly public, these include technical institutes and centers and military academies. On the private side, I give little attention to seminaries and other highly specialized institutions not usually considered part of the national higher education system (though *system* is often a nebulous concept in higher education). Additionally, I concentrate on "first-degree" (or undergraduate) education, deleting detailed analysis of graduate (*posgrado*) education, which is growing fast but was marginal until recently, and of separate research institutions (for example, Argentina's Di Tella Institute), as opposed to research undertaken within multipurpose universities. This is not to say that I ignore all such activities and institutions but that I invoke the usual excuses of limited time, space, and other resources to justify limiting the study's scope. Similarly, to discuss individual universities, let alone types of universities, is often to make simplifying abstractions, since few universities (especially public ones) speak with one united voice; I try to identify specific actors as frequently as possible.

Perhaps the most significant conceptual limitation concerns the private-public balance. As mentioned at the outset, the public sector receives somewhat less consideration than the private sector, despite the former's remaining the more important sector, especially regarding factors related to its two-to-one lead in enrollments.[35] Two major reasons account for the degree of imbalance. First, however lacking is the literature on public higher education, it dwarfs the literature on private higher education in Latin America (as it usually does outside the United States). This is true whether one focuses on the nature of autonomy, recruitment to State and private employment, student activism, or indeed most topics relevant to this study. Not surprisingly then, especially given an overwhelmingly public tradition, awareness of the private sector's importance and distinctiveness from the public sector requires documentation built almost from scratch. The sections on public higher education can more often rely in part on previous works and footnotes. Therefore, more effort must be devoted here to the private sector just to help achieve a greater balance of understanding. Second, the private sector generally proves to be more interinstitutionally diverse than the public sector. While great dangers naturally exist in generalizing about either sector, the public sector typically shows more standardization, often tied to an overarching State role. For example, almost all public institutions in Latin America are financed overwhelmingly by the State, while private income profiles are much more institutionally specific.[36]

All that said, the book's focus remains systemic much more than single sectoral.[37] Systemic statements encompass the two sectors together or compare them. And harkening back to the section on extant literature, even the public sector is treated more extensively here than elsewhere on many issues, especially in cross-sectoral as well as cross-national context. In sum, an effort is made toward substantial intersectoral comprehensiveness without reaching for full symmetry sector to sector.

Regarding geographic coverage, the twenty republics fall into four categories. The first includes Brazil, Chile, and Mexico—each given a separate chapter and each illustrating one of the three principal private-public patterns characterizing Latin American higher education. The second category includes Argentina, Colombia, Costa Rica, Peru, and Venezuela. I have drawn widely on these nations in developing the principal themes. The third category trails only by a matter of degree. It includes Bolivia, Cuba, the Dominican Republic, Ecuador, Guatemala, and Uruguay. Finally, the fourth category includes El Salvador, Haiti, Honduras, Nicaragua, Panama, and Paraguay. I have tried to incorporate just enough on these small countries to achieve reasonable regional coverage.[38]

Finally, having highlighted the major phenomena and issues as well as the concepts central to the organization and theoretical significance of this study, chapter 1 now concludes by peering briefly at the chapters that follow. Chapter 2 explores how and why dual sector growth has occurred, giving special emphasis to the disproportionate private surge of recent decades. It also extracts the three key evolutionary waves that have led to the private-public patterns dominant in Latin America today.

Chapters 3 through 5 explore in depth the three major contemporary private-public patterns, moving closer than the other chapters can to the complex richness of detail that usually marks Latin American private and public higher education. Had size alone been the criterion, these chapters would have covered Brazil, Mexico, and Argentina, but the desire to offer the clearest case of these three patterns argued for Chile instead of Argentina. Chile best typifies the first pattern—private-public homogeneity. Homogeneity is, however, an important subpattern throughout most of Latin America. Once especially notable for homogeneity based on the degree of publicness characterizing both sectors, Chile since its right-wing military coup of 1973 became notable for homogeneity based on an unprecedented crusade for systemwide privatization. In contrast, the most noteworthy pattern in most of Latin America, where great social-class stratification is salient, is a private-public distinctiveness with a strong elite private component. Mexico comes closest to full private-public distinctiveness along these lines, allowing us to see the operation of two sectors that have evolved differently and are financed, governed, and functionally oriented very differently. Additionally, Mexico is Latin America's largest nation aside from Brazil, with the largest higher education system outside Brazil. Brazil itself is the only clear case of a third major pattern (with Costa Rica since 1976 coming next closest), where private-public distinctiveness based on private inferiority is dominant. But Brazil's enormous size makes this pattern important, and the pattern is also subsectorally important even in most nations where the Mexican pattern dominates.[39] In short, while there is no typical case in that one system represents a miniature of the whole region, each of the three cases chosen approximates one of three basic private-public patterns that are found in different blends in different systems and together best cover Latin America. Furthermore, the three cases themselves combine to account for fully half the region's enrollments.

Chapter 6 provides a regional overview, drawing on information from individual nations. It weighs the three principal patterns, discussed consecutively in chapters 3 through 5, with some reference to the previously dominant public monopoly pattern. Where do the patterns hold, predominantly and subsectorally? What variations and blends are most salient? If chapter 6 thereby serves as a substantive summary of empirical findings, chapter 7 synthesizes the private-public findings on each of the concepts identified in chapter 1 and subsequently pursued, especially those regarding the State and the private sphere. In short, each chapter tries to make political, economic, and social sense out of the powerful forces that have been transforming Latin American higher education.

2 Private versus Public Growth

ANALYTICAL CATEGORIES

The incredible rise of the private sector—from nonexistence through most of the nineteenth century, to marginality until near the mid-twentieth-century mark, to great significance since then—obviously warrants explanation; in this chapter, therefore, I focus mainly upon it. Nonetheless, the public sector is still the more important one and has itself expanded to an unprecedented degree since midcentury. Moreover, private growth has been integrally related to public growth, so we cannot properly understand the growth of either sector without understanding the growth of the other.

As I pursue middle-range generalizations for analytical purposes, the categories distinguish, more than reality, between the determinants of sectoral genesis and sectoral growth and, subsequently, among the various determinants of sectoral growth. Thus, the categories do not substitute for actual case studies; they build upon them and, in return, should add meaning to them. Dismembering real-world cases allows us to explore each determinant both in depth and cross-nationally. The use of analytical categories should also facilitate future cross-field comparisons (e.g., to secondary education or health care). In this connection, the choice of analytical categories derives largely from emerging theories of why nonprofit organizations arise and grow; one key concept used here can be called "government failure" or "public sector failure," but more on that later. Following the analytical efforts made here, the initial sections of the ensuing three chapters provide three national case studies of sectoral genesis and growth that blend the analytical categories back into real-world contexts.[1]

Chapter 2 is structured around five "waves" of sectoral evolution.[2] For each, both sectoral creation and subsequent growth are considered. The five are as follows: the rise of fused private-public colonial universities; the rise of public monopolies; the rise of private, religious universities; the rise of secular, private, elite universities; and the rise of secular, private, nonelite institutions. I refer to the three waves of private growth as wave I (Catholic), wave II (elite), and wave III (demand absorbing).

There is some evolutionary flow through the five waves, although I hasten to add that this does not imply a fixed order. Fused private-public universities generally arose in the colonial period, giving way to public monopolies during the nineteenth century. Until well into the twentieth century the major exceptions to public monopolies were several Catholic universities, some of which, especially over time, provided only limited distinctiveness from the public sector. Therefore, private-public distinctiveness arose mostly with the emergence, particularly since the early 1960's, of secular, private institutions. Elite alternatives to the public sector have been most important, but another wave of private institutions has offered lower-quality alternatives. This wave has usually begun shortly after the elite wave, but the two tend to grow simultaneously. Again, the five waves map out a general trend, not a predetermined nor a definitive route for each nation; exceptions as well as more typical cases are discussed throughout this chapter. That said, most nations have consecutively experienced most of the waves.

The different waves discussed in this chapter will logically determine the structure of subsequent chapters because the waves have strongly influenced contemporary private-public patterns (in finance, governance, and function). Different patterns are associated with different blends of waves. Consequently, we will understand the cross-national variation in contemporary private-public patterns largely in terms of the relative strength of different waves in different nations.

The first two waves produced the historically dominant patterns. The colonial universities created as fused private-public entities dominated higher education for centuries. Similarly, the public monopoly pattern dominated throughout most of the nineteenth and part of the twentieth century. However, because the second pattern replaced the first, and because only Cuba and Uruguay retain a public monopoly today, these two patterns do not merit a separate chapter here. The three basic patterns that do (chapters 3 through 5) will each be understood largely in terms of the special importance of a particular private wave; however, most nations are found to show somewhat mixed patterns that are understood by blends of waves. The three basic patterns analyzed in this work are crucial—partly because they are dominant in certain systems, partly because they are subdominant in others. The public-monopoly pattern, by definition, is not subdominant in any nation. Nevertheless, the rise of public monopolies has left a vital imprint on almost all national systems, for these systems still have important public sectors. If contemporary patterns apparently depend on subsequent private waves, it is because the public sector became omnipresent early on, though of course the public sector's continuing evolution has also shaped contemporary private-public patterns.

In sum, as almost all Latin American contemporary higher education systems are characterized by private-public distinctiveness, the nature of that distinctiveness depends greatly on the different waves of growth. This chapter analyzes why and how each wave arose and spread. As such, it sets the stage for ensuing chapters to pursue what sorts of systems these waves have helped shape.

The Genesis of Public and Private Sectors
Private-Public Fusion

Spanish America's colonial institutions of higher education were neither private nor public according to contemporary terminology. The key factor in preventing either privateness or publicness from dominating these institutions was the Church-State relationship. Only when a far greater degree of differentiation was achieved between these two central institutions would our terms *private* and *public* become meaningful. Few people in either the university, the Church, or the State believed that a basic private-public cleavage existed or should exist. This colonial perspective may be understood by what many have referred to as the holistic or corporatist or organic-statist nature of Spanish America's colonial societies.[3] To generalize broadly, the guiding colonial notion was that the driving forces toward the good society should not be competing organizations, plural groups, free-market mechanisms, or class conflict as much as State action united with Church action.

Spanish America's universities were created to serve the Church and State simultaneously. They often functioned by the authority of papal bulls and royal charters. First to receive the papal bull was the University of Santo Domingo (1538); first to receive royal authorization was Peru's University of San Marcos (1551); and first to open was Mexico's Royal and Pontifical University (1553). It was common for the Crown to authorize the creation of universities that were then retroactively sanctioned by the Pope. Sometimes the sequence was inverted. More important, religious groups and the Crown generally worked together to create universities, regardless of which authority gave first official sanction. If some of Europe's early universities were largely self-created, Spanish America's were created by the State united with the Church.

Naturally, the character of Spanish America's colonial universities was strongly influenced by the mother country's universities. The first Peruvian and Mexican universities, which themselves became models for subsequent colonial universities, were closely patterned after the University of Salamanca. Beyond the importance of Spanish institutions among Europe's leading higher education centers, especially once Spain became the world's leading power (and colonized the New World), I emphasize here their organic ties to both Church and State. Lanning describes the University of Salamanca as both "royal" and "essentially a cathedral school . . . little less than the oracle of Catholic Europe"; the word *claustro* (cloister), used for its academic community, "testifies to the ancient connection between Spanish universities and cathedrals."[4]

Although the State granted the legal authority, indeed owned the colonial universities, religious authority was also manifest. Such authority was often expressed through the *maestrescuela*, a liason officer between the university and the Church. The maestrescuela had certain powers, surpassing even the rector's, over examinations. In other matters he was a sort of second in command behind the rector. Nearly all rectors were clergy. Most of the universities were organized by religious orders, especially Jesuits and Dominicans, and these orders provided not only most of the administrators but also most of the teachers. Students were prepared primarily for either of two employment posts—the State bureaucracy or the priesthood. Graduation was a religious as well as an academic event. Compared to Spain's mother institution in Salamanca, theology played an even greater role in the colonies, law a lesser role. Some fused private-public universities actually grew out of sectarian institutions (e.g., the University of Santo Domingo grew from a Dominican institution). Sánchez sums up the general picture by depicting a unified trio of "Viceroy, Archbishop and Rector, as if to say, Power, Dogma and Knowledge."[5]

Surely conflicts arose between Church and State, just as they arose between Church and university, and State and university. I briefly mention five qualifications to the State-Church-university trinity image: (1) The university was one of the few colonial institutions to be granted autonomy, though both Crown and Church frequently violated it. (2) Rivalries occurred among religious orders as well as between the orders and both the State and the dominant Church itself. (3) While most of the major universities had State and religious affiliations, some of the minor ones were more tied to either the Crown or the Church (or religious orders); numerous seminaries were, of course, more religious than State oriented. (4) The Crown generally held the upper hand in most major universities, at times even tampering with clerical monopolies in high administrative positions and asserting itself when push came to shove, suggesting that it was the stronger partner even when State-Church harmony held. (5) As we will see, Church influence began to wane in the last few decades before independence.[6] Nonetheless, these qualifications did not generally raise questions of separation between a private religious realm and a public

29

secular realm, as would arise in the nineteenth century. In contrast to later periods, there was little perception of separateness. If Spain's colonial institutions of higher education existed primarily to foster religious training, this was regarded as a service to the State; religion was a holy bond cementing the Church-State-university trio. These societies were, after all, more fused than those that were to follow them. Nurturing a relatively homogeneous elite for one purpose was simultaneously nurturing it for an entwined network of purposes. Nothing could more parsimoniously symbolize the State-Church-university tie than the very nomenclature of most of the major universities: Royal and Pontifical (e.g., of Mexico, of San Francisco in Bolivia, of Santo Domingo, of Saint Xavier in Panama, of Caracas). In sum, to call these colonial institutions either private or public would probably confuse more than it would describe. Private-public was not a major concern.

Two and one-half centuries elapsed between the opening of the first royal and pontifical university and the end of the Spanish colonial era. By the end, Spanish America had roughly twenty-five universities—ten "major" and fifteen "minor." Much depends on definitions: a few of the latter were universities in name only, while certain "colleges" could grant degrees, and naturally there were many seminaries. Mexico, for example, had about forty college seminaries, but only one degree-granting university.[7] Political independence from Spain would mark a major turning point. Fused universities would give way to public universities.

Private-Public Separation: Public Monopoly

Whereas Spain provided the model for the colonial universities, France provided the major European inspiration once the colonies gained independence. The French Revolution had attacked centuries of Church monopoly in French higher education. Napoléon then established the very public university form that bears his name. In fact, French influence preceded Spanish America's independence period, and by the late colonial period private-public consciousness and conflict grew beyond the embryonic stage. The 1767 expulsion from Spanish America of the Jesuits, leaders in education, was accompanied by some increase in academic freedom but, mostly by Carlos III's increased State control over the university. The State assumed a more active role in choosing administrators, curricula, textbooks, and so forth, as it moved toward standardizing, centralizing, and bureaucratizing higher education. "The university and seminaries took bifurcating roads, following the pattern of Church-State tensions."[8] Especially with the coming of national independence, the universities plunged headlong toward publicness.

30

Private versus Public Growth

A major battle of nineteenth-century Spanish America, waged in nation after nation, pitted liberals against conservatives in respectively promoting and opposing secularism. Education was one of the most crucial institutional arenas in which this battle was fought. Liberals were strongly influenced by the North American and especially the French revolutions, by the Enlightenment, and by a new faith in reason rather than in faith itself. They advocated State control over education and repeatedly demanded the banishment of Church influences. They wanted public universities as organizational alternatives to seminaries, but mostly as alternatives to fused private-public universities. This stand was particularly championed later in the century by Radical parties associated with Freemasonry. Also later in the century the philosophy of positivism powerfully reinforced the notion that scientific progress was inherently incompatible with religious interference. Traditional conservatives, on the other hand, generally wanted to preserve clerical influence and maintain the close Church-State-university nexus. They generally lost.

Public universities were created throughout Spanish America. Ecuador's three colonial universities, each founded by a different religious order, became one public university. The University of San Carlos in Guatemala, created by the Crown and retroactively recognized by the pope, transformed itself into a public institution (1832), although it underwent a brief religious restoration before being designated the national university. Within Central America, Nicaragua and Honduras followed similar paths.[9]

Clerics were often purged from the professoriate; faculties of theology were closed. National universities were publicly funded and controlled. They were oriented to the professions, and increasingly toward secular ones such as civil law. The earlier trio was becoming a State-university duo. The State had changed, and it tried to recreate the university in its own image—an image that no longer fit the Church's. All these changes followed the Continental model. As García Laguardia has summarized the change from the colonial to the independence era: "The colonial universities disappeared violently or slowly during the nineteenth century and were replaced by federal schools, tied to the central government's program of national unity, abandoning theology as the center of interest, and substituting the liberal professions. . . . As long as the liberal regimes maintained their purity, the State exercised an educational monopoly and closed the door to the different religious orders."[10]

The national universities generally became the State's higher education arm. In Central America, for example, the universities of Costa Rica, Guatemala, Honduras, and Nicaragua all held State monopolies on the authority to grant academic degrees and professional licenses. Where professional colleges existed they were linked to these universities and relied on

31

their degree- and license-granting authority. Beyond this, national universities frequently functioned as State educational ministries. Uruguay's University of the Republic, created in 1833, supervised all educational levels until 1877, and only in 1935 lost its authority over the secondary and preparatory (preuniversity) levels.[11] Still today some universities control the preparatory level.

For nearly a century and a half public predominance was overwhelming and sometimes practically unchallenged. Even when public monopolies finally faced serious challenges, the claim to "national" status provided a weapon in rearguard efforts to deny places to aspiring private institutions. However, just as there were some qualifications to fused private-public predominance, so there were some to public predominance as well. First, several newly independent nations did not create universities for some time. Honduras's National University did not open until 1881. At the extreme, Haiti did not boast a university until 1944. Second, in certain nations, such as Mexico and Venezuela, the national universities were sometimes closed down. Third, the university reform movement begun in Córdoba, Argentina, in 1918 sometimes pressed for university autonomy. Where this reform took hold, partial substitution of autonomous governance for statist governance became the rule. Fourth, two Catholic universities (Chile's and Peru's) and two secular universities (Colombia's) were created in the period between 1810 and 1930. Fifth, seminaries and private colleges were widespread. In fact, "universities" did not dominate Peruvian higher education, for example, until the second half of the nineteenth century.

A sixth qualification is that the Church retained a role in the established universities of a few countries. In Guatemala, the conservative restoration of 1839 led to a concordat (an agreement between the Vatican and a State regarding the regulation of ecclesiastical matters) and the 1855 redesignation of the Pontifical University of San Carlos, although the triumph of Guatemala's liberals later in the century brought the institution its "national" status under State control. But it was Colombia that provided the prime example of extended Church authority in higher education.

Even allowing for all relevant qualifications, the shift from the fused private-public to the public-monopoly pattern was widespread both in structural and geographical scope. As the State separated itself from the Church, so the concepts of private and public became relevant. Universities became public. But this destruction of the privateness which had previously blended so naturally with the publicness sowed the seeds for the eventual emergence of truly private institutions. If the Church-State separation gave rise to a private-public distinction, it remained for the private sector to be allowed its own institutional expression.

The Catholic Reaction: Wave I

The Church was slow to achieve this institutional expression, to work its way back into the university sphere. It was the major force in the creation of Latin America's first private universities, but there were few private universities. Even by liberal count, only six Latin American private universities predated this century. Only two existed outside Colombia—one in Bolivia and one in Chile. By 1920 only eight had been created, by 1930 only eleven—and still only four countries were represented.[12] But these figures include three universities (one Bolivian, two Colombian) that either did not function in the twentieth century or became public. So the picture was even more exclusively public than these figures imply. Outside Colombia, Latin America entered the twentieth century with only one private university (the Catholic University of Chile, 1888); only one other was added prior to the 1930s (the Catholic University of Peru, 1917). Not until the 1930s, when fundamental political-economic changes swept several nations, and not until later in most nations did the Church cease relying principally on its seminaries for its higher educational needs. For subsequent decades and its "reopening to the world," the Church would need institutions devoted to a wide set of academic disciplines and to religious influences on, or integration with, other pursuits. It would need universities.

The reopening was made possible in part by changes in the Church inspired by European developments; even in France the Church (by 1850) had regained some of its higher education power previously lost in the revolution. Also important, however, was the changing role of the State. Catholic universities were able to emerge partly because supportive conservative political forces were still strong but also partly because liberals had won enough victories so that religious higher education no longer posed a great threat. Church and State were substantially more separate than in the colonial era; while the Church still had enough strength to sustain a university sector, it could no longer seriously rival the dominant public sector.[13] Similarly, as our three main cases and others will show, Catholic universities were often "second-best solutions" once backers gave up on securing sufficiently Christian public universities.

Church initiatives were spurred and ironically aided by the ascendance, within the public sector, of progressive forces basically antagonistic to the Church. The Córdoba reforms beginning in 1918 indirectly facilitated the creation of Catholic universities. Even if autonomy was not an initial preoccupation, it came to be identified with Córdoba movements, and some national universities became more private in governance; equally important, the proponents of choice and pluralism in higher education received a major boost. Prospective founders of private-Church institutions would have a symbolic precedent with which to petition liberal political regimes, as traditional governance patterns came into question. Any retreat from the Continental principle of purely public systems dependent on national ministries was a potential victory for private higher education. For decades, that usually meant Catholic universities.

Whatever the paradoxical role of progressive politics in promoting Catholic university creation, the Church obviously was the central institutional actor. Seen in the context of more than a century on the defensive, Catholic universities were organized religious responses to the secular nature of the State's public universities. Ecuador provides a good example. The liberal revolution of 1895 achieved Church-State separation and subordinated the Church to the State in educational policy. As late as 1945 the constitution provided for secular education and contained strong antiprivate provisions; moreover, 1945 saw constitutional adoption of Córdoba-style reforms. An immediate backlash followed in 1946. The 1946 Constitution supported parents' rights to choose their children's schools, allowed an increased Church role in primary and secondary education, and opened the way for public funding of private schools. And against the opposition of the Left, led by the national university and the Liberal and Communist parties, the Conservative party and the Church won an important battle: the Catholic University of Ecuador was established (in Quito, 1946) to immunize students from the "virus of atheism" that had triumphed in the public university.[14]

Although religious factors were the most important in the founding of the first wave of private universities, other factors were at work as well. These first private universities were the result of reactions against the secularization not only of the public university but also of the State's role in society. Certainly this was explicit in the founding of Chile's (1888) and Argentina's (1959) first Catholic universities. Reflecting the "born-again" character of postindependence Catholic universities, some were self-conscious descendants of colonial ancestors.

The Colombian case is interesting, both for its atypical and typical features; after deviating significantly from regional patterns, it came to parallel many of them. Political independence had sparked the usual efforts to replace fused colonial universities with public ones. One product was the University of Cauca (1827). But the kingpin public liberal institution, the National University, could not be firmly implanted until 1867. Nor was public predominance insured at that point. Instead, reflecting the well-known strength of the Colombian Church, a concordat was established providing that public education at all levels be geared to Catholic dogma and that, for example, bishops could chose school texts for each diocese. Daniel

Levine has called this concordat, not dissolved until 1973, "a model of the traditional ideal of Christendom—complete Church-State integration."[15] In a sense, then, fused private-public universities survived Colombia's colonial era, although there was now definite awareness that private and public were relevant and separable concepts, pointedly mixed more than naturally blended. This unusual State posture understandably provoked an unusual private initiative. Colombia's first truly private universities would not be Catholic reactions to the dominance of truly public universities; instead they were laical anticlerical reactions to the persisting dominance of fused universities. The Externado University was established (1887) just shortly after the concordat; it was closed by the State in 1895, but reopened in 1918. It was followed in 1923 by the Libre University.[16]

Only when Colombian Church-State relations moved a little closer to the regional norm did Colombian higher education do likewise. In 1930 the Liberal party rose to power for the first time in a half century. President Alfonso López soon amended the 1886 constitutional provisions facilitating Church control in education. Immediately the Church reacted by creating its own universities. The Javeriana University was reopened in the 1930s, more than 150 years after the fateful Jesuit expulsion. The new Javeriana's main mission was religious service through the study of theology and canonical law. The founding decree of the Bolivariana University, created in response to rising alienation from the public Antioquia University, declared: "There is an urgent need to create in our Republic of Colombia a fully Catholic center of education that juxtaposes the light of truth and Christian consequence to the cloud of errors and impieties that today threaten not only peace and social tranquility, but society's very existence, and that tend to turn our homeland into a lake of tears and blood." Between 1933 and 1936 the private sector's share of total enrollments jumped from 12 to 35 percent, where it more or less held for two decades.[17] Plainly, the creation of Colombia's Catholic universities was the Church's response to its failure to preserve its influence within the public sector. This response also plainly illustrates how the creation of Catholic universities might reflect declining as much as increasing Church influence with the State. The private wave that swept Colombian higher education starting in the 1930s was not truly its first, but the characteristics strongly paralleled those found in the first private waves occurring simultaneously in sister nations.

Data contrasting "early" and "late" private universities show how much Catholic universities constitute a first wave. In Bolivia, Panama, and Paraguay, the sole private university created was Catholic. Ecuador's first two were Catholic (1946–62), but two of its next three were not (1966–71). Venezuela simultaneously created a Catholic and a secular university (1953), followed by four secular ones (1965–79). Eleven of Brazil's first twelve private universities created before 1962 were Catholic, and the twelfth was Protestant; yet each of the next nine (1962–70) was secular. The first private universities of Nicaragua, Guatemala, and the Dominican Republic were Catholic, but at least the next two, three, and six, respectively, were not. Chile's first private university was Catholic (1888), but only two of its next five were (1919–56). Peru's first private university was Catholic (1917), but only one of its subsequent eleven was (1958–69). Six of Argentina's initial seven (1959) were Catholic, but only five of its next seventeen were (1960–68).[18]

Except for Colombia, Mexico, and Costa Rica, all private university sectors in Latin America began with Catholic universities.[19] Moreover, the concept of a Catholic first wave makes sense not only because the first private universities in almost all nations were Catholic, but also because so few of the private universities created after the first wave have been Catholic. An indicator of the movement from wave I toward wave II lay in the creation of private universities with only limited ties to religious orders, relegating "Christian inspiration" to one goal among several. The crest of wave I—based on Catholic universities with formal ties to religious organizations, most often the national Church, and frequently also the Vatican—occurred in the 1930s through the 1950s, spilling over into the early 1960s. Such universities have not been created since.

The nature of the dialectic process through which Latin America's private sectors developed from fused settings may be nicely summed up by quick contrast to the emergence of U.S. private and public sectors. As in Latin America, U.S. colonial higher education institutions were basically fused private-public. Again, when one sectoral tendency began to emerge and assert itself, it triggered a defensive reaction by the excluded tendency. A major difference was that in the United States, privateness gained the early lead and triggered a public reaction (later followed by a more explicit and self-conscious private reaction to public sector development). In Latin America the dialectic worked in the other direction—and was much clearer. Latin America's fused private-public period lasted considerably longer, followed by a far stronger domination by one sector, in this case the public sector. In turn, the second sector, in this case the private sector, had a much more difficult time initially establishing itself, and then it much more clearly grew in opposition to the existing sector.

Public Sector Evolution: Toward Perceived "Failure"

Once created, private institutions can grow from many of the same social and demographic forces that fuel public sector growth. However, I concentrate more on the distinctive causes of sectoral expansion, especially private expansion. These distinctive causes have been responsible for the creation of many private *institutions*, even though they were not as important as religion in the original creation of private *sectors*. Employing the concept of "public sector failure," the religious factor could be seen in terms of actors' disenchantment with a failure to provide sufficiently spiritual education. The more general social failure considered below is the perceived failure to maintain the degree of class differentiation that elites demand; subsequently, perceived political and economic failures are analyzed.[20]

Theories of public sector failure are especially appropriate here because I am dealing with an empirical change in preferences for sectors, not "explaining" the rise of one sector merely by the "failure" of another to emerge. Government failure and market failure are often invoked as nonempirical explanations for why one sector rather than another exists; failure in such cases refers to being uninvolved (e.g., market failure to explain why policing is a public function), not to trying and losing. In contrast, what follows specifically concerns a shift from one sector (public) to another (private). Moreover, the shift explains the rise of the private sector not just (negatively) by perceived failures in the public sector but (positively) by identifying the actors (students, Church, businesses, government) involved in creating the private alternatives.

To look at the proportional share of enrollments absorbed by the private sector is to see only part of the story. To be sure, Spanish America's private sector nearly tripled its share of total enrollments from 1955 to 1975 (7 to 19 percent). It is startling, however, that the sector would even maintain its percentage during a period of unprecedented growth in the public sector. Newly mobilized groups come from less-privileged economic backgrounds and go overwhelmingly to the (free) public universities. Most Spanish American private sectors that have at least held their proportional shares of enrollments have done so via a massive shift from the social sectors that have for some time counted on public higher education as their privileged domain. It is this shift that basically explains the private sector's ability to expand significantly in absolute terms, and proportional growth is especially remarkable.

This dialectical approach to explaining sectoral growth demands analysis of changes in the public sector to understand private sector evolution. The main roots of Spanish America's private sector growth are found in prior and coterminous public sector growth. Only when the public sector itself changes dramatically does a strong felt need for private alternatives arise. I first consider the previous elite functioning of the public sector and then its spectacular transforming growth.

Traditional Public Sector Exclusiveness

Higher education systems are generally established, in part, to nourish elites. In the Spanish American colonies especially, this process had a religious component overlapping the socioeconomic status (SES) component. Although Spanish America's newly independent nations built monopolistic public systems, jettisoning the religious orientation, their universities clearly still catered to only a small SES range. "Public" universities directly served only a fraction of the public at large. For all their antipathies, the sometimes violent nineteenth-century struggles between Liberal and Conservative parties were basically intraclass. The (upper-class or sometimes upper-middle-class) elite had, in the public university, an institutional vehicle for its maintenance and reproduction. Only later, after its exclusive claim on the public university ended, would it feel compelled to seek alternative, private institutions to maintain class differentiation. Free choice became a preoccupation only when the public sector became less effective for the elites.

Throughout the nineteenth and into the twentieth century, Spanish America's public universities provided elite certification for social status and economic reward in much the manner widely described in European contexts. Max Weber noted how the university was the nineteenth-century equivalent to the outdated "proof of ancestry" and how degrees solidified "claims for connubium with the notables. . . . and, above all, claims to the monopolization of socially and economically advantageous positions."[21] Just as Fritz Ringer argued that the European university often became the main instrument for preindustrial or early industrial elites to transfer high status to their offspring in industrial society, so Rudolph Atcon observed for Latin America that professional diplomas "served both as a key to all dominant positions in the civil service and as an effective block to close these same opportunities to all non-holders of such a title. *A new oligarchy was thus established based on the university degree*" (Atcon's emphasis).[22]

A true measure of the elite mission of Latin America's public higher education is revealed in enrollment figures. As late as 1950, when the United States enrolled 1,740 students per 100,000 inhabitants, Latin America enrolled only 167. Latin American higher education did not have to perform a SES differentiation function since that had already been accomplished at lower educational levels. Only 3.1 percent of the cohort group was enrolled in higher education as late as 1960. Even secondary education was quite exclusive, with only about 15 percent (1960) of the relevant age group enrolled. (See tables 2.2 and 2.3 below.) The more European orientation was very important because secondary education was traditionally distinct from primary education and scholastically rather than practically or technically inclined; its major function was preparation for higher education, a luxurious route reserved almost exclusively for the elite.

Additional protection was afforded by the dual, private-public, secondary structure. Class differentiation by utilization of private alternatives certainly manifested itself at the primary and secondary levels before it did so at the higher education level. Many parents "saved" their children from the perceived inferior quality and/or lower-class composition of public schools. Indeed, whereas the elite could count on free public higher education, it often relied on relatively expensive private secondary education. The private sector has much stronger historic roots in Spanish America's secondary rather than higher education, partly because public secondary education could not always be as elite as public higher education. What better evidence that public higher education served the elite than that families willing to pay for an alternative to even the markedly elite public secondary system would feel comfortable with the public higher education system? And even though many of the private primary schools established as religious sanctuaries from public secularism were not superior in academic quality, overall private sector superiority has been the rule at that level as well.

The private sector not only guaranteed class differentiation at the secondary level itself, it reinforced institutional tracking patterns toward higher education. In fact, both private secondary and even primary sectors clearly funneled the elite toward the top. Colombia's less than 20 percent of primary enrollments in the private sector provided the majority of university entrants; the two most prestigious private universities, Los Andes and the Javeriana, drew more than 85 percent of their entrants (1964) from there. Even Colombia's National University drew more than 60 percent from both private primary and private secondary backgrounds. In Uruguay, where only about 14 percent of the secondary school enrollment was in the private sector, 28 percent of the entering (public) university class came from that sector.[23]

Thus, only recently was there much felt need in Latin America for sectoral differentiation in higher education. Even in Argentina, boasting one of the region's most developed higher education systems, it was not until the 1960s that invidious institutional differentiation clearly broke a tradition of relative interinstitutional similarity.[24] In most of the region, higher education remained almost exclusively for the elite well into this century. Universities required only narrow, moderately deep bases of support. Political regimes were either authoritarian or democratic with rather narrow bases; usually only a small percentage of the population was politically influential.

Equity was certainly not a major issue in higher education. And until the social base expanded, elites felt little need for private-public choice.

Public Sector Growth

Public sector exclusiveness was transformed under a torrent of expanding enrollments. While the transformation hit different nations at different times and with different intensities, its regional impact was obvious. The great boom clearly came after 1940, overlapping the period of private boom.

According to UDUAL data, nearly 60 percent of the 174 public universities in existence by 1970 were created after 1940, nearly 50 percent after 1950, and 30 percent after 1960. Private university proliferation was even sharper. The comparable figures for the 113 private universities are an impressive 90 percent, 80 percent, and more than 50 percent. Data on institutional proliferation are paralleled by data on enrollment growth. We have seen that only 167 students per 100,000 inhabitants were enrolled in 1950, but that figure already represents "takeoff." As late as 1890 the figure had been 33, and by 1940 still only 85; thus the figure nearly doubled in the 1940s alone. By 1960 it reached 250, and by 1970, 469.[25]

Table 2.1 shows that, as late as 1965, Latin American enrollment rates barely exceeded those for the developing world in general and were but a fourth of European rates. By 1980, however, Latin American rates exceeded twice those for the developing world and approached two-thirds of

Table 2.1 Worldwide Higher Education Enrollment Ratios, 1960–1980

Year	Latin America	Europe	Developing Nations	Developed Nations	World
1960	3.0	10.2	2.1	13.1	6.2
1965	4.2	16.5	3.3	19.6	9.0
1970	6.4	17.5	4.4	23.4	11.2
1975	11.8	20.4	6.1	28.3	13.5
1980[a]	14.9	22.8	7.2	31.0	14.5

SOURCE: UNESCO, *Statistical Yearbook 1981* (Paris: UNESCO, 1981), pp. II 35–II 36.

NOTES: UNESCO bases ratios on the total higher education enrollments divided by the total population in the five years beyond the normal graduation age for secondary school students. See p. II 3 for further notes. These comparisons should be handled with some skepticism. Different nations define higher education more strictly than others. Some Latin American nations probably include "short courses" not generally included by European nations. Also, "easy access" can "inflate" Latin America's first-year class, many members of which will not remain enrolled for long or will not attend courses.

a. Many of the component national figures predate 1980; UNESCO used them in the absence of 1980 data but they naturally underestimate growth.

Europe's. While European rates had slightly more than doubled from 1960 to 1980, Latin America's had jumped fivefold. Of course Latin America started with a smaller base (although larger than that for the rest of the developing world). Latin America did not catch up to Europe in quantitative terms only because European growth was also remarkable, albeit less so. Nonetheless, Latin America's kaleidoscopic change not only narrowed the gap but also represented a greater SES transformation.

In fact, as table 2.2 shows, several Latin American nations now either hold their own by European standards or come close. We also see that enormous variation remains within Latin America regarding the percentage

Table 2.2 Higher Education Enrollments, 1960–1979

Country	1960	1970	1975	LAD[a]
Argentina	11.8	15.2	25.3	21.9 (1978)
Bolivia	3.6	7.5	11.0	12.6 (1976)
Brazil	1.6	5.2	11.2	11.0 (1977)
Chile	4.0	9.8	14.9	11.9 (1979)
Colombia	1.7	4.7	8.0	10.2 (1979)
Costa Rica	4.8	10.2	16.5	24.4 (1979)
Cuba	3.3	3.7	11.0	19.2 (1979)
Dominican Republic	1.3	6.5	10.0	—[b]
Ecuador	2.6	7.6	8.7	—[c]
El Salvador	1.1	3.3	7.0	7.9 (1978)
Guatemala	1.6	3.7	4.3	5.5 (1978)
Haiti	0.5	0.2	0.4	0.9 (1978)
Honduras	1.0	2.0	4.6	8.0 (1979)
Mexico	2.6	6.1	9.0	11.8 (1978)
Nicaragua	1.2	5.7	6.7	—[b]
Panama	4.6	7.2	19.8	20.4 (1978)
Paraguay	2.4	4.3	6.3	7.7 (1978)
Peru	3.6	11.0	15.1	16.5 (1978)
Uruguay	7.8	9.8	12.9	17.8 (1977)
Venezuela	4.3	10.1	19.5	21.1 (1978)
Latin America	3.1	6.8	11.7	—

SOURCES: For 1960–75, James W. Wilkie, ed., *Statistical Abstract of Latin America* (Los Angeles: UCLA Latin American Center Publications, 1980), vol. 20, p. 123. The latest available data come from UNESCO, *Statistical Yearbook 1981* (Paris: UNESCO, 1981), pp. III 46–III 56. UNESCO also shows 1970 and 1975 data, and these differ slightly from data in table 2.2; thus, comparisons between 1975 and LAD are hampered.

NOTES: Enrollments are indicated as shares of the population aged 20 to 24. The source for 1960–75 refers to "students enrolled," which could include some in the age cohort group (20–24) enrolled at the secondary level; but the source draws on U.N. data which (as in our own LAD column) make clear that only students at the indicated level are included. The figures in table 2.2 are extremely close to those found in U.N. publications.

a. Latest available data.

b. No data listed after 1970.

c. UNESCO gives a 34.7 percent figure, which must be ignored.

41

of the relevant age group enrolled, ranging from Argentina's 25.3 to Haiti's 0.4 percent (1975). However, except for Haiti, every nation's 1975 ratio exceeds the 1960 regional average; in fact, all at least nearly match the 1960 leaders, save Argentina and Uruguay.

One of the main causes of this mostly public boom is population growth. Although it does not by itself explain cohort percentage growth, it obviously produces an impact on higher education enrollments, thus jeopardizing any elite flavor that depends on small size. Latin America's population increased from roughly 125 million in 1940 to over 200 million by 1960, to over 250 million by 1970, and to over 300 million by 1975 (with roughly 350 million by 1980).[26] At least in the 1950s and 1960s, Latin America was the fastest growing region in the world. More specifically, enrollments of pre-university-age youth soared, as table 2.3 shows. Compared to 15 percent for 1960, 42 percent of youth aged fourteen to nineteen were enrolled in 1975. However unimpressive the 1975 figure remains, it reflects the huge increase in Latin America's pool of potential university students. From 1960 to 1977,

Table 2.3 Secondary School Enrollments, 1960–1975

Country	1960	1970	1975
Argentina	27.4	38.1	48.3
Bolivia	11.6	13.0	18.7
Brazil	13.6	32.7	61.8
Chile	25.6	25.0	32.3
Colombia	12.5	25.9	40.5
Costa Rica	18.4	32.8	49.5
Cuba	14.4	29.6	50.4
Dominican Rep.	13.0	19.4	26.8
Ecuador	12.6	28.5	38.9
El Salvador	11.5	17.0	31.0
Guatemala	6.4	10.9	15.8
Haiti	3.8	5.1	5.0
Honduras	6.8	13.3	17.2
Mexico	11.9	22.5	33.2
Nicaragua	6.3	18.9	23.0
Panama	29.8	43.0	57.6
Paraguay	11.6	17.6	20.6
Peru	16.1	35.6	49.3
Uruguay	38.0	60.8	66.8
Venezuela	21.1	35.8	36.6
Latin America	15.0	28.7	42.0

SOURCE: See table 2.2

NOTES: Enrollments are indicated as shares of the population aged 14 to 19. See *Notes* of table 2.2.

enrollments doubled at the primary level, increased fivefold at the secondary level, and increased eightfold at the higher level (which naturally started with the smallest base). Whereas higher education comprised only 1.8 percent of total educational enrollments in 1960, it comprised 5.4 percent by 1977 (4,267,000/78,658,000). Education has expanded even faster than population, and higher education has expanded even faster than education in general.[27]

The growth in public enrollments at all levels stemmed not only from population increases but also from economic development and the supportive tenets of human capital theory (predicting excellent rates of return on expansion). All this proved especially relevant to the middle classes. They demanded inclusion in the traditional privileges provided by the public universities. Thus it was that Argentina, often cited within Latin America for its relatively early and strong middle-class growth, would develop easily the largest university system, holding more than one in three Latin American enrollments even as late as 1955. Put succinctly in class terms, the public university became predominantly middle-class oriented. Contemporary analysts have estimated that roughly 85 to 90 percent of Latin America's public university students come from the middle class, although such findings obviously depend on definition.[28] This broadening has followed a bumpy course, but the 1918 Argentine student movement provides a benchmark. The ensuing Córdoba reforms are consensually seen as expressions of the rising middle class. Increasingly important in many nations, the middle class represented a strong force for expanding public education, and thus its own opportunities. Whereas nineteenth-century liberals had supported public education but were chiefly concerned with the elite, twentieth-century liberals, supported by Radical parties, pressed for great expansion of coverage by the public sector. Especially since World War II, ideologies of development identified education as a key component of the program for progress toward the good society. Put pejoratively, the "mass university" often became, in Stephen Spender's words, "a status symbol not only for students but for countries: like space rockets for the two great powers and airlines and dams for the small ones."[29] States and societies in general, and the higher education field very much in particular, became committed to "democratizing" ideologies. By the 1960s, rhetorical commitment to working-class entry became common, but policy results occurred only in certain pockets. Despite limits, however, equity considerations became policy relevant. If higher education had been effective for a tiny minority, the new hope was to make it effective for the middle class as well. This shift in focus from a very small to a sizeable minority would have profound educational, social, and political ramifications.

43

Institutional Proliferation

As others have argued, a system's growth in numbers can stimulate structural differentiation, including institutional proliferation.[30] Throughout Latin America, growth indeed stimulated structural differentiation, including the creation of new faculties and institutes within universities. Only Uruguay avoided institutional proliferation. Proliferation affected both private and public sectors, provided of course that a private sector already existed or was created. (See Appendix C.) In another sense, however, institutional proliferation carried sectorally specific connotations.

Much of the institutional proliferation occurred on the geographic periphery as alternatives to the central public universities. Some of these alternatives are private but most (in Spanish America) are public provincial institutions. Provinces and municipalities want the prestige of having their own universities. The provinces of Argentina, Colombia, Mexico, and Peru have lobbied central governments effectively for "theirs." Indeed, one of the most common self-criticisms heard about Latin American higher education systems is that they have grown so "politically," based on demands more than on rational central planning. Most Latin American nations have seen public proliferation without formidable central regulatory restraint. In the Colombian case, total enrollments shot up three and one half times during the 1960s, while the national universities only doubled their enrollment. (And private institutions were created without the need to meet any licensing or any legal norms at all.) According to Pelczar, what occurred in Colombia was "unplanned and haphazard differentiation," as student pressures forced the State's hand.[31] Such accounts should not suggest, however, that the State is powerless. Even though its autonomy may be restricted, the State is not often a completely dependent actor with regard to expansion. For example, the Venezuelan and Peruvian States sometimes assumed the initiative, to bolster their legitimacy, in establishing provincial institutions.[32]

Whatever the complex blend of causes, traditional Latin American corporatist beliefs in the creation of carefully centralized systems, so prevalent with the Continental model of a supreme national university, caved in under an avalanche of pluralist institutional proliferation probably more akin to the historical U.S. than Spanish American mode. No longer could opponents of private sector growth invidiously contrast the supposed ivory-tower order, harmony, and unity of an existing, centrally planned, public system to the alleged dangers of a widely uncontrollable private sector. Thus, proliferation within the public sector undermined the sector's defense of its unisector monopoly or near monopoly.

Although proliferation holds dangers for the public sector's dominance over the private sector, the public sector cannot easily escape proliferation. After all, proliferation is a logical consequence of enrollment growth. This growth, in turn, is the logical outgrowth of social, economic, and political forces that rarely have been squelched except under extremely repressive political regimes. If enrollment growth is allowed, the State has two fundamental alternatives—and both generally favor disproportionate private growth.

One option is to maintain the orderly, elite, exclusive character of the public system. To accommodate growing enrollments, new institutions—private ones—must be allowed to emerge and expand. The private sector becomes the nonelite or "mass" outlet, as in the wave III growth discussed below. The second option is to accept huge growth within the public sector. Insofar as the public sector then tries to "protect" its flagship universities by funneling growth into new institutions, it runs into the dangers inherent in proliferation. On the other hand, insofar as the public sector accepts huge growth and change in its flagship institutions, it accelerates the elite's flight toward the private sector. For not only the public sector in general but its leading universities in particular lose much of their previous claim to effectiveness. In practice, most systems have funneled new growth into both existing and proliferating public institutions. I will discuss an elite exit from the beleaguered public sector, but for the sake of simplicity my discussion assumes it is immaterial whether that sector has been transformed through proliferation or growth within established institutions.

FROM PUBLIC FAILURES TO PRIVATE ALTERNATIVES
Social-Class Failure: Declining Elitism

The second growth option is, in fact, the principal one exercised in Spanish America; the public sector, not the private sector, absorbs the bulk of new demand. While private enrollments have grown proportionately faster than public ones, the latter have increased more in absolute size. Empirically, the 1960s show no significant deviations from either the absolute or the relative intersectoral growth pattern among Spanish American national systems.[33] Although I refer here mostly to secular elite universities—the second private wave—many points also apply to the growth of elite Catholic universities.

The impact of unprecedented growth socially transforms the public sector. Its elite nature is smashed. As table 2.1 shows, there has been a remarkable increase from 3 to 15 percent in the cohort group attending higher education. Notably, the new percentage is the one used by Martin Trow to define the transition from "elite" to "mass" higher education. For Latin American public universities the change represents a shift from an overwhelmingly elite to an overwhelmingly middle-class constituency (with some lower-middle elements but hardly an egalitarian upheaval). Thus the elite have opted to reestablish themselves in newly exclusive private universities.[34] Change within the public sector, followed by client exit decisions and the creation of organizational alternatives, represents a clear case in which perceived public failure explains the rise of private institutions. Because the public sector no longer exists exclusively for them, many of the elite seek to preserve social-class differentiation through a sectoral bifurcation of higher education. Whereas the public sector has come to rest on an increasingly broad base, the private sector would not rest on such a widespread base of legitimacy—or on such a widespread constituency. Its sustenance comes from a narrow but deep base—those able to choose universities with more stringent academic and financial requirements. This constituency is drawn from the upper and, increasingly, upper-middle classes.

Here, then, is the crux of the middle class's changing attitude toward the State and public activity. As it makes its way into the political system, the middle class strongly supports equity and the expansion of State services; as it consolidates its position, however, the middle class becomes increasingly ambivalent about both. Some groups now put the doctrines of private choice above those of State responsibility. In higher education, upper-middle-class groups, joined by some of the middle-middle class, assume a proprivate posture. This reflects, for example, Luis Ratinoff's findings on the Latin American middle class at different stages of its development: "During this rise to power, the middle classes openly identified themselves with different forms of state control, but during the phase of consolidation . . . they tended to lay stress on the rights of ownership and on individual guarantees."[35]

Evidence of a major class-based exit from the public sector, based on a reaction to declining SES, can be found in every large Spanish American nation except Chile (and to a lesser extent Argentina). For Peru, Drysdale and Myers show how not only the middle but the lower-middle classes made strong inroads into the public sector, stimulating the private sector backlash, most notably from the previously esteemed San Marcos University. Peru's pontifical university benefited from the exit, although it probably has a mixed SES base; the secular elite universities are most limited in SES, some attended only by the academic elite (e.g., the Cayetano Heredia and Pacific universities), while others are attended by lower achievers (e.g., the Lima University). Similarly, in Colombia the traditional constituency felt threatened as public higher education was opened to the middle and even the lower-middle class; members of the elite left the public sector for private universities of unquestionable social prestige. Additionally, several Central American private universities were founded in the late 1960s and 1970s by a select SES group educated at private secondary schools and seeking to reestablish elite sanctuaries; the financially deprived student who manages to get into these private universities is rare indeed—a token.[36]

Of course, exiting elites have not generally proclaimed that they have been running away from association with less-privileged aspirants. Nor, in fairness, should we assume that snobbish elitism has been the chief social factor behind the sectoral crossover. For as booming enrollments have meant lowered average SES, so they have also meant lowered average quality of student preparation, student/instructor ratios, job prospects, and other indicators. However speculative statements about educational quality tend to be, a marked public sector decline during the 1960s is almost consensually acknowledged, whether in Argentina, Colombia, Ecuador, Mexico, Peru, or Venezuela, with the big debate hinging on the causes of decline. But a discussion of quality, as well as citations on its multifaceted, intricate, and elusive nature, is left for chapters 3 through 5 and especially chapter 6.[37]

Declining SES and declining academic standing together produce a crisis of "credentialism." Educational institutions may or may not provide the knowledge necessary for better jobs but they surely provide the requisite credentials for these jobs. Contemporary experts on credentialism have emphasized the continued relevance of Max Weber's concept of "status groups" that use cultural resources to solidify class power.[38] In Latin America, public universities traditionally served as the highest institutional bastion in education for the top status groups. Soaring enrollments, however, destroyed boundary maintenance between these and rising groups. A new, private sector therefore became necessary to retain separateness and superior social status. Moreover, rising groups increasingly obtained the same credentials as traditionally privileged groups. As the bulk of literature on credentials and stratification predicts, the traditionally privileged groups tried to maintain their invidious lead over other groups. In fact, Ronald Dore has suggested that educational certification for job placement is even more important in late-developing than in early-developing societies, often leading to intense demands for certification and producing runaway degree inflation. To cite just one Latin American example, by the 1950s Colombia's booming secondary and higher education enrollments destroyed the elite's automatic privileges via academic credentials, and as competition and "devaluation" intensified, so did privatization.[39]

In sum, public institutions were failing to ensure the social-class distinctions and privileges that the elite had previously enjoyed and still demanded. As the public sector responded to demands for expansion and equity, it became a less effective tool for the elite. And so the elite increasingly exited into private alternatives.

Seen alongside U.S. experiences, sectoral evolution has served particularly inegalitarian ends in Latin America. Primary and especially secondary education expanded belatedly in Latin America. By early in the twentieth century, when the public sector had become dominant in U.S. primary and secondary systems, Latin America continued to maintain significant private sectors. Compared to the U.S. pattern, Latin American education remained private at lower levels, even as it was emphatically more public at the tertiary level. Because Latin American higher education was available to so few, the public monopoly (publicly funded) was for the elite: later, when Latin American enrollments increased markedly, private sectors emerged as elite sanctuaries. Of course the United States has also used private sectors, at each educational level, to provide elite sanctuaries. But Latin America has relied more on private sanctuaries, and has done so even while systemic enrollment rates have been lower.[40] In higher education, Latin America has established much sharper intersectoral social-class divisions than found in the United States.

Political Failure: Politicization

Related to the perceived social-class failure of the public universities was a political failure to prevent intense "politicization."[41] In reaction, upper- and upper-middle-class students and their families increasingly sought alternative institutions.[42] This pattern of SES and politically stimulated exit from the public sector naturally goes far toward explaining why the private institutions would generally be depoliticized; indeed, depoliticization was part of the basic raison d'être, especially for secular institutions created in the 1960s and 1970s. Those students likely or eager to be activists would naturally choose the public sector. Moreover, even if some students at private universities would be disposed to political activity, private universities would rarely tolerate it.

The roots of public sector politicization can be traced to the 1918 Córdoba reform. We have already seen how such reforms aided the creation of private sectors by weakening State predominance. But the main impact from the reforms came from the politicization they promoted. Although this impact proved variable, depending on nation, regime, and other factors, the general orientation was clear. Students demanded sweeping changes not only in the university itself but in society at large. Progressivism or leftism was the dominats,ing ideology. One manifestation was a strong antiprivate bias. Student politics often became inextricably linked with national politics and often served as a conduit to national office, including top leadership positions. Some major political parties actually emerged in the public university. One prominent example was Peru's APRA party; its leader for decades, Víctor Raúl Haya de la Torre, had been president of the San Marcos Federation of Students. While the institutional role that students came to play in public university governance will be discussed in chapter 6, suffice it to say here that the role changed markedly. Moreover, the democratization encompassed professors as well. Leftist professors could even be elected to top administrative positions, including the rectorship itself. The gap between university policy and State and especially private enterprise policies increased enormously, leading to serious confrontations. Thus, as public universities became more autonomous (or private) in their governance, they paradoxically provoked the establishment of private university alternatives.

It comes as no surprise, then, that the private sector grew more spectacularly in the 1960s than in any previous decade. As this was the decade of the most intense politicization in the history of Latin American universities, it was the first decade of major institutional proliferation that saw the creation of more private (fifty-eight) than public (fifty) universities.[43] Table 1.1 shows that in this decade the private sector doubled its proportional share of total enrollments (15 to 30 percent).

Let us briefly consider a few Andean and Central American cases. Peru's 1960 University Law encouraged the creation of private institutions as a possible hedge against the outcome of the simultaneous enactment of many of the Córdoba reforms, including cogovernment, in the public universities. From eight universities in 1960, Peru could boast thirty-three in 1970. Whereas only one private university existed by 1960, as many as twelve existed by the end of the decade; politicization is generally seen as the most direct impulse. The establishment of the Cayetano Heredia University was a clear reaction to disorders wracking medical studies at the San Marcos University. More generally, as Sánchez wrote, many businessmen viewed the public sector as ridden with anarchism, communism, radical ideologies, and guerrilla activity.[44]

Even though Colombia allowed more private influence in higher education earlier than did any other major Spanish American nation (both within the public sector and then in a separate private sector), public sector politicization nevertheless contributed to private sector growth. Liberal rule from 1930 to 1946 favored the public sector while allowing private growth as well. As Colombia descended into a period of extraordinary internal strife (the *violencia*), the stage was set for the emergence (1953) of Gustavo Rojas Pinilla's repressive dictatorship. In opposition, Colombian students became more politically active. But this was only the beginning. In the 1960s, after democracy replaced dictatorship, Colombian students became more active than ever. Marxist and guerrilla influences were strong. Even the student organizations themselves often could not control the ensuing violence.

49

Some of the protest was directed against U.S.-aided "modernization" efforts; one notable episode centered on ousting the Ford Foundation presence from the National University's sociology department.[45] Increasingly potent radicalism in the 1960s and 1970s provoked a potent backlash; one manifestation of the backlash was to bypass the more-politicized public sector for the less-politicized private sector.

In Ecuador, according to Martz, students form the nation's "most eloquent, dramatic, and militant pressure group."[46] And the student federation, very involved in both university and national political issues, has been generally leftist. Indeed student activity has been heavily politicized at all public universities in Ecuador, and leftists have risen to high administrative positions.

At first glance it might appear strange that depoliticized private sectors were deemed necessary in much of Central America (outside Costa Rica). After all, the region has generally been ruled by rightist dictatorships naturally hostile to public sector politicization. But the Rojas-Colombian case has shown that such politicization may occur despite the efforts of right-wing regimes. Ironically, student politics has sometimes assumed extra significance in Central America, as other potential actors (e.g., unions, parties) have been blocked from organizing effectively. Thus, student politics has often had a chance to make a stronger impact in these countries than in more developed ones. Additionally, as in the Andean cases, leftists could sometimes gain administrative posts within the public universities. Public politicization has contributed to reactions not only by the State but by private enterprises. As Mayorga describes the prevalent reaction: "But above all other factors was the 'anti-communist' obsession, in the face of increasing infiltration of Marxists into important academic and administrative posts in these [public] institutions." The phenomenon continues. In the 1970s and early 1980s Guatemala's San Carlos University remained a major center for opposition to the dictatorship; in turn, right-wing groups have viewed San Carlos as subversive, and death squads have done their ugly business there. In Honduras, the National University has remained a violent Left-Right battleground, leading to harsh criticism and to private alternatives such as the José Cecilio del Valle University.[47]

El Salvador and Nicaragua provide two further examples of how public sector politicization reached great heights, provoking conservative reactions. After El Salvador's national university regained its autonomy (1950), it grew increasingly apart from the regime, resulting in serious conflicts. By the decade's end, problems occurred over rector selection. Soon the university became the center of leftist agitation; the regime responded with repression, including police actions involving the arrest of the rector and many students. A major backlash set in against "communist subversion," and the national university was viewed as "a microcosm where one could find concentrated in extreme form virtually everything thought to be wrong in El Salvador." Furthermore, all this followed a decade in which enrollments had doubled and costs had quadrupled. An elite exit, led by parents of private school graduates and by the Catholic church, culminated in the mid-1960s with the creation of the (Jesuit) José Simeón Cañas University; this institution then grew in importance as the national university reflected the nation's tragic political fate.[48]

Earlier, but in a similar fashion, political conflict in Nicaragua stimulated impassioned efforts to create private alternatives. As one Catholic leader pleaded, "Nicaraguans: we still have time to save Nicaragua from the claws of the Moscovite bear. The Catholic university is the only strong barrier that can stop the communist advance in Nicaragua. Help to found it, help to sustain it. . . . God willing the day will not arrive when you say: We are lost. It is too late to save Nicaragua from communism."[49] In Nicaragua, as in Peru, the legal opening for the private sector occurred simultaneously (1958) with the State's decision to grant increased public university autonomy. Despite strong public university opposition, the Central American Catholic University in Nicaragua, Central America's first private university, was created in 1960. It proclaimed its commitment to Christian education, but was soon followed by secular universities providing further private alternatives to public sector politics.

For a final example, from the Caribbean, let us consider events in the Dominican Republic. Until its demise in 1961, Trujillo's dictatorship had suppressed Córdoba-like reforms in the public Autonomous University of Santo Domingo. Subsequently, however, student and faculty participation increased. The first private university was founded in 1962 by Dominican bishops. Then, sparked by the U.S. armed intervention of 1965, political divisions within the public university reached a high conflictual level. A conservative group decided to bolt the institution. Helped by the business community and U.S. foundations, it established the Pedro Heríquez Ureña University. Explicitly banning cogovernment, it substituted the "vía academicista" for politicization. State subsidies for the public university declined,[50] and other depoliticized private alternatives quickly ensued.

Economic Failure: Modernization and Dependency

Connections between the perceived political and economic failures of the public universities are clear. Politicization has hurt institutional capacity to perform economic functions such as technical training. It has weakened student preparation for the job market. Strikes are only the most dramatic indication that too little classroom education takes place, and student activ-

51

ists sometimes proclaim that the prime role of the university is not to give such education but to change society. Economic elites perceive disorder, not modernization, as the chief outcome of reformist campaigns waged by moderates as well as radicals. Naturally, the price tag for all this soars as enrollments soar. When, as in Peru, expanding public universities promote access to the political system for the middle and lower-classes, elites may preserve their hold on the economic system partly through private universities.

Meanwhile, if economic change often stimulates the rise of new educational institutions, the point is especially relevant where dissatisfaction is widespread. When Latin America's elite look at the public university they see not only dangerous politics but also irrational economics. Many believe that inadequate attention is given to job-relevant fields and instructional methods. Public universities ostensibly become less effective just when economies place increasing demands upon higher education.

Evidence of the perceived public sector failure to provide desired personnel comes from even the least modernized nations. The founders of Central America's private sectors have basically held this view of the public sector: "Except for some of their faculties—typically in medicine—higher education in these universities was seen, in general, by the dominant sector, as technically mediocre and decidedly deficient."[51] Carlos Tünnermann writes that, in addition to expanding enrollments, declining elitism, and increasing politicization, the needs of industrialization contributed to the private sector's rise. For example, the Central American Common Market's efforts at industrialization required technical personnel, and "private universities were an answer to this need."[52]

Thus, business naturally plays a visible role in both founding and funding private universities. It has been particularly helpful in providing capital expenditures. Moreover, it offers job incentives since it tends to see private university graduates as better, safer bets for employment. Prospective job opportunities therefore help attract some students to private universities. This fact is not lost on public university students. A major reason for the fierce opposition of Bolivia's public university students to the creation of a private university was fear of marked deterioration of their own already dubious job possibilities.[53] They especially feared competition for strategic posts in industry, planning, and even politics.

One need not accept the claim that private universities teach more material of direct relevance for private sector jobs, though they often do. Sufficient is the indirect preparation of students, from families screened by tuition, who are disciplined to attend class, complete assignments, and conform to established standards. Beyond this, critics argue that the rise of private universities is inextricably tied to economic dependency. Crude versions malign the private university as a significant cause of dependency.[54] More sophisticated versions hypothesize the ways in which the private sector especially, but both sectors somewhat, may be integrated into a pattern of dependent development.[55]

Whether one calls it dependency or modernization, foreign interests have clearly supported those trying to mold Latin America's universities toward U.S. models. Where this has involved increased tuition or increased revenues from private foundations such as Ford or Rockefeller, many institutions have seen a privatization of public structures. In fact, both U.S. foundation and government aid has gone to public as well as private institutions. One major effort, briefly alluded to above, was made in Colombia in the mid-1960s. Private foundations, transnational corporations, AID, UNESCO, and the IDB were all involved in trying to create "centers of excellence." This manner of promoting university development was essentially an "elitist strategy," similar to the capitalist model of economic development in that it reinforced the "haves," hoping there would be a "trickle down" benefit; if "modernization" was the rage, "this usually meant 'modelling' the North American University.[56] While such policies are theoretically neutral as to private versus public, they directly favor the more modern, efficient, and politically receptive institutions whose rectors are dynamic or powerful enough to avail themselves of the opportunity to use funds effectively. Consequently, such modernization policies probably favor private universities.

In sum, economic factors, like social-class and political factors, have provided specific reasons for private sector growth based largely on perceived public sector failures. We have already seen how the social-class factor was far more potent, in establishing sectoral distinctiveness than in the United States. The same could be said even more strongly for the political and economic factors. That is, neither factor contributed very distinctively to private rather than public growth in the United States. U.S. universities have rarely been as politicized as Latin American ones, and the politicization that has existed has not been overwhelmingly concentrated in one sector. Nor has the U.S. private sector, any more than the public sector, grown in order to fulfill unmet business needs. By comparison, then, one appreciates how powerfully the social, political, and economic factors have led to the growth of a distinctive private sector in Latin America.

The Wave II Backlash to Wave I

I have depicted the rise of secular private universities as a reaction to perceived social-class, political, and economic failures in the public sector. An effort at still greater parsimony could try to reconceptualize these three

53

failures as part of a general social-class failure. Private institutions arise as the traditional elite monopoly on public institutions fades. Class composition becomes more heterogeneous and higher education loses its special capacity to recertify the elite while excluding others. Expansion may also entail the admission of less-prepared students, while it certainly threatens to lower effectivensss by straining resources. Newer groups are more politically disruptive, and falling standards create further tensions. The elite therefore see their privileges threatened by (1) social interaction and sharing with lower classes; (2) increased politicization that tilts the university away from the status quo, as it also disrupts orderly learning and socialization; (3) challenges to job and status superiority as other classes now receive the same credentials previously reserved for them. Private institutions become logical choices not just because they can be less politicized and academically superior but also because they can be separate.

In sum, within the public sector lies the overwhelming explanation for the secular, elite private growth. Nonetheless, this analysis ignores a major question: Why has the existing private sector not provided a sufficient outlet for the public sector exodus? In fact, the second private wave (creation of secular, elite, depoliticized, rationalized institutions) has represented a rejection of the first private wave (Catholic universities). The difference between the two private waves often reflects the difference between traditional conservative coalitions, epitomized by the Church, and modern capitalist coalitions, epitomized by private enterprise. (Again, however, several Catholic universities have most elite traits.)

There are two principal reasons for the two-wave private pattern. First, the perceived need for distinctive alternatives to the public sector grows as that sector increases in size, mixed SES composition, political activity, and economic inadequacy for the productive apparatus. Second, Catholic universities have sometimes offered only limited distinctiveness from public universities. As the demand for choice grows, Catholic universities provide less and less. This limited choice is analyzed in the next chapter on Chile and the sixth chapter on Latin America generally. Here I will simply highlight the evolutionary pattern as it relates to the rise of wave II.

Most Catholic universities are created as religious alternatives to the secular public universities. From the outset, however, some offer only limited distinctiveness on other dimensions. This varies by nation. Certain Catholic universities are created by the national Church and for some time serve almost as the "national" private university, seeking to grow more than secular elite institutions would, although much less than the dominant public institutions. (Cleavages based on Jesuit, Dominican, or Franciscan denomination do not begin to offer the sort of diversification afforded by religious-oriented U.S. higher education.) The main point is that the first private universities often seek political and academic legitimacy by copying the public universities. Created primarily in order to offer religious alternatives, they may self-consciously try to offer little else in the way of distinctiveness.

Catholic universities may offer more distinctiveness where religion overlaps other motivations in the first wave. One cannot always find clear-cut divisions between the first two waves. As a rule, Catholic universities created prior to 1960 were meant to provide dual religious and social-class alternatives, while Catholic universities created later often prominently included the rationalization motivations (depoliticization and economic utility). The multiple motivation behind the more recently created Catholic universities is well reflected in Central America and the Dominican Republic. For example, the Dominican Republic's first private university, the Catholic Madre y Maestra (1962), tried to copy "modern" and U.S. models and was tied to business interests.[57] Similarly, Bolivia's Catholic university (1967) deviated from the traditional Catholic universities that often tried to attract students interested in a Catholic flavor to offerings otherwise found in the public sector; instead, it emphasized business-related courses not offered in that sector. Thus, many of Latin America's Catholic universities created early in the region's private sector history were never meant to offer the same across-the-board alternative to the public sector that many of the subsequent secular universities would.

Furthermore, many Catholic universities have not maintained whatever degree of distinctiveness they originally sought. Core distinctiveness diminishes insofar as *university* is increasingly emphasized more than *Catholic*. Also, *Catholic* has taken on new meanings as the Church itself has changed. This change is of course rooted in Vatican II and ensuing movements to involve the Church in progressive socioeconomic struggles. As Levine describes it, the Second Vatican Council (culminating in 1965) "marked the opening of a period of deep change for the Church, but its impact on Latin America was perhaps even more profound." It was "a major attempt to rethink the nature of the Church, the world, and the proper relation between the two."[58] It moved toward a greater concern with material issues of this world. Of special relevance to higher education, Vatican II called for Catholic universities to open up, declaring that each discipline should develop according to its own methodologies and freedom of research. Of course, this would presumably result in the happy conclusion that "faith and reason lead to the same truth."[59]

At Medellín, Colombia, in 1968, Latin America's bishops took major strides toward adapting Vatican II to their special regional concerns. But even earlier (1967), at a CELAM meeting in Buga, Colombia, delegates (rectors, professors, and students) from Catholic universities met with other

55

religious thinkers to consider how Vatican II could be adapted to higher education. A powerful attack on the Catholic university status quo was unleashed. Accelerating trends already underway, Catholic universities pledged themselves to reform both their governance structures and missions. Key concepts included social consciousness, self-criticism, academic freedom, dialogue with secular universities, and a decline of the inward-looking defensiveness that shields faith from science and worldly problems. Several other conferences in Latin America and beyond (including two in Rome, in 1972 and 1975) addressed similar themes and contributed to evolving thought.

All of this is far from saying that the entire Latin American Church has abandoned traditional conservatism for social reform. But the change has been widespread, usually resonating in Catholic universities. Indeed, it has often found leadership there. Catholic university students, and even professors and administrators, have frequently become politicized. As Marxist influences have grown (e.g., in Ecuador), pressures have developed to attract a broader SES student base.

Consider first the Peruvian case. The Catholic university created in 1917 was to provide a religious and depoliticized alternative to the public sector. In practice, however, it remained marginal for decades as the State relinquished less control than dual sector appearance might suggest. The Catholic university remained dependent for admissions, structure, curriculum, exams, and degrees on the State and its public San Marcos University. Only in 1949 did the Catholic university receive from the State the autonomy requisite for distinctiveness; it had become pontifical earlier in the decade. By the 1960s, however, there were fresh signs of a degree of convergence. Leftist professors and especially students (full partners in the Peruvian Student Federation) became increasingly active. If the Catholic university had been expected to remain pure and isolated from the political currents swirling in the public universities, it failed. "It was natural," therefore, that private economic groups "would seek new channels to train the qualified personnel that their modernization required." Business interests helped create a number of private institutions that had much-diminished or nonexistent religious involvement.[60]

A wave I–wave II pattern occurs even in Central America, where the first private universities did not emerge until the 1960s and were motivated by political and economic as well as religious and social-class factors. Before long, Marxism made inroads, sometimes actually gaining ascendency in the Catholic institutions. Marxists allegedly controlled Nicaragua's Central American Catholic University for two years. In some cases, such radicalism was quashed by a depoliticizing backlash. In others, it spurred the founding of wave II alternatives. As Jesuits engaged in social activism, even in direct

56

opposition to the government, business interests withdrew their support from Guatemala's Catholic Rafael Landívar University and, backed by the Chamber of Industry, founded the Francisco Marroquín University; the Marroquín prohibited student politics. A second secular private university (del Valle) was founded in conjunction with U.S. interests. Similarly in Nicaragua, business turned from the Catholic university toward private secular alternatives.[61]

The data presented earlier on the primacy of the religious factor in the first wave of private development are relevant here. The second wave is thereby shown to be overwhelmingly secular. Time lapses between the two waves depend mostly on how early the first wave arrived. Where it arrived late, there was often only a short period before the second wave approached. Furthermore, given the diminished religious orientation of some Catholic universities, it is possible that the same universities, if created today, could be created as secular universities. In other words, the basic motivation to preserve class privilege has increasingly coupled itself with (political-economic) modernization more than with religious factors.

State Support for Private Alternatives

A final consideration relevant to waves I and II concerns the chief organizing forces. I have dealt more with explaining why and how the demand for private higher education arises and grows than with describing who actually creates the structures to meet that demand. In fact, much of the answer is obvious. Focusing on institutions rather than students and their families, the Church is the main power behind wave I and business the main power behind wave II. A less obvious but vital actor is the State. It plays a role in each wave. While only wave I requires explicit State support—to strike down existing legislation guaranteeing public monopolies—even wave II generally has the State's at least tacit support. This apparent betrayal of the public sector makes sense when we realize that the State's own interests, including its class interests, are often better served by the private sector (see chapter 7). To keep the issue in perspective, however, the State often continues to go far in supporting the public sector, even as it is also facilitating private alternatives.

To be more specific, it is tempting to associate the creation and growth of private sectors with certain types of government. This proves elusive, however, because private growth occurs nearly everywhere in Latin America, across a range of regimes. Still, some tendencies are observable.

Rightist dictatorships naturally have supported depoliticized options that carry no price tags and that themselves support the elite and sometimes the Church. Thus, Central America's private universities, both religious and secular, were actively promoted by dictatorships in the 1960 and 1970s; Somoza had a variety of reasons for aiding the creating of Nicaragua's private universities. Velasco Ibarra supported the creation of Ecuador's private sector in 1946, just as Pérez Jiménez did in Venezuela in 1953. In 1960, Peruvian dictator Manuel Prado joined with the decreasingly progressive APRA party to support private growth.[62]

Although the explanations are more complex, less rightist regimes, whether populist or democratic, have also encouraged private growth. At least this has been true once private sectors have been created. Consider two important ways in which less rightist regimes have helped. First, no democratic regime has blocked the growth of existing private sectors. Even a neutral or laissez-faire policy in effect supports such growth by giving powerful societal actors freedom of choice. Beyond this, many democratic regimes, like the rightist dictatorships (though to differing degrees), have also been favorably disposed toward depoliticized, money-saving sectors that protect the elite and perhaps the Church. Post-Peronist Argentina offers one example of democratic support for private creation, while Peru under Belaúnde (1965–68) illustrates democratic encouragement of private growth.

A second factor is the indirect or paradoxical way in which nonrightist regimes promote elite private growth. By supporting public sector growth and democratization, the regimes increase the elite's zeal to find private sanctuaries. This is true of democratic regimes, such as Venezuela's, and of somewhat "populist" governments, such as Mexico's under Luis Echeverría (1970–76). When public sector expansion is directly promoted, the elite private option is indirectly promoted. Rare exceptions involve the coercive denial of private choice. Pending the Sandinista course in Nicaragua, Communist Cuba is the only Latin American nation that has successfully implemented and sustained a strong antiprivate policy after private institutions were already in place. Perhaps Peru under the military is the next closest example, yet not a strong one. After nine private (fifteen public) universities were created in the 1960s, none (three public) were created in the 1970s, but private enrollment growth did not slow.

The other side of the paradox is that certain rightist regimes may logically forestall elite private growth. A key is regime policy toward the public sector. If the regime places tight controls on the sector and limits its expansion, then consequently the regime dilutes the felt need for elite private alternatives. In fact, public sectors vary enormously according to how much they have been transformed and even radicalized. On the other hand, this dynamic applies to traditional dictatorships only to the extent that they have controlled their public sectors, an extent generally falling far short of that fashioned by modern authoritarian regimes. If these latter regimes depoliticize, rationalize, and even "reprivatize" the public sector while reintroducing exclusiveness, they smother much of the rationale for elite private exits.[63] Instead, they may either block enrollment growth in the private as well as public sectors, as in Chile; or bolster nonelite private growth by allowing expansion but mostly not in the State-funded public sector, as in Brazil; or permit the private percentage to increase but only amid stagnant total enrollments, as in Argentina. Meanwhile, military rule in Uruguay did not spawn a private alternative. For the most part, then, Latin America's modern authoritarian regimes have not promoted a growth of private elite subsectors comparable to those flourishing in much of the rest of Latin America. A potentially important aside, therefore, is that the redemocratization of several Latin American nations in the early 1980s does not necessarily portend diminished privatization, even though that may occur in individual cases (e.g., Argentina, 1983).

Nonelite Private Alternatives: Wave III

The secular private reaction discussed thus far is mostly an elite reaction to perceived failures in public sector (and Catholic university) performance. Additionally, a different kind of secular private response has occurred—a nonelite response to the failure of the public sector to meet the growing demand for higher education. Here I use *public failure* in the loose sense of avoiding tasks. Because Brazil is the only Latin American nation (save Costa Rica) where the nonelite secular subsector clearly dominates private higher education, this evolutionary pattern is most closely considered in chapter 5. Nonetheless, the broad rationale should be set forth here, since it is reflected to one degree or another in the private subsectors of all major Spanish American nations. In several cases wave III becomes the single largest wave within the private sector, but it is "demand-absorbing" in its dynamics whether or not it results in a massive phenomenon.

Like the elite reaction, the nonelite reaction has its roots largely in the extraordinary growth of population, secondary education, and demand for higher education. It may even emerge partly from a preoccupation to maintain SES differentiation through sectoral distinctiveness. Again, private growth is shaped by the State's response to increasing demand. But here the State's response is different. It tries to "protect" the public sector.

The hypothetical extreme would be for the State to maintain the sector's historical exclusiveness. The empirical extreme occurs when the State restrains public growth enough for the private sector to become the larger sector—as happened in Brazil, and later in Colombia. More often, the State allows unprecedented public expansion that still falls short of booming demands. Fully open admissions for secondary school graduates has not been a widespread reality, rhetoric nonwithstanding. In some cases, there has been government control, while in others the universities or individual faculties have imposed admissions requirements. Medicine is the faculty where restrictions have been most common. Moreover, even where "open admissions" has been allowed, accepted students have sometimes had to wait years until space was available. Thus, notwithstanding great public growth, some individuals have either not been absorbed at all or have not been absorbed in keeping with their career plans.[64]

Additionally, some States that long tolerated massive public growth have recently restricted that growth. The most dramatic examples have occurred where modern authoritarian regimes have replaced more open regimes, but even some of the more open regimes such as Venezuela's have moved from unconcern to policy restriction. In sum, many different forms of public restrictiveness have led to nonelite private growth.

As with the elite wave, the third private wave is a reaction mostly to the public sector but to the existing private sector as well. While Catholic universities generally grow to accommodate some of the increased demand, they never assume burdens comparable to those characterizing the national universities. More important, even after the first or "national" Catholic university is joined by others, the religious-oriented subsector generally does not succumb to institutional proliferation to the degree that the public (and eventually the private secular) sector does.[65]

Nonelite growth is also a response to private elite universities. By definition, wave II elite universities cannot accommodate excess demand. The third wave fills a gap left unfilled by both the public and the first two private subsectors. Nevertheless, the I-II-III sequence is only the most common one, and there are exceptions. Most important, growth overlap occurs, even where the nonelite subsector emerges after the elite subsector is already established. Moreover, some institutions lie ambiguously between the elite and nonelite categories, at least in certain respects. For example, some technically and commercially oriented institutions created to meet the needs of modern capitalist enterprises do not attract the most privileged students.[66] While some wave III institutions principally absorb excess demand for the traditional professions, others concentrate on newer fields of study.

Table 2.4 sketchily summarizes how the three waves of private growth have manifested themselves throughout Latin America. Obviously, my data are more complete for some nations (e.g., Peru more than El Salvador). Just as obviously, some cases lend themselves to neater and surer categorization than others (e.g., Colombia more than Argentina). Categorizing individual institutions is not always easy, let alone aggregating for national summaries. Catholic institutions may resemble wave II or wave III institutions, and the very designation Catholic is not clear-cut. Some institutions are not affiliated with the Church or any religious order but do claim Christian inspiration. I have tried to include all institutions for which religion was at least an initial central concern, excluding only those that encompassed such inspiration as but one among many concerns. Also, some secular institutions combine elite with demand-absorbing characteristics. Nonetheless, the clear majority of institutions appear to fall comfortably into one of the three waves. Moreover, the categorization proves easier to apply to the causes of growth than to the institutional characteristics that have ensued; the latter issue is considered in subsequent chapters.

Table 2.4 Balance of Three Private Waves in Latin America

| | | Mixed Growth[c] | | |
No Private University	Wave I Only	Wave III Subordinate[d]	Wave III Holds Numerical Edge but Otherwise Subordinate[j]	Wave III Dominant
Cuba	Bolivia	Argentina[e]	Colombia	Brazil
Haiti[a]	Chile[b]	Ecuador	Dominican	Costa Rica[k]
Uruguay	Panama	El Salvador[f]	Republic	
	Paraguay	Guatemala	Peru	
		Honduras[g]		
		Mexico		
		Nicaragua[h]		
		Venezuela[i]		

NOTE: Assessment based on the situation as of 1980 or the latest available information and on associating waves with the institutions they produce, as follows: wave I = Church or religion-affiliated; wave II = secular elite; wave III = secular demand-absorbing.

a. See chapter 1, footnote 2.

b. Unique case with no genuine wave II or III, at least until 1980, but where secular institutions evolved; the other three private sectors in this category have only Catholic universities.

c. Continuum based on the balance between waves II and III, while wave I is prominent in all these nations, except Honduras and Costa Rica, but varies in proportional size and in whether it approximates wave II or III.

d. Most of wave I can be associated more with wave II than wave III, and waves I plus II combined are larger than wave III, if there is any wave III at all.

e. See chapter 6, footnote 116.

f. See chapter 1, footnote 2; wave I is dominant.

g. At least the two principal private universities are secular.

h. Based on the situation at least until the Sandinista takeover.

i. High-quality Catholic and wave II universities still hold half the private university enrollments, but to include nonuniversity growth is to give wave III a majority.

j. If we apportion the growth of elite Catholic universities to wave II and the growth of nonelite ones to wave III, wave III would be larger than wave II, but wave II would be more important, at least in academic, political, and economic influence.

k. The one private university claims Christian inspiration.

It is difficult to predict the future of nonelite relative to elite growth. On the one hand, the experience of regions outside Latin America might argue against increased momentum for nonelite growth. Among developed nations, only Japan has a major private sector that is less elite than its public sector. Moreover, very few of these nations have large private sectors of any sort. Such sectors, largely nonelite, are much more prevalent in less-developed nations (India, the Philippines, Turkey). Explanations for the proportionally large private sectors in less-developed countries include the State's inability to finance adequate public sectors and the colonial legacy; colonial rulers did not build major public sectors, and therefore private sectors were often large when independence came. Consequently, insofar as Latin America may be becoming more developed, one might expect it to harness the third wave.

On the other hand, our analysis of Latin America's distinctive causes of sectoral and subsectoral growth suggest that the nonelite subsector may grow substantially. Public sector growth is likely to continue but there are indications that many States will not accommodate the full extent of population- and development-pushed demand for higher education. Especially, but not exclusively, with the right-wing political shift of the 1970s compared to the 1950s and 1960s, official concern over higher education's economic cost increased. And there is growing chagrin over the public sector's declining effectiveness. Expansion by the nonelite private sector could relieve the public sector of a considerable financial, social, and academic burden, all within a depoliticized setting.

Growth in the nonelite subsector may depend partly on future trends in the elite subsector, but these are not easily predicted. The creation of secular elite universities has often depended significantly on international finance, which was seriously jeopardized by the worldwide economic crisis surfacing in the late 1970s and early 1980s. Additionally, deep domestic economic crises could drastically affect support from the national bourgeoisie. Even such established leaders as Colombia's Los Andes have suffered. Beyond this, elite growth may have peaked in many nations, at least in proportion to enrollments. The wave II alternative was meant to serve an elite, by definition a relatively small percentage of the population. Should an increasing demand for this subsector be accommodated, there would be the danger that elite distinctiveness would suffer, as happened earlier with some Catholic universities. Even so, substantial room might be left for elite expansion. If a nation's elite private institutions (including elite Catholic ones) account for about 10 to 15 percent of total enrollments, and if only 10 to 15 percent of the cohort is enrolled, then these institutions might be catering to roughly a 2 percent elite. Naturally, this does not mean that prestigious private universities have enrolled students only from the top 2 percent in SES terms, but they are drawing on a very limited pool.

In sum, if the private sector continues to gain a greater share of system enrollments, the nonelite subsector will probably also gain a greater share of those enrollments, even if the elite subsector also gains; it certainly will do so if the elite subsector does not sustain its proportional growth. The Catholic subsector probably will not expand through institutional proliferation, while growth within some existing Catholic institutions could further blur the lines between waves I and III. Additionally, a brief reference to the United States suggests further that nonelite growth might at least retain its momentum in Latin America. Because the U.S. private sector was established as early as or earlier than its public counterpart, the private sector could grow from sectorally nondistinctive causes. That is, students could choose given institutions, regardless of their private or public status. By contrast, in most of Latin America, only public sectors were in place when the big increase in demand for higher education initially occurred. Even when Latin America's private sectors first emerged, most students could not meet their religious, academic, or financial (tuition) requirements. The situation is different, however, where nonelite private subsectors have also developed. While these grow from certain distinctive causes, they grow from relatively nondistinctive causes as well. They grow because many students choose institutions on other than a private-public basis and because the nonelite private subsector does not generally bar them. They grow, in large part, because they are already there.

Finally, the entire discussion on the future balance of different waves of private growth should be seen within the context of continued strong but proportionally slowing growth in each sector, as pointed out in chapter 1. Also, whatever the future holds for nonelite private growth in Latin America, both the elite and nonelite subsectors have been growing dramatically to the present. For example, we have seen how the Dominican Republic's first two private waves emerged, but the impact of booming enrollment also launched a major demand-absorbing subsector. In fact, higher education enrollment grew from roughly 3,500 in 1960 to roughly 90,000 by 1979. The public Autonomous University of Santo Domingo still held onto greater than half the total, but during the 1970s alone, perhaps ten private higher education institutions were added, and twenty more were already asking for permission to function. The average expenditure per pupil in the system is roughly half the Latin American average. At least until 1978 the State "has held a laissez-faire position," allowing new private institutions to multiply. A move toward insistence on systemwide standards could retard the nonelite private growth, but tightening the public sector could promote it.

Probably only three private universities (the Madre y Maestra, the Henríquez Ureña, and the Technological Institute of Santo Domingo) fall outside the third wave category, giving that wave (1979) roughly two-thirds of private enrollments.[67]

The major Spanish American example of private nonelite growth is found in Colombia. By 1975, Colombia became Spanish America's only nation in which the private sector overtook the public sector. By 1981 the private sector held not only 59 percent of total enrollments but 64 percent of first-year enrollments, indicating continued growth. As discussed, Colombia developed its private sector relatively early. Thus, a private sector had already been established when the big demand came in the 1940s, 1950s, and 1960s; it was not just an emerging exit option. Rather, illustrating the point just made above, the private sector grew, in part because it was already there. Most important, however, was that Colombia did not open its public sector as widely as most sister republics did. By 1946 a *limitacionista* policy was implemented. The national university never became gigantic. Not until the late 1970s did it reach twenty-five thousand enrollments, leaving it still only half the size of Venezuela's national university, the UCV. This means that the former holds roughly 10 percent, versus the latter's 20 percent, of national enrollments. In fact, national enrollments have been almost equal, despite Colombia's much larger population; table 2.2 shows that Colombia's cohort enrollment rate is only half Venezuela's. To have a proportionally small public sector within a comparatively small system is to have a truly limited public sector. Moreover, those who expected Liberal president Alfonso López Michelsen to promote great public expansion in the 1970s were mistaken. Instead, the López position was sometimes viewed as proprivate for holding the public sector comparatively small, restricting both institutional proliferation and enrollments. The public sector does not even fill its allotted quota because not enough students can meet admissions standards, especially at the top public universities, and some will not then settle for public provincial institutions. Data from 1981 echo 1960s data showing rejection rates higher in the public than private sector. The private sector's 64 percent share of first-year enrollments was drawn from only 45 percent of the applications (1981). Also, echoes of 1960s data showed the private sector far ahead in night-course offerings. Pointing to a lack of State funds, the public sector, even in the late 1970s, still hesitated to expand night courses for workers, while the private sector, mostly for commercial reasons, welcomed this demand. Meanwhile, the State backed plans for loans to private sector students. In short, the public sector left a major share of the demand unattended, making it a low financial risk to open private institutions. While the public sector held nearly three-fourths of enrollments in 1935 and continued to do so in 1950, it then lost ground quickly. The private sector has grown much faster both in terms of new enrollments and new institutions. And as Rama shows, the Catholic share of private growth has diminished over time, as Colombia has lost "the atmosphere of religious polarization that explains a preference for that institutional type." Rama sums up the importance of State restrictions (and third-wave growth) by asserting that lifting public barriers would mean that a "considerable number" of private universities "would disappear shortly."[68] Actual policy, however, had led to a demand-absorbing boom that makes a sizeable part of Colombia's system resemble Brazilian patterns.

ENTRÉE

Empirical counterparts to the analytical categories of sectoral growth will be pursued, with three case studies spaced over the ensuing three chapters. Chile, Mexico, and Brazil all show spectacular public sector growth. All, especially Chile and Brazil, have undergone some form of significant wave I religious reaction. Mexico offers the clearest example of a major wave II elite reaction, Brazil of a massive wave III nonelite growth.

Mostly, however, the ensuing three chapters are case studies of the contemporary behavioral patterns that flow from the major waves of sectoral evolution. The study of sectoral evolution, therefore, has been a necessary preamble to an analysis of private-public patterns of finance, governance, and function. Public sectors, nearly everywhere, have been fundamentally transformed. The first private wave has led to some private-public differentiation, but also to substantial homogeneity. This homogeneity is explored as the dominant Chilean pattern and then as a subdominant Mexican and Brazilian pattern. The second and third private waves have each produced profound private-public distinctiveness, respectively displayed in the Mexican and Brazilian cases. After these three chapter-long studies, chapter 6 returns to Latin America inclusively, analyzing how and where the major patterns of private-public finance, governance, and function manifest themselves.

3   Private-Public
Homogeneity: Chile

THE CONTEXT

Rarely are private and public sectors thoroughly distinct from one another in evolution, finance, governance, and function. Overlap commonly exists and often increases with time. In fact, some intersectoral homogeneity is found in nearly every dual sector system in Latin America (and beyond). Therefore, while most of this book focuses on the region's notable intersectoral distinctiveness, this chapter focuses on homogeneity.

Chile has been Latin America's most striking national example of similarity between sectors, notwithstanding some private-public differences. As Latin America now has only two single sector systems (Cuba, Uruguay), Chile emerges as the logical nation from which to gain insight into the general phenomenon of system homogeneity. But while the Chilean system may be unique in Latin America, patterns and dynamics of homogeneity are widely found subsystemically. Moreover, some of these patterns and dynamics have had a historical importance that would be understated if we focused only on the more intersectorally distinctive systems.[1]

Chile's homogeneity has been forged on two very different bases. The first and major one is publicness. Chile's public sector shows many similarities to public sectors elsewhere, while Chile's private sector resembles public sectors more than their private counterparts. A key factor is that the first private wave (Catholic universities) drifted even further than usual in Latin America, yet it yielded to no strong second wave of conservative business-oriented universities to rejuvenate the system's private-public distinctiveness. Nor did any separate third wave of low-quality institutions arrest the waning privateness. The second, much less certain basis of Chile's intersectoral homogeneity moves toward stunningly different ground. Especially in finance and function, both sectors have been pushed brusquely toward privateness.

Each basis of intersectoral homogeneity in Chilean higher education

66

should be understood within the broader political-economic context of State-private relations. Most fundamentally, the Chilean State has long assumed an unusually active role in society and the economy. One root of the State's strength came from the rapid postindependence success of civilian leaders in centralizing political power. This strength was sustained by long periods of political stability. State activity increased notably as reformists replaced the oligarchy in the 1920s, followed by a popular front in the late 1930s. In health and social services, Chile became a leader in Latin America. Even when increasing State involvement in industrialization became common in Latin America, Chile's was "striking," and the Chilean Development Corporation (CORFO), created in 1939, became the region's most influential development agency.[2] The State assumed important roles in industry, finance, foreign trade, planning, banking, and credit.

Clearly, the tradition of an active State preceded the last two civilian administrations, which then greatly intensified the tendency. The 1964 triumph of Eduardo Frei and the Christian Democratic party (PDC) represented a fortified State commitment to promote equity and economic development. Although private enterprise was still assigned an important role, the PDC distanced itself from what it considered the amorality of capitalist materialistic development. Undertaking certain new roles, the State sometimes pushed aside private and foreign actors, as with the Chileanization of copper. Nonetheless, the PDC "Revolution in Liberty" was considered much too limited and sluggish by its successor. Victors in the 1970 presidential elections, the Marxist Popular Unity (UP) coalition headed by Salvador Allende was naturally very State oriented. To be sure, there were many restraints on UP members who sought to supplant private with State action across the board. Some coalition members were moderate, public opinion was terribly polarized, the legislature was controlled by the opposition, economic power remained largely in hostile hands, foreign companies and the U.S. government tried to undermine the regime, and the military ultimately monopolized the coercive apparatus.

Whereas Chile had long been a Latin American leader in State activism, it abruptly became *the* leader in a campaign to diminish the State role when the military ousted the UP (1973). Headed by Augusto Pinochet, the junta immediately turned to the "Chicago Boys" (economists trained at or influenced by the University of Chicago's economics department) and their doctrine of a minimalist State. Many State-run enterprises were returned to private hands. "It falls to the State directly to assume only those activities that by their scope or nature are impossible for individual persons or intermediary groups to handle."[3] *Privatización* became one of the most widely used terms in Chilean political-economic affairs. Most attention initially focused on economic fields such as industry and agriculture, but the philosophy also applied to social areas such as health, social security, and education. State activities were turned over to not only private for-profit but also private nonprofit organizations. In short, modern authoritarian policy tried to combine increased State political repression with privatization in economic and social fields. A long tradition that regarded an active State as essential to expanding real freedom and choice as well as effectiveness and especially equity was brutalized by an antistatist ideology that proclaimed the tradition to be detrimental to each of those ends.

Higher education has been an ideological focal point both for State activism and privatization.[4] Few Latin American nations have experienced a more rapid and fundamental change in dominating ideologies about the State's role generally nor about its higher education role specifically. But while publicness was the dominant policy orientation for over a century, privatization has been pushed toward center stage for only one decade; deeply ingrained fact versus grand experimentation is the difference here. Although privatization quickly put severe dents in the statist tradition, the future remained uncertain by the time this analysis terminated (1984). Among the obstacles were a severe economic crisis undermining the Chicago Boys' ideology, difficulties in adapting market principles to higher education, and the continued force of a statist tradition. Whatever the future, however, Chile under the junta made Latin America's most determined effort (with some results) at privatizing an entire higher education system, an effort oriented by a general push to restructure State-private relations. That effort therefore merits analysis here; partisans of divergent views will draw "lessons," just as they have drawn lessons from the broader authoritarian experiment and from the preceding Marxist experiment. How striking it is, nevertheless, that Chile itself offers a much more established and enduring example of statist rather than privatized higher education and of private sector emulation of the public sector. Thus, this chapter emphasizes the private-public homogeneity associated with Chile's ingrained statist tradition.

EVOLUTION
Estado Docente

Nearly two centuries passed between the founding of Latin America's first universities and the founding of Chile's first. Unlike Mexico and Peru, Chile was not one of Spain's "poles of development" in the New World. While there were some religious institutions of higher education, no university existed until Santiago's municipal government (*cabildo*) helped create the Royal University of San Felipe. Though the Crown granted authorization in 1738, the university did not start functioning until 1757.

The new university fit our notion of a fused private-public institution. Only by emphasizing certain characteristics to the exclusion of others could one declare the institutíon truly private or public. The public hue could be related to the relatively late colonial creation. By the mid to late eighteenth century, many of Latin America's fused institutions began to look increasingly public. Social thought had changed in the centuries since the region's first universities were created and so had the power relationships between Crown and Church. Compared to earlier Latin American universities, the Royal University of San Felipe was born into a more liberal environment. In fact, it was something of a secular alternative to existing seminary education. Notably, this would not become a royal *and pontifical* university.

On the other hand, authors such as Silvert and Reissman have emphasized the university's private hue. The philosophies of St. Augustine and St. Thomas were fundamental. The distribution of the university's graduates, between its 1757 inception and its 1839 closing (620 philosophy, 569 theology, 526 law, 33 medicine, 40 mathematics) "makes evident the religious character of the institution, for even the law graduates were trained in canonical and ancient law only."[5] Thus, precisely because a case can be made either for a public or private tendency, neither single characterization rings true.

Typically for Latin America, political independence strengthened publicness in higher education, a trend that paralleled broader trends in Chilean educational politics. From 1830 to 1860, under the leadership of Diego Portales, Francisco Bulnes, and Manuel Montt, the State assumed an unusually stable and respected role. Political stability created an excellent climate for the influx, permanent or temporary, of many of Latin America's leading educational innovators.[6] Often inspired by European liberalism, they supported public education against clericalism, but even conservative political power did not preclude a growing State—certainly not in education. In any case, by later in the century positivism came to be a decisive current.[7] Positivists promoted State over Church influence in education and fought hard to beat back an 1872 Freedom of Education Decree giving degree-granting powers to private schools.

The close association between the State and education, reflected in the slogan To Govern is to Educate (promoted by positivist philosopher and university rector Valentín Letelier), rested on an increasingly sturdy legal and structural base. The 1833 Constitution (in effect until 1925), discussed responsibility for "national education." A key concept was the *Estado Docente* (teaching state). In fact, this would be a key concept in much of Latin America. The Estado Docente regarded public education as a "preferential activity of the State." According to its champions, only the Estado

Docente could provide liberal choices of values and professions, equity for those unable to purchase higher education, effectiveness for a progressive system, and freedom from religious dogma. Despite the consequent proportional growth in public primary and secondary education, however, private education also remained important. Moreover, no "true educational system" took hold nationally until the State delegated responsibility over Chilean education to its own higher education institution.[8]

The roots of the University of Chile (UCH), founded in 1842, are found in the National Institute, formed in 1813 from a fusion of different institutions, including the Royal University of San Felipe. But the new university would be no mere extension of the colonial university. Instead, it broke with Spanish colonial ways and founded its sixteen initial chairs largely around secular fields such as political law and chemistry. The new university was a strikingly public institution, an integral part of the State apparatus. Its wide powers were rooted in the 1833 Constitution and foreign influences, including the Napoleonic University. Indeed, the key figure in creating the UCH was himself a foreigner, Venezuela's Andrés Bello. Bello worked closely with the education minister Manuel Montt and was himself named the first rector. His appointment and those of the first professors were made by the State. (The UCH's role as the State's regulatory arm in all educational policy will be considered in the governance section.)

Just as the State's roles grew in education generally and in higher education specifically, so a challenge to these roles arose in each. In the former, "peaceful coexistence" gave way to a "violent polemic concerning the role of the State and the private institutions."[9] Much of the tension obviously arose from the growing State threat to private education, as Domingo Sarmiento and others of the influential Generation of 1842 pushed their anticlerical positions. Already by the 1850s, conservatives increasingly looked away from the Estado Docente, toward "freedom of instruction." In higher education, the challenge to the State's role would lead to the creation of a private sector.

Dual Sectors and Homogenization, 1888–1973

Chagrin over the State's higher education monopoly was most keenly felt by the Church; the institutional alternative would be a Catholic university. Chile thus illustrates—indeed foretells—the typical Latin American first-wave phenomenon whereby the first private universities were Catholic reactions to the growth of public, secular control. The Church was naturally backed by conservative interests similarly averse to the liberal enemy, the UCH.

The Chilean case also illustrates how the creation of a Catholic alternative reflected not only Church power but also a weakness in relation to the State with which it had previously been integrated. Obviously, the UCH's (nearly half-century) monopoly on Chilean higher education was already one proof of the Church's subordination to the State, given the Church's lack of influence within the UCH. Heartened by the European Catholic church's late-nineteenth-century reassertion of its social role, some Catholic leaders spoke of "reconquering" the UCH or at least its Faculty of Theology—a theology faculty in name only.[10] It became clear, however, that practical efforts had to focus on establishing an alternative institution. In 1888 Monsignor Mariano Casanova, archbishop of Santiago, signed the founding decree for "the Church's answer to the University of Chile, with its increase in 'free thinkers,' atheists and masons who endangered the Christian culture of our people."[11] The Catholic University of Chile (UC) soon began functioning, becoming Latin America's first Catholic university (with only a very questionable Colombian exception).

This Catholic alternative signified not only that the Catholic leadership could not repenetrate the nation's major educational institution but that the political climate was changing unfavorably for the Church. Liberals were giving ground to even more staunchly anti-Church elements. Radicals (and Freemasons) and positivists were clearly more statist than the more laissez-faire liberals. The Liberal party would soon be closer to its traditional rival, the Conservative party, than to the Radicals. In the 1920s under President Arturo Alessandri, the Radicals mandated compulsory primary education, despite a conservative opposition basing its case on the sanctity of individual freedom. Furthermore, Chile's 1925 Constitution emphasized that the State (not just the government) was the guarantor of this provision. The new constitution also explicitly insisted on the separation of Church and State. At times, the Church's university felt so beleaguered that its seriously considered incorporation into the UCH.[12]

In sum, Chile's first wave of private creation presaged the general Latin American pattern in many respects. Typically, Chile's first wave was Catholic and largely a defensive reaction against liberal, secular, public dominance. Atypically, however, Chile's Catholic University preceded the 1930s and indeed inaugurated Latin America's first wave. Like the second Catholic university, in Peru, it was thus condemned to many decades of marginality, a weak island surrounded by the public's near monopoly.

As with other Latin American nations, both what is typical and atypical in contemporary private-public patterns can be understood largely in terms of the relative strength and juxtaposition of different waves. The atypicality of Chile's patterns stems more from the nature of its next six universities than from its first two. Typically enough, two of the five new private ones would be Catholic, three secular. But atypically, the secular subsector developed

71

early. Only Colombia had previously created secular private universities. More important, Chile did not emerge along the usual lines later found in Latin America's elite second wave or demand-absorbing third wave. Part of the explanation lies in the early development of these private institutions. Chile's private sector was born prior to the perceived "massification," and lowered elite composition, academic deterioration, and radical politicization of the public sector. By the time these perceptions materialized (and they did not go as far in Chile as in many nations), two sectors had been firmly in place and were both affected, albeit not equally.

As proliferation proved limited, we can easily bring the remaining universities into our analysis. Chile's first private secular university was the University of Concepción (1919). Its creation provided no comfort for the Catholics and their UC. On the contrary, Concepción represented hostility. Fundamentally a Masonic university, it was dedicated to the "free development of the spirit," often code words for anti-Catholicism. Thus the new university was more like the public UCH than like the private UC. Whatever privateness it developed evoked second-wave elite images more than Catholic ones. Neither public nor Church funds, but other private funds, primarily built the new university. There was also a secular governing board and some effort to bypass semiautonomous professional faculties by establishing departments and institutes.

Yet in other ways the University of Concepción does not conform to our second-wave elite pattern. For one thing, it represented a liberal rather than conservative alternative to the UC. This fact can be related to the early creation of this secular wave, many decades before the UC would itself liberalize. Further showing that Concepción did not conform to the second-wave pattern, its creation was not fundamentally a response to public sector failure. Instead, Concepción was an odd private-public hybrid from the outset. Fernando Campos writes that it was probably only a quirk that Concepción was born a private university.[13] A major initial booster was the UCH. The government went along in principle but, lacking the ready financial resources, let the proposal sit. At this point private groups, mostly business groups, took the initiative and created the university. Their central motivation was not to establish a private alternative to the public UCH but to give one of Chile's major cities, their own, a deserved institution. More than privateness, regionalism was a motivating force in creating a university five hundred kilometers south of the UCH. Indeed, until 1960 the UCH served as something of a model.

Nor would a private backlash to the public sector be the principal cause for the creation of subsequent private institutions. While seventy-seven years elapsed between the creation of independent Chile's first and third universities, the other five were created within a twenty-nine-year span—

72

1928 to 1956. In each of the four private cases, regionalism would again be at least as important as private-public inclination. Chile's fourth university was the Catholic University of Valparaíso, created in 1928 by the bishop of the port city. To be sure, this new institution was something of a private religious alternative to the secular UCH. Dictator Carlos Ibáñez was persuaded to support and then officially recognize it largely by a friend in the priesthood. But also important was Ibáñez's appreciation of Valparaíso's importance. This importance was similarly felt by private interests, including one crucial benefactor—Señora Isabel Cacés de Brown. After all, along with Santiago and Concepción, Valparaíso was one of Chile's three chief urban centers. Yet it had been suffering from the rerouting of international shipping in the wake of the Panama Canal's opening. Chile's second Catholic university, much less than the UC, was created as a religious or political alternative to the UCH.[14]

Valparaíso's prestige received another boost just three years later (1931) with the creation of the Federico Santa María Technical University (UTSM). Here was a private university very different from both the existing public and private universities. The primary distinction lay in its technical orientation. So explicit was the idea to deviate from established Chilean models that provision was made for courses to be taught only by foreigners for the first ten years of the UTSM's existence. The specific model copied was the German technical school. In some ways the UTSM fit the second-wave category. Donations from the city's private interests were even more crucial than for the city's Catholic university. Most notable was an eccentric millionaire, long involved in Valparaíso's development, whose 1925 will in effect created the university that bears his name.

That there was nothing intrinsically private about a technical university in Chile was proven in 1947 with the creation of a State Technical University (UTE). Until the founding of UTSM, Chile's technical education had existed only at the primary and secondary levels. The UTE's antecedents went back to 1849 when President Bulnes, concerned about the need for technicians in the mining and industry crucial to the young nation's economy, established Chile's first technical schools. Many such institutions were subsequently created in the provinces. Not until 1940, however, was the School of Industrial Engineering formed for their graduates; it was followed by the Pedagogical Institute to train teachers for the technical schools. Finally, at the higher education level, many of the technical schools were merged to form the UTE.

The last two universities founded in Chile were explicitly regional institutions—the South or Austral University (1954) and University of the North (1956). The latter was created as a regional dependency of the Catholic University of Valparaíso. Local clamoring for these universities must be understood in terms of Chile's unique geography, which is remarkably long and narrow, imposing great distances between its extremities and its Santiago center. Many prospective students were simply too far from the UCH. In the 1960s a major solution was the creation of regional campuses, chiefly of the UCH. But until that point the major remedy was creation of provincial private universities. Had such regional institutions been created a decade later they might well have been branches of existing universities. As it was, the UCH played a major role in the creation of the private Austral University and subsequently maintained strong ties.[15]

Both the Austral University and the University of the North were intended to serve, in only a very limited fashion, as second-wave private alternatives to the dominant public sector. They were concerned less with expanding choice for students who already had access to public institutions than with providing equitable access to students who lived in deprived regions. The Austral University (at Valdivia) met the need to have an institution of higher education located somewhere between Concepción and the southern end of the country. It set aside 80 percent of its places for students from the Bío-Bío region on south. Similarly, the University of the North (at Antofagasta) served the country's other extreme. It set aside 85 percent of its places for students from Tarapacá and Coquimbo. As with its mother institution and the UTSM, one benefactor (Berta González Vda. de Astorga) played a crucial role. The University of the North achieved statutory independence in 1964, although ambiguity as to its religious ties remained. Some have stressed its status as a separate institution, while others have stressed its parental heritage from the Catholic University of Valparaíso, which passed along its own heavy Jesuit influence. Because it has remained juridically Catholic, I group the University of the North with Chile's two older Catholic universities for subsequent data analysis but note that it has rightfully been seen as only marginally Catholic, even compared to its counterparts.

Thus, until the military usurped power, only one public and five private universities had been added to the UCH and the UC (see table 3.1). Compared to other major Latin American nations, Chile had effectively restricted institutional proliferation, thereby maintaining some semblance of a system, perhaps even of a public nucleus, though one institutionally outnumbered by the private sector. Remarkable in the Latin American context was the nonproliferation of both public and private demand-absorbing institutions. Instead, the further structural differentiation of Chilean higher education came from the creation of regional colleges associated with the existing universities. And the great majority of these were tied to the two public universities, especially to the UCH. So the private sector's proliferation nearly culminated in 1956—an abbreviated growth phenomenon compared to private sectors elsewhere and to Chile's own public (regional college) proliferation.

Modeled in large part on the University of California's junior college system, the UCH's plan aimed at decentralization, modernization, and increased opportunity within the public sector.[16] Admissions were less rigorous than at the parent institution. More emphasis was placed on technical and local needs, reflecting the equity as well as public sector considerations that insured Communist party support despite the U.S. model and the financial involvement of the Ford Foundation and the IDB. The plan could also be interpreted as the UCH's attempt to shore up its waning status as the national university. Except for the consolidation of technical schools into the UTE, no public university had been created since 1842. Regionalization seemed like a good way to extend the public sector while preserving effective coordination. The UTE soon created its own regional college network to reinforce its stature as the national technical university. While the private sector did not sit by idly, it created a much smaller network of associated regional colleges.

Such was the institutional evolution of Chilean higher education until 1973. Only the UC back in 1888 was created largely in opposition to the public sector. And no private university was created fundamentally as an institutional alternative to a failing public sector. Although some very important private-public differences persisted into the 1960s, the point here is that the private-public division was limited, even initially, paving the way for the homogeneity in finance, governance, and function that will be explored more closely. The early creation of private universities meant not only that the private sector became rather large, holding roughly one-third of total enrollments while private sectors were just beginning elsewhere; it also meant that the private sector grew and transformed itself under many of the same pressures that affected the public sector. The Chilean case shows how limited distinctiveness attracts nondistinctive growth, i.e., students

Table 3.1 Evolution of Chile's University System, 1842–1980

University	Year	Juridical Type
University of Chile (UCH)	1842	public-secular
Catholic University of Chile (UC)	1888	private-Catholic
University of Concepción	1919	private-secular
Catholic University of Valparaíso	1928	private-Catholic
Federico Santa María Technical University (UTSM)	1931	private-secular
State Technical University (UTE)	1947	public-secular
Austral University	1954	private-secular
University of the North	1956	private-Catholic

choosing institutions for reasons not fundamentally related to private-public issues. Of course, some nondistinctive growth occurs even where there are far greater intersectoral cleavages. It is a matter of degree, and Chile's substantial nondistinctive growth best shows how such growth naturally erodes the intersectoral distinctiveness that does exist.

Proliferation and Retrenchment, 1973–1983

To complete the discussion on evolution and to be ready to explore finance, governance, and function in detail from the 1960s on, two final factors must be addressed. One is that, until 1981, the junta followed what we might soberly call a neutron bomb policy—not destroying most structures even while brutally assaulting personnel as well as programs. With its 1981 legislation, however, the junta brought about substantial institutional proliferation.[17] The only requirement for opening an institution was to lodge an application with but bare educational guidelines; such applications were to be automatically approved if not rejected within ninety days. A system of eight separate institutions quickly grew to roughly fifty. Regional campuses and some professional schools were ripped away from the two public universities, forming "derived" regional universities and professional institutes. On the private side, the six traditional universities remained largely intact, but three new universities were born (Gabriela Mistral, Diego Portales, and Central), six new professional institutes opened, and numerous technical training centers were opened or elevated to higher education status. Universities were defined by their right to offer the licenciatura (and higher) degrees and to license for the practice of any profession, while institutes could not confer such academic degrees and therefore could not license for any of twelve specified professions (see footnote 34 below), and centers could offer only studies of two years or less. (Academies, usually pedagogical, were treated like institutes, so I subsume them under the latter term.) Thus, the picture as of 1982 is shown in table 3.2; it surely would prove partly transitory as some institutes became universities, private institutions were created and closed at a dizzying pace, and "privatization" was reassessed, but the picture suggests the zeal of the junta's attempt to transform the structure of Chilean higher education.

The last factor that must be addressed here concerns enrollments. Note the sharp authoritarian reversal which, unlike institutional proliferation, began immediately after the coup. But also note the previous long-term growth. Table 3.3 shows the magnitude of Chile's systemic growth and reversal. Cohort enrollments jumped from 4 to over 16 percent from 1960 to 1974, before falling back to 11 percent by 1980. The system grew 69, 84, and 91 percent in three respective quinquennia from 1960 to 1975 and then

76

shrank 19 percent from 1975 to 1980. Yet the private share of enrollments remained remarkably stable—between 34 and 38 percent—throughout the entire 1960–80 period of rapid growth and sudden reversal. The sectors were similarly affected by the powerful external forces that shaped higher education. After 1980, data became more difficult to compare. The 1981 figure for the eight traditional universities fell under 100,000, but that did not include the derived institutions ripped away from them.[18]

Within two years, however, many aspects of the new system were very much in question, just as the junta's overall antistatist thrust was in question. In a flash, the regime reshuffled the education ministry, at least temporarily banned the creation of new careers, then new institutions, and announced that yet more legislation would be forthcoming. For one thing, free-market policies had allowed a sudden surge in first-year enrollments. While some State officials spoke about working out anomalies, others railed against the ineffectiveness of irresponsible competition—and called for rational planning. However structural differentiation may develop, more definitive conclusions can be drawn about the private-public patterns of homogeneity established over a long evolutionary process.

FINANCE
A Public System

That Chile's public sector has relied directly on the State for nearly all its funds is but typical for Latin America. More dramatic has been the overwhelming public subsidy for the nominally private sector. Many factors, such as progressive political ideology, may help explain this State role. One important factor is the early development of the private sector. Chile is the

Table 3.2 Chile's Institutional Structure, 1982

Juridical Institutional Type[a]	No.	Popular Private-Public Nomenclature
Traditional public universities	2	public
Derived regional universities	8	public
Derived professional institutes	8	public
Traditional private universities	6	private-public
New professional institutes	6	private
Technical training centers[b]	15	private
New universities[c]	3	private

a. *Traditional* = existing pre-1973; *derived* = carved mostly out of traditional public universities; *new* = not part of the higher education system pre-1973.
b. See footnote 18 for more recent data.
c. Two of these did not begin classes until 1983.

most striking Latin American case where a private sector initially supports itself but later relies increasingly on the State. While some sister nations have already moved in this direction in more limited ways, many others have or may soon debate whether the State should undertake any such financial role. How then has State financing of the private sector developed and operated in Chile?

Chile's private sector moved slowly from self-financing to State subsidization. For many years private universities scrounged for their subsidies while their public counterparts received legally guaranteed subsidies.[19] A significant feature of Chile's early State subsidization, however, was that it involved the private sector generally, not just the Catholic subsector.

A major breakthrough for the concept of State subsidization of private education came in 1920 when Alessandri's reformist government decided that compulsory primary education could work only if the State subsidized private as well as public schools. Subsidization greatly increased in the 1950s. One aim was to promote consumer or parental choice. Another was to promote effectiveness or educational quality throughout the system. But possibly the major goal was equity—to increase and equalize educational opportunities. Therefore, much more would be given to the tuition-free than to the tuition-charging private institutions. By 1970, 75 percent of private students at the primary and 40 percent at the secondary level were in tuition-free schools; private primary education came to be more than 80

Table 3.3 Chilean Higher Education Enrollments, 1935–1981

Year	Enrollment	% of Cohort Group	Private % of Enrollments
1935	6,283	1.4	27
1945	8,893	1.8	26
1955	19,749	3.5	31
1960	24,703	4.0	37
1965	41,801	5.6	37
1970	76,979	9.2	34
1974	144,523	16.4	34
1975	147,049	16.2	35
1976	134,149	14.3	35
1977	130,676	13.3	38
1978	130,208	12.7	37
1979	127,446	11.9	37
1980	118,978	10.8	37
1981[a]	118,984	10.5	38

SOURCE: Rafael Echeverría, "Evolución de la matrícula en Chile, 1935–1981," a PIIE working paper, November 1982, pp. 22–23, 114–17, 120.

a. Data for 1981 are not fully comparable with earlier years. See footnote 18 for estimations regarding the early 1980s.

percent State subsidized, private secondary education about 40 percent.[20] While substantial State subsidization of private schools is possible without similar subsidization of private universities, the former may weaken political barriers to the latter. In cross-national perspective, Chile's preuniversity private education received unusually substantial State subsidization.

Two initial breakthroughs in higher education itself occurred almost simultaneously at the two first private universities. Because the University of Concepción was created as a private institution partly by chance, it was not the sort of antithesis to existing public universities that ideologically precluded State aid, even initially. As mentioned, the State supported creation of the new university, although not strongly enough to finance it directly. It therefore sought an intermediate mechanism—a lottery. Revenues represented a type of State aid that permitted greater freedom than ministerial subsidies generally did. Additionally, the State gave some direct aid to supplement the university's private income.

Another big breakthrough came at the UC, 1923, when the legislature granted more aid to it than to the University of Concepción.[21] This was interpreted as acceptance for the religious university that had been regarded as a pariah by the public sector. State subsidies would fluctuate and even fall significantly in the 1930s, but the diminished gap between the UC and secular society would ensure a stable State role by the 1960s.

To the extent that Chile's four more recent private universities were created only secondarily as private organizational alternatives to public universities, they were logical recipients of State subsidies in ways that the UC and Latin America's other first-wave private universities initially were not, and as most Catholic and nearly all secular private universities still are not. Special laws financed each of the four.[22] Like the University of Concepción, the Austral University received lottery money.

Another significant piece of legislation came in 1954. It earmarked 0.5 percent of all revenue from fiscal taxes plus duties and customs for a fund created primarily for the construction of research facilities. The fund would be run by the Contraloría General, a public agency with a wide administrative and juridical role in State finance. A specific formula regulated distribution of the fund: UCH 10/18, UTE 1/18; UC and University of Concepción 2/18 each; the other three (the University of the North was not yet operating) 1/18 each. Thus the private sector would receive 7/18 of this State funding.

More important, however, was the State's increasingly solidified role in providing regular subsidies for general private university expenditures. By the 1960s the private sector approached the public sector in its State/total income percentage (see table 3.4 below). Serious doubts about private eligibility arose only with the election of Allende's Marxist coalition (1970). A major congressional debate developed over the applicability to private higher education of a law prohibiting State subsidization of private schools that were neither nonprofit nor tuition-free. In the end, universities were simply exempted from this measure. Against the backdrop of new laws that

Table 3.4 Self-Generated Income in Chilean Universities, 1965–1977

	1965[a]	1970	1973	1974	1977	Five-Year Total
U. of Chile	12,1983	175,507	221,835	321,727	611,088	1,452,140
(UCH)	815,393	1,687,585	1,798,017	3,505,121	2,852,882	10,658,998
	15.0%	10.4%	12.3%	9.2%	21.4%	13.6%
State	5,714	21,165	14,045	31,144	374,441	446,509
Technical U.	156,456	316,672	507,080	701,815	1,074,549	2,756,572
(UTE)	3.7%	6.7%	2.8%	4.4%	34.8%	16.2%
Catholic U.	58,909	67,687	85,958	153,675	440,381	806,610
of Chile	148,032	350,415	494,068	879,260	1,190,625	3,062,400
(UC)	37.8%	19.3%	17.4%	17.5%	37.0%	26.3%
Catholic U.	9,530	8,985	4,131	10,212	41,704	74,562
of Valparaíso	45,743	101,830	148,303	238,949	254,080	788,905
	20.8%	8.8%	2.8%	4.3%	16.4%	9.5%
U. Concepción	4,447	0	18,590	29,301	130,985	183,323
	170,901	386,156	547,565	721,861	702,850	2,529,333
	2.6%	0.0%	3.4%	4.1%	18.6%	7.2%
Austral	3,812	13,577	42,962	34,833	91,058	186,742
University	41,932	143,759	193,330	258,935	310,287	948,243
	9.1%	9.4%	22.2%	13.5%	29.3%	19.6%
U. of the	3,177	3,195	6,403	12,021	38,096	62,892
North	15,884	92,845	182,797	208,146	304,863	864,535
	20.0%	3.4%	3.5%	4.5%	12.5%	7.3%
Technical U.	6,988	6,589	4,544	18,753	40,104	77,008
Santa María	36,213	65,491	116,701	216,990	231,779	667,174
(UTSM)	19.3%	10.1%	3.9%	8.6%	17.3%	11.5%
TOTAL	214,560	296,705	398,468	611,646	1,767,857	3,289,286
	1,430,554	3,144,753	3,987,861	6,791,077	6,921,915	22,276,160
	15.0%	9.4%	10.0%	9.0%	25.5%	14.8%

SOURCE: Ministerio de Hacienda, "Análisis financiero de la educación superior chilena: Período 1965–1978," Santiago, 1978, Appendixes 4–17.

NOTE: Data deal with annual subsidies, not income for capital expenses. Each set of information includes self-generated income over total income, followed by the former's share of the latter.

a. Data from UDUAL, *Censo universitario 1962–1965* (Mexico City: 1967), pp. 359, 371, 347, 377, 333, show the following percentages for 1961: UCH 21, U. Concepción 8, UTSM 33, Austral 15, with no data for the other four.

pledged certain percentages of the public purse to the public universities, private universities successfully demanded that they too receive guarantees of stable State financing.[23] Such victories should be seen in the context of general legal guarantees to preserve democratic freedoms that the powerful opposition parties insisted on from Allende's government. Ironically, then, the Marxist electoral triumph indirectly moved to new heights the Chilean policy of State support for the private sector.

Pushing Dual Sector Privatization

Immediately upon seizing power, the junta proclaimed that a drastic privatization would occur in higher education finance. On the one hand, both the goal and the ideological zeal with which privatization was pursued appear unprecedented in Latin American history; on the other, many regimes have tried to impose some increased self-financing on the universities. But because the effort produced inconclusive results in its first decade, and because the junta's financial policy has been analyzed elsewhere, this section merely outlines the efforts.[24] A salient point for this study is that intersectoral homogeneity persisted. No thought was given to making only the private universities truly private; rather, the idea was to move the whole system toward the private pole. A model of State financing of dual sectors was targeted to become a model of private financing of dual sectors.

Higher education presented a particularly attractive target for the broad privatization and austerity policy pushed by the Chicago Boys. After all, State financing and its allegedly accompanying ills in waste and lack of competition characterized not one but both sectors. Compared to this effectiveness argument, an equity argument probably influenced policy less but was as loudly proclaimed. Chile's educational system was considered unduly top-heavy, and empirical studies had particularly questioned the distributive effects of higher education.[25]

Before long, however, privatization was in trouble. Strong opposition came not only from middle-class groups but even from several military rectors defending "their" institutions. A cornerstone argument, shared by many in the army, was that education remains a State responsibility (Estado Docente). Additionally, myriad technical problems arose, as did disputes among proponents themselves about the meaning of self-financing. As the concept became diluted, officials issued denials—demonstrably false—that it had ever been intended as an absolute. In any case, by the late 1970s the junta tried to reinvigorate privatization, this time with much less extreme goals but more detailed planning. The 1981 legislation (in severe trouble by 1983) fixed State subsidies at 1980 levels for each university (and its derived institutions); from there the subsidies were to be reduced by 50 percent within five years. The difference would be funneled into a fund of indirect subsidies available through interinstitutional competition involving the top 20,000 students (of roughly 120,000 applicants, 30,000 were admitted) as identified by aptitude tests adapted from U.S. models, thus reinforcing Chile's self-conscious pursuit of effectiveness through U.S. competition rather than Continental criteria. By placing a cap on subsidies, the regime hoped to pressure institutions to raise private funds and to restrict enrollments. At the same time, systemwide expansion would be pushed toward the new institutions, privately funded. Reflecting the junta's astonishing zeal for privatization, the centers and institutes among these institutions can be for-profit organizations, in stark contrast to the long-established rules for Chile's private universities—indeed for private higher education in Latin America generally.

In summary, several points can be made about the effects of a decade of attempted privatization. Policies changed in important ways, though far less than originally intended, and the ultimate extent of privatization remained uncertain. The junta was not only quicker but more resolute in slashing subsidies than in imposing tuition or, at least for several years, any other new formula. A precipitous fall in subsidies by 1976 was followed by some recovery.[26] However, substantial tuitions were not implemented in the early years; later they amounted to only a few hundred dollars annually, high compared to Chilean living standards. Each university boasted its own ameliorating measures. But the regime was painfully slow with its ballyhooed loan plans. Then, just as Chile's economic crisis deepened in the early 1980s, tuitions jumped to roughly $800 per year or more, depending on university and career, paralleling private norms elsewhere. Tuitions in the new private universities soared way beyond these, matching U.S. ceilings of only a few years back. The Gabriela Mistral charged roughly $5,000 per year in 1982, while offering fields relatively inexpensive to teach and not offering exemptions or loans.

Financial data confirm not only intersectoral homogeneity but also its movement away from the pre-coup public pole. Assuming that "self-generated income" equals not only tuition but service fees, contract research, and international aid, table 3.4 shows that, even by this overly liberal definition, private sources accounted for only 15 percent of the system's funds by 1965. The figure hit its low point in the early 1970s, before the junta brought it to new highs.[27]

Throughout these periods of substantial increases and then decreases in State subsidization, intersectoral differences have remained remarkably small. In 1965 there was still a hint of distinction, as the private sector drew 19 percent of its income from nonstatist sources compared to 13 percent for the public sector. But even that minimal gap narrowed, and in 1977 State funds accounted for a smaller share of public than private sector income. Averaging the five years included in table 3.4, the public sector drew 14 percent of its income from non-State sources versus a system average of 15 percent. Moreover, the UCH consistently lay near the system average. Only the UTE, as is typical for public technical institutions, had been especially dependent on State funds, until the junta ruled. On the other side, the UC provided the most private flavor to its sector, although even that was limited by 1965 and then much diminished by 1970. The Austral was also on the private side within Chile's statist context. But the other four private universities were even more State-dependent than Chile's systemic norm. The University of Concepción in particular stands out as a secular private university, relatively large and prestigious, that has depended overwhelmingly on State funds. Even as the junta made Chile's public sector unusual for its degree of private finance, Chile's private sector remained much more unusual for its degree of public finance. And intersectoral homogeneity proved to be deeply rooted.

GOVERNANCE

Chile presents Latin America's clearest profile of private-public homogeneity not just in finance but in governance as well. As the system modernized in the 1950s, and as a far-reaching reform swept the system in the late 1960s, differences in governance continually diminished and the UCH lost its supremacy over the rest of the system. Military rule also fundamentally changed governance patterns systemwide without igniting profound private-public distinctions; as in finance, that such dramatic changes befell different universities in many similar ways reflected the high degree of previously established homogeneity. After the coup the entire system became more public in the sense of State domination, although initiatives in the early 1980s pushed toward some U.S. forms. Before the coup the major trend had been toward institutional autonomy.

The National University as State Regulator

The UCH was founded as the national university. Adopting the Napoleonic model, its monopolistic control over university education was indisputable, and it enjoyed certain statist powers over national education at all levels. The young UCH, not an education ministry, ran Chilean education. Although this direct supervision ended in 1860 for primary education and 1879 for secondary education, a major UCH role persisted subsequently. The UCH rector sat on important committees and joined with the education minister in making important decisions. He had, for example, the authority to nominate (to the president of the republic) candidates to head the public *liceos*.[28] Reciprocally, and also illustrating the State-UCH nexus, the education ministry and its primary and secondary school directors were represented at the UCH.

Predictably, the UCH's identity with the State proved especially persistent in higher education. From the outset the UCH was accorded monopolistic authority to certify professional elites, and 1879 legislation underscored its central role. But a few chinks began to appear in its monopolistic control. Primarily, the UC was emerging at this time. While legislation still insisted that only the UCH could give valid exams, grades, and degrees for professional practice, exceptions were made. The UC, based partly on canon law, could authorize degrees for employment outside the "public sphere." It could also grant degrees in fields not offered by the UCH.[29]

The fall of the UCH from its peak authority represented an end to undisputed public sector supremacy in Chile. It more sharply represented the redistribution of authority from one institution to many, thereby illustrating a common tendency in twentieth-century Latin American higher education.

Ambiguity, which reigned for decades after the first private universities were created, was unrelieved by further legislation (1927). Private universities established some governance patterns similar to those operating in the national university; the venerable institution was branding its mark on new institutions. This insured a UCH leadership role and a significant degree of system homogeneity, but it also legitimized the new institutions (all boasting official recognition by the State). A somewhat nervous national university reasserted its prerogatives in new legislation (1931). Its regulatory authority was reaffirmed, and it was pointedly labeled the supervisor of Chilean higher education. Only on this basis were the degrees given by each university officially deemed to be of equal value. Moreover, the State agreed to consult the UCH before sanctioning the creation of any new institutions. In reality, however, some additional universities were created without such consultation, and certain UCH supervisory prerogatives on curriculum and degree granting were widely ignored. The 1931 law remained so ambiguous that the private universities' power easily outstripped the authority that the legislation probably had envisioned.[30] Whereas they could originally grant degrees only where specifically permitted (e.g., engineering and architecture), they subsequently did so except where specifically prohibited. By the 1960s, only medicine and some areas of biology were off-limits, still dependent on the UCH's programs and exams.

The progressive extension of private university autonomy from the UCH inevitably was a conflictual process. By early in the twentieth century, and especially by the 1920s, the UC complained about State discrimination against private universities. Private interest groups successfully pressured the State, arguing for the virtues of free choice.[31] Supporters of public universities fought back, arguing that only with adequate authority could the UCH effectively represent the State, coordinate higher education policy, and maintain quality. Later it was likewise argued that the UTE should be the State's representative in technical higher education. The Communist party emerged by midcentury as the most ardent statist voice. It advocated not just holding the line against further private gains but sometimes even the reassertion of the earlier UCH regulatory powers.

Efforts to transform higher education's institutional structure, discussed under the PDC and UP but pushed more authoritatively by the junta, showed how much resonance was still left in the controversy. The junta's initial idea was to create from eight separate universities, with many regional campuses, one unified system. Heated protest came quickly from the UCH. Fifteen of the institution's eighteen deans proclaimed that theirs was the "national" university, the State's university, the supervisor of the system: "The private universities have been born and created as subsidiary and cooperative organizations of the University's activities." One dean added a metaphorical touch: "The University is the biggest ship and the others are small frigates at its side." And a professor summed things up this way:[32]

> We have here an ideological controversy with two positions
> about education. On one side the laical tradition of masons,
> radicals, and some rightists among others who think that
> since education is a national good of prime necessity it should
> be preponderantly in State hands. The University [UCH]
> would be the most important instrument to fulfill this State
> function. On the other side is the economic team and the
> Ministry of Education, with people mostly from the Catholic
> universities, who tend to favor private action, where the
> criteria of efficiency and free educational competition reign.

The proprivate position, in the professor's opinion, would lead to onerous elite "university-enterprises." Predictably, private universities responded harshly to the UCH's assertions. They insisted that only the State, not any single university aspiring to hegemony, is responsible for the system.

There was more form than substantive reality in much of this debate, however, because the UCH was no longer the monopolistic institution nor even the system's supervisor. But something was still at stake here, something definitely sensed by partisans. The UCH had remained the nation's foremost educational institution—first among equals even in the most cautious estimation. The junta seemed intent on reducing it to the status of just one university among others. Until the turn of the decade the junta, while progressing with regionalization, had fallen far short of its much ballyhooed plans. The principal modifications came with the consolidation of campuses within the same region. Ironically, several representatives of the frustrated national university invoked choice and free-market economics arguments against the junta and its imposed coordination. "If there is one place where competition is valid, it is in the universities. If there is only one university per region, academic competence and improved teaching and research are not guaranteed."[33] Indeed it was at least equally ironic to hear the junta echo the cries of its PDC and UP predecessors against uncoordinated proliferation.

In practice, regionalization and proliferation policies struck much harder at the preexisting public than private sectors. Except for the UC network, few private regional colleges existed. Moreover, mostly because of regime wariness about the Church, the UC retained its own campuses. Meanwhile, the two public universities were dismembered into the derived institutions discussed earlier. The UTE was renamed the University of Santiago, signaling its loss of national status as the State arm in its field. Chile no longer had a clear national university and, in fact, the UC (retaining its regional campuses) could mischievously stake some claims to that status.[34]

Another aspect of the erosion of UCH authority, which was connected with the regionalization and proliferation policies but also initiated before the coup, involved efforts to strengthen Chile's Council of Rectors. The very concept of such a council, originally charged to coordinate science and technology policy and to forge a university system, cuts against UCH claims to be the national university, properly entrusted to secure system effectiveness. From its inception in 1954, however, the council has been notoriously weak. Where interinstitutional coordination has been achieved, as in admissions policy, the council has provided support more than initiation or coercion. Chile's successes in interuniversity coordination have been attributable more to the limited number of universities and their relative homogeneity than to an active council.

There are several reasons for the council's traditional weakness. One has been the possibly inevitable resentment between the biggest university and the others. If a council should exist, the UCH has held, it should be headed by the UCH. Other universities favor a more equal distribution of power, despite their lesser size and prestige, even if they acknowledge that the UCH is the most important single partner. Another major obstacle to council strength has been the sometimes antagonistic ideologies of the constituent rectors; during the UP years, for example, two of the eight rectors were Communists.

An early attempt to strengthen the council came during the years of PDC rule. Leftists complained that the government was using the council to diminish the UCH and to promote the private universities. The Christian

Democrats were themselves caught between their quest for coordination and their priority on choice and voluntary action. Nor did the UP achieve much.[35] Even the junta had great difficulties. In desperation, it stripped the UCH rector of his council chairmanship, replacing him wit the minister of education. The change was a culminting symbol of the substantial shift of authority away from the UCH, but it hardly guaranteed effective council power.[36]

The UCH has fallen far from its original status as the national university. The junta's anti-public sector policies have accelerated that fall even beyond the movement that began, albeit slowly, back in the nineteenth century. The UCH, which had previously wielded State authority over higher education—once predominantly and then partially and ambiguously—now has, at most, a very limited supervisory role.

Institutional Governance

While an explicitly coordinated higher education system has been illusory ever since the UCH lost its position as the State's supreme representative, remarkably similar governance patterns came to characterize the individual institutions. We can trace the evolution of homogeneity in governance, culminating in the 1967–68 reform. This evolution has also been characterized by expanding institutional autonomy, so much so that Chileans have often referred to a "privatization."[37] *Autonomy* is a better term for our purposes, however, because it focuses on governance and encompasses not only increased public university freedom from the State but also increased private university freedom from its initial controllers, including private actors as well as the UCH. At any rate, we again see that the Continental model weakens. The decline of the national university as the State's delegate is accompanied by other movement from State control toward public university autonomy. Both tendencies find substantial parallels elsewhere in Latin America.

Some important cross-institutional differences manifested themselves for many years, despite the UCH influence. This was particularly true for the UC, as an alternative to the UCH. The UC's highest authority was the grand chancellor, who was the archbishop of Santiago. He chose the rectors, prorectors, and deans (from the rector's recommendations). From the outset, however, the leading lay advocate of the UC's creation was named to the high post of secretary general.[38] The UC continued to have priests as rectors until 1967, although its deans were increasingly drawn from laical ranks.

The laical University of Concepción also showed certain governance patterns distinct from the public UCH mode, but hardly similar to the UC mode. It was ruled by a six-member board of trustees. Both in composition and function it was influenced by U.S. counterparts.[39] Limiting institutional autonomy, extrauniversity influence was considerable, often by private financiers. Nonetheless, Concepción largely followed the UCH in academic structure and policy.

State authority was probably greatest at the public UTE. Its University Council included many direct representatives of the president of the republic. A distinctive extrauniversity influence was exerted by groups especially concerned with technical education: CORFO, the Association of Industrial Engineering, and labor unions. Nonetheless, governance at the two public universities was more similar than governance at the two major private universities, Catholic and laical. The main private-public distinction—an important one—rested with the State's direct representation and appointment powers only in the public universities.

Private-public differences in autonomy illustrated basic Latin American patterns, though in milder form. The main challenge to private university autonomy came from Church or business groups. The main challenge to public university autonomy came from the State. For example, while private universities generally owed less accountability than public ones for State subsidies, these same private universities could dangle on tight strings pulled by their private sources. So if *degrees* of institutional autonomy did not necessarily vary that much between private and public sectors, the *contours* of autonomy did. Moreover, intrainstitutional power hierarchies varied. The UCH's was probably the "flattest," with considerable control in the hands of (chaired) professors; the UC's, the "steepest." In this sense, academic freedom may well have been greater at the public UCH than at the private UC.

Yet even authors who identify interinstitutional differences also emphasize major structural similarities.[40] Much of the similarity predictably stemmed from the tendency of new institutions to copy the established UCH. But part resulted from the UCH's relatively hierarchal pyramid, compared to some public universities elsewhere in Latin America. However powerful professors became within UCH faculties, wresting some influence from central university administration, a good deal of power remained high in the pyramid. Only over time did the right of Chile's president to select professors from lists of three proposed by professorial councils become a mere formality. Naturally, the president was more influential in administrative appointments. Even when the 1931 statute increased institutional autonomy from the State, leading to greater faculty power and greater university freedom to distribute lump-sum annual grants, Chile's president continued to name the UCH's rector and faculty deans, albeit from professors' nominations. He also named its school and institute directors, from the rector's nominations, and he had a freer hand in firing. Moreover, students did not gain the degree of power they enjoyed in many sister republics. Nor was the UCH one of the region's major political battlegrounds. An exceptional period would be 1923–33, when the UCH had nine different rectors; but one rector then held office for the next twenty years. However, showing typical Latin American private-public contrasts and reflecting typical private sector hierarchy, rector stability was even greater at the private universities. Monsignor Carlos Casanueva held the UC rectorship from 1920 to 1953, and one of his own prorectors, Monsignor Alfredo Silva Santiago, then held office for some fifteen years, until the reform. The University of Concepción's Enrique Molina Garmendía served for thirty-seven years.[41]

In the 1950s "university modernization" began to alter the structure of Chilean higher education. One effect was to make the system more homogeneous. Foreign influence, including recommendations from the U.S.-oriented report by Rudolph Atcon, penetrated not just the private University of Concepción, where Atcon was primarily based, but the public UCH as well. More departmentalization and more centers of science and research at the expense of traditional concentrations in the professions were among the changes.

But probably the single biggest event leading to homogeneity was the late 1960s reform. Changes accelerated in such modernizing directions as departmentalization, unified teaching and research, curriculum flexibility, core courses, and electives; what most separated the reform from a mere continuation of the modernization process, however, was a notable redistribution of intrauniversity power. Democratization favored junior professors and students. This, then, was something of a delayed Córdoba reform, similar to reforms that were just then sweeping much of Western Europe. The analogy is appropriate because Chilean universities had maintained themselves closer to the European oligarchic norm than to the more participatory norm found in those Latin American universities previously more affected by the Córdoba reform.

Change would be greatest in those universities that had previously allowed the least degree of internal democratization. The public UCH had already distributed power more widely than had the private University of Concepción and the UC. Reform brought an end to Concepción's distinctive pattern of governance by a private board of trustees. For the UC it brought greater freedom from the Church. No longer would archbishops appoint rectors; a committee of professors, students, and university functionaries would do so. Together with a superior council, also composed of university personnel, the committee and rector would be the universities' supreme authorities. Thus, the private universities gained far greater autonomy from their respective extrauniversity authorities. But two trade-offs were clear. First, like the UCH and public universities in much of Latin America, the private universities would be more vulnerable to the consequences of widely distributed freedom and power. Second, also like public universities, they would be significantly dependent on the State (which had itself promoted the reform).

Authoritarian Control and U.S. Models

The reform received substantial support from both leftist and centrist political movements, although there was continual disagreement between the two groups over its nature and scope. Allende's election intensified the split. Rightists and centrists feared a Marxist design to supplant autonomy with unchecked State control over education. As with the controversy over Marxist financial policies, most of the battle explicitly concerned primary and secondary schools; but clear parallels to higher education intensified an already furious opposition.[42] Consequently, the legislature demanded constitutional recognition of university autonomy, within the 1971 Law of Democratic Guarantees. Actually, these provisions only confirmed existing legislation in terms of academic and administrative as well as financial freedoms; now, however, these freedoms were constitutionally consecrated so that breaches could be more severely punished. Yet whether it lacked the strength or the inclination or both, the UP government did not launch a major, systematic assault on university autonomy.

Instead, devasting destruction of university autonomy by the State would come with military rule. Little could be done contrary to State policy, and much had to be done actively to support it. The State came to abuse university autonomy more than at any time in Chilean history, just as it abused a broad range of societal freedoms in unprecedented form. The higher education reversal was especially sharp after the reform had greatly augmented the participatory base. In fact, the dividing line between State and university policy often became an arbitrary one as purges and top-down appointments placed the State's own personnel in most crucial decision-making centers within the universities. This included the installation of military officers—some retired, some in active service—as rectors of all eight universities, an example of blunt State control unequaled in Latin American history.

Several accounts have documented the junta's repression of Chilean higher education.[43] Concerning personnel matters, universities suffered from the effect of imposed hiring of top- and middle-level officials, and widespread purging of professors and students as well as an increased State

90

role in admissions. Regarding freedom to participate in academic policy, the junta, repressively intolerant of dissent, abolished most student representation and activities. "Responsible" and safe associations were the only sanctioned alternatives, though corporatist attempts failed and students remained a notable protest group. Similarly, repression affected professorial participation. Regarding the substance of academic policy, disciplines and research were reoriented, "undesirable" departments and faculties cut back or even dismantled, and the interinstitutional framework coercively undone and redone. Also, as we have already seen, the regime tried to impose its new financial policies in an authoritarian style. Overall, repression went beyond undoing the reform or restoring some previously reigning university model.

Yet even within this context of repressive State control—the most extreme analyzed in this book—there were significant qualifications. One concerned the substantial autonomy of several small research institutes aided by international finance, some offering nondegree courses and many under the Church's umbrella.[44] More generally, regime effectiveness was reduced by a lack of sustained priority and by incompetence, added to the opposition of many independent professors and students (and even administrators) who remained in the system. Another factor was related to the regime's internal divisions. The free-market recipe for effectiveness suggested some policies contradictory to centralized political imposition; a State-market tension ran through much of higher education policy. At least during the first decade of military rule, however, the authoritarian-statist orientation clearly predominated over the market orientation in most cases of discrepancy.[45]

A major attempt to pursue a more free-market and U.S.-style governance pattern was an integral part of the 1981 legislation. The attempt is worth considering for its ostensible push toward privatized governance. While architects of the new model publicly claimed that they drew upon studies of the world's leading universities, they privately admitted that they self-consciously pursued U.S. models deemed most successful in academic, economic, and political effectiveness.[46]

A quick view of the 1982 UCH statute and its provisions concerning the appointment of policymakers and their authority shows how the move toward U.S. modes still had to be reconciled with the regime's authoritarian concerns.[47] Supreme authority was divided between the rector and a board of trustees (*junta directiva*). The idea for the board obviously reflected U.S. influence: the rector/board combination was meant to parallel the U.S. president/board combination. Some board members, within certain limits, were to be selected by the University Council; others were to be selected by the president, possibly in consultation with the rector. The board would supposedly fix general orientations and resolve intrainstitutional conflicts, but its authority was shared with a rectorship largely dependent on the president and forceful enough in appointments and other areas that other actors would remain decidedly subordinate.

Such were the rough guidelines for the eight traditional universities, public and private, with some modifications for the derived institutions, including the advent of the first (post-1973) civilian rectors.[48] Similarly, the first new university's rector was a civilian: she had been neither a military officer nor a professor. These guidelines fit the Gabriela Mistral's *estilo americano*, complete with its board of trustees.[49] Ironically, however, most of the other new and nominally private institutions—the technical training centers—were not granted the autonomy legally accorded all the traditional universities and derived institutes. Instead, strong supervision over academic affairs was left to the education ministry. Thus, while private in finance, these centers were clearly not private in governance, even formalistically. A further restriction was placed on the autonomy of all new institutions of higher education, including the universities; each had to choose one of the eight traditional universities as a five-year supervisory institution. For example, the Gabriela Mistral chose the UCH, and the UCH (oddly restored to a bit of its old regulatory role) showed little inclination to go easy on the new university.

The reconstituted governance structure could be seen as an attempt to move beyond the blunt State control characteristic of the first eight years in order to institutionalize a trustworthy (antireform) system. In selecting U.S. models, leaders claimed to opt for anti-State innovations, challenging the bureaucratic inertia born of excessive centralism or inward-looking rectors. Nonetheless, innovations did not soon alter the martial command structure dominant in the major institutions. The major features of governance since 1973 could still be summarized as follows: For all its talk of free-market economics, the junta ruled higher education through unprecedented State control. The State fixed appointive, academic, and financial policies, either ignoring, repressing, or coercively changing the university's own preferences. It forcibly opened the universities to certain private actors, such as business, while limiting the role of others, such as the Church. But to the extent that university privateness relates to autonomy, the Chilean university became less private. The newly limited State discovered in financial policy found little parallel in governance. One striking similarity between governance and financial policy, however, was that drastic changes hit both traditional sectors almost equally. As these sectors moved from overwhelmingly public to mixed private-public financing, they lost autonomy to State control. Intersectoral homogeneity survived, but in radically different form.

FUNCTION

Compared to most dual sector systems, Chile's interinstitutional differences in function are limited, although perhaps not as much as those in finance and governance. Moreover, Chile's differences do not fundamentally form along private-public lines. Instead they form more along religious-secular and technical-nontechnical lines. While both overlap the private-public dimension, neither mirrors it. In fact, much interinstitutional variation forms ad hoc along none of these dimensions.

Religious Orientations

At least until the UTE's creation in 1947, religious versus secular orientations provided the major cleavage among Chilean universities. This cleavage has obvious private-public relevance as no public university is religious. Yet half of Chile's private universities have no religious roots either, and no Chilean university has a more adamantly secular heritage than the private, Masonic, University of Concepción. Believers, be they students, professors, or administrators, once had no place in this institution. In any case, with the reform, most remnants of the strong religious-secular divisions were swept away.

Historically, the religious core formed at the UC. The UC's declining distinctiveness from the UCH (for it was certainly not the UCH that remade itself on the UC model), is worth examining as a fairly typical case of how Latin America's first wave has turned away from original religious missions. Such declining distinctiveness is a key to much of the homogeneity seen in Latin America's higher education systems.

To insure piety, the young UC wanted students home by ten o'clock at night and forbade them to leave Santiago without special authorization. Symbols, ceremonies, conferences, confessions, and some curriculum gave the university a distinctive religious flavor. Moreover, UC graduates had a tough time finding State employment. But it would be inaccurate to concentrate exclusively on distinctiveness. From the beginning, many of the new university's policies replicated those of the UCH. The basic idea was to achieve legitimacy and effectiveness by providing much the same studies found in the nation's established institution but with the significant exception of providing a religious choice and fortifying the faith deemed necessary for good Christian citizens. Of the new university's 249 students in 1900, more than half were in law; the rest were in civil, electrical, and chemical engineering.[50] Course content differed between the two universities, but not drastically. Incredibly, the UC began without a theology faculty. Only after nearly a half century was one added. Moreover, the regulations that insured

UC dependence on UCH personnel and standards in governance further promoted program similarity.

In any case, whatever the early degree of UC distinctiveness from the UCH, it strongly declined in the mid-twentieth century. Vatican II was decisive. The Church and its universities, previously associated with agrarian and other conservative interests, would be more concerned not only with temporal affairs but with material progress and equity. The UC would downplay alleged incompatibilities between Catholicism and pluralism. Few Protestant or Jewish students would shun the UC for fear of discrimination or discomfort. So weak was the Catholic orientation by the late 1960s that the last pre-coup UC rector was not a priest but a laical architect and a leftist at that. Nor were other top administrative positions held by priests. A reflection of new orientation could be found in evolving partisan ties. Although the Conservative party had given valuable support to the UC's creation, by the 1950s a major debate arose within the UC over the extent to which ties should be maintained.[51] Continued conservatism provoked the resignation of the vice-rector and several professors, including future PDC president Eduardo Frei. Christian Democracy would soon be ascendent at the UC. Much the same was true of the Catholic University of Valparaíso, where the rector had been among the first to call for Chilean higher education to turn from elitism to reformism.[52] Indeed this university pioneered in the reform.

Change from more to less traditional religious orientation came intermittently. Declarations from the UC's rectors often appeared orthodox in the 1950s and early 1960s, sometimes more than in the 1920s. "A Catholic university goes beyond the search for truth and development of sciences or training of professionals; it should be a true Christian community in its spiritual, moral, and extrauniversity supernatural life."[53] Even today religious symbols adorn the UC. One sees portraits of popes, plaques to archbishops, and holy inscriptions in Latin. But substantive functional differences between Catholic and secular universities largely disappeared by the mid-1960s. As a well-known rector of the Catholic University of Valparaíso unhappily summed up the Latin American situation from his Chilean vantage point: "The 'Catholicism' of the Catholic universities is not 'integrated' into the faculty, the school, the department, the institute, the chair. It is an 'addition' that is given in order to justify the Catholic nature of our universities." Although these universities were intended as distinct alternatives, the rector continued, they have resulted only in "the frustrations of great hopes." Pedagogy is similar to that found in the public universities—mostly "indifferent," sometimes even hostile to Christianity. Those few required religious courses that still exist are often below general university quality and isolated from the students' basic program. "Catholic universities continue to accomplish valuable missions, but they do so more as universities than as Catholic universities."[54] Although a reassertion of religious orientation arose in the 1970s, this was more a means to combat the junta's control than a revival. Chilean higher education no longer offers the institutionalized religious choice it once did.

Finally, it is worth noting that the UC did not shift directly from traditionalism to reformism. Instead, U.S.-sponsored modernization began in the 1950s (as the UC finally expanded significantly) and accelerated in the 1960s. The Ford and Rockefeller foundations played important roles, the UC's development plan drew on U.S. higher education models, and the controversial Chicago connection developed. University of Chicago economists, beckoned by the U.S. ambassador to Chile, were first rebuffed at the public UCH but then eagerly received at the Catholic UC, which was converting its accounting and financing programs into an economics faculty.[55] Perhaps the UC's modernization helped limit a potentially perceived need to create a separate second-wave alternative. More certainly, the reform following that modernization pushed the UC away from the conservative second wave surging elsewhere in Latin America. Yet no secular elite institutions arose to redefine and rejuvenate privateness. This lack of a distinctive second wave helps explain the lack of private-public differentiation found in the issues explored forthwith: partisan political orientations, career orientations, socioeconomic orientations, and academic quality.

Partisan Political Orientations

There have been important links between religious and political orientations. For decades the major private-public political difference was that the UC was substantially to the right of the UCH. However, declining religious distinctiveness went hand in hand with declining conservatism in the UC and brought it close to the evolving political mainstream, though some conservative-liberal gap has always persisted.

By the end of the 1950s, the UC's student movement aligned itself with the PDC, against conservative students who regarded their first mission as being good Christians and their second as being cultured professionals. Moreover, as noted earlier, activists at the Catholic universities pioneered in Chile's reform. Still, the Right probably remained stronger in the Catholic rather than in the secular private universities and definitely remained much stronger than in the public sector. The "Left" in the Catholic universities and the UTSM usually backed PDC reforms since the Left itself was small and the rightist opposition represented the greater of two evils. Similarly, rightists in the UCH were so weak that they supported the PDC, since leftists represented the most potent evil. In general, student activism at the UCH was much more pronounced and leftist than at the UC; fewer UC than UCH activists had personal or family experiences with student activism, and fewer had ties to political parties or plans for political careers, while many more had religious affiliations.[56] Furthermore, the UC's leftward drift slowed by 1968, when counterreformist students overtook reformist students. By 1971 several major centers of opposition to the UP government developed. Prime examples were found in economics and political science. After leftist students at the UC broke from the main part of the PDC because the PDC's Christianity was insufficiently oriented toward solving material problems, the new splinter group—the Movement of United Popular Action (MAPU)—remained much weaker than the centrist PDC it disavowed.

Communists enjoyed by far their greatest strength at the two public institutions. Yet, as Socialists rarely gained influence in higher education, it was the Leftist Revolutionary Movement (MIR) that became the most potent representative of the extreme Left. With Socialist support, the MIR at the UCH formed a revolutionary front, actively opposing the *vía electoral* (electoral route) espoused by the Communists. Yet the MIR itself was strongest at the private University of Concepción.[57] This university's leftism alone destroyed any simple notions of private university conservatism versus public university leftism.

Most of the political generalizations to this point hold specifically for student movements, which themselves largely shaped the universities' political profiles. Additionally, professorial inclinations often followed similar interinstitutional lines, albeit less extremely. And after 1967 many administrators were popularly elected by the students and professors, thus reflecting their views.

Having sketched the political orientations of Chile's major universities, it is interesting to explore their relations with the three very distinct regimes in office since 1964.[58] Each regime had better relations with certain universities than others. Some private-public tendencies emerge, but simple hypotheses that each regime's positions on a Left-Right continuum would determine propublic sector or proprivate sector positions prove risky, not only because of the complexities of Chilean politics but also because the private-public juridical breakdown fails to represent a clear Right-Left division.

The PDC faced a major dilemma in fixing the State's role during its six-year rule (1964–70). On the one hand, its commitment to institutional pluralism, freedom, diversity, choice, and religious values may have argued for a fairly limited State role. On the other, its general belief in the State's responsibility to promote equity and its specific belief in the State's responsibility to increase educational opportunity and quality argued for a larger role. On balance, the latter tendency proved stronger. The PDC strove to move public primary and secondary education toward the standards of good private schools. Public expansion was enormous. Many in the Church charged "betrayal."[59] Yet Frei also faced charges that he favored private over public higher education, partly because State activism included increased subsidization of the private sector. At the same time, however, Frei's political problems with the Left at the UCH rarely rivaled the problems he faced with the Right at the UC, for although the reform had early roots at the UC, it met strong opposition there. The rector, in power since 1953, believed fervently in hierarchical control. His exalted post, he thought, made him the university's eminence of knowledge. Finally conceding increased powers to professors, the UC administration continued to oppose student participation and demands for further change. Frei insisted that the conflict be solved, appointed Santiago's archbishop to the task, and supported his decision in favor of the students. The rector was replaced. According to the archbishop, Frei had made it clear that continued disorder would have led the State to take over the university.[60] Only by assuming missions of social change could the UC count on support from the PDC administration.

UP ideology might presumably favor the public sector. But while many within the UP coalition saw private education as a manifestation of bourgeois reaction and wanted to substitute the unified school system for a plural system, it was unclear how their orientations would translate into higher education policy. One obstacle to antiprivate policies lay in the UP's weakness and internal splits. A strong UP branch stressed the need for coalition politics based on progressive PDC support: What could be worse than to attack private higher education and the Church? Also important, however, was the changing political profile within higher education itself. Private universities could not easily be identified as rightist; in reality, it was even difficult to say how they could be identified as private by that time. Antipathy to truly private institutions did not necessarily mean antipathy to Chile's six "private" universities. The private University of Concepción housed a leftism unsurpassed at any Chilean university. Although the public UCH had a strong Communist movement, the PDC gained the upper hand within the university's student movement during most of the UP era, and Rector Edgardo Boeninger was a Christian Democrat, a major figure in the progressive opposition. Paradoxically, Rector Fernando Castillo of the UC, although also a Christian Democrat, was more to the left and a personal friend of Allende.[61]

As the junta favored antistatist values, it sought alternatives to Chile's heretofore uniquely public system. Parallels could be found to the creation of second-wave alternatives elsewhere in that rightist forces held the public sector responsible for leftist politicization, waste, and declining effectiveness. The big difference, however, was that the Chilean junta also found the private sector guilty. Therefore, it launched a dual sector reaction, concentrating on the public sector only to the degree that it still lay to the private sector's left. Possibly least affected by the junta's initial wrath was the private UTSM, perceived as a small technical center of quality, while reports conflict on the immediate impact at the two small regional universities (the Austral and the North). Probably hardest hit by initial junta policies were the private University of Concepción, stronghold of the extreme Left, as well as the public UTE, stronghold of the Communist party. The UTE was so thoroughly remade that a certain calm set in compared to the situation in its sister public university and in the two main Catholic universities.[62] Control of the UCH largely passed to rightist professors who had led the anti-UP fight. These professors retained a degree of influence over even the imposed military rectors. By 1976, however, it was clear that purging the Left was not considered sufficient. More Christian Democrats and even rightists were forced out by true believers. This "second coup" exemplified how the UCH bore much of the brunt of harsh junta policies, accelerating the institution's fall from system leadership. Subsequently, the 1981 legislation led to the UCH's loss of more than half its twenty-four faculties.

Meanwhile, no major university escaped the junta's wrath as lightly as the private UC, though repression also came in stages there. Explanations for this special, but not so special, treatment go far to demonstrate the distinctive, but not so distinctive, character of this institution. The UC had been the leading university bastion of the anti-UP struggle, and the bulk of its student body and professoriate was Christian Democrat or rightist. Most important, the UC economics school was the intellectual headquarters of the Chicago Boys and the influence of such controversial figures as Arnold Harberger and Milton Friedman. It was no accident that the navy was "given" the UC (an admiral was appointed as rector), since the navy was especially partial to free-market economics. "Young-boy" (*lolocracia*) contacts were established between the UC's new leadership and regime authorities.[63]

Another factor protecting the UC was its link to the Church. Few in the junta wanted to antagonize the Church more than necessary, especially given the strong Church-State tensions that resulted from Church denunciations of the regime's human rights and social policies. This helps explain why only the UC had but one rector, thereby reinforcing comparative continuity in the decade since the coup, while the UCH and other universities had several. The Church made clear that it still considered the UC to be its institution and would try to assert its right to appoint the next and all future rectors. Similar assertions were heard at the Catholic University of Valparaíso. The regime responded, bluntly, that heavy financial dependency—statism—obliterates such freedom from the State. Still, the regime moved more hesitantly in the Catholic subsector than elsewhere. Unlike the UCH, the UC retained its faculties in fields such as pedagogy as well as its regional campuses.[64]

But neither its Church ties nor its political ideologies fully safeguarded the UC from regime repression. For one thing, the pre-coup UC was no longer merely a conservative institution. Many Christian Democrate, especially social scientists, were ousted in 1974. By 1975 possibly 20 percent of the UC's personnel had been directly affected—half were forced out and half found their time commitments reduced—while others were pushed into nonideological fields.[65] Furthermore, as the Church itself had become a major critic of authoritarianism, repeated conflicts ensued between the regime, represented by the rector, and the Church, represented by the archbishop of Santiago. Confrontation reached new heights in 1979 when the Church demonstrated solidarity with protesting students at the theology faculty and asserted that theology must be the crowning glory and soul of a Catholic university—the critical conscience that defends Christian values and freedoms before any encroachments, including the State's. The rector replied that he was aware of his university's Catholic status in an essential, not just decorative, honorific way.[66] Nevertheless, the Catholic orientation that had once distinguished the UC from other Chilean universities obviously had greatly diminished even before the coup.

Data on enrollments and State subsidization (table 3.5) broadly corroborate the general discussion. By far the most important differences are systemwide. PDC and UP policies amply supported enrollment and financial expansion at all universities; junta policies abruptly reversed the trends.[67] Only within that powerful context should intersectoral differences receive attention. From 1965 to 1970 the public sector's share of State funds fell significantly, as the PDC's funding of private universities brought intersectoral homogeneity to a climax. But since overall subsidies nearly doubled, even the public sector's resources grew enormously. Then, under the UP, the public share of subsidies continued to decline somewhat, but the striking fact (even more than with the PDC) was how both sectors grew similarly both in size and State resources. At least as striking was how the two sectors declined together under the junta, though with a definite anti-public emphasis.[68]

Field and Job-Market Orientations

Apart from religious and political dimensions, the functioning of private and public sectors can be compared on certain economic dimensions. A quantifiable issue that is economically important concerns the subjects that students study. While there is no guarantee that graduates will work in the fields they studied, the professional faculty, rather than U.S.-style general liberal arts focus, suggests some link. Moreover, this study is obviously interested in what the universities themselves do during their students' tenure. Table 3.6 shows each university's distribution of students by field of study. The inclusion of three separate years provides a check on the durability of interinstitutional patterns. The table shows the earliest and latest data available to me, at intervals long enough to assume different student cohort groups. It also offers the chance to check the patterns' durability while regime power has passed from the PDC, to the UP, to the military. In fact, most major patterns have been durable.

These patterns include important differences among universities; but instead of analyzing each institution separately, my concern is to discover the most significant clusters. Thus table 3.7 focuses on private-public, technical-nontechnical, and Catholic-secular splits. Table 3.6 remains useful for its breadth of information and for further references to individual

Table 3.5 Chilean Regime Policies toward Sectors, 1965–1980

Year	Public Enrollments		Subsidies of Public Sector[a]	
	#	% of System	Amount	% of System
1965	26,355	63	862.8	78
1970	50,867	66	1,526.7	67
1974	95,792	66	4,065.8	64
1977	80,993	62	2,890.2	58
1980	75,209	63	—	36–56[b]

SOURCES: See table 3.3 on enrollments. On finance, Ministerio de Hacienda, "Análisis financiero de la educación superior chilena," (Santiago, 1978), Appendix 3; for 1980, "4 universidades concentran," *El Mercurio*, May 20, 1982.

a. In millions of December 1977 dollars; these are "fiscal" subsidies, both running and capital. The data in table 3.4, dealing beyond fiscal with all ongoing sources of State funds but not including capital funds, suggest a smaller decline in the public sector's share of total subsidies from 1965 to 1970.

b. Refers only to the direct, not indirect, subsidies described in the section on finance. The UCH and UTE share of direct subsidies was supposed to remain at 36 percent, at least for 1981–85, but the eight traditional universities captured only 80 percent of the new system's total. The 1982 percentages were 28 UCH, 8 UTE, 14 UC, 10 Concepción, 6 University of the North, 5 each Catholic University of Valparaíso and Austral University, and 4 UTSM, with the derived institutions (mostly public) sharing the other 20 percent.

institutions. For simplicity's sake, and because table 3.6 has suggested longitudinal stability, table 3.7 focuses on 1980.[69]

Startling private-public parallels can be seen in table 3.7. In none of the nine fields does proportional enrollment differ intersectorally by more than 5 percent. The greatest public advantages come in the health sciences (13.6 to 10.0 percent), engineering (31.7 to 26.7 percent), and the social sciences (13.4 to 10.8 percent). Basing my comparisons on Spanish American data found in chapter 6 (see tables 6.13 and 6.14), the engineering advantage is fairly typical, but the medical one is unusually small. The social science edge reflects Chilean higher education's emphasis on basic social sciences such as sociology rather than on areas such as business and administration, where Latin America's private sector leads overwhelmingly. Chile's lack of substantial commercial enrollments, either within the social sciences or in a separate category, relates to the absence of second- and third-wave private institutions. The private sector advantage in humanities is large (5.9 to 1.4 percent), while the edge in education is small; both follow Latin American norms. It is the private edge in agronomy (6.9 to 3.7 percent) and the natural sciences (4.3 to 2.0 percent) that is most unusual and noteworthy. In systems with private-public distinctiveness, the public sector characteristically dominates these fields.

A much wider split runs along the technical-nontechnical than the private-public cleavage. By itself the UCH resembles Chile's larger private universities more than its one public partner. Whereas the UCH distributes its students widely across nine fields, the UTE is highly concentrated in one field. Engineering alone has held roughly two-thirds of all UTE enrollments. Furthermore, its next largest field is education—training teachers for technical schools. In practice the UTE has been the capstone of Chile's technical education, a system that has grown up completely independent of the academic schools, according to some observers.[70] The academic schools have been conduits to the nontechnical universities, while technical schools have trained most of their students directly for the job market, with access to higher education only in certain fields. Still, the *private* UTSM has concentrated the highest percentage of enrollments (over 90 percent) in engineering. Thus, the two technical universities together, with one-fourth of total enrollments, hold three-fifths of all engineering enrollments (1980). But even while the technical-nontechnical cleavage overshadows the private-public cleavage, the first also helps to define the second since the UTE's share of the public sector is much greater than the UTSM's share of the private sector.

The other cleavage displayed in table 3.7 is the Catholic-secular one. This cleavage may suggest stronger private-public effects than does the technical-nontechnical cleavage because all Catholic universities are private. But

Table 3.6 Enrollments by Field of Study in Chilean Universities, 1967–1980

University	Year	Soc. Sci.	Law	Hum.	Ed.
U. of Chile	1967	6,436	1,576	624	7,938
(UCH)		(22.6)	(5.5)	(2.2)	(27.9)
	1974	9,999	2,287	1,265	22,571
		(15.8)	(3.6)	(2.0)	(35.6)
	1980	6,362	1,528	1,022	16,830
		(13.0)	(3.1)	(2.1)	(34.5)
State Technical	1967	163	0	0	2,070
U. (UTE)		(1.9)	(0.0)	(0.0)	(24.3)
	1974	2,186	0	0	6,046
		(6.6)	(0.0)	(0.0)	(18.3)
	1980	3,730	0	0	3,953
		(14.1)	(0.0)	(0.0)	(15.0)
Catholic U.	1967	1,112	572	237	2,197
of Chile (UC)		(16.6)	(8.5)	(3.5)	(32.8)
	1974	1,594	476	623	4,736
		(12.4)	(3.7)	(4.9)	(37.0)
	1980	1,343	488	891	5,907
		(9.9)	(3.6)	(6.5)	(43.2)
Catholic U.	1967	570	374	171	1,226
of Valparaíso		(16.7)	(11.0)	(5.0)	(35.9)
	1974	1,091	279	198	2,211
		(15.6)	(4.0)	(2.8)	(31.5)
	1980	950	290	1,022	1,331
		(14.0)	(4.3)	(15.1)	(19.7)

three of the five secular universities are also private. Additionally, the Catholic-secular division is not nearly as sharp as the technical-nontechnical one. The Catholic institutions' weakest areas, compared to the secular institutions, are health studies and engineering. In fact, the latter "weakness" really relates only to comparisons with the UTE, since the Catholic universities more than hold their own within the nontechnical sector. Moreover, they are proportionally overrepresented in the natural sciences. Indeed, the two regionally based Catholic universities make distinct contributions to their locales in science and technology (e.g., the Catholic University of Valparaíso in oceanography). Although the Catholic sector holds the edge in each of the six other fields, that edge is substantial only in the humanities. Generally, the Catholic-secular cleavage does not produce major private-public differences.

Just as the Chilean case illustrates only moderate distinctiveness between Catholic and public universities in fields of study, it also illustrates how the degree of private-public distinctiveness elsewhere may well depend on the secular private institutions. Whereas secular private institutions in most of

Table 3.6 cont'd

Art. & Arch.	Engin.	Agric.	Nat. Sci.	Health[a]	Total
1,970	3,026	1,564	731	4,565	28,430
(6.9)	(10.6)	(5.5)	(2.6)	(16.1)	(99.9)
4,022	6,774	3,751	1,536	11,216	63,421
(6.3)	(10.7)	(5.9)	(2.4)	(17.7)	(100.0)
3,115	6,160	2,211	1,488	10,118	48,834
(6.4)	(12.6)	(4.5)	(3.0)	(20.7)	(99.9)
33	6,246	0	0	0	8,512
(0.4)	(73.4)	(0.0)	(0.0)	(0.0)	(100.0)
548	22,245	1,772	134	119	33,050
(1.7)	(67.3)	(5.3)	(0.4)	(0.4)	(100.0)
308	17,683	551	1	119	26,375
(1.2)	(67.0)	(2.1)	(0.0)	(0.5)	(99.9)
319	1,217	329	237	478	6,698
(4.8)	(18.2)	(4.9)	(3.5)	(7.1)	(100.0)
856	2,594	530	472	929	12,810
(6.7)	(20.2)	(4.1)	(3.7)	(7.3)	(100.0)
760	1,990	573	614	1,094	13,664
(5.6)	(14.6)	(4.2)	(4.5)	(8.0)	(100.0)
158	621	294	0	0	3,414
(4.6)	(18.2)	(8.6)	(0.0)	(0.0)	(100.0)
351	2,207	667	8	0	7,012
(5.0)	(31.5)	(9.5)	(0.1)	(0.0)	(100.0)
356	1,678	723	415	0	6,765
(5.3)	(24.8)	(10.7)	(6.1)	(0.0)	(100.0)

Spanish America have grown as distinct elite or demand-absorbing alternatives, these rationales have been subordinate in Chile. In this regard the single most important institution to consider is the University of Concepción. More than four times larger in 1967 than the other two private secular universities combined, more than three times larger in 1974, and still a little larger in 1980, Concepción's enrollments have been widely and impressively distributed for Latin America's secular private institutions. As table 3.6 shows, Concepción's three principal fields have been education, health studies, and engineering, the last related to its regional function in mining. The large health share, well above the system norm, is very unusual for private universities, especially secular ones. Concepción has also held its own in the typically public areas of agronomy and the natural sciences. In short, Concepción has been strong in fields often bypassed by Latin America's secular private institutions.

The three smallest private universities have more concentrated field enrollments, but only the UTSM has a single field that contains more than half its institution's total enrollments. It is only the UTSM which, by field

Table 3.6 cont'd

University	Year	Soc. Sci.	Law	Hum.	Ed.
U. of	1967	468	431	281	492
Concepción		(9.0)	(8.3)	(5.4)	(9.5)
	1974	2.310	565	369	4,779
		(13.5)	(3.3)	(2.2)	(28.0)
	1980	544	451	220	3,064
		(5.6)	(4.6)	(2.2)	(31.3)
U. Austral	1967	0	0	0	284
		(0.0)	(0.0)	(0.0)	(27.6)
	1974	103	0	43	1,187
		(2.9)	(0.0)	(1.2)	(33.6)
	1980	374	0	443	1,416
		(8.5)	(0.0)	(10.0)	(32.0)
U. of the North	1967	194	0	0	580
		(14.7)	(0.0)	(0.0)	(44.0)
	1974	1,046	0	29	2,105
		(17.4)	(0.0)	(0.4)	(34.9)
	1980	1,284	0	0	1,309
		(23.2)	(0.0)	(0.0)	(23.7)
Technical U.	1967	0	0	0	0
Santa María		(0.0)	(0.0)	(0.0)	(0.0)
(UTSM)	1974	0	0	0	0
		(0.0)	(0.0)	(0.0)	(0.0)
	1980	240	0	0	0
		(6.7)	(0.0)	(0.0)	(0.0)

SOURCES: UCH, *Antecedentes e informaciones universitarias* (Santiago, 1975), pp. 124–31; Consejo de Rectores, *Anuario estadístico 1980* (Santiago, 1981), p. 28. The fields identified below follow the Consejo de Rectores categorization. From left to right are social sciences, law, humanities, education, art and architecture, engineering (tecnologías), agronomy, natural sciences (and mathematics), health sciences, and total.

distributions alone, might look like a second-wave secular private alternative to the public sector. The University of the North also concentrates on engineering (especially oriented to its regional specialties in oceanography and geology) but on education and the social sciences as well, while the Austral combines education principally with agronomy and health studies, both atypical of Latin America's private universities and reflecting the university's regional functions in Chile's agricultural south. The Austral has also held its own in the natural sciences, partly substantiating its ex-rector's exuberant claim that the university "has perfectly delineated its areas of excellence in biological sciences and related areas."[71]

No Chilean private (or public) university has concentrated its enrollments in only those fields that are least expensive to teach. Instead, three of the six private universities offer nine of nine possible fields of study, while

Table 3.6 cont'd

Art. & Arch.	Engin.	Agric.	Nat. Sci.	Health[a]	Total
176	588	228	152	769	5,192[b]
(3.3)	(11.3)	(4.3)	(2.9)	(14.8)	(100.0)
100	3,309	745	755	4,137	17,069
(0.6)	(19.4)	(4.4)	(4.4)	(24.2)	(100.0)
18	2,169	565	453	2,307	9,791
(0.2)	(22.2)	(5.8)	(4.6)	(23.6)	(100.0)
0	10	488	4	242	1,028
(0.0)	(1.0)	(47.5)	(0.4)	(23.5)	(100.0)
142	64	1,070	299	622	3,530
(4.0)	(1.8)	(30.3)	(8.5)	(17.6)	(99.9)
122	89	1,038	182	762	4,426
(2.8)	(2.0)	(23.5)	(4.1)	(17.2)	(100.1)
0	531	12	0	0	1,317
(0.0)	(40.3)	(0.9)	(0.0)	(0.0)	(100.0)
34	2,495	116	198	0	6,023
(5.7)	(41.4)	(1.9)	(3.2)	(0.0)	(100.0)
1	2,389	109	228	213	5,533
(0.0)	(43.2)	(2.0)	(4.1)	(3.8)	(100.0)
50	428	0	0	0	478
(10.5)	(89.5)	(0.0)	(0.0)	(0.0)	(100.0)
0	1,840	0	106	0	1,946
(0.0)	(94.6)	(0.0)	(5.4)	(0.0)	(100.0)
0	3,350	0	0	0	3,590
(0.0)	(93.3)	(0.0)	(0.0)	(0.0)	(100.0)

a. In 1967, 587 students (399 in health sciences and 188 in social sciences) are listed under the National Health Service, which I do not include here and which is almost never included with Chilean higher education data.

b. In 1967, 1,607 (31.2 percent) of Concepción's students were listed as unspecified.

another two come close. There has been no demand-absorbing subsector, at least not until the institutional proliferation of the early 1980s.

The findings based on enrollments are confirmed by data concerning degrees granted. Table 3.8 shows the breakdowns for 1957–74 inclusive. These data offer the advantages of inclusive coverage from an early date and of more direct links to employment than seen in enrollment data. On the other hand, the total numbers are smaller, and even those who do not complete degree requirements nonetheless are "ahead" of the nonstudents and are often oriented to the field they had studied. Again most major interinstitutional differences do not fall along the private-public axis, as only two private-public differences exceed 2.2 percent; again the Catholic-secular axis is less decisive than the technical-nontechnical one.

In sum, with specified exceptions, Chile's private sector has not offered a major alternative to the public sector in fields of study. Choice has not operated principally on a sector-versus-sector basis. Instead, Chile's private sector has tended to provide choice much as the public sector has—by incorporating it within most institutions. This proves quite a contrast to Latin America's intersectorally distinctive systems.

A final question on fields of study is whether the junta's introduction of new institutions in the early 1980s, including new private ones, could lead to significant private-public contrasts and perhaps to field profiles consistent with the regime's development model—what critics called "the University at the service of private enterprise"—especially since table 3.6 shows surprising continuities for 1974–80.[72] In fact, private-public contrasts immediately emerged, but the junta quickly disapproved of the field profiles they reflected. Each institutional type behaved "perversely." Traditional universities, at least briefly forced to compete for the top twenty-thousand students, expanded their quotas in those fields such as medicine where they could attract those top students, regardless of whether desired employment would be available there. An especially rankling abuse was the immediate enrollment jump in fields eligible for special subsidization (before the junta abandoned that incentive), for this jump resulted from opportunistic face-lifting, as when low-prestige technological careers suddenly become "civil engineering."

Table 3.7 Focused Field Comparisons of Chilean Enrollments, 1980

Institutional Type	Soc. Sci.[a]	Law	Hum.	Ed.	Art & Arch.	Engin.	Agric.	Nat. Sci.	Health	Total
Private[b]	4,739	1,229	2,576	13,027	1,257	11,665	3,008	1,892	4,376	43,769
	(10.8)	(2.8)	(5.9)	(29.8)	(2.9)	(26.7)	(6.9)	(4.3)	(10.0)	(100.1)
Public	10,092	1,528	1,022	20,783	3,453	23,843	2,762	1,489	10,237	75,209
	(13.4)	(2.0)	(1.4)	(27.6)	(4.6)	(31.7)	(3.7)	(2.0)	(13.6)	(100.0)
Technical[c]	3,970	0	0	3,953	338	21,033	551	1	119	29,968
	(13.2)	(0.0)	(0.0)	(13.2)	(1.1)	(70.2)	(1.8)	(0.0)	(0.4)	(99.9)
Nontechnical	10,861	2,757	3,598	29,857	4,372	14,475	5,219	3,380	14,494	89,013
	(12.2)	(3.1)	(4.0)	(33.5)	(4.9)	(16.3)	(5.9)	(3.8)	(16.3)	(100.0)
Catholic[d]	3,581	778	1,913	8,547	1,117	6,057	1,405	1,257	1,307	25,962
	(13.8)	(3.0)	(7.4)	(32.9)	(4.3)	(23.3)	(5.4)	(4.8)	(5.0)	(99.9)
Secular	11,250	1,979	1,685	25,263	3,593	29,451	4,365	2,124	13,306	93,016
	(12.1)	(2.1)	(1.8)	(27.2)	(3.9)	(31.7)	(4.7)	(2.3)	(14.3)	(100.1)

Source: Consejo de Rectores, *Anuario estadístico 1980* (Santiago, 1981), p. 28.

a. See table 3.6 for field abbreviations.

b. Private = all universities except the University of Chile (UCH) and the State Technical University (UTE).

c. Technical = the State Technical University (UTE) and the Santa María Technical University (UTSM).

d. Catholic = the Catholic University of Chile (UC), the Catholic University of Valparaíso, and the University of the North.

Table 3.8 Chilean Degrees by University and Field of Study, 1957–1974

	Soc.[a] Sci.	Law	Hum.	Ed.	Art & Arch.	Engin.	Agric.	Nat. Sci.	Health	Total
U. of	8,156	2,721	1,247	12,467	1,407	3,273	2,193	715	11,946	44,125
Chile (UCH)	(18.5)	(6.2)	(2.8)	(28.3)	(3.2)	(7.4)	(5.0)	(1.6)	(27.1)	(100.1)
State Technical	271	0	0	3,538	0	4,847	7	0	0	8,663
U. (UTE)	(3.1)	(0.0)	(0.0)	(40.8)	(0.0)	(56.0)	(0.1)	(0.0)	(0.0)	(100.0)
Catholic U.	2,246	1,136	488	6,320	521	1,475	768	292	643	13,889
of Chile (UC)	(16.2)	(8.2)	(3.5)	(45.5)	(3.7)	(10.6)	(5.5)	(2.1)	(4.6)	(99.9)
Catholic U.	885	240	42	2,428	248	895	289	87	0	5,114
of Valparaíso	(17.3)	(4.7)	(0.8)	(47.5)	(4.8)	(17.5)	(5.7)	(1.7)	0.0)	(100.0)
U. of	851	797	18	3,042	1	913	292	179	1,920	8,013
Concepción	(10.6)	(9.9)	(0.2)	(37.9)	(0.1)	(11.4)	(3.6)	(2.3)	(23.9)	(99.9)
U. Austral	0	0	0	240	0	6	463	9	372	1,090
	(0.0)	(0.0)	(0.0)	(22.0)	(0.0)	(0.5)	(42.5)	(0.8)	(34.1)	(99.9)
U. of the	177	0	0	1,132	0	171	3	1	0	1,484
North	(11.9)	(0.0)	(0.0)	(76.3)	(0.0)	(11.5)	(0.2)	(0.1)	(0.0)	(100.0)
Technical U.										
Santa María	68	0	0	0	36	998	0	0	0	1,102
(UTSM)	(6.2)	(0.0)	(0.0)	(0.0)	(3.3)	(90.6)	(0.0)	(0.0)	(0.0)	(100.1)
Total	12,654	4,894	1,795	29,167	2,213	12,578	4,015	1,283	14,881	83,480
Private[b]	13.8	7.1	1.8	42.9	2.6	14.5	5.9	1.9	9.6	100.1
Public	16.0	5.2	2.4	30.3	2.7	15.4	4.1	1.4	22.6	100.1
Technical	3.5	0.0	0.0	36.2	0.4	59.9	0.1	0.0	0.0	100.1
Nontechnical	16.7	6.6	2.4	34.8	3.0	9.1	5.4	1.7	20.2	99.9
Catholic	16.1	6.7	2.6	48.2	3.8	12.4	5.2	1.9	3.1	100.0
Secular	14.8	5.6	2.0	30.6	2.3	15.9	4.7	1.4	22.6	99.9

Sources: UCH, *Titulados de las universidades chilenas desde 1957 hasta 1970* (Santiago, 1972), pp. 2–33; Consejo de Rectores, *Anuario estadístico 1975* (Santiago, 1976), pp. 227–34.
    a. See table 3.6 for field abbreviations.
    b. For delineation of all six university categories (e.g., "private"), see table 3.7. I have obviously deleted the raw numbers for the three clustered comparisons.

Worse yet, Chile took a giant step toward creating demand-absorbing institutions. Because many institutions had little chance for State aid, logical market behavior was to push growth into inexpensive fields, creating additional ones and expanding existing ones. This third-wave growth occurred principally in new institutions, and it sharply broke with Chile's heritage of interinstitutional homogeneity. Many derived institutes were tied to a particular profession, and the new training centers had profoundly circumscribed functions. However blithely the regime had launched its free-market experiment in interinstitutional competition, it almost immediately denounced the practical results when it at least temporarily banned further field and institutional proliferation.

Considerable interest was shown in the fate of new universities, heralded as effective links between useful fields of study and the job market, as potential, secular elite private institutions. By the late 1970s the Chicago Boys made progress toward establishing business universities, and the 1981 legislation (further cutting the size and limiting direct subsidies for the traditional universities) seemed to be a major victory. At least two major business universities were planned, but one (San Felipe) folded when indirect State subsidies became unavailable. Until that point (1982) the regime, specifically its ministers of finance and interior, had been very supportive of the business universities. Naturally, enthusiastic backing came from the business world. The failed university was to have represented the powerful Cruzat group, some of whose members then decided to help the Finis Terrae University, scheduled to open in 1983. In fact, Finis Terrae appointed its rector in anticipation of opening. He was Pablo Barahona, former dean of the UC economics school and former head of the Central Bank under the junta. Barahona had also been promoted as the Chicago Boys' choice to be Chile's first post-1973 civilian president—eventually. The Finis Terrae counted on the business community for financial support and for part-time professors. It planned to offer courses only in economics and law but to consider subsequent additions. Even its modest hopes were frustrated, however, not only by the junta's decision against subsidization but more emphatically by the deepening economic crisis, the Cruzat group's near collapse, and internal dissension.[73] With the Finis Terrae effort dormant at best, the Gabriela Mistral was the sole private university to function prior to 1983, followed soon after by the Diego Portales and Central universities. While the Gabriela Mistral's extraordinary tuition could qualify it as socially elite, it had neither the strong business support nor the academic prestige to qualify as a bona fide second-wave university. Critics saw it more as a demand-absorbing institution. That judgment appeared overly harsh, but the university initially offered only economics, law, psychology, and education.[74] After a decade of rightist rule, Chile still had not established the sort of second-wave business alternative that had become so important elsewhere.

Clientele and Social Class

Searching for the most significant difference between Chile's private and public sectors, many experts have suggested social class. It is therefore especially relevant to find that even here differentiation is comparatively limited.

Chile follows, though in diluted form, the Latin American norm in which the public sector is the socially less elite one. The public UTE makes the strongest equity claims, having had the highest working-class percentage, even before the rapid UP acceleration. Generally, as privileged groups have enrolled disproportionately in private institutions at the primary and secondary levels, evidence exists for some enrollment continuity to private higher education, especially for the UC. But even the UTE does not fully escape the elite mold. And since the public sector's major university (UCH) draws disproportionately on private secondary schools, one is struck by the large share of total higher education openings that these schools capture.[75] Putting aside the many religiously affiliated tuition-free private schools, the favored status of the elite private schools becomes especially striking. So does the elite status of higher education, regardless of sector.

A good, summary generalization is that considerable homogeneity in SES composition exists across Chile's eight universities, allowing for exceptions at the UC and the UTE. Reflecting both some residual interinstitutional invidiousness and Chile's ingrained sensitivity about social justice, people affiliated with the UC tend to minimize the institutional differences, while UTE counterparts point with pride to their more progressive SES profile. In fact, major differences in SES occur less across the eight universities than between them and the affiliated regional colleges. It is largely because the great majority of these colleges have been public that a private-public profile SES gap arises. With the interinstitutional reorganization of the early 1980s, many of these colleges became separate institutions and were joined in the lower SES range by the private training centers (to which the junta did not extend its tuition loan program). However much junta policy may have heightened interinstitutional differences, the main equity effect of tightened admissions and increased tuition was that Chilean higher education as a whole became more socially restrictive.[76] For many, this reflects the junta's disdain for equity.

Quality

As usual, social class and institutional prestige are correlated; furthermore, so are prestige and quality, but I leave a fuller analysis of this relationship for chapter 6. In any case, what is striking in Chile is the substantial intersectoral homogeneity in both prestige and quality. Chile has achieved greater systemwide parity than has any other major Latin American nation with dual sectors. Even a nation such as Argentina, with a historical inclination toward centralized authority to guarantee parity, has developed many clearly superior and inferior universities, and parity is more often lauded than achieved elsewhere in Latin America. But in Chile, allowing for great differences in institutional size, all eight universities have usually enjoyed considerable prestige. No binary technical-nontechnical division terribly upsets this uniformity. Though the UTE often ranks a bit lower, it has been

109

recognized for excellence, even superiority, in some fields, and certainly ranks closer to the other universities than do most technical institutes in other systems. Besides, prestige is not the same as quality, and parity may be greater for the latter. Quality distinctions have emerged more prominently within the eight universities (across fields) than across them.

Chile's ability to minimize distinctions despite the presence of dual sectors, and despite intersectoral differentiation at the primary and secondary levels, stems from a few factors. One is the limited number of institutions. Another is the network of regional colleges, channeling perhaps inevitable differentiation away from the university level. Stripped of its regional campuses, the UCH could be seen to occupy the top prestige spot. A third factor is the historical absence of a true second or third wave.

Common statistical indicators of quality confirm impressions of substantial intersectoral homogeneity. Referring back to table 3.5, for example, the public sector's enrollment share has never varied from its share of State subsidies by more than 5 percent, at least from 1965 to nearly 1980. Data on total expenditures per student closely parallel these data, with the UTE ranking low but the UCH ranking about average.[77] Similar results are found for student/full-time professor ratios. The 1975 system average was 13:1, with 12:1 in the private sector versus 14:1 in the public sector. By itself, however, the UCH ratio was lower than those in the three largest private universities and higher than those in the three smallest ones. Finally, private universities are slightly more likely to have classes with thirty or fewer students; while the UTE is least likely to have such small classes, the UCH ranks centrally among the other universities.[78]

As no significant consistent private-public gap existed in quality before the 1973 coup, so military rule has affected quality similarly in each sector. Supporters emphasize academic seriousness, discipline, toughened standards, and increased competition. Critics emphasize the loss of many top students and especially professors, repression of originality and critical thought, devastation of certain fields of study, and resource restrictions—all of which may have disastrous long-run as well as short-run consequences. Supporters claim that the whole system improved, critics that the whole system deteriorated. There might be agreement that the public sector lost some ground to the private sector, but this factor would be marginal compared to either side's systemic evaluation. And this debate about post-coup quality parallels the debate about pre-coup quality. Critics of the junta argue that quality had improved or held its own systemwide. The junta argues that quality had fallen drastically, with the private sector declining only marginally less than the public sector.[79] Not until the 1981 legislation was the path opened for greatly increased interinstitutional stratification, partly along private-public lines. The junta argued that the new system would promote consumer choice and free-market competition in place of State-imposed bureaucratic standardization. One cause of steepened interinstitutional hierarchy was the regionalization policy. Whereas the UCH, for example, had previously been composed of its higher-prestige Santiago campuses and lower-prestige regional colleges, the latter became separate institutions. A major purpose for attaching the regional colleges to major universities had been to minimize the quality lag for locales that could not draw equally on the nation's centralized human resources. Again, the junta apparently rejected such equity considerations.[80]

Furthermore, junta policies promoting competition soon led institutions into advertising once regarded as unseemly and alien to intellectual pursuits. Even in the midst of their own advertising, different institutions accused others of debasing the enterprise. The UCH in particular affected an air of superiority. It claimed to advertise less than its competitors, merely stressing its tradition, high prestige, and employment prospects. A key slogan read: "The UCH: The Choice for the Best." Yet newspaper readers, pedestrians, and subway travelers were continually confronted with propaganda from all major institutions.[81]

Competition proved especially difficult for the derived and new private institutions—the junta's own brainchildren—which had to allow relatively low entrance standards. The training centers suffered a double burden. Their low status not only left them at a disadvantage in open competition but also subjected them to ministerial supervision. They could award only technical titles, not the licenciatura. Additionally, even the new universities faced considerable difficulties since their inferior status was underlined by the five-year probationary dependency on an established university. Consider the plight of the Gabriela Mistral University. The UCH's rector forbade any of his professors to teach part time at the prospective university, which itself felt compelled to postpone continually the promised announcement of its preliminary faculty roster. Moreover, when the State denied indirect subsidies, the Gabriela Mistral had to charge far more than the tuition at competing Santiago universities.

What, then, happened to market competition? Partly, it was eviscerated by statist opposition and traditional political power bases. Partly, it persisted, not spurring all system components to higher quality but stratifying the system far beyond the pre-1980 situation. New institutions could compete only because post-coup enrollment restrictions left many thousands unable to fulfill their hopes of attending the established universities, their choice limited to lower-quality higher education or no higher education. Long known for its homogeneous system, Chile found itself embarked on an alien pattern of differentiation. Excess demand was funneled into less prestigious private institutions, lowering private sector quality as it increased the private sector's enrollment share. "Brazilianization" arose.[82] As in Brazil, a paradox of free-market privatization was that it condemned the more truly private institutions to inferior status. Even the junta soon acknowledged the trend and decided to reconsider its policies. No one could know how far Brazilianization would go to undermine Chile's long notable systemwide parity.

CONCLUSION

Seen in a broad Latin American context, Chile has illustrated a strong statist tradition and, since 1973, novel but uncertain efforts at privatization. The statist tradition has been based on a combination of a rather typical public sector and an atypical private sector. With the UC's creation in 1888 came a first major chink in the Estado Docente's armor. Yet the UC example showed how limited the distinctiveness born of Latin America's first-wave challenge could be. Until the 1950s the UC played a relatively marginal role in Chilean higher education and society. Moreover, as the UC grew in importance, it epitomized the Catholic subsector's diminishing distinctiveness from the public sector over time. What has proven extraordinary about Chile's private sector is that ensuing private universities have not offered a distinct alternative to the public sector. Especially since the 1960s, Chilean higher education has shown remarkable homogeneity in finance, governance, and function. Choice has not essentially depended on private-public differences.

As the Chilean case illustrates strong tendencies toward private-public homogeneity, it likewise suggests by omission how crucial secular private institutions are to private-public distinctiveness. The absence of such institutions appears to be as important to private-public homogeneity as is the transformation of the Catholic subsector. Therefore, to understand the private-public distinctiveness that is more common than private-public homogeneity elsewhere in Latin America, I must devote particular attention in the next two chapters to the patterns produced by Latin America's second and third waves.

The Chilean case also illustrates that transformations in higher education, including those involving privateness and publicness, need not be sectorally based. So similar are the two sectors that none of the three ideologically divergent regimes analyzed most closely here formulated, much less implemented, policies largely dependent on sector. Even the junta's attempted transformation was basically directed at the entire preexisting system. Still, no other Latin American nation has seen such a drastic, parallel, and simultaneous effort to transform both sectors. Instead, the less dramatic but nonetheless important system changes elsewhere have turned much more heavily on intersectoral differences; evolving public sectors have been challenged by growing private sectors that offer clear social, political, economic, and educational alternatives.

4 Private-Public Distinctiveness: Mexico

Shifting our attention to nations in which substantial intersectoral differentiation is found, Mexico comes to the fore. There may be no national system of higher education anywhere with more salient private-public distinctiveness. It is especially notable for such distinctiveness to hold over time, and Mexico's has lasted for a half century. Unusually clear alternatives face the clientele, participants, policymakers, and scholars of the system.

The Mexican case illustrates in striking form many of the basic patterns found in Spanish America. The Mexican private sector's 15 percent share of enrollments (118,999/785,419 in 1981) is fairly typical; in fact, this share has held fairly steady from the mid-1960s, when it matched Spanish America's private share, to the present, in which it trails only slightly.[1] More significant, Mexico's private institutions have grown mostly as elite reactions to changes—"perceived failures"—in the socioeconomic composition, politics, quality, and job relevance of a rapidly growing public sector. Emerging alongside a religious subsector, itself approximating elite much more than demand-absorbing characteristics, Mexico's secular elite subsector is larger and more important than any other in Latin America. It accounts for the majority of Mexico's private enrollments. The subordinate growth (wave III) of private institutions based on excess demand for higher education also follows the Spanish American mode, although this growth has been limited in Mexico. Chapter 6 explores the Spanish American mode more generally, but it is worth analyzing one fairly typical case in depth. Intersectoral distinctiveness and sheer numbers make Mexico the logical choice.[2]

To analyze higher education within Mexico's broader State-private context requires recognition of the following basic paradox: The Mexican State is powerful and active but private enterprise enjoys a central and privileged role in national development. The roots of this paradox are found in the institutionalization of the revolution that erupted in 1910.

114

The revolution produced a strong State. Two decades of violence culminated in a remarkable consolidation of political power, with State control. The State coopts mass participation and concentrates power in the presidency. Economically, the Mexican State is properly considered "atypically and forcefully interventionist," as compared to other States in Latin America.[3] It has long been the nation's key entrepreneur. It owns the principal industries such as oil, controls the distribution of many important resources and credits, and enjoys wide regulatory authority over private economic activity. The 1982 nationalization of all domestic private banks pushes State authority still further. Moreover, the revolution has produced a continually proclaimed ideological commitment to a strong State role in the social-welfare field. Indeed, Mexico's constitution goes well beyond the U.S. Constitution in pledging the State to promote the general welfare directly and actively.

The paradox emerges because the revolution also culminated in a conservative State that has left wide latitude to private enterprise. Mexico's development model emphasizes, above all else, political stability and economic growth. By insuring political stability, the State provides a secure and profitable environment for private interests. By controlling the "popular sectors," the State promotes policies that are very favorable to business. For example, wages are low and social-welfare lags, even in comparison to other Latin American nations with similar levels of economic production. Furthermore, Mexico offers attractive incentives for both private investment (domestic and foreign) and private savings. Yet the State often maintains the appearance of distance, sometimes coolness or open hostility, beyond what the real degree of State-private conflict would suggest. In return for its privileges, private enterprise is expected to produce the economic growth desired both as an end in itself and for its contribution to the State's political stability. Mexican development—for all the statism both real and affected—is therefore characterized by a State-private alliance that is deep, if largely undeclared. The alliance is continually reaffirmed by policies though obscured by rhetoric.

The ensuing analysis of Mexican higher education explores how both the private and public sectors figure into this alliance. An important point to remember throughout is that generally this alliance has been notably successful on its own terms, despite the severe economic crisis of the early 1980s. Based largely on decades of strong economic growth, the regime has enjoyed the greatest stability in twentieth-century Latin America. As one consequence, there has been comparative continuity in State-private relations, notwithstanding the bank nationalization. In higher education as well, changes in private-public patterns have never approximated the degree of transformation seen after Chile's 1973 coup; this stability facilitates intensive analysis of Mexican patterns. And a major policy corollary of the alliance's success and stability is that higher education has found secure niches within the alliance. The private sector has found a particularly gratifying niche, for it has played a significant role within this compatibly conservative State-private alliance.

EVOLUTION
From the Private-Public to Mostly Public

The Royal and Pontifical University of Mexico, the first (1553) functioning university in the Americas, helped establish the dominant pattern for subsequent universities in the region. Its very genesis strongly suggests its fused private-public character. When Mexico's religious leaders issued the first call (1536) for a university, they foresaw an institution dedicated both to clerical (the training of priests) and secular pursuits.[4] In 1539 the municipal government (*cabildo*) of Mexico City formally requested the Spanish Crown to create a university. A royal decree establishing the university under the legal and financial patronage of the Crown was issued in 1551. The pope bestowed the Vatican's authorization in 1595, and the Church assisted the Crown in financing the institution. Fused privateness-publicness was further epitomized in the office of *maestrescuela*, the direct representative of both Crown and Church. Student graduation ceremonies were religious as much as academic events.

Anyone who insists on identifying and separating privateness from publicness in the Royal and Pontifical University of Mexico should attribute more weight to publicness. The same could be said for much, but not all, of colonial Latin America. It could also be said for Mexico's second university, the Royal and Literary University of Guadalajara (1791). However, if higher education is defined broadly, it clearly could not be said for many institutions run by Franciscans, Dominicans, Augustinians, and Jesuits (e.g., the Jesuit College of San Ildefonso, ancestor of the prominent National Preparatory School ultimately connected to the National University).

Publicness supplanted private-public fusion in the first century of independence, but the process was neither quick nor painless. One side, more identified with liberalism, pressed for a thorough eradication of the fused Royal and Pontifical University, arguing that true national independence should mean the rejection of the Spanish Crown's influence and the Church's influence at all educational levels. French and U.S. models of secularism and rationality were held up as desirable substitutes. A public university should replace the fused university. The other side, more identified with conservatism, argued for the preservation of fusion, traditional culture, and clerical and humanistic influences, even if alongside moderniz-

116

ing and scientific influences. When one side captured the State apparatus, it closed the fused university. When the other side captured the State apparatus, the university was reopened. The most emphatic shutdown came in 1867, under Benito Juárez's reform, after three openings and closings. But liberals could not successfully substitute a public university for the vanquished private-public one, and for almost a half century no university functioned.[5]

As in Chile, public sector expansion received a boost when positivism became increasingly powerful in the second half of the nineteenth century. As enemies of "irrationality," positivists went beyond liberals. Effectiveness became the dominant value. Gabino Barreda convinced Juárez to found the National Preparatory School, which relegated the study of religion and humanities so thoroughly that only the seminaries saved them. Under the presidency of Porfirio Díaz it was easy for another leading educator, Justo Sierra, to launch a positivist university. Sierra spoke bluntly on the inauguration day of his institution: "The pontifical university is not the antecedent, it is the past. . . . The Mexican university that is born today has no genealogical tree." Although his idea of a positivist university to serve "Order and Progress" was quickly undermined by the eruption of Mexico's protracted revolution, no new university law would be promulgated until 1929, and the positivists' statutes remained in effect for two decades. Their National University was definitively public, an appendage of the State, with ministerial appointment of the rector and other top university authorities and with public financing and control. Its explicit function was to meet public needs. In fact, most changes that occurred from 1910 to 1929 reinforced university publicness, even to the point where the university became, as seen earlier in Chile, a "University Department" serving in effect as a ministry of education, with supervisory powers over education at all levels. Ultimately, the university itself was most instrumental in creating a ministry (1921), whereupon Rector José Vasconcelos immediately left the university to become the first minister.

But the university soon found itself imperiled by a ministry stressing equity, and therefore public primary schools (a sharp break from positivist priorities), and by a revolutionary antagonism to any autonomy appearing to create a "State within a State," a shield for privileged pursuits. Revolutions, after all, are commonly based on the consolidation of public power. The new regime hoped to reorient policy, even at the expense of freedoms cherished by much of the university community. By 1929, however, the regime was seeking to institutionalize itself, largely by quelling sources of instability. The university had been a battleground, and national leaders sought to defuse the situation by granting partial autonomy. The reformed university of 1929 was a hybrid, "half autonomous, and half of the State."[6]

117

But unlike the fused private-public institution, it was a tense hybrid in which distinct private and public features confronted one another. Moreover, the public "half" seemed larger than the private "half."

In 1933 Mexico's National University was dramatically transformed into an essentially private institution for the first and last time in its history. Turmoil had not subsided after 1929, and the regime desperately wanted to rid itself of what it regarded as a perpetual time bomb. If the university could not effectively and peacefully serve the State, why should the State maintain responsibility for the university? To support private functions with public funds was outrageous; the State pledged only a small sum to help the university establish an endowment and declared that there would be no more annual subsidy. Nor was there State supervision of the university budget, or appointment of officials, or veto power over university resolutions. Nonetheless, harrassment did not cease. A 1934 constitutional amendment established that State education would be socialist.[7] Moreover, the (1937) National Polytechnic Institute (IPN) could easily be seen as a very public alternative to the private university. The State would fund it, appoint its officials, set its curriculum, and charge it with the mission of applying technology to development needs. However, undoubtedly the main pressure on the university was the lack of funds; the university soon looked for compromise, pledging itself to revolutionary public functions. Freedom without an economic base had proven ephemeral. President Lázaro Cárdenas then granted some funds but held firm that any resumption of basic State responsibility would be contingent on university willingness to subordinate private autonomy to public revolution.

A solution—still in effect—came only with what most observers call the end of the revolutionary era, about 1940. The revolutionary drive to control institutions slowed significantly, as did the official concern for equity. Mexico's university once again became heavily public, especially in financial matters. Annual public subsidies soon accounted for one-half to two-thirds of total income. The National Autonomous University of Mexico (UNAM) regained legal status as a "public corporation"—a decentralized organ of the State, explicitly charged to devote itself to national problems—but now, unlike 1910 and even 1929, the university was also granted considerable freedom in governance.

The Rise of Private Alternatives

During the public university turmoil of the 1930s the first private university was created, and, more important, only after the revolution became "institutionalized," or stagnant, did a major private sector develop. No such sector was feasible while revolutionary politics reigned. The regime change by no means marked the end of public sector development, however. Remarkable expansion of UNAM, and especially of the state university system as well as the public technical system, dialectically stimulated private sector growth. The new public universities fundamentally copied UNAM's financial, governance, and secular (often politicized) orientations. A major public sector change, however, was that SES broadened markedly as enrollments soared. While political stability, economic growth, and educational reform helped enhance quality in the 1950s and into the early 1960s, at least at UNAM, expanding enrollments and politicization then contributed to a perceived public sector decline.[8] Therefore, as new groups entered the public sector, much of that sector's established clientele exited in search of private alternatives. Mexico thus classically illustrates the Spanish American pattern of elite private growth in response to perceived public sector deterioration.

As in the discussion of Chile's private sector evolution, the determinants developed in chapter 2 are viewed in specific cases. I focus on the most important institutions illustrating each determinant, except the very general political one. Public sector politicization has been a powerful determinant in the creation and growth of all of Mexico's major private universities and many of its minor ones. Conservatives continually charge that public universities brandish an "unmistakable red color." Thus one hears public university officials continually defending themselves against charges of promoting chaos, subversion, delinquency, and unscrupulous young politicians.[9]

Politicization has generally blended with the other factors considered forthwith. In analyzing them, the sequence of evolutionary waves proves important. While Mexico has experienced all five elaborated in chapter 2, a deviant Mexican feature is that religious institutions did not precede secular institutions. Seen against the general Spanish American context, Mexico's religiously oriented universities were not especially "late," but its first secular ones were notably "early." Additionally, Mexico's creation of private institutions slowed after an initial spurt and did not reach a frenetic pace until the 1960s, when Latin American private higher education was already becoming more secular.[10]

Social class. Mexico's first private university (1935) was the Autonomous University of Guadalajara (UAG).[11] Conflict over the regime's effort to control the National University and to impose Marxism also affected the state University of Guadalajara. UAG's founders thus claim that autonomy with choice and academic freedom, not privateness per se, was their main goal. But UAG would stand for something more—a network of conservative social and political values.

An unusual constellation of forces struggled over UAG's creation. Un-

119

like most secular private universities, UAG did not receive a huge business boost, and unlike most initial private universities elsewhere, it was not Catholic. There was even some Jesuit opposition. Still, it did draw support from traditional Guadalajara Catholic and bourgeois elites. More striking was the lack of opposition from certain other quarters. Despite UAG's antistatist orientation, the Cárdenas administration did little except protect it from the hostile Federation of Socialist Students, and the state government only sporadically hindered UAG. Moreover, if swirling forces within the State led mostly to inaction, swirling forces within the National University were weighted toward an anti-State coalition (among liberal, religious, and business interests) that provided strong support for UAG, as well as other private initiatives, into the 1940s. Indeed the National University's first rector under the privatizing 1933 statute was the founder of PAN (National Action party), destined to become the bourgeoisie's major opposition party. His two successors similarly supported private development. Only after UNAM itself became more public again would it throw much of its institutional weight against private sector growth.[12]

Social conservatism became a more important factor in Mexican private development in the 1960s, as average SES and prestige declined in the rapidly growing public sector, while the size of the middle class able to afford private higher education expanded with Mexico's steady economic growth. The Anáhuac University, created in 1964, is a good example. Surely there were important religious, political, and economic determinants, but Anáhuac's highly exclusive SES and conservative values were also evident, and students were recruited largely from well-to-do neighborhoods in the western part of Mexico City. A Mexican religious order, the Legionnaires of Christ, was especially instrumental. A priest who had founded the Legionnaires (1942) helped secure contributions from the organization's businessmen. Anáhuac could be seen as a second-wave reaction to a decreasingly conservative first-wave institution, the Iberoamerican University.

Religion. The creation of the Iberoamericana, Mexico's first and still most prominent university with a religious identity, must be analyzed against the backdrop of prolonged, sometimes violent (especially 1926–29), conflict between the revolutionary State and the Church. This conflict had made it impossible to create any Church university. Naturally, the State's push for Marxist education stimulated Catholic opposition in the 1920s and 1930s; for example, the National Union of Catholic Students (connected to the Church hierarchy though not always in agreement) joined in efforts, paralleled elsewhere in Latin America, to combat Marxism in public universities.[13] Yet a university with a religious identity became possible only after Church-State conflict diminished. When Cárdenas's successor Manuel

Avila Camacho declared "I am a Believer," a modus vivendi was sanctioned. Still, unlike Chile, Mexico had no pontifical university—no university structurally tied to or governed by either the national Catholic church or the Vatican.

The Iberoamericana was created in 1943, building on various centers that the Jesuits had been establishing since the 1930s. As with UAG, Ibero was created in part as an alternative to UNAM's politicization. Also as with UAG, it was created with UNAM's help. UNAM's rector met frequently with the director of the National Union of Catholic Students, a friend from law school days. Noting the lack of a pontifical university since the nineteenth century, he offered UNAM's umbrella to incorporate and legitimate a new, religious university.[14] In the 1960s Ibero joined the socially progressive surge that, alongside many of Latin America's churches and Catholic universities, turned disaffected financial and religious groups toward the Anáhuac, Panamerican, and other conservative universities.

The second major institution in the religious category, La Salle University, adopted neither Ibero's progressive nor Anáhuac's conservative reputation, but it did closely approximate Ibero's early evolution in many ways, including UNAM's assistance. The most important similarity obviously was the religious inspiration. Jean Baptiste de la Salle himself, the university's spiritual father, came from France to Mexico in 1905, whence the *Lasallistas* and the subsequent urge for a university true to their purposes. Actually a preparatory school since 1938, La Salle did not become a university complete with professional studies until 1960. La Salle leaders suggest New York's Manhattan College as a good institutional parallel in founding purposes and operation.

Economics. Mexico's, indeed Latin America's, most important economics-oriented private university, the Monterrey Institute of Higher Technical Studies (ITESM), was created in the same year as Ibero. Political and social conservatism figured in its founding, but economics was the foremost determinant. Businesses in the nation's industrial center wanted well-trained and reliable graduates from useful fields of study. ITESM therefore adopted the Massachusetts and California institutes of technology as their models. As with UAG in Guadalajara, regionalism also played a role, although ITESM now has many campuses outside the Monterrey and Nuevo León locale, in places where the bourgeoisie is also strong. Still, this locale has nine private institutions (with nearly fifteen thousand students, 1981) besides ITESM.[15] Unlike UAG, ITESM grew in at least tacit alliance with the State as part of the broad State-private sphere alliance formed by 1943.

Mexico's foremost economics-oriented private university, the Auton-

121

omous Technical Institute of Mexico (ITAM; 1946), did not achieve economic primacy as immediately as ITESM. Again an initial trio of conservative political, social, and economic factors figured in its founding, but until the mid-1960s ITAM's economic role lay mostly in granting undistinguished degrees for jobs in fields such as accounting. ITAM failed to attract much financial support from big business, despite the addition of business administration courses in 1958.[16] By 1965, however, ITAM's economics school had become the outstanding one in Mexico.

The University of the Americas, with 68 percent of its (1978) enrollments in engineering, business, and economics, could also be added to the economic category. Americas has prided itself on its self-consciously U.S. orientation to education and its value on the job market. Created as Mexico City College in 1940, the university took form in 1963 to serve both Mexican and U.S. students in a depoliticized, secular environment that would foster international ties through bicultural, bilingual education. Its distinctive mission required an elite niche that only the private sector could provide.

The ensuing account of finance, governance, and function will give particular attention to these seven institutions—which until recently have held more than half Mexico's private enrollments—grouped into social (UAG, Anáhuac), religious (Ibero, La Salle), and economic (ITESM, Americas) categories. UAG, Ibero, and ITESM are the most important institutions in each category and perhaps the three most important private universities in Mexico. The other four rank next or close to next, partly depending on whether one chooses to relegate the compact ITAM and Americas behind larger but less prestigious universities.[17]

This categorization of individual institutions should not obscure the presence of multiple determinants in each university. Specifically, just as all seven universities have been political alternatives to the public sector, at least six of the seven are strongly oriented toward private enterprise, each with the majority of its field enrollments in administrative, economic, and engineering fields (while UAG has but one-fifth of its enrollments there). Instead of placing six institutions in the same ("economic") category, however, I separately categorize three in which economics appears especially blended with social (Anáhuac) or religious (Ibero, La Salle) orientations. The religious category could more accurately, but inelegantly, be labeled economic-religious, if not political-economic-religious. Table 4.1 gives a brief profile of the seven major institutions under consideration.[18]

Focus on the seven "name" institutions underplays the numerically typical institutions. Although four of the seven have fewer than five thousand students (1981), most private institutions are much smaller still. The average size of the remaining 115 private institutions is only one-tenth (626) the average size of the seven. Overall, the private sector's 15 percent of total enrollment is dwarfed by its virtually 50 percent of total institutions (1981). Even the largest private university, UAG, trails its state university by a four-to-one gap that is growing.

Focus on the name institutions likewise understates the importance of demand-absorbing institutions. Some third-wave growth has occurred within existing demand-absorbing institutions; by far the biggest example is the University of the Valley of Mexico, which shot from under four thousand to over eleven thousand enrollments between 1978 and 1981, before curbing its expansion. But most third-wave growth has occurred in new institutions. However, unable to examine third-wave institutions individually, I resort to generalization. The third wave has gained significance in recent years as system enrollments have continued to soar, as public but especially prestigious private universities have insisted on enrollment ceilings, and as economic crises drive students toward commercial pursuits. Reflecting the fact that not all institutions fall neatly into waves II and III, perceived public failures in quality, job relevance, and social-political orientations have also been relevant. Many students who are rejected by their first-choice private institutions opt for other private rather than public

Table 4.1 Seven Key Private Institutions in Mexican Higher Education

Institution	Year of Foundation	Distinctive Growth Cause[a]	Enrollment[b] 1978	1981
Autonomous University of Guadalajara (UAG)	1935	social	15,047	15,555
Anáhuac University	1964	social	2,945	4,061
Iberoamerican University (Ibero)	1943[c]	religious	6,803	7,844
La Salle University	1960[d]	religious	4,363	4,446
Monterrey Institute of Higher Technical Studies (ITESM)	1943	economic	9,348	12,555
Autonomous Technical Institute of Mexico (ITAM)	1946	economic	1,289	1,734
University of the Americas	1963[e]	economic	1,172	2,298
TOTAL			40,967	48,493

SOURCES: See accompanying text. Also, ANUIES, *Anuario estadístico 1978* (Mexico City: ANUIES, 1979), pp. 244–46; ANUIES, *Población de licenciatura en México 1981* (Mexico City: ANUIES, 1982), pp. 61–255.
a. See text; "political" could easily fit all seven, "economics" all except UAG.
b. The chapter rests mostly on both 1978 and 1981 data, as explained in footnote 1.
c. Reached full university status in 1953.
d. Preparatory school since 1938.
e. Evolved from Mexico City College, created in 1940.

ones. Probably the most powerful consideration is economic—to steer oneself toward a job, albeit not the elite ones available via the name institutions. But while Mexico's third wave typifies Spanish America's in some ways, there are notable differences. Most important, Mexico's third wave remains comparatively small. As late as 1968, just four of our name institutions held half the private sector's twenty-five thousand enrollments. Ten years later our seven accounted for 53 percent, before dropping to 41 percent by 1981.[19] And substantial (though unspecified) numbers of the remaining share are also in prestigious institutions, especially when compared to most public institutions.

Considering that the character of the private sector has not fundamentally changed in recent decades, the sector's ability to maintain (or even slightly increase) its proportional size is impressive. For the public sector, as mentioned, has been growing at an extraordinary pace. Whereas only 2.7 percent of Mexico's cohort group attended higher education in 1960, this percentage doubled by 1970. It almost doubled again, to 10.4 percent by 1975, as Mexico was passing the point of taking in one-hundred-fifty thousand new students each year.[20] Groups that were not higher education bound in 1960 have come to provide most of the students, and the expanded SES base is naturally directed predominantly to the more open and virtually free public sector. Only a very substantial exit decision by privileged groups could account for the present private share.

As expansion continues apace and some projections point to another doubling of total enrollments during the 1980s, even possibly reaching the two million mark by the turn of the century, it is uncertain whether the private sector will maintain its proportional size.[21] If it does, growth will probably have to occur through a hefty jump in the demand-absorbing subsector. In any case, a secular elite subsector continues to dominate the private sector. Ramifications for freedom, choice, equity, and effectiveness can be appreciated in the strong private-public differences that have consequently characterized finance, governance, and function.

FINANCE

Mexican private higher education is privately funded, and Mexican public higher education is publicly funded. Rarely can such generalizations be made so neatly, with so little reservation. Among private institutions, ITESM receives the most financial support from the State, and yet this accounts for less than 4 percent of ITESM's income. There are very few additional examples of private institutions receiving any annual State subsidy. In further contrast to the Chilean case, Mexico's private universities have not even requested such subsidies.[22]

I have elsewhere explored how Mexico finances the public sector, including the frustrated effort to introduce a significant private contribution.[23] Just a sketch will serve here as a basis for comparison with the private sector (leaving aside the issue of control through finance, which will be discussed in the governance section). Over 95 percent of public sector income comes from the State. University students, viewing tuition or other private income as capitalist intrusions, have beaten back attempts to diminish the State's proportional burden. Moreover, the public's technical subsector is nearly 100 percent financed by the State, through the federal government. Overall, increased enrollments have meant increased State expenditures, whether measured in absolute terms or as percentages of university income or national education budgets. The public sector's reliance on State subsidies almost unrelieved by tuition has been justified but also criticized on grounds of equity.[24]

Tuition

By contrast, private sector income comes overwhelmingly from tuition. Most private institutions declare no outside income, and most others rely on tuition (and fees) for at least three-quarters of their income. A three-way division of the private sector (largely overlapping waves III, I, and II respectively) helps identify the picture more specifically. Institutions located at the bottom and even the middle of the academic prestige ladder tend to rely fully on tuition. Funding is only somewhat different for the more prestigious social and religious universities. Ibero meets between 80 and 90 percent, La Salle 100 percent, and the socially conservative UAG 85 percent of ongoing costs through tuition.[25] Tuition is less important, though still the major income source, at the prestigious economic institutions, with ITESM at roughly 70 percent, ITAM 50 to 80 percent, and Americas 60 percent.

Administrators at many private universities proclaim the desirability of keeping the tuition share as high as possible to maximize academic freedom. Nevertheless, they also try to keep tuition low to minimize the stigma of elitism (and to attract applications). Both these general preferences apply more to the religious than the economic institutions. Administrators often claim that their competitors in *other* private universities understate the real level of tuition (to appear more equitable and exaggerate tuition's share of total income (to appear free from business donors). Personnel at the economic institutions may express opinions ranging from regret to fact-of-life acceptance to pride in high tuition as an indicator of academic status. Defensiveness about elitism frequently trails off into disdain for the public sector's claim of "free" education, paid for by a poor society at large and by sacrifices in effectiveness.

125

Private institutions point to their scholarship programs. Some religious institutions lament their inability to do more, given intractable inequities. "The Iberoamerican University, because of its tuition, is inevitably within reach of only a privileged minority. This situation is not consistent with the *Ideario*" (guiding ideas).[26] In principle, the State requires that the private institutions provide need-based scholarships to at least 5 percent of their students, but it does little to guard against abuses (e.g., scholarships awarded on the basis of favoritism to students who could well afford to pay). Overall, then, scholarships do not undo the substantial financial barrier that tuition represents in a highly stratified society. Nor do they greatly dilute a major intersectoral distinction. By 1975, while public students were still paying nominal fees of $10 to $50 per year, private counterparts were already paying over $500, usually closer to $1,000 or more, with total expenses running higher. Tuition variation within the private sector is dwarfed by the difference between sectors.[27]

The Nonprofit/For-Profit Connection

The financial profile of Mexico's private institutions is more complex than shown by tuition alone. At least some private universities, to hold down tuition, maximize effectiveness, and minimize dependency ties on business donors, would like to generate their own alternative income (e.g., as Aná-huac tries to with its computer facilities).[28] In practice, however, their nontuition income overwhelmingly derives from business donations, thus raising thorny questions about the relationship between for-profit and non-profit organizations. Aside from secretarial, language, and other commercial schools not properly included as higher education, all or nearly all the institutions in Mexico's private sector are nominally and legally nonprofit. They do not, at least admittedly, pursue lucrative ends nor distribute profits among their owners; they are "civil associations." How behaviorally non-profit the private institutions are remains less certain. This issue was not significant until recently in the Chilean context, since all six private universities have clearly been nonprofit—the characterization of *private* proving much more dubious than that of *nonprofit;* the private universities' relationship to the public and private financial worlds was similar to that of the public universities' relationship to those worlds. Mexico's private institutions, in contrast, have been unquestionably private, while sometimes questionably nonprofit.

Two broad categories of institutions could be considered. First, there are the scores of small, low-prestige institutions of the sort traditionally not allowed to sprout up alongside major universities in Chile. Such third-wave institutions are much more dominant in Brazilian than Mexican higher education, however, so this suspect side of the nonprofit/for-profit question is better explored there; suffice it to say here that critics, not just from public but also from prestigious private universities, decry mercantilistic missions. Second, there are the high-prestige institutions, especially dominant in the Mexican private sector. I now explore the nonprofit/for-profit connection of these institutions, aware that some aspects would prove relevant to less prestigious institutions as well.

Nonprofit status is obviously important. It carries with it the tax exemptions that constitute indirect State support for the private sector. But various factors limit the impact of nonprofit status for private universities. For one thing, public universities also receive tax exemptions. Beyond this, there are neither exemptions nor tax credits for those, parents or students, who pay tuition; so enrollees in 'the private sector "pay twice," in tuition for their education plus taxes for the public sector they forgo. Double payment can therefore lessen the inequities associated with Mexican private higher education. Additionally, the salaries paid to professors in either sector are not exempt from taxation. On the other hand, Mexico's nonprofit educational institutions are generally exempt from taxes on income and educational materials, including books and laboratories. In both state and national contexts, property is the main area in which exemptions are contested, as reflected in the national legislature's periodic votes that are divided but mostly support tax breaks. The official Institutional Revolutionary party itself (PRI) has been split, with a majority allied with the more rightist parties, backing exemptions, and a minority allied with the Marxist parties in opposition. Advocates of exemptions invoke principles of pluralism, choice, and constitutional guarantees for private education. They could also point out that the Mexican State heavily subsidizes noneducational private concerns, including even the Monterrey group, suddenly staggering in the early 1980s; only some of these concerns can reasonably claim to perform basically public functions. The private sector itself pushes for exemptions, partly for obvious financial reasons, partly as a token of political legitimacy from the State, a hedge against potential insecurity. However, opponents call exemptions for private higher education antidemocratic subsidies in favor of profiting businesses, and some inveigh against the clergy.

Even those who accept the principle of exemptions for private nonprofit organizations may question the eligibility of many private universities. Some elite institutions allegedly violate at least the spirit of the law by making "profits" that are squandered on luxuries unrelated to education.[29] But the main issue surrounding the integrity of the private sector's nonprofit status concerns the relationship between the educational institutions and those who own them. Businesses and foundations account for the bulk of the private sector's nontuition income. Their contributions help defray costs other than ongoing salaries, which means that the contributions are especially significant in those universities with the physical facilities necessary for academic quality and/or luxury. Donor funds are important in physical creation, expansion, or transplantation (as when Ibero and Americas moved to their present sites) and in buying and maintaining buildings, laboratories, and computers.

Who are the donors? Foreign interests, private and public, play a role. The Ford, Kellogg, and Rockefeller foundations on the private side and U.S. AID on the public side have been among those active in Mexico. AID, for example, has helped significantly in the construction and reconstruction of campuses for UAG and Americas, granting grace periods and low-interest loans.[30] Such foreign roles require more research. They may be blurred by ties to Mexican affiliates (as in aid to the Americas University from Unión Carbide Mexicana and Sears Roebuck de México). But our main attention here focuses on Mexico's foundations and businesses.

Although Mexico lacks a powerful foundation world comparable to that in the United States, there are several Mexican foundations active in higher education. The Mary Street Jenkins Foundation (MSJF) easily heads the list. The success story of businessman-philanthropist Williard Jenkins would not be so exceptional if it had happened in the United States, where Jenkins was born. But it is exceptional for Latin America. After moving to Mexico early in the century, Jenkins amassed a fortune from investments in movie theaters and other industries. He turned some of his profits back into charity and, when he died in 1968, left an unusually large private foundation. The MSJF is devoted overwhelmingly (perhaps 90 percent) to higher education and is the leading foundation in Mexican education. The state of Puebla, now home of the Americas, has been a particular target of interest. Overall, the MSJF has been active in the Americas, Anáhuac, Ibero, ITESM, and others. For example, Anáhuac's campus was built with a $2.5 million matching fund grant from the MSJF, and in 1975 the foundation granted a similar sum for a library, computer, and medical school.[31] Direct links between the MSJF and Jenkins Enterprises have raised questions, again more common in the United States, about the relationship of philanthropy to profits. The MSJF is managed by a board of trustees, chaired by Manuel Espinosa Yglesias, head of Bancomer, a major banking conglomerate.

Because private banks have been heavily involved in the private universities' financial base, the State's 1982 nationalization is obviously a serious concern. Grounds for speculating on the variable impacts for different institutions naturally relate to the institutions' dependence on banking interests.[32] All other things being equal, the less tuition-based universities are more vulnerable. More generally, however, most are threatened by the harsh economic facts of the early 1980s, including a huge foreign debt, zero growth, soaring inflation, repeated and severe devaluations, and the financial plight of the Monterrey group. But whatever the outcome, and few predict wholesale private university financial collapse, we must understand the financial relationship that has existed between the private universities and private enterprise (including but certainly not limited to banking).

Extraordinary power is concentrated in a few "groups," characteristically conglomerates involved in an impressive array of economic activities. The Monterrey group of industrialists is by far the most powerful; more precisely, it is divided into a few groups. It epitomizes Mexico's business- and industry-oriented development model. For some, it also epitomizes salient inequities in Mexico's development model; whatever the group touches is tainted or at least suspect. It has been estimated that the group's roughly two hundred families account for at least 15 percent of Mexico's total production.[33] The group's roots can be traced to late in the last century when Eugenio Garza Sada and his brother Roberto built an industrial empire based on beer, cartons, chemicals, glass, packaging, processing plants, and then metallurgy, banking, textiles, tourism, entertainment, and other concerns. As president of the Alfa industrial group within the Monterrey group, Eugenio was kidnapped and murdered in 1973. Roberto became the symbolic if decreasingly active leader until his death in 1979, after which his son assumed Alfa's presidency. The VISA group within the Monterrey empire is one of Mexico's largest holding companies. Formed in the late 1960s, it controlled the Banca Serfin, which itself was one of Mexico's biggest private financial institutions, as well as eighteen corporations.[34]

Among other major business groups important in financing private higher education are the Monteczuma group and the Continental group. Again we see the importance of family networks; again in fact we see power pass from father to son, in the Monteczuma group; again, a brewery. Yet Monteczuma (one of Mexico's biggest breweries) represents but a core around which diversified industrial and banking concerns have developed. Among these banking concerns, Banca Cremi has been strongly associated with ITAM and Ibero. The Continental group, prominent in a number of states and the federal district, runs businesses, banks, industries, Coca-Cola bottling, plastics, and the Banco Continental, S. A. (a multiple banking institution whose assets have grown enormously in the years prior to nationalization). This group has been particularly associated with the Americas University.

Business's clearest contribution to the private university lies in the area of financial aid. Such a contribution has historically been alien to Mexico, and to Latin America generally, for higher as well as for primary or secondary education. It is interesting therefore to analyze the local adaptations of U.S.

business-university practices that have evolved. Crucially, in the absence of a tradition of spontaneous foundation or individual giving, more predictable, explicit, direct, and even paternal patterns are found. At the extreme, but not uncommon, a single business group creates a *patronato* (parent foundation) which itself creates a university or assumes financial responsibility for an existing one. Osborn calls this pattern "a substitute for philanthropy" as well as for widespread endowments (funds established to yield income and handled by the universities themselves).[35] Sponsorship is only a little less direct when a few businesses operate jointly. Of course, some U.S. businesses give to only one university and some U.S. universities depend almost exclusively on one business concern, while some Mexican businesses and foundations give to various institutions and some Mexican universities rely on multiple donors. In general, however, one-to-one relationships are more characteristic in Mexico than in the United States.

Where the relationship between a Mexican business group and a university is especially close, the group may guarantee to make up whatever deficit is left when expenditures exceed tuition income. ITESM had such a guarantee for at least its first twenty years from a group of forty businesses in the Monterrey group. Americas has had a similar arrangement, once actually a written agreement, with the MSJF, and the need has been constant. Such guarantees can, at their best, promote a financial security that, in turn, can promote effective educational and administrative risk taking.

The art of soliciting charitable donations has come into practice either to fulfill such guarantees or just to provide the funds needed by private universities. In ITESM's early years, the Garza Sada family made plain just how much it expected from different constituent businesses of its Monterrey group. Their emissaries were not sent to expound the philosophical blessings of philanthropy. They were sent to collect. But more open campaigns are characteristic elsewhere. For example, the powerful businessman who heads the Directive Council at Americas initiated the 1978 Business-University Campaign, explicitly emphasizing how his university serves private enterprise.[36] And procedures are also more open where a university's financial foundation is less tied to any specific business group. UAG is a notable example, though identified with what might be called the Guadalajara group. UAG's financial board pursues potential donors dispersed in the business community. UAG has therefore put together a sophisticated how-to book on fund-raising, complete with psychological techniques and records on who has contributed previously. UAG does engage in broad philosophical discussions of the blessings of philanthropy, often directed through its alumni association (also alien to Latin America's public sector tradition, while common in the United States in both sectors). Its fund-raising guide implores: "We want to underscore the preponderant value that higher education plays in aggrandizing the national economy and private enterprise. . . . With this participation we will be in better shape to train high quality professionals on whom private enterprise can rely fully."[37]

To this point, whatever reservations one may have about private business investment in universities, the nonprofit/for-profit relationship appears clean. Nonprofit foundations or nonprofit universities themselves raise funds from the for-profit enterprises on behalf of the nonprofit universities. For-profit enterprises donate to their nonprofit foundations or directly to the universities. This procedure obviously holds for simple donations. It also holds when foundations buy land and donate to their university either the appreciated land or what would otherwise be "profits" from it. Beyond this, however, doubts arise. Some argue that businesses use their nominally nonprofit foundations for profit. As suggested earlier, the foundations may reinvest "profits" not in educational quality but in luxury, nepotism, and personal salaries and privileges, or they may actually pursue profits by charging the universities for use of land or buildings, usurping what would be profits at the university level (so that universities always remain with pious nonprofit deficits). Some businesses allegedly use the funds they accrue at the foundation level, from professors' pension funds for example, to invest as only the wizards of the business world know how.[38]

It is not possible simply to prove or disprove such charges. That officials at some private universities say the charges apply to other private universities (ITESM is often mentioned) gives only indirect testimony. Probably these charges apply much more to some universities than others, such as the religious ones. Beyond this, there seems to be enough leeway within the law on nonprofit institutions to satisfy the major aims of business actors involved with the prestigious universities. This becomes clearer as we more on to assess both the control exercised by business over university governance and the functions (other than possible profit making) that the private universities perform for private businesses. Beside such control and functions, any possible profits surreptitiously plucked from the universities might seem trivial.

GOVERNANCE
Profiles of Private Power

To what degree, then, does private enterprise control Mexican private higher education? It turns out that the degree is variable but substantial, operating chiefly through private university administrations. It is in fact between the financiers and the university administrations that the private sector's power fulcrum lies. This is not just because the State plays such a limited role but also because a top-down hierarchical pattern of private university governance allocates little power to professors and students.

A few comparisons help take us beyond the correct but nebulous assessment that private enterprise is influential but not all powerful in Mexican private higher education. The first comparison, compelling if obvious, is that business is much more influential in private than public higher education. Its impact on the latter is largely limited to its influence through the State and to insidious actions (e.g., hiring thugs to disrupt leftist activities). A second comparison is that business has long been the main external agent in Mexico's private sector, whereas the Church has filled that role in some other Latin American nations, especially until the 1960s and 1970s. A third comparison is that business is much more influential in setting "policy thrusts," as the cliché goes, then in determining daily decisions for the academic understructure. Thrusts include the institution's size, the timing and orientation of its expansion, tuition levels, expenditures on quality versus luxury, student-teacher ratios, courses offered, graduate fields offered, general bounds of academic freedom, and the institution's basic rules. Over such matters Mexico's donors are very influential. The interface between institutional autonomy and legitimate external influence naturally becomes a source of conflict. So do trade-offs between educational effectiveness and economic efficiency. Business and academic personnel frequently draw the lines in different places. A fourth comparison deals with those institutions relying on a single foundation run by a single business group and others usually suffering less business interference. The former might be pejoratively referred to as "kept" institutions. Overlapping this consideration is whether the institution relies on business donations not only for capital expenditures but also for an important share of recurrent expenditures. Such reliance especially characterizes institutions linked to a given foundation and its controlling business group.

Another overlapping comparison deals with economic and religious universities. Americas, ITAM, and ITESM are more hierarchically tied to business donors than are Ibero and La Salle. Anáhuac is tied to mixed economic-religious interests, while UAG is a distinct case. The ensuing analysis follows the economic-social-religious distinction.

As already noted, Americas is one of the universities that most depends on business finance. Very influential in Americas' affairs is the Continental group; its chairman of the board heads the executive committee of the university's governing board. And this committee is the university's chief policy-making body. It nominates the rector (to the whole governing board). The committee's head is the rector's boss, more than the rector would like.[39] Overall, the university's power structure resembles that of many nineteenth-century U.S. liberal arts colleges or some usually low-quality twentieth-century ones. Professors are responsible to departments headed by deans appointed by the rector. The Academic Council is not particularly powerful, though the administration usually accepts the professors' expert judgment on matters of professorial appointments and course curriculum. Professors are definitely responsible to deans, who are definitely responsible to the rector, who is definitely responsible to the governing board and its executive committee. Students have no role in governance. Their associations at best provide feedback and organize activities such as dances, poetry readings, and sports events. No graffiti appears on the University of the Americas campus.

Turning briefly to other economic institutions, ITAM depends on the Asociación Mexicana de Cultura foundation, which in turn depends mostly on the Monteczuma group for its finances. The asociación appoints the rector for an indefinite term. Again, struggles occur between the rectorship and the financing foundation (or the "beer people," as some disgruntled academics call them). One well-known observer has labeled ITAM "an academic appendage to Banca Cremi," connected to the Monteczuma group, but that seems like purposeful overstatement.[40] At ITESM, one advantage of the understructure is that the institution is too large for the close personal rulership found in some smaller private universities. Nonetheless, ITESM remains Latin America's most significant example of financial-governance ties between business and university. Among the Monterrey group's sponsoring businesses, the VISA group is especially powerful. The rector, handpicked by the business leaders, has a major role in setting general academic policy.

The more socially oriented institutions, Anáhuac and UAG, resemble the economic institutions in that they are run by rigid hierarchical authority. Both are also similar in that they depend heavily on business, but they differ by relying less on any one business group.

Anáhuac's owners, the Legionnaires of Christ, a wealthy organization satirized as the "millionaires of Christ," may serve as a buffer between donors and academic personnel, yet they themselves execute the general wishes of the donors through their oversight of academic policy. Priests occupy key administrative positions, except for some temporary loosening in the early 1970s. Anáhuac's executive committee, headed by the rector, includes strong representation of the legionnaires. In turn, the committee names the rector for an indefinite term. Predictably, the rector names his directors. There is no academic senate. Professors, even the full-time ones, have little role in university policy making.

UAG does not depend on any fixed business group, despite its important associations with one or two families, the Bacardi company, Sauza (the world's largest tequila producer), and especially the MSJF. UAG prides itself on having been created more by students than business and on resisting subordination to any foundation or other outside group, even though, its officials like to point out, there have been numerous offers both from domestic and U.S. financial groups.[41] Acknowledging there had been some drift in the wrong direction, UAG purportedly rejected the foundation pattern characteristic of Mexico's economic private universities and instead, in the mid-1960s, created a Directive Council. It cited the U.S. board of trustees as the model. The council's first president emphasized that the university itself should raise its own income. That, then, is the council's main task. Composed of thirty community representatives, it adds the experience of businessmen to that of the additional members, the rector, and two alumni representatives and maintains good relations between the university and its regional and national community. The council's power beyond this advice function is difficult to assess. Theoretically, the University Council is the chief academic body, and the Directive Council has only one vote in forty-five on it. Administrators, professors, and students each command one-third representation on the University Council, and the proportions hold for all its votes. Thus, the heads of the student associations of each academic division of UAG sit with the president of the alumni association and all of UAG's directors. On paper, UAG appears unique among Latin America's private universities in its degree of cogovernment. There are, however, significant counterindications.

The first concerns the rector's power. While the University Council formally appoints the members of the Directive Council, it does so from a list presented by the rector. And while it formally appoints the rector himself, Luis Garibay has had successive six-year terms since at least 1961. His personal authority is paramount, except for how it may be shared with the vice-rector, Antonio Leaño, who critics see representing a major intrusion from the business world. Many observers in other private as well as public universities, and in the Mexican polity at large, believe that UAG is unusually hierarchical, with tight control over hiring, firing, admissions, and academic orientations. Student demonstrations are flatly forbidden. Sanctions are swift and harsh. All students are advised to attend "orientation" and "encounter sessions." In any case, the hierarchy hardly ever is faced with open power challenges.[42]

Turning to religious institutions, La Salle is also run very much from the top, with a governing board of thirteen as supreme authority. But business and banking representation is limited compared to the economic universities' pattern. No financial group or (nonprofit) board is comparable to ITESM's, ITAM's, or Americas'. La Salle draws all its recurrent income from tuition, and when it needs capital funds it draws ad hoc on its own land holdings or bank loans or donations. Only four or five of the thirteen board members come from outside the university, and they represent not just business but the professions as well. The center of board power resides with the Lasallistas, one of whose officials is the board's president. Other board members include the rector and some of the university's top administrators, posts also held by Lasallistas. There are neither professor nor student representatives. The board names the rector and, from the rector's recommendations, also appoints the directors. The directors, in turn, formally name the professors, with the rector's approval. In some ways, therefore, while not tied to the Catholic church or Vatican and while controlled by Lasallistas instead of Jesuits, La Salle's governance pattern is closer than that of Mexico's other private universities to the pattern found in most of Latin America's Catholic universities. While the academic hierarchy is top-heavy, La Salle's governance rests more with academically trained priests than with external business interests.

Ibero is perhaps the most exceptional case. To be sure, the MSJF and banking and other financial interests have played important roles in that institution. But Ibero's authority pyramid is flatter and less hierarchical than that of any other major Mexican private university. Only after thirteen years of financial difficulties did Ibero call upon external groups to create a nonprofit financial patronato (1956). Among FICSAC's (Promotion of Research and Advanced Culture, Civil Association) eighty-four founders, private enterprise loomed large. The Monteczuma group and Banca Cremi have been notable, but along with the Bank of London and Mexico and the First National City Bank of New York, they have shared power with the religion affiliated businessmen who have also contributed. Furthermore, FICSAC's Directive Council functioned as the university's governing board only until 1968. Then, while most of Mexico's private sector was proclaiming its disgust with the "democratizing" pressures convulsing the public sector, Ibero was also democratizing. It created an Academic Senate, freely elected by the university community, to replace FICSAC's Directive Council as the governing board. Although the rector still has to deal with FICSAC, the university's new governance structure promotes (partial) autonomy from business control. To rein FICSAC's influence further, a separate academic board composed of Jesuits was created. Their role is that of moderator in case of business-academic difficulties. Moreover, the Academic Senate is the university's supreme academic authority. It is supposed to set the university's general course, fix tuition levels, approve budgets, and name and remove rectors (though in consultation with the Iberoamerican University Civil Association). Rectors, in turn, name and remove directors.[43]

135

The senate's thirteen members include two members from FICSAC, two from the academic board, the rector, two directors, one alumnus, two students, two professors, and one from service personnel. The administration thus maintains its numerical superiority, though not overwhelmingly, over representatives from the understructure. But the senate delegates academic power largely to the University Council, composed, one-third each, of directors, professors, and students. This is a startling case of private sector cogovernment without the hierarchically guaranteed consensus found at UAG. Ibero students have elected their own representatives since 1969. As is characteristic of the public universities and not of other private universities, political petitions and posters (e.g., solidarity with Nicaragua's Sandinistas) adorn bulletin boards, though without the radical graffiti seen at many public universities. Predictably, associated financial groups insist on certain parameters, but the frustration of some has already been suggested by their withdrawal from Ibero and their shift to other universities.

State Licensing

The preceding analysis has considered private university governance with particular reference to its main external powers, usually business and sometimes religious groups. Any discussion of the State's role is conspicuously absent, mainly because the State does not play an active role in private university governance. A potential exception lies in the State's constitutional authority to license private institutions and their programs, reaffirmed by the 1973 Federal Education Law. This law also reaffirms the State's right to revoke the license, not subject to judicial review, of any violating institution. Public universities, by the very act of their creation, automatically have the legal right to function and to grant degrees valid for professional practice. Private institutions must secure such rights from the State. This private sector dependency might raise the spectre of corporatist ties between the State and its societal institutions, but closer analysis leads to a very different assessment.

"Opening a private university is as easy as opening a tortillería," some observers have wryly said. Just as the State only loosely enforces the constitutional provision proscribing religious entities from establishing schools, so it is lax in enforcing regulations on private higher education. Naturally, the State's standby authority is a ready fountain of State power— an institutionalized threat to private sector freedom. Just as naturally, UNAM has been dissatisfied with its diminished status as "national" university and as the State's regulatory arm in higher education. Since I have detailed a national university decline in the Chilean case, little will be added here. Note, however, that the issue was more potent in Chile, where the national university was well established by the 1840s, whereas Mexico's was not securely established until the 1920s or 1940s.

Obtaining the licensing necessary to grant valid university degrees is difficult in only two respects, albeit sometimes important ones. The first is that the process may take years. The second is that private institutions must affiliate with the national government, usually the Ministry of Education (SEP), or with UNAM or the IPN, or with official counterparts in their own state; only through such auspices can students gain degrees. This affiliation presupposes copying significant features of the public sector's curriculum. But the overall restrictiveness of "incorporation" is debatable. It does not disturb the lower-quality private institutions that seek to absorb excess demand nor the higher-quality ones that really seek distinctiveness from the public sector in social differentiation or academic quality more than in academic content. Beyond this, the rigidly defined bureaucratic guidelines are not stringently implemented. The ideology of State supervision outstrips the reality. Excessively detailed regulation by remote bureaucracy does not generally have great impact. Although UNAM formally sets forth detailed curriculum plans, down to appropriate readings, such details would be so ludicrous to impose and monitor that they are frequently disregarded even within UNAM itself. To take one important example, UAG's incorporation to UNAM has limited its academic flexibility but, as in the case of health sciences, not very much.

The major difficulty with initial or subsequent affiliation lies in academic change, especially change to curriculum or procedures that lie outside the existing public sector range. Private officials tell different tales of public sector or State reaction to proposals for change—tales ranging from denial to long waits to smooth acceptance. Approval is of course facilitated wherever, as in Puebla, the government may in fact "privately" prefer effective alternatives to its "own" politicized universities. Private university flexibility is also enhanced by the possibility of affiliating different programs with different public institutions.[44]

One route to fuller institutional freedom from the State lies open for private institutions, but few are permitted to follow it. As of 1982, only eight institutions were granted presidential decrees freeing them from incorporation. The largest institution is ITESM. Most other "free-private" (*privado-libre*) institutions are very small. Among them are ITAM, El Colegio de México, and the Free Professional Schools of Law, Municipal Engineering, and Homeopathy. Some other private universities, such as Americas and La Salle, aspire to freedom from incorporation, but not all share the aspiration. Incorporation carries with it an open expression of legitimacy by the State,

137

important because one legacy of the revolution is an unshakable fear within Mexico's private sector of a potential populist or demagogic assault on "elitist private" institutions. It is not so surprising, therefore, that the rector and other top officials of a rightist university such as UAG would declare their preference for continued affiliation with UNAM rather than free status. Of course nobody is offering them a choice.

The State's licensing role, indeed its overall policy toward the private sector, includes a subtle blend of indifference, even disdain, and tacit support. It is largely a laissez-faire policy. Despite variation by specific administrations, a significant irony in State-university relations generally holds.[45] Although laissez-faire policies deny the private sector both material and overt symbolic support, they also spare it from many of the regulations and vicissitudes of the federal and state political arenas. Private institutions remain private. And because Mexico's private higher education has been perfectly capable of providing for itself, attracting students as well as financial support, laissez-faire policy has been favorable policy. A more active State role carries risks for the private sector. Thus some fear the consequences of the 1979 law that provides for greater central coordination of the entire higher education system, especially through the National Association of Universities and Institutes of Higher Education (ANUIES). Many private institutions have been part of ANUIES for some time, but now it may be changing from a voluntary to a quasi-government organization. To date, however, private universities have been so private in governance that they feel compelled to proclaim ostentatiously their loyal cooperation with the State, lest they be considered illegitimately isolated. Public institutions, on the other hand, often find it necessary to proclaim their autonomy, lest they be considered subservient to the State. They openly promoted the move, successfully culminating in 1980, to write autonomy into the constitution. Private universities are much more autonomous from the State, but very few include the adjective in their name, while all but four state universities do.

Thus, although a greater State role could undermine the safety enjoyed under laissez-faire policy, it is not so simple. Indeed, more State inspection may be a blessing for the private sector.[46] Insofar as quality is high, or, at least, public sector curriculum is copied, and insofar as the State really lacks the technical means for massive and careful evaluations, most of the private sector can easily pass its tests. Legitimacy is enhanced—academic legitimacy in the lower-quality institutions and political legitimacy throughout the private sector. So the private sector contemplates the uncertain trade-offs between more explicit recognition and the dangers of a closer State. And the State itself contemplates whether the private sector performs more effectively, and appears better subordinated, by cold-shoulder but benign neglect or by visible supervision.

Comparing Private to Public Governance

With the State's role kept minimal and the power of professors and students pointedly restricted, the locus of private sector power clearly resides with the university administrations, along with the business or religious groups that sustain them. Mexico's public universities are generally much stronger at the top (the State) and bottom (faculties, professors, and students) and correspondingly weaker at the middle or university-wide tier. Detailed analysis of public university governance was delineated in a previous study, allowing here for succinct sectoral comparisons organized according to structural levels.[47] One caveat however: While there is a great variation both within and among public universities, I must generalize and stick close to the norms.

Compared to its role in the private sector, the State is extremely important in the public sector. The contrast is an enormous but far from all-or-nothing one, since State control is limited if compared to its role in many of Mexico's other societal institutions or to the higher education role of Latin America's modern authoritarian regimes. Note, moreover, that control is a tricky concept, and that while several public universities produce strong opposition to the State, several others (usually more technocratically oriented) march in concert; in any case, most are significantly divided internally.

The State has been trying, in recent years, to increase its control over the public universities. For instance, the 1979 law tightened controls over research and new programs and created a network of planning agencies from the institutional through the state, regional, and national levels. It is too soon to judge the probability of major change. Skeptics easily point to one grand plan after another that has failed.[48]

To this point, the State's major leverage has been financial.[49] It formally fixes subsidy levels or, in effect, the public university's income level. It can hold the level steady or drop it below the inflation rate. It can vary recurrent subsidies, but especially capital and research funds, according to compliance with its policies (usually informally communicated) or according to political caprice. Certain state governments are more prone than others or than the national government (under almost all recent administrations) to use the financial weapon coercively. But empirical evidence establishes fundamental limits to the notion of systematic financial control, even though it surely rules out neither important instances of such control nor threats that would be difficult to measure.

First, since the State-university modus vivendi of 1945 was implemented, contrasts to the financial policies of earlier governments show how comparatively safe the contemporary universities have been. Second, the subsidy level is not really set by the State alone. Rather, the State is forced by students and the middle class to provide nearly the entirety of the public universities' income. The amount allocated to each university often results from bargaining, not simple State decree (nor simple requests from all-powerful universities), and many public universities, especially UNAM, have powerful bargaining chips. Furthermore, at least some data show that recurrent subsidies do not vary in statistically significant ways according to compliance or defiance of State policy preferences, for example, by achieving favorable distributions of students by field of study or by avoiding political disorder. Instead, the sheer number of students, not set by State policy, is the overwhelming determinant, especially if linked to fixed costs such as professors' salaries.[50] Third, recurrent subsidies follow statistically predictable much more than variable patterns over time. From 1959 to 1975, counting each year at each state university as a case, federal funds declined in only 2.4 percent of the cases, state funds in only 6.5 percent, and almost never in significant amounts. UNAM's federal funds declined just once, slightly, compared to seven times from 1912 to 1933. The growth of federal subsidies to state universities has increased in a linear pattern, and public higher education's share of the federal budget has been stable. Fourth, several public universities retain considerable freedom in distributing the funds they receive. They initially make their requests in gross categories, difficult to disaggregate for careful review, and they receive lump sums from the State. Only sometimes are formal pledges made concerning which faculties, schools, or activities will get what, and there is little subsequent program accountability. Again, all this evidence does not deny a major State role, but it shows that important limits exist, even regarding what is generally seen as the State's most potent weapon.

Appointment of university administrators is perhaps the State's other most potent means of influencing public university governance. Again, the State's public sector role is limited, even though it is profound compared to its virtually nonexistent private sector role. State influence can come through governing boards, but only about half the public universities have them. When UNAM instituted the first governing board (1944), explicitly acknowledging U.S. models and praising their effectiveness, the shift was widely denounced as a move toward not State but private control—toward "gringo" notions of external private representation versus traditional Euro-Latin traditions, a move that "beheaded" freedom and self-government. In practice, public governing boards have been more open to the community than have other public university organs, but this community includes business much less often than does the private university community.[51] If governing boards have assaulted public university freedom, the main assailant is the State, not private enterprise. Yet some governing boards are

140

elected from within the university itself, and only some include State representatives; thus board members may be respected academics. In turn, the governing boards (where they exist) appoint the rector through variable *auscultación* (consultation and informal polling) of the university community and sometimes of the State authorities. Overall, the State is one actor in the process, varying in influence depending upon institution and government administration. By comparison, as in the U.S. private sector, the State role is negligible in appointing private rectors. Private boards also consult much less with the university understructure and much more with their "unrevolutionary families" of business and/or religious groups.

A related private-public difference concerns rector tenure. Private university rectors may be appointed for indefinite terms, serving at the pleasure of private governing boards. Even when the term is fixed, reappointment often leads to impressive continuity; for example, UAG has had only three rectors in nearly a half century. Public university rectors are appointed for fixed terms of usually four years, with reelection sometimes proscribed and often rendered irrelevant by the fact that many fail to survive politically. Even the "orderly" change of public university administration, like the orderly change of Mexico's national administrations, generally means wholesale personnel shifts at the top. It may mean policy discontinuity. The greater stability of private university administration, on the other hand, both reflects and promotes the greater private effectivenss at this middle level of governance.

Faculties are important in much of the public sector. Authority may be derived from the university-wide administration above, as in the private sector, but it is often derived from below as well. Professors have more clout in the public than the private universities. They have a larger role, voting and otherwise, in choosing their administrators. A typical struggle for the directorship of a UNAM social science faculty, for example, may involve four or five aspirants; the winner will be the one who conciliates the broadest spectrum of constituent interests.[52] The faculty and university-wide councils on which professors and their elected representatives serve are stronger than in private universities, largely because the administration that sits above them is weaker. Following the U.S. model, more private universities are organized by departments, which is conducive to effective university-wide coordination. More public universities are organized by faculties and are therefore supportive of professorial power, at least for senior professors. In this sense, academic freedom may be greater in Mexico's public rather than in its private universities; conservatives frequently charge that academic freedom is too wide and is therefore ultimately abused in the public universities.

A more fruitful comparison concerns not the extent of academic freedom but the source of challenges to it. The challenge from the State is minimal for private institutions, limited for many public ones, but substantial for other public ones. Restrictions from business groups are fundamental in many though not all private universities, but only indirect in public universities. Private university administrations are more likely than their public counterparts to impose stringent limits on free speech. Professorial and student intolerance can be found in each sector. The main difference is that it usually comes from the Right in private universities and from the Left in public ones; also, battles among university groups, much more salient in public universities, often create precarious environments for academic freedom.

Finally, the gulf between student power in private versus public institutions is immense. Of those private universities analyzed, only in Ibero (unless one debatably adds UAG) was student participation notable. By contrast, students are a major force in many public universities, usually much more so than even at Ibero. Most private universities grant students no representation on governing bodies. Most public ones allow some governing bodies to consist of at least one-fourth students. Much more important, however, only public university students hold the viable threat of disruption. This means that they can more freely express their feelings, demonstrate, or even challenge the authorities in ways that would spell sure expulsion from the private sector.[53] It also means that they can shape policy by blocking State or university administration initiatives. Tuition, admissions, exams, personnel policy, and curriculum are examples. Decisions about tuition levels and admissions standards are made at the top in private universities, while in the public sector student power has often spelled inaction—";choice" for the students, ineffectiveness for administrators. Certainly in the public sector State and student interests partly overlap; where they do not, repression (and the threat of it) limits student power. But repression may involve great cost to the State and rarely leads to coherent policy implementation. Moreover, as students became less active in the 1970s then in the 1960s, university worker unions became very formidable forces. A good example of official frustration with student and worker power surfaced in 1979. The government proposed legislation to limit solidarity strikes—strikes undertaken by groups to support protesters at different public institutions. The proposal itself prompted a wave of strikes that led to a government retreat.

Overall, then, Mexico's public sector is characterized by a wide distribution of power at many different levels, while its private sector concentrates power much more at the university-wide level, in conjunction with its sponsors. The latter parallels many hierarchical U.S. liberal arts colleges more than Mexico's public universities parallel patterns found in U.S. public institutions. Mexico's public universities are not run by separate state governments as in the United States, nor by the national government to the extent seen in modern authoritarian regimes, nor by university-wide administration as in U.S. or Mexican private universities, nor by senior, chaired professors as in the Continental model, nor by students to the extent found in Latin America's truly cogovernment universities, nor by workers. Instead, each of these layerings shares power. On the other hand, this means that the national government, students, and workers are far more influential in Mexican public universities than in U.S. public or private ones.

In comparative perspective, then, the wide distribution of Mexico's public sector power appears notable for the understructure's strength. Notwithstanding cross-national perspectives, my main comparison is, of course, to Mexico's private sector, and generalization easily overrides qualifying detail there. In dealing with the center of gravity of each sector, however, we should not forget that differences between, for example, Ibero and UNAM may be smaller than those between UNAM and those radical (or conservative) state universities where government and students continually (or rarely) clash and the university center cannot hold (or holds without challenge). What remains remarkable, nonetheless, is how relatively little variance exists among so many private institutions. Almost all conform to a pattern that is sharply distinct from most public universities'. It is also sharply distinct from the public's technical subsector; this subsector narrows the private-public gap in hierarchy versus freedom of participation, but it widens the private-public gap in State control. Overall, the private-public gap is huge.

FUNCTION

So distinctive are Mexico's private and public university sectors that clear differences arise not only in finance and governance but even in the generally fuzzier category of function. The principal values in Mexico's private universities remain remarkably faithful to those for which they were created as alternatives to the public universities. How each sector serves the public and the State is an intriguing and complex matter, while the private much more than the public sector serves conservative values and private enterprise, often through highly esteemed education.

Values: Religious, Political, and Nationalist

At least three factors have limited the importance of religion in orienting the private sector. One, mentioned earlier, concerns the antireligious component of Mexico's revolution; this factor rules out any university officially tied to the Church or Vatican or any university in which personnel act primarily as priests rather than as educators and administrators. Article three of the 1917 Constitution declares that all education, private or public, must be laical and that no religious corporation can establish a school. In keeping with the general laxity with which many antireligious laws have been enforced, however, some institutions at all levels have religious affiliations, principally with the Jesuits. While La Salle University emphasizes its freedom from Church control, it also emphasizes that it has the hierarchy's confidence, and it proudly (though unsuccessfully) invited Pope John Paul II to the campus during his 1979 Mexico City visit. So Mexico's revolutionary heritage restricts religious influence but does not negate it.

A second factor limiting religious orientation is that most of Mexico's private universities have been created for nonreligious social, political, and economic reasons. One estimate puts the Catholic institutions' share of private enrollments at around one-fifth.[54] Even the "religious" universities have been created for multiple reasons. Mexico has never had the equivalent of Chile's Catholic University of Chile. It has no university with the words *pontifical, Catholic,* or *saint* in its name. Only La Salle (joined recently by a small Lasallista university in Guanajuato) bears the name of a religious group. Compared to Chile, Mexico's historic fault line has been private-public much more than religious-secular. Nonetheless, a third factor limiting religious orientations is that, as in most of Latin America, such orientations have weakened since the principal religious universities were created. For example, less than 1 percent of Ibero's students specialize in faculties of religious sciences; yet that percentage comprises the total number of students (fifty) in all Mexican higher education (1978) who study in this area. Additionally, there are only twenty-six students specializing in theology in Mexico. Only 1.5 percent of Ibero and La Salle students combined specialize in philosophy, though Ibero at least has other students in letters, history, sociology, and anthropology, where Christian thought may orient disciplinary content. No Anáhuac students specialize in religion or philosophy. Furthermore, general religious requirements are not all rigid. The universities are generally open to Protestant and Jewish students and professors, though preferences and especially national demographics keep Mexico's religious universities basically Catholic in composition. There are neither obligatory religious services nor compulsory religious courses. La Salle has an institute for "comprehensive development" in which a team of professors concentrates on humanities with religious content; in its advanced semesters, Catholicism is presented as the optimal solution to human needs. Ibero is even less strict in promoting religious values. More than two years of reflection (in the 1960s) led to a reformulation of Ibero's ideals. Not a conventional Catholic university, it is a university of "Christian inspiration." That is, most of the university community, certainly the most dynamic

144

part, should be personally committed to Christian principles and act upon them, but individual students and professors may hold opposing beliefs and even criticize Christianity (though they must do so "respectfully and not aggressively").[55] Only vaguely guiding or restrictive, Ibero's doctrine of Christian inspiration nonetheless separates it from the secular universities, private and especially public.

Except for Ibero, the major private universities approximately reflect the position of Mexican private enterprise on a left-right political spectrum. This puts the private sector as a whole far to the right of the public sector as a whole. Private enterprise villifies public universities for their alleged Marxism, disorder, and immorality. It espouses values such as a limited State, economic growth over distribution, financial stability, technocracy over populism, restrictions on labor organizations, social conservatism, and hierarchy.[56] Naturally, different private universities and their owners are more associated with some of these political beliefs and less with others. Even the progressive Ibero is not to the left of most public institutions, although its sense of Christian social responsibility makes it unusual within the private sector. Most other universities either do not take seriously the idea that students should contribute their services to the needy or they postpone "social service" until graduation. Ibero tries to integrate social service into the student's program, awarding academic credit for it. Aside from the testimony of disinterested parties, one possibly compelling sign of Ibero's dedication is its sober analysis of the very limits of its progressivism. This university acknowledges the high SES and unenthusiastic approach to self-sacrifice of many of its students. Moreover, with its pockets of radical departments and socialist Christians, Ibero finds itself in the unique position, within Mexico's private sector, of denying that it is communist and of chastising those who foolishly but spontaneously see red whenever there is any concern for social justice.[57]

Newer religious universities have done less in pursuing social justice. An important example, despite Jesuit administration, is Guadalajara's Western Institute of Technological and Higher Studies. Opened in 1958, it is Mexico's fourteenth largest private institution (1981).[58] On the far religious Right are institutions under Opus Dei influence. Most of these—the Panamerican University is widely thought to be one—are small. More important is the extent of very rightist penetration, where some charge Opus Dei influence and others deny it, in larger institutions. All I can responsibly say here, however, is that some of these institutions represent a religious Right associated with social exclusiveness.

UAG is the main social institution. Indeed, because it alone has accounted for nearly one-fifth of the entire private sector, it is crucial to examine the values UAG promotes. Ruled by laymen, UAG is a bulwark of

Mexican conservatism. The writings of powerful rector Luis Garibay are unabashed diatribes—albeit literary ones—against radicals, Marxists, Freudians, "Janefondistas," sexual licentiousness, and other permissiveness. They are also firm statements of how a university should face such problems. Consider these respective samples from Garibay's "The Romantic Protest" and "A Policy for Youth."[59]

> The key word in decoding this enigma is *irresponsibility* [Garibay's emphasis]; irresponsibility hidden behind new attitudes, myths, illusions, and above all, behind the proclamation, suspiciously noisy, of responsibility and involvement. This is the group to whom everything has been offered and of whom nothing has been asked.
> We cannot continue to contemplate those avalanches of extenuated youth, already indifferent to good and evil, their consciences more tattered than their clothes! We cannot allow that an idea of decadence convert us into living a life of decrepitude, establishing a vicious circle between disaster and a "philosophy of disaster." Neither can we resign ourselves only to teach our young people to live in a rotten society, as some perhaps with good intentions but with cloudy judgment claim, supposing that the conversion can start with confusion.

Many of Garibay's essays have been delivered as "First Lessons" at UAG's orientation sessions. Students are indoctrinated in the UAG vision of how the university has evolved, where it is going, and what the proper student role is within it. There are also ongoing seminars on UAG values, at which student attendance is strongly recommended.

UAG places tough limits on undesirable behavior. It tolerates no political demonstrations. It tolerates no marijuana smoking. Either spells eviction, and students may initiate punitive action against their peers. Freedom of classroom speech is obviously greater than freedom of protest, but all such freedoms are fragile in this environment. As suggested earlier, UAG avoids serious internal conflicts, partly through careful hiring and admissions procedures (at least for its Mexican students). Seasoned UAG sources fervently deny charges that they use restrictive and secret criteria, including the need to believe in God and to eschew political activism, especially involving Marxism.[60] Again, a key seems to be self-selection. Few activists or ardent atheists would want to attend or teach at UAG. Anyone who chooses UAG, or most private institutions, has chosen to forgo certain freedoms.

Critics also denigrate UAG as antinationalistic and antipublic—an unfortunate example of a private university prostituting itself to U.S. interests and modes. In fact, UAG is more involved than any other Mexican university in international education associations. These associations are perceived by some Mexican experts on higher education as tied to U.S. models of finance, governance, and function, and as holding conferences that are overly patronized by figures from the Western industrialized countries. UAG defenders factually point out that the associations, and their governing boards, are made up overwhelmingly of Latin Americans. But they do not shy away from applauding UAG's internationalism and the prestige of its international collaborators, emphasizing the need to learn from others ("just as the Japanese have done") and to train more Mexican talent in fields such as educational policy and administration. They also emphasize the participation of Latin America's public as well as private universities in some of these organizations. UAG claims to have historically preserved its integrity in the face of multiple foreign solicitations to orient and patronize the university, just as it has claimed to preserve its self-governance. UAG's rector describes the arrangment for bilateral programs this way: "The role of North American universities would be that of midwife. They would aid in the birth of a program of university reform, without altering its essential aspects, or [having] paternity rights over the benefited institution. . . . The new university . . . . will still be authentically Mexican and work in harmony with our social-cultural characteristics and entities."[61] And UAG participates in international programs with not one but many nations, including several in Latin America.

UAG's single most important international connection, however, stems from its medical faculty. UAG is often called the largest U.S. medical school in the world, with approximately three thousand U.S. citizens enrolled and three hundred receiving degrees each year.[62] It is therefore maligned for subsidizing the United States by training its students, meeting a demand avoided by the U.S. American Medical Association, and relieving the U.S. government of the high financial burden of U.S. medical education (largely federally funded). In return for this service, most graduates simply return to practice in the Colossus of the North. UAG responds that it gives away nothing. After all, tuition from U.S. medical students helps to finance the multiple functions of this *Mexican* university. Besides, Mexican youth study in the United States. UAG confidently sees such Mexican-U.S. ties as mutually beneficial, fostering both choice and effectiveness as well as understanding, and scoffs at knee-jerk perceptions of inherent inequities and dependency in U.S.-Mexican bilateralism.

The Americas University, however, is the one that has been, by design, most associated with U.S. orientations. "Mexicanization" became a major goal only after the university's difficulties in the mid-1970s, followed by a commitment to the Spanish language, an 80 percent Mexican professoriate and a 90 percent Mexican student body. Not until 1975 did Americas appoint its first Mexican rector. One effort to reconcile its northward leanings with Mexican needs is the Americas' offering of quality programs on U.S. policy and philosophy to better enable Mexico to understand and thereby deal better with its neighbor. Although a university's character and especially its image does not change overnight, and although Americas acknowledges its continuing vulnerability on the bicultural issue, important change has taken place. As Americas evolves, its special functions have been partially picked up by the the International University of Mexico. Founded a decade earlier, this university did not function seriously until 1981, whereupon it pledged itself to U.S. style and quality. Its main language is English, since the children of U.S. executives and other foreigners are especially targeted.

Thus, the private sector battles stereotypes of being "gringo" just as the public sector battles stereotypes of being "red."[63] Similarly, the private sector defensively claims legitimacy based on its public national functions. The so-called private university is really public if open to the general public, is nonprofit, and produces social benefits; it merely uses private finance and ownership to pursue public ends.[64] While UAG can stress its contribution to meeting social demand, smaller institutions such as Americas must stress the public benefits from the "externalities" or "trickle-down effects" of quality education for the elite. Some private universities are careful to mix pre-Colombian images into their catalogues, though photographs of students often depict the less *mestizo* ethnicity found at most private compared to public universities.

But there is the rub. Pablo Latapí forthrightly declares that neither sector can afford to feel superior when it comes to such public functions as serving the poor, serving the least-developed regions, promoting social service, or simply bettering Mexico.[65] The leftist rhetoric found in much of the public sector has not routinely translated into effective action. While the public sector probably does more than its private counterpart, at least directly, the evidence remains unimpressive, the issue cloudy. Private university policy is directly oriented to promote private ends—sometimes religious but especially social (elite) and economic. How well it serves the public interest depends on how well these private ends add up to the public interest. An analysis of fields studied and jobs assumed helps us specify where each sector truly concentrates its efforts.

Fields of Study

Although the distribution of students by field of study gives important measures of what the sectors do differently, interpretation of how distribution should be associated with privateness or publicness is trickier. One hypothesis would link the self-financed institutions with fields of study that

148

are less expensive to offer. These would include humanities, law, social science, and business and administration more than engineering, medicine, and the exact sciences. Another hypothesis would link these institutions with fields that their financiers desire. Business and administration is an obvious choice for private enterprise, and engineering might suit the needs of contributing industrialists. But the situation is more complicated: most private university income derives from student payments; and students may want prestigious careers, or any career with job prospects, or any career that offers good chances of easy graduation and some credential.

It has been possible to put together nearly comprehensive data on Mexican higher education for analysis by field of study. Fortunately, ANUIES gives the data separately for each institution and each specific career of study. Thus, I have been able to (1) show data by sector; (2) group the careers by fourteen fields of study, avoiding the more common and grossly aggregate categories such as "social science and administration" or "engineering," including architecture. Table 4.2 presents the results for Mexico's more than six hundred thousand students (1978).

Probably the most significant private-public difference is the private concentration in business and administration (30 percent private versus 16 percent public). Adding the related communications category, the private sector has such a wide lead that it holds only a slight proportional edge in only three other fields, while trailing in nine. It has a small edge in basic social sciences but trails in economics and law. Significant variation would be hidden by a gross category such as "social science and administration."

The public sector leads where expected, but the margin is surprisingly small in medicine and agricultural sciences (though ample in veterinary studies). The biggest public lead is in engineering, 24 to 17 percent. It is interesting to juxtapose these figures to the nearly identical 6 percent each sector has in architecture; again, disaggregation proves worthwhile. The biggest proportional public edge is in the exact sciences, 4 to 1 percent.

There is ample confirmation of the private sector's link to private enterprise in its business and administrative concentration.[66] That concentration also tends to confirm the hypothesis that the private sector teaches mostly the inexpensive fields. The sector's low enrollments in engineering and exact sciences also point in that direction, while its share of medical students casts doubt on it. The hypothesized private tendencies are particularly strong in the demand-absorbing subsector, as we can see by comparing our sectoral data with data drawn mostly from the prestigious institutions.[67] Disaggregation proves useful within sectors as well as within field categories.

Probing within the public sector, we can separate out the technical subsector, which holds nearly one-fifth of that sector's enrollments. The IPN, the main institution, is joined by a broad network of regional technical

Table 4.2 Mexican Enrollments by Field of Study, 1978

Sector	Business & Administration[a]	Communications[b]	Economics	Basic Social Sciences[c]	Law	Humanities[d]	Education
Private	23,351	2,364	1,772	5,958	4,747	987	941
	(30.0)	(3.0)	(2.3)	(7.7)	(6.1)	(1.3)	(1.2)
Public	86,948	3,531	19,171	30,858	49,371	10,975	3,203
	(16.0)	(0.6)	(3.5)	(5.7)	(9.1)	(2.0)	(0.6)
TOTAL	110,299	5,895	20,943	36,816	54,118	11,962	4,144
	(17.7)	(0.9)	(3.4)	(5.9)	(8.7)	(1.9)	(0.7)

SOURCE: Calculations from data on individual careers found in ANUIES, *Anuario estadístico 1978* (Mexico City: ANUIES, 1979), pp. 13–322. My fourteen-part categorization is adapted largely from ANUIES, *Catálogo de carreras* (Mexico City: ANUIES, 1973), pp. 12–15.
a. Accounting; business administration; commercial relations; computer studies; industrial relations; public administration (except where listed as "political science and public administration"); tourism.
b. Communications studies; journalism.
c. Anthropology; area studies; international relations; political science; psychology; social work; sociology.

institutes and a newer network of agricultural technical institutes. This subsector is supposed to break traditional university patterns and meet national development needs as determined by the State. Tables 4.3 and 4.4 provide relevant data.

As table 4.3 shows, public technical institutes predictably concentrate in engineering. Half their enrollments are in that single field. The technical profile is weakened somewhat by concentrating another fourth in business and administration, but both fields together perhaps comprise a modern, development-oriented profile. Thus the technical subsector reduces the

Table 4.3 Mexican Enrollments by Field of Study: The Public Technical Subsector, 1978

Sector	Business & Administration	Communications	Economics	Basic Social Sciences	Law	Humanities	Education
ITR[a]	4,417						
	(17.4)						
ITA[b]							
IPN[c]	20,645		3,823	999			
	(28.1)		(3.8)	(1.4)			
TOTAL	25,062		3,823	999			
	(24.9)		(3.8)	(1.0)			

SOURCE: See table 4.2.
a. Regional technical institutes.

150

Table 4.2 cont'd

Medical Sciences[e]	Nursing	Veterinary Studies	Agricultural Sciences	Exact Sciences[f]	Engineering[g]	Architecture	Total
15,136	119	630	3,192	1,009	12,893	4,687	77,786
(19.5)	(0.2)	(0.8)	(4.1)	(1.3)	(16.6)	(6.0)	(100.1)
110,135	1,563	14,287	28,014	22,086	132,649	31,557	544,348
(20.2)	(0.3)	(2.6)	(5.1)	(4.1)	(24.4)	(5.8)	(100.0)
125,271	1,682	14,917	31,206	23,095	145,542	36,244	622,134
(20.1)	(0.3)	(2.4)	(5.0)	(3.7)	(23.4)	(5.8)	(99.9)

d. Fine arts; geography; history; letters; linguistics; literature; philosophy; religion.

e. Dentistry; health specialist; medicine; nutrition.

f. Actuarial sciences; biology; chemistry; earth sciences; mathematics; oceanography; physics; statistics.

g. Specializations include clinical, civil, electrical, extractive, industrial, and mechanical engineering; military studies.

overall private-public gap a bit. As table 4.4 shows, a larger gap would otherwise exist in seven of the nine fields where the public sector leads, with economics almost unchanged and engineering proving exceptional. Another conclusion that could be drawn, however, is that the public technical sector does not alter the overall private-public balance very much, again except in engineering. The public technical subsector is distinct from the rest of the public sector, but it is also distinct from the private sector. It provides a separate set of choices.

Disaggregating further, table 4.5 shows the private-public breakdown in

Table 4.3 cont'd

Medical Sciences	Nursing	Veterinary Studies	Agricultural Sciences	Exact Sciences	Engineering	Architecture	Total
					21,015		25,432
					(82.6)		(100.0)
		516	1,238		55		1,809
		(28.5)	(68.4)		(3.0)		(99.9)
5,749	8			1,284	30,511	10,528	73,547
(7.8)	(0.0)			(1.7)	(41.5)	(14.3)	(100.0)
5,749	8	516	1,238	1,284	51,581	10,528	100,788
5.7	(0.0)	(0.5)	(1.2)	(1.3)	(51.2)	(10.4)	(100.0)

b. Agricultural technical institutes.

c. National Polytechnic Institute.

151

Table 4.4 Mexican Enrollments by Field of Study:
Deleting the Public Technical Subsector, 1978

Sector	Business & Administration	Communications	Economics	Basic Social Sciences	Law	Humanities	Education
Private	23,351	2,364	1,772	5,958	4,747	987	941
	(30.0)	(3.0)	(2.3)	(7.7)	(6.1)	(1.3)	(1.2)
Public	61,886	3,531	15,348	29,859	49,371	10,975	3,203
	(14.0)	(0.8)	(3.5)	(6.7)	(11.1)	(2.5)	(0.7)
TOTAL	85,237	5,895	17,120	35,187	54,118	11,962	4,144
	(16.3)	(1.1)	(3.3)	(6.9)	(10.4)	(2.3)	(0.8)

SOURCE: See table 4.2.

Mexico's principal geographical centers. I confine my observations to salient deviations from the national pattern. In the federal district, the private-public gap in business and administration, 43 to 16 percent, is even larger than it is nationally. More important, a big private-public gap, 8 to 18 percent, emerges in medicine. And it is in Jalisco that we see the root of Mexico's odd medical pattern. Because of UAG, Jalisco's private sector holds a whopping 57 to 19 percent lead. Fully two-thirds of the nation's private sector medicine is found in Jalisco alone, without which Mexico would not deviate from the predicted public dominance in this field. Largely because medicine holds more than half of Jalisco's private enrollments, and because UAG does not conform to Mexico's economic category, the state's private business and administration percentage is unusually small.

As Jalisco attracts attention for its unusual pattern in medical studies, Nuevo León does the same in engineering. Whereas the public sector holds a big advantage nationally, the private sector has a 32 to 23 percent lead in Nuevo León. Indeed, the state enrolls two-fifths of all private sector engineering students. The explanation is simple. Nuevo León is the home of the Monterrey group, making its greatest educational impact at ITESM.

The last geographical category merely aggregates all states outside the federal district, Jalisco, and Nuevo León and is therefore atypically weighted toward poorer Mexico. Here the private sector captures only 6 percent of the enrollments. Most patterns parallel national ones, with a major private advantage in business and administration contrasting with a major public advantage in engineering. The most significant differences involve the diminished private shares in medicine and engineering. Yet despite sure overlap, it would oversimplify to equate private higher education in these states with the demand-absorbing subsector. For one thing, some quality institutions not discussed here figure in the overall picture; for

Table 4.4 cont'd

Medical Sciences	Nursing	Veter- inary Studies	Agri- cultural Sciences	Exact Sciences	Engi- neer- ing	Archi- tecture	Total
15,136	119	630	3,192	1,009	12,893	4,687	77,786
(19.5)	(0.2)	(0.8)	(4.1)	(1.3)	(16.6)	(6.0)	(100.1)
104,386	1,555	13,771	26,776	20,802	81,068	21,029	443,560
(23.5)	(0.4)	(3.1)	(6.0)	(4.7)	(18.3)	(4.7)	(100.0)
119,522	1,674	14,401	29,968	21,811	93,961	25,716	521,346
(22.9)	(0.3)	(2.8)	(5.7)	(4.2)	(18.0)	(4.9)	(99.9)

another, fully 10 percent of these enrollments are in regional ITESM campuses.

To check the basic patterns found for 1978, I similarly analyzed 1971 data. Table 4.6 shows the national pattern, while the geographical patterns appear in Appendix D; Appendix E provides a focused 1971/1978 comparison based on only those institutions listed in both years, thereby deleting institutions established since 1971. The 1971 choice makes sense because ANUIES probably did its most careful data compilation in that year. Also 1971 is far enough away from 1978 to provide a distinct enrollment group, guarding against any single-fluke cohort pattern. Overwhelmingly, the private-public contrasts are confirmed.[68]

However elaborate its coverage, such quantitative analysis does not convey the whole story. Although it shows very striking private-public differences, it underestimates them. Even my fourteen-part categorization lumps together some disparate areas. For instance, private engineering is much more likely to relate to civil or mechanical than to petroleum, textile, or mining specializations, just as law is disproportionately likely to mean fiscal law, and administration to mean business administration rather than public or *ejidal* (communal) administration.[69]

Most important is that even the same subject title often means very different things in the two sectors. Economics is a good example because, unlike the exact or medical sciences, its subjective content varies enormously, and unlike sociology or political science, it has a significant presence in the private as well as public sector. A careful study by LaBarge and Osborn describes ITESM's economics as the antithesis of UNAM's. ITESM's is strongly laissez-faire and U.S. oriented, geared to serve the desires of Mexican business. UNAM's is heavy on Marxism, with little microeconomics, mathematics, or statistics, even at the master's level. Like

Table 4.5 Enrollments by Field of Study in
Mexico's Principal Geographical Centers, 1978

Sector	Business & Administration	Communications	Economics	Basic Social Sciences	Law	Humanities	Education
			Federal District				
Private	11,042	965	819	1,809	2,662	587	453
	(42.6)	(3.7)	(3.2)	(7.0)	(10.3)	(2.3)	(1.7)
Public	32,164	2,550	11,241	17,596	14,504	6,368	292
	(15.8)	(1.2)	(5.5)	(8.6)	(7.1)	(3.1)	(0.1)
TOTAL	43,206	3,515	12,060	19,405	19,405	6,945	745
	(18.8)	(1.5)	(5.2)	(8.4)	(8.4)	(3.0)	(0.3)
			Jalisco				
Private	1,980	375	117	1,073	408	78	0
	(11.2)	(2.1)	(0.7)	(6.1)	(2.3)	(0.4)	(0.0)
Public	10,246	0	1,361	577	4,613	739	0
	(21.4)	(0.0)	(2.8)	(1.2)	(9.6)	(1.5)	(0.0)
TOTAL	12,226	375	1,478	1,650	5,021	817	0
	(18.7)	(0.6)	(2.3)	(2.5)	(7.7)	(1.2)	(0.0)
			Nuevo León				
Private	4,724	541	485	1,133	452	284	298
	(28.7)	(3.3)	(2.9)	(6.9)	(2.7)	(1.7)	(1.8)
Public	4,347	318	190	2,197	3,751	505	180
	(13.1)	(1.0)	(0.6)	(6.6)	(11.3)	(1.5)	(0.5)
TOTAL	9,071	859	675	3,330	4,203	789	478
	(18.3)	(1.7)	(1.4)	(6.7)	(8.5)	(1.6)	(1.0)
			All Other States				
Private	5,605	483	351	1,943	1,225	38	190
	(31.6)	(2.7)	(2.0)	(10.9)	(6.9)	(0.2)	(1.1)
Public	40,191	663	6,379	10,488	26,503	3,373	2,731
	(15.5)	(0.3)	(2.5)	(4.0)	(10.2)	(1.3)	(1.1)
TOTAL	45,796	1,146	6,730	12,431	27,728	3,411	2,921
	(16.5)	(0.4)	(2.4)	(4.5)	(10.0)	(1.2)	(1.1)

SOURCE: See table 4.2.

ITESM, ITAM boasts a curriculum more like that of a U.S. university.[70]
Prospective economics students and employers have substantial choice
between the two sectors.

Furthermore, notwithstanding subsectoral probes, the analysis has
understated differences between "typical" private and public institutions.
Just as medicine is an unusual field for private institutions other than UAG,

Table 4.5 cont'd

Medical Sciences	Nursing	Veterinary Studies	Agricultural Sciences	Exact Sciences	Engineering	Architecture	Total
			Federal District				
2,142	0	0	0	403	3,488	1,562	25,932
(8.3)	(0.0)	(0.0)	(0.0)	(1.6)	(13.5)	(6.0)	(100.2)
37,002	320	3,499	85	13,448	44,971	20,075	204,104
(18.1)	(0.2)	(1.7)	(0.0)	(6.6)	(22.0)	(9.8)	(99.8)
39,144	320	3,499	85	13,851	48,459	21,637	230,036
(17.0)	(0.1)	(1.5)	(0.0)	(6.0)	(21.1)	(9.4)	(99.8)
			Jalisco				
10,100	29	0	0	180	2,203	1,107	17,650
(57.2)	(0.2)	(0.0)	(0.0)	(1.0)	(12.5)	(6.3)	(100.0)
9,111	0	1,790	4,254	310	12,601	2,202	47,804
(19.1)	(0.0)	(3.7)	(8.9)	(0.6)	(26.4)	(4.6)	(99.8)
19,211	29	1,790	4,254	490	14,804	3,309	65,454
(29.4)	(0.0)	(2.7)	(6.5)	(0.7)	(22.6)	(5.1)	(100.0)
			Nuevo León				
663	82	583	1,176	106	5,202	716	16,445
(4.0)	(0.5)	(3.5)	(7.2)	(0.6)	(31.6)	(4.4)	(99.8)
8,345	287	278	2,192	1,710	7,530	1,246	33,076
(25.2)	(0.9)	(0.8)	(6.6)	(5.2)	(22.8)	(3.8)	(99.9)
9,008	369	861	3,368	1,816	12,732	1,962	49,521
(18.2	(0.7)	(1.7)	(7.0)	(3.7)	(25.7)	(4.0)	(100.2)
			All Other States				
2,231	8	47	2,016	320	2,000	1,302	17,759
(12.6)	(0.0)	(0.3)	(11.4)	(1.8)	(11.3)	(7.3)	(100.1)
55,677	957	8,720	21,483	6,618	67,547	8,034	259,364
(21.5)	(0.4)	(3.4)	(8.3)	(2.6)	(26.0)	(3.1)	(100.2)
57,908	965	8,767	23,499	6,938	69,547	9,336	277,123
(20.9)	(0.3)	(3.2)	(8.5)	(2.5)	(25.1)	(3.4)	(100.0)

so conventional social science is limited outside Ibero. Instead, many private institutions are even more commercially oriented than thus far suggested, even more than most of the prestige universities with their impressive (1978) percentages for business and administration plus economics: ITAM 93, Anáhuac 49, ITESM 39, Americas 36, Ibero 34, La Salle 29, and UAG with its very unusual total of only 9. But at an extreme, as their very

155

Table 4.6 Mexican Enrollments by Field of Study, 1971

Sector	Business & Administration	Basic Social Sciences	Law	Humanities	Education	Medical Sciences
Private	14,538	2,482	1,738	1,085	2,093	4,947
	(39.8)	(6.8)	(4.8)	(3.0)	(5.7)	(13.5)
Public	41,363	13,984	22,263	6,199	6,111	37,781
	(18.8)	(6.3)	(10.1)	(2.8)	(2.8)	(17.2)
TOTAL	55,901	16,466	24,001	7,284	8,204	42,728
	(21.8)	(6.4)	(9.3)	(2.8)	(3.2)	(16.6)

SOURCE: ANUIES, *La enseñanza superior en México 1971* (Mexico City: ANUIES, 1974), pp. 59–140.

NOTE: See table 4.2. There are a few small categorization differences, however. For 1971 I put communications under the business and administration category. Economics was categorized according to the faculty it appeared in, usually administration or social sciences; if it appeared as a separate

names hint, many small private institutions can be fully devoted to business and administration, as are the Commercial and Banking School (enrollment 1,531), the Institute of Advanced Commercial Studies (739), and the Institute of Administrative, Economic, and Social Sciences (337). So are others not indicated by name, such as the Latin University (307) and the Mexican Technological Institute (85). Others, such as the University of the Valley of Mexico (3,847) and the Technological University of Mexico (1,689), have at least the majority of their enrollments in business and administration.

However, business and administration have also grown rapidly in the public sector, certainly compared to law and the basic social sciences. Accounting and administration together represented only 2 percent of the degrees issued by UNAM from 1945 through 1950, and still only 6 percent from 1961 through 1965, but 9 percent from 1966 through 1970 and 25 percent from 1971 through 1975.[71] This suggests that the private sector is specializing in growth fields. Moreover, it holds several comparative advantages in those fields over the public sector. One is a lesser commitment (interest, responsibility, or capability) to more costly and research-oriented fields. Another, related, is the flexibility to specialize. State universities are constrained to offer the range of at least all the traditional professional careers (engineering, law, medicine) and some social and exact sciences; none could match the 50 to 100 percent business-oriented profiles of most small private institutions. Private sector expansion more freely focuses on new concerns.[72] Even most of the sector's major institutions bypass medicine. Another contrast is that the public sector must be much more preoccupied with access. Thus, for example, it provides much greater geographical coverage, partially sustaining the claim that it better serves less-privileged

Table 4.6 cont'd

Nursing	Veter- inary Studies	Agri- cultural Sciences	Exact Sciences	Engi- neer- ing	Archi- tecture	Total
20	79	819	725	6,545	1,446	36,517
(0.1)	(0.2)	(2.2)	(2.0)	(17.9)	(4.0)	(100.0)
365	3,458	3,894	7,573	69,556	7,681	220,228
(0.2)	(1.6)	(1.8)	(3.4)	(31.6)	(3.5)	(100.1)
385	3,537	4,713	8,298	76,101	9,127	256,745[a]
(0.1)	(1.4)	(1.8)	(3.2)	(29.6)	(3.6)	(99.8)

faculty it was put under social science. When law and social science were listed as one entity, they went under social science (unless the entity was a law faculty).

a. I have found the field category for 256,745 students of the 256,752 overall figure given by ANUIES. The private sector has 14.2 percent of the total.

regions. In 1981 all thirty-one states offered public higher education versus eighteen for the private sector.[73]

Employment: Private Enterprise or the State?

The distribution of students by field of study tells us a good deal about private-public differences. In terms of subsequent employment, however, these distributions could be considered only as inputs, if jobs obtained are the outputs. As usual, outputs (jobs) are unfortunately more difficult to measure than inputs (fields of study), and no major data bank on job placement has been compiled and analyzed by any State or university bureau. Nonetheless, this chapter can go further than the previous one. Furthermore, Mexico's fundamental private-public cleavages herald several basic Latin American ones, so the analysis here is elaborated in chapter 6.

We have seen the much greater private university affinity for commercially oriented subjects. While many professional schools, such as the Free Law School, do not by name suggest a special affinity for either private or State employment, many commercial schools do (e.g., the Commercial and Banking School). Then too, field of study may be more important than private or public educational status; for example, a private manufacturer may well prefer a public engineering student over a private philosophy student. But there are strikingly different field distributions by sector; as now discussed, field of study is only one factor shaping the links between private higher education and commercial employment on the one hand and public higher education and State employment on the other.

Following the typology in chapter 1, there are four conceivable linkage types: (1) public higher education to State employment; (2) private higher education to State employment; (3) private higher education to private employment; (4) public higher education to private employment. By restricting private employment to private enterprise, I exclude private professional practice (as well as employment by private voluntary organizations). I simply observe here that field distributions showing 54 percent of public enrollments in the big three professions (engineering, law, and medicine) moderately substantiate images of the traditional, Continental university for professional training, especially if architecture and some small professional fields are added. Leaving aside this sort of public-to-private link, I disregard type 4 here, partly because some private businesses are skeptical about public university students and partly because little information is available on this link. Still, some private businesses do hire public university graduates. This is obviously the case where business demands skills from fields offered overwhelmingly in the public sector, as with veterinary specialists for the Purina Company.[74] Also, many students in the public as well as the private sector work part time for private enterprise, while others from both sectors work part time for the State.

Public higher education to State employment. The State is dissatisfied with the field specializations of public sector students. Too many study social science, law, architecture, civil engineering, and, probably, medicine. Too few study most types of engineering, agronomy, and exact sciences. The State is upset because the oversubscribed fields lack adequate employment channels. Also, the State itself has often functioned as employer of the last resort. Thus State preferences do not necessarily reflect employment opportunities for graduates.[75]

The relationship between several professions and State employment has been changing. Although many public professional school graduates continue to enter private practice, an increasing number have joined the State apparatus. Consider the evolution of UNAM's School of Architecture. When the school was small, most students prepared for private practice, which notably included the design of homes for the wealthy. However, as the school grew in size, student SES composition changed and proportionately fewer sought such work. Besides, only so many wealthy families are clamoring for architects. The school radicalized, specialties such as "social architecture" arose, and more graduates found employment in the Ministry of Public Works, including its division of human settlements. Veterinarians have taken a similar path into State employment; roughly 70 percent now work for the State, especially in the Ministry of Agriculture.[76] These surges into State employment echo the historical path of lawyers into the bureaucracy. Physicians now also split between private practice and State employment, whereas agronomists are overwhelmingly tied to the

State. If graduates of private professional studies stick closer to private professional practice while their public counterparts move toward State employment, this would be an important private-public difference.

Leaving aside the bureaucratic majority in State employment, I now concentrate on a much smaller but critical group—the political leadership of the State. Fortunately, this is an area in which solid data already exist. In fact, Roderic Camp and Peter Smith have provided better documentation of the connection between public universities and political mobility in Mexico than exists for any other Latin American nation. I focus especially on Camp's most comprehensive work on the subject.[77]

Camp proves that the public university is *the* major center for political recruitment. Roughly 80 percent of the State's political leaders (1935–76) obtained a university education, the great majority from UNAM. Of all the organizations (bureaucracy, local government, unions) over which the public university predominates in political recruitment, perhaps the most striking two are the private university and the official party. Despite its quality, the former simply has not had a major function in political recruitment. "It is difficult, if not impossible, for a graduate from a private institution to break this pattern . . . not one graduate from the prestigious Ibero-American University (an institution graduating many PAN leaders) or Monterrey Institute of Higher Studies (financed by the powerful Monterrey industrial group) has ever succeeded in reaching the top."[78]

Regarding the official party's role, a youth sector handles recruitment. In some states, university students join the PRI and, upon graduation, move directly into political positions with the party or the State. But even this may depend as much on being in the university as on being in the PRI.[79] Long associated with the status quo, the PRI does not inspire the sort of loyal party following that has characterized student politics in Chile, Peru, or Venezuela. Yet the PRI lacks a sufficiently conservative image to recruit many private university students.

Consequently, to study political recruitment is to focus largely on public universities. Within those universities, the two major, and related, routes to political positions are student politics and clientelistic recruitment. Larissa Lomnitz has written a vivid account of student politics that identifies "political" types, as opposed to "academic" and "professional" types.[80] Either through official or disruptive channels, the political types demonstrate key political skills (recruitment, mobilization, organizational cunning, intelligence, bargaining) and thereby demonstrate their worth to those who recruit for careers in local or national politics. Herein one finds a principal reason for the lack of a private university role: if a campus has no student politics, there is no stage on which students can audition for political leadership beyond the campus. The phenomenon is self-perpetuating.

159

Those youngsters disposed toward participating in politics choose the public universities.

Especially because political mobility in Mexico is notoriously based on clientelistic contacts more than policy beliefs, the contacts made at the university are crucial. Student-student contacts, most tied to student politics, flourish, and students form networks.[81] As an ex-student achieves prominence in politics, he recruits his colleagues from school days. The most famous recent case was President Echeverría's appointment of his old UNAM friend and traveling companion José López Portillo as treasury minister and ultimately as president.

A second link, probably the most important, involves professor-student contacts. This link is strong because the large majority of professors teach only part time; their principal employment is often with the State.[82] Nor is it unusual for wholesale recruitment to take place. State officials may draw heavily on a particular school, such as UNAM's engineering school, linked to the Ministry of Public Works and PEMEX (the State's oil enterprise). Finally, there are student-professor contacts, important where a student achieves political prominence and then recruits the professors who had helped or impressed him.

Private higher education to State employment. Filling both mid- and high-level State positions has historically been the almost exclusive function of public not private universities. A major private-public cleavage will undoubtedly continue along these lines. But cracks in the monopoly have begun to appear, and it is not rash to proclaim their significance.

Even strictly political positions within the State and PRI elite have allowed for private penetration. For example, President Echeverría selected a former ITESM head as his education minister, an ideologically sensitive post. Moreover, we see definite increases in participation by private graduates in the 1982 legislative elections and in the executive branch that serves new president Miguel de la Madrid (1982). Whereas private graduates accounted for possibly less than 1 percent of the governmental elite between 1935 and 1982, they account for possibly 6 percent in the new administration.[83]

While a private penetration of the mainstream political elite bears ongoing scrutiny, penetration of the State's top technical posts is far more established. As Mexico follows the path characteristic of Latin America's most industrial nations, the country is experiencing an increasing demand for technocrats. Call it development, bureaucratization, technification, or rationalization, traditional politicians have given ground to technocrats, notably so by the time of the López Portillo administration.[84] This penetration by *técnicos* provides a sure opening for private universities, with their business and client finance, conservative governance, and applied fields of study. Their graduates are competing successfully for good jobs in the State's technical, financial, and planning fields. The trend is naturally strong within those ministries and public decentralized agencies or enterprises associated with conservative economic policy, those that basically push the private over the State role in economic development. Consequently, penetration can be especially intense in State enterprises such as PEMEX and the Bank of Mexico and in ministries such as Treasury and Programming and Budget. Ministries with a more statist outlook, such as National Patrimony, may be less open, but inroads have been made there as well. Significantly, there are powerful indications of a shift of political power toward those structures most permeated by private graduates. Illustratively, Presidents de la Madrid and López Portillo (1976–82) emerged from the stewardships of Programming and Budget and of Treasury, respectively, whereas their two immediate predecessors, indeed most of their predecessors, emerged from the quintessentially political (as opposed to technical) Ministry of Gobernación. Both López Portillo and de la Madrid had pointedly technical rather than political careers compared to those who previously had ascended to the presidency. De la Madrid, although a UNAM law graduate, as all but one of the last five presidents have been, became the first president to have earned a U.S. graduate degree (Harvard University, public administration, 1965); as suggested below, Mexican graduate students in the United States come disproportionally from Mexico's private universities.

Changing State needs that alter the balance of tapped fields of study could significantly diminish the public university's predominance. Law alone contributed more than half the university graduates to the political elite from 1935 to 1976. UNAM's law school obviously held center stage, while the Free Law School accounted, by itself, for more than half of all the private sector's graduates who made it to the political elite. Medicine and engineering, second and third after law, both have been historical public university pillars, while respective private strongholds at UAG and ITESM have not been traditional recruiting grounds for the State. But economics is the newest of the "big four" fields for political recruitment. In fact, as Camp writes, it is the one with *"proportionately the greatest percentage* of graduates in public life" (Camp's emphasis); the representation of economics graduates doubled in each administration since 1952 until it reached 18 percent under Echeverría.[85] Moreover, harkening back to our field comparisons, private economics graduates are usually more suitably trained than their public counterparts for positions in a State that is much more strongly inclined to mainstream Western than to Marxist economics.[86] So UNAM law has predominated, but the rise of economics opens space for private graduates.

Even where the State's needs remain the same, the private sector will probably increasingly penetrate because of changes within higher education itself. Camp's data deal with political positions from 1935 to 1976, thereby in effect covering an earlier university training period (since it usually takes some time to climb to Mexico's political elite). Camp acknowledges that UNAM's past educational preeminence may lead to an exaggerated image of its present political influence. Just as UNAM usurped the recruitment role of its National Preparatory School earlier in the century, he writes, state universities can now pick up UNAM's slack.[87] This will happen, but the way is also open for the private sector to encroach. Only the small Free Law School existed before 1935, and only it and UAG before the mid-1940s; UNAM's prestige was still rising in the 1940s and 1950s. Only later was UNAM perceived to slip, stimulating prodigious private growth. The availability of private graduates from recent decades finally provides a necessary condition for recruitment to the State. Taken together with evolving field orientations and State needs, it becomes a sufficient condition.

State officials cannot openly declare a preference for private graduates, but officials and students in both sectors definitely sense the shift. Public university officials may sadly accept the change as reflecting deep-seated public sector problems, or they may see the State's preferences as confirmation of its underlying rightist, proprivate values. What more colorful litmus test of underlying perceptions is there than the propensity of top political leaders to send their children to private universities, just as they have frequently sent them to private schools?[88] Presidents Echeverría, López Portillo, and de la Madrid have sent their children to private universities, as has Hank González, governor of the State of Mexico and federal district regent during the first two of those presidencies.

Within the federal district, private penetration of the State is notable at each of the four prestige institutions closely analyzed. Most striking, especially given its small size, is ITAM. ITAM has probably attracted proportionally the greatest share of the children of politically prominent families. Its secularism helps it achieve public legitimacy, as reflected by the State's grant of free-private governance status. But most important is its devotion to high-quality, applied economics. ITAM graduates are getting jobs as technicians and even high level advisors to politicians in powerful ministries such as Treasury and Programming and Budget, as well as the Bank of Mexico. ITAM shows that part-time professors who hold important State positions are no longer teaching exclusively at the public universities. The clientelistic recruitment line to high State employment is now being established in the private universities, even if the student politics line will not be.

Anáhuac has also done well, especially under López Portillo, whose own son was given high public office, thus strengthening links with his university. Additionally, Anáhuac was asked to provide special training courses for officials of the Ministry of Education. Most of all, Anáhuac students in actuarial sciences for example, have gone "right to the apex" in ministries such as Programming and Budget and in the State's banking institutions.[89] But the Ibero and La Salle universities, despite the potential liabilities of religious symbolism, have made much more serious inroads than the Anáhuac. This is especially true of Ibero, under presidents as different as Echeverría and de la Madrid. La Salle has special indirect ties to the State through its preparatory school. Many of the school's graduates who want political careers switch to UNAM for their professional degrees, the path followed by de la Madrid.

Nor is the hiring shift limited to private universities in the federal district and national politics. There are similar trends in Baja California, Guadalajara, Puebla, Sinaloa, and Sonora. Even so visibly rightist an institution as UAG could reap (for its medical school graduates) high positions in the Mexican Institute of Social Security under López Portillo.

In the absence of more structured data, I conclude for now that, particularly in technical areas, high-prestige private universities are penetrating the State. This constitutes an important change in established private-public distinctions. It does not by any means stifle distinctiveness, however. First is the matter of degree—the public sector remains more important in recruitment to the State. Second is the matter of target—the private sector usually penetrates certain types of positions in the State.

Private higher education to private employment. Private sector ability to penetrate State employment might be greater than first appears, once one controls for student preferences. If all students sought State employment, and if all succeeded, then 15 percent would represent the private universities' proportional share. In reality, however, most private university students seek private employment. Reciprocally, there are many reasons that private enterprises often prefer these students, and they need not disguise their preferences the way State officials must. Entrepreneurs claim that private students compete effectively because of field and curricula orientations and especially because of the excellence of their education.[90]

Tight recruitment links exist between private universities and private enterprise. Businessmen teaching part time in the private universities recruit business administration and economics students into private enterprise. Thus, alongside public links between UNAM's engineering and PEMEX, there are private links between Anáhuac's, Ibero's, and ITESM's communications sciences and the Televisa (television) enterprises. Additionally, if business has unmet needs, it can create new fields of study.[91] Perhaps the most revealing, direct form of enterprise recruitment occurs when industrialists and other businessmen send their sons to Americas, Anáhuac, Ibero, and ITESM, absolutely sure of bringing them right back into the family business.

Most private universities measure their effectiveness largely by the number of students offered jobs, the number of jobs offered to each student, and the level of pay obtained. Public officials must consider such factors as only one measure of success; some even argue that it is an irrelevant or negative or capitalist measure. They could rarely unabashedly boast, as Americas does, that their business administration students are finding good jobs with multinational corporations, nor, as ITESM does, that a university should be evaluated by the rewards of the free market—what they regard as a U.S. norm alien to mainstream thought in Latin America's public universities. While the private sector's lesser institutions do not realistically aspire to the higher rungs of private enterprise, many do define their success largely in terms of finding decent-paying employment for their graduates.[92]

These findings on links between universities and both private enterprise and the State tend to substantiate Smith's basic argument that Mexico has two fundamentally distinct power elites. The mobility path of the political elite, mostly from middle-class backgrounds, runs through the public university. The mobility path of the economic elite, mostly from more privileged backgrounds, runs through the private university.[93] One significant qualification to this distinct private-to-private, public-to-public pattern that has characterized Mexico for decades is the private university's increasing penetration of important technical, economic, and advisory positions within the State. No comparably increasing public university penetration of private enterprise exists; instead, public university graduates are becoming less competitive there, unless they have added a private sector or a U.S. graduate degree. Mexico's private and public universities have generally served different private and State employment functions.

Quality

Graduates of Mexico's private universities usually get better jobs than their public counterparts—partly because they have studied more job-relevant fields, partly because they are better connected and trusted, and partly because they are more highly educated. The view is widespread that Mexico's private sector upholds, on balance, a higher quality than the public sector (promoting the elite transfer from public to private sector discussed earlier). As Osborn summarizes that view: "In the 'conventional wisdom' the private universities are believed to produce the 'best' college graduates in the Republic. This applies particularly with regard to the larger of the private institutions, but the impression spreads to many of the smaller ones as well."[94] Such assertions require important qualifications, however, most generally and fully elaborated in chapter 6; here I sketch some case study specifics.

A first qualification to the generalization is that the evolution of Mexico's private sector in the decade since Osborn wrote has included a notable growth of commercial institutions, some responding to unattended demand and not achieving respectable quality. A second qualification is that there is overlap in quality. Institutional overlap occurs, with the best public universities generally better than many private institutions. Additionally, overlap by field of study occurs, with one institution superior in a given field and another in a different field. Among the major centers of excellence within the private sector are ITESM in engineering, ITAM in economics and administration, Ibero in anthropology, architecture, and law, La Salle in medicine and accounting, Anáhuac in business, UAG in medicine, and the Free Law School in law. The public sector tends to be superior in the expensive fields, such as exact sciences, medicine, and some types of engineering. It is often superior in basic social sciences and humanities as well.

The great comparative advantage and disadvantage of UNAM and the major state universities is that they may excel in some fields even while they simultaneously suffer in others. If a university's quality is to be measured by the number of fields in which it excels, then UNAM is still Mexico's foremost university, easily. And what holds for fields of study, holds for professors and students. UNAM is far ahead of any competitor in having most of the best. It is when one considers average quality that the public sector falls behind the private. UNAM has some of the best and some far removed from that. In other public universities, there is usually less of the best and proportionally more of the least qualified. Finally, overlapping quality also characterizes graduate education, where Mexico's public sector probably maintains a diminishing advantage, and research, where it probably clings to a sturdier advantage.[95]

In any case, easily quantifiable indicators of sectoral quality tend to favor the private sector. Most, however, could be considered more as inputs that perhaps should promote quality than as measures of quality output. An exception might be the percentage of graduates continuing on to graduate school. Unfortunately, no sectoral compilations have been made, but isolated data confirm perceptions of private superiority on this score.[96] Such superiority assumes great significance as graduate study, especially at U.S.

165

universities, is becoming a common route to elite jobs including many in politics.

Fuller data are available on the expenditure/student ratio. García and Hernández find a slight private edge, confirming Osborn's conclusion, though Osborn found the relationship reversed in the federal district, no doubt because of UNAM's status and research.[97] So the private sector may spend more per pupil even though it does less research, offers less expensive fields, and perhaps spends money more efficiently. One component of the higher private expenditures is higher salaries for full-time professors. A few private universities claim that their privateness also gives them flexibility to offer differential salaries and therefore to outbid competing public universities tied to bureaucratic wage-scales. But realistically, competition is not a big factor since most professors teach part time and neither sector can often match the salaries paid by the State and private enterprise.[98]

Another indicator that favors the private sector is the student/professor ratio, but contradictory data appear on percentages of full-time, part-time, and hourly professors;[99] moreover, it is specious to equate full-time status with quality where so many eminent professionals teach only a few courses. This is not to rule out any relationship between full-time status and quality, a relationship that may hold for some of the best institutions such as ITESM, but too many cross-cutting factors keep us from inferring much from available data.

What is really more important than continuing to search for quantifiable ways to document a private-public quality gap is seeking to understand it. While not much debate has been heard as to the existence of private sector advantages, even from its critics, there is great debate as to the gap's roots. Although the private sector's probable edge in resources may contribute, basic factors include institutional size, admissions policy, SES, and institutional rigor. Most of these remarks presage more general ones for Spanish America inclusively, but in addition to case study specificity we deal here with a private-public gap wider in Mexico than it is cross-nationally. Mexico's private and public universities generally have different orientations toward size and exclusiveness. The public universities are much more heavily tied to access and meeting booming demand for higher education. These policies of course have been fundamental to the sector's transformation in recent decades and thereby to perceived public failure followed by elite exit. Even when they feel their quality jeopardized, public universities have been able to do far less than private universities to protect themselves. Many still tend toward an open admission policy for secondary school graduates, though screws have been substantially tightened.[100] UNAM generally grants automatic access to applicants from its own preparatory schools; in the past these students have accounted for the majority of UNAM's incoming classes. Public universities demand admissions exams of applicants from private institutions, but in practice most graduates of these institutions either prefer private universities or enjoy a competitive advantage, by SES background and education, on the public exams.

Mexico's private universities have not only the right but the will to be small. In most prestigious ones, officials make it clear that they seek influence through quality and not quantity. They set ceilings on how large their institutions should grow: "We want to be the Harvard of Mexico," say officials at Americas, pledging to hold enrollments under five thousand (the same figure Anáhuac projects for itself). ITAM sets its ceiling at two thousand. It and Americas believe that their secular orientations give them advantages in serving as creative models for the public sector. But both La Salle and especially Ibero, which also have ceilings in mind, similarly strive to be influential models.[101]

Most major private universities have competitive exams; indeed they boast of high rejection rates that often exceed 50 percent. Even the progressive Ibero takes pride in its rigorous selection process, despite the fact that choosing Mexico's best-prepared candidates means choosing disproportionately from privileged backgrounds. At the most elite universities, such as Anáhuac and Americas, the high SES is reflected in clothing, cars, and even ethnicity. Thus, in the public sector one hears derisive remarks about snobbery in the private sector.[102]

To draw on privilege the private sector in particular relies on a sectorally stratified school system. In fact, a wave I–wave II phenomenon has developed to parallel that found in higher education in many Spanish American nations. After Mexico's Church became increasingly active in providing low- or no-cost private schooling to the poor, secular elite institutions showed the most dynamic growth (1970s) within the private school system. Private universities surely have a wide base of privilege from which to recruit, since the private share is proportionally larger at the secondary than at the higher level (26 versus 14 percent).[103] As Latapí sees it, the best public universities can probably draw most of the best secondary students from the lower-middle, perhaps even middle-middle, class; but a disproportionate number of the best students come from the upper-middle and upper class, and they overwhelmingly attend the private universities.[104] Thus, probably the foremost explanation for Mexican private universities' apparent superiority is the ability to draw the best-prepared students. If the private sector boasts "better" products, it is more difficult to know how responsible it is for producing them.

Mexico's private sector can, however, reasonably claim at least some credit for its status. Its privateness helps it subordinate pressures that handicap the public sector. Even many officials in the public universities acknowledge the inefficiencies of large scale, which they seek to combat through inter- and intrainstitutional decentralization. Moreover, evidence indicates that the private sector should be credited with structural innovation and efficiency through discipline. Departmentalization, regular classroom attendance, and "efficiency" in graduating admitted students may be good examples.[105] Again, however, the roots and limits to private superiority are pursued more extensively in chapter 6.

CONCLUSION

Although intersectoral overlap can be found even in Mexican higher education, intersectoral distinctiveness is much more notable. The two sectors have grown from distinct roots. They are financed differently. They are governed differently. They perform different functions. The public sector, for all the confusion reflected in its internal governance conflicts and functional complexities as well as in its simultaneous service and antagonism to its sponsoring State, remains clearly the more public sector. This is true especially in finance but also in governance and function. The private sector, which has arisen as an alternative, has remained remarkably private. Private finance is accompanied by private governance and functioning. Mexico's private universities are not sham private institutions. However much the public sector's relative autonomy from the State may defy some theories about the Mexican regime exercising authoritarian-corporatist control over Mexican society, the evidence is overwhelming for the private sector and the State.[106] The State does not finance private universities, does not appoint their leadership, does not set their internal policies, and does not coordinate them according to any systemizing policy. (A broader discussion of privateness and corporatism is left for the final chapter.)

The State's policy toward the private sector is best understood not in terms of any single concept such as corporatism or pluralism, though I would find the latter more accurate, but in terms of Mexico's tacit State–private enterprise alliance described at the chapter's beginning. The State cautiously, even pointedly, keeps its distance from the private sector but nonetheless provides the basic conditions that the sector needs to flourish. Indeed, closer involvement might only necessitate interference and restrictions, especially given the State's revolutionary posture, or posturing. The State has not created private universities or openly blessed them, but it has been lax since 1935 in imposing regulations (whether based on secularism, revolutionary statism, or academic quality) that would restrict their creation. While not directly subsidizing private universities, the State allows easy nonprofit deductions. Most of all, the State guarantees the economic development model that promotes prosperity for the social classes that attend the private universities and for the businesses that financially support those universities. Although the State promulgates regulations that could control academic policy, these are usually more formal than applied. Instead, the State trusts private groups and privileged classes to govern the private universities in ways that, in practice, generally please the State. Thus the State leaves the private sector free to pursue the functions that the sector itself chooses; these functions, in turn, serve the State, mostly by serving the private interests with which the State is allied.

In sum, there are four crucial (albeit highly generalized) similarities between the State–private higher education alliance and the more general State-private alliance in Mexico. First, the State often leaves the private higher education sector alone where that sector wants to be left alone. Second, the State insures the basic environmental conditions that the private sector needs. Third, the State maintains a formal coolness. And, fourth, in return for the first two policies, the State benefits from what the private sector does, which sometimes contrasts sharply to what the State reaps from its "own" public universities. After all, the Mexican State can hardly be considered leftist, let alone revolutionary. Politically, the private sector is relatively free from disruptions. It satisfies the elite that would be dissatisfied, perhaps dangerously so, if confined to the public sector. Economically, tuitions and business donations save the State from higher social-welfare costs. Additionally, the private sector trains commercially and technically oriented personnel for private enterprise (counted on by the State to maintain economic growth) and even, increasingly, for the State itself. In the latter capacity, private universities are playing a crucial role in the changing *técnico-político* relationship widely viewed as crucial to Mexico's political economy. And the private sector makes a special contribution by training high-quality personnel.

There is, however, at least one interesting difference between the broad State–private sphere alliance and the State–private sector alliance. The State administers key areas of the economy but leaves the bulk of economic activity to private enterprise. By contrast, the public sector administers the bulk of higher education, but the private sector administers a disproportional share of the key institutions. As the State plays a vital role in the general economy, so the private sector plays a vital role in higher education. Despite being small compared to the public sector, and despite being very different from the public sector, the private sector is no marginal sector in the context of either higher education itself or Mexican politics and society more generally. Instead, the very distinctiveness, or privateness, of Mexico's private universities is basic to the sector's significance. The private sector has found an important and secure niche within Mexico's relatively stable State–private sphere alliance. It has done so mostly by serving the State indirectly and private enterprise directly. The public sector has found a niche less by serving private enterprise than by serving the State, and even there its performance has brought mixed reviews.

5 Private-Public Distinctiveness: Brazil

Sheer size—1,345,000 enrollments by 1980—gives Brazil the single most important higher education system in Latin America. The region's largest nation has had the largest higher education system ever since its enrollments overtook Argentina's in the late 1960s. Brazil now holds roughly 30 percent of all Latin American enrollments, dwarfing even the next largest system (Mexico's). Brazil also merits close study because it illustrates a distinct private-public pattern. As a rule, Spanish America has not relied, as Brazil has, on a private sector considered generally inferior to the public sector. Nor has any Spanish American nation relied so heavily on a private sector to meet its multiplying demand for higher education. More than three-fifths (63 percent; 1980) of Brazil's enrollments are in the private sector. This combination of system size and high private proportion means that Brazil accounts for more than half of all private enrollments in Latin America.[1]

Thus, even if Brazil's private-public pattern were irrelevant elsewhere, there would be powerful reasons to study it in depth. But many of the features that are dominant in Brazil do manifest themselves elsewhere, especially in low-prestige private subsectors that absorb demand. This applies to several Latin American cases, most notably that of Colombia but also those of Peru, the Dominican Republic, Mexico, and others. Furthermore, while Brazil has been the only Latin American nation where the private sector has been clearly larger than the public sector, several Asian nations (India, Japan, the Philippines, Thailand) follow the pattern, with others, such as Turkey, having important demand-absorbing private subsectors.

As with the Chilean and Mexican cases, private-public sector relationships can be seen in the context of State-society relationships. In Chile the active State role in economic and social affairs has helped explain the

171

historically limited arena for truly private universities to flourish. Mexico pointedly exemplifies a widespread Spanish American phenomenon in which the State fuels huge public sector expansion and change but also guarantees plenty of room for private alternatives, alternatives that largely express the State's own class interests. In Brazil the State has never allowed an equal transformation of the public sector, instead using the private sector for ends different from those served in most of Spanish America. Two keys lie in the late development of the Brazilian State and in the institution of military rule before the higher education enrollment crunch.

Brazil's singular importance stems from the colonial era. Spain's American empire divided into many nations while Portugal's formed only one. Also, Portugal never developed the same tight control that the Spanish Crown exerted; indicatively, Portugal did much less than Spain to implant a New World replica of its higher education system. Although the independence won in 1822 brought about a Brazilian empire, it was based on a weak central government, with considerable power left in the hands of provincial oligarchs. By late in the century, Comtian positivism exerted a major influence over Brazil, and its emphasis on rationalism and science to overcome obstacles to development suggested moves to shape an enlightened, active State. Nonetheless, a strong State did not develop under the 1889–1930 republic. Instead, national politics were dominated by elites in the states of São Paulo and Minas Gerais. Contrast this with the early (postindependence) and subsequently intensified growth of the Chilean State and with the Porfirian and revolutionary growth of the State in Mexico.

The Revolution of 1930 overthrew the Old Republic and brought Getúlio Vargas to power. Vargas greatly increased the central government's power and in 1937 proclaimed the Estado Novo—a "New State" inspired by both Portuguese fascism and the U.S. New Deal, widely divergent experiments to be sure but each based on the expansion of the State. Brazil's rural oligarchs lost power to the urban industrialists, the middle class, and the workers. The State bureaucracy grew enormously. Activities previously left to individual or local authority now depended on the centralized State. Employment expanded, tied to the State bureaucracy. More public goods and favors were distributed, with patrimonial strings tied to the State. Worker rights, unionization, and social security were established and expanded, tied to the labor ministry. In short, the Estado Novo promoted corporatism in State-society relations. As Skidmore writes: "The state was elevated to the role of a powerful director of all major economic and social activities."[2]

Vargas's fall from power, starting in 1945 but arrested from 1951 to 1954, climaxed with his (1954) suicide. But his fall did not signal the dismantling of corporatist structures nor disaffection for active statism. Instead, the democratic rule of Juscelino Kubitschek in the 1950s saw further State growth, including attempts at economic planning. State activism was symbolized by the construction of Brasília, the new national capital boldly placed in Brazil's interior. The early 1960s witnessed the brief and ineffectual rule of Jânio Quadros, followed by João Goulart's attempts to expand State activities still further in response to the needs of Brazil's lower class and impoverished northeast. Perceiving a leftist or populist State dramatized by expanding and radicalized mobilization, various powerful interests clamored for a forced reversal. This the military effected with its 1964 coup.

Presaging the Chilean coup of 1973, the Brazilian military was committed to changing the system, not to immediately turning back power to civilians. Like its Chilean counterpart, the Brazilian military greatly expanded the State's repressive apparatus and functions. But whereas the Chileans, at least until 1982, pledged to remove the State from many of its socioeconomic activities, the Brazilians were much more reserved about privatization. Initially, the military was "avowedly pro private enterprise and antistatist," denouncing those leftist rulers who had expanded the State and hurt private and foreign interests.[3] Nonetheless, the State's share of national economic activity increased; although State enterprises were "rationalized," they were not turned over to private hands, as in Chile. Brazil's civilian technocrats pressed effectively for antipopulist policies, engendering opposition from some military statists, but policy debate focused less on private-public issues than in Chile. If the State has been proprivate, it has been so mostly through its political decisions on savings, investments, and income distribution as well as through the stability generated by repression of popular demands—all of which broadly parallels the Mexican case. As Cardoso writes, the State has "mushroomed" while "civil society has contracted."[4] So even if one considers only the State role in the economy, military rule did not bring the same antistatist fervor seen in Chile. If one broadens the question to include the State's political control, particularly with the crackdown on political unrest in the late 1960s, then one could hardly speak of a shrinking Brazilian State.

Finally, the Brazilian regime became much less repressive after the mid-1970s, and significant redemocratization, including the election of a civilian president, was achieved by the mid-1980s. Even before the mid-1970s, Brazilian military rule was far more favorable to the middle class than was Chilean military rule, partly because the former did not dismantle a similarly developed network of State subsidies for middle-class institutions, including universities.[5] But as in Chile, the deep economic crisis of the 1980s threatened middle-class as well as other institutions.

EVOLUTION
Retarded Public Sector Development

If, to adapt language used in dependency theory, Spanish America was an early developer and English America a later developer of higher education, then Portuguese America was a late, late developer. Spanish America had some full-fledged universities in the sixteenth century, and many in the seventeenth. English America boasted prestigious colleges in the seventeenth, and many in the eighteenth. Portuguese America had nothing comparable. Only in the twentieth century did bona fide universities arise.

Unlike Spain, Portugal saw insufficient reason to create colonial institutions of higher education. Colonial elites would be trained in Portugal, at the University of Coimbra. No colonial infrastructure of higher education arose. There is a sense, then, in which colonial Brazil resembled colonial Africa more than colonial Spanish America: Britain and France did very little to establish institutions of higher education in Africa prior to World War I (with notable exceptions, such as in Nigeria), and Belgium and Portugal did much less. To keep the Portuguese-Spanish comparison in perspective, remember that Spain itself had a much larger population and a much larger and more prestigious higher education system. Portugal had less to offer. One might also argue that Portugal tried to integrate Brazil into its empire rather than to create separate Brazilian institutions. The reality, however, was that Brazilian educational development was ignored just as the overall development of Brazil was ignored. Almost everything of value, people and goods, were to be extracted for Portugal's benefit.

All attempts to establish a local university were thwarted. Jesuits petitioned for one, and lost, as early as 1592.[6] When the Jesuits were expelled (1759), what "higher education" had existed suffered greatly, for Jesuits had played a major role in seminary education, indeed in most of Brazilian education. An attempt to create a domestic university on the Coimbra model was crushed in 1789. And so throughout the nineteenth century, Brazilian higher education consisted of some isolated professional schools expected to serve a national population of millions. Sluggish development continued even after Brazil became the seat of the Portuguese empire (1808), with Napoléon's humbling of the mother country, and even after Brazil became politically independent (1822). At the same time, Spanish America's newly independent nations were busily constructing formidable public university systems. In comparative terms, then, Brazil's slow development meant slow development of the public sector.

The lack of a strong public role was in fact generalizable throughout Brazil's educational system. Reformers spanning diverse eras tried repeatedly to activate the reticent State. As in Spanish America, efforts to

174

place Crown clearly above Church in education date back to the late eighteenth century. Portugal's prime minister, the Marquis de Pombal, preached reforms (1772) to free the State from ostensible Church domination, to create a secular political-administrative elite, and to modernize the university. He blamed Church control of education for Portugal's backwardness within western Europe. But secular reforms obviously went much further in revolutionary France than in Portugal, and Brazilian students (in the nineteenth century) increasingly went to France for their university studies. Brazilian political independence spurred the growth of Freemasonry, just as establishment of a republic (1889) spurred the growth of positivism; both ideological movements were strongly anticlerical. As time passed, anticlerical motives combined with other European and then U.S. influences to inspire twentieth-century efforts at strengthening public education. A grand goal of the New School movement was to provide a standard education and expanded opportunities culminating with the public university. A central State role would be essential. To their ardent supporters, leaders such as Anísio Teixeira were modernizing crusaders; to their ardent enemies they were communists.

The New School movement, like other efforts to strengthen public education, produced mixed results, depending largely on the sympathies of the national government. Only after decades of struggle was the movement's Law of Directives and Bases of National Education promulgated, and then in much diluted form. In fact, the two decades immediately prior to the 1964 coup saw the State promoting a strong private role in education, especially secondary education. As Teixeira himself wrote, Brazilian policymakers traditionally believed that education existed for the individual, perhaps for society, but not for the State. This belief relegated the State role to the promotion and regulation of private initiatives.[7] A strong private school tradition thus dates continuously from colonial days; it was finally joined, but not supplanted, by public school development in the twentieth century. The sluggish development of public higher education must be understood in this context of a minimal State role at all educational levels as well as in the broader context of a late-developing State.[8]

Various nineteenth-century attempts to establish a university failed. The privileged few who went on to higher education in Brazil attended isolated professional schools. Near the end of the century, hopes for a public university soared when liberal military officers established the republic and encouraged congressional promulgation of a constitution (1891) mandating a federal role in secondary and higher education. Pressures for public universities grew, but still none appeared in the ensuing decades. Attempts in both 1909 and 1912 failed.

Many observers fix the date of Brazil's first university from the 1920 establishment of the University of Rio de Janeiro, uniting the three traditional professional schools of law, medicine, and engineering. Others maintain that a true university did not develop until the 1930s with the University of São Paulo, a mobilized reaction of São Paulo's elite to their political defeat by Vargas and his centralizing movement, and with the University of the Federal District (soon closed, however). Major sociopolitical changes encouraged university development. The coffee boom, import substitution, industrialization, European immigration, and then the 1930 revolution helped break the traditional oligarchy. Modernizing Brazil would need a viable higher education system. The advent of Vargas's corporatist Estado Novo meant an activated State reaching into many socioeconomic fields. Yet the Estado Novo also posed serious challenges to the liberal orientation of the New School movement.[9] State-funded public education meant different things to different supporters. By 1937 Brazil had four universities, but perhaps we should say *only* four.

Although compared to Spanish America the development of Brazil's university system was clearly belated and slow, some institutions of higher education existed prior to 1920. Cunha has shown how critics generally exaggerate Brazil's sluggishness. Several institutions, not called universities, including some prestigious ones, would have been considered universities in sister republics. Unlike many Spanish American countries, Brazil required the joining of three faculties, with specific requirements concerning inclusion of health or natural sciences, for a university to be formed. Nonetheless, it is with some reason that most Brazilian commentators have referred to the "original sin" of having no university.[10] The frustrating struggle to create a university was a central preoccupation of Brazilian intellectuals. In comparative terms, several true universities, in addition to single-faculty institutions, existed in Spanish American nations. Even back in the sixteenth century, and certainly before the twentieth, these universities included diverse faculties and had identities and wielded power as universities. Finally, regardless of institutional types, Brazil's *total* "higher education" as of 1920, indeed as of 1960, was extremely small in terms of cohort enrollments, lagging far behind most Spanish American nations.

Creating the Private Sector

While the public sector was finally establishing itself, the private sector was following close behind. Catholic intellectuals pressed for the expansion of religious education, in opposition to the New School movement's emphasis on public education. They insisted that Brazil must avoid materialism, whether U.S. (individualistic, Protestant) or socialist in style. They spoke of the family and the Church as being legitimate educational supervisors along with the State. Some argued further, against the New School movement, that although two-thirds of the nation was illiterate, good Catholics and good Brazilians depend on good souls, not on reading or writing. Thus Catholic intellectual leadership was ambivalent about educational expansion per se but clear that it should not be secular. From the 1920s through the 1940s this leadership mounted an intense fight against the New School movement—a fight really dating back to the Catholic reaction to the 1891 Constitution and the dominant positivism that had all but ostracized the Church.[11]

Some Catholic leaders tried to build their movement on an alliance between the Church and the masses, while others emphasized strengthening Church-elite ties; the latter group concentrated on higher education. A Catholic university was needed to train elites faithful to Christian principles, for the "moral reunification" of Brazil. Theirs was a crusade to re-Christianize society and the State. They decried the technocratic, pragmatic, materialistic, "scientistic," secular nature of Brazilian higher education and accused it of being "French." They argued that Brazil's universities, by not being Catholic, were lessened as universities.

The Revolution of 1930 did not necessarily identify the Church within the traditional oligarchy it set out to attack. Instead, Church influences actually increased because the new regime lacked homogeneity and needed all the support it could get. Anticommunist support was especially welcome. In return for its support, the Church demanded recognition of its quasi-official status, the continued illegality of divorce, and reintroduction of religious education. As early as 1931 the State gave the Church its big educational prize—the return of religious education into the public school after forty years of laicism.

Energies then turned increasingly to higher education. Here, however, Catholic intellectuals soon despaired of penetrating the public structure. Previously, many had doubted the desirability of separate, private, Catholic institutions. Such institutions might have low academic quality; priests would have to spend time teaching many essentially nonspiritual courses; a terrific financial burden would be incurred; besides, Brazil was a sufficiently Catholic nation that even public institutions could really be Catholic.[12] In fact, Catholic higher education had to be restricted to isolated schools until the increasingly alien ideological direction of the public university in the early 1930s proved decisive in encouraging a private university. The creation of the (public) University of the Federal District (1934) was denounced by some Catholics as an attempt to communize Brazilian public higher education. As communists defeated Catholics in competitions for chairs in political economy and law, the only adequate response was to create an institutional alternative, a distinct Catholic choice.

177

The First Catholic Congress of Education (Rio; 1934) called for the establishment of a Catholic university "as soon as possible." An effort was made to build upon institutions established in 1929 and 1932 and to join together existing professional faculties. Jesuits assumed most of the relevant pedagogical and administrative responsibilities, while a civil association was formed to raise necessary funds. And so in 1940 the Catholic University of Rio became Brazil's first private university, receiving official authorization from the Estado Novo. Instruction began in 1941. Only in 1946, however, did the institution meet the final official requisites for full-fledged university status, and only in 1947 did the Vatican bestow pontifical status. Before long, Brazil had pontifical Catholic universities (known as PUCs) in São Paulo, Porto Alegre, Recife, and Belo Horizonte. In 1952 the Mackenzie University was created from a college founded by U.S. Protestant missionaries (and once related to New York University).

Brazil's first private wave had arisen for much the same major reason operating elsewhere in Latin America—State toleration of a Catholic reaction to public secularism. Also typically, this reason was combined with others. Chapter 2 identifies some of the contributing social, economic, and political factors. In the Brazilian context, a certain demand-absorbing function might also be noted, given restricted public sector admissions. But one of the most salient comparative points is that Brazil's private universities arose at chronologically the same time or even earlier than private universities in most of Spanish America. Brazil's first wave of private creation paralleled Spanish experience in a way that its later private waves would not.

Private versus Public Growth

Brazil's retarded university development thus refers only to the public sector. Consequently, a critical contrast between Brazil and Spanish America is the chronological gap between the origins of public and private sectors. Only twenty years elapsed in Brazil between the creation of the first university and the first private university, if we use the 1920 and 1940 dates for quasi universities; only twelve years elapsed if we use the 1934 and 1946 dates for bona fide universities. In Mexico four centuries elapsed, elsewhere generally more than three centuries. Even between the first truly public and first private university, the Spanish American gap was usually greater than a century. By the time its private sector was sanctioned, Argentina already had more than 150,000 public sector students, roughly 800 per each 100,000 population. For Brazil the comparable figures were roughly 30,000 and fewer than 50.[13]

Because of its unique development pattern, therefore, Brazil never had the kind of predominant public sector characteristic of most of Latin America. By 1955 more than four in ten of Brazil's higher education enrollments were already in the private sector—a share higher than all Latin American nations except Colombia and the Dominican Republic have ever had and a share far exceeding Spanish America's 7 percent for 1955. Brazil's slow educational development meant that by the time massive growth in demand arose, a substantial private structure was already in place. In 1960 Brazil trailed Latin America as a whole by roughly two to one in proportional enrollments; Brazil had 1.6 percent of its cohort group enrolled, Latin America 3.1 percent; Brazil had 137 higher education students per 100,000 population, Latin America 250.[14] Because a proportionally strong private sector was in place "early," it could share in the enrollment boom to come.

The timing of private versus public sectoral development is therefore crucial. Too much work on the shift from elite to mass systems focuses on the effects of enrollment growth on institutional form, without giving sufficient attention to the effects of established institutional form in shaping the growth.[15] In a sense, Brazil's private-public development resembles the United States's more than Spanish America's. The bulk of Spanish America's enrollment boom occurred in the public university because it was either the only or the predominant institutional form. Brazil, like the United States, had two sectors of relatively equal size ready to absorb the huge influx. Brazilian private higher education would grow by leaps and bounds in the 1960s and 1970s largely because it was already there when the crunch came.

The crunch has been impressive, as table 5.1 shows. From under 100,000 in 1960, enrollments jumped to over 1 million by 1975. The biggest boom came between 1968 and 1974. First-year openings (*vagas*) give the clearest indication of change. From 1960 to 1968 they grew by fewer than 50,000, from 1968 to 1974 by more than 200,000. Whereas Brazil could claim only half the cohort enrollment percentage shown by Latin America as a whole in 1960, the difference dwindled to 11.2 versus 11.7 percent in 1975. The causes of Brazil's phenomenal enrollment growth include substantial economic growth, increased middle-class mobility and demands, the changing status of women, primary and secondary school expansion, a decreasing utility of secondary school degrees on the job market, and the belief that Brazil's relative backwardness could be overcome with more education.[16] The accelerated boom starting in the late 1960s was largely a response to middle-class demands for expansion: "Mais verbas e mais vagas" (more subsidies and more first-year university slots).

Whereas Brazil's *numerus clausus* (quota) had been "extremely demanding,"[17] the State now faced increased political pressures for relaxation. An especially severe political problem arose over the growing number of *excedentes,* secondary school graduates who passed admissions exams but

179

Table 5.1 Brazilian Private and Public Enrollment Trends, 1940–1980

Year	Total Enrollment	% Growth	Private Enrollment	Private, % of Total	Total First-Year Quotas	% Growth in Total First-Year Openings
1940	27,671	—	—	—	9,200	—
1950	48,999	—	—	—	14,600	—
1954	64,645	—	26,905	41.6	—	—
1955	72,652	12	30,755	42.3	—	—
1956	78,659	8	38,362	48.8	—	—
1957	79,505	1	38,051	47.9	—	—
1958	84,481	6	37,570	44.5	—	—
1959	87,603	4	38,562	44.0	—	—
1960	93,202	7	41,287	44.3	39,781	—
1961	98,892	6	43,560	44.0	43,240	9
1962	107,299	9	43,275	40.3	47,000	9
1963	124,214	16	47,428	38.2	51,751	10
1964	142,386	15	54,721	38.4	57,990	12
1965	155,781	9	68,194	43.8	57,469	−1
1966	180,109	16	81,667	45.3	60,137	5
1967	212,882	18	91,608	43.0	80,915	35
1968	278,295	31	124,496	44.7	88,588	9
1969	342,886	23	157,826	46.0	117,229[a]	32
1970	425,478	24	214,865	50.5	145,000	24
1971	561,397	32	309,134	55.1	202,110	39
1972	688,382	23	409,971	59.6	223,009	10
1973	772,800	12	472,721	61.2	282,333	27
1974	937,593	21	596,565	63.6	309,448	10
1975	1,072,548	14	662,323	61.8	348,227	13
1976	1,044,472	—[b]	648,862	62.1	382,418	10
1977	1,137,070	9	708,554	62.3	393,560	3
1978	1,267,559	11	779,592	61.5	405,367[c]	3
1979	1,298,331	2	808,253	62.3	—	—
1980[c]	1,345,000	4	852,000	63.3	—	—

SOURCES: Enrollments, 1940–50, and first-year quotas, 1940–67: José Veiga Simão, "General Aspects of Brazilian Higher Education," a working paper of the Higher Education Research Group, Yale University, July 1978, p. 16, based on MEC data. Enrollments, 1954–75: Pedro Lincoln Carneiro Leão de Matos, "Políticas do governo federal na expansão de ensino superior no Brasil," master's thesis, School of Public Administration, Fundação Getúlio Vargas, 1977, table 5, based on MEC data. Enrollments, 1976–80: MEC-SESU, *Boletim informativo* (Brasília), March 1981, p. 17. Note that MEC-SESU gives a 1975 figure of 61.1 percent compared to our 61.8 percent from Matos. Thus there is some discontinuity in switching sources in 1976. However, Matos gives only estimates for 1976–77 and nothing after that, while offering the advantage of starting back in 1954. Moreover, the 1976–77 estimates in the Matos data show discrepancies of only 0.1 percent in each year from our MEC-SESU data; the main problem in continuity is not the private percentage but the different total figures found in the two sources, even though both sources derive from MEC itself. Also note that table 1.1 (OAS data) shows consistently higher private percentages than those found in table 5.1. See MEC, *O ensino superior no Brasil 1974–1978* (Brasília: MEC, 1979), p. 26, on the first-year quotas, 1968–78; because the 1969–75 figures found here fall short of those found in the Simão source I use through 1967, another discontinuity may exist, despite common MEC roots and a common 1968 figure.

a. Possible discontinuity because of switch in data sources.
b. Discontinuity because of switch in data sources.
c. Estimated.

exceeded the allotted number of vagas. Thus there were two intertwined problems. Exams were considered too exclusionary and, even at that, the system did not find a place for all who passed. The State's dual response was to relax standards somewhat in the public sector and, more important, to allow uncontrolled private sector growth. That massive private growth resulted from excedentes reflects its demand-absorbing nature.

Private enrollments soared even faster than public enrollments, quite unlike the situation in Spanish America, where public enrollments grew far more in absolute terms, even while private growth was proportionally greater. From the mid-1950s to the end of the 1960s, Brazil's private/total share had held fairly constant at roughly 44 percent, but by 1970 that share jumped to over 50 and soon to over 60 percent. Even when the State offered more *vagas* (places), it clearly hoped to limit the growth of *verbas* (subsidies) by funneling new enrollments disproportionally into the private sector. Thus, Brazil's isolated schools or establishments (*estabelecimentos isolados*), lacking multiple and linked faculties, expanded greatly, where the private sector was dominant, to meet demand not accommodated by the universities, where the public sector was dominant. From 1968 to 1974 the number of public institutions grew by 88, but the number of private ones grew by 388, producing "profound heterogeneity."[18]

So far, this account has tied Brazil's private growth largely to extraordinary growth in demand, combined with the early development of the private sector relative to the public sector in the preboom period, and has hinted at the State's proprivate role. The last point must be made more explicit. Although the new military regime immediately broadcast its proprivate ideology, its actions, as shown, have not followed simply from that declaration. In fact, higher education offers a stunning example of where the regime has allowed great public expansion. This again forms a stark contrast to the Chilean, Argentine, and Uruguayan freezes of or cuts in their public sectors and surely reflects Brazil's less severe authoritarianism on issues of concern to the middle class. On the other hand, the Brazilian military took power before the enrollment boom, while neighboring militaries took power after years of booming growth; one could say that there was still more room for growth and that there was less against which to react. Equally important, the Brazilian military arrived in time to shape the enrollment boom.

For example, the regime called on expert foreign consultant Rudolph Atcon to help shape the university's role in capitalist modernization.[19] The hope was that rationalization could be effected within the public sector, minimizing the degree to which privileged interests would have to abandon the public sector for private sector alternatives. If the regime was not repressive enough to deny the demands for increased higher education, the regime was not open enough to accommodate most of that demand within its public sector. The Brazilian regime permitted neither the degree of change (political, socioeconomic, academic) within the public sector nor the same rise in the State's financial burden that less authoritarian regimes were permitting elsewhere in Latin America. Moreover, the Brazilian regime was able to "protect" many leading public universities, funneling public growth primarily into new public institutions. Although significant Spanish American growth went into proliferating public institutions, the leading universities also grew prodigiously. Brazil's largest universities did not similarly transform themselves by growing to gigantic proportions. Even the largest federal universities, such as the one in Rio, have "only" about twenty-five thousand students, and most have considerably fewer. Partly because of federalism and the late development of an active central State, and partly because leading public universities did not throw their doors wide open during the enrollment boom, Brazil's public sector was never transformed through phenomenal growth in its national or leading universities the way Chile's, Mexico's, Venezuela's, and most of Central America's public sectors were. However great Brazil's public expansion, the comparative point here is that it was shaped and limited when measured against the demand it faced.[20] Furthermore, the State directly aided private sector growth not only through the very loose sanctioning of new private institutions but also through a series of tax exemptions, credits, and other stimuli. In sum, the State role should not be seen as fully dependent on demands for expansion; while its hand was pushed, the State actively sought to parlay expansion into political legitimacy, and it actively directed the enrollment flow toward the private sector.[21]

Fearing negative effects from higher education expansion, the State initiated a slowdown policy in 1972 and especially 1974.[22] MEC (the education ministry) strongly suggested that the FCE (Federal Education Council)—the agency charged to supervise the private sector—fix priorities for the authorization of new courses and institutions. This had some effect but did not curtail enrollments in existing structures. Moreover, the policy addressed only the private sector, where the bulk of expansion had been occurring. A 1981 presidential decree was much broader and more explicit. Restrictions were extended to enrollments and to both sectors.

Both the ministerial (and even presidential) involvement and the increasingly high rejection rates show that Brazil's slowdown resulted from a political decision.[23] What, then, were the causes of the political decisions to curb expansion? While concern over rising State costs for the public sector was one cause, the main causes lay in the private sector. There had in fact been a continual debate within the military regime about the advantages of satisfying demand versus the dangers of plummeting quality. By 1972, and increasingly over the next decade, the pendulum shifted to those concerned

182

about quality; other concerns included the relative neglect of basic education and mounting evidence of unemployment among higher education's
graduates, especially during the economic crisis of the early 1980s.[24] Thus,
the State responded to market as well as political pressures.[25]

The slowdown had strong systemic and private-public effects. Whereas
the number of institutions doubled in the 1968–73 quinquennia, the increase
slowed to 12 percent in 1973–78. The impact on enrollment was delayed and
weaker but still strong. First-year enrollments grew 219 percent in the first
period as compared with 44 percent in the next; total enrollments, growing
at an annual average of over 20 percent in 1965–75, grew only 3 percent
annually for 1978–80. However, it was precisely in the private isolated
schools that most of the enrollment increase continued—63,430 of the total
77,401 growth for 1978–80; while the public sector grew but 1 percent,
private universities grew 4 percent, and private isolated schools grew
12 percent.[26] On the other hand, because private enrollments had been
expanding so much faster than public ones, the slowdown powerfully
affected the private sector. Then, by the early 1980s, Brazil's economic crisis
added to the slowdown.

But the slowdown had not begun until well after rapid expansion had
changed the face of Brazilian higher education, especially private higher
education. While hundreds of new private institutions were born, few new
PUCs were created. Eleven of the thirteen PUCs functioning in 1979 had
been created by 1961. Considering the much smaller representation
(9 percent) of Catholic institutions among the isolated schools than universities, expansion clearly was a secular phenomenon as opposed to the first
wave of private growth (1940–61). Existing PUCs grew, but only one grew to
over twenty thousand students; private growth occurred predominantly in
newly formed isolated schools. Meanwhile, PUCs held 24 percent of Brazil's
university enrollments in 1977, just as they had in 1961.[27] In sum, while
Catholic institutions held their own in the university sphere, they lost out
overall as isolated secular private schools met most new demand.

Enrollment growth was just too strong to implement statutory law (1931),
reinforced by 1961 legislation, mandating that the university should be the
higher education form. As of 1980, 53 percent of higher education enrollments were in isolated schools. The private sector had 86 percent of these
enrollments, compared to roughly 39 percent of university enrollments.
While only 32 percent of all universities were private, 78 percent of the
isolated schools were.[28] If the two most important dichotomies in Brazilian
higher education have been the private-public and the isolated school–
university phenomena, the two overlap considerably.[29] Privateness has been
a fundamental, not incidental, characteristic of the demand-absorbing institutions neither subsidized nor closely regulated by the State. Therefore,

the great proportional growth of the secular private subsector has represented a demand-absorbing dynamic. Meanwhile, the first private wave has stagnated. And no strong private elite subsector has developed. Finance, governance, and function have all been very much shaped by the evolution of a huge private sector composed of a fairly typical Catholic subsector alongside a mammoth demand-absorbing subsector.

FINANCE
The Private Sector

The State restricts its role in higher education by allocating only limited funds to the massive private sector. While Spanish American counterparts usually avoid major financial responsibility for less than 20 percent of their higher education enrollments, Brazil avoids more than 60 percent. As Brazil's unusual intersectoral balance leads to unusual private-public financial patterns, it strongly affects policy considerations turning on such issues as equity and choice.

Unfortunately, no comprehensive data exist on private higher education income in Brazil; even government officials cannot get reliable figures from individual institutions. Nonetheless, we know that private institutions finance very little of their ongoing costs through State funds. A common estimate is that the private sector receives only about 1 percent of all federal subsidies (overwhelmingly targeted to salaries) that go to higher education.[30] State aid to these institutions has been greatest where graduate studies and research are strongest. Like the U.S. federal government, Brazil's government is basically indifferent to the private-public distinction when it comes to these privileged areas. This attitude accounts for the very uneven allocation of public funds to the private sector. Because few private institutions boast graduate or research programs, few receive any aid at all. Only about 10 percent of the private isolated schools make the financial list. Most do not even have the gall to solicit funds. Yet possibly all private universities receive some public funds. Criteria for support include academic quality, research, graduate education, and, of course, political pressure. State agencies such as FINEP (Corporation for Financing Students and Projects) and CAPES (Campaign for Improvement of High Level Personnel) give funds for research and support of graduate students.[31] PUC-Rio probably gets the most public funding of any private institution, largely because it has an unusually good research center in engineering, a considerable expense. Thus the financial picture is uneven not just across but within institutions. Also, funds are often given for unforeseen or new needs. And there are indirect forms of aid, including salaries to public sector professors who also teach part time in private institutions; perhaps most important, however, is a government loan program established in 1976 that, like U.S. counterparts, benefits mostly the private sector.[32]

A key private-public difference in finance concerns annual MEC subsidies for undergraduate education and general purposes. Brazil's secular, then positivist, then New School traditions were fundamentally opposed to State subsidization of any private schools. As Florestan Fernandes expressed it: "Such a State would not be 'democratic,' but a Frankenstein, a monster incapable of autonomous existence."[33]

But the majority of private higher education institutions have been eager for annual public subsidies, pressing hard by the late 1970s and into the 1980s. While no constitutional provisions have stood in the way, even the thirteen Catholic universities collectively receive less from the ministry than do any of the twenty-five individual public universities.[34] PUCs have led the fight for public funds for private universities as a group, and even led the fight somewhat for the private sector overall. In fact, all five ensuing arguments apply not only to the Catholic subsector but, with qualifications of the first, third, and fourth, to the demand-absorbing subsector as well. Thus, it is worth examining the case for State subsidization because it is based on rationales characteristic of educational systems (including but not limited to higher education systems) with these subsectors and large private sectors overall.

First, PUC rectors argue, present tuitions no longer cover basic costs. Big deficits have been accumulating as expenditures, especially salaries, have skyrocketed from the 1970s. Internal solutions based on improved efficiency are no longer sufficient. Reform and sacrifice can no longer substitute for significant ministerial aid. As a corollary, PUC rectors point out that State aid has declined. Table 5.2 was prepared by PUC rectors to dramatize their plight. It is actually misleading, basing yearly averages of public income on nonweighted averages among universities and not computing in early years when subsidies might have been zero. Consequently, averages for the late 1960s are terribly inflated to dramatize a 1970s decline. I reproduce the table here partly to present the PUCs own case, however exaggerated. More important, the basic decline is corroborated by reliable data,[35] and the table presents rare data on ministerial funding for private institutions. Also, it shows powerful declines in the percentage of subsidies drawn from the ministry for several prominent PUCs (e.g., São Paulo) and allows for reasonable comparisons between 1975 and 1978, showing that eleven of thirteen universities received a smaller share of their income from State subsidies in the later year. Mostly, it shows how limited State subsidization has been even for PUCs. No PUC received as much as 15 percent of its annual income from State subsidies for 1977–78. Finally, the table illustrates, though less precisely, the notable proportional drop around 1970 when the State faced an accelerating public burden.

Second, PUC rectors argue that to raise tuition to meet costs would be an unforgivably elitist policy. Currently, the private sector caters to many less-privileged students who cannot gain access to the public sector. In this light, tuition has already gone up too much.

Third, problems with income would inevitably lead to lowered quality. Even the best PUCs would lose good and full-time professors. Facilities would deteriorate. Pressing needs would have to be ignored. (Moreover, because the State is legally committed to favor universities over isolated schools, both private and public universities, which offer quality and a range of fields, including expensive ones not found in the isolated schools, should be subsidized.) To preserve quality without increased subsidization inevitably requires increased tuition. However, even if enough students could pay and the universities were willing to incur charges of elitism, the State actually imposes barriers to this solution. Specifically, State approval of tuition hikes is required. Criteria include the institution's operational costs and quality, but there are political considerations as well. Playing for middle-class support rather than risking unpopularity among affected students and their families, the State is reluctant to authorize increases at PUCs and private isolated schools.

Table 5.2 Percentage of Income for Brazil's Catholic Universities from MEC, 1960–1978

Catholic University of	Founding Year	60	61	62	63	64	65	66
Rio	1964							
São Paulo	1946			76.4	33.3	23.2	23.9	29.7
Rio Grande do Sul	1948							
Pernambuco	1956							
Campinas	1955	31.6	25.6	32.3	28.2	7.5	22.5	28.9
Minas Gerais	1958							
Goiás	1959		97.0	42.0	35.0	73.0	90.0	65.0
Paraná	1960							
Pelotas	1960						30.0	21.9
Salvador	1961							
Petrópolis	1961							
Rio dos Sinos	1969							
Santa Úrsula	1975							
Average[a]								

SOURCE: Reitores, *As universidades católicas no momento atual* (Belo Horizonte: FUMARC, 1979), p. 55.

186

Fourth, the private sector claims to perform basically public functions. The PUCs' religious orientation is quite limited, more so than that of many private secondary schools receiving State support. Aside from indirect contributions to a better society for all, PUCs perform direct nonprofit services such as administering hospitals. Additionally, the private sector helps meet societal demand for higher education.

Finally, if the State does not bail out the PUCs, and even the private isolated schools, it could face far greater financial burdens. Due to greater efficiency, costs per student are lower in the private than public universities. Beyond this, the State would eventually have to take over private institutions, thereby assuming not partial but full financial responsibility.[36] The threat to "go public" is a dramatic political tactic to garner more funds. Your money or our life is the primary message, but it is embellished with the spectre of political-economic fallout that also touches on a your-money-or-your-life theme. Hence, the rectors asked for 3 percent of MEC's budget in 1979, steadily increasing to 10 percent by 1983.

The State has had some positive reactions. Until 1979 no annual subsidies were distributed for general purposes in first-degree education; but the ban was then lifted, with small subsidies flowing through the Program of Financial Aid to Non-Federal Institutions. For one thing, the PUC rectors were making several valid points. For another, private institutions are so widespread that they pack considerable political support from their middle-class

Table 5.2 cont'd

67	68	69	70	71	72	73	74	75	76	77	78
								10.4	4.6	6.8	5.4
10.4	25.4	18.0	16.8	8.9	6.1	4.1	3.0	4.2	4.6	5.6	3.6
	20.1	25.8	22.0	14.2	11.9	10.2	5.7	5.2	6.2	5.3	3.2
		55.3	32.3	49.6	25.6	16.6	11.2	13.1	14.2	8.9	6.1
26.4	28.8	19.9	7.2	13.3	9.4	5.9	4.1	3.6	4.3	3.6	2.8
	30.7	31.0	14.9	16.9	11.7	7.6	6.0	5.0	3.9	3.1	4.7
55.0	54.0	52.0	37.0	46.0	24.0	16.0	10.0	11.0	6.0	11.0	8.0
					33.9	38.0	8.3	10.7	7.0	7.5	6.5
35.1	39.1	37.2	15.5	37.3	15.2	6.8	9.3	14.6	8.2	7.7	6.1
	25.9	27.0	24.6	12.3	7.0	6.5	6.6	2.9	8.4	8.4	
	62.7	54.3	26.8	26.1	19.4	14.2	9.8	11.1	9.9	6.4	4.6
			5.1	5.6	2.9	0.7	1.5	4.6	2.3	1.8	0.4
	3.3	—[b]	0.1	0.0	0.9	—[b]	0.0	0.0	—[b]	0.1	0.3
31.7	33.0	35.5	18.6	22.0	14.4	11.5	6.3	7.7	5.9	5.9	4.6

a. The averages are deceiving.
b No figures shown.

187

constituencies and from senators, governors, and others who recognize the institutions' regional importance (or who in some cases actually own them). Opposition might well have been more intense when the PUCs were more oriented to religious purposes. Now they are committed to much the same missions as the public universities and are fulfilling those missions better than most public isolated schools. Moreover, the military regime had some ideological affinity for promoting private higher education and showed in other fields its willingness to use State resources to promote private activities, demonstrating neither indifference toward their fate nor reservations about undermining privateness through State "contamination." Critical, however, would appear to be the State's fear of the potential financial burden posed by a failing private sector. It is not hard to see the private sector's point about partial subsidies to protect private solvency versus full subsidies for students closed out of the private sector.

Nevertheless, State aid has not progressed very far. The PUC petitions, after receiving initially positive reactions, ran into a net of obstacles. Foremost was the severe economic crisis inflamed by the jump in world oil prices. Within the context of austerity for State agencies, increased aid for the private sector was not only economically difficult but politically unfeasible. Public university rectors, who might have otherwise offered less resistance, saw fit to oppose the initiative just as strongly as their private counterparts supported it. Finally, as the powerful planning ministry opposed any such measure to increase the State's social-welfare expenditures, the education ministry worried about the degree of accountability it could have for funds turned over to the private sector. However, the private sector plan is not clearly defeated. Rather, it lies ready for consideration when current events are more favorable or when the private plight degenerates to where its needs are undeniable.[37]

For at least some considerable time, though, Brazilian private higher education income will probably have to depend chiefly on private sources, as it always has. Analyzing these, we see first that, beyond tuition, they are limited. Brazilian private enterprise lacks a tradition of giving to causes that cannot yield clear and immediate profit. Multinational corporations tend to rely on research done in the developed world. Furthermore, important areas of the economy are run by State enterprises, such as Petrobrás (petroleum), and they tend to conduct their own research where necessary. Some donor foundations are involved in education, but these are few. Most corporate giving is concentrated on a very small number of the best institutions. The Getúlio Vargas Foundation in São Paulo, for example, receives donations from its state's entrepreneurs. The main branch of the Getúlio Vargas Foundation (Rio), a quasi-private institution, receives roughly 10 percent of its income from donations, but this could well be one of the highest figures for any Brazilian higher education institution.[38] Additionally, some of the best institutions gain income through contract research. Overall, however, the lack of corporate support for private higher education reflects the absence of an elite subsector comparable to those found in Mexico and several other Spanish American nations. Indeed, those few Brazilian private universities that approach the elite model most closely (e.g., the Mackenzie University) stand the best chance of receiving corporate support.

Because most private institutions rely on tuition, the university–isolated school dichotomy is important. Students in private isolated schools usually pay practically the full cost of their education; students in private universities may pay half of theirs by the best, albeit very rough, estimates.[39] The highest tuition for 1979 was that of the Gama Filhol University, where medical students paid at least $1,750 per year. The same university's engineering students paid the most in their field, at least $1,100, while the highest fees in letters, at the Santa Ursula University, were probably only half as much. In 1982 the average national tuition for medicine was just under $2,000.[40] By U.S. private higher education standards, then, tuitions are not very high, partly because of State regulation. They tend to be highest at those institutions that most closely resemble the elite model and probably are somewhat higher at the PUCs than at most, but not all, isolated schools. This comparative breakdown parallels the dominant Spanish American pattern, except that Brazil's expensive elite institutions are so few compared to the demand-absorbing institutions. Thus, more than elsewhere in Latin America, many students in private higher education pay less than students at even the private primary level. After all, the private primary students are disproportionally in the elite sector at their level; private higher education students disproportionally are not.

Focusing on financing for the private isolated schools, serious questions arise regarding nonprofit status. Such questions have arisen for low-prestige private institutions elsewhere, but they reach their greatest salience in Brazil. These institutions often charge higher tuitions than their educational expenditures justify. Because advantages flow from legal nonprofit status, including tax exemptions on income and investments, private isolated schools do not distribute income above educational expenditures as profits. But there are other ways of realizing what are essentially profits. High salaries, fringe benefits, nepotism, and luxurious facilities are common examples in Brazil. There are also ways to transfer profits outside the nonprofit school to the *sociedade mantenedora* (patron foundation) that ultimately controls the isolated school.[41] While the schools often show deficits, their patron foundations often enjoy profits.

Profits are also transferred within the nonprofit institutions, taking from

189

faculties that do well to subsidize faculties that operate at a loss. A related "Robin Hood" approach is found in the Cândido Mendes institutions, where lucrative first-degree offerings subsidize the high-quality, but expensive, research-oriented IUPERJ (although most IUPERJ funds come directly from State grants for research and graduate education). The ways in which "profits" are manipulated raise questions about the concept of trust as a widespread rationale for supporting the nonprofit sector.[42] Many of Brazil's private, nonprofit isolated schools seek to maximize income and minimize educational expenditures. They are able to get away with it largely because of the otherwise unmet demand for higher education, which limits consumer bargaining power.

The Public Sector

Public higher education in Brazil is virtually free. This holds not only for the federal but also for almost all of the state universities. Two state universities in Paraná charge fees, and some municipal institutions also have limited charges. But even São Paulo, the richest state, with the most prestigious public sector, does not impose tuition in its state universities, in contrast to the situation in its private institutions. Thus, allowing for very limited exceptions, Brazil's rule is: "Public institutions are free for the students."[43] Even though official policy is supposed to discourage isolated schools and encourage universities, the State almost fully finances public isolated schools while not giving direct annual subsidies to private universities. As in Spanish America, the big variable within the public sector is not the percentage of State versus total income but simply the amount of State subsidy. As of 1977 the five major recipients of central government funds were the federal universities of Rio, Minas Gerais, Paraíba, Rio Grande do Sul, and Paraná.

Free public higher education has not gone unchallenged. Groups in the military and other quarters have opposed this "indiscriminate" subsidy, making clear that the State cannot meet its primary and secondary school commitments while still saddled with the burdens of public higher education. They have called for increased tuition and university responsibility to seek alternative outside funding. They have argued that the search for such funding, thus avoiding full State subsidies, would help overcome bureaucratic inertia by providing incentives for reform.[44]

Tuition reform is backed by many independent researchers. They believe that public primary and secondary education are a national disgrace, that primary teachers often do not receive even the minimum wage, and that teachers are very poorly trained. Scathing editorials in *O Jornal do Brasil* have pointed out that higher education cohort enrollments are reaching proportional equivalence with much of Western Europe, while primary and secondary levels are neglected in quantitative and qualitative terms alike. Prominent officials in education, such as the University of Brasília's rector, have written repeatedly on the subject.[45]

Thus far the protuition case may sound very much like that heard in Chile as well as in Mexico and much of Spanish America, but Brazil's massive private enrollments present important twists. In one way, the issue is less salient because more than three-fifths of all students are actually attending tuition-charging institutions. In another way, however, the issue is more salient because the public sector attracts the most privileged students—those most able to pay. The issue is therefore critical from the point of view of equity. A double negative is operating here, and it does not make a positive. Children from privileged backgrounds, who attend exclusive primary and secondary schools and do well on university admissions tests, generally choose the prestigious public universities. In Spanish America, public university students are generally from lower socioeconomic backgrounds than their private counterparts and get a free ride at lower-prestige institutions; private university students pay tuition. Brazilian students in the private sector also pay tuition but they receive less than their public counterparts, who can afford more. This is not to say that Brazil's private sector students are poor, just that the majority are less privileged than their public sector peers.

Whereas Spanish America's elite private higher education draws heavily on private secondary education, in Brazil public higher education does the same. Brazil's private primary and secondary schools are generally far superior to its public ones. The burden of providing access falls largely upon the public sector at these levels. Therefore, while enrollment expansion has occurred disproportionally in the private sector at the higher level, it has occurred disproportionally in the public sector at the primary and secondary levels. Between 1960 and 1975 private secondary enrollments, despite growth, fell from 70 to 40 percent of the secondary total. The result is a special pattern of privilege in which private schooling culminates in free public higher education. If Florestan Fernandes is correct that public facilities do not serve socialism but privilege in societies controlled by upper classes, his observation is more relevant to Brazilian than Spanish American public higher education.[46]

The double negative effect on equity has apparently been aggravated by the proliferation of *cursinhos*—cram courses designed to help students pass their entrance exams. Such courses are common in systems as diverse as the Greek, Japanese, and Chinese, where openings for public higher education fall far short of demand. In Brazil, all or almost all the cursinhos are offered in private schools, subject only to minimal State regulation. These are for-profit institutions often engaged in intense competition with one another. Fees are high. Monthly costs could approach three-fourths of a minimum wage; the examination inscription fee could approach one-half of such a wage. Some secondary schools, mostly private, work out arrangements to substitute a cursinho for the senior year. If one accepts reports that cursinhos have been efficiently run and effective, at least in their first decade of rapid expansion, then perhaps the cursinhos have given an extra boost to those who could afford them, often a boost into the elite, free, public universities.[47]

Opposition to tuition has been just as intense and self-righteous in Brazil as in sister nations, where public students are generally less privileged than private students. Tuition, critics charge, would be a regressive policy, unfortunately consistent with Brazil's capitalist-dependent development, a show of good faith to foreign capital, and another example of spending "more resources on arms and less on education." Loans would only be attempts to "buy off" the students who oppose such "privatization" even when they can afford it.[48] Thus the military regime's initial attempts to impose tuition led to strong student reactions. Persistent attempts risked invigorating the outlawed student movement. Yet the regime did not give up completely. A 1971 law provided for tuition in public secondary education. But a 1972 plebescite of University of São Paulo students showed 95 percent opposed to public university tuition. And student opposition to tuition was a major rallying cry as students began reorganizing in the late 1970s. There were even demonstrations against tuition at several private institutions (e.g., PUC-Rio; March 1977). In 1979 Brazil's new student union reasserted that 95 percent of the thirty-five thousand students participating in its plebiscite opposed tuition.[49]

Many public university administrators have joined the opposition. One reason that they opposed the 1960s creation of *fundações* (less-centralized public universities) was that these institutions might pioneer in public sector tuition. A fear is that any diversification of funding sources would make MEC's subsidies less reliable and income more variable, thereby placing considerable burden on the public universities themselves to search for funds.[50] On a less self-interested basis, other critics of tuition argue that, however appealing the vision of non-State financing, such income could never cover costs in expensive fields; thus, lowered State subsidization would lead to lowered quality and overall effectiveness.

The State's obvious solace in not being able to impose tuition has been that the public sector is proportionally the smallest in all of Latin America.[51]

192

Enrollment expansion inevitably took its financial toll, but the State lessened the pressure by leaving major responsibility to the private sector. With the region's proportionally largest private sector, which has depended relatively little on State funds, Brazil has clearly had the most private system of higher education finance in all Latin America. Annual State subsidization of the private sector remains a possibility, but it has not yet occurred, despite private university quality, despite the private sector's contribution to public functions such as access, despite the private sector's deteriorating financial situation, and despite the spectre of private collapse leading to a vastly expanded public sector burden. Similarly, public sector tuition remains a possibility, but it has not been implemented, despite certain State initiatives in the 1960s, despite substantial political authoritarianism and economic conservatism, and despite the straining of State resources amid the economic crisis of the late 1970s and early 1980s—a crisis that followed upon the enrollment and therefore financial surge in the public sector in the 1960s and 1970s. However great many of the differences between Brazilian and Spanish American private-public patterns, both patterns are characterized by private financing of the private sector combined with State financing of the public sector.

GOVERNANCE

In governance as in finance, Brazil parallels Spanish America in that the private sector is tied chiefly to private interests while the public sector is much more directly tied to the State. Again, however, these are generalizations that require much more factual specificity as well as qualification. A central question here will be the degree to which the State's power actually approaches its formal authority over both sectors. As in many Continental and Spanish American systems, the education ministry has enormous bureaucratic authority, leading to striking centralism and conformity on the books. Naturally, the centralist tradition has strong roots in the Estado Novo just as contemporary Italian centralism has strong roots in Mussolini's corporate structures.[52] The Estado Novo set a single model for all public universities in Brazil.

Reflecting the late development of central government authority, the Brazilian education ministry dates back only to 1930, but it has grown quickly. Today, prime responsibility for public higher education falls to MEC's Secretariat of Higher Education (SESU), which replaced an earlier Department of University Affairs (DAU). Relations between the State and private higher education fall more under the official purview of the Federal Education Council (FCE), which also has some responsibilities in the public

193

sector. The FCE's twenty-four members are nominated by the president of the republic. It has some authority, with the MEC, in accreditation of new institutions, curriculum requirements, admissions policies, student and professor discipline, and interinstitutional coordination. The rector of the University of Brasília has gone so far as to declare that, of the two extremes characterizing the world's systems, Brazil comes closer to the centralized communist system than to the decentralized U.S. system.[53] Still, as in many Continental and Spanish American systems, no matter how elaborate the formal structure of central authority, a wide gap emerges between that central authority and the realities of who governs and how. Partly because the center tries to reach so far, that is, to reach in from so far away, considerable power may be left to the academic underbrush. This gap will be investigated in the Brazilian case while focusing on three aspects of governance: (1) State control over student movements, (2) State control over institutions, and (3) State attempts at public sector reform.

First, however, a word is in order concerning the state universities. The very existence of these institutions suggests a limit to centralism, even at the formal structural level. Important state roles survived the Estado Novo, the nationalization of several state universities, and MEC initiatives to create one national university as a structural and governance form for all others. Notwithstanding all this, the 1946 Constitution still stressed the states' role, and as late as 1973, the states held roughly 10 percent of total enrollments; municipalities held another 5 percent, versus roughly 24 percent for the federal government.[54] Although the states and municipalities are far more important at the primary and secondary levels, they are, in comparative perspective, important at the higher education level as well. At the same time, MEC wields considerable formal authority over the state and local institutions in terms of structure, organization, and curriculum, and the FCE's authority generally supersedes that of state education councils. Again, however, such formal authority may mislead us as to the real exercise of power in policy making. The ensuing account includes only limited references to the state institutions, especially considering that there is more interinstitutional variation among state than federal universities. Within São Paulo alone, the USP (University of São Paulo) was established in the 1940s and reflected significant French influence; the state university at Campinas established its structure much more on a U.S. model, although it has contracted many ex-USP professors; a third institution is really a university umbrella for scattered offerings in São Paulo's interior. Castro concludes that "no generalizations are possible" across the state subsector,[55] and we cannot here substitute in-depth studies of individual state institutions. Some, like the two in Paraná, appear to be patterned largely after federal institutions, but others are not.

194

Students and the State

Under both the Estado Novo and military rule, there were corporatist attempts to tie student movements to the State. At least two factors have spurred such attempts at corporatist encapsulation in Latin America. One has been the great propensity for student activism, which threatens political stability; another has been the frequency of repressive regimes squelching freedoms. Although Chile's very repressive regime failed to construct viable corporatist student movements, it could be argued that Chile lacked Brazil's corporatist tradition and that, in the specific case of the student movement, Chile's corporatist attempt followed decades of independent activity and freedom. Brazil's Estado Novo characteristically incorporated newly formed and potentially disruptive groups and attempted to do so with students starting in 1938. This was twenty years after the Córdoba movement got underway in Argentina and other countries, yet it was only a few years after Brazil established its first universities, and it was still many years before massive expansion in Brazilian higher education.

In textbook corporatist fashion, the Estado Novo created a National Union of Students (UNE) and guaranteed it State financial support, with a legal representational monopoly for organizational activity among students. Nonetheless, the initiative was ineffective. Separate student unions remained independent of the UNE, sometimes even defiant of it. Philippe Schmitter called this institutional reality a form of "unbalanced corporatism," as State controls lagged despite the official financial and representational monopoly.[56] Moreover, except in the 1940s, the State did not control even the UNE. And the UNE gained strength under the democratic administrations between the Estado Novo and the military coup. Its activities multiplied especially quickly during the Goulart years, immediately preceding the coup, when the UNE found the nation's president supportive of its leftist positions on populism, mobilization, and nationalization.

Therefore, the new military regime (1964) tried to replace the UNE with a National Student Directory (DNE), a more truly corporatist structure. The DNE was to be tied to higher authorities even on matters such as its own elections. As an officially sanctioned corporatist body, "the DNE had everything going for it—except the allegiance of university students."[57] It never gained importance. Not excluding the toughest years of military rule, the regime had even less success than the Estado Novo in building a corporatist student movement.

The military rulers had more success in curbing free student politics than in imposing a corporatist alternative, a contrast paralleling the Chilean case. But there was more student activity at least until 1983 in Brazil than in Chile. This reflects the long duration of Brazilian military rule and its periods of

195

more lenient rule than seen in the first decade of Chilean military rule. Hardly any student protests took place immediately following the 1964 coup, but the UNE remained alive; by summer 1965 it held an important meeting in São Paulo. By late in the year newsworthy protests occurred at the University of Brasília, and by early 1968 Brazilian students were active. Flynn concludes: "Of all the opposition groups the students were the most vocal and most conspicuous."[58] In response, the regime initially mixed repression with dialogue and reconciliation; soon, however, repression intensified, and the late 1960s–early 1970s formed the closest parallel to Chile in terms of State controls over students. One cause was the ascendency of hardliners within the regime, and another was the strength shown by students in demonstrations over vagas, verbas, and AID. Decree Law 477 (1969) clamped down on free speech and strikes. By the mid-1970s, however, the regime's "opening up" (*abertura*) allowed independent student activity to gain momentum. Starting in the late 1970s, demonstrations became common. Students revitalized the UNE and demanded a greater role in university life. Five thousand delegates met in Bahia (1979) to reorganize their free union.[59] Even while maintaining the UNE's illegality, the State permitted many of its activities and met with student leaders.

Private university students are actively involved in the new freedom movement. This can be understood in terms of sectoral and subsectoral growth. Brazil's private sector has not grown chiefly as an elite, depoliticized alternative to a politicized public sector. Its students are therefore different from those in Spanish America's depoliticized private sector. Specifically, no strong Brazilian parallel exists to Spanish America's secular elite private subsector. Instead, most private universities are found in the Catholic subsector, identified at several points in this book as the private subsector most prone to activism.

Following typical Latin American patterns, Catholic student groups were more devoted to Catholic action than political action in the early decades of Brazil's first wave. However, their public counterparts did not generally form a potent political force at that time either. In the late 1950s and early 1960s, when the Catholic student groups became politically active, they assumed leadership positions in the increasingly vibrant UNE, cooperating with Communists—and leaving the Church aghast. Military rule subsequently further diminished the private-public student politics gap by repressing student freedoms across the board. Then by 1977, as authoritarian controls weakened, student demonstrations erupted mostly at public universities but also at the PUC-Rio and the PUC–São Paulo. Reflecting the increased student activity, even the Mackenzie University was ultimately involved—but this was unusual, the first major demonstration in its history—while PUCs have been repeatedly involved.[60]

196

Intersectoral and intrasectoral patterns tell us much about not just the degree but also the type of politics manifested. Students in public universities and PUCs are by far the most involved in national political issues. They are the ones who took on the military regime and pressed strongly for *abertura*. Activism in the private isolated schools, except for the few high-quality ones, more often concerns particularistic issues involving students at those institutions. The most common issue is the tuition level (e.g., at the Souza Marques School of Medicine; 1979). In other words, Brazil's subsectors show patterns of inactivity and activity associated with those subsectors in Spanish America. The key difference is that this implies a huge subsector concerned only with particularistic issues, only a tiny depoliticized elite subsector, and a rather large Catholic subsector that most closely approximates the public sector in terms of political activity. Furthermore, no gap is obvious between the PUCs and the public universities in student propensity to participate freely within the classroom itself. Finally, the preceding analysis should not imply that university demonstrations and other signs of independence from the State have been limited to students; for example, widespread strikes by professors and workers have occurred in federal universities amid the State financial stringency of the early 1980s.

Institutions and the State

Just as the State has not extended its effective power over students nearly as far as formal provisions would allow, so it has been with State control over institutions. But the question of institutional autonomy is much more complex than the question of student autonomy from the State. Widespread criticism from opposition figures, independent experts, and certainly from State officials themselves gives ample testimony that excessive bureaucratic rigidity by the State and its education ministry hampers initiative, flexibility, and efficiency. Even public university rectors, at least since 1972, have joined a chorus calling for more decentralization.[61] Many observers believe that the public universities are just as bureaucratically crippled from innovation as are other parts of the State bureaucracy. In short, indications are strong that pervasive State bureaucracy is not simply a formal artifact, irrelevant to higher education policy. Still, analysis shows a wide gap between formal authority and actual power; it shows gaps whose extent and shape vary greatly both across and within sectors.

In addition to the state universities and the isolated schools, the public sector is chiefly divided into *autarquias* (traditional federal university structures) and *fundações* (federal universities formed since the 1960s, largely with the intent of achieving greater flexibility). As usual, interinstitutional heterogeneity is much greater within the private sector. Some PUCs, such as

PUC-Rio, have formal structures similar to the federal universities, while others, such as PUC-Bahia and PUC-Pernambuco, are very different. A major intersectoral division in structure reflects the fact that most private institutions are isolated schools, not universities. More important, differences in institutional-State ties are greater than differences in formal structures within institutions. The State bureaucracy tends to pervade the fundações less than the autarquias, but a more substantial division exists between the public sector overall and the private sector, the latter enjoying greater freedom from the State.[62] This broad statement becomes clearer through more specific reference to control over expenditures, appointments, admissions, and academic content, including course offerings.

The State's bureaucratic control over institutional expenditures falls most heavily on the autarquias. These institutions are locked into civil service and other rules reigning in the federal bureaucracy and have very limited freedom. They must pay their personnel according to wage slots set by ministerial regulations. There is no room for performance-based incentives or sanctions to attract or encourage, let alone to dismiss. Fundações can offer competitive salaries and allocate received resources in freer fashion; but strong restrictions are found even there, and not all fundações use their authority, instead lapsing into more familiar bureaucratic habits. In general, rigidity in planning and implementation is found in the public sector's budgeting process.

A pattern of mutually reinforcing inertia develops between most public universities and the State. The former cannot or do not choose to innovate, but the State too is restricted by its own procedures. Aware of the constraints, both public rectors and the MEC have sought pockets of flexibility. Rectors dutifully submit the form sheets associated with "scientific administration," but some also pursue a "bureaucratic activism" in which hired representatives figure out what might be available, what issues are popular that year, and what strategies might work. A favorite strategy is "creative crisis management," wherein potential student disorders are used, or even encouraged, to solicit State funds for particular purposes. It appears that strong rectors have become adept at obtaining extra funds. It also appears that fundações have exercised more initiative than autarquias, and to better results. On the other hand, that very flexibility has encouraged the MEC to convert particular autarquias into fundações; so if fundações are less tied to bureaucratic restrictions, cause and effect are difficult to establish. Finally, MEC subsidies do not seem to vary according to institutional quality but, based on equity criteria, may slightly favor poorer institutions. Mostly, MEC subsidies to public institutions are determined by fixed or incremental factors. For example, the great majority of MEC funds are automatically allocated according to fixed salaries.[63]

198

Whatever the limited flexibility involved in determining subsidy levels, the issue of limited institutional freedom in spending received funds remains. Room for flexible policy-making in resource distribution is much less when dealing with the basic MEC structure itself than with the newer, smaller units within it (e.g., CAPES) or outside it (e.g., FINEP). Private institutions derive very little of their annual income from the ministry and therefore are not nearly as restricted as public institutions by its bureaucracy. Their limitations in distributing resources stem much more from inadequate resources, lack of initiative, and private donor strings than from statist requirements.

Similar public-private differences appear in the control of appointments. The State role is decisive in selecting the autarquias' chief executives. The president of the republic chooses from a list of six candidates proposed by the institution's council. In fact, the president's preference is often made clear in advance and his wishes honored in the list of six. On this score, fundações have not achieved greater autonomy from the State. On the contrary, the procedure was the same until 1980 and then became less autonomous, at least briefly, as fundação heads were named directly by the president. The State's power was further suggested by the absence of a fixed term for these heads. They could be fired, or they could remain indefinitely. By comparison, autarquia rectors were given four-year terms. Appointment policy was in turmoil, however. Amid reinvigorated student politics since the late 1970s, direct State appointments sometimes sparked strong protest (e.g., at the Uberlândia University). The national clamor for direct election of the president of the republic had its higher education counterpart in widespread demands, by students and professors, for election of university rectors (both public and private) by their university communities. Before long, the State role in choosing fundação heads became less direct, more like its role in the autarquias. Still, because of the importance of certain rectorships, such as Brasília's, the regime was reluctant to open things up very far. Similarly, governors wanted to maintain a role in state universities that was broadly parallel to the president's role in federal universities. Also, other government officials had turf to protect, since public rectors were often selected through political deals struck with legislators.[64]

One of the reasons State appointment of rectors is critical is that rectors are generally powerful within their institutions. Except in some of the largest universities where rectors may have additional power bases, their strength usually derives from the State; some rectors relied heavily on the military to run their institutions. In turn, the State sometimes plays upon the rectors' apparent power for its own political ends, telling students that it sympathizes with their positions but must respect the rectors' autonomous authority. One difficulty in evaluating rector strength is that rectors are often selected because of their conformity with regime policies and there-fore do not pit their strength against the regime's. It is also difficult to weigh the rectors' powers in appointing subordinates against the persistence of the traditional Latin American mode in which a rector's power is eroded be-cause individual faculties maintain considerable autonomy from central university administration. Brazil's rectors tend to be stronger where facul-ties are weak, sometimes new. Formally, the top policy-making authority may still be the university council, based on representation from below. At least one analyst confirms the reality of rector power but cautions that, below the rector, power resides with officials not directly appointed by the State and often not in step; consequently, the widespread purges of the late 1960s often saw dissidents replaced by less famous dissidents from below.[65] On the other hand, the rector's strength increased under military rule. Moreover, the rectors and the State appoint faculty directors, albeit upon variable consultation with faculty members. Also, the enormous counter-vailing power of the chaired professors, once notoriously strong even within the general Latin American context, has been abolished. Although public university professors are still appointed as civil servants, no longer does a constitutional provision safeguard those Ribeiro called "feudal lords" who, once appointed, had "absolute power in university life."[66]

By contrast, the State has no direct role in naming private chief execu-tives. Private institutions name their own rectors, with variable Church or proprietor influence, depending on subsector. Control over appointments is especially significant because, as in the general Latin American pattern, rectors are typically more powerful in private than public institutions. Many matters that are determined by State regulation in public institutions are decided by the rector in private ones. And whereas the president has a role in appointing the public sector's faculty directors, he generally has no parallel role in the private sector. Reflecting their strong hand, private chief executives are usually appointed without a fixed term. Although it is tricky to compare the degree of verticality between the federal universities and the PUCs, most PUCs have historically been more vertical. Some changes have occurred within this subsector, however, and signs of further democratiza-tion have been noted in such important institutions as PUC–São Paulo. What is clear is that verticality is often greatest in most private isolated schools, as is the rule in demand-absorbing institutions, where appoint-ments and related decisions are fashioned from the top down.

A poignant illustration of the private sector's greater autonomy from the State regarding personnel issues arose during the military regime's most repressive stage, as Costa e Silva and the hard-liners replaced Castelo Branco. Public sector purges fell upon such respected figures as Mário Schenberg, Leite Lopes, Herman Lent, Fernando Henrique Cardoso, and

200

Florestan Fernandes. At the same time, comparatively few purges were carried out in the private sector. Although one could argue that fewer leading leftists could be found there, many of those purged in the public sector were hired by the private sector, notably by the PUCs. Obviously the regime was capable of imposing blanket blacklists on the entire higher education system, but State control over personnel decisions in the private sector was just as obviously considered a less legitimate, more extreme measure.[67]

Finally, alongside personnel decisions concerning rectors, directors, and professors lie decisions over student admissions. In fact, the State has traditionally held important powers over admissions in both sectors, insofar as it must approve all increases or decreases in quotas. This is a real limit on institutional freedom in the private as well as the public sector. But this limit does not involve criteria used by the institutions to select within their quotas. During the enrollment boom of the 1960s, the State became preoccupied with unregulated criteria, particularly in the faster-growing (private) sector. Here then is one area in which the State has attempted systemwide standardization to make the whole system more public and to diminish private distinctiveness.

Private universities were strongly urged to join in a new comprehensive testing and admissions network. Some complied while others, especially the good ones, stayed out so that they could continue to choose their own students.[68] Another reason to stay out was that administration of the examination process was financially profitable. The State forced all the reluctant public institutions into the network but not the reluctant private ones. Although the State harrassed some reluctant private institutions by reviewing their academic facilities, it never exerted sufficient pressure to standardize the admission process. Its chief threat was that it would use cooperation as one criterion in reviewing all private requests for funds, but the State itself feared that full private compliance could lead to immensely burdensome requests for public funds. Better to tolerate private autonomy in admissions. Better to exert only indirect control. Furthermore, the financial carrot and stick was never persuasive for the majority of self-financed, private isolated schools. By the mid-1970s even some PUCs came to feel that the State funds in question did not equal what they could extract in exam fees; a big blow to plans for systemwide standardization was the partial pullout of PUC-Rio in 1976.[69]

The private-public distinction also holds, but less clearly, in the area of State regulation of academic content. Private institutions do need State sanction, via the FCE, for their degrees to have national validity. Leaders of the first PUCs resented this requirement but nonetheless had to accept it as part of a compromise that underwrote the viability of their institutions.

Meanwhile, leaders of the public school movement denounced what they saw as an altogether too easy process of State validation leading to private degree equivalency. State accreditation then became a relatively trivial formality during higher education's boom period. Private isolated schools, with little legitimate claim to meeting minimal educational standards, spontaneously grew by the hundreds. Some offered diplomas without FCE recognition, hoping that lax standards and political pressures would subsequently bring such recognition. With the ministry's enforced slowdown in the mid-1970s, however, accreditation once again has become an important State function.[70]

Since most private institutions created during the boom have rather easily received accreditation equivalent with public institutions, has the State then carefully regulated their ongoing academic activities? After all, some cross-national evidence suggests that States will allow less autonomy in academic affairs if they do not appoint the (trustworthy) chief executives.[71] Within Brazil's public sector, the fundações enjoy more academic autonomy from the MEC than do the autarquias, but the fundações' rectors have sometimes been more directly appointed by the State. One might hypothesize that Brazil's private sector suffers special State interference in academic affairs because it is not headed by rectors of confidence. And one specific indication that State regulation is more severe in the private than public sector is that each private institution has assigned federal inspectors; the public ones have none. However, inspection usually involves very limited requirements, such as verifying that as many students are properly enrolled as the institutions claim. Ironically, gross distortion may be more common in the public institutions, where such distortion costs the State more in subsidies. But the State does not extend similar inspection to public institutions, part of the State's family.

Overall, private institutions must accept some academic standardization mandated for the public system, and even some extra measures of State vigilance, but it is a matter of degree in which the private sector enjoys more autonomy from the State than does its public counterpart. The private sector accepts a degree of State authority that, as it knows, is mostly exercised in a ritual, formalistic way. More serious limits on private institutions' autonomy have come from Church officials in the more traditional PUCs and especially from owners of isolated schools.

That such elaborate statist procedures for the private sector would be bypassed by the reality of substantial academic autonomy reminds us how autonomy can sometimes flourish in the public sector as well. In general, the state universities fall under the same broad MEC rules and regulations regarding structure, organization, and curriculum that hold for the private sector. Again, however, many such rules are either circumvented or allow for substantial academic autonomy. For example, curriculum guidelines are so broad, so vague, or so difficult to enforce that the great bulk of policy-making power over classroom matters resides with faculties, departments, and individual professors. At least in São Paulo's state universities, the government role in academic policy-making is preponderantly a state role, not a federal one, despite provisions for nationwide standardization. As usual, autonomy probably reaches its height at the most prestigious institutions, such as USP. Thus, universities may be granted greater freedom from bureaucratic vigilance than granted to isolated schools. This could be one reason that the Cândido Mendes chain of schools has petitioned for university status. The major safeguards of freedom from State control for most isolated schools lie in their collective proliferation and their individual insignificance.

If private institutions maintain more autonomy than public ones from the State in ongoing academic policy-making, they may still be subject to special vigilance when attempting any institutional changes. In practice, they may have more difficulty than public ones in obtaining State approval for curriculum changes or added fields of study. Big federal universities sometimes have such great political power that a ministerial challenge would be a bad risk. Mostly, however, federal universities are less likely to run into trouble because they are less likely to attempt innovation.[72] That the State is not the major obstacle to academic change is suggested when newer, more flexible, public universities go ahead with reforms while older ones languish; this sometimes reflects the fundação-autarquia split. At least one study finds that State criteria for authorization of new courses are neutral as far as private versus public is concerned. Criteria instead revolve around a loose blend of factors such as institutional (financial and administrative) capacity, professional quality, and the necessity or usefulness of the proposed course. Good quality alone usually has been sufficient. When growth was intense, course approval was common regardless of institutional affiliation, though a major complaint even then concerned the ministry's sluggishness. State approval may have been merely a formality, but institutions could wait years for it. Between 1962 and 1973, 79 percent of all proposals were approved. Then came the enforced slowdown. Whereas 278 proposals were approved in 1972, only 86 were approved in 1975.[73] The change fell principally on the private sector because that was where the most rapid growth had occurred.

In sum, there is insufficient evidence to conclude that the State regulates academic change more significantly in the private than public sector. Broadening the question to academic policy in general, the private sector is more autonomous because it need not comply with so much of the standardization mandated for the public sector. Adding such findings to evidence on control over expenditures and appointments leads to the strong conclusion that Brazil's private institutions are fundamentally freer from State control than are Brazil's public institutions, even though the latter are much freer than bureaucratic formalities would indicate.

Public Sector Reform

Discontent has been widespread over the governance structure in the public sector, the paradoxical combination of excessive bureaucratic centralism on the books, and the ineffective, ad hoc policy-making in reality. Many of the key reforms proposed and attempted would make public sector governance a bit more like private sector governance. Brazilian attempts to increase public flexibility in an overbureaucratized public system are somewhat reminiscent of French efforts in 1968. Other European efforts, or the Venezuelan attempt to create public experimental universities, could also be cited. Brazil's push for public sector reform illustrates well the growth of U.S. over traditional European influences in Latin American higher education, as noted in chapter 1.[74]

The main push for reform came with the creation of the first public fundação, the University of Brasília (1962). One major goal was to weaken both the administrative bottom and top while strengthening the middle, a move away from the Continental and toward the U.S. model. Thus chairs would be abolished and departments would substitute for faculties. Departments would be much more interrelated and much more tied to a general university structure, whereas faculties had been isolated, inward-looking entities. Students would be admitted to the university, not to one of its individual faculties, and would be required to take a basic course of study before choosing their field of specialization. University administration would therefore have greater responsibilities and would pull from below and from above the powers to meet them. Illustrating this change and paralleling recent European efforts in this direction, rectors would be managers, not just senior professors drawn from the faculties. Tasks previously handled here and there throughout the university would now be centralized. This centralization within the institution was geared toward a decentralization of the higher education system by transferring some ministerial bureaucracy to institutional bureaucracy, thereby increasing the latitude for institutional choice. Needless to say, the attempt was denounced by critics as an effort to Americanize and privatize Brazilian public higher education. While the second part of the charge is subject to varied interpretations, the first part is clearly correct, reflecting the important influence of collaborative work between Brazil's education ministry and AID, and then reflecting the consulting efforts of "modernizer" Rudolph Atcon.

The fundação idea has in fact yielded partial success. Although the

University of Brasília ran into early political problems with the military because of involvement with pre-coup leftism, the university served as a model for other new institutions. Most of the intended structural reforms were implemented, though to varying degrees. Thus Brazil's public sector developed an alternative to its Continental model of uncoordinated, autonomous, professionally oriented faculties. In 1966 another reform law pushed further for institutional centralization and flexibility. Although fundações were explicitly created as alternatives to traditional public sector structures, the reform was aimed with varying degrees of intensity throughout the public sector. Autarquias were supposed to modernize themselves, and even the state University of São Paulo consequently altered its credit, chair, and department structures. Still further afield, the private sector was involved. For example, PUCs were enjoined to alter their traditional structures in step with the reforms. Such alterations complemented the changing complexions of many PUCs.

The exact extent of implemented reforms in these different institutions is not clear. In general, there have been mixed results. The idea of greater autonomy from the State obviously became a carefully circumscribed one post-1964. Thus, for example, the University of Brasília could hardly count on its fundação status to protect itself from the regime control and purges of the late 1960s. From the institutions' end, many reforms were pursued much more in word than deed. Such was the case with the new "departments" supposedly replacing traditional faculties.

Considering that a modern authoritarian regime took power in 1964, it may be surprising that reforms backed by the State would be so sporadically and ineffectively implemented in the public sector, indeed that institutional autonomy would not have been much more thoroughly undone. Clearly, the regime was not as unrelentingly repressive in higher education policy as was its Chilean counterpart. For one thing, the Brazilian regime did not move immediately into its full-blown hard-line posture. For another, its repression abated a bit by the mid-1970s with abertura, and certain prominent opposition figures, such as ex-rector Darcy Ribeiro, were allowed back into the country. As the decade ended and the 1980s began, the abertura widened considerably, as reflected in renewed student politics.

Even in its more repressive period, the Brazilian regime never tried to remold higher education policy on the ostensibly rationalized and antipublic design pursued in Chile.[75] Its rationalization attempt started with a shift of power from the education to the planning ministry, but so stiff was opposition by students, media, and the middle class in general that the planning ministry soon gave up and turned its attention to secondary education. Leftist students and many faculties claimed that the modernization or Americanization of Brazilian public higher education would transfer power from traditionally strong faculties to those modern ones in step with the desires of multinational corporations, precisely when the concern should be democratization and equity. Here then was a classic confrontation pitting domestic and foreign capitalists, supported by the State, against a coalition of university interests defending traditional values enshrined in many public universities in Latin America. For a regime basing its legitimacy and strength largely on middle-class support, the costs of forced imposition would have been too great. The regime's retreat was facilitated by two factors: leftist or populist interests had not previously controlled Brazil's public sector for as long as they had controlled Chile's or even Argentina's, and the regime could push majority enrollments into a private sector run in a fairly conservative manner—a sector that did not subsist on State funds. The existence of such important private-public differences from pre-coup days helps explain why the Brazilian regime, unlike the Chilean regime, concentrated its repressive efforts more on the public than the private sector. Even in the public sector, however, there was no basic change of structure, no imposition of tuition, and no enrollment and subsidy freeze at all comparable to the Chilean case. Instead, enrollments and expenditures soared, and Brazilian universities entered perhaps their "golden age" in social sciences. Political science took hold in places such as the state universities of USP and Campinas in São Paulo and the federal universities of Minas Gerais and Rio Grande do Sul. And the dominant school in Brazilian social science is Marxism, however loosely construed.[76]

Despite its failures to rationalize "undergraduate" education, or partly because of them, the regime (with support from many academics) has effectively insisted on enclaves for graduate education and research. But in addition to the enclaves within universities, most of which are public, such activities have moved increasingly into separate institutes, most of which are private and many of which are substantially autonomous from State control.[77]

Overall, then, efforts at reform have produced only mixed results in moving the system away from the stultifying effects of bureaucratic centralism. Some success has been achieved within the public universities, particularly by fundações, and some has been achieved outside the university structure. More important, however, statist regulations have not proven as stultifying in practice as they appear on the books. Many public universities have achieved significant degrees of autonomy from the State in determining what to teach and whom to hire below the rectorship level. It remains the private sector, nonetheless, that has offered the quantitatively most important organizational alternative to the statist pattern. More than public institutions, private ones have exercised autonomy from the State in allocating their resources, appointing their personnel, selecting students, setting work conditions, and, to a lesser extent, in setting their substantive academic policy. All this offers no small contribution to values of societal autonomy from the State.

FUNCTION

Compared to the pronounced private-public differences in governance, and especially in finance, differences in functions pursued and achieved are, as usual, somewhat narrower. Even to the extent that he who pays the piper calls the tune, nothing prevents separate pipers from calling similar tunes. One indicator of a degree of private-public homogeneity is personnel overlap. Many professors work part time in both private and public institutions. Additionally, the Council of Rectors of Brazilian Universities, a private organization composed of the chief executives of all Brazil's universities, presses for mutual interests. Another factor limiting private-public distinctiveness has been the comparative absence of a secular elite subsector. This absence reflects the fact that the public sector never transformed itself through massification, radicalism, and slipping prestige in the same way that many Spanish American counterparts did; as a result, there has been less felt need to create an elite backlash private alternative. It was largely the lack of an elite private subsector that was crucial to Chile's private-public homogeneity in function. In Brazil, however, a distinctive secular private subsector did develop. Insofar as this subsector seeks legitimacy and enrollments more than explicit distinctiveness from a failing public sector, it does not offer the sort of choice boasted by elite subsectors; a private sector based on Catholic and demand-absorbing subsectors is not likely to be as functionally distinct from the public sector as is a private sector with a strong elite subsector. But this lesser distinctiveness is still substantial. Moreover, the shape of private-public distinctiveness tends to be different in Brazil as compared to Spanish America. We can explore the actual degree and shape of Brazil's private-public distinctiveness in function by focusing on religious orientations, fields of study and job-market orientations, and academic quality.

Religious Orientations

As in Chile, and indeed in much of Latin America, private-public distinctiveness in function is narrowed insofar as Catholic universities have rarely pursued religious orientations to the degree envisioned by their creators and insofar as even their rather limited religious pursuits have declined over time. In Brazil, however, such factors assume special significance because Catholic institutions account for seventeen of twenty private universities.[78]

207

The decline of religiousness in the Catholic subsector can be traced, as in much of Latin America, to environmental stresses and organizational responses. The environmental stresses have included both ecclesiastical and secular currents. Vatican II represented a major turning point in ecclesiastical thinking, away from some of the more orthodox beliefs that had originally led to the creation of Brazil's private higher education sector. Church liberalization narrowed the gap between Church and secular society.

From the secular side, significant changes in society at large, including rising concern over national development, conceived in materialistic terms, also undermined the Catholic leadership's rationale for distinctive institutions. At the primary and secondary levels, there was even some thought of turning Catholic schools over to the public school system.[79] Fewer and fewer students chose Catholic universities specifically because the universities were Catholic or because they themselves were Catholic. An additional environmental stress on the PUCs was that the public sector, even as early as the 1940s, was not offering sufficient places to meet the demand of qualified secondary school graduates; the PUCs consequently attracted students who cared little about any distinctly Catholic alternative.

Instead of resisting such environmental stresses in order to preserve distinctive religious choice, the PUCs generally adapted to them. As fewer nonreligious students refrained from applying to the PUCs, so fewer were prevented from entering. Agnostics and atheists were acceptable. This opening up occurred not just in student admissions but also in the appointment of professors and even administrators. The professorial change naturally came first in fields such as mathematics and the exact sciences, proceeding to fields in which religious orientations might once have been stronger. A good early example was the creation (1948) of a polytechnic school at PUC-Rio. The school offered strictly technical courses without Catholic orientations. PUC-Rio opened the school at the request of professors at the National School of Engineering, then the only such institution in Rio; the professors pointed out that they simply could not meet growing student demands.[80]

PUC-Rio, one of the most important Catholic universities, also illustrates lay penetration all the way to administrative ranks, although this penetration is still circumscribed. Going by identified listings in the university's catalog, the rector and either three or four of the five vice-rectors are priests. Similarly, the heads of the university's six centers include four priests; the four include both the theology-humanities and social science heads but not the biology-medicine head. As one goes further down the administrative hierarchy, however, lay representation increases sharply. The rector's cabinet, involved with juridical, planning, and other administrative functions, has no priests among its six members. Very few of the university's twenty-five department heads are priests. Only five members of the seventeen-member university council are priests, including three vice-rectors and two Church representatives. On the individual councils of the six centers are a total of ninety-four members, only thirteen of whom (14 percent) are priests, including the deans' memberships. Even in the theology-humanities center priests are in a small minority.[81] Note further that most of the priests execute their university duties as administrators or professors first, as priests only thereafter. Of course, the university's grand chancellor is Rio's archbishop, but the former has become largely a figurehead role.

Along with personnel changes, there have been equally profound accommodations in curriculum. Most PUCs still require certain theology and philosophy courses, and these are rarely taught by atheists. But they are generally taught "openly," like the social science courses. Professors who insist on "old-fashioned approaches" are spurned by most students. Moreover, as with Catholic universities in much of Latin America, Brazil's PUCs engage in much curriculum copying from the public universities, outside the most religiously sensitive fields. This copying has been based partly on convenience, partly on the need to achieve legitimacy and attract students, and partly on the need to conform to the State's system-wide bureaucratic provisions.

In short, the evolving function of the PUCs reminds one of Jencks and Riesman's famous account of the shifting role of U.S. Catholic institutions in the "academic revolution." Salém has written that the PUCs, in pursuing a "highly respectable teaching staff, have guaranteed their success as centers of excellence but, on the other hand, and in a paradoxical way, ended up by betraying their goal of serving as evangelical vehicles." No special Catholic elite would be trained, and the envisioned "confessional profile" would not emerge. "The initial project conceived for the PUCs . . . never could even be tested." Instead, PUCs were set within various environmental pressures "that upset the ideal route proclaimed at their creation."[82]

The original dream of Catholic universities to re-Christianize State and society has been dead for some time. This death is implicitly recognized by the lost desire, even prior to the military coup, to create new PUCs. Chapter 2 shows that Brazil's first twelve private universities (1930–61) were religiously affiliated, the next nine (1961–70) secular; additionally, the explosion of private isolated schools has been overwhelmingly secular. Here is a reflection that the PUCs have formed a typical Latin American first-wave phenomenon—a very diminished proportion of the private sector now has a religious affiliation. Moreover, those Catholic institutions in existence never did, or at least do not today, offer many effective religious alternatives to the public sector. The religious issue no longer raises the same high-pitched discord it once did, despite occasional faint echoes of outbursts against "the priests" or against the "godless sector."

Field and Job-Market Orientations

Where the religious-public dichotomy came to have diminished importance in most of Latin America, a second wave of private universities generally arose with a dedication to secular modernization reflected by field and job-market orientations. But despite some partial exceptions, Brazil produced few such universities; instead it developed its very large subsector of demand-absorbing institutions. Partially offsetting this, Brazil's Catholic subsector is rather large and parallels the field patterns generally found in Spanish America's academically creditable Catholic universities. What results, then, is a degree of private-public distinctiveness in Brazilian field distributions that does not markedly deviate in most respects from that dominating in Spanish America but which is shaped by somewhat different factors. The Mexican case showed that two preoccupations of the private sector were to offer inexpensive courses and courses related to private enterprise. The two overlapped considerably; where they did not, cost tended to be a more compelling factor, especially in the demand-absorbing subsector. As the Mexican case also suggests, but as will be shown much more substantially in chapter 6, the Catholic subsector tends to be less influenced by these two factors and therefore offers the least field distinctiveness from the public sector. On the one hand, Brazil's and Spanish America's subsectors show notable similarities in function; on the other hand, the relative importance of the subsectors varies. Overall, private-public distinctiveness proves ample in Brazil, despite the Catholic subsector's importance and the elite subsector's unimportance, because of how the large demand-absorbing subsector differs from the public sector.

Brazil's most lamented problems regarding the distribution of students by field of study are hardly unique. Too many students are in human and social sciences, too few in natural and applied sciences, most observers agree. Also common, from the Continental legacy, is early specialization. Most students are already on a career track in secondary school. Although higher education reforms establishing one or two years of basic study have helped, they have not changed the picture fundamentally. At first, the military regime hoped to reshape field distributions, but its acquiescence to booming expansion dashed those hopes. Most expansion shot into the private isolated schools, where distributions were off target.[83]

Given the reasons for its growth, Brazil's private higher education sector could logically be expected to present a "less desirable" field distribution profile than does the public sector. Brazil's private sector is its "mass" sector, and most of its students are unlikely to jump into demanding academic programs. Moreover, they cannot afford to pay their way through more expensive courses of study. This atypical factor of having less-privileged students in the private sector must be added to a more typical one in Latin America—private institutions must generate their own income and thus have a strong built-in tendency to offer inexpensive fields. Finally, to generate their own resources many private institutions, especially the behaviorally profit-making ones in the group, try to attract as many students as possible. Consequently, many private institutions concentrate on offering courses that appeal to students, whether or not the courses also please private enterprises.[84] This is not to say, however, that private institutions fully gratify student demand. For example, medicine is the most desired field, but it is expensive to offer, so the private sector forces students to settle for fields such as business administration. Brazil's private sector gratifies demand for some higher education, but it is Brazil's public sector that more fully gratifies those students it does accept. Brazil's public sector offers the most desired fields, thus compounding its quality and no-cost advantages. In fields of study as well as in evolution, there is some reason to associate Brazil's private sector with access and its public sector with choice. As chapter 6 elaborates, these dynamics are different in Spanish America.

Available evidence, shown in table 5.3, substantiates hypothesized private-public differences based on cost. Private enrollments concentrate most heavily in the "human sciences" (social sciences) and letters. In these fields three-fourths of the enrollments are private; in no other fields do private enrollments reach that sector's share (64 percent) of total enrollments. Lest its respectable 57 percent of exact sciences and technologies be deceiving, Schwartzman points out that Brazil's "mathematics" refers basically to training secondary school teachers and therefore should be grouped more with education than applied sciences.[85] Private enrollments are especially low in the agricultural sciences as well as in biology and health professions. It seems clear that the private sector emphasizes the less expensive fields.[86] Still the private sector holds a substantial share of every field category except for agriculture. As the last column shows, private-public percentages are much the same for graduated as for enrolled students (except in the arts).

If we explicitly categorize "more desirable" and "less desirable" fields according to widely used criteria of national development needs and allow for gross oversimplification, the public sector shows a favorable 54 to 46 percent breakdown versus an unfavorable private 37 to 63 percent breakdown.[87] This sharp invidious contrast is sustained by the public sector's combination of three advantages—less preoccupation with cost, no tuition, and greater exclusiveness in admissions (or attention to quality).

Private-public field differentiation is mostly based on the university–isolated school cleavage. Cunha finds that, within the public sector, universities attracted most engineering and medicine students while isolated schools attracted most humanities and social science students in the 1970–72 enrollment boom.[88] The private-public distinction is sharp because the public sector is primarily composed of universities, the private sector of isolated schools. Whereas the schools often concentrate on just one field, universities have traditionally been expected to offer at least law, medicine, and engineering, and now to offer courses in at least four "basic areas."[89]

Private-public differences are far smaller within the university than within the whole higher education system. We get some indication from available data on Catholic institutions. These enrollments are overwhelmingly (71 percent; 1977) in the university sector. Catholic institutions comprise 24 percent of the university sector compared to 16 percent of higher education overall. For 1977, Catholic institutions claimed anywhere from 22 percent to 24 percent of Brazil's total first-year offerings in engineering, general sciences, and biological sciences as well as in physics, architecture, and urban studies. As is nearly always the case for Latin America's private institutions, medicine (9 percent) and dentistry (12 percent) are underrepresented. Yet the Catholic subsector is proportionally overrepresented in engineering and scientific fields where Brazilian private institutions as a whole are underrepresented.[90] Finally, basic similarities in enrollments by field of study are reinforced by similarities in curriculum content among universi-

Table 5.3 Brazilian Enrollments by Field of Study, 1980

Field	Private	%	Public	%	Total	% in Private Sector	Graduates[a]
Human sciences	536,736	60.6	183,347	37.2	720,083	74.5	(77.5)
Letters	54,677	6.2	28,354	5.8	83,031	65.9	(73.1)
Exact sciences and technologies	195,266	22.1	145,841	29.6	341,107	57.2	(58.2)
Arts	13,707	1.5	13,428	2.7	27,135	50.5	(71.8)
Biology and health professions	71,834	8.1	93,974	19.1	165,808	43.3	(38.9)
Agricultural sciences	4,320	0.5	27,149	5.5	31,469	13.7	(13.2)
Basic cycle	8,514	1.0	139	0.0	8,653	98.4	—
Total[b]	885,054	100.0	492,232	99.9	1,377,286	64.3	(66.4)

Source: Raulino Tramontin and Ronald Braga, "O ensino superior particular no Brasil," in Cândido Mendes and Cláudio de Moura Castro, eds., *Qualidade, expansão e financiamento do ensino superior privado* (Brasília: Educam ABM, 1984), pp. 41, 43.
 a. Private sector percentage of 1979 graduates.
 b. Figures differ slightly from those cited in footnote 1.

ties. Specializing in law or biology in a public university is like specializing in law or biology in a Catholic university. Such similarities reflect both bureaucratic standardization and the limited religious orientation of Catholic universities.

Notwithstanding the Catholic subsector's contribution, the State is understandably concerned about the concentration of first-degree enrollments in inexpensive and less-desired fields. The problem is compounded by an unusual public sector configuration—the absence of a dual university-technical structure comparable to those found in most of Latin America—although technical studies are taught within some universities and although some isolated schools resemble small technical institutes. Lacking the same sort of private elite or distinct technical sectors found elsewhere in Latin America, Brazil has instead made special efforts to insure that graduate education meets basic development needs.[91]

Unable to claim the distinctive function of serving modern development through its field distributions, the private sector must emphasize its extraordinary contribution in providing access to higher education. The contribution cannot be questioned, especially when more privileged students tend to concentrate in the public sector. Nonetheless, the private sector does not especially serve Brazil's poorer regions. On the contrary, whereas 46 percent of all public institutions are in the prosperous southeast, 75 percent of private ones are there. Stated differently, 83 percent of the southeast institutions, compared to only 18 percent of institutions in the impoverished northeast, are private. As usual, the isolated school phenomenon plays a major role. The five states of São Paulo, Rio, Rio Grande do Sul, Minas Gerais, and Paraná housed 652 of the 822 (79 percent) listed isolated schools in 1980. Not that much private-public difference existed among isolated schools: of the private ones, 83 percent were concentrated in the five states; of the public ones, 69 percent were thus concentrated. Yet the private concentration by region holds among universities as well. Whereas 14 of 45 public universities (31 percent) were concentrated in São Paulo, Rio, and Rio Grande do Sul, 14 of 20 private universities (70 percent) were concentrated there.[92]

The strong tendency of the private sector to respond to demand, but only in limited, inexpensive ways, shapes not only field and regional distributions but also employment. In most of Latin America, private sector graduates have an edge on the job market, but not in Brazil. Graduation from the private rather than the public sector is at best a neutral factor, leaving job placement to depend on field specialization and institutional quality. Neither works to the private sector's advantage. While quality will be analyzed shortly, we have already seen that the private sector is underrepresented in fields such as exact sciences as opposed to human sciences. The

213

private sector starts with a decided disadvantage because its enrollments concentrate in isolated schools offering fields already glutting the job market.

In short, the public diploma generally goes further than the private one on the job market, public or private.[93] Where Latin America's private sectors have penetrated State employment, they have generally done so based on their prestigious universities. Thus we would not expect such private penetration in Brazil; instead, historical evidence points to the traditional Latin American pattern of recruitment from public universities, through student politics, into public political life.[94] On the other hand, Brazil does not have the sharp ideological private-public differentiation, found in Mexico and elsewhere, that can be an obstacle to private access to State positions; conservative rule has often minimized ideological obstacles to private access. In any case, where the State has not felt itself adequately served by its public universities, for the most part it has not responded by turning toward the private sector. Rather, it has tried to fortify graduate education and has relied heavily on its own schools to train needed personnel. The most famous, or infamous, case is obviously the Superior War College, instrumental in preparing the armed forces to feel competent to take and maintain political power.[95] Other important programs include the Itamarati, or foreign service institute, and aeronautical and engineering institutes, as well as an administrative school tied to the treasury ministry. And as noted earlier, Petrobrás is an example of a State agency that carries out research functions.

More striking, even private enterprise has not relied principally on the private sector, defying a Spanish American pattern. By the late 1970s there was a marked tendency for many businesses to train their own people. Financially capable, these businesses could spend lavishly on facilities and offer good salaries for instructors—thereby worsening teaching quality in higher education institutions, which, because of their low salary scales, have great difficulty competing with State salaries and attracting good full-time personnel. Private enterprise need not depend on either private higher education or public higher education for its work force. The point is illustrated by a quick comparison between São Paulo and Mexico's Nuevo León. Both states are leaders in industrial and commercial activity. Their economic elites have both effectively engaged in politics primarily to influence important decisions concerning their economic interests.[96] Both have also linked their work force needs to the higher education system. But whereas Nuevo León's economic elite pointedly relies on its own private higher education system, the São Paulo elite is not as overwhelmingly tied to any one sector.

On the other hand, a vital link exists between Brazil's private sector and employment. The great majority of its students, more than in the public sector, are employed before entering studies, and many work while studying. They are seeking, often through night school, to buoy their prospects for better work. In some respects, then, the threat facing them is underemployment or job dissatisfaction more than unemployment.[97] Such points bear attention when considering Spanish America's demand-absorbing subsector.

QUALITY

A major obstacle to preferred employment, and one faced more by private sector than public sector graduates, is low educational quality. It is not surprising that Brazil's private sector is academically inferior to its public one, given growth based on public sector exclusiveness and private sector absorption of leftover demand. Mass sectors are likely to be inferior academically. A cycle then develops in which inferior institutions generally attract inferior students and professors.[98]

Most, though not all, of Brazil's private-public quality gap has to do with the isolated school–university gap. Roughly 40 percent of all students enter private isolated schools that have weak financial, laboratory, library, and instructional resources. These schools have a disproportionally high percentage of Brazil's nighttime and working students.[99] Most offer just one or two fields of study.

One could consider a number of indicators of public superiority in academic quality, for example, public preponderance in graduate studies[100] or expenditure per pupil. The public sector spends much more than the private sector. Even focusing on universities alone, the difference in expenditures is three to one. Of course, as in Mexico, there are difficulties with this measure. Public universities offer more of the expensive professional studies. And private universities claim to be more economically efficient, a claim probably supported by most experts.[101] Private institutions are clearly cost conscious. More than in public institutions, students and professors must show up for class, and administrators take a greater role in enforcing efficient procedures throughout the institutions. At the extreme, profit-making isolated schools may operate like factories, with very rigid procedures—including punch-in clocks for professors. Discipline along with outside work obligations may also help explain the slightly higher dropout rate in private, rather than public, institutions.[102]

Another possible indicator is the student/professor ratio. Before the boom, private and public institutions were well matched—4.1:1 in the private sector versus 4.5:1 in the public. Then with private deterioration under the weight of enrollment increases, the balance changed. By 1981 it was 18.0:1 private versus 8.4:1 public. Additionally, private institutions employ fewer than 20 percent of Brazil's full-time professors, and roughly 70 percent of professors holding the M.A. or Ph.D. teach in the public sector.[103]

Public superiority is also suggested by indexes of selectivity. Public institutions are far more selective, accepting (1982) only one of six applicants while private ones accept one of three. Moreover, those differences hold even though the public sector gets applications from students who score higher on admission exams; of course the tuition gap helps make the public sector more attractive.[104]

All that said, no comparison of private and public quality should overlook the key factor that average quality, or at least prestige, is decreasing in both sectors, notwithstanding advances at the forefront of many fields, for example in the social sciences. Whereas in Spanish America elite private sectors have developed as sanctuaries from the perceived deleterious effects of system expansion, in Brazil that role has been left more to the public sector. But this is an inherently difficult role for public sectors. While Brazil could push most new enrollments into the private sector, it could not prevent massive growth in the public sector as well. It is easier to deviate from the dominant Spanish American pattern by having relatively inclusive private sectors, or subsectors, than to deviate by preserving relatively exclusive public sectors. Furthermore, lack of exclusiveness probably implies declining quality when the higher education system rests atop a very weak secondary system in which only a restricted subsector provides top-notch graduates. In both higher education sectors, expansion has merely "postponed students' professional frustration for a few years. Instead of frustrating them at the point of entrance, the frustration now occurs after graduation." Meanwhile, the system's student/teacher ratio has risen steadily, from 4:1 in 1962 to 13:1 by 1979.[105]

Even in the absence of a well-defined sector of excellence, the system has developed definite interinstitutional differences. This is not a system of uniform calibre. Private and public quality overlap according to institution, with some public advantage probably even within the university sector. Brazil's best university, judged by reputation, staff, and articles published in internationally recognized scientific journals, is USP (the State University of São Paulo).[106] Indeed, regional factors figure in private-public overlap. The richest states have some good private and public institutions as well as many inferior ones, while the poorest states often do not have similarly high-quality institutions in either sector. São Paulo certainly leads, with the Mackenzie University, the state universities of USP and Campinas, and the PUCs of São Paulo and Campinas. The best federal universities are mostly in the biggest states, such as Rio and Minas Gerais. Within the public sector, fundações are generally considered superior to the autarquias. Within the

216

private sector, the Mackenzie University and the PUCs in Rio and São Paulo stand out, but not the PUCs of Bahia and Pernambuco. Even the nonuniversity sector has its elite institutions; however, they are often research oriented. Among these are the School of Medicine in São Paulo, the Getúlio Vargas Foundation, and certain parts of the Cândido Mendes network, most notably the IUPERJ. Additionally, different institutions hold distinct advantages in certain fields even while they are inferior in others. For example, in Rio the federal university is considered better than the state university, but the latter probably holds the edge in law. Finally, an important and increasing degree of quality as well as SES stratification is accomplished by allowing only the best students into certain fields while forcing others to accept less prestigious ones, such as medicine versus letters. This sort of quality stratification reinforces the tendency toward public superiority, since the public sector offers many more positions than the private sector in the prestigious fields.[107]

IMPLICATIONS

Brazilian experience shows that private sectors need not be small, exclusive, or superior to public ones. They need not necessarily blossom principally as effective, elite, depoliticized alternatives to ballooning and slipping public institutions. They need not provide privileged choice, even where there is intersectoral distinctiveness. It is noteworthy, nonetheless, that many of the characteristics normally associated with private sectors find expression. Various actors—students, professors, researchers, private enterprises, the State—create functional differentiation somewhere within the higher education system. Indeed chapter 7 briefly considers whether a logical affinity exists between private sectors and many of the traits empirically concentrated in that sector in most of Spanish America but not in Brazil. At any rate, the Brazilian case affords an in-depth look at some very different relationships among evolution, finance, governance, and function, from those found previously.

Despite the important differences between dominant Brazilian and Spanish American patterns, private-public distinctiveness is fundamental to understanding higher education in both settings. In degree, this distinctiveness is less in Brazil than in Mexico, but not clearly less than in many other Latin American nations. In shape, private-public distinctiveness is largely parallel between Brazil and most of Spanish America in some areas, especially financial ones. In other areas, especially those involving functions, the shape of private-public distinctiveness diverges between the two regions.

Both what is typical and what is atypical by degree about Brazilian private-public patterns can be understood at least partly in terms of the

State's role. The late development of an active Brazilian State promoted the development of an extraordinarily large private sector, which was reinforced by the military's control of the State when massive enrollment growth occurred. The shape of private-public distinctiveness in finance, governance, and function stems largely from this private-public evolution. But the Brazilian State–higher education relationship has not been a product merely of historical circumstances. Rather, the State continues to use and mold private-public distinctiveness to its own ends. This is just what the Mexican and other States have done, but the different private-public configuration in Brazil naturally means that the State uses different policies. For example, it looks mostly to the public sector to meet trained work force and other quality needs, while using the private sector largely to limit its own financial burden, to meet politically important demands for access, and to protect the public sector from the full impact of those demands. The Brazilian State can be most appropriately and generally viewed, at least in terms of its higher education policies, as neither inherently proprivate nor propublic but prepared to use dual sectors to meet diverse needs and face diverse challenges.

Finally, the special private-public configuration found in Brazil has been understood in the context of our evolutionary waves and ensuing subsectors. However different Brazil is from the dominant Spanish American tendencies, the difference lies less in the existence of wholly unique features than in very different balances of features found elsewhere. Specifically, the private-public patterns found in Brazil, whether we are dealing with finance, governance, or function, are based on the enormous size of the demand-absorbing sector, juxtaposed to a moderately large Catholic university subsector, a tiny secular elite subsector, and a comparatively restrictive and prestigious public sector.

Just as Chile was used partly to highlight the dynamics of Catholic subsectors, and Mexico, more so, to highlight the dynamics of secular elite subsectors, so Brazil has been especially helpful in probing demand-absorbing subsectors. Having studied markedly different sectors and consequent private-public patterns in depth, we can now consider subsectoral as well as intersectoral balances in evaluating private-public patterns beyond these three nations.

6 Overview of Latin America

The three case study chapters have provided in-depth analyses of the major patterns of evolution, finance, governance, and function. At least two formidable and interrelated problems block our advance from those analyses to an empirical overview for Latin America. The first is that we must establish the relative weight of each pattern throughout the region. The second is that the patterns are clearer in the three case studies than in Latin America generally. This is true for Chile's private-public homogeneity, based largely on the private universities' approximation of their public counterparts; for Mexico's private-public distinctiveness, based on the secular elite universities' clear dominance within the private sector; and for Brazil's private-public distinctiveness, with its unusually large demand-absorbing private subsector. Whatever the qualifications already made in each case study, further qualifications are necessary as we move into wider and more complex terrain. At the same time, the three cases prove to be useful guides in understanding most systems because either the systems or especially their subsectors approximate the three types. Thus, the cases, and the patterns they illustrate, help us structure the analysis and findings concerning Latin America in general.

FINANCE

The three national cases have revealed three different private-public financial patterns. These can be labeled homogeneous (Chile), dichotomously distinctive (Mexico), and qualified distinctive (Brazil).

In Chile, since the 1960s the private sector has relied virtually as much as the public sector on State finance. But since the rightist military coup of 1973, the existing private and public sectors alike have been forced to rely on mixed State-private finance; only the creation of new private institutions

219

that receive no State finance has begun to replace private-public homogeneity with some distinctiveness. In contrast, no major changes have affected the Mexican private-public balance in the half century since the private sector's creation. The private sector has continued to draw its income almost completely from private sources. Meanwhile, the public sector has moved beyond predominant to nearly absolute dependence on State funds. Private-public distinctiveness has also characterized Brazil, but with exceptions. While the private sector has not received State finance for the basic annual costs of undergraduate education, the situation is different for expenses related to plant facilities, graduate education, and research; all this has meant State aid for private universities (rather than private isolated schools), and these are mostly Catholic. The State has even considered direct, annual subsidization of the private universities. Until now, however, finance has depended overwhelmingly on the private-public sectoral distinction, especially as the isolated schools have held most of the private enrollments.

Table 6.1 sketches these three private-public financial patterns. Note that the public sector always relies chiefly on the State. Private-public variation, therefore, depends mostly on the private sector's income source.

The three private-public patterns provide a framework within which to extend the financial analysis to Latin America inclusively. I intend to establish the relative weight of each pattern and to see how well the three together cover regional variation. After a brief look at the only available aggregate

Table 6.1 Three Financial Patterns in Latin America

| | Private Sector's Major Income Source | | | |
Type of Pattern	Basic Annual Costs	Capital Costs	Research and Graduate Costs	Public Sector's Major Income Source
Homogeneous (Chile)[a]	State	State	State	State
Dichotomously distinctive (Mexico)	private	private	private	State
Qualified distinctive (Brazil)	private	mixed[b]	State	State

SOURCE: Chapters 3–5.
a. The Chilean pattern differs before the 1960s and after the 1970s.
b. The State may supplement private sources for the Catholic universities, but not for demand-absorbing isolated schools.

220

data, the analysis turns to accumulated evidence on public sectors and on each private subsector (Catholic, elite, demand absorbing).

The only data purporting to cover Latin America inclusively come from UDUAL for 1962 and 1971. While the public sector is easily more than 80 percent dependent on the State, the private sector's dependence is less than 30 percent. Table 6.2 shows the figures, but unfortunately the categories in table 6.2 are not well defined. Apparently, "private" refers to donations and "own income" refers to tuition and other charges. "Other" should refer to non-State income but could sometimes refer to indirect State subsidies. In any case, the private-public sectoral differences are clearly fundamental. Furthermore, there is no evidence of diminishing distinctiveness, at least in the 1960s.

Yet even these figures seriously underestimate private-public distinctiveness. Some private universities underreport their private income, either to minimize evidence of privilege or to plead convincingly for State funds. More important, UDUAL data are based on universities, not on all institutions of higher education (see Appendixes A and B). The single major omission concerns the majority of Brazil's private institutions. Also, data are compiled only from those institutions that respond to census queries. All this leaves out many more demand-absorbing institutions than Catholic or elite universities. As indicated below, demand-absorbing institutions are the least likely to receive State funds.[1]

The Public Sector

The aggregate data provide a general but very inexact orientation. A fuller view comes from examining the different sectors more closely. The public sector's income profile is less complex than the private sector's. The State dominates. Argentina is a leading example of this extreme. Its national universities have received 99.75 percent of their income from the State and a mere 0.25 percent from "specific sources." Tuition has been free, for foreign students as well as Argentines. Among nations associated with less statist profiles, a trend in recent decades has been (as in Mexico) from dominant to more dominant State financing. Even the most academically and socially exclusive of the new, alternative, public universities have depended overwhelmingly on the State. For example, Venezuela's Simón Bolívar University charges its students little more than they would be charged in the four traditional public universities—much less than in all (especially three of four) private ones.[2] Additionally, there is simply no significant Latin American tradition of philanthropic or alumni donations to public universities, including the historically most prestigious, such as Argentina's UBA. More important is foreign aid. This has been the case in Colombia (in the 1960s) and in much of Central America; foreign aid for Honduras flows into a context in which tuition has been limited and the role of private enterprise is "nil."[3]

Despite the near State monopoly on public sector finance, variations within the State–public funding pattern should be considered. For instance, funds sometimes come from special taxes and dispersed State sources rather than from general appropriations and the education or treasury ministry. A good example is Ecuador's petroleum and rent tax, of which 10 percent is earmarked for the public universities, 1 percent for the private ones.[4] Another variation occurs when public universities are financed by state or local governments. Both Mexico and Brazil have been significant cases, but Latin America provides few others. Neither Argentina nor Venezuela, despite nominal federalism, delegates the national government's financial burden. Although Colombia formally delegates responsibility (for its public "departmental" universities) to regional departments, the national government itself shoulders the great burden.[5] In sum, nonministerial and nonnational funds have been limited both in cross-national scope and absolute amounts. Their effect on the decentralization-centralization aspect of finance is minimal. There is no effect on the private-public aspect.

Some variation arises between those nations where the State assumes almost the full responsibility and those where it assumes "only" the overwhelming role. Until the Chilean privatization experiment, Colombia had made perhaps the best-known attempt to restrict State responsibility. Chap-

Table 6.2 Sources of Finance in Latin America

Sector	# of Universities	State	Private Donors	Own Income	Other	Total
			1962			
Private	21	27.4%	6.0%	65.5%	1.1%	100.0%
Public	103	84.1	1.8	12.6	1.5	100.0
Total	124	79.0	2.2	17.4	1.4	100.0[a]
			1971			
Private	61	27.9%	0.6%	62.8%	8.7%	100.0%
Public	130	87.3	2.3	6.4	4.0	100.0
Total	191	79.9	2.0	13.4	4.7	100.0[b]

Source: UDUAL data as reported in Juan F. Castellanos et al., *Examen de una década* (Mexico City: UDUAL, 1976), pp. 215–16.
a. The 1962 total = 223.7 million dollars.
b. The 1971 total = 888.0 million dollars.

ter 2 shows how Colombia has taken more measures to curb public enrollment growth than generally seen in Spanish America; this has limited the State's financial burden. Beyond that, tuition plans have been fashioned. The idea has been to give part of the savings in public sector subsidies to the loan agency ICETEX, thus insuring that students can afford tuition in either sector. But tuition plans have not gotten very far, and the State remains the almost unrelieved financier of the public sector.[6]

In most nations, tuition is nominal. Argentina, Bolivia, Peru, Venezuela, and Uruguay are among the South American examples.[7] Donations are also nominal. Data suggesting that the State provides less than 90 percent of public sector income are based partly on the universities' miscellaneous service charges, partly on complex or ambiguous accounting procedures. There is less deviation from the State financing rule than first seems apparent.

If tuition is usually nominal, the next question is whether the State goes further and directly subsidizes students' living expenses. In keeping with Communist policy elsewhere, Cuba provides the widest benefits, including small stipends for personal and boarding costs. Benefits progressively increased during the 1960s, while enrollment growth was restrained; special consideration has been given to the poorer and more revolutionary students.[8] Benefits vary in the rest of Latin America, as in Western Europe. It is not uncommon, however, to see the State subsidizing student health care, housing, food, transportation, and social activities.

The big variable in public sector finance has not been the private-public balance as much as the sheer level of State expenditures. Like enrollments, expenditures have soared faster in higher than primary or secondary education in recent decades. In some cases, higher education has claimed 40 percent of the national education budget, with roughly 25 percent a more typical figure. Growth has stemmed largely from ideologies linking development to education and according higher education a leadership role in fostering economic growth, modernization, social change, and even redistributive policy. In the 1960s international organizations such as UNESCO and CEPAL (Economic Commission for Latin America) set goals for higher education/national budget or GNP ratios. Even earlier, many Latin American nations wrote minimum standards directly into their constitutions. Colombia and Costa Rica fixed higher education/education ratios, while several Central American and Caribbean nations fixed national university/ national budget ratios. These were not always fulfilled in practice, and soaring costs led to some revisions or indirect State financing, as in Costa Rica. The biggest backlash to the growing State financial role occurred within the modern authoritarian context, most notably in Argentina and Chile.[9]

Overall, however, increased doubts about the desirability of the State's financial role have rarely reshaped that role and even less frequently have expanded the private role. Thus, almost all of Latin America follows the rule established in Chile, Mexico, and Brazil—nearly complete public sector dependence on State financing.

The Catholic Subsector

Except in the dichotomously distinctive cases, such as Mexico, the private sector is not as privately financed as the public sector is publicly financed. The greater complexity of the private sector income profile can be best understood by focusing separately on the three different private subsectors.

Chilean private-public homogenization has been based partly on increased Catholic university reliance on State funds, while Brazil's Catholic universities have experienced some such reliance, but much less so. Although Mexico has had no Church-run universities (which is one reason that its private sector continues to be fully private in financing), its religious institutions have not received State aid. Thus, Chile and Mexico have represented the extremes of State versus non-State financing, with Brazil falling much closer to the Mexican pattern.

On the whole, Catholic universities elsewhere in Latin America approach the (Mexican) private-financed much more than the (Chilean) State-financed pole. Yet they fall in between, even to the statist side of Brazil's religious universities. In fact, State financial support for religious universities varies greatly in Latin America. Some States follow the Mexican course and give no direct annual subsidies. Examples include Argentina, Panama, and Venezuela and sometimes involve constitutional proscriptions.[10] Yet aid to Catholic universities is significant in Ecuador, Peru, and some Central American and Caribbean nations. Often combined with the large Catholic subsectors in these nations, this aid accounts for the comparatively high private sector dependence on public funds there. Two decades after its creation, the Pontifical Catholic University of Ecuador received nearly 30 percent of its income from the State (1965). Similarly, the Pontifical Catholic University of Peru draws roughly half its income from the State. The only other Peruvian private university heavily dependent on the State is the Cayetano Heredia, that special case dedicated to medicine.[11]

Rationales for State aid—heard not only in the nations where aid already is common but also in nations such as Argentina, Colombia, and Venezuela—have depended very much on the reorientation of missions described in chapter 2. Some Catholic universities still solicit State funds by invoking arguments based on choice—families have the right to opt for religious education. Octavio Derisi, rector of Argentina's first (and very traditional)

Catholic university, goes so far as to ask for State funds without strings because an overwhelmingly Catholic nation should facilitate such student choice.[12] But, as in Brazil, most Catholic universities now emphasize their similarities to the public sector. Access generally outweighs religious distinctiveness. As Catholic universities are often the largest private institutions and their SES constituencies are not uniformly exclusive, it becomes increasingly difficult to meet costs through tuition and Church funds alone, at least without raising tuition to plainly elite levels.

More powerful, however, is an efficiency argument. Either the State assumes part of the financial burden for the Catholic subsector, which is reformed and serves public functions, or it may well face the full burden of an expanded public sector. And this efficiency argument clearly relates to an effectiveness argument—the Catholic universities are academically superior to most public ones and produce better-prepared personnel. Thus, Peru's pontifical university began to receive greatly increased State support since the 1950s because it greatly improved its quality, surpassing the bulk of a declining public sector. Similarly, quality has been the principal factor in State aid for Brazil's Catholic universities.

Bolivia provides a striking example of how State financing may be used to counter the public sector. Until 1971 the State granted no subsidy to the Catholic university (opened 1967). Things changed however, as military regimes robbed the public universities of their autonomy, reincorporating "autonomy" into a university system with a Council of Rectors including all universities; the Catholic university assumed a prominent council position. The public universities were "persuaded" to give 2 percent of their State subsidy to the Catholic university—a sum that totaled one-third of the latter's income.[13] Immediately upon restoration of institutional autonomy in the late 1970s, however, the public universities successfully demanded that the eight-year dual sector subsidization pattern end. The Bolivian case suggests that some governments might like to favor relatively modern Catholic universities, distinctive from the public sector; alongside cases involving older, evolving, Catholic universities, it also suggests that a key is academic distinctiveness without much religious distinctiveness.

Whatever the exact dimensions of State aid to Latin America's Catholic subsector, it is clear that private finance continues to be much more important. Even where State subsidies are most significant, they usually amount to far less per capita than State subsidies for the public sector. No case has approximated the homogeneous pattern found in Chile. Instead, most Catholic universities still rely overwhelmingly on student fees. Church donations and donations from churchgoers are variably important. A major hidden support (e.g., at Argentina's Catholic University of Santiago del Estero) is the willingness of professors and administrators to contribute their services for little remuneration. Another income source, more sporadic than systematic, involves donations by international, mostly European, Catholic organizations.[14] Finally, Catholic universities that grow as mixed wave I Catholic–wave II elite institutions often receive the business donations characteristic of the secular elite subsector.

The Secular Elite Subsector

Shifting from the Catholic to the secular elite universities, we see that, following the Mexican pattern, exclusively private financing is salient. There is no State subsidy for the secular elite subsector in such nations as Argentina and Venezuela. In other nations, only limited State aid is available, less than aid given to those nations' Catholic universities. Direct annual subsidies are rare. In fact, this is the subsector that has been least disposed even to solicit State aid.[15]

Corporate and foundation donations are much more significant for the elite subsector than for the other private subsectors (or for the public sector). Here is where the historic lack of a Latin American donor tradition has been most convincingly undone. A common pattern of U.S. corporate philanthropy has been to subsidize existing universities, although, of course, there are important historical cases where philanthropy made possible by corporate wealth has helped establish universities (e.g., Carnegie-Mellon, the University of Chicago, Duke). Because Latin American capitalists have viewed even their nations' major public universities largely as failures, they have inclined heavily toward creating their own private universities—and retaining tight links to them. This phenomenon was examined closely in the chapter on Mexico. A parallel lies with Venezuela's powerful Mendoza Foundation, based on industrial wealth, and the Metropolitan University it finances. There are also major examples in Colombia. In Central America many fund-raising campaigns have been launched to attract personal and business donations; one important aspect is the purchase of needed land. Nor does corporate and foundation giving end once the elite universities are functioning. Peru's Pacific University reportedly counts on donations for 21 percent, foundations for 12 percent, and investments for 10 percent of its income.[16] And as shown in the Mexican case, the major role of donations does not lie in annual subsidies. It lies instead with capital costs (periodic or sporadic) for physical creation, grants, and maintenance.

Elite universities are in the best position to attract major donations. They maintain high quality and prestige, their students have the wealthiest parents and other relatives, with the best business connections, their graduates are similarly wealthy and well situated, and many can solicit private donations by emphasizing, even boasting, that they have no alternative State finance. Yet not only the most renowned universities receive donations. In Argentina, for example, the founders of the John F. Kennedy University (1964) donated money at the inception and during the first years.[17]

The elite subsector has also been the special target for international financial donations. Even more than domestic donations, these are primarily targeted for capital, not for annual running expenses; for example, international aid was important in helping construct Central America's private universities. International aid for Catholic universities (other than aid from Catholic organizations) is found mostly where Catholic universities hold second-wave business characteristics; thus, the Dominican Republic's Madre y Maestra University has received support from AID, Ford, and UNESCO. International targeting of elite institutions is logical insofar as these institutions maintain quality and orient themselves more than the others to the "modern" and applied fields of study favored by multinational corporations and international organizations. It is also logical given that the public sector is often perceived as a failure both by domestic and international elites. Furthermore, even where international agencies might be disposed to assist public institutions, they sometimes must contend with ideologies and student movements antagonistic to "dependency" or "imperialism"; Colombia provides an instructive case.[18]

All these patterns of domestic business and international assistance to elite universities follow the pattern described at greater length in the Mexican case. As in that case, donations remain subordinate to tuition, and tuition is the overwhelming source for annual running expenses. Even in the elite subsector, there are very few institutions (Peru's Pacific University is one) in which tuition does not cover the majority of these expenses. A more ominous parallel between Mexico and several other nations is the effect economic crisis may have on the financial fate of some elite universities.

The Demand-Absorbing Subsector

Predictably, qualifications to tuition's dominance exist even in demand-absorbing institutions—qualifications that follow those elaborated in the analysis of Brazil. On the private side, some of these institutions are at least initially promoted by enterprises, including family-owned ones. Motives may include vanity, finanical gain, the desire to train technicians for private enterprise, or the desire to offer educational opportunity. On the public side, the State makes two indirect financial contributions. One is through the institutions' use of professors or other employees who draw their principal salary from their State jobs, often in public universities. The other is through the tax exemption apparently accorded to virtually all private institutions. As in Brazil and Mexico, a serious policy issue is the extent of

227

the exemptions. In the 1960s the Peruvian government encouraged private growth through expanded tax incentives. Critical among these were exemptions on rent. The advent of leftist military rule in 1968 led to the repeal of many tax incentives, subsequently reinstated. The point is that the degree of tax benefits offered to Latin America's private nonprofit sectors has been an instrument of State policy that has significantly affected that sector's financial position.

If States manipulate tax policy toward nonprofit institutions, the institutions themselves can be more manipulative, or abusive. This may have been the case in Peru, partially justifying the junta's crackdown on exemptions. As the Brazilian case suggests, substantial room for abuse occurs when a powerful, almost desperate demand is created for higher education. It is not surprising, therefore, that charges of abuse are heard frequently in the only nation in which the demand-absorbing subsector comprises the entire private sector. Critics claim that Costa Rica's UACA, like the U.S. Oral Roberts College, is really a nonprofit umbrella for a conglomeration of for-profit constituent colleges. The ownership foundation, the "university," is allegedly formed as a cover to receive the tax breaks given to nonprofit institutions. UACA's law school is most widely attacked, while deans of several of the constituent UACA colleges are said to be paid handsomely for notoriously little work. Such alleged abuses have led critics to argue that the nonprofit label allows demand-absorbing institutions an indirect source of income that they do not deserve. UACA dismisses its critics as frustrated statists and sees profits to constituent colleges as proof of market success.[19]

All these possible sources notwithstanding, analyses of Brazil's demand-absorbing institutions, as well as of Mexico's, suggest that such institutions are financed almost completely out of private funds and that the composition of those funds is less complex than in the other subsectors. This pattern holds for demand-absorbing private institutions throughout Latin America. Tuition generally covers ongoing annual costs, while capital costs are held to a minimum. Good libraries, good laboratories, and impressive buildings are rarely found in these institutions, which receive significant donations from neither domestic business nor foreign interests. Nor do they receive direct State aid. Thus, they lag behind the other private subsectors in their percentage of income derived from every source save tuition. For example, Peru's demand-absorbing subsector relies on tuition for perhaps 99 percent of its income; moreover, this tuition dependency occurs within a private sector that not only attracts private donations but also receives a notable 10 percent of its income from the State.[20]

It is now possible to make general comparisons about tuition in the different subsectors. The highest tuitions are found in the elite subsector.[21]

Academic prestige, related to social prestige and future economic reward, allows this. Demand-absorbing institutions simply do not offer enough to warrant high charges. The same holds for the unprestigious Catholic universities. As Jencks and Reisman found in the United States, Catholic institutions that are neither very good nor distinctive would lose students if they raised tuition.[22] Furthermore, some Catholic universities are truly restrained by concerns about equity. I would guess that they charge more on the average (as the prestigious ones certainly do) than do demand-absorbing institutions. Venezuela's Catholic Andrés Bello charges more than most or all of the nation's nonuniversity private institutions, but the elite Metropolitan and Rafael Urdaneta universities charge the highest tuitions. Even at Colombia's top Catholic university, Javeriana, the average charge is less than the minimum at the secular elite Los Andes. Similarly, Argentina's Belgrano charges about double that charged at the most expensive religious university (Salvador).[23] These secular elite versus religious comparisons confirm our Mexican patterns.

Also confirming these patterns, tuition is the major income source in all three subsectors. In fact, it comprises its smallest percentage of income in the elite subsector, even though its absolute amount is highest there. This results mostly from the greater ability of this subsector to attract private donations. Thus, Colombia's Los Andes draws roughly two-thirds of its income from tuition, while the respective figures for the religious Javeriana and La Salle universities are roughly 80 and 90 percent.[24] Table 6.3 gives a simplified comparative summary of which subsectors receive the most from different sources. It shows that the demand-absorbing subsector has the weakest income base. Yet it should not obscure all the subsectors' principal reliance on tuition. Nor should it obscure the major tuition comparison, which is intersectoral. Private tuitions often parallel those found in U.S. public and even some private institutions, while public tuitions remain virtually nil. Considering all private and public funding sources, Latin America's nominally private and public sectors are empirically quite private and public, respectively, with regard to finance.[25]

GOVERNANCE
The Public Sector: Autonomy and State Control

The analyses of public sector governance in Chile, Mexico, and Brazil reveal many similar patterns. The most significant variation was produced by differences in regime type. And the most significant single regime transformation clearly occurred in Chile. Just a few years after the university reform had expanded university autonomy and especially the scope of student and professorial participation in governance, the junta imposed a degree of centralized State control previously unknown in Chilean higher education. Brazil's turn to military rule in 1964 also led to increased State control. But even before the abertura relaxed controls somewhat by the late 1970s, the Brazilian State never crushed either autonomy or decentralized governance as much as did the Chilean. Mexico's transformation from a more revolutionary to a more status quo regime around 1940 set the general limits to State control, though some power was simultaneously squeezed from professors and students into university administration. The governance of Mexican public higher education has been based on greater autonomy and dispersed political power than in Brazil. Still, the greatest autonomy, and especially participatory power, was found in Chile in 1967–73.

In this section I identify where the locus of power lies in other Latin American public sectors. One major issue is the degree of State control. Another is the power distribution (centralization-decentralization) among all the actors "below" the State in the authority structure. Subsequently, the same issues are probed for the private sector, thereby establishing the cross-sector contrasts in governance.

Latin America's public universities are rooted in a Continental heritage involving strong but often ambiguous State control. The rise of nation-states in Europe had led to the fusing of State authority with traditional professorial control, thus creating subtle mixtures of State control and self-regulation. Good examples occurred wherever chaired professors transferred their power upward into national curriculum or research councils that were the State's policy-making bodies for higher education. Even when guilds declined in most of society, they retained importance in the university, where new capitalist forms did not destroy them. In contrast, U.S. higher education was born and developed without similarly strong guild control and with much more capitalist influence. Latin America, with its colonial ties, followed European patterns more closely. After independence, fused private-public universities were replaced by public universities, meaning that State and guild activity would no longer share the scene with strong Church authority. By the end of the century, as Hanns-Albert

Table 6.3 Income Sources for Latin America's Private Subsectors

	State	Donations	Tuition
Catholic	1[a]	2	2.5[b]
Secular elite	2	1	1
Demand absorbing	3	3	2.5[b]

a. 1 = the subsector receiving the most income; 3 = the least.
b. I have not established a rule as to which subsector charges more.

230

Steger writes, nearly all Latin American nations had structurally similar universities.[26]

Striking similarities can be found in nineteenth-century governance structure between most Latin American and European universities. In both, State control was apparently paramount but modified by the delegation of authority to the university itself, agent of the State. It was also modified by the enormous power vested in chaired professors. Still, regulations about appointments, curricula, exams, professional degrees, and so forth were fixed and standardized systemwide by the State. Professorial power vested in the chair, and in derivative control over the faculties, represented some decentralization of power, but it also reflected the lack of university-wide power to counterbalance State power. Whatever the degree of professorial academic freedom, there was only limited institutional autonomy from the State.

Major Latin American movements to achieve university autonomy from the State, often invoking the 1918 Córdoba reform, have achieved significant success. But just as that success has not spread uniformly across nations, neither has it been unidirectional. Once achieved, autonomy has frequently been lost. Nor is there a clear dividing line around which to define universities as autonomous or nonautonomous. The State's legal grant of autonomy is but one, formal criterion. Relevant dates include Argentina 1918, Bolivia 1930, Colombia 1935, Costa Rica 1949, Cuba 1933, the Dominican Republic 1961, Ecuador 1938, El Salvador 1927, Guatemala 1928, Honduras 1957, Nicaragua 1958, Panama 1946, Paraguay 1929, Peru 1931, Uruguay 1951, and Venezuela 1936.[27] Some cases are ambiguous even in terms of legal dates, either because the State has recognized autonomy through a combination of different laws (as in Colombia) or because (as in Mexico 1929, 1933) grants of partial autonomy were followed by fuller grants (e.g., Ecuador 1925, 1938, 1945; Nicaragua 1958, 1966; Peru 1931, 1946). Sometimes the word *autonomy* is mocked by the law itself, as with Velasco Ibarra's "disciplined autonomy" in Ecuador (1971). Autonomy is frequently reaffirmed after it is dissolved de facto, sometimes even de jure, with the advent of hostile regimes (e.g., Bolivia 1971, Guatemala 1931, Peru 1948, Venezuela 1948).

Obviously, State grants of autonomy only sometimes indicate reality. The degree to which the governance of Latin America's twentieth-century universities can be distinguished from their nineteenth-century ancestors, or from the Continental model, depends largely on how much institutional autonomy has really been achieved. As one scholar wrote in 1963: "If a foreign observer, especially a European, looked at the University of Uruguay in recent years, two facts would catch his attention. First, he would be surprised to learn of the almost total absence of ties between the central government and the university administration." (The second surprise, considered below, is that students participate significantly in the administrative hierarchy.)[28] The applicability of such assessments naturally depends on the scope of autonomy where it does exist and on the frequency or infrequency of its existence.

The three case studies of public sector governance specify how wide ranging autonomy can be in regard to such issues as student admissions, professorial and administrative appointments, and setting policy concerning curriculum, exam, and degree requirements. To help assess the parameters of autonomy, I look here at extreme facets. First, it is often argued that the public university's financial dependence on the State infringes on all facets of autonomy. "In the last analysis almost everything came down to the one constraint, i.e., shortness of funds."[29] To be sure, financial dependency does limit autonomy. Drawing empirical evidence from Mexico, however, I argue that many public universities maintain considerable autonomy, even autonomy over distributing funds, despite almost full dependence on State finance. Many of the variables involved in the Mexican case are broadly applicable in Latin America's public sectors, except in several cases of very authoritarian regime rule.[30] The point is that autonomy has included at least some important financial as well as administrative and academic components.

Possibly the broadest threat to autonomy comes with attempts to impose systemic unity via coordinating councils (found in some form throughout the region). At the extreme, as in Bolivia, Ecuador, and Peru at various points in the 1970s, autonomy is formally displaced from individual institutions to a system. More often, councils of rectors or other national councils seek to fix some systemic policies, leaving fewer decisions ad hoc to multitudinous points within separate institutions. Some nations, such as Chile, Mexico, and Venezuela, include both sectors under one umbrella while others, such as Argentina, have separate councils for each sector. Without discussing various experiments in depth, I venture these hypotheses: (1) most have accomplished relatively little, partly because of national university reticence (e.g., in Chile and Argentina); (2) dual sector councils tend to have even less control over their private than public constituents; (3) whether one compares across nations or over time within nations (e.g., Mexico or Colombia), there is a strong correlation between council influence and State involvement; (4) however, as in Chile (and Argentina) in the 1970s, even repressive regimes may largely bypass councils, instead imposing their wills directly on institutions; and (5) extreme experiments where autonomy is formally displaced from individual institutions to a system are usually short lived.[31]

Turning to the other extreme, many observers have pointed to "extraterritoriality" as evidence of startling or even excessive autonomy from the State. Extraterritoriality refers to self-policing, beyond the State's security forces. This issue was not treated in the case studies, though it could have been mentioned that Eduardo Frei's decision to send Chilean police on campus to pursue revolutionary leftists breached extraterritoriality. It is nevertheless amazing how widespread the norm of extraterritoriality has been; although many governments have violated the norm, others have respected it even when facing circumstances that would provoke their incursion into other geographical or institutional spheres. In any case, the concept has become decreasingly potent.

Venezuela is probably the major nation where extraterritoriality remained a highly visible issue in recent decades. For roughly a decade after 1958, extraterritoriality had constitutional sanction, offering legal sanctuary, even against a background of violent attacks on the State. A court order was needed for State security personnel to enter the campus. A 1970 law finally dissolved extraterritoriality, specifying that such unbridled autonomy should apply only to classroom activity. Nonetheless, the State remained reluctant to send its security personnel onto the public-autonomous campuses.[32] In Ecuador the military abolished extraterritoriality in 1964, although civilian rulers at least temporarily revived it a few years later.

Paradoxically, extraterritoriality never has been relevant to Latin America's private sector, even though the concept perhaps goes beyond autonomy to independence or "privateness." In fact, few private universities would dare claim extraterritoriality, lest they seem to defy the State's legitimate authority. Mostly, however, the issue is academic since the State rarely faces severe political disruptions in the private sector. Venezuela's extraterritoriality policy, for example, has been most important at the public UCV.

If autonomy, where achieved, has had great but not unrestricted scope, the next question is how often it has been achieved. One major variable has been the form of government. Autonomy has usually been achieved under democratic or open regimes in the twentieth century but only sporadically under authoritarian ones. Even legal autonomy, which has clearly been granted much more easily than real autonomy, is correlated with regime type. Autonomy was first granted, or reinstated, by Cuba's Auténtico party (1933), Argentina's Radical party (1918), Venezuela's Democratic Action party (1958), the Dominican Republic's successors to Trujillo (1961), and so forth. Nevertheless, cases exist where democratic political parties have been reticent to grant autonomy while they themselves were in power, e.g., Colombia's Liberals in the 1930s. Moreover, some dictatorships have granted autonomy (e.g., Bolivia's military regime of 1930), and many more have refrained from declaring autonomy illegal.[33]

Differences among regimes become more significant when considering real autonomy. After a setback stemming from its 1933 military coup, Uruguay achieved progressively greater university autonomy under democratic rule; in the mid-1960s Solari could write that "the University of Uruguay is, almost certainly, the most autonomous of all State universities in Latin America."[34] That statement would have to be almost completely reversed after the 1973 military takeover. With parallels to Brazil in 1955–64, Argentina's golden age of autonomy—at least since the 1920s—occurred in 1958–66. And it began to revive immediately after Raúl Alfonsín's Radical party replaced military rule in 1983. Costa Rica and Venezuela have probably preserved autonomy as broadly and consistently as have any other Latin American nations from the 1950s to the present. By contrast, sudden changes from autonomy to increased State control, as in Brazil 1964 and Chile 1973, have occurred with the assumption of authoritarian rule (Argentina 1966 and 1976, Guatemala 1931, Peru 1948, Venezuela 1948). Still, some authoritarian regimes have permitted substantial autonomy, unwilling or unable to have it differently. Mexico might be the most prominent contemporary example, but there are numerous historical examples. Moreover, even where authoritarian regimes have not permitted the degree of institutional autonomy found in nonauthoritarian settings, they have often allowed more autonomy for the university than for most other social-economic-political institutions. As Parker wrote in 1964: "Central America's five universities are her greatest bastions of freedom. By tradition and legal standing they all have privacy through autonomy."[35]

This is not to minimize the precarious fate of autonomy within authoritarian settings. The historical preservation of autonomy under authoritarian regimes must be understood in the context that these regimes were generally conservative and determined to preserve the status quo; their nonrevolutionary ends did not require them to extend State control over all of society. A major change has occurred since the 1960s with the advent of several authoritarian regimes dedicated to remaking society.

Cuba presents probably the most obvious, though distinct, contemporary case. As Hugh Thomas describes it, the university had once been "the only place where political meetings could be freely held": young Castro himself spent considerable time in political activity at the University of Havana. In 1960 a strong-armed student-regime takeover led to the departure of much of the faculty. A new governing board of four students and four professors replaced university councils and faculty boards. By 1961 the State absorbed all private education, and by 1964 the once autonomous Higher University Council was replaced by a Centralized National Council of Universities responsible to the Ministry of Education. A vice-minister of higher education was appointed. Nonetheless, there have been problems in governing the university as a pawn of the State, leading to revolutionary campaigns against dissident, unsocialized, or homosexual students and intellectuals, leading in turn to charges that the regime is striving for "Stalinist" control. In any case, Cuba's leaders leave little doubt about the proper nature of the State-university relationship. Raúl Castro (1960): "To assert an artificial separation between the interests of the people, finally represented by the revolutionary government, and the university, which is paid for by the people and which should serve it, is nothing more than to revive old patriarchal and contemptuous concepts." Fidel Castro (1971): "I don't remember if, legally, there is or isn't autonomy in the University of Cuba. I do know that it is a problem I haven't heard anything about for around ten years."[36]

That a revolutionary leftist regime dedicated to a maximalist State should grant the university no autonomy is one thing. That counterrevolutionary conservative regimes should expand State control over the university is another. Yet that has happened recently with modern authoritarian regimes. Of course the degree varies, as shown by the much tighter State control found in Chile than Brazil. The Argentine and Uruguayan cases more closely approximate the Chilean. After decades in which periods of Peronist and military rule had overwhelmed periods of democratic rule, the 1976 attack on Argentine university autonomy was not altogether new. By comparison, Uruguay's military ended an extended period of democratic rule and substantial university autonomy. Some autonomy was maintained in the first military year (1973), but purges and repression intensified and hard-liners bent on purification (reminiscent of Chile 1976) assumed control. Departments were abolished in such fields as sociology, political economy, and the history of ideas. State security agents kept watch from within the university. The Federation of University Students was declared illegal. In other countries, such as Peru, efforts were also made to extend State control greatly, and these efforts substantially reduced university autonomy (in appointment of officials, restrictions on curriculum, student admissions, and so forth), but not on anything like the Argentine-Chilean-Uruguayan scale.[37] Democracy returned to Peru in 1980, although, as in Colombia, political and economic conflict did not provide a secure environment for autonomy.

The Public Sector: Institutional Decentralization

A strong relationship exists between the degree of institutional autonomy from the State and the degree of decentralized power within the university itself. Nevertheless, the correlation is not perfect. An institution's freedom from external authority is not the same as democratic participatory freedoms for those within the institution. A very centralized, hierarchical institution can be autonomous from the State, while a more decentralized, internally democratic one may be more vulnerable to State control. In practice, however, not only has traditional university autonomy been accompanied by relatively decentralized institutional governance, but where a change to heightened State control has occurred it has usually been accompanied by a marked centralization in institutional governance.

Again it is useful to describe the Latin American public university as similar to the Continental university. A major parallel has been the highly decentralized nature of the faculty structure. Although "superior councils" have been variously comprised as well as variably powerful, they have often drawn from within the faculties. Administrative dependence is further illustrated where the rectors are selected by and beholden to these influential structures. As Russell Davis aptly writes: "Presiding over this motley of *facultades* and *institutos* and *escuelas* was a rector who had no tenure, and who had to politic with the *consejos* of the powerful old facultades, including student representatives, to survive"; nor did the rector have a governing board to support him.[38]

In other cases, the rector has been appointed by the government or by a university governing board, as in Mexico, which may or may not have State representation. Often the rector is appointed from a list of three names presented by one authority to another, for the latter's final decision. The deans themselves may be strong figures, representing strong faculties, or they may remain dependent on the chaired professors who select them. As chair-centered power has declined significantly in recent decades, deans and faculties may have become more prominent. The relationship of the faculties (often oriented around a given profession) to the central university institution has been variously described as fieflike, decentralized, and centrifugal. The phenomenon has often been both reflected and reinforced by the physical separation of different professional faculties in different buildings throughout a city, as with Argentina's UBA. Additionally, schools, institutes, and departments have emerged alongside or within faculties. To think of Latin America's traditional public university in terms of a national political system is to think of a relatively weak chief executive, responsible to implement the decisions of a more powerful legislature, and of a federalist system in which the states and localities retain considerable power. In its foreign affairs, this nation is financially dependent and quite vulnerable but has achieved considerable sovereignty nonetheless. All of this, however, is variable across given nations, institutions, and time periods.

Thus, we again find broad parallels in the internal governance of the traditional public university in Latin America and Europe, although it is difficult to identify exact similarities and differences while speaking so generally. Most observers who have attempted such comparisons have emphasized the parallels. Although research and full-time teaching have been much more common in Europe, probably making chair-oriented power greater there, that power has been significant in both areas and has declined seriously in each. Major differences in intrainstitutional governance stem from the Córdoba reform. As Latin America's public universities became more autonomous, so they generally became internally more participatory, divisively politicized, and decentralized, in a way uncharacteristic of the European experience until the late 1960s. And the single major difference concerned student power.

Whereas chapter 2 considered how student politicization stimulated private sector growth, here I consider the actual degree of representation and power that students have achieved in the public sector. The Córdoba reform pushed cogovernment, with one-third student participation on university councils. Remarkedly extensive results were soon achieved in internal governance in many nations, such as Peru, Bolivia, Honduras, and Uruguay. Some universities restricted student representation to certain decision-making bodies while others allowed a much broader range, extending even to decisions over administrative appointments. Writing in 1960, Havinghurst found that student representatives were included on the governing bodies of Latin American universities "with only a few exceptions."[39] Of course, most individual students have not been active, but majority participation is no requisite for strong movements. Furthermore, student politics have often been accompanied by professorial (and even university worker) politics. As in Chile in 1967–73, a broad participatory base may be involved in campaigns for many university positions (e.g., Uruguay 1958–73, and Costa Rica and Venezuela for decades).

The relationship between student governance and national regime type has been described elsewhere.[40] Suffice it here to note that most modern authoritarian regimes have smashed traditional student power, whereas students have played important roles under both democratic or reconciliation regimes and even under oligarchic ones. These roles have often been tied to national policy and political parties. Regarding university policies, students have often been influential through their institutionalized participation and even more through their power to disrupt and therefore to block decisions. Returning to the analogy between public universities and national political systems, student power may resemble power to the people, possibly the ultimate in decentralized power.

However much student power and other factors contribute to public university decentralization, there is a danger of forming an exaggerated image. My analysis has been based on comparisons with other systems, not on ideal types of decentralization. Beyond this, modern authoritarian systems have imposed greatly increased centralization. Moreover, as with Brazil's fundações, new public universities have been established to curb centrifugal forces and build tighter institutions. Some reforms have reduced student and professorial authority, giving it instead to administrators or even to the State. Nor are such reforms restricted to authoritarian cases. Venezuela is a good example. In the late 1960s and early 1970s "a spate" of educational decrees was passed "with higher education regulated to an unprecedented extent."[41] Most laws involved the creation of new public institutions, which clearly would have neither the institutional autonomy nor the institutional decentralization still found in the traditional four public universities; for example, the Ministry of Education would select the rectors and vice-rectors of the public experimental universities.

In other Latin American nations, centrifugal tendencies have been attacked even in the traditional universities. Some efforts are reminiscent of the 1945 Mexican plan, creating governing boards to select rectors and to resolve intrauniversity disputes. Among the widely successful measures have been the destruction or limitation of the chair and the construction of "university cities" or campuses in place of scattered faculty buildings. Other reforms have generally been less successful. One is the attempt to replace semiautonomous faculties with departments more tied to the central university structure. Resistance to such measures comes from those with entrenched power (e.g., deans) and those who distrust U.S. or private sector models based on strong university-wide administration. By contrast, many private universities have been created with numerous reforms built in; this relates at least partly to an intrainstitutional centralization rarely found in the public sector. First, however, I consider the private sector's interinstitutional decentralization.

The Private Sector: Autonomy from State Control

The Mexican case and (with modification) the Brazilian case indicate that the State plays a much more limited role in private than in public sector governance. On the other hand, the Chilean private sector approximates the public sector in terms of State control, though major differences held until 1967. Most nations provide evidence for generalizing from the Mexican and Brazilian cases: the State plays only a limited role in the private sector.

Colombia offers a good illustration. Compared to public institutions, the private ones are more juridically autonomous from the State. More important, the differences are not only juridical but behavioral. Each private institution is individually responsible for its own personnel, whereas public personnel are grouped as State civil servants, and rectors of some public institutions are appointed by the State. Furthermore, the State assumes less control over how funds are spent in the private than in the public sector. And whatever the difficulties of establishing strong interuniversity coordinating councils, Colombia's public sector maintains a greater degree of uniformity in governance than is found in the nation's private sector. For example, alumni are strong at Los Andes, while some Catholic universities come under direct ecclestiastical control, and the Santiago University of Cali allows wide intrainstitutional participation.[42] In sum, as is generally true in Latin America, there is much more institutional pluralism within the private than public sectors. This pluralism is feasible largely because the State imposes fewer uniform policies on the private than on the public sector. Instead, more freedom of choice is allowed at the institutional level.

It would be relatively easy, but repetitive, to accumulate the evidence nation by nation. It is more instructive to analyze the extreme national cases before analyzing the limited State role that exists in most nations. The most extreme cases (at least outside Cuba) probably involve the modern authoritarian regimes, where we might expect State control oblivious to the niceties of private-public distinctions. The Chilean case post-1973 has epitomized blanket State control. But two factors should be considered. One is that Chile's 1981 legislation has opened the possibility for a degree of autonomy, albeit limited, in the new (private) institutions. A more established factor is that before 1973, the nominally private sector was already governed in much the same way as the public sector. By comparison, Brazil experienced strong private-public governance differences prior to its 1964 coup, and the military regime subsequently exerted less control over the private than the public sector.

Since Uruguay has never had a private sector, the major remaining modern authoritarian case is clearly Argentina. The level of societywide repression was broadly comparable to that found in Chile, although floundering rather than reinstitutionalization characterized the Argentine military's higher education policy. But prior to the inception of the first (1966) and second (1976) modern authoritarian regimes, private-public distinctiveness already existed, and State control subsequently varied greatly according to sector, thus following the Brazilian more than the Chilean pattern. This was shown most clearly in administrative autonomy. The government appointed the UBA's but not the private universities' rectors. The private sector Council of Rectors retained a level of Church support as a buffer against State repression. Most interesting was the hiring of purged professors. No private sector had been in place when Perón first became strongman in the 1940s and immediately purged those UBA leaders who had opposed him. The tables were turned in 1955 when many Peronists were purged from the universities; within a few years, however, some found employment with the creation of a private sector, traditionally anathema to

239

most Peronists. Again in 1966 and 1976, military rule led to widespread public purges, mostly of leftists. Again many found employment sanctuary in the private sector they had opposed.[43] Private universities also served as sanctuaries after the Peronist-led public sector purges of 1972. They provided safety nets from variously motivated purges. And they helped save many from economic as well as political hardship when severe regime cuts in public sector funds necessitated major cuts in personnel; private sector budgets were not subject to the same devastating blows. Similarly, the post-1976 regime severely curtailed public enrollments but, despite some disposition to do so, did not similarly curtail the private sector. Thus, the private sector not only retained its own clientele but formed a safety net for students as well as professors. Compared to its Chilean counterpart, Argentina's private sector grew both in proportional and absolute terms during the last military tenure.

Bolivia, during its harsh authoritarian rule in the 1970s, provides a final, related example. President Hugo Banzer initiated probably the most potent State intervention ever in Bolivia's public sector, robbing the universities of their autonomy. The Council of Rectors usurped considerable power over academic, administrative, and financial matters. Although the Catholic university was included in the council, its autonomy was not similarly quashed. Its rector was not named by the government. As in Argentina, many of the better professors purged from the public sector found employment in the private sector. Governmental restraint was based on a combination of faith in the Church's governance policies and a respect for the Church's legitimacy and power.

Thus, evidence from Bolivia, Argentina, and Brazil indicates that the private-public division often makes a significant difference in terms of institutional autonomy from the State, even under harshly authoritarian regimes. Both sectors lose autonomy, but the private sector loses much less.[44]

Switching the focus from extreme to more typical contexts for State action, let us consider other possible limits to generalizations about private sector autonomy. As there is little State subsidization and as the State rarely plays an important role in appointments, the main area of interest concerns autonomy in academic affairs. The Mexican and Brazilian chapters analyze the issue of State recognition and accreditation. In Mexico, opening a private institution is not difficult. While all must affiliate with a public university or other State agency, the restrictions have been limited. Until the 1970s Brazil imposed even fewer constraints on opening new private institutions, as these could be "isolated" rather than affiliated. Then, however, Brazil changed from a laissez-faire to a supervised policy that was more of a ban on any new creation than a case-by-case evaluation process.

240

Concerning the degree of institutional dependency on the State for ongoing accreditation in the existing institutions, the situation has been ambiguous in both countries. However formidable the State's authority, its use of that authority has been much less formidable.

For most of Latin America a modified laissez-faire policy turns out to be common in the creation of new institutions. This approximates Mexican policy more than Brazil's recently restrictive policy.[45] There is variation of course, but the norm is that the State imposes very few obstacles to private initiative. This market freedom, or anarchy, clearly complements our earlier discussion (chapter 2) of private growth and institutional proliferation. State control has been minimal where there has been wanton proliferation, with massive third waves. Although institutions created by private initiative often require legal recognition (whereas public universities are created by law), this dependency is only minimal. The Dominican Republic and Peru are two national examples that join pre-1970 Brazil in illustrating the pattern. Except in certain years, Peru has had no requisites beyond executive authorization for new private institutions, while proposals for new public institutions have required legislative debate and approval. Nations such as Argentina and Venezuela have more constraining regulations on the books, but even these are usually minimal. Colombia shows that some nations with comparatively impressive formal regulations have really pursued modified laissez-faire policy; while ICFES has held the authority to decide whether new universities meet basic requirements and to fix six-month trial periods, private institutions have often proliferated freely, as seen in chapter 2.

Here, then, is an impressive demonstration of the privatization of Latin American higher education. Whereas bitter battles were fought in many countries over the initial creation of private sectors, most countries have subsequently allowed the almost unimpeded creation of private institutions within those sectors.

The next question is the degree to which private institutions, once created, remain dependent on State accreditation and supervision. At an autonomous extreme, we could imagine institutions that need not conform to any basic State regulations, free to develop their own policies and criteria leading to degrees useful in professional practice. Far from that extreme, other institutions might perform their academic activities only in compliance or partnership with State agencies. Again following Mexican and Brazilian patterns, the general rule is that there is much less restrictiveness than suggested by legal provisions. This still leaves room for some restrictiveness, however, as the provisions themselves frequently reflect statist traditions.

Fighting a rearguard action against the private surge, many national universities have argued that private institutions should be dependent on national university authorization. As Davis explains this phenomenon to a

241

U.S. audience, "It is as though the University of Massachusetts has veto powers over Harvard program developments. Instead of being answerable in some cases to the Commonwealth of Massachusetts, Harvard would be subject in all things to the University of Massachusetts."[46] The analogy is useful, but there are at least three provisos. First, the U.S. parallel would place venerable institutions under the control of less venerable ones, contrary to the Latin American pattern. Second, formal dependence on public university authorization does not necessarily translate into power or policy. Third, while authorization for private sector functioning is often linked to the public sector, it is also often linked directly to the State. Public university officials argue that they represent the State's higher education arm, but private university officials respond that authorization for each sector should ultimately depend on the State, just as private primary and secondary schools are generally inspected by ministerial not public school officials. Drawing on Central American experiences, we see that national university claims to authority have often proved unenforceable.[47]

In practice, while the private sector's legal dependence on the public sector or the State varies, it usually varies from minimal to ambiguous. Once established, Peru's private universities need no further or renewed accreditation. Ambiguity arises where State regulations stipulate that private institutions must at least partly copy the public structural or curriculum model. In Paraguay all curriculum should be "comparable" to the national university's, and the ministry retains the right to "review" the private university's teaching staff qualifications, exam systems, and so forth. Moreover, as in Brazil, so in Argentina and other nations, State or public university bureaucracies may long delay or even stifle private efforts to create new curriculum, fields of study, and faculties. Nonetheless, enforcement of restrictions often falls far short of what formal authority might allow.

Expanded potential for State supervision may come in the aftermath of widespread third-wave (unregulated) growth, as we have seen in Brazil. In 1980 Colombia's ICFES undertook not only to restrict the creation of additional institutions but to evaluate new programs in existing ones. However, while the 1980 legislation looks tough on the books, whether it can really curb the ad hoc proliferation discussed earlier remains to be seen.[48]

Paradoxically, while some private universities seek the fullest possible juridical freedom, many welcome and even exaggerate their legal dependency on either the public university or the State in matters of academic policy. There are several reasons: (1) it provides firmer legal footing; (2) it provides greater public or populist legitimacy to institutions regarded as

242

particularistic or elitist; (3) it provides some academic legitimacy and guidelines for low-quality or noninnovative institutions; and (4) it allows private sector administrators to avoid responsibility and blame. Mexico's UAG poignantly illustrates the first two reasons. Mexico's demand-absorbing institutions illustrate the third, as would many demand-absorbing and some Catholic institutions in several nations; indeed, the obstacles to greater pluralism in the private sector may stem as much from a lack of private initiative as from explicit public or State restrictions. The fourth reason is well illustrated by the declarations (about Costa Rica's main public university) of one of the founders and deans at Costa Rica's private university: "Everything that's wrong with Costa Rican higher education is the UCR's fault. . . . The UCR imposes the models and has too much weight for an independent institution to buck it."[49]

The Private Sector: Institutional Centralization

The State's only very limited role in private university governance does not guarantee private university autonomy. Much less does it mean that private universities are democratically run by their constituencies. One must consider the role of extrauniversity authorities other than the State in limiting autonomy as well as the power distribution among administrators, professors, and students within the university.

As shown especially in the Mexican case, private financiers play a role in university governance. Usually this role concerns broad directions of university policy, and usually the institutional vehicle for such influence is a board of trustees, sitting "above" the university, or a governing board, sitting within the university but with significant external representation. These generalizations hold for most of Latin American private higher education. Thus, the frequent assertion that such boards of laymen are found only in the United States (and perhaps Canada and Great Britain) is simply untrue.[50] Nonetheless, Latin Americans, including those who criticize the boards as undemocratic and those who hail them for minimizing State power while maximizing effectiveness in meeting the functions freely chosen by certain societal actors, properly and closely identify them with the U.S. model. Boards of trustees are rarely found in the Continental/Latin American public tradition, while they have always been a defining characteristic of U.S. higher education, especially in the private sector. Although recent years have seen an increase in Latin America's public sector governing boards, these are still less common and have much less significant external (non-State) representation than do their private sector counterparts. Typically, Latin America's private boards have wide powers to shape general orientations in finance, governance, and functions. They work closely with the administrative officials, especially with their own appointed rectors.

One of the most significant variables among Latin America's private boards concerns the composition of external interests. Differences between the Catholic and secular institutions are notable. Catholic universities traditionally vest ultimate authority in the Church; if pontifical, the Vatican has a role. Most boards are made up principally, if not exclusively, of clergy. In fact, many of Latin America's Catholic universities are registered in the Congregation of Seminaries and Universities of Rome.[51] Moreover, the city's archbishop is generally the grand chancellor, as found in Chile, Brazil, Argentina (e.g., Salta's archbishop and the University of Patagonia), and Paraguay (Asunción's archbishop and the Nuestra Señora University).

Secular institutions have lay boards, frequently dominated by businessmen. As in Mexico, so in most of Latin America, prominent businessmen generally work with the elite universities, while demand-absorbing institutions may depend more on local businessmen. Colombia is typical in that directors and members of foundations and corporations assume the role of maximum authority fulfilled by religious in the Catholic subsector. And logically, mixed religion-business composition is common where universities were created in a wave I–wave II overlap (e.g., Bolivia's Catholic university) and where several traditional Catholic universities have reformed over time.

The three-part subsectoral division is useful not only in identifying major external authorities but also in assessing the degree to which those authorities determine university policy. Influence may be comparatively limited in those Catholic universities that have evolved away from their earlier religious dogma. The stigma of abusing academic authority is further diminished where religious personnel have strong academic credentials, characteristic of the Jesuits. Such personnel sometimes blunt the edge of interference by other external authorities. Where the Catholic university and the national or local Church itself are less reformed, the limits on academic authorities are greater. Few, if any, Catholic universities have ever evolved as far as Chile's UC, with a leftist lay rector preceding the coup (and a military officer following it). Nonetheless, Church influence has been increasingly limited to top-level administrative appointments and to maintaining some broad academic and social guidelines. In some institutions, such as Panama's Antigua University, most of even the top positions are held by nonreligious. Beneath the very top levels, as seen in Brazil, there is variation in whether most personnel are lay or religious. Colombia illustrates that the Church or founding religious order often remains the supreme authority but leaves academic affairs largely to academic officials.

The Ecuadorian case also exhibits the sort of mix often found. Wilson writes that archbishop–grand chancellors have "little direct administrative control over university operation" but that it would be "naïve" to overlook their "commanding voice" in the formulating of "basic policies." In fact, however, the Catholic university at Guayaquil has broken all but formal Church ties, and the Catholic university at Cuenca never had strong ties; that leaves the senior Catholic university, in Quito, with the strongest ties, but even there Jesuit administration maintains "a tenuous relation with the Hierarchy." In sum, there is movement toward the autonomy and "pluralism verging on anarchy" that Jencks and Reisman find for the great majority of U.S. Catholic colleges in relationship with the Church, although most of Latin America's Catholic subsectors still fall considerably short of that.[52]

Within the secular subsectors, the academic prestige of the elite institutions sustains a greater degree of university autonomy than found in most demand-absorbing institutions, but probably more external influence exists than in most Catholic universities. Nonetheless, at least one significant type of exception can be found in each secular subsector. In the elite subsector, not all universities are strongly tied to business. In the demand-absorbing subsector, not all institutions are autocratically administered by their owners; instead, many owners care less about the substance of educational policy than about the prestige or financial assets involved in ownership.

The affirmation that the private sector substantially substitutes extrauniversity religious and business influence for State influence provides a background against which to focus more directly on the distribution of power at lower university levels. Obviously, the role of boards of trustees, the representation of extrauniversity interests on university governance bodies, and the appointment of rectors by external authorities all blur distinctions between intra- and extrauniversity, but significant private-public differences emerge at both the higher governance levels and the lower ones—those that lie more clearly within the university.

As found most assuredly in Mexico, but also in Brazil and in pre-1967 Chile, power is much more restrictively centralized within private than public institutions. Even choosing the Colombian case, where the public structure has been molded to minimize the perceived problems of decentralization, one finds basic private-public contrasts. We have already seen that there is more interinstitutional differentiation within Colombia's private than public sector, especially because the State is far less powerful there and does not impose uniformity; now attention focuses not across but within institutions. Compared to most public institutions outside modern authoritarian systems, Colombia's allot more authority to administration, representing both the State and even private external interests, and less to professors and students. Nevertheless, compared to Colombia's own private institutions, the public ones give far less power to private external interests and university administrators. Just the opposite holds for professors and students (and the State), who are clearly more powerful in the public sector. In other words, the private governance locus is tightly packed around owners and their administrators while public power is distributed among several actors. As Franco and Tünnermann conclude, governance "varies notably" between the sectors.[53] Table 6.4 highlights the contrasts in governance.

Table 6.5 strengthens the findings by depicting the more dispersed representation in public rather than private governing bodies. Private external interests and university administration account for 85 percent of private membership versus 40 percent of public membership, while the State plus university community categories total only 8 percent in the private sector versus 60 percent in the public sector.

Thinking of a structural hierarchy in which the State is the top and the university community is the broad bottom, power in Latin America's private

Table 6.4 Typical Power Distributions in Colombian Institutions

Actor	Private Institutions	Public Institutions
1. State	Limited role; despite some representation since 1975 and increased ICFES authority.	Greater role than in most nations; appoints rectors; increased ICFES role.
2. Governing boards	Like U.S. private governing boards; *the* locus of power; overwhelming representation of private external interests, including alumni; composition varies according to subsector; appoints rector.	"Hybrid of U.S. board of trustees and the classic Latin American university council"; "legitimacy problem" weakens power; "very heterogeneous" and variable composition,[a] with State official presiding.
3. Rectors	Based on delegated authority from (2) above; otherwise, very powerful, more so than in public sector; stability of rulership.	Variable strength resting on different constituency and authority bases, often competing; instability.
4. Professors	"Minimal or non-existent"[a] role, compared to both (2) and (3) above and to role in public sector.	Significant role in "directive councils" that help set academic policies but weaker viz (1–3) above than in most public sectors.
5. Students	See (4) above.	Limited representation compared to most public sectors, but greater than in private sector; main power through direct action.

SOURCES: Adapted from Augusto Franco Arbeláez and Carlos Tünnermann Bernheim, *La educación superior de Colombia* (Bogotá: Tercer Mundo, 1978), pp. 290, 292, 295, 298–301, 339; Germán W. Rama, *El sistema universitario en Colombia* (Bogotá: Universidad Nacional, 1970), pp. 144, 211–14.

a. Quotations from Franco and Tünnermann, pp. 298, 299, 300.

Overview of Latin America

Table 6.5 Representation on Colombia's Chief Governing Bodies

Representatives	Sector	
	Private (%)	Public (%)
State[a]	0	23
Private external[b]	64	27
University administration[c]	21	13
University community[d]	8	37
Other	7	0
TOTAL	100	100

SOURCE: Compilations from Jaime Rodríguez F., "Universidad y sistema científico-tecnológico en Colombia," in CPU, ed., *Universidad e integración andina* (Santiago: CPU, 1974), p. 241. No exact date is shown, but context indicates roughly 1970. Rodríguez has data on thirteen private and fifteen public universities.
a. Representatives of ministries or other government agencies.
b. Alumni, Church, cultural and professional organizations, labor and economic groups.
c. Rector, secretary general, deans.
d. Professors, students, University Council members, workers.

sectors is clearly concentrated neither at the top nor the bottom but in the middle. This pattern of a strong middle level of governance was put forth (chapter 1) as one of the essential defining differences between U.S. and Continental models. It is especially associated with the U.S. private sector. Thus, here again, Latin America's private sector follows U.S. patterns while its more venerable public counterpart remains more wedded to Continental patterns, despite recent reforms.

The strength of the private university's administrative level is illustrated by several factors of the sort discussed more specifically in the case study chapters. For example, there is much greater stability in the private than the public rectorship. No parallels can be found to the volatility seen at Ecuador's (public) Central University, where even more rectors (twelve) came and went between 1919 and 1939 than that unstable nation had presidents; rectorship instability has continued for decades. Colombia's National University had thirty-one rectors from 1936 to 1969, not counting interim rectors. The recent average tenure in the public sector overall is probably two to three years, possibly less. Moreover, in those nations where public university rectors have more often served their entire terms, these terms are usually limited to three to five years, sometimes with reelection prohibited.[54] Yet it is not unusual for rectors in Latin America's private sector to hold office for decades. One reason is that they are much less likely to be selected from below by students and professors divided among themselves or in open conflict with the State; rather, they are almost always appointed from above by a fairly coherent religious or business board. A corollary is that private rectors are likely to accumulate greater administrative experience than their public counterparts. In fact, they may start with greater experience, to the point that their academic credentials are sometimes more suspect than their administrative credentials. This too constitutes a (U.S.-style) reversal of the Continental model wherein the rector is "merely" an academic type, a senior professor selected from among his academic peers. Private rectors are selected for administrative reasons because the rectorships are important organizationally, and the skills they bring to the task may reinforce the powers of the rectorship. How different all this is from traditional views of Latin American universities as "composed exclusively of a restricted number of semi-autonomous professional schools, and nothing else," with each feudal unit headed by a "ducal" dean accountable to his professional class, not (upward) to a "King-Rector."[55] Largely because the private university is less constrained by the State's national or civil service policies, but also because it does not allow power to spin centrifugally around dispersed intrauniversity loci, the private university is generally capable of charting and implementing its own defining policy directions. Its harmonious power structure, based on a strong administrative or managerial middle tied to higher external authorities, is frequently put forth as a major reason for private sector effectiveness.

What at first seems like the most apparent exception to the private sector–university centralization rule turns out to be only a partial exception, albeit an interesting one. Costa Rica's UACA prides itself on its decentralized power structure, on what it likes to call its "traditional Cambridge model." (Cambridge has allegedly become too centralized in recent decades.) This model is based on separate colleges, highly autonomous in academic, administrative, and financial affairs. Colleges are incorporated into UACA by a pact that binds them only to UACA's broad guidelines; then the colleges enter a two-year trial period. But each college has its own Administrative Entity, or board of trustees, which appropriates and allocates funds. Each has it own deans, at least statutorily selected from within the college, and these deans are powerful. UACA's Academic Senate is made up mostly of the deans of the constituent colleges.[56] The central UACA administration is thus limited in its role. It insists that no college have more than one thousand students nor fewer than five fields of study. It also claims to guarantee quality by monitoring appointments and even by closing negligent colleges. Still, the central administration usually boasts not of its wide powers but of its limited powers.[57] It claims to prefer having scarce rather than abundant resources at its disposal.

248

But a weak central administration does not necessarily promote a widespread distribution of power. UACA limits student and professorial freedoms. Each college has a dean of students, a maestrescuela reminiscent of the colonial university's Church-State disciplinary officer. As the deans have great authority over the professors, so the maestrescuela has great authority over the students. Without his explicit permission, no student resolutions can be published, no books, papers, or propaganda can be circulated, and no media can attend student meetings. Either he or a professor can refuse to admit any student to class or can decide to expel him, without any explanation. As UACA's rector explains it: "We give the students an economic vote but not a political vote; both would make them the university's owners."[58]

Beyond Costa Rica, many of Latin America's private sector leaders similarly argue that they have adopted a U.S.-style market mechanism wherein universities are properly accountable to their "consumer public" of students and their families (rather than to the State); to do its job the university cannot let its policies be disrupted by student politics. Here again the link is made between private sector governance and effectiveness. The private sector should provide institutional choice, but it should also responsibly restrict the students' freedom to undermine the chosen institution's effective pursuit of its goals.

There are several routes to private limits on student power. Much stems from the self-selection process by which many students choose private sectors precisely to escape public sector politicization. Another factor is strict university policy both in terms of punishment for disruption and (excepting many demand-absorbing institutions) stern academic requirements. Private universities are more likely than public universities to require class attendance, insist on more rigid course selection, and give more demanding exams.

Evidence of restricted student politics accumulates from almost all private sectors, though certain individual institutions are exceptional. Few nations have experienced more student political turmoil than Venezuela, but the private sector usually remains isolated from it. Panama is a strong parallel, where private university protest has been very belated and mild compared to public university protest. Much the same can be said for Peru, even though the public San Marcos University, like Venezuela's UCV, has had a profound politicizing influence on the provincial public universities. As a Peruvian rector boasts of his university: "Since its creation, the Pacific University has never seen its institutional life disturbed nor interrupted as a result of strikes, protest work stoppages, or any other manifestation of party politics, and it is our hope to maintain this record." Student participation on governance bodies is limited to one representative with only voice, not vote,

249

this deemed sufficient for a "permanent dialogue." Colombia's Los Andes University does not allow student representation on its governing board nor in academic and administrative matters. According to Molina, this is Los Andes's "golden rule": "The administrator administers, the professor teaches, and the student studies."[59] One observer has summed up the private-public differences throughout Latin America by condemning the public sector for its excessive chaos and the private sector for its excessively hierarchical restrictions on student participation.[60]

Of the three private subsectors, the Catholic one most often violates the depoliticization dictum. This obviously relates to the reformist evolution, and chapter 2 discusses how Catholic student activism helped evoke a secular private backlash. The 1967 Buga conference of Latin American Catholic university representatives drafted a document emphasizing the value of student dialogue, academic freedom, and autonomy, all juxtaposed with a monopoly of external control. For many this was the Catholic university parallel to the Córdoba reform. It was greatly praised by Church reformists, greatly feared by Church traditionalists.[61] In terms of not just student power but the broad distribution of power, evidence from nations (such as Bolivia, Colombia, Peru, and Venezuela) with overwhelming private-public distinctiveness in governance shows that the Catholic subsector often avoids the extreme private pole of vertical autocratic governance. Sometimes it reaches a midpoint between the private secular and public norm, precisely as in Mexico's Iberoamerican University. Rarely, however, and possibly nowhere outside Chile, do even the Catholic subsectors approach public sector norms. For example, when activism at Bolivia's Catholic university reached unusual heights for the private sector, in 1979, it was still no match for Bolivia's public sector activism. Although students are unusually represented in Ecuador's Catholic universities, this too falls short of public sector norms. Moreover, students are more likely to achieve representation in assemblies than on governing boards; the former are more powerful in the public universities, the latter in the private ones.[62]

Thus, limitations concerning our generalizations about private sector governance are less profound than our limitations (reforms, and especially the recent modern authoritarian changes) concerning public sector governance. Allowing for such limitations, it is possible to conclude the section on governance with strong generalizations. These generalizations best follow the Mexican case, where comparatively few exceptions arose, but they follow the Brazilian case as well, and even the Chilean case prior to 1967.

First, the private sector is truly much more private than the public sector. This statement is made in terms of the contrasting degrees of State control. Second, institutional autonomy is not clearly greater in either sector, but third, the authorities that impinge both on institutional autonomy and

250

individuals' freedom are very different. For the public sector that authority is largely the State, while for the private sector it is largely business and Church groups. Fourth, there is much less distribution of power and freedoms within the private institutions. Public institutions are usually governed from plural power centers, including the State, university administration, professors, and students, and even sometimes workers; private institutions allocate much less power to the "top" (the State) or the "bottom" (professors, students, and workers), instead concentrating power with the owners and university administration. Each of these four generalizations places Latin America's private sector closer to the U.S. governance pattern, especially to many U.S. private colleges, while placing Latin America's public sector much closer to the Continental pattern.

A fifth generalization is that Latin America's private universities have achieved many of the reformist goals that the State has sought in public sector governance. Some success has been realized in the traditional public universities and some in the newer ones, but the greatest public sector transformation has occurred under modern authoritarian rule. Despite even this last phenomenon, the public sector has generally fallen short of the private sector on many governance policies that the State itself has acclaimed or tacitly pursued. Naturally, this does not mean that most States have wanted public sector governance to become a carbon copy of private sector governance but only that there are important elements of desired convergence. Many of these involve building strong university administrations. For example, central campuses may be established, and rectorships may be strengthened and entrusted increasingly to full-time "administrative types" rather than to "amateur" professorial types. Such attempts to strengthen university administration often involve weakening other actors, mostly those from below. The student power base may be eroded, and department power may replace faculty power. Whereas faculties have derived most of their power from their constituent chairs, departments derive more power from their ties to the administration "above." In practice, most public universities have gone further in strengthening the rectors and weakening the chairs than in weakening the students, or in departmentalization.

FUNCTION

The three case studies show that function is a more complex category to analyze than governance or, especially, finance. Yet they also show some consistency across these three dimensions. As there was great private-public homogeneity in Chile's finance and governance, so there was in its functioning. As there was great private-public distinctiveness in Mexico's and Brazil's finance and governance, so there was in their functioning, even though this distinctiveness assumed different forms in the two nations and was more marked in Mexico. All three case studies considered similar dimensions of functioning; these will be reformulated for Latin America inclusively in categories of religious missions, political ideologies, economic orientations, and quality.

Religious Missions

Common to all three case studies, religious values are no longer as salient as they had been when Latin America's first Catholic universities were created. Chile's UC, the oldest Catholic university in Latin America, maintained a core religious orientation, though not what its founders had envisioned, until the mid-twentieth century. Brazil's Catholic universities, not created until the 1940s, were never very oriented to religious matters, and Mexico allowed the creation only of Christian-inspired institutions, not bona fide Catholic universities. In all these cases, the decline of religious orientation has involved market factors, such as the inability of the Catholic universities to attract students and professors with primary allegiance to Catholicism. There have also been broader societal factors, illustrated by Vatican II and the societal secularism accompanying modernization. Because religious orientation is limited in each of our three divergent cases, it comes as no surprise that this finding is generalizable for Latin America.

Limited religious orientations stem from a combination of limited original orientations and declining orientations, depending on the university. Usually, the older Catholic universities (pre-1960; e.g., Ecuador's at Quito, 1946) initially had more decidedly Catholic missions than the newer ones (post-1960; e.g., Ecuador's at Guayaquil, 1962); the latter increasingly substituted Christian inspiration and loose ties to religious organizations for more binding ties to the Church. Argentina's (unsuccessful) Catholic university opened in 1910 with the stated core purpose of providing education "within the doctrinal unity consecrated by the Catholic church" to defend Catholicism "in all spheres of human activity."[63] Argentina's first successful Catholic university (UCA), created in the 1950s, modified this confessional approach only partially, but others (created in the 1960s) relegated Catholicism from centrality to one mission among many. And while newer institutions generally have been less confessional than older ones, many of the older ones have evolved and liberalized. The locus of conservatism has passed from the Catholic subsector to the secular elite universities, as analysis of the wave I–wave II transition found.

Expectedly, the move to reorient the Catholic universities' missions has not proceeded at the same pace everywhere in Latin America. Beyond different universities beginning at different points, additional variation has evolved over the years. Fortunately, some typologies help order the variation. For example, Pablo Latapí writes of "pastoral," "apostolic," and "open" Catholic universities.[64] The *pastoral* is the highest education arm of the Church hierarchy, officially dependent in mission as well as governance. It is dedicated to showing the divine harmony between faith and science and to crowning the university with theology and divine knowledge. The cultivation of good Christians, which is fundamental, must be realized not only through formal education but also through continued campus interaction with religious personnel and events and through banning any teaching antithetical to that end. Some academic freedom is sacrificed for religious effectiveness. The *apostolic* university, more autonomous of the Church hierarchy, is less committed to the direct cultivation of good Christians and concentrates instead on integrating Christian values into the general culture. Though run mostly by priests, not all administrators (nor professors nor students) need be believers, nor even Catholics. Priests function as individuals more than as Church personnel and are judged primarily by academic standards. The Church can, however, supervise the university's moral teaching. Finally, the *open* university does not even make an institutional commitment to specific doctrine. Individuals should act as good Christians by performing whatever earthly duties serve humankind. That an administrator or professor may be a priest is incidental, except insofar as his work gives personal testimony to Christ. The open university postulates no definite relationship between faith and science, instead emphasizing full academic freedom in the pursuit of truth. In fact, it goes beyond accepting the heterogeneity, which the apostolic (though not the pastoral) does, and actively seeks it out to maximize dialogue and interaction.

Most other typologies can be related reasonably well to this three-part one. Some authors have written of "confessional" or "traditional" rather than pastoral universities and have related the idea of "Christian inspiration" to the apostolic type, while others have related it to the "open" category. Predictably, some have argued that the open universities are non-Catholic. The lines between pastoral and open are clear, but blurring occurs between each and the apostolic type. Those who describe their own universities' missions sometimes do so in ways that defy easy categorization into one of the three types.[65]

Floating between the pastoral and apostolic types, but closer to the former, are the statements of Octavio Derisi, rector of Argentina's UCA and longtime head of the Organization of Catholic Universities of Latin America. Derisi presents his own typology of Catholic universities, from most to least Catholic, and the typology parallels Latapí's in important respects. But Derisi proceeds to specify his own requisites for a truly

Catholic university. Revealed truth, "scientifically elaborated" by theology, must be at the core of all university studies, not just isolated in a theology faculty. This is a Catholic university "responsibility" because "supposedly scientific conclusions are not that, since scientific truth cannot contradict revealed truth."[66] Thus, attacking the Jesuit model, Derisi insists on pervasive references to Jesus and the Church. The Catholic university should not even include other religious thought since, as a private university with a distinctive mission, it accepts only those professors and students who by choice commit themselves to the Catholic university model. Though not all students, professors, nor even administrators must be believers, they must (1) not express their atheism or opposing religious beliefs, and (2) understand that the Church hierarchy, however involved it may or may not be in day-to-day university affairs, always retains the right to denounce and reverse university deviations from the Church mission. Autonomy, Derisi argues, does not mean freedom from the authority and mission of the university's founding institution.

More important than categorizing the declarations of Catholic leaders is categorizing the real funtioning of their universities. Although this is extremely difficult without close analyses of individual institutions, some generalizations are possible. While certain universities still aspire to pastoral status, the aspiration usually goes unfulfilled. The Church may retain formal governance authority, but it cannot insist on a strong value commitment from the university community. In this category are several Catholic universities (e.g., some in Argentina) dependent on traditional national or local churches. More Catholic universities approximate the apostolic model. Toward the open end of the spectrum one might place some of the Jesuit institutions, such as Argentina's Salvador University (in sharp contrast to Derisi's UCA). Indicatively, Jews who attend the private sector probably concentrate in the open as well as in the secular elite universities. The nature of religious commitment makes for a deep and emotional split within Argentina's Catholic subsector.

Another institution leaning toward the open end might be Bolivia's Catholic university: few students choose the university for reasons related to Catholicism, very little theology is taught, minimal Catholic influence is detectable in the coursework, even most top administrators are lay personnel, and, overall, the Bolivian Church wonders what contribution "its" university has made. Similarly, Chile's Catholic subsector accelerated its slide toward the open end with the 1967 reforms. Brazil's Catholic universities might well be apostolic in declared mission, but they are increasingly open in practice. Mexico's principal religious universities have long labored uphill to retain some Christian inspiration. To generalize, many religious universities in Latin America increasingly approach the tendency commonly found in U.S. institutions, where even the official mission now emphasizes intellectual understanding and broad moral concerns over a distinctly Christian approach or evangelicalism.

However one labels them, most of Latin America's Catholic universities now do relatively little to foster identifiably Catholic missions. Some insist on a few required courses or try to keep some Catholic content, at least spirit, in other courses. Another way to pursue religious missions is to accept only true believers, but this policy is now very uncommon with regard to students and even professors. Many professors work simultaneously in Catholic (usually Jesuit) universities and secular ones, private or public. All this often renders the religious missions largely symbolic. For example, religious statues oversee many campuses; for another, written correspondence even from institutions not formally tied to the Church ritually include religious salutations (such as "Science and Faith" at Ecuador's Catholic university in Guayaquil). Generally, the religious mission is probably stronger in those nations where the Church itself has been stronger (e.g., in Colombia more than in Venezuela).

To summarize, most of the Catholic subsector in Latin America retains only a diluted religious mission, doing little through curriculum, pedagogy, control over personal values, or other means to promote the faith, let alone to insist on it. Even the diluted mission is only partially and variably realized. Yet, there is one persuasive reply to this whole critical evaluation of the Catholic universities' mission: most Catholic universities still do more than secular universities, private or public, to promote religious missions.

Political Ideologies

Catholic universities are not the only ones that have undergone severe identity crises. Many public universities too have wrestled hard with their fundamental values. Moreover, their struggle is frequently more complex insofar as they have lacked the degree of central inspirational focus that many Catholic universities have had, and especially insofar as their less hierarchical power structures have allowed more actors to struggle over the universities' hearts and souls. In any case, many Catholic leaders have eagerly argued that almost all universities promote some ideological values (some say "confessional" ones) rather than the pursuit of neutral academic freedom and that at least the Catholic universities acknowledge their values.[67]

The secular elite universities have rarely undergone equally severe identity crises. Instead, they have been remarkably effective in pursuing the

255

missions set forth when they were first created. This generalization holds for fields of study and job orientations, social privilege, and academic quality. They have also been strikingly effective in avoiding political disruption.

Private-public ideological differences were much more evident in Mexico than in Chile or even Brazil, partly because of the repression of dissenting political expression in the two South American nations, but also because only in Mexico has the elite subsector been dominant within the private sector. Even in Chile, however, some private-public distinctiveness withstood the Catholic university estrangement from its conservative roots. Brazil also experienced a diminished private-public gap as the Catholic subsector evolved; however, a dual sectoral comparison there would have to consider the ideological bent of the demand-absorbing subsector. While this subsector is probably conservative, its political role is neither very prominent nor easily discernible.

In general, Latin America's elite subsector is politically conservative. This political conservatism is expressed intrainstitutionally in curriculum, governance hierarchy, and prohibitions on leftist activity. It is also evident from the ideological bent of many families that send their offspring. In terms of broad political-economic orientations for society, the elite subsector tends to favor free enterprise, only a limited State welfare role, strong restrictions on leftist or populist political mobilization, and pro-Western foreign policy. This fits, for example, Albornoz's characterization of Venezuela's "bourgeois" Metropolitana, just as it fit our earlier view of most of Mexico's major private universities.[68] Indeed the rightist political-economic label would be broadly appropriate for Colombia's Los Andes, Peru's Piura, Central America's secular private institutions, and so forth. This does not, of course, imply homogeneity among or within institutions. To illustrate, many sociology and economics professors at Los Andes would defy the conservative label.

How much these generalizations should be modified for the demand-absorbing subsector is open to further investigation. As in Brazil, many institutions are individually too insignificant for their political profile to have an impact beyond their own restrictive locales. Probably most universities that hover ambiguously between the elite and demand-absorbing subsectors are conservative. Certainly Costa Rica's UACA is far to the right; its critics charge it with being neofascist, its rector with eulogizing Franco. Yet the rector himself argues that he is only one man, that other administrators are more liberal, and that UACA is open to plural values.[69] He even asserts that Marxists would be free to open colleges within UACA, though critics regard this as nonsense. UACA's conservatism contrasts starkly with the UCR's strong social democratic bent and with the second biggest public university's more leftist bent. Still, where there are both demand-absorbing and elite subsectors, the former may well be the less conservative of the two. After all, the class base is not as privileged, and it lacks ties with its nation's powerful business enterprises. Thus, Colombia's Libre University can be juxtaposed with the elite Los Andes. The Libre University was created by the left wing of the Liberal party while Los Andes has had ties to the Colombian Association of Industrialists.[70]

The degree to which rightist political ideology should be identified with the Catholic subsector often depends on where the individual universities locate themselves within the schema used in discussing their religious values. The pastoral or traditional universities are conservative, while those inclining toward openness or Christian inspiration may be centrist or even somewhat leftist. Note, however, that even the pastoral universities tend to be conservative in a different sense from the secular elite ones. They are not so free-market nor U.S. oriented, though they are anticommunist and similarly favor restrictions on leftist political mobilization. The secular elite–pastoral split reflects the split between modern, capitalist, techno-cratic, "U.S." orientations and Catholic, traditional, spiritual, "colonial Spanish" orientations. But most Catholic universities are no longer strictly traditional, so the private sector's conservative political center of gravity has shifted toward the secular elite institutions.

Yet most of the Catholic subsector still appears to fall somewhere be-tween center and right when the public sector is added to the picture. Consider first El Salvador, where the leftward first-wave drift analyzed in chapter 2 has been especially notable. According to its own rectors as well as other supporters and critics, the Jesuit José Simeón Cañas University explic-itly turned away (in the 1970s) from its conservative founding ideologies. It came to be an advocate of political compromise rather than right-wing military victory in the nation's civil war. In this connection, it became a target of right-wing venom and violence, and President Alvaro Magaña warned that it was looking increasingly like the national university. Yet the private-public contrast remained striking. The José Simeón Cañas con-tinued to operate within permitted parameters (e.g., no political graffiti), whereas the national university was shut down for years starting in 1980. Additionally, Bolivia's Catholic university has sometimes been a mediator between the "establishment" regime and the "antiestablishment" public sector. In Ecuador's Catholic universities (1960s), "modernization" repre-sented a leftist or progressive force backed by students and some professors dissatisfied with the institutions' professionalist orientation; in Ecuador's public Central University, on the other hand, "modernization" represented conservatism, pushed by the administration, while many radical students and professors called for a "revolutionary university."[71] Whatever the dif-ferences between Venezuela's Catholic Andrés Bello and business-oriented

Metropolitana, both lie much to the right of most Venezuelan public universities.

It is not just that the major private universities have often been to the right of the State. It is also that the public universities have generally been to the left—or even far to the left—of the State. Even through their administrators, as well as professors and students, many public universities have repeatedly called for "social change," a greater State role in the economy, greater distribution of wealth, political mobilization of underrepresented groups, and less support of the United States. A good Peruvian example during much of the first half of this century would be the importance of Mariátegui's revolutionary theses in the public universities, while the pontifical university represented something of an antithesis. Moreover, Latin America's public universities have frequently been major centers of leftist political and ideological opposition to the State. The major exceptions have come in revolutionary or quasi-revolutionary settings (e.g., Mexico in 1929–40, and Chile in 1970–73), where universities perceive that leftist regimes threaten academic freedom and pluralism, and in counterrevolutionary contexts (e.g., Chile after 1973 and Brazil after 1964), where regimes forbid leftist dissent (though universities may still be centers of whatever opposition exists). Other prominent examples of the counterrevolutionary context include Argentina and Uruguay (after 1976 and 1973 respectively).[72]

The generalization that the public university has been politically to the left of the private university is supported by the relationship between the different universities and the party systems (where there have been dual sectors and where parties have been allowed to function). Conservative parties, sometimes allied with Liberal parties, pushed for the establishment of Catholic universities and stood by them—unless the universities transformed themselves greatly. Especially where transformation has occurred, Christian Democracy has become the major pillar of party support. Along with Chile, Venezuela offers a good example. Thus, COPEI is identified with the Andrés Bello University, while the AD remains much stronger in the public UCV; amid the tumult of the 1960s, the chief alternative to COPEI at the Andrés Bello was not the AD but independents generally to the right of COPEI.[73] Latin America's Radical parties, however centrist or even rightist they have become, have usually maintained their pro–public sector posture (though Argentina's Radical party split over the issue in the 1950s). Elite universities characteristically rely more on the political-economic influence of their business supporters than on specific political parties, though they sometimes draw support, at least tacitly, from parties on the right to the center. The demand-absorbing institutions also depend mostly on the influence of their individual supporters, but possibly also on the political influence of whatever parties advocate increased access to higher education, regardless of sector. Finally, public universities have generally relied more than private universities on party support and have enjoyed their greatest backing from social democratic parties (e.g., APRA Peru, AD Venezuela) and more leftist parties (Socialist and Communist).

Economic Orientations: Fields of Study

As strong private-public differences characterize political-ideological functions, so they characterize economic functions. If the gap is smaller on the economic end, it is nonetheless demonstrably wide. In fields of study the two sectors show divergent patterns, with the private sector much more oriented toward business-related and especially toward inexpensive fields. Such patterns follow the Mexican and Brazilian examples. The Mexican case best illustrates the business factor chiefly because secular elite institutions have predominated in Mexico's private sector. The Brazilian case study best illustrates the differences based on inexpensive fields of study chiefly because Brazil's predominant private subsector is demand absorbing. The Chilean case best shows the effects of private-public homogeneity, partially limiting interinstitutional differences but mostly locating them along dimensions (e.g., technical institution versus university) other than the private-public one. Notably, however, some such homogeneity was also found in the religious subsectors of Mexico and Brazil. To explore how these different private subsectoral patterns manifest themselves in Latin America inclusively is a major challenge, crucial to understanding private-public differences.

First, however, it is useful to establish traditional public sector patterns. Probably the most common criticism made by observers of varied political persuasions concerns the public orientation toward traditional professions (especially medicine, law, architecture, and civil engineering) to the relative neglect of more "modern" or "development-oriented" fields (e.g., administration, agronomy, business, computer sciences, and economics). Everyone wants to be a doctor is a common refrain, even if a nation is surfeited, at least in the urban areas toward which most doctors are destined. The professionalist emphasis follows the Continental heritage, based on the incoming students' immediate and rarely revised entrance into a fixed field of study rather than into a U.S.-style liberal arts or general education. Moreover, Latin America's public sector heritage derives from Catholic rather than Protestant European modes, with the former, as Max Weber explained, less oriented to technical, industrial, and commercial studies and to business-oriented middle-class ways of life.[74] Risieri Frondizi reported that from 1901 to 1940 (a period in which Argentina's higher education system was generally considered Latin America's leader), Argentina graduated more students in law than in all other fields combined.[75] As late as 1977 Uruguay still had a classic fully public system, with nearly two-thirds of all enrollments in just two traditional fields, law and medicine (see table 6.14 below).

For the most part, however, public sector enrollments are no longer so overwhelmingly concentrated in the traditional professions. Cuba has made the biggest break, predictably, but important changes may also be achieved wherever nonuniversity technical higher education has become a priority.[76] Duly noting the extremes found in Cuba and Uruguay, the overall picture of the contemporary public sector can be appreciated in comparison with the private sector. However much public sectors have evolved, higher education's human resource profile now depends heavily, as in Mexico and Brazil, on private-public contrasts. These contrasts typically follow certain basic patterns.

Most important, private sectors have much lower percentages of enrollments in medicine and the exact sciences and much greater percentages in inexpensive business-related fields. Yet even the broad intersectoral contrasts really understate private-public differences significantly; the chapter case studies show how categories such as "social sciences" and "engineering" comprise very different balances of careers, and also how substantive content often differs between two similarly titled *carreras* (careers or courses of study) in the different sectors.[77]

Unfortunately, there is no established inclusive Latin American data base for private-public field enrollments. At least data exist on the number of professional carreras. Table 6.6 shows that the private sector has extraordinary concentrations in the economic, administrative, and social sciences as well as in the educational and human sciences. These categories hold nearly two-thirds (65.2 percent) of the sector's careers. They also account for nearly half (48.1 percent) the public sector careers, but so do the exact and health sciences (43.1 percent). By contrast, the private sector gives fewer offerings (26.8 percent) in these latter fields. In any event, these data must be used with great reservation. They tell nothing for certain about enrollments. Moreover, the data are derived from UDUAL and therefore have all the problems discussed in Appendix A; crucially, they greatly underestimate the demand-absorbing private subsector and, therefore, private-public differences.

Fortunately, it has been possible to compile ample enrollment data for sixteen of our twenty nations. I include a separate table for each nation that has had at least one hundred thousand total enrollments by 1975: besides Chile, Mexico, and Brazil, this adds Argentina, Colombia, Ecuador, Peru, and Venezuela. To save space and because the general patterns soon become clear, the text here elaborates individually only Argentina and Venezuela, for which we have complete data. Tables on Colombia, Ecuador, and

Peru are found in Apendixes F through H; Appendix I includes data on eight smaller systems.

Table 6.7 shows the intersectoral contrasts for Argentine higher education inclusively (87 percent of the total are in "universities"). The data on this third largest Latin American system (second until the late 1970s) bear out the major private-public generalizations made above. Private institutions, which hold 15.5 percent of this total, are overrepresented in the social sciences and humanities. Much clearer than the orientation toward business fields (e.g., administration) is that toward inexpensive fields. The private sector concentrates on the social sciences and humanities, is severely underrepresented in the basic sciences and technologies, and is almost nonexistent in the medical sciences. Note also that the private sector matches the public sector in architecture but trails badly in engineering (5.3 to 14.8 percent). Only 18.3 percent of the private sector versus 49.5 percent of the public sector is found in the medical and basic sciences and technologies.[78]

Much the same picture arises, using 1975 data, within the university portion of Argentine higher education. In this year the university portion represents 92 percent of the public sector and 76 percent of the private sector. When nonuniversity enrollments are removed, meaning largely humanities (mostly education), the predominance of social sciences in the private over the public universities shows up starkly (61 to 33 percent).

Available data allow an even closer look at Venezuela. Tables 6.9 and 6.10 show the major private-public differences for both university and total higher education. In Venezuela there are yet fewer compelling contrasts between the university and total higher education private-public pictures

Table 6.6 Number of Professional Careers in Latin American Universities, 1971

Field	Private	%	Public	%	Private/Total
Economic, administrative, and social sciences	344	34.6	500	24.3	40.8
Educational and human sciences	304	30.6	488	23.8	38.4
Arts and architecture	60	6.0	144	7.0	29.4
Exact and natural sciences	191	19.2	551	26.8	25.7
Health sciences	76	7.6	334	16.3	18.5
Other	19	1.9	37	1.8	33.9
Total (N = 3,048)	994	99.9	2,054	100.0	32.6

SOURCE: Juan F. Castellanos et al., *Examen de una década* (Mexico City: UDUAL, 1976), pp. 177–81. Only the licenciatura level is included.

261

than in Argentina. This is despite Venezuela having gone further than most Latin American nations toward imposing "planned diversity" by creating various types of nonuniversity institutions, hoping to reshape the traditional field patterns found in the public-autonomous university. This makes it especially noteworthy that Venezuelan private-public differences remain salient, both in university and higher education comparisons.

As table 6.9 shows, the most striking private-public difference lies in the economics and social science category. More than half the entire private sector is concentrated there, compared to less than one-fourth of the public sector. By contrast, the public sector is much more devoted than the private sector to the health and basic sciences. As usual, the private sector is more

Table 6.7 Argentine Enrollments by Field of Study, 1977

Field	Total	Private #	Private %	Public #	Public %	Private Share of Field
Social sciences	171,777	35,008	42.2	136,769	30.2	20.4
Law	61,597	14,190	17.1	47,407	10.5	23.0
Administration	102,851	17,544	21.2	85,307	18.8	17.1
Other	7,329	3,274	3.9	4,055	0.9	44.7
Humanities	109,286	29,312	35.4	79,974	17.6	26.8
Philosophy & letters	10,982	2,528	3.0	8,454	1.9	23.0
Educational sciences	68,871	19,156	23.1	49,715	11.0	27.8
Other human sciences	22,473	7,210	8.7	15,263	3.4	32.1
Fine arts	6,024	280	0.3	5,744	1.3	4.6
Music	936	138	0.2	798	0.2	14.7
Medical sciences	64,469	637	0.8	63,832	14.1	1.0
Medicine	56,117	637	0.8	55,480	12.2	1.1
Dentistry	8,352	0	0.0	8,352	1.8	0.0
Basic sciences & technologies	175,179	14,500	17.5	160,697	35.4	8.3
Agricultural & veterinary sciences	28,287	1,842	2.2	26,445	5.8	6.5
Engineering	71,602	4,372	5.3	67,230	14.8	6.6
Architecture	31,625	4,564	5.5	27,061	6.0	14.4
Exact & natural sciences	20,391	2,003	2.4	18,388	4.1	9.8
Chemistry, biochemistry & pharmacy	23,274	1,719	2.1	21,555	4.8	7.4
Miscellaneous specialities (not pedagogical)	15,739	3,454	4.2	12,285	2.7	21.9
TOTAL	536,450	82,911	100.1	453,539	100.0	15.5

SOURCE: Calculations from data in MCE, *Estadísticas de la educación 1977* (Buenos Aires, 1977), pp. 7–8.

NOTE: Higher education inclusively; the university total = 465,167.

Table 6.8 Argentine Enrollments by Field of Study, 1975

Field	Private Higher Ed.	Public Higher Ed.	Private University	Public University
Social sciences	46.2%	30.6%	60.5%	33.3%
Humanities	32.7	17.9	15.5	11.6
Medical sciences	1.7	16.0	2.3	17.4
Basic sciences and technologies	16.6	34.6	21.8	37.7
Miscellaneous specialties (not pedagogical)	2.7	0.9	0.0	0.0
TOTAL	99.9%	100.0%	100.1%	100.0%
	(73,082)	(523,654)	(55,804)	(481,155)

SOURCE: Calculations from MCE, *Síntesis 1971–1975* (Buenos Aires, 1975), pp. 143, 162.

oriented toward inexpensive fields. Since these enrollment comparisons could be misleading, owing to the major share of the public sector lodged in the "basic cycle," table 6.10 shows the figures for those who graduate (thus eliminating the basic cycle). The prior patterns are confirmed.[79]

The compound field categories in table 6.9 can be dissected, revealing some interesting differences. For example, two-thirds (66 percent) of the private university's engineering, architecture, and technology students are in civil engineering versus only 14 percent for the public universities.[80] But, as table 6.11 shows for economics and social sciences, some other intracategory contrasts are not overwhelming; others are not even predictable. In fact, among its economics and social science students, the public sector has a higher percentage than the private sector in administration, though *administration* may have different meanings in the two sectors. The substantial private edge in law is also surprising. On the other hand, the private edge in economics and the wide public edge in basic social science are expected. Note also that the public experimental subsector is very much responsible for the public edge in administration, while it has lowered the public percentage in law, economics, and basic social science. Here the alternative public institutions do make a difference. Finally, and importantly, the public edge in administration within the economics and social science category does not mean that the public sector enrolls a greater percentage of its students in administration than does the private sector. Quite the contrary: 25 percent of the private university's students are in administration compared to 12 percent of the public's.

263

Table 6.9 Venezuelan Enrollments by Field of Study, 1978

	Economics & Social Science		Humanities & Letters		Teacher Education	
	#	%	#	%	#	%
Private universities	12,114	63.1	538	2.8	1,192	6.2
Public universities	45,466	22.8	3,169	1.6	20,834	10.5
Private higher education	14,782	57.4	538	2.1	2,286	8.9
Public higher education	51,095	21.3	3,169	1.3	39,548	16.5

SOURCE: Calculations from data in OPSU, *Matrícula estudiantil* (Caracas: CNU, 1978), p. 92.

A more compelling analysis should consider private as well as public intrasectoral differences. Venezuela's four private universities (1978) can be classified by subsectoral type: Catholic = Andrés Bello; elite = Metropolitana and Rafael Urdaneta; demand-absorbing = Santa María. Table 6.12 shows how both the Catholic and demand-absorbing institutions concentrate overwhelmingly on economics and social science, along with some of the traditional professions. On the other hand, the elite subsector centers two-thirds of its enrollments on engineering and technology; there is no private sector architecture. Moreover, while all engineering in the Catholic and demand-absorbing subsectors is civil engineering, the figure is only one-fourth in the Metropolitana and zero in the Rafael Urdaneta.[81]

Table 6.12 also illustrates vividly the degree to which private universities often concentrate their enrollments in just one field. Each of the four universities has at least 64 percent of its enrollments in one field, while not one of the four public-autonomous universities has more than 36 percent in any field. The situation in the public-experimental universities varies. Two have very dispersed enrollments while four have concentrated ones, but none has the degree of concentration found in every private university.[82]

Table 6.10 Venezuelan Graduates (Egresados) by Field of Study, 1977

	Economics & Social Science		Humanities & Letters		Teacher Education	
	#	%	#	%	#	%
Private universities	1,053	64.6	54	3.3	135	8.3
Public universities	2,848	32.3	202	2.3	1,645	18.6
Private higher education	1,441	61.4	54	2.3	249	10.6
Public higher education	3,212	32.7	202	2.1	1,869	19.0

SOURCE: See table 6.9.

Table 6.9 cont'd

Engineering, Architecture & Technology		Health Sciences		Basic Sciences		Basic Cycle		Total Enrollment	
#	%	#	%	#	%	#	%	#	%
3,976	20.7	916	4.8	71	0.3	386	2.0	19,193	(99.9)
29,572	14.8	24,824	12.5	12,295	6.2	63,039	31.6	199,199	(100.1)
5,269	20.5	1,105	4.3	71	0.3	1,705	6.6	25,756	(100.1)
35,669	14.9	24,824	10.3	14,794	6.2	70,816	29.5	239,915	(100.0)

With the addition of two in-depth national studies to the three established in previous chapters and with accumulated data on eleven more cases (Appendixes F through I), the overall Spanish American picture can now be presented. Regrettably, my Brazilian data do not come in comparable categories, thus hindering a truer Latin American overview. However, it appears that the Spanish American results at least broadly parallel those identified in chapter 5 for Brazil. If Brazil were added to the Spanish American nations covered here, our field-of-study data would include nations holding 96 percent of Latin America's total enrollments (shown in the latest available data column of table 1.1); as it is, I must settle for roughly 95 percent of Spanish America's enrollment. Analyses of individual cases have yielded significant advantages in terms of interpreting data in context, counting on nearly complete data and avoiding the aggregation of field categories that differ somewhat among nations. The following composite tables not only exclude four small nations (Dominican Republic, El Salvador, Nicaragua, Paraguay) but work with incomplete data (though always better than 90 percent) from some others. Yet it is mostly because of the aggregation problem that the cross-national data should be interpreted with

Table 6.10 cont'd

Engineering, Architecture & Technology		Health Sciences		Basic Sciences		Total Enrollment	
#	%	#	%	#	%	#	%
240	14.7	141	8.7	6	0.4	1,629	(100.0)
1,855	21.0	1,656	18.8	616	7.0	8,822	(100.0)
398	17.0	200	8.5	6	0.3	2,348	(100.1)
2,109	21.5	1,656	16.9	770	7.8	9,818	(100.0)

Overview of Latin America

Table 6.11 Enrollments within the Economics and Social Science Category in Venezuelan Universities, 1978

Sector	Adminis-tration[a]	Eco-nomics	Basic Social Science[b]	Law	Total
Private	39.4%	18.5%	6.3%	35.8%	12,114 (100.0%)
Public	50.1	14.4	14.7	20.8	45,466 (100.0%)
Public autonomous	42.0	16.8	16.4	24.8	38,122 (100.0%)
Public experimental	91.8	2.1	6.1	0.0	7,344 (100.0%)

SOURCE: Calculations from OPSU, *Matrícula estudiantil* (Caracas: CNU, 1978), p. 99.
  a. Administration and accounting, managerial and administrative sciences, social communication, statistical and actuarial sciences, and industrial relations and technical courses.
  b. International studies, political and administrative studies, geography, psychology, sociology and anthropology, and social work.

reserve and discretion. Now, instead of placing data into the field categories provided by the relevant nation, I must place data into my own categories, which obviously cannot be identical to those used in every nation. (See Appendix J.) It would have been reasonable to stick with several of our individual national cases, foregoing aggregation.

Tables 6.13 and 6.14 are built from nation-based tables found thus far in the text and from Appendixes F through I; there are indications (in the notes to table 6.13) of how modifications were introduced to allow aggregation of nonidentical categories. Given that field aggregation (greater here than in individual national cases) leads to major underestimations of intersectoral differences, those major differences that do appear are especially noteworthy. Considering first the fields in which the private sector concentrates

Table 6.12 Enrollments by Subsector in Venezuelan Private Universities, 1978

University	Economics & Social Science	Humanities & Letters	Teacher Education	Engineering, Architecture & Technology
Catholic				
Andrés Bello	64.0%	2.4%	12.6%	16.3%
Metropolitana	7.4	16.8	7.3	67.7
Rafael Urdaneta	21.3	0.0	0.0	67.6
Santa María	78.0	0.0	0.0	11.1

SOURCE: Calculations from OPSU, *Matrícula estudiantil* (Caracas: CNU, 1978), p. 93.

266

more than the public sector, the major difference is found in business and administration.[83] This is by far the largest field in the private sector. The small communications category could logically be added, and the proportional private advantage there is greater than two to one. More important, economics could likewise be added, and the private advantage there also exceeds two to one. Thus, adding communications and economics to business and administration, the private sector has 30.7 percent compared to the public sector's 17.8 percent.

Less predictable is the private edge (7.0 to 5.1 percent) in the basic social sciences. There may be several explanations. One is that the different interinstitutional meanings of basic social sciences could well have a patterned sectoral bias. Another is that the public share would rise slightly, to 5.5 percent, if the comparison were based only on nations with dual sectors. Note also the smaller private edge in basic social sciences than in economics; it was not possible to separate out economics from basic social sciences in many nations, thus distorting results somewhat. Critical, however, is the cost factor. The public sector does not hold the edge in *any* inexpensive field. The private sector leads even in law (11.0 to 7.3), one of the traditional professions. Similarly, the private sector holds an edge in education (11.5 to 9.3) and the humanities (6.5 to 3.7).

As the private sector leads in seven fields, so the public sector leads in six, with one field even. Most telling is the 14.3 to 6.5 public lead in medical studies. The gap would be still greater except for the unusual Mexican university (UAG) discussed in chapter 4, which attracts many U.S. students. Outside Mexico, the private sector has only 3.5 percent of its enrollments in medical studies (versus 12.2 percent public). In the fields related to medicine, Spanish America again shows a decided public advantage, more than two to one in nursing and nearly five to one in veterinary studies.

Veterinary studies are also related to agricultural studies, where another large public advantage exists, 4.6 to 1.8. Further overlap occurs between

Table 6.12 cont'd

Health Sciences	Basic Sciences	Basic Studies	Total	
0.0%	0.0%	4.7%	8,284	100.0%
0.0	0.8	0.0	2,014	100.0
0.0	11.2	0.0	484	100.0
10.9	0.0	0.0	8,411	100.0

267

Table 6.13 Spanish American Private Enrollments by Field of Study, 1977–1980

Nation	Business and Administration	Communications	Economics	Basic Social Sciences	Law	Humanities	Education
Argentina (1977)[a]	17,544	0	0	3,274	14,190	10,156	19,156
Bolivia (1978)	200	250	400	300	0	170	0
Chile (1980)[b]	3,320	0	0	1,419	1,229	3,199	13,027
Colombia (1977)	24,336	998	10,684	6,463	15,225	4,748	1,708
Costa Rica (1979)	934	0	51	14	738	167	0
Cuba (1978)	0	0	0	0	0	0	0
Ecuador (1977)	4,269	0	1,268	2,051	1,480	2,208	7,724
Guatemala (1977)	762	0	729	162	610	1,403	355
Haiti (1978)	0	0	0	0	0	0	0
Honduras (1979)	0	0	0	0	0	0	0
Mexico (1978)	23,337	2,364	1,767	5,958	4,739	987	941
Panama (1977)	460	0	0	185	217	112	0
Peru (1977)	14,665	750	7,251	8,049	2,406	3,163	1,824
Uruguay (1977)	0	0	0	0	0	0	0
Venezuela[c] (1978)	6,814	621	2,240	766	4,341	538	2,286
TOTAL[d]	96,641 (23.6)	4,983 (1.2)	24,390 (5.9)	28,641 (7.0)	45,175 (11.0)	26,851 (6.5)	47,021 (11.5)

SOURCES: See tables 3.6, 4.2, 6.7, 6.9, and Appendixes F through J; these show the field percentages for each nation, by sector.

NOTE: Certain changes had to be made to adapt the tables on Chile, Argentina, and Venezuela (3.6, 6.7, 6.9) to the form I used for most nations (see notes a–c below).

a. The Argentine data do not allow us to break down the social science enrollments beyond administration and other social sciences; there is no separate listing for economics. Nor do the data allow us accurately to separate agricultural from veterinary studies, so I simply distributed the enrollments equally between the two.

b. I did not have the data to break down certain Chilean categories sufficiently for the present table, but I did have full 1977 Chilean data. The fields in question were social sciences, which I broke down into basic social sciences and administration, and art and architecture, which I broke down into its two separate components. I used the 1977 private-public percentages in the divided fields to divide up the double categories shown in the 1980 data (table 3.6). I got the 1977 figures from Consejo de Rectores, *Anuario estadístico 1977* (Santiago, 1978), pp. 14, 106–7, 111–15.

Table 6.13 cont'd

Medical Studies	Nursing	Veterinary Studies	Agricultural Studies	Exact Sciences	Engineering	Architecture	Miscellaneous	Total
637	0	921	921	3,722	4,372	4,564	3,454	82,911
0	150	0	0	0	0	0	0	1,470
4,376	0	0	3,008	1,892	11,665	634	0	43,769
4,374	363	0	170	3,795	16,546	5,127	3,315	97,852
120	0	0	0	0	38	290	0	2,352
0	0	0	0	0	0	0	0	0
345	321	0	225	635	1,790	792	576	23,684
31	0	0	0	0	1,034	50	150	5,286
0	0	0	0	0	0	0	0	0
0	0	0	0	0	0	0	0	0
15,136	119	630	3,192	1,009	12,893	4,687	0	77,759
0	0	0	0	8	279	32	0	1,293
676	0	0	0	3,041	3,963	1,502	840	48,130
0	0	0	0	0	0	0	0	0
1,105	0	0	54	17	4,913	356	1,705	25,756
26,800 (6.5)	953 (0.2)	1,551 (0.4)	7,570 (1.8)	14,119 (3.4)	57,493 (14.0)	18,034 (4.4)	10,040 (2.4)	410,262 (99.8)

c. For Venezuela, working from table 6.9, I had to separate architecture from engineering, nursing from medicine, agricultural from exact sciences, and veterinary studies from agricultural studies; the economics and social science category had to be broken into economics, administration, law, and basic social sciences. Data from OPSU, *Matrícula estudiantil* (Caracas: CNU, 1978), pp. 99–107.

d. Cuba and Uruguay have no private sectors. See Appendix I, note d, on the omission of private figures on Haiti and Honduras. I omitted the Dominican Republic, El Salvador, Nicaragua, and Paraguay because I could not gather anything close to the 90 percent or greater coverage (judged against separate sources, mainly table 1.1) that we have on other nations and sectors. Although UNESCO data achieve broad national coverage, they show no sectoral breakdown and are therefore inadequate for our purposes where two sectors exist. The omission of these four cases contributes to an underrepresentation of the private sector in tables 6.13 and 6.14. According to the "latest data" column in table 1.1, these nations held 5.2 percent of Spanish America's total enrollments, but 8.8 percent of Spanish America's private enrollments. The major omission is the Dominican Republic.

agricultural studies and engineering, where the public edge is 20.0 to 14.0. Additionally, engineering is a category that encompasses many subtypes, so I would expect several larger private-public gaps in them. In fact, architecture is sometimes lumped in with engineering, but there, where costs are lower, the sectors are about equal (4.4). Cost is certainly one factor behind the public lead in exact sciences, although the 5.7 to 3.4 difference is smaller than I would have guessed. Few universities in either sector enroll many in this area.

Spanish America's private-public differences can be explained in several

Table 6.14 Spanish American Public Enrollments by Field of Study, 1977–1980

Nation	Business and Administration	Communications	Economics	Basic Social Sciences	Law	Humanities	Education
Argentina (1977)	85,307	0	0	4,055	47,407	30,259	49,715
Bolivia (1978)	4,222	226	0	5,844	3,452	922	201
Chile (1980)	8,263	0	0	1,829	1,528	2,786	20,783
Colombia (1977)	7,663	620	2,842	13,624	4,443	7,242	8,840
Costa Rica (1979)	0	0	0	11,003	0	3,134	3,918
Cuba (1978)	20,059	2,541	0	698	3,320	4,157	25,000
Ecuador (1977)	19,217	0	8,473	7,417	8,733	8,538	26,195
Guatemala (1977)	0	91	6,513	3,451	2,164	1,206	0
Haiti (1978)	94	25	0	493	168	109	28
Honduras (1979)	5,518	0	2,322	1,197	2,103	114	277
Mexico (1978)	86,903	3,531	19,171	30,858	49,371	10,975	3,203
Panama (1977)	9,355	525	1,759	2,478	649	1,678	1,920
Peru (1977)	23,484	295	9,240	13,227	5,415	653	13,106
Uruguay (1977)	4,133	196	0	259	12,894	1,178	0
Venezuela (1978)	23,754	1,532	6,556	8,226	9,442	3,169	39,201
TOTAL	297,972 (14.5)	9,582 (0.5)	56,876 (2.8)	104,659 (5.1)	151,089 (7.3)	76,120 (3.7)	192,387 (9.3)

Sources: See table 6.13.

ways. These ways are interrelated, however. A central consideration is that each sector responds to controlling groups but that these groups are different in each sector. This consideration can be related to cost and employment factors.

Cost has emerged as the most obvious factor responsible for the private-public field differences. Each of the seven fields where the private sector leads tends to be less expensive than each of the six where the public sector leads. None of the former generally require much heavy capital or plant costs, while the latter often do. Medicine is obviously expensive to teach,

Table 6.14 cont'd

Medical Studies	Nursing	Veterinary Studies	Agricultural Studies	Exact Sciences	Engineering	Architecture	Miscellaneous	Total
63,832	0	13,223	13,222	39,943	67,230	27,061	12,285	453,539
9,662	0	0	504	6,874	10,512	2,527	0	44,946
10,237	0	0	2,762	1,489	23,843	1,689	0	75,209
10,147	2,091	2,728	4,421	13,051	27,652	2,202	693	108,259
2,914	0	0	2,292	3,031	2,423	2,422	13,778	44,915
13,998	0	0	13,003	6,198	39,006	5,034	0	133,014
17,279	175	1,129	6,054	8,016	25,223	6,453	9,283	152,185
5,415	0	607	1,551	985	3,366	1,334	2,551	29,234
984	0	0	139	152	1,562	0	432	4,186
2,426	402	0	1,694	1,025	4,187	0	101	21,366
110,135	1,563	14,287	28,014	22,086	132,616	31,557	0	544,270
1,859	963	281	99	2,082	1,140	1,180	2,724	28,692
9,924	4,320	4,067	8,080	5,492	40,851	2,907	983	142,044
11,963	0	0	3,825	1,319	1,524	1,645	456	39,392
24,494	330	2,084	8,221	4,841	30,986	4,741	72,338	239,915
295,269 (14.3)	9,844 (0.5)	38,406 (1.9)	93,881 (4.6)	116,584 (5.7)	412,121 (20.0)	90,752 (4.4)	115,624 (5.6)	2,061,166 (100.2)

and there the public sector holds its largest lead; even in Chile, where private-public homogenization has gone furthest, medical studies showed a typical public advantage. As Peru's Cayetano Heredia is a rare case of private concentration on medicine, so it is a rare case of a private institution financed mostly by the State. Owners of private universities are generally responsible for their expenses—and therefore seek to minimize them. To do otherwise would require even higher tuition or higher business, Church, or individual donations, or less profitability. Something similar might hold for the State and the public sector, except that the financial burden is not nearly so immediately and squarely focused, and the State finds it harder to set policy in the public sector than private owners do in the private sector. Moreover, as long as the private sector does not assume responsibility for fields (e.g., medicine) essential to virtually any conception of the national interest, the State can hardly avoid the expensive fields. This helps explain why private enrollments are often concentrated in only a few fields, while public enrollments much more characteristically are spread over many fields. In Argentina, for example, only two of more than twenty private universities have more than ten faculties, while most public ones do. Also, the past naturally shapes the present in that public sectors assumed certain responsibilities before private sectors existed. Private inaction means continued public responsibility.[84]

If expenditures form the input side of the economic ledger, graduates form most of the output side.[85] Thus, a logical link exists between private governance and strong concentrations in business and administration, communications, and economics. To the chagrin of many State officials, however, the link between the State's field priorities and public enrollments is weaker, as indicated earlier. State bureaucracy often expands to employ public sector graduates; here, however, the State often reacts to demands while those who govern the private sector more characteristically set its policies.

Both cost and employment thus relate to selectivity. Private owners are able to restrict their institutions to fields that are inexpensive and whose graduates they require. Much more heterogeneity generally characterizes those who in the aggregate, but frequently not in concert, govern public institutions. The relationship between governance and functional selectivity and the ramifications for choice and effectiveness are pursued in the next chapter. Suffice it here to conclude by placing the cost and employment factors into subsectoral context, which reflects the case study findings. Lacking conventional elite and demand-absorbing subsectors, Chile has not produced conventionally wide private-public differences, whereas both Mexico and Brazil, with their respective concentrations in these subsectors, have produced such differences.

272

Data on the field distributions in individual nations generally show Catholic subsectors to be the least distinctive from public sectors. Although not offering as many fields as national universities, Catholic universities may offer as many as provincial public universities. They offer more than the secular private ones. The two Argentine private universities offering ten or more fields are the religious UCA and Salvador universities. The Catholic posture has to do partly with the greater heterogeneity in governance found in certain reformed and comparatively recent religious institutions. Even in the traditional ones, however, the road to legitimacy often involved establishing fields already found in the public sector. Consequently, traditional Catholic universities have often been associated with the "nonmodern" field profiles commonly found in the public sector. Moreover, Catholic institutions are not usually as economics-oriented as secular private ones and so do not fully share the preoccupations of employers and financiers. They are more likely to weigh cost against other goals, such as social legitimacy; in turn, if these goals are achieved, cost problems may be alleviated by State aid. All this fits Peru's pontifical university and its unusual concentration in exact sciences.

Elite universities have a stake in effectively producing highly trained graduates, which leads to some activity even in fairly expensive fields. Note that engineering is much more common than medicine; this probably relates to the elite subsector's ties to manufacturing interests. But cost is such a vital consideration that it pushes most enrollments toward fields that are inexpensive as well as suitable to business needs. Economics and business and administration are good examples.

Cost is an even more powerful consideration in the demand-absorbing subsector. Wherever this subsector holds the majority of private enrollments—in Brazil, Colombia, Costa Rica, and Peru—the inexpensive fields are especially dominant. To be sure, some demand-absorbing institutions aim to meet both cost and employment considerations while others make cost paramount to the point of appearing unconcerned about employment. Although most nations have allowed public institutions to proliferate, creating a parallel to the private demand-absorbing institutions, the former (as shown in chapter 2) are often politically bound to serve a region by offering many of the fields given in the capital city and for which there is substantial popular demand; private institutions grow largely in major urban centers and do not carry equal responsibilities. Thus, juxtaposed to the public sector, the two secular subsectors together are often primarily responsible for the profound private-public distinctiveness found in field distributions.[86]

Private-public distinctiveness would be far greater if the public sector really conformed to certain stereotypes of it. Examination of the strongest stereotype shows that the sector is not overwhelmingly tied to the traditional professions. Engineering holds one-fifth of all enrollments, medicine less, and law well under one-tenth. What really characterizes Spanish America's public sector is its wide enrollment spread and the degree of choice it offers. This follows the rule established in Chile (excepting the UTE), Mexico, and Brazil. The public spread is much greater than the private spread in all three nations. And so it is for Spanish America generally. No single field holds more than one-fifth of total public enrollments, and only three hold more than one-tenth. The public sector has moved into new fields, albeit less resolutely than the private sector has. Of course the public sector's breadth is exaggerated by looking at aggregated cross-national data; if each individual nation concentrates on only certain fields, but the fields vary across nations, aggregate data will falsely suggest a spread. But previous analysis of individual nations showed this spread to be characteristic, even at the individual institutional level. It is in the private sector that such aggregation gives a false sense of dispersion; most private sectors, certainly most private subsectors and institutions, focus on just a few fields, overwhelmingly the inexpensive and often the business-related ones.

Economic Orientations: The Job Market

Analysis of fields of study is important not only for the information it gives us about the universities themselves but also for the information it gives us about their ties to the job market. These ties are imprecise, however. Graduates of law faculties, for example, may not work as lawyers. Yet fields of study give some ideas about the ties because such fields are mostly offered in professional faculties, as opposed to the preprofessional departments (associated with U.S. higher education) that typically shun specialized training, often leaving it to graduate schools. A rare cross-national survey indicates that perhaps three-fourths of Latin America's university graduates believe they will enter occupations in their specialized fields.[87] Moreover, impressions of some strong patterns are commonly affirmed both by those who approve and those who denounce the patterns. Unfortunately, statistical data on the subsequent jobs actually held by graduates are almost nonexistent for Latin American higher education in general, let alone for comparative analysis of private and public sectors.

Often-heard generalizations about Latin America's university-employment patterns follow those made about field distributions. Again many do not fit the private sector, but they at least help establish the traditional public pattern. As Robert Scott has written: "Until very recently the university's principal recognized function was professional training, particularly in the traditional fields of medicine, law, and engineering."[88] Following the Continental model, each faculty represented a profession, and its graduates could practice that profession upon receiving a license from the State. Argentina was perhaps the single most important example during the past and into the present century; even its provincial public universities, created partly to be modern alternatives, soon followed the traditional pattern. Throughout Latin America, historically and into the present, public graduates have frequently entered private professional practice. But others have availed themselves of what has been widely regarded as a "right" in Europe and Latin America—the right of any public university graduate to a job in the State bureaucracy. In Ecuador, for example, there is no doubt of the State's role as major employer.[89] This forms a strong parallel to the Mexican case and indeed to the Continental model, as elaborated in Suleiman's study of the tight link between public higher education and State employment in France.[90]

A common assessment is that field-job links once fit their given societies, albeit in a conservative sense resistant to social change, but that today's public universities do not adequately serve even the given economic order. Despite increases in the number of accountants, agronomists, or natural scientists produced, Latin America's public university remains more tradition bound than its U.S. counterpart, "an object of concern to States throughout the region."[91] By no means have the State's "own" public universities effectively produced graduates that meet State development goals. Some public technical institutes have done better, but without parallel to the French grandes écoles (e.g., the Ecole Nationale d'Administration), which recruit privileged students for high-level training and, ultimately, top jobs in the State bureaucracy. If public universities have largely accommodated student demand, that demand has not neatly fit market-oriented notions that it should rationally follow the job supply. At the same time, the career orientations of public university graduates have satisfied private enterprise less than they have satisfied the State.

Considerable but scattered testimony complements our findings on fields of study by showing that private universities have been better oriented to the job market and certainly to private enterprise.[92] The private sector attributes much of its success to an ability to innovate in fields of study. It claims to meet the needs of changing societies, while public universities allegedly talk more about social change but do less to produce it. In truth, some Catholic and demand-absorbing institutions really copy the public sector more than they innovate, especially in traditional fields. But other institutions, especially in the elite subsector, have taken the lead in nontraditional fields such as business and administration. There are numerous examples where private sectors have pioneered in new fields with good prospects, e.g., Venezuela's technical electronics and Argentina's business administration, communications, short courses, and other areas. Naturally, such innovation is

275

not necessarily good, and the public sector does not covet all of the private sector's laurels, yet there is little doubt that the private sector's innovations have pleased private employers.

Generalizations about the private sector and the job market are best pursued by subsector. The Chilean and Brazilian cases suggest that the Catholic subsector is less different (than other private subsectors) from the public sector. The Brazilian and Mexican cases suggest that demand-absorbing institutions are oriented mostly toward lower-level positions in the job market—some assumed after technical training, some after traditional professional training. The evidence was strongest, however, for the elite subsector, dominant in Mexico; here, cost considerations are less likely to dilute employment goals. Graduates find good positions in private enterprise, though they now also penetrate technical positions in the State. On the other hand, no Mexican or Brazilian subsectors, especially not the demand-absorbing ones, have come close to the public sectors in State employment; probably Chile's unique private-public homogenization narrowed the gap before the (private) UC's Chicago Boys actually forged a startling private advantage under the junta.

What generally happens in the Catholic subsector may depend on the degree to which Catholic universities have copied the public universities (e.g., in curriculum). If the coloration is not that distinctive from the public sector's, then differential job placement depends largely on academic prestige. This prestige, in turn, depends on a combination of academic quality and privileged clientele. Thus, Colombia's Javeriana and Bolivariana do very well, especially in private enterprise but also even in State positions. As Lebot laments, the "oligarchy" sends its children to the exclusive private universities—the Catholic Javeriana as well as the secular Los Andes—for elite reproduction and recruits its personnel from there; the Bolivariana does particularly well with the regional industrial and commercial elite in Medellín, while less prestigious private universities (Santo Tomás, La Salle, San Buenaventura) train technical personnel for middle levels.[93] The plight of Peru's San Martín University confirms that employment prospects are not so bright where universities blur waves I and III. On the other hand, Catholic universities that were really created for elite as well as religious reasons, blurring waves I and II, approximate the elite subsector's enviable employment profile. Graduates of Bolivia's Catholic university can expect top jobs in private enterprise. They can also expect top jobs with the State, as the planning and finance ministries fill many of their desirable economic and technical positions with these graduates. And while the Bolivian private sector is smaller than Mexico's, the private sector–State link is vital insofar as the State runs much of the economy. Moreover, links between quality Catholic universities and high-level State employment apply not just to recent universities created in a wave I–wave II blur. They also apply to once traditional institutions that have upgraded and reformed themselves academically, as has happened with Peru's pontifical university. Interestingly, this Catholic institution provided leftist sociologists for the reform-oriented ministries' post-1968 programs as well as economists for the democratic regime reinstalled in 1980.

Compared to the complexity of factors operating in the Catholic subsector, the employment picture is clearer for the secular elite subsector. This makes sense in terms of everything learned so far about this subsector, including its genesis, its SES and the prestige it attracts, its financial and governance links to private enterprise, its depoliticization, its field-of-study orientations, and its success in Mexico. It also makes sense in terms of findings, from a multination study, that strongly correlate high SES with plans to enter business, while lower SES strata plan much more on State employment.[94] The link between Los Andes and Colombia's industrial complex, as well as multinational companies, is a prime example. In a poll, students at Los Andes expressed much more assurance than their National University counterparts about obtaining their preferred employment.[95] Another example is the Metropolitana's close employment links to Venezuela's industrial complex. Still other Andean examples are found in Peru. The Pacific University has good ties to the business world, domestic and foreign. Together with the Piura, it has done well, while the demands of Peru's industrializing economy have not been adequately met by the public sector (whose degrees declined drastically on the job market). The Lima University does not quite match the Pacific or perhaps even Piura University in quality, but it too has strong ties to private enterprise; its open university is oriented to business administrators, accountants, and industrial engineers.[96] Moreover, the Peruvian case reaffirms that the elite subsector, as well as the Catholic subsector, can penetrate the State, especially when the State is conservatively oriented (as when Peru's reformist fervor faded in the mid-1970s). An obstacle in Peru, even when the State wants private graduates, is that it cannot always pay well enough to compete for these privileged personnel.

Less can safely be generalized about the demand-absorbing institutions. Graduates from Peru's large de la Vega and Ricardo Palma universities do not do well on the job market. As in Colombia, some job notices in newspapers and elsewhere pointedly ask for graduates from only certain universities, usually elite private ones. On the other extreme are the lowest-quality institutions interested more in attracting students than in their subsequent job placement. Only if much tighter regulations were in effect or if much more free-market information to the consumer (student) were available, amid less pressing demand for any higher education, could one assume that a lack of job opportunities would seriously diminish demand for such institutions. Unfortunately, deception of students is notoriously common in demand-absorbing institutions cross-nationally. Other demand-absorbing institutions, however, maintain decent quality or at least orient themselves directly to the job market's needs, mostly in the private sphere. This seems to be so for Costa Rica's UACA, which claims good employment success. Furthermore, in-depth investigation of the Brazilian case, where the demand-absorbing subsector is most prominent, suggests that these institutions may enroll many students who already have jobs and seek better ones.

So much then depends on quality and SES composition, both of which vary within the Catholic and demand-absorbing subsectors but are consistently high in the elite subsector. Where the public sector maintains a general edge (Brazil, Costa Rica), public institutions produce many of the best-trained students, who then obtain top positions in both the State and private enterprise. Moreover, even where the private sector holds an average quality edge, some public institutions will be competitive. The issue becomes even more complex when considering not just institutional prestige but varying faculty prestige within institutions.

This is not to overlook frequent entrepreneurial biases for private sector graduates or State biases for public sector graduates. It sometimes takes a decided private sector edge to gain access to top State positions. As discussed for Mexico, there is the issue of political legitimacy and also of inertia, with much hiring done through personal contacts. Especially where the public sector has long dominated, part-time public university professors have held influential positions in ministries and bureaus, often shifting back and forth. Without doubt, the UBA law graduate working in a given Argentine ministry can give an edge to a UBA law job candidate, particularly if the candidate is his own student or the student of a close colleague. Such contacts are also important for jobs in private professional practice and in private enterprise. It is in the latter that the private sector has often been developing superior personalized recruitment links.[97]

Finally, this section on the job market concludes by looking most closely at one specific case. Venezuela is a good choice because we have examined fairly thorough data on its fields of study.

Orlando Albornoz has probably written more than any scholar on the relationship between higher education and employment in Venezuelan development. Though describing his normative values as pro–public sector, he vividly portrays the public sector's declining position in the job market. Its graduates are oriented toward service rather than productive fields. Worse yet, the majority "are incapable of performing a task effectively." As against a "long-standing tradition that members of the elite graduate from the Central University," the daily newspapers' social pages show that "the politicians and other influential men are graduates of the Catholic University [private] and Simón Bolívar [public-experimental]." The UCV recruits an increasingly "higher proportion of the population who do not form part of the dominant elite. They belong to the majority of the population absorbed into the public sector of society and wish to support themselves by providing services within that public sector."[98]

The apparent failure of the UCV, as well as the entire public-autonomous subsector (which still accounts for half of Venezuela's total enrollments), has been partially ameliorated by the role assumed by newer public institutions. Among the public experimental universities, the Simón Rodríguez (created in 1972) is traditional in that it trains professionals, but novel insofar as it attempts to reach the popular strata and to stress careers not emphasized in the public autonomous institutions. The Simón Bolívar trains high-quality engineers and achieves an employment record much more typical of the private than public sector. Indeed, according to Albornoz, the whole public experimental subsector was created largely to meet the needs of private enterprise; but the Simón Bolívar stands alone in the success achieved in high level jobs.[99] Beyond the university realm, other public (and private) institutions have been created to meet the otherwise unmet needs of technical and industrial development. Some would be public parallels to job-oriented demand-absorbing institutions and may be partially comparable to U.S. community colleges.[100] Many new public institutions have been designed primarily to meet regional employment needs, be they in the private or State job market. For the most part, however, it is the private sector that has gained where the traditional public universities have lost. Certainly the private sector does especially well in private enterprise's top positions.[101]

Furthermore, Venezuela's private sector is penetrating the State. This penetration follows the Mexican (and the Bolivian, Colombian, and Peruvian) pattern in many respects. It is based on perceived public sector failure alongside private sector quality and pertinent field orientations. It is also based on the existence of mixed enterprises and a "third sector" that is publicly owned but administered in decentralized fashion, emphasizing "modern" tasks and practices. In both Venezuela and Mexico, oil has expanded the State bureaucracy, maintaining opportunities for public university graduates, and at the same time contributed to the State "technification" that favors private university graduates. In one important sense, however, private penetration of the State has gone further in Venezuela than in Mexico. Venezuela's private sector graduates have for some time obtained clearly political positions, in addition to economic, technical, planning, and advisory positions. There are at least three major explanations. One is that Venezuela does not share the revolutionary legacy that can make such private penetration appear illegitimate. Related to this, Venezuela has a truly Catholic university (Andrés Bello), as Mexico does not; most political penetration in Venezuela has come from this institution, not the elite (business-oriented) subsector. Third, one of Venezuela's two major political parties is the Christian Democratic COPEI, and it naturally has some ties with the Catholic university. Compared to Mexico, Church orientations are more accepted in Venezuela in both higher education and politics. Thus, for example, a former Catholic university dean was Venezuela's minister of education in the late 1970s. The Catholic university has done better under COPEI than AD rule but has achieved some top positions under both.

Quality and Prestige

The final topic treated here is quality or, often, prestige. In truth, not all institutions make high quality a central pursuit. Nonetheless, quality tells us something inherently important about how the private and public sectors perform. And quality affects how effectively the two sectors pursue their other functions, some of which are particularly private or public in nature.

The Chilean case shows a considerable degree of standardized quality. Furthermore, the interinstitutional differentiation that we found does not depend principally on a private-public split. The Mexican case shows enormous differentiation, which depends very significantly on the private-public split. However, important provisos deal with intersectorally overlapping quality. The Brazilian case also shows strong private-public quality differences, with more important provisos, but this time the public sector holds the general edge. Exploring further into subsectoral differences, additional findings emerge. The Catholic subsector appears relatively equal or superior to the public sector. The elite subsector, dominant only in Mexico, is clearly at the prestige pinnacle. But the demand-absorbing subsector appears either inferior to the public sector or relatively equal to most of it, depending on whether one draws more on the Brazilian or Mexican case. The subsectoral patterns are suggestive for Latin America as a whole, though the provisos must be elaborated and the explanations for the patterns explored.

However desirable it would be to determine the quality of institutions through systematic procedures, there are severe problems. In terms of statistical measures, one problem concerns the availability of data. Accumulating some national data is easier than finding broad cross-national data. Another problem is data reliability. Perhaps even more fundamental is the relationship between hypothesized indicators and quality. In the extreme cases, where the private (Mexico) or public (Brazil) sector is far superior, conventional statistical measures of quality tend to confirm consensual impressions. Nonetheless, it is very difficult to rely on such measures for Latin America inclusively, with all its varied cases. The following paragraphs consider some conventional statistical measures of quality, but I emphasize my strong reservations about the inferences that can be drawn.

One indicator commonly used is the percentage of full-time professors. But this indicator, as in Mexico, is terribly confusing in Latin America generally. Many of the best professors, in terms of ability to teach and to help place their students in good jobs, work principally in State ministries, hospitals, law firms, and so forth. Even the very designation *full time* is vague. Many full-timers, ostensibly working forty "university hours," also work elsewhere. The percentage of designated "exclusive-time" professors is very small. Moreover, "hourly" contracts may refer to sizeable commitments of time or to only one course a year.

In any case, the fullest data I have are from UDUAL. They reportedly cover 88 percent of Latin American universities in 1962 and 68 percent in 1971, but we know that they cover a much smaller part of higher education institutions, especially poorer private ones. Naturally, the data aggregate vastly dissimilar cases, both in terms of percentage of full-time professors and in terms of the private-public balance.[102] Table 6.15 shows mixed results. In 1962 the private sector leads in the exclusive and full- but not half-time categories, while it leads only in the full-time category in 1971. More revealing is the overall increase in work-time commitments in both sectors. But more revealing still is the continued dominance of part-time professors.

A related measure is the student/teacher ratio, but this suffers from many of the same problems as the previous measure. To be meaningful, data would have to be converted into full-time equivalents, which is rarely done.

Table 6.15 Professors' Work-Time Obligations in Latin America's Private and Public Sectors

	1962		1971	
	Private	Public	Private	Public
Exclusive dedication	3.2%	2.7%	3.5%	9.8%
Full time	12.9	10.7	19.8	12.6
Half time	4.4	13.1	8.9	11.7
Weighted total[a]	18.3	20.0	27.8	28.3

SOURCE: Adapted from Juan F. Castellanos et al., *Examen de una década* (Mexico City: UDUAL, 1976), p. 213.

a. Weighted total = exclusive + full + half of the half-timers.

Moreover, the OAS and other organizations generally count twice those who teach in both sectors, regardless of how much time they spend in each. For what it is worth, OAS data allow us to add seven cases to our three discussed in chapters 3 through 5. Argentina and Panama show wide private advantages, Nicaragua and Venezuela slight ones, while Paraguay shows a wide public advantage, and Colombia and El Salvador show small ones. Separate data show decided private advantages in Ecuador and Honduras and a public one in Peru.[103] All this can be added to the private advantages found in Chile and Mexico and the public one in Brazil. Out of thirteen cases, then, there is a private advantage in eight. Since typical private-public patterns are inverted in Brazil, and since Peru and especially Colombia have unusually large demand-absorbing subsectors, only the Paraguayan and Salvadorean results are unexpected (though mildly so). Still, I find the measure conceptually flawed and dependent on questionable data.

It is no easier to draw conclusions from data on expenditures per pupil. Higher ratios may indicate either quality or inefficiency—or student concentrations in fields that are expensive to teach, or diseconomics of scale, or major expenses on research. Each of these factors, assuming undergraduate quality to be standard, would be expected to push the public ratio higher than the private one. As with other measures, there are great differences among and within nations. If the measure is deemed worthwhile, then subsectoral patterns should be analyzed instead of just private-public comparisons. In Argentina, for example, data indicate that the secular private universities spend per pupil almost three times what the Catholic universities do; however, several factors (e.g., donated services) other than quality could account for the gap. Similarly, comparisons within the public sector could focus on experimental versus traditional universities or on state versus federal ones. In any event, a broad UDUAL private-public comparison for Latin America shows the public sector to spend more per pupil.[104]

Another facile indicator is the percentage of students in university versus nonuniversity intitutions. There are proportionally more quality universities than "other institutions," but there are also poor universities and good nonuniversity institutions. Many new public institutions use the university designation as a way of proclaiming their aspirations to match their predecessors' prestige; on the other hand, many private nonuniversity institutions choose names that reflect their specialized, selective missions and course offerings. We already know that the public sector holds a marked edge here, as gross enrollment data showed greater private enrollment in "higher education" than in university education. In Argentina, for example, the private sector holds only 18 percent of the university but 32 percent of the nonuniversity enrollments (1982), while in Colombia the respective figures are 57 and 75 percent (1981).[105]

Surrendering hopes of establishing statistically based conclusions on quality, I rely largely on the opinions of experts and "users" of higher education. This approach has obvious limitations but carries special weight when, as in our three case studies, there is consensus—even amid great disagreement over the roots or desirability of the situation. Such is the situation in most of Latin America. More fruitful than a mere conclusion concerning which sector is superior, however, is the identification of patterns of perceived superiority and inferiority. When discussing perceptions, I am not pretending to deal with provable, objective quality but more with prestige. Even regarding prestige, I am uncomfortable with unqualified conclusions on which sector leads. The identifications should be sensitive to national, institutional, and subject-matter variation. It is more useful to show quilted patterns than to declare one sector superior, even in prestige.

In most dual sector systems, the private sector is considered generally superior to the public sector. Yet much of what follows tempers that assessment. The huge Brazilian case alone would be sufficient to shatter assumptions that private sectors are inherently superior. But again it is the Mexican case that points the way toward much of the rest of Latin America, although it requires fewer reservations than typically needed for the region. All three cases show important overlap—each sector has some of the system's better and lesser institutions—although Chile's overlap is limited by substantial inter-institutional parity. Outside Brazil and Costa Rica, however, either no clear sectoral edge can be distinguished or that edge goes to the private sector.

Disregarding the two nations with only one sector, and momentarily leaving aside all with fewer than one-hundred-thousand students in 1975, there is a perceived private edge in five systems (Colombia, Ecuador, Mexico, Peru, Venezuela), rough parity in two (Argentina, Chile), and private inferiority in one (Brazil). Of the cases with under one-hundred-thousand students that I could bring in with reasonable confidence, three show private advantages (Bolivia, El Salvador, Honduras) while one shows private inferiority (Costa Rica). Most other small systems probably fit the private edge group, with Panama questionable.[106] Therefore, the private sector may well hold a perceived edge in somewhere up to fourteen of the eighteen systems with dual sectors, while the public sector has a clear edge in only two.

The private edge depends largely on the good reputation of most Catholic universities, especially where the Catholic subsector constitutes a major part of the private sector, as in Ecuador. To quote Wilson, "Ecuador's leaders in higher education are its two Catholic universities," and "the serious Ecuadorian student favors studying at the Catholic universities instead of the public universities," while public university administrators are

283

concerned even if they do not openly admit it.[107] Although not all Catholic universities have achieved the level of Ecuador's Quito or Guayaquil universities, Colombia's Javeriana or Bolivariana, Chile's UC, Peru's pontifical, or Venezuela's Andrés Bello, most have achieved respectability. Bolivia's and probably Paraguay's Catholic universities do well within the context of their higher education systems, as does El Salvador's alongside the crippling repression of the public sector. Catholic universities save Brazil's private sector from almost utter disrepute.

Increasingly, however, the private sector's prestige rests on the secular elite as well as on the Catholic subsector. Notwithstanding its pontifical university, Peru's private sector prestige now probably depends more on the Cayetano, Pacific, and other universities. Los Andes has the highest prestige in Colombia, just as the Belgrano may have in Argentina (within the private sector). Although further examples could be added, the importance of the elite subsector never quite equals that found in Mexico; this helps explain why the private edge is rarely as clear as in Mexico, despite significant parallels elsewhere.

Although not crucial in Mexico, the biggest factor diluting a generalized Spanish American private edge is the size of the demand-absorbing subsector. Most assessments of sectoral quality ignore this subsector, which is, after all, less important in most respects (economic and political) than in enrollment weight. Demand-absorbing institutions thus have something in common with U.S. "invisible colleges"—nonprestigious private liberal arts colleges that are often overlooked when conclusions about private sector quality are based on the Harvards and Dartmouths.[108] If the private sector is evaluated by giving full weight (proportional to enrollments) to the demand-absorbing subsector, then the private edge is seriously diminished, as in Colombia, Peru, and the Dominican Republic.

The significance of the demand-absorbing modification to private superiority obviously depends on the relative size of this subsector (see table 2.4). It also depends on just how poor the quality is (e.g., probably worse in the Dominican Republic and Peru than in Argentina and Venezuela). Finally, this modification must be measured against the size of the public sector's demand-absorbing institutions. In fact, most public institutions have been partly demand absorbing, driving down average quality, and some have been at least as essentially demand absorbing as those in the private sector. An important example is the set of Colombia's departmental (regional) universities, which offer few fields of study and lack finances, laboratories, and libraries.[109] In other words, a full evaluation of private-public quality or even prestige would have to compare the bottom as well as the top of each sector.

Further to illustrate perceptions about private-public and subsectoral

284

quality differentials, consider the experience of CINDA (Interuniversity Center for Andean Development), an international organization concerned primarily with fostering linkages between universities and centers of economic production—private and public, rural and urban—especially with regional development foci. It seeks member institutions, irrespective of sectoral affiliation, based on the feasibility of establishing these linkages. It explicitly favors innovative and high-quality institutions of manageable size, receptive to pilot projects. In practice, this results in the involvement of few public universities, either somewhat atypical (e.g., Costa Rica's UCR) or very atypical (Venezuela's Simón Bolívar). Nor are any demand-absorbing institutions included. The overwhelming majority of members are elite universities (e.g., Argentina's Belgrano) or high-quality Catholic universities (e.g., Ecuador's Catholic University of Guayaquil). CINDA's fifteen-member board of directors (1982) includes three at-large country representatives, eleven private university representatives (rectors, vice-rectors, and directors), and one ex-rector of a public university.[110]

A few national examples may be helpful here. Venezuela typifies general private sector superiority, with reservations. The Catholic Andrés Bello is still quantitatively the most important bulwark of private quality, although the secular Metropolitana may have overtaken it in prestige; the secular Rafael Urdaneta and Tecnológica are also rising. One of the public experimental universities, the Simón Bolívar, shares the pinnacle with these private institutions, but the other public experimental universities do not. While there are both private and public nonuniversities of varying quality, the only nonselect private university is the Santa María. In short, allowing for exceptions, the private edge already came to be widely acknowledged by the 1960s, as the public sector was academically, socially, and politically transformed. On the other hand, despite an institutional slide based on trends in fields such as education and economics, the public UCV still maintains its position at or near the prestige pinnacle in fields such as dentistry and architecture.[111]

Colombia is generally characterized as having unusually great overlap, but still with a private edge. Molina writes that "heterogeneity appears to be the rule that best characterizes Colombian higher education," and Rama finds that Colombia differs from most of Latin America in that quality varies even more in the private sector than the public sector; the private sector occupies both the top and bottom. In numerical terms, the demand-absorbing institutions dominate the private sector.[112] San Buenaventura, Santo Tomás, and the Libre University parallel Venezuela's Santa María in being rather unprestigious private universities, while Colombia's Valle University parallels Venezuela's Simón Bolívar as a prestigious public university more inclined toward the U.S. than the traditional Latin American model. But demand-absorbing institutions abound in both sectors. The influence of Los Andes, Javeriana, and (to a lesser extent) Bolivariana and others, helps make the private sector better regarded than the long-beleagured public sector. As de Zubiría reports, the private edge is recognized by State agencies as well as private enterprise.[113]

Much the same principles hold in Peru. Most observers, participating and disinterested, think that the private sector is superior. In fact, the Peruvian private-public gap is considered wide. Typically, however, the tendency is to point to the best private institutions, the pontifical, Cayetano, Pacific, Piura, and perhaps Lima universities. Less is said about the Santa María and Women's Sacred Heart universities, which are not as good, nor especially about the low-quality San Martín, de la Vega, and Ricardo Palma universities. If the pontifical, Santa María, San Martín, and Sacred Heart universities are taken as Catholic, then that subsector holds 46 percent of private enrollments; but it is very mixed in prestige, so it might be divided into the other two subsectors to assess sectoral quality.[114] This could yield a very prestigious level with 17 percent, followed by a reputable level with 28 percent, and a low level with 55 percent. Given perceptions of an abysmal public sector, we are left with seven of the private universities appearing generally superior to the public sector. Still, because all the low-quality institutions are large, the majority of the private sector, in enrollment terms, is unenviable. The private sector's lead is thus easily exaggerated. It rests on most of its institutions' reputations but not on most of its enrollments. Nonetheless, the private sector has certain very important advantages. First, the majority of its institutions are at or near the top, while most public institutions are far from it. Second, even where the public sector has centers of excellence, the private sector may lead (e.g., Cayetano over San Marcos in medicine). Third, while the private sector has slightly over half its enrollments in low-quality institutions, these are sadly dwarfed by public enrollments.

Argentines are divided over which sector is superior, partly because the private-public issue can still stir historic passions. Also, the equation has been in flux. The public sector probably held a strong prestige edge as late as 1966 and probably even retained some edge until at least 1976, despite military and Peronist-led purges. The second modern authoritarian experience may have changed this, as the public sector was hurt far worse than the private sector. Unfortunately, the private gain had more to do with public decline than private improvement, although the latter occurred and the two were related (e.g., hiring purged professors and attracting students who once would have preferred the public sector). Still, the Argentine case shows how far ahead the public sector could be before the private one was even created. Prestige feeds on itself, and most top students continue to prefer the public UBA and La Plata universities. Yet student choice does not prove quality. Graciarena believes that the private sector really caught up in the 1960s and that the students' public sector preferences subsequently stemmed from the tuition gap and a quality-prestige lag.[115] Just as social exclusiveness often leads to a larger private edge in prestige than quality, so tradition can do the same for the public sector. In any case, by the time a civilian regime retook power (1983), a subsectoral analysis could suggest that the private sector had probably achieved rough parity with the public sector.[116] Whereas Chilean private-public parity has been based mostly on the minimization of private-public distinctiveness, Argentine parity continues to be based more on countervailing distinctive factors.

To illustrate intersectoral overlap (in both quality and prestige) more broadly, we might imagine a relatively typical Spanish American system with 20 percent enrollments in the private sector. Put another way, this is not so much a typical system (since there is no single modal type) as it is a composite picture based on an aggregation of Spanish America's systems. The system might be divided into (1) a pinnacle, of roughly the top 5 percent; (2) its prestige core, of perhaps the next 15 percent; (3) the mediocre bulk of roughly 40 percent; and (4) the low-prestige bulk of about 40 percent. The private sector would at least hold its own in the top category, probably better. It would achieve great overrepresentation in the second. It would be significantly underrepresented in the other two, but perhaps not as significantly as some might guess.

Additional features partially counterbalance this private edge in average quality, however. These features are found, as they were in Mexico, even where the private sector is generally more prestigious than the public sector. A major example is research. Traditional Catholic universities have not generally regarded research as fundamental to training good Christians, while modern enterprises are more often tied to imported technology than to domestic research. But the biggest obstacle to private research is cost. There is simply no strong Latin American parallel to the early and sustained U.S. research relationship between philanthropy and private universities; instead research has depended on State funds. Exceptions involve foreign funds and social science research institutes, especially noteworthy where authoritarian regimes have knocked such research out of the university system. Overall, however, most research is done in the public universities, increasingly within their protected institutes. The private sector has made inroads in only a few areas, usually in applied research. UDUAL data indicate a public edge both in terms of the proportional number of researchers and the percentage of the university budget devoted to research. Some would minimize the research factor, arguing that little research is really done (or even should be done) in Latin America, anyway. Yet what is done is greatly concentrated in the university, more so than in other regions.[117] Relatedly, graduate education has been minimal until recently (and not deeply analyzed in this study), but it has been concentrated in the public sector; here, however, recent private inroads are significant.[118] Moreover, it appears that (following the Mexican case) private sector students are much more likely than their public counterparts (e.g., in Peru) to pursue graduate education abroad (mostly in the United States).

Aside from research and graduate education, the public sector also holds qualitative (as well as quantitative) advantages in many fields of under-graduate study. The private sector only sporadically contributes to the agricultural, medical, or exact sciences; for example, despite the average private edge in Peru, the leader in agronomy is the public Molina University. The private sector is also frequently weak in the basic social sciences. Additionally, the national treasure of fine arts (music, dance, theatre, poetry) generally reaches its heights in the public sector. Superiority in the law, engineering, and architecture can be found in either sector. So much depends not only on national and sectoral variation but on institutional variation as well. Even where one sector is usually inferior in a given field, some institutions defy the rule. For example, Argentina's private Salvador and Córdoba universities are highly rated in medicine and the Mendoza University in law, even though the public sector is more renowned overall in these fields. The broad point here is that much intersectoral overlap occurs by fields, much of it patterned, some of it random. One strong point in the public sector's favor is that it generally holds a proportional edge over the private sector in certain fields, such as medicine and exact sciences, that often attract the best students. Another is that some public universities, particularly national ones, have on their staffs many of the most prestigious professors.

Furthermore, some observers draw distinctions turning on values. The social sciences provide interesting illustrations. Even where the private sector teaches more economics and places graduates in higher positions, the public sector may be "better" if one prefers theoretical or Marxist to mainstream Western economics. Many charge that the private sector is inferior in terms of critical and antistatus quo dialogue and true freedom of expression. This point applies to the humanities as well as the social sciences. As usual, greater distinctiveness is found between the public sector and the elite subsector than between the public sector and the Catholic subsector.

But normative differences do not preclude shared perceptions of facts. It is possible to identify surprising bases for consensus, albeit far from complete, about private and public prestige. This consensus emerges largely because, as in Mexico, critics of the private sector give the devil his due and concentrate instead on crucial reservations. They also emphasize the roots of the private edge, about which there is great disagreement, or at least greatly different emphases, with antagonists often talking past one another.

The private sector emphasizes its claim to efficiency and superior policies. Much of this is related to the innovations in governance (debureaucratization, depoliticization, departmentalization, academic requirements) discussed earlier and to further claims about functional innovations (general studies, ties to private enterprise, direct job preparation). I have generally inclined toward granting the private sector an edge in innovation. In some of the specific areas cited the edge appears clear, but a definitive general statement would require more research on this issue than has been done here or elsewhere. In one sense, the issue is simple: The public sector has represented the established patterns, so an alternative sector's policies are often innovative in that they are different. Of course, some public institutions, such as Colombia's Valle University, have broken the traditional model, but such breaks are much more characteristic of the private sector. Whether innovations really lead to extra quality is harder to assess. For what it is worth, given its biases, the published testimony of most foreign observers is affirmative. Typical is Wilson's view of Guayaquil's Catholic university in comparison with Ecuador's public sector: "Uninhibited by tradition, this school has demonstrated its willingness to experiment with new methods and programs in an effort to achieve educational excellence."[119]

In response, critics of the private sector emphasize one factor above all others—elitism. In short, the private sector's quality edge rests largely on the better-prepared student it attracts. Even if the private sector is credited with attracting quality, it may not hold as much of an edge as it claims in "value added."

The private sector's ability to attract the elite has already been explained (chapter 2). A related characteristic is institutional size. As in the United States, the private proportion of institutions outstrips the private proportion of enrollments. Even UDUAL data, which exclude many hundreds of small private institutions, show private-public differences; in 1971 the average private institution had 2,765 students while the average public institution had 7,127. Or, to use OAS data found in table 1.1 and Appendix C, Spanish America's private sector (1975) has 19 percent of enrollments versus 39 percent of institutions. These aggregate data have their flaws, but private institutions are smaller in every nation for which we have reliable data. Restrictiveness is, of course, especially characteristic of the elite subsector. Typically, the Dominican Republic's Technological Institute of Santo Domingo declares its intention to train a few people of high quality and to remain small and not compete with the public university.[120] This clearly parallels evidence accumulated for Mexico. Few public universities have similarly held down their numbers in recent decades. But quality and size are related only to a point. As shown in Brazil, average private size is smaller even where the sector is inferior.

Perhaps it then seems odd that scattered data show private and public universities rejecting similar percentages of applicants, even where the private sector is more prestigious.[121] One interpretation is that such statistical indicators ignore self-selection. Many students do not apply where there are insuperable academic and financial requirements. Much more telling data deal with the percentage of private secondary school graduates. Private secondary schools hold a clear edge over public secondary schools in most of Latin America, as measured for example by the percentage of graduates proceeding to higher education. Chapter 2 has already provided data. To add one case, nearly all Venezuelan private secondary graduates can go on to higher education, and a disproportionate share choose private universities.[122] A corollary indication is the frequency of entrance exams (also discussed briefly in chapter 2). In Ecuador all private universities have such exams, while only one public (polytechnic) institution does. In several nations, including Venezuela and Ecuador, student activists in the public universities fight attempts to impose such "private" policies.

Restricted size joined with rigorous academic and financial requirements clearly favor the privileged classes, whether or not this is an explicit goal. Naturally, students with the highest SES backgrounds are found in the elite subsector, again as shown in the Mexican case. The most prestigious Catholic universities may trail slightly, while others trail substantially, and the demand-absorbing institutions attract mostly a different clientele. Unusually good data on the Colombian case support these generalities. Beyond the data in chapter 2 on the top private institutions' large edge over the top public institutions in attracting the highest SES students, additional evidence can be found. It is unclear whether the public sector really offers much more opportunity for the lower classes, though that sector probably offers more opportunity for the lower-middle classes. What is clear is that the public sector is especially attentive to the middle-middle class. It is also clear that several Catholic universities offer more opportunity for this class than do the elite institutions. But the most prestigious Catholic universities (especially Javeriana) approach Los Andes at the SES pinnacle. Expectedly, the demand-absorbing institutions, such as the Libre University with its nighttime and part-time studies, attract many working- and lower-middle-class students. Although a few public universities (including the National and the Antioquia) draw from the SES pinnacle, the point is that they simultaneously draw a more heterogeneous clientele than do the most prestigious private universities.[123]

In sum and in the absence of broader and more reliable data, evidence suggests that the private edge is partly based on privileged SES recruitment. The elite subsector has the highest average SES, followed by the prestigious Catholic universities. The national public universities, like the former two types, also draw from the very top but, even more than the Catholic universities, they simultaneously draw largely from the middle and lower-middle class. Even most demand-absorbing private institutions draw off groups that are atypically privileged within the general population but not within the higher education population. Most regional and other public institutions draw off the least privileged within the higher education population.[124] However elite the overall higher education profile, patterned variation occurs both within and across sectors.

Similarly, such variation characterizes quality and prestige issues in general. Despite this, it has been possible to identify certain patterns of superiority and inferiority. Much as in the case of U.S. private and public schools, these complex patterns, and the controversial explanations for them, prove far more interesting than the simple conclusion that the private sector holds an average edge in quality and a wider edge in prestige.[125]

CONCLUSION

In a sense, this chapter represents the book's summary. It has evaluated the relative weight of the principal patterns of finance, governance, and function discovered in the three major case studies. The idea has been to establish the best empirical generalizations possible while making order out of the major qualifications. This, then, has been the empirical overview for Latin America.

Great private-public distinctiveness can be seen in all three areas—finance, governance, and function. This distinctiveness tends to follow the Mexican pattern more than the Chilean or Brazilian one, but all three patterns, and variations on them, help form the overall picture. Although subsectoral analysis shows major pockets of homogeneity, especially between Catholic and public universities, this homogeneity does not match that found in Chile; moreover, the Catholic subsector is diminishing in relative importance in favor of the two secular subsectors. Following the Brazilian pattern, there is important distinctiveness between the private demand-absorbing and public institutions. And following the Mexican pattern, there is a different but even more important distinctiveness between the private elite and public institutions.

7 The Consequences of Privatization: Reconceptualizing

The preceding chapter, in showing how the three case-study patterns manifest themselves throughout Latin America, went far toward concluding this book. But an important challenge still remains: revising basic conceptualizations of higher education and its relationship both to the State and society, in light of the enormous changes that have emerged during decades of privatization. Such an effort pushes the analysis to a level of generality exceeding that found in previous chapters. Also, whereas those chapters dealt with higher education inclusively, drawing conclusions bracketed by sector but also identifying intrasectoral variation and systemwide tendencies, this final chapter devotes special attention to what can be concluded about the nature of private-public interfaces.

The scope of documented change wrought by privatization is such that once valid ways of thinking about Latin American higher education no longer suffice. After all, the private sector has exploded from near nonexistence to where it now holds one-third of all enrollments. Its profile—in evolution, finance, governance, and function—is largely distinct from the public sector's. As this distinct profile has developed in intense interaction with various classes, groups, and interests, it has remolded not only higher education itself but relationships between higher education and its environment. Thus, this final chapter seeks broad ways of understanding the consequences of privatization. First it summarizes the extent and shape of private-public contrasts within higher education, showing how each sector can usefully be compared to contrasting foreign models and how the concepts of privateness and publicness are truly relevant. It then shows how privatization affects different conceptions of success and failure for higher education in relation to society at large. Finally, it considers how privatization reshapes State–higher education relations and, as a result, the usefulness of different concepts (such as corporatism and a generalized privatiza-

292

tion of Latin America's political economy) for understanding the recast mold.

PRIVATE VERSUS PUBLIC
Sector versus Sector

The private-public distinction matters. Evidence accumulated throughout this book adds up to enormous and patterned intersectoral differences on most of the major dimensions considered. Basic questions demand contrasting answers depending on sector, notwithstanding overlap. While regional patterns, variations, and qualifications were elaborated in the previous chapter, this section confines itself to a summary statement on the extent of intersectoral differences in finance, governance, and function. Admittedly, this does not do justice to identified complexity; however, the private-public distinction matters too much to bypass in conceptualizing about Latin American higher education.

If privateness and publicness in finance depend on the ratio of State to total income, then Latin America's private sectors are truly private and its public sectors are truly public. Most private institutions are completely financed through non-State sources. Significant differences in income sources usually involve not the State but balances among various private actors, including students, alumni, churches, and businesses. The major exceptions to private financing involve Chile's private universities, several Catholic universities (which nonetheless derive the bulk of their income from private sources), and indirect State support granted through tax exemptions for nonprofit institutions. Yet, however private one sector is, the other sector is even more public. Tuition and donations have rarely been more than token supplements to State subsidies in the public sector. Latin America's private and public institutions are indeed financed differently, with different burdens placed on clients and external financiers, including the State and its taxpayers.

Similarly, if privateness and publicness in governance depend on the State's share of political control, then the private sector is generally quite private and the public sector appears substantially public in comparison. As a rule, the State has much more control in the public than private sector over resource distribution, administrative and academic appointments, and the content of academic policy. But in governance, unlike finance, the State is not the only major actor in the public sector. Instead, both sectors distribute power among several actors. One crucial contrast is that the power distributions typically involve different actors in the two sectors. Another is that public institutions typically distribute power more widely. Compared to public institutions, private institutions concentrate authority and have steeper, more hierarchical power structures. All this makes for interesting differences. On the one hand, the private sector is more decentralized than the public sector. This is largely because individual private institutions have their own financiers and authorities while the State plays a significant role in most public institutions. On the other hand, individual private institutions are more centralized than individual public institutions. This is because private institutions usually concentrate power in fewer hands. Along with the university administrators they appoint, "external" actors (principally business and religious groups) run the private institutions. These actors are much less powerful in public institutions. University administrators also tend to be less powerful in the public sector, partly because they share more power with professors, and especially with students, than do their private counterparts. Broad participation is much more common in the public than in the private universities. This private-public gap is greatest when it deals with autonomous public universities under relatively open political regimes. It diminishes both under modern authoritatrian regimes, where the State increases its control over most actors, and in nations where Catholic universities have moved away from traditional hierarchy. As a rule, however, the private and public institutions are governed very differently.

It remains more difficult to compare sectors on the basis of privateness and publicness in function than in governance or especially finance. This analysis has considered services performed for private enterprise and the State as private and public, respectively, but it has also included different functions performed by each sector regardless of whether those functions could clearly be labeled private or public. Religious groups are served much more by Catholic than other universities, be they secular private or public, although that service has been transformed and rendered less direct over time. Private enterprise has increasingly been served more assuredly by private than public universities. This is seen, for example, in fields of study and in employment patterns. At the same time, public university graduates are likely to find State employment, though both sectors prepare students for private professional practice.[1] Politically, the private sector has served conservative parties and their supporters much more than the public sector has. In sum, the private and public institutions perform different functions, serving different interests.

These findings on substantial private-public differences are especially pertinent given various tendencies to minimize such differences. Most specifically to this study, these tendencies exist in the field of Latin American higher education. The effort to minimize is usually couched in terms of the broad, laudatory functions that universities generically perform.[2] Thus, supposedly all universities pursue truth, the growth and dissemination of knowledge, academic quality, student development, national development, more rational relationships between higher education and the productive apparatus, social justice, the public interest, and so forth. But two fundamental issues are sidestepped by such nebulous claims. One is that these general missions have all sorts of meanings in different universities. Throughout this book, certain religious, social, political, economic, and academic factors have been treated far more closely than would have been possible in a mere listing of normative goals. The other issue is that even the truly and identically pursued goals are achieved in very different degrees and forms across institutions and sectors.

Although the claim of private-public similarity is most often based on normative pursuits, it is sometimes based on empirical overlap. While the major proponents of the former argument are partisans concerned about invidious perceptions of private illegitimacy or public inferiority, even many disinterested observers emphasize overlap in behavior. Most broadly, Marxists and others often argue that universities inevitably reflect their own societies. No findings from previous chapters contradict this assertion. The point is, however, that the societies in question are complex, composed of very different classes, groups, and interests, and different types of universities vary greatly in the shape and degree to which they serve different parts of these complex societies. Even if one believes that all universities serve the dominant class, there is still great latitude for differences in how and how much. Beyond this, while each chapter has elaborated major qualifications to the findings on intersectoral differences, such qualifications are the natural by-products of generalizations about complex phenomena, and the generalizations on private-public differences stand by the overwhelming weight of the evidence. Empirical overlap does not dissolve empirical tendencies.

Furthermore, the findings on substantial intersectoral differences tap into literatures beyond Latin American higher education. As noted in chapter 1, there has been considerable uncertainty and disagreement as to whether the private-public distinction matters. In fact, policy analysis has often cast doubt on whether different organizational forms, be they social institutions or political structures, including even political regimes, produce significant policy differences. In the Latin American context in particular, socioeconomic level or dependency or the omnipotent State are sometimes regarded as the crucial factors next to which different organizational forms produce little effect.[3]

This book's findings are obviously derived from analysis of only one field—Latin American higher education. A key factor here is that the private and public institutions have usually arisen for distinct reasons, the private ones often as religious, SES, economic, political, or academic alternatives to existing public institutions. But another reason for the conclusions about the great extent of private-public difference derives from the emphasis on in-depth analysis of complex issues. Note, for example, how sterile an exclusive focus on available quantitative measures of quality would be, or how quantitative measures of gross field categories would have understated private-public differences. In any event, different readers will make different judgments concerning how much to generalize about the private-public distinction on the basis of Latin American higher education. A possible attraction of this study is that it has treated multifaceted components of the private-public question, across many nations and higher education systems, and has dealt mostly with sectors that are truly private and public more than torturously ambiguous. Clearly, however, better understanding of private-public issues can be achieved only through an accumulation of studies dealing with different subject areas.[4]

Stereotypes, Foreign Models, and Comparative Perspectives

Decisive differences between private and public sectors, along with the substantial size and importance of the former, render inaccurate many popularized notions about Latin American higher education. To reconceptualize, different sectors can fruitfully be compared to contrasting foreign models. Unfortunately, most extant notions are based on outdated and stereotypic views of the public sector alone. Rare and limited exceptions include some Spanish-language sources on specific private institutions. U.S. perspectives are particularly colored by the most prolific literature on Latin American universities, that on student politics (mostly in the 1960s). Although this literature has helped counter popular misconceptions that most individual students are activists, it has also promoted the image that student associations are very active, very leftist—and very powerful. Largely by omission, it has given the impression that the State, other external entities, and university administrations are not as important as they are. This is a misleading impression of public autonomous universities, but it is an even more misleading impression of public universities under modern authoritarian rule. Beyond this, the stereotype has never properly characterized the private sector. The private sector's students have been neither active, nor leftist, nor powerful; power lies elsewhere.

Even beyond the student politics literature, most generalizations about Latin American higher education have been based only on the public sector. Consider some of the principal traits that the influential Atcon report finds typical of what he calls "the" Latin American university.[5] In terms of governance, Atcon's rector is weak and usually selected from below. The key powers from below are (1) the students, who riddle the institutions with their partisan politics, (2) the chaired professors, civil servants who form the basic organizational units of university governance, and (3) the deans, loyal to clans of chaired professors and antagonistic to efforts to centralize university structures that are incredibly decentralized (despite State-imposed structural uniformity for higher education nationwide). While some of these traits have characterized or even still partly characterize the public sector, none has characterized the private sector. Turning from governance to function, Atcon refers to the monopoly of the professional school form, to the dominance of medicine, law, and engineering, and to the socially elite student body. In reality, all three traits have become less characteristic of the public sector than they once were. More striking, the first two traits have not been nearly as pertinent to the private sector. Atcon also harps on the gap between university functions and the national productive apparatus, whereas the private sector has frequently oriented itself directly to the job market. Finally, even regarding the most easily assessed facet of all— finance—Atcon's generalization proves fundamentally wrong for the private sector, even as it remains fundamentally right for the public sector. "It is valid to generalize stating that *all universities* in Latin America are subsidized wholly or in part *by the state*," that universities lack clear financial policies, and that private finance is "insignificant" and "mostly window-dressing" (Atcon's italics).[6]

Erroneous extant notions about Latin American higher education stem partly, and understandably, from the fact that much more U.S. literature was written in the 1960s than the 1970s.[7] Public sectors have since evolved, and private sectors have grown to where generalizations that fail to account for them prove much less adequate in the 1970s and 1980s than they did in the 1960s or especially in the 1950s or 1940s. Therefore, attempts to think of contemporary Latin American higher education in terms of any one foreign model necessarily exacerbate the unfortunate stereotyping. Because of this, and because of the tendency of the few comparisons to focus on only the Continental model, this study has considered U.S. models as well. Not to do so would again reflect inattention to Latin America's private sector. Granted, this attempt to see Latin American practices in very broad comparative context is not free from facile parallels and contrasts. The hope is that it brings us closer to the mark and is particularly helpful for readers more acquainted with European and U.S. than Latin American higher education. In any case, drawing on the foreign models outlined in chapter 1, the following section summarizes the approximations discussed throughout the book.

In the area of finance, Latin America's public sectors closely resemble the Continental model in that they draw their resources almost exclusively from the State, usually from the national government. This holds for relatively new, alternative, public institutions. The U.S. public model, based on state government financing accompanied by business, endowment, individual (including alumni), and client financing, is emulated only in small bits and pieces. But as Latin America's public sector is more public than the U.S. public sector, so Latin America's private sector is more private than the U.S. private sector. Here it is the Continental model that is irrelevant. Even the U.S. private *university* model is appropriate (outside Chile) only to the limited extent that some private universities in Latin America receive national government help for research and graduate education and that some quality universities, mostly Catholic, receive direct State subsidies. State subsidization of Latin America's private universities remains much less important than State subsidization of U.S. private universities. It is the U.S. private liberal arts college, which receives little or no State aid, that provides the closest approximation for the Latin American private norm. These colleges, like Latin America's private institutions, especially the lower-quality ones (in both regions), rely mostly on tuition, with religious ones also counting on Church as well as other voluntary assistance. Like higher-quality U.S. liberal arts colleges and universities, many of Latin America's prestigious private universities draw substantial corporate or foundation aid.

Concerning governance, chapter 6 in particular suggests several comparisons with foreign models. Tying them together here, albeit sketchily, Latin America's public sector continues to approximate the Continental model better than any U.S. model, although the parallel is much more restricted than in finance. The main similarity is that the State plays an important role. Certain differences arise concerning how that role is limited. Most of Latin America's public universities have been granted some real as well as formal autonomy in many policy areas, such as resource distribution and administrative appointments, and State control has been further restricted by student power. In the Continental model, the main check on State power has involved neither student power nor even institutional autonomy as much as the chaired professor. This check has also been manifest in Latin America, but less so because of the atypicality of full-time professorial status and the lack of an institutionalized research base even remotely comparable to Europe's. Where State power has gone comparatively unchecked in Latin America under modern authoritarian regimes, one would have to reject the Continental model, perhaps looking more to an East European model in certain respects.

Latin America's private sector differs from the Continental model, and its Latin American public approximation, on every fundamental aspect of governance just discussed. The State is much less important while other external actors are much more important. Professors are considerably weaker than in the Continental model, while the main contrast in student power remains that between Latin America's own private and public sectors. The minimal State role in Latin American private universities is much closer to that found in the U.S. private sector, except where statewide coordinating boards, regulations, and guidelines for federal funds have increased the U.S. governmental role or where ingrained statist norms contribute to restrictive bureaucratic practices in Latin America. Similarly, the powerful role of other external actors in Latin America approximates U.S. private models. The Church role has diminished in the Catholic institutions of both regions, though remaining more active in Latin America. Also in both regions, some prestigious institutions are more likely than others to achieve relative autonomy from trustees and businesses. But less autonomy is the tendency in Latin America; there, even prestigious institutions may be tightly tied to one or a few business concerns. Professorial power is substantial only in the esteemed U.S. institutions, where academic freedom is greatest. Organized student political power is minimal in both private sectors.

Perhaps the most suggestive focal point for summarizing these governance tendencies is university administration. The Continental model is noted for the weakness of this level, reflecting the weight of the State above and the chaired professors below. Latin American public universities have also had weaker university administrations than those found in the private universities, but often stronger ones than in the Continental model; this strength may be seen where there is relative autonomy from the State or where university administrations are backed by modern authoritarian regimes. On the other hand, Latin America's public university administrations are often severely weakened by student power and partisan political conflict. Largely because Latin America's private universities have not suffered these constraints, they have had stronger administrations than their public counterparts. Power is derived from and shared with the non-State external authorities above, not the university community below. This approximates certain U.S. private norms, particularly those in some liberal arts colleges.

Functions seem too varied and complex to allow for cross-national approximations that are as clear as those found in governance and especially finance. Nevertheless, focusing on religious, political, economic, social, and academic functions, Latin America's public sector closely resembles the Continental model in many ways, while its private sector does not. Instead, its private sector closely resembles U.S. models.

Latin America's public sector follows the Continental and also the U.S. public model in terms of secularism. Latin America's private sector, like its U.S. counterpart, is split between religious and secular institutions. Although the balance is more heavily weighted on the religious side in Latin

America than in the United States, religious orientations have declined in both settings. Politically, Latin America's public sector generally inclines leftward more than its Continental or certainly its U.S. counterpart, while its private sector inclines more rightward than any other sector, best approximating only some U.S. liberal arts colleges, usually religious ones. Economically, a parallel in employment patterns exists between Latin America's public sector and the Continental model. Both place graduates into the State apparatus as well as into private professional practice, but graduates of Europe's public universities rarely face major competition from private graduates when seeking jobs in private enterprise. Latin America's private sector also is oriented to private professional practice, but it is much less oriented to State employment and much more oriented to private enterprise. Parallels in employment of U.S. college graduates are dubious, partly because U.S. undergraduate education leaves much of the professional orientation to the graduate level. Beyond this, the Latin American pairing off of the public sector and the State versus the private sector and the private sphere goes far beyond any such U.S. private-public distinction. A similar comparison could be drawn concerning which social groups are served. For all the exceptions, especially regarding the demand-absorbing subsector, private-public distinctiveness based on elite private sectors is more pronounced in Latin America than in the United States. Latin America's public sector follows the European precedent in moving from traditional elite patterns to increased heterogeneity. Finally, Latin America's public sector has frequently endorsed Continental principles concerning standardized functions and quality, although it obviously has fallen short in practice. Such orientations contrast with U.S. preferences for competition, based on pluralism and specialization, especially (but not exclusively) in the private sector. In Latin America the private sector has brought higher education closer to U.S. norms and at the same time has destroyed any pretense at standardization in functions and quality.

In brief, while neither the private nor the public sector in Latin America fully mirrors any foreign model considered, the public sector still shows some prominent similarities to the Continental model while the private sector inclines much more toward U.S. models, particularly of the U.S. private sector and many of its liberal arts colleges. Unless one is broad, bold, or reckless enough to generalize so widely as to cover European and U.S. experience simultaneously, generalizations about Latin American higher education should at least be sectorally bracketed.[8] To make the point another way, intersectoral distinctions, whether in finance, governance, or function, are much more central to understanding Latin American than U.S. higher education. For one thing, the U.S. private-public enrollment ratio is roughly one to four, while the Latin American ratio is roughly one to two. More important, Latin America's public sector, like the Continental model, is more markedly public than the U.S. public sector, while Latin America's private sector is more markedly private than the U.S. private sector.

Privateness versus Publicness

Our effort to conceptualize the revamped nature of Latin American higher education should consider not only private and public sectors but also privateness and publicness. Fortunately for the clarity of analysis, Latin America's nominally public sector proved to be truly public in most respects, and its nominally private sector proved to be even more truly private. Thus, privateness and publicness have usually been investigated even while focusing directly on private and public sectors. For example, the enormous intersectoral gap just summarized and related to foreign models was discussed in terms of privateness and publicness. All this has been fairly clear. The issue becomes thorny when attention turns to "associated traits"— traits observably and logically linked with privateness (or publicness) but not intrinsic to our definition of it. The lines between nonassociated, associated, and definitional (intrinsic) traits may be thin, ambiguous, subjective, or even variable according to policy field. While privateness and publicness correlate extensively with our private and public sectors, it remains difficult to assess the nature and depth of these associations.

If one concept is pivotal in understanding the traits associated herein with privateness as opposed to publicness, perhaps it is focus, or alternatively, coherence, specialization, or narrowness.[9] The concept could be reduced to focused power. Private universities are responsible to fixed, identifiable, narrow constituencies. Because these constituencies are narrow, the universities can concentrate nearly full power in few hands, usually the chief business or religious groups in conjunction with their appointed university administration. Public university power is more characteristically variable, ambiguous, and dispersed. Although theoretically the State could be analogous to the private organizations that concentrate power, the analogy generally falters in practice because the State itself is usually a variable, ambiguous, and dispersed entity, much larger and much less coherent than individual private organizations. It pursues myriad purposes and includes diverse groups—even "the public," however vague the concept. In Latin American higher education, the State may encompass, or share authority with, the education ministry, related ministries, professional groups, students, the middle class at large, and several private groups outside the university itself. Only in very authoritarian (or revolutionary) contexts does the State, by excluding many actors, sometimes approach the coherence of certain private groups. Even then, the approach is generally neither close nor sustained. In sum, the power and constituency bases of private universities usually are both observably and logically more focused, narrow, and deep than those of public universities. And focused power makes choosing and pursuing tasks easier and freer from conflict, opposition, and obstacles.

Strongly related to the concept of focused power is the concept of selectivity. Like focused power, selectivity seems to be highly associated with privateness. Private universities have the right and the will to choose and exclude. They can choose, for example, to be small in size. Smaller institutions, in turn, usually can be more focused than larger institutions in pursuing their limited purposes. They innovate more easily, with fewer entrenched groups in opposition. And they can choose to be small in scope by admitting fewer students or by offering only certain fields of study. By selecting the students they want, many of Latin America's private universities help insure a certain SES level, private financing, depoliticization, academic standards, academic quality, and good employment connections. They can ignore the desires of nonselected students and the interests they represent. Instead, they tailor themselves to their selected groups, just as they select groups that suit their tailoring. Private universities set the orientation and then attract and accept those students and groups that fit and reinforce it. Most public universities are less selective and must respond to broader groups and purposes; the less selective constituency itself helps to shape the institution.

The relationship between focused power and selectivity is one key aspect of a broader relationship between governance and function. Focused power makes it possible to choose focused functions. Focused functions make focused power more feasible. For example, private entrepreneurs are generally more successful than the State in achieving their desired distributions in fields of study. More broadly, our findings show a strong internal consistency among function, governance, and finance in the private sector, more than in the public sector. Illustratively, the privateness of the private sector has been manifestly and equally clear in finance and governance, whereas the publicness of the public sector is manifest in finance but ambiguous in governance. Who pays is clear in both sectors, but who benefits and especially who governs are generally clearer in the private sector. The private sector would approximate a single all-encompassing private ideal type more closely than the public sector would approximate a single all-encompassing public ideal type.

It is therefore the public sector that conforms to important cross-national conceptualizations about the inherent ambiguity and even anarchy of universities as compared to other organizations.[10] Among the roots of this ambiguity are the lack of explicit and meaningful organizational goals, the

302

plethora of organizational goals espoused by diverse constituencies, and the relatively flat governance structure based on the power inherent in both expertise and liberal participatory norms. By contrast, ambiguity is considerably reduced in Latin America's private universities. These universities have a clearer, narrower, and more hierarchical authority structure choosing more explicit and limited goals and financing endeavors through payments by those who support those goals and that structure. Another way to portray the private decisiveness is that private financiers have relatively clear ideas about functions and about the appropriate governance means to achieve them. In comparison, the State has neither the consensus, coherence, ability, nor will to impose similarly fixed governance and function profiles through its financing of public universities.[11] If the State charges public universities with tasks as clear as those a foundation gives its private university—which is uncommon—it is the private university that is more likely to be ready and able to fulfill its charge. It is also the private university that is much more likely to face severe punishment from those who hold financial and political power if it does not fulfill its charge. To sum up, a State–public university tension contrasts with a comparatively greater private sphere–private university harmony.[12] Another way to sum up is to take conclusions reached earlier about governance and relate them to function as well: (1) the private sector achieves greater pluralism than the public sector, while (2) individual private institutions are generally less pluralistic internally than are their public counterparts. (The first conclusion but not the second clearly applies to finance as well.) Still another way to sum up, this time using the terminology of organizational theory, is that the private university basically operates within a much narrower environment and is less ecologically constrained than the public university by the numerous forces that lie outside that environment. Each of these summations about Latin American higher education emphasizes contrasting conceptualizations, depending upon sector.

However deeply privateness and publicness may be tied to private and public sectors, respectively, public policy can try to alter the ties. Predictably, there have been attempts to make one sector more like the other. Two types of private-public inversions are possible. One would put definitional elements of publicness into nominally private sectors or elements of privateness into nominally public sectors. The findings on the strong privateness of private sectors and publicness of public sectors show that such inversions have been limited, although several significant exceptions emerge. Finance offers the clearest illustration of sectoral purity. Little publicness (State subsidization) is found in most private sectors, and even much less privateness (non-State funding) is found in public sectors. Attempts to inject the definitional characteristics of one sector into its very distinctive counterpart have generally met powerful opposition. To the extent that such inversions occur, they obviously produce sectors that are less private and public respectively.

Also attempts have been made to implant traits associated with one sector into the other. It is more difficult to evaluate how far this second type of inversion has gone in practice, but again the strong intersectoral differences suggest that event this type of inversion has not been widespread. More specifically, certain attempted inversions can be scrutinized. The private sector has sometimes copied the public sector, for it has not sought distinctiveness in everything. Institutions seeking distinctiveness on some dimension, such as religion, may simply seek legitimacy on others, such as course content in nonreligious fields. Nor need it be a matter of private choice; statist regulations frequently mandate considerable copying of public sector procedures. Subsectorally, the private demand-absorbing institutions' pursuit of numbers, or access, may also weaken some traits, such as selectivity, associated with the private sector; altering usual private-public contrasts in size (both institutional and sectoral) diminishes certain differences associated with privateness and publicness.[13] Private-public differences tend to be greater and clearer in those nations, such as Mexico, where the private sector is relatively small than in those with large private sectors based on large demand-absorbing subsectors. Nonetheless, most traits associated here with privateness characterize nonelite as well as other private institutions. Thus, one sees private income, selectivity in fields of study, and focused power with limits on participation. Additionally, chapters 4 through 6 show that private sectors not only in Mexico but also in Colombia and even Brazil restrict themselves, much more than public sectors, to the relatively developed regions.

Turning to the public sector, attempts to create public alternatives to the established public universities deserve more attention than they receive here. The public sector is too important, even to disillusioned elites and middle-class groups, for them, let alone the State and society as a whole, to write the sector off in wholesale resignation. Besides the importance rooted in State finance, influential politics, and so forth, the public sector is vital because many students have no private option, either because they cannot gain entry to the private sector or because that sector's narrow functions do not include the desired ones. Moreover, there surely can be plural institutional options within the public sector. These options include revamped universities, new universities, junior colleges, regional institutes, technical institutes, and research centers. But scattered findings, especially from Argentina, Brazil, Costa Rica, Ecuador, Mexico, and Venezuela, have suggested only mixed results. Although public alternatives have often achieved a degree of distinctiveness from public predecessors, they have usually fallen far short of projected distinctiveness. Technical institutes have probably become more distinctive than new university forms, such as Brazil's fundações and Venezuela's experimental universities. Among the difficulties in pursuing public alternatives, the lack of the same focused power and selectivity found in the private sector figures prominently. Thus, for example, there is strong student, professorial, or even ministerial opposition to many forms of change.

Two related problems concerning public alternatives are as follows: One is academic drift—the tendency of higher education institutions to slip from their original purposes to pursue more prestigious norms found elsewhere in the system. Drift is especially likely where different actors even within institutions pursue different goals and where the finance-governance-function relationship lacks the internal consistency found in the private sector. It is also likely where traditions normatively favor systemic standardization. More generally, a second problem is that it may be harder to plan plural diversity within statist systems than to encourage some traits usually associated with privateness in less statist systems, such as the U.S. or British systems.

Even when public alternatives do achieve some distinctiveness from the established public mainstream, this distinctiveness does not basically resemble private-public distinctiveness. Consequently, it does not provide strong empirical evidence of public substitutability for private universities. For example, while some public institutes minimize the problems of political disorder and employment opportunities that are found in public universities, the institutes characteristically differ from the private sector in many other ways—more than the public universities do. Generally, the institutes are the most fully State-financed institutions, have the least autonomy from the State, and have lower SES and prestige levels than the public universities. They also tend to be more community or service oriented. Additionally, evidence from certain nations suggests that the public sector's technical institutes may have field distributions further removed from private than from public university profiles. However, this study has not tackled counterfactual scenarios; it cannot tell us to what degree public institutions would assume traits associated with the private sector were there no existing private sector.[14]

Concluding this section on privateness and publicness, I decline to minimize the private-public gap found throughout this study and summarized in this chapter. First, whatever its roots, the gap is fundamentally wide and deep. Second, the private sector is truly private and, despite more exceptions, the public sector is truly public, at least according to the definitions of privateness and publicness proposed in chapter 1. Third, many traits not definitionally tied exclusively to one sector or the other are in fact both observably and logically associated with one. Fourth, attempts at private-public inversions appear to have had only limited success. To think about Latin American higher education is to think about two sectors that are substantially distinguished by sturdy differences in privateness and public-ness.

EVALUATING PRIVATIZATION

While the entire study has investigated the scope and contours of the private-public gulf, it has also, if less explicitly, identified many factors upon which invidious intersectoral evaluations can be made. The ensuing section suggests how we may think about the relative successes and failures produced by the intersectoral split. Inevitably, this section moves into more subjective terrain than that crossed in most of the book. Of course one could emphasize different findings, give different interpretations to the findings, or explain the findings differently—in each case coloring the evaluation differently. What follows might legitimately be judged unduly propriivate, unduly propublic, or unduly preoccupied with restrictive evenhandedness. It first considers the successes of privatization, next the problems with those successes, and finally the contrasting performance of the two sectors on four selected values.

The Success Story

The private sector is a striking success if judged by its own goals. Intersectoral distinctiveness is already one strong indication of this success since the private sector has grown mostly in order to offer an alternative to the public sector. Of course, being different from the public sector is not necessarily being different in envisioned ways, but in practice the private sectors have generally been fulfilling the purposes—in finance, governance, and function—for which they were created. And fulfilling intended purposes is one important basis on which to evaluate success. This is especially true given at least two factors. One is perceived public sector failure—a perception held not only by propriivate partisans but also by many who are ideologically neutral in sectoral preference, and even by some who ideologically support public over private sectors yet find present public reality wanting. The other factor is that private sector promoters include many of societies' most powerful interests, from elite social groups to churches to private enterprise. This does not make the private success desirable, but it helps make it politically significant. I begin, therefore, by evaluating each wave of private creation and growth in terms of fulfillment of its own goals.[15]

Wave I, the Catholic wave, is probably the least successful, based on a comparison of its mixed success-failure and the general success of the other two waves. Many Catholic universities only partially perform the religious missions for which they were created. Some barely pursue these missions even from the outset, while others lose much of their Catholic essence over time. In fact, the liberal evolution of several Catholic universities has helped provoke the genesis of wave II and its secular elite universities. In any case, most Catholic universities do not attract students or professors chiefly on the basis of Catholic missions, little effort is made to fortify religious feeling or practices, and only a few course requirements are relevant to the religious orientation. Theology does not penetrate the myriad faculties, institutional ties to the Vatican and national churches have weakened, and many professors and even administrators are not priests, or their priestly status is subordinated to their professional academic status. Of course the ways and degrees that Catholic universities pursue Catholic missions vary greatly; several universities, including most limiting themselves to "Christian inspiration," have never undertaken to fulfill primarily distinctive Catholic roles. Therefore, they should not be labeled failures by goals that were never theirs. Moreover, one finds decidedly defensive orientations in the creation of most Catholic universities; in practice, they have at least helped shield students from the antireligious atmosphere sometimes found in the public sector.

Beyond the religious realm, most Catholic universities have done well in their other goals. They have provided alternatives to the public sector's changing social-class profile, declining credential value, growing employment problems, and increasing politicization, even though important limits to these Catholic successes have helped explain the emergence of the secular elite wave. Additionally, most Catholic universities have achieved a major success related to their major failure. The decline of traditional Catholic missions has been accompanied by increasing academic prestige. This is not merely a fortuitous by-product but a consciously pursued policy. Most Catholic universities began to emphasize *university* over *Catholic*, as Vatican II and subsequent Catholic university conferences moved their institutions away from defensive dogmatic faith toward objective and open searches for scientific truth through increased academic freedom. Catholic universities in Bolivia, Brazil, Chile, Ecuador, Peru, and Venezuela, among others, have achieved enviable levels of academic quality within the context of their national systems. In other words, universities can change their goals, or the priorities among their various goals, and the Catholic universities have been more successful pursuing the quality than the primordial religious goals. Of course, any successes in the Catholic subsector are crucially restricted by the lack of institutional creation there since the 1960s. Also, where existing Catholic universities expand, distinctiveness may diminish;

this is particularly noteworthy in nations such as Ecuador, where the Catholic subsector continues to account for the majority of private enrollments.

Against this mixed Catholic record, the secular elite wave is probably the most successful, judged by its own purposes. It has satisfied an exclusive socioeconomic class. It has groomed its students for economically and socially rewarding employment. It has been very disciplined and politically tranquil. And it has distinguished itself with academic prestige. Therefore, it has effectively provided an alternative to the public sector, mostly for the academically and financially privileged. One of the most striking facets of this organizational distinctiveness is its endurance over time. For example, Colombia's Los Andes and Mexico's Technological Institute of Monterrey (ITESM), two of Latin America's earliest secular elite universities (both created in the 1940s), have successfully perpetuated their salient characteristics. Such persistence makes for a revealing contrast to the academic drift from original purposes seen in many Catholic universities.

Wave III has also been successful on its own terms, although this is obviously a much easier success than that found in the second wave. Perhaps the success of the third wave seems tautological, insofar as the demand-absorbing institutions are observed to absorb demand. The point is that they were created for the purpose of absorbing demand, and they have generally fulfilled that purpose. Putting the demand-absorbing function in more positive terminology, the third wave (through creation of new institutions and through expansion of existing ones) has helped provide "access" and higher educational opportunity for many who might not otherwise have found a place within the public sector or elsewhere within the private sector. In more crass terms, many institutions created less to offer access or choice than to bring financial reward or social attention to their founders and owners have likewise achieved their ends. Diluting the third-wave success, especially compared to the second-wave success, some individual institutions have failed even while subsectors have succeeded.

Another way to look at the private sector's success, very much related to its success in meeting chosen goals, is to see how well the sector has satisfied certain social groups and organizations. (Although these groups and organizations do not necessarily reflect the will or the good of society at large, neither does the State, especially in nondemocratic settings.) We have already concluded that most Catholic universities, and especially the secular elite universities, have satisfied privileged student clienteles and their families, mostly an upper- and upper-middle-class constituency. Similarly, international agencies have had reason to be pleased.[16] It is more difficult to generalize about the social class served by the demand-absorbing institutions. Shifting the focus from classes to organizations, the Church has clearly

308

been served by the Catholic universities more than by any other type of university, whatever its disappointments and however much looser the ties between Catholic universities and Church have become since the 1960s. And clearer success has been achieved by business organizations. The secular elite universities have trained top-level personnel, disciplined and socialized, in fields (such as business administration, accounting, actuarial studies, computers, and communications) of great interest to private enterprise. Even the demand-absorbing institutions have contributed by training personnel in applied and commercial fields for middle-level positions. Sometimes the public sector has followed the private example, though rarely matching its commitment. Even bitter critics of these "successes" should have little difficulty acknowledging that they exist, that the private sector has substantially pleased its constituency.

In pleasing its constituency, the private sector can claim to pass "market tests" of its success. Market tests may be especially legitimizing, or at least eye-catching, where little chance exists for policy evaluation based on adequate data or on other criteria that are widely accepted. Although generally associated with for-profit private institutions, market tests may also be useful in evaluating private nonprofit organizations, despite the absence of a clear and measurable goal comparable to profit. Enrollments and finance provide perhaps the most obvious market tests.

The data show that the private sector has not only survived but flourished in proportional as well as absolute enrollments. In addition, the private sector continues to draw the overwhelming bulk of its funds from students and private enterprise—their direct and indirect consumers. Of course, the public sector has also experienced staggering growth, but students do not pay tuition and private enterprise very rarely contributes. Nor does State financing of the public sector necessarily constitute the equivalent of a market test. Although the State preserves a range of autonomous initiative, its subsidies could be viewed as bureaucratic responsibilities as well as discretionary support. And the State is under more direct political pressures to maintain its finance than are private actors, even if it does not give its recipient universities high marks. Sectoral persistence and growth may result from the lack of competitive market forces as well as from market success. Surely competition may be limited in the private sector also, but there real challenges in enrollments (with tuition) and finances can be found. A more substantial reservation about the market tests is that they are not so tough, even for low-quality institutions, where student demand greatly exceeds institutional supply and where institutions require only small budgets. Yet however limited they may be, market tests tend to sustain the conclusion that the private sector has fulfilled most of its goals and has thereby satisfied its main constituencies not only within the higher education institutions but beyond. On these terms, the private sector may be thought of as successful.

The Negative Side

Such findings, however, do not compel us to rest with the notion of private success. Even accepting the findings, one can legitimately question their desirability and scope. Evaluation based only on fulfillment of the chosen goals of particular institutions and their constituencies is an incomplete and biased evaluation. To achieve one's chosen goals is not necessarily to do well from other perspectives. To serve the desires and interests of particular individuals, classes, groups, and organizations is not necessarily to serve society. This is perhaps the most important general critique of pluralism— that the aggregated interests of the most active groups do not define societal interests. No "invisible hand" coordinates diverse political and economic interests into a coherent and worthy whole. The problem is especially severe when it disproportionally concerns elite groups—those that most powerfully shape policy toward their own ends. And if this critique is applicable in terms of serving society in its present forms, it is much more potent if one hopes for fundamental social change. Critics of the private sector can concede that the sector serves the status quo well yet regard this very success negatively.

Our findings could support certain fundamental normative arguments against the private sector. First, private finance may undermine State responsibilities and equal access. Similarly, private governance denies democratic principles of community self-rule while fostering control by private enterprise, conservatism, and an apparent depoliticization that substitutes autocratic politics for more progressive participatory politics. Finally, private functioning directly serves privileged classes, private enterprise, and the powerful, allegedly at the expense of the more open public sector serving wider interests. Even within the private sector itself, representatives of certain types of institutions have fundamental, normative reservations about other institutions. The secular subsectors often reject Catholic traditionalism, while many in the Catholic subsector reject what they see as narrow, materialistic means and ends. Naturally, many in both the Catholic and secular elite subsectors disavow the demand-absorbing approach to education.

Less often discussed but no less important than such normative questions, the private sector success is limited by severe substantive considerations. Granted, it is difficult to speak of failures when the private sector does not

310

do things that it has not set out to do; if one values the omitted goals, however, their absence contributes to normative reservations. In any case, they represent objective limits to the scope of private success. A key is selectivity. It obviously relates to the previous discussion associating selectivity and focus with privateness. In fact, most of the ensuing remarks concerning objective limits relate to that discussion.

The private sector tends to choose only those means and ends that suit its interests, regardless of wider societal interests or demands. Private institutions may remain small, selecting students and functions by their own academic and financial criteria. If we draw on the education literature that has gone furthest in exploring the causes of high achievement (the literature on U.S. schools), a central observation is that student SES background is critical. Schools that take in the best prepared students subsequently boast the best graduates—quality in, quality out. Moreover, even controlling for an individual student's SES, the amount learned correlates with the abilities and commitments of classmates.[17] Such factors clearly help make selective institutions look successful. Just as clearly, these institutions can claim credit for attracting the "best."

The substantive limitations involved in the successful performance of carefully selected ends is further illustrated by summarizing the conditions under which Latin America's private sector has so strikingly sustained self-financing. Some institutions, especially Catholic ones, rely heavily on donated services, such as those received from priest-professors. Many private universities have elite financial profiles in that they accept only students who can afford to give their institutions a solid tuition-income base. Less elite private institutions count on excess demand for higher education, as some secondary school graduates seeking a higher education feel compelled to purchase that education. Additionally, most private universities greatly limit their functions, spurning costly ones. They concentrate instead on commercial studies, economics, law, humanities, or architecture—areas that usually require merely students, professors, and classrooms. They forsake medical studies and exact sciences, which require laboratory facilities. Nor do many pursue research, at least not in costly fields. Most professors are part time, often poorly compensated, relying principally on income drawn elsewhere. A clear example of self-financing through restricted functions is found at one of Argentina's most prestigious private universities, the Belgrano University. It began with but four rooms, a faculty in each. Courses were offered only in law, economics, and the humanities, with architecture and then communications added subsequently, as the university prospered and bought more land and buildings. The Belgrano does no research, except contract research, has very few

311

full-time professors, and pays low salaries. Such are some of the restrictions freely acknowledged by the university's own officials.[18] An essential component of the private sector's ability to manage self-financing is its ability to select and limit its goals.

Moreover, the private sector's ability to select and limit its goals is related to the public sector's less-restricted character. The private sector can function successfully within its chosen and limited scope largely because the public sector assumes higher education's wider and more difficult burdens. It is the public sector, notwithstanding the importance of several private demand-absorbing subsectors, that offers higher education to more students in all nations except Brazil and now Colombia as well; even in Colombia the public sector probably offers more access for all but the elite. Widespread parallels exist to the public burden of compulsory education at the primary and secondary levels, leaving private sectors free to choose. The private universities minimize costs because public universities accept students who cannot pay and offer more fields of study in more regions. In some nations, such as Venezuela and Costa Rica, the public sector pays full-time salaries to professors who then sell their services cheap for extra teaching in the private sector. One must also consider the State contribution through tax exemptions for private (nonprofit) universities.

It is easier to fulfill goals successfully when those goals can be chosen, and chosen by criteria related not just to valued goals but also to feasibility and cost. The public sector must respond to a broader constituency and raison d'être. The private sector has the luxury of relying parasitically on the public sector to do the dirty work. Private sector success depends on public sector maintenance.[19] It may even depend on a degree of public sector failure, explaining the exodus of elite groups from the public sector to the private sector and explaining the private sector's consequently strong support among privileged groups.

Because private sector success is substantively limited, even those who normatively favor the private over the public sector cannot logically deduce the public policy assumption that privatization should be further pushed. Such a conscious push to increase private over public sector size could well result in only limited expansion for Catholic and elite universities, with the major growth found in lower-quality institutions. In other words, public policy designed to expand a highly regarded private sector could run the risk of altering that very sector in undesired ways—a common intersectoral policy problem in education and beyond. Suggestively, most nations with large private sectors have large demand-absorbing subsectors (Brazil, Colombia, the Dominican Republic, Peru). To rate the private sector more successful in its undertakings than the public sector is not necessarily to rate the private sector higher nor necessarily to favor its expansion.

312

Freedom, Choice, Equity, and Effectiveness

Obviously, then, this study produces no simple verdict as to which sector is "better." Less grandiose but more reasonable conclusions could emerge in reviewing the evidence on separate values, indicating where each sector excels and fails. One could consequently compare sectors according to the weight one attaches to the different values. What follows is a summary statement of how each sector handles the four basic values—freedom, choice, equity, and effectiveness—introduced in chapter 1 and used throughout to orient intersectoral comparisons. Predictably, the web of answers and patterns developed in chapters 2 through 6 is here reduced to only certain salient tendencies. The most critical loss is that, by highlighting the intersectoral contrasts, this section does not reevaluate the substantial intrasectoral variation found; that would require a lengthy analysis, repetitive of conclusions drawn in other sections.

Freedom has been considered in regard both to institutional autonomy and academic freedom. The State–public sector interface is mixed, with the State exercising both direct and indirect controls but also responding to varied public sector demands. Ample evidence shows that the private sector achieves autonomy from the State both more often and more extensively. Even under modern authoritarian regimes, where autonomy hits its nadir systemwide, the private sector generally retains a marked edge; an exception is Chile, where private-public distinctiveness had already faded before the coup. The private edge is probably smallest under open regimes that allow considerable public university autonomy, yet even there the private sector enjoys greater autonomy in decisions over finance and appointments. Additionally, the existence of private sectors relatively autonomous from the State has increased the freedom of various societal actors to establish institutions that please them.

But autonomy from the State is only one concern, albeit a critical one. Just as the private sector is more autonomous from the State, so it is less autonomous from external private organizations; the public sector faces much less pressure from the Church or private enterprise. Indeed, private sector autonomy from the private sphere (external actors other than the State) might be more restricted than public sector autonomy from the State. The catch is that conflicts of interest are much less common between the private sector and the private sphere than between the public sector and the State. In other words, there are two sides to these autonomy relationships. On the one side, private sectors are so constituted that (compared to the public sectors) they are less likely to be asked to do things against their will. The bounds of their autonomy are less likely to be tested. On the other side, if conflict does arise they are less able to assert their autonomy.

As with institutional autonomy, useful intersectoral comparisons concerning academic freedom show the different contours of freedom more than they show where freedom is absolutely greater. Again there is the issue of how frequently the boundaries are probed. Dissidence arises less often in the private sector. Its students and professors are less prone to claim wide freedoms to speak and act. This is only logical considering the greater degree of homogeneity and selection, including self-selection, found in most private institutions. Consequently, in this limited sense the private sector's students and professors are less likely than their public counterparts to be coerced into submission. Those counterparts more often cross the tolerated boundaries and run the attendant risks. Nevertheless, and critically, the parameters of their academic freedom are usually demonstrably wider. They can go further before they are coerced. They enjoy much greater latitude for institutionalized political participation in university governance and for dissent from the university and its major external authorities than do private university students and professors. Thus, private authorities explicitly criticize the public university "excesses" allowed under the banner of academic freedom. Their main argument is that such "anarchy" contributes to ineffectiveness. They also point to a paradox of academic freedom: allowing too much freedom to "radicals" infringes on the freedoms of the majority. A common manifestation is seen when leftist student movements restrict the freedom of nonleftists in the public universities. This is but one example sustaining the conclusion (weakened under modern authoritarian regimes) that freedom for leftists is likely to be greater in the public sector and freedom for rightists greater in the private sector. A broader conclusion is that academic freedom is a more salient issue in the public sector, exercised much more energetically, and consequently more often openly challenged.[20]

Choice clearly overlaps freedom, as choice implies the freedom to select among alternatives. At first glance the private sector might seem to have an unassailable claim here. Even critics acknowledge that the private sector offers distinct choices. Students, families, and various groups and organizations can choose options that go well beyond what the public sector alone provides. These range from Catholic options to politically quiescent and highly specialized technical institutes to exclusive prestige universities. If choice is related to diversity, then the private sector contributes to both, not just by offering alternative functions but also by offering alternative financial and governance patterns. The range of options has been amply established in previous chapters. The range is diluted wherever homogeneity predominates, but aside from Chile, homogeneity is only a subordinate tendency where two sectors exist.

314

One public rebuttal that could draw on this study's findings is to deny not the fact but the desirability of the choices provided by the private sector. These choices may pervert or undermine worthy public purposes. For example, the choice of religious, conservative, job-oriented, or elite quality alternatives may impede national homogeneity, liberalism, fundamental economic change, or equal opportunity.

Beyond these normative reservations are limits on the scope of private choice. The main consideration is that observers often give the private sector high marks for choice because they take the public sector as given and then see the private sector as an addition. This of course relates to the public burden discussion above; the private sector often looks good because the public sector is doing the heavy work, even the dirty work. To illustrate, the private sector can provide added student choice among institutions because the public sector bears the main responsibility for access. Similarly, the private sector increases choice by offering certain fields of study not offered, or not offered in innovative or prestigious ways, in the public sector, but the public sector covers the range of basic fields.

In reality, comparing each sector as it is—not giving the private sector special status as the fortuitous addition, and not opening the difficult issue of how either sector might expand its range were the other sector to contract or disappear—one might think of the public sector as the one that offers greater choice. Additionally, the issue is clearer at the institutional rather than at the sectoral level. Most public institutions provide considerably more choice than most private ones. Drawing again on the example of fields of study, students may choose among more fields in the public than the private sector, and the gap is substantially larger if the comparison deals with individual public and private institutions. More broadly, on many facets of function and governance, private institutions offer choices that are quite narrow compared to those available in public institutions. Again, the basic point relates integrally to earlier assertions associating privateness with selectivity and focus. Again, as shown most clearly in Brazil, these tendencies hold even where the private sector is composed largely of non-elite institutions.

Despite the perhaps surprising strength of the public sector's case, related evidence helps shore up private claims. For one thing, the very nature of the private sector renders the interinstitutional comparisons less appropriate than the intersectoral ones. Most private institutions are narrow. Substantial choice emerges not because individual institutions are broad but because they are different from one another and because the private sector is pluralistic. Individual private institutions are tied to different external actors, whereas public institutions are generally tied at least partly to the

State and some consequent bureaucratic or civil service standardization. Furthermore, as individual institutions protect their rather narrow foci, they insure the sanctity of choice; that is, when students or others choose a given private institution, they count on that institution's profile not being muddled by the seemingly incalculable pulls and tugs associated with the wide and less-defined breadth characteristic of Latin America's public institutions. To opt for a public institution is to face greater uncertainty though to leave open greater possibilities of shaping choice after entry. Another factor that must be considered in evaluating the degree of sectoral choice is sectoral size; Latin America's public sectors are generally much smaller than their public counterparts, so in the aggregate, less choice could be expected. But the most persuasive, though circumscribed, case for associating the private sector with choice remains the dual sector one—taking the long-standing public sector as given and then showing how much additional choice the newer private sector provides.[21]

As private sectors zealously assert their superiority in fostering choice, so public sectors zealously lay special claim to providing access and equity. Such is the rule in U.S. higher education, and such proves to be the rule in Latin American higher education. Indeed, a major argument against private sector choice is that it undermines public sector equity. The choice of a private university is viewed as a classic liberal choice for the elite, since these universities draw disproportionally from high SES groups and graduates of privileged, usually private, primary and secondary schools. Similarly, private universities count on and sustain the privileged groups that become donors and employers. While some socioeconomic strata exercise their choice and exit options, leaving the public universities, most cannot. As a result, the range of choice for the majority is not left unaffected but is diminished as opportunities open mostly for their private competitors. For example, public university graduates have less choice in selecting their employment positions because private university graduates have special opportunities.

In fact, this study leaves little doubt that Latin America's private sector caters directly to the highest SES clientele more often than the public sector does. However, a private defense on this score can be based on three findings. One is that the private demand-absorbing subsector is not very elitist; its leaders might even welcome such "flattering" charges. Instead, this subsector increases the system's access. Whether or not public sectors could conceivably pick up the slack themselves, the reality is that the State has sometimes placed strong limits on public growth and left the degree of access dependent on private activities. A second point is based on the notion that a good offense is a good defense, that the public sector is also vulnerable. All higher education in Latin America is still socially exclusive compared to the average citizen's plight; the great majority of the region's youth have no prospect whatever of attending a university. Within this context, the private sector adds an increment of inequality that may be more than counterbalanced by the fact that its students, and the private orgnizations it serves, pay for their privileges, thus bringing greater resources to education. Only minimal payments are made in the public sector. Third is the facts-of-life argument, heard most commonly in the elite subsector. Inequities are natural for quality institutions in highly stratified societies; primary and secondary schools are perhaps the more critical filters of privilege. More speculatively, given societal inequities, one sector alone might face pressures to promote intrasectoral differentiation by institution, field, or other invidious "tracking" mechanisms. Actually, sharp SES differentiation already appears within the public sector (e.g., by fields in Brazil's public universities), even where there are two sectors. This point parallels one repeatedly heard about U.S. elementary schools: the public elementary schools stratify through the neighborhood school concept and classroom tracking and might stratify themselves much more were they to take on the private sector's pupils. Additionally, if Latin America lacked the institutional stratification promoted by the private sector, many elite students might study abroad, possibly deepening dependency. Mexico's elite subsector has helped to keep the bulk of privileged students at home, and a parallel role is played by Colombia's Los Andes University.[22] Just as some positive features found in the private sector are not created by that sector, so it is with some negative features. And just as the private sector's clear successes are based largely on public burdens, so the private sector's demonstrated ability to satisfy powerful privileged groups may help the public sector to be comparatively open to less-privileged groups.

Concerning effectiveness perhaps even more than the other three values, certain factual conclusions can be shared by those drawing divergent interpretations from them. The discussion of effectiveness is already advanced because basic findings were presented when summing up privatization's success story and its related shortcomings. In brief, if effectiveness means success in carrying out selected goals, then the private sector has been strikingly effective. This study has produced much evidence to temper that assessment but more to sustain it. Nevertheless, critics can find evidence to show the comparative ease of fulfilling carefully selected goals, especially where those goals are backed by a restricted, focused power structure. They can also emphasize how limited the goals are. And they can deny the desirability of this private sector effectiveness for society generally (and for the public sector specifically).

This work has devoted somewhat less direct attention to public than to private sector effectiveness. In its continual pursuit of private-public comparisons, however, it has often found the public sector to be less effective in pursuing goals. Particularly striking was the picture of perceived public sector failure, with dissatisfaction expressed not only by exiting elites but also by the State and even by some advocates of public sector dominance. At least three major countervailing considerations exist. One involves persistence. If we follow organizational sociologists who see effectiveness as securing the support necessary for survival, not to mention great expansion, then almost all public universities qualify. This is a major sense in which private demand-absorbing institutions have also been effective. A second consideration involves the record of public sector accomplishment in matters ranging from social access and mobility, to knowledge dissemination, to political change and legitimacy, and beyond. Finally, the third consideration relates to selectivity and focused power. The public sector's goals are complex and inherently difficult to fulfill. Moreover, they are often contradictory, since no one voice speaks for the public sector. The power structure tends to be more open and less cohesive than in the private sector. So even if we discuss goals desired by key State actors and achieved more fully in the private than the pubic sector, it does not necessarily follow that the public sector is ineffective in achieving its goals. In this context, invidious comparisons to private sector effectiveness are inherently biased. On the other hand, an inability to fix clear goals can itself be considered a sign of ineffectiveness.

Whatever one makes of it, the private sector has successfully implemented certain goals pursued but also opposed, or in any case often ultimately frustrated, in the public sector. These include legitimizing new fields, relating course offerings to employment opportunities, implanting departmental organizations and more centralized university administration, imposing tuition, raising external funds, and minimizing political disorder. It remains difficult to assess how often private sector effectiveness has lit a path that the public sector has followed.[23]

As this overall evaluation has not attempted to say which sector is better, it has not even strained to conclude which is better on each of the four considered values. Rather, it has tried to show the different ways in which these values are promoted in the two sectors. It has presented substantive findings that even antagonists may agree upon and has proceeded to identify some ways in which their interpretations of these findings could reasonably differ. It has tried to suggest how each sector may be superior, in what ways, and for whom.

Almost inevitably, much depends on what one chooses to bracket. Those who accept the status quo can easily conclude that the private sector promotes freedom, choice, effectiveness, and even equity within it. If one assumes that State resources for public higher education would not go

318

beyond present levels even were there no private sector, then the private sector clearly adds quality and even access. The private case is more empirical, based on observable facts. The public case is more hypothetical, based on how the public sector might improve were there only one sector, diminished societal inequality, more funds, more progressive political regimes, and so forth. Yet this juxtaposition does not reflect the ultimate weakness of the public defense as much as it reflects the power of those groups behind the private sector's ability to shape reality (to create the status quo context from which factual observations emerge).

Finally, a tolerant view of the status quo might well evaluate both sectors positively. Each sector accomplishes something distinctive, something better than the other sector, something that certain groups want and that satisfies their notions of desirability. Such a tolerant view has more often been forwarded by those defending the private sector, especially where that sector's legitimacy is questioned. But it proves equally relevant as a defense of the public sector, especially as the private sector grows at the public sector's expense and achieves higher prestige. This analysis suggests, for example, that those who support maximum choice and diversity in Latin American higher education may be logical supporters of dual sectors. Such views could be acceptable to those who see the tasks each sector is performing as useful or who emphasize the negative consequences sometimes associated with single sector monopoly, inertia, or repression. Such views cannot, however, satisfy those who interpret the private sector's successes as negative developments (serving the elite, private enterprise, conservatism, and U.S. models, while perverting public purposes).

There are, then, many approaches to evaluating the privatization that has transformed Latin American higher education. Those mentioned here have identified strongly patterned private-public differences. They have provided substantiation as well as challenges for contrasting normative interpretations.

THE STATE AND HIGHER EDUCATION

The preceding evaluation demonstrates how the rise of powerful and truly private alternatives to the public sector forces revisions of extant views concerning not only higher education itself but also relationships between higher education and society. Until now, however, the analysis has not suggested how we might reconceptualize the relationship between higher education and the State. To tie together comments on that relationship as cohesively as possible, the State was deleted in the evaluation of the sectors' services to different classes, groups, and interests. Consequently, this section considers how each sector serves the State. It then assesses the ade-

319

quacy of competing concepts for understanding the broad State–higher education relationship.

Serving the State

This study confirms the usefulness of considering the State and the public sector as distinguishable entities. While it is clear that the private sector, much more than the public sector, has served various parts of the private sphere of organized interests such as private enterprise, it is not clear that the public sector holds the edge in serving the State. Overall, the strongest link is that between the private sector and the private sphere, the weakest between the public sector and the private sphere, while the links between each higher education sector and the State occupy intermediate positions.

The traditional public university, following the Continental model, had an enshrined purpose of serving the State, so much so that distinctions between the two entities were once harder to make. National universities were established as State arms—the State's representatives in higher education or even all education. But while national universities are still the single most important higher education institutions in many countries, they hold near monopoly control in very few, and their ties to the State are variable. The State–public university nexus was weakened by the autonomy movements that reverberated in most nations sometime during the twentieth century. This privatization of governance, coupled with refortified State financing, was supposed to promote State interests indirectly, through university policies. And it often has. But the State has also subsequently shared much of the widespread perception of public sector failure. It has often indirectly and directly stimulated alternative private initiatives, and it has continually advocated public sector reform. Much of this reform would implant into the public sector traits intrinsic to or associated with privateness. Yet results have fallen far short of satisfaction, being almost nil on some issues such as tuition, disappointing on others such as making curriculum more relevant to the productive apparatus, and mixed on others such as depoliticization or shaping field orientations. That the public sector does not dutifully serve the State is integrally connected with our findings on governance. Only in exceptional circumstances have regimes fully or almost fully controlled the public university, instead usually sharing power with divergent groups pursuing interests often not consistent with the regimes.'

One of the principal ways that the public sector does serve the State concerns political order. This assertion may seem a bit paradoxical, given the public sector's propensity to be involved in political disorder. But satisfying the demands of relatively influential groups, mostly middle class, is critical to the State's legitimacy and stability. These groups benefit through access to public higher education and through increased social, economic, and political mobility—all fully subsidized by the State. The State, in turn, uses figures on growing public enrollments and expenditures to buttress its legitimacy. Additionally, the State is often served by the political and bureaucatic recruitment lines established between itself and the public university. On the other hand, whether the political socialization transmitted at the public universities is, on balance, positive or negative for the State is difficult to determine; answers obviously vary according to nation and regime.

Finally, the public sector clearly performs many tasks thought necessary for society's well-being and therefore, indirectly, for the State's. Many of these tasks, from research to the training of doctors and scientists, are more commonly performed in the public than the private sector. Also in this category are numerous social-welfare tasks, sometimes directly oriented toward helping the masses; examples include community extension programs in nonformal education, nutrition, housing, and social organization.[24]

The private sector serves the State in ways that are often less apparent, less discussed, and even less direct—yet no less important. In fact, the private sector–State relationship can be more harmonious than the public sector–State relationship because it often lacks a similarly strong conflictual side. Nevertheless, some possible liabilities should be considered. States visibly tied to private sectors are vulnerable to populist charges of conservatism, foreign influence, illegitimacy, and disdain for the public sector. In practice, Latin America's successful private sectors appear to weaken public sectors by draining talent, privilege, and resources more than they help by setting examples. To the extent that the public sector serves the State, forces that weaken that sector may present a problem. Dissatisfaction over declining quality, credentials, and job prospects could even promote political disorder in the public sector. Nonetheless, most States have successfully maintained a purposeful, if sometimes limited, outward distance from the private sector, a sector they generally neither finance nor govern. Besides, another side to the private sector's effect on the public sector is cited above in the normative discussion of privatization. Because the private sector performs special tasks for privileged groups, it allows the public sector to function as it does. Were there no private sector, the public sector might have to attend to, and pay for, many additional students, which would either raise costs or push out other students (or stratify them within the public sector), thereby restricting the public sector's openness and legitimacy. Perhaps the public sector can better serve the State politically because the private sector exists. Furthermore, since the State can count on a measure of elite satisfaction, political order, job training, and academic standards in the private sector, it may feel less constrained to use force to push those ends in a partly disappointing public sector. In other words, the State often achieves many of its ends simply by allowing freedom and choice for privileged alternatives rather than by having to "rationalize" the public sector through exclusion and coercion.

More important to the State than any liabilities the private sector may pose are its positive contributions. These were explained most closely in the chapter on Mexico, our most typical case study in terms of private-public distinctiveness with majority enrollments in the public sector; some of those contributions can be generalized and summarized here.

One way to appreciate the private sector's service to the State is to note how its service to its own constituencies naturally benefits the State. By satisfying the demands of privileged groups for a social-class alternative with high status, credentials, and quality separate from the increasingly heterogeneous public sector, the private sector (at least its elite subsector and much of its Catholic subsector) placates even more powerful groups than does the public sector. These are precisely the groups that are most crucial to political stability, given the nature of most Latin American States. If the private sector's drain on public sector talent and resources sometimes contributes to dissatisfaction and disorder within the public sector, that effect appears minimal (with regard to order) when compared to the elite satisfaction produced. The private sector's perceived quality edge is also welcomed for the innovation, reform, and effectiveness it adds to the higher education system. At the same time, the demand-absorbing subsector joins many unprestigious public institutions in "cooling out" the very heated-up demand for expanded access; candidates need not be fully denied access nor provided a costly slot within the public sector's academic mainstream.[25]

Politically, each private subsector (though to differing degrees) places itself on the conservative side of the public sector, and this suits most States. Political disorder is minimized, again without need of direct State repression or even administration. Economically, the State derives several benefits from those gained by privileged groups and private enterprise. First, it is relieved of a major financial burden since the most immediate beneficiaries pay their own way. Second, the State itself is directly served by the recruitment of well-trained graduates into high level technical, sometimes even political, positions within the State. We have seen evidence of this in Mexico, Venezuela, Colombia, Peru, Ecuador, and Bolivia—evidence that also relates to what has been variously called the modernization, rationalization, or technification of the State. More broadly, all Latin American States outside Cuba have been tied to capitalist development models for most of their recent histories, so to serve private enterprise is, in large measure, to serve the State.[26]

Thus, while each sector serves the State in distinct fashion, the private sector holds several clear advantages in economic terms. As long as these States remain more concerned with the effectiveness of the basic political-economic order and less concerned with issues such as equity, they are likely to be especially gratified by the private sector's role. Naturally, the public sector (by definition) remains the one more closely tied to the State in structural terms. It also is more closely tied by the most obvious financial relations, although not necessarily by more subtle economic relations. But the private sector challenges its public counterpart concerning the strength of functional ties. Moreover, the public ties, especially in finance and governance but also in function, are often felt like dead weights by the States, burdening the budget, presenting administrative and political problems, and swelling its bureaucratic job ranks. Overall, while the relation of the State to each sector obviously varies across nations, most States have seen their self-interest promoted by supporting dual sectors as opposed to the greater systemwide homogeneity once more characteristic of Latin American higher education.

Corporatism?

How then should the important but variegated ties between higher education and the State be understood? As chapter 1 suggests, relationships between the State and civil society are often conceptualized along the lines of two ideal types—corporatism and pluralism. In the 1970s several leading works on Latin American politics argued that corporatism was easily the more relevant concept for the region. While different authors have defined corporatism in different ways, it is possible to identify widely cited organizational characteristics. And since corporatism has often been explicitly defined as pluralism's opposite, I do not here elaborate two separate definitions.

Ten salient definitional characteristics (somewhat overlapping) of organizations in corporatist relationship with the State, which focus on what Schmitter calls "state corporatism," are as follows:[27] (1) Organizations must be recognized (officially licensed and chartered) and even created by the State; they cannot emerge spontaneously. (2) The State grants a structural and representational monopoly to these organizations. (3) Consequently, the number of these organizations is centrally limited as well as regulated. (4) Membership in these organizations is therefore compulsory for all who operate in the fields they cover. (5) Another corollary is that the organizations are not competitive with each other. (6) Instead, they are functionally differentiated and coordinated. (7) The State subsidizes the organizations, thereby manipulating them. (8) It also exerts strong control over the selection of leadership, through which the organization's members act. (9) The State also exerts explicit control over the organization's internal governance policies and demands. (10) The organizations are governed hierarchically. Additionally, beyond such a structural picture some also assert that significant support exists in Latin America for corporatist ideology. Advocates of corporatism believe that explicit coordination, centralism, and direction best produce harmonious public interests—clearly a rejection of pluralist beliefs in optimal results through open, liberal, voluntary, spontaneous, competitive, autonomous organizations.

The literature on corporatism surged partly as a result of dissatisfaction with modernization theory's failed visions of development via Western pluralist models. Much of the new literature tied corporatism to authoritarian regimes, although some of it pointed out that corporatist relationships and policies were also associated with nonauthoritarian regimes. As often happens in scholarship, a tide of overreaction, straw men, revisionism, and then calls for greater specification ensued.[28] It now seems fair to say that, despite strong disagreements on the roots and "naturalness" of modern Latin American corporatism, there has been a wide belief in its relevance to State-society relations. Some argue that it is easily the dominant mode, others that it is at least more characteristic than pluralism. Others (whom this study tends to support) cautiously emphasize that corporatism is variably mixed with pluralism in ways that can be established only case by case, field by field, nation by nation, however tediously.

Strongly related to corporatism in many respects is the concept of organic statism. Here the State's importance is definitionally paramount; private activity is decidedly limited. According to Stepan, the organic State is "clearly interventionist and strong," playing an "architectural role" in pursuit of its notions of the common good, rejecting the class antagonisms furthered by the liberal State and "classic capitalism." Moreover, the "concern for the pursuit of the common good leads to a de-emphasis or rejection of . . . the legitimacy of 'private interests' even if these private interests represent the majority." Private organizations are allowed, but according to a "principle of subsidiarity," the rule is subordination and even significant absorption into the State. Moreover, organic statism, while clearly an ideal type, is held to be particularly relevant for Latin America, where certain strong normative and empirical traditions run counter to pluralism.[29]

As foretold in the case studies and substantiated in the regional overview, this work emphasizes trends that run fundamentally counter to the basic postulated characteristics of corporatism and organic statism. These characteristics are found only variably even in the State's relationship with the public universities.[30] The two concepts certainly do not prepare us for the presence of powerful, vibrant, private institutions substantially autonomous of the State and the public sector.

These broad statements can be elaborated by specific reference to the ten definitional characteristics enumerated above. First, although public universities are recognized by the State (often even considered part of the State), in recent decades many have been spontaneously created through student, regional, or other demands to which the State then reacts. Greater deviations from postulated norms are found in the private sector since State restrictions on private institutional creation are usually minimal. Second, whereas many national universities once held State-granted monopolies over higher education, both private and public institutional proliferation demolished monopolistic structures in almost all nations, especially the larger ones. Third, because the number of institutions has not often been closely regulated by the State, it is no longer limited. The private sector in particular is now often composed of multitudinous small institutions. Fourth, proliferation has also destroyed traditions of mandatory student entry into any given institutions and has likewise contributed to profound limits on interuniversity umbrella organizations requiring the membership of all universities. Fifth, while the degree of interinstitutional competition is variable, it is not fully negated by State fiat. Instead, some strong private-public competiton exists as private universities attract privileged groups away from the public sector. The corporatist norm of systemic uniformity (e.g., in prestige), pursued more successfully in some European countries, is increasingly violated in Latin America. Sixth, despite continual State pleas and endless rhetoric, planned functional differentiation and coordination hardly exist. Councils of rectors have been notoriously unimposing in the public sector and less effective still in the private sector. Seventh, while the State subsidizes the public sector, it does not influence financial distributions or other policies as much as corporatist concepts would have it. Moreover, the State finances only a small share of the private sector; instead, "consumers" make private payments for expected private returns. Eighth, State controls on leadership selection are variable in the public sector, and in any case, university constituencies frequently act apart from, even blatantly against, the leadership. The private university constituency is more tied to its leadership, but the State's role in appointing that leadership is usually either limited or negligible. Ninth, much the same could be said of the State in relation to each sector and control over internal governance and academic policy; that is, the State role is variable in the public sector and less important in the private sector. However, corporatism fits well where the State enforces certain systemwide norms, as in curriculum. Tenth, hierarchical structuring dominates in some public institutions but not in others. This postulated corporatist trait is more commonly found in the private institutions, where verticality usually characterizes internal structures and connections to private external owners. But less than with public institutions does the hierarchy point upward, as corporatist concepts suggest, to tie the private institutions directly to the State.

Clearly, corporatism of the sort defined here does not characterize State–higher education relations, despite the strong links between the State and both sectors. Even more clearly, the concept of organic statism provides a poor orientation for the reality portrayed in this book. Private activities and interests are not only allowed but encouraged to flourish well beyond any notion of subsidiarity or subordination. Only by stretching the concept of the State quite far could one argue that the State absorbs the private sector or preserves its own strongly interventionist and architectural role. Rather, what emerges in these relations is something of a liberal State, manifestly class based. This does not mean that the State is weak but that it promotes its strength through a less directly active role than the organic-statist concept suggests. For simplicity, and because the organic-statist concept is so clearly inappropriate, the ensuing discussion refers more to corporatism than to organic statism.

Our evidence permits us to say less about normative preferences than actual practices. Indications are that considerable support exists for many corporatist norms, at least in the public sector, but that more powerful reasons for flouting them prevail. This is especially true for privileged groups. Whatever values might be rhetorically espoused, behavioral patterns in both sectors show that several pluralist practices are ascendent. Much of public policy, if one can discern it, is the sum of innumerable uncoordinated decisions; these decisions are based less on encompassing societal or moral views than on self-interest, expressing and reinforcing class-based divisions.[31] Even the religious subsector, often associated with a corporate-oriented Church, operates more on these pluralistic bases; this is even more true for the secular elite and demand-absorbing subsectors. Therefore, State–public sector relations themselves would only partially— and decreasingly—sustain corporatist concepts, and the public sector accompanied by a private sector offering limited distinctiveness would deviate still further. Beyond this, however, the private sector is very distinctive from the public sector—very private in finance, governance, and most aspects of its functioning. Such factors push State–higher education relations closer to a pluralist than a corporatist pole. This does not mean, obviously, that no corporatist features can be identified in the public sector especially nor that State–higher education relations are adequately conceptualized by pluralism. It does mean that corporatism fails even as an ideal type and that, at minimum, the corporatist-pluralist mix has changed substantially under the impact of privatization.

Several possible explanations account for the inadequacies of corporatism as an ideal type. Most broadly, some of the corporatist literature since the late 1960s may have exaggerated the preponderance of corporatism over pluralism in Latin American politics generally. Analysis of State–higher education relations lends support to those who have raised such doubts.[32] These doubts have focused largely on the relationship between corporatism and regimes. For example, if corporatism is associated with State-society relations under modern authoritarian regimes, such regimes do not rule all Latin America; the early 1980s saw the balance swing from modern authoritarian toward more democratic regimes (typically less tied to corporatism though not free from it). Furthermore, corporatism does not in practice characterize all the critical State-society relationships, even under modern authoritarian regimes. O'Donnell points out that one of the modern authoritarian regime's major supporters, the upper bourgeoisie, resists corporatism for itself, spurns incorporation into the State. Similarly, Cardoso stresses the modern authoritarian regime's tendencies, unlike those of truly corporatist regimes, to permit "the representative organizations of liberal-capitalist classes to survive without organic bonds with the State."[33] Therefore, the regime's corporatist possibilities must be weighted against its neoliberal possibilities.

While the relationship between corporatism and regimes requires more research, so does an equally critical factor in corporatism's variability, a factor central to our study. This is the policy field under consideration. Related to the policy field is the social class under consideration (and this relates to our preceding comments on the bourgeoisie). Corporatist literature has concentrated on trade unions and the working class, while higher education's privileged constituency surely helps explain the relative freedom from corporatist control.[34] The public sector's constituency is basically middle class; the private sector's is still higher. Insofar as nearly all Latin American States are substantially class based, the classes with influence do not characteristically subject themselves to corporatist control. Pluralist modes, in democratic or nondemocratic societies, can function notoriously well to protect privilege.[35] Decentralized power and opportunity, options for those with resources, interinstitutional hierarchy, and so forth may uphold privilege just as surely as they uphold freedom and choice. While these traits are found in the public sector, they are especially pronounced in the private sector. To the extent that States want to preserve privilege, they may employ substantially more corporatism for the disadvantaged, whom they seek to control more than protect, than for the elite, whom they seek to protect more than control. All this obviously suggests a powerful functional tie, albeit without a structural corporatist base, between the State and privileged organizations such as private universities.

Privatization

The concept of corporatism has proven decreasingly adequate for understanding the relationship between higher education and the State, largely because of changes wrought by privatization. Indeed the concept of privatization itself has become increasingly important in understanding the relationship. Consequently, the final section of this book reflects on privatization—how the State has supported this trend as well as to what extent it has occurred both within higher education itself and in relation to potentially more general political-economic trends.

As not only public but private higher education serves the State, so, logically, the State serves not only public but private higher education. The State has not been merely a dependent or passive beneficiary but an important actor promoting policies favorable to the private sector. Chapter 2 discusses the State's role in creating private sectors. The first essential step was to lift prohibitions on private initiative. Subsequently, different regimes have given various blends of tacit or active support. Just as private sectors have served different regimes in different ways, so different regimes have sought different means of helping private sectors. State support has gone beyond private sector genesis to ongoing assistance. Most States have granted easy recognition to the private institutions that proliferated after private sectors were initially created. This has been the case in nations such as Colombia and Peru as well as in Mexico and Brazil. Some States, not all, have granted financial assistance. The assistance has been more substantial for Catholic than secular institutions, especially low-quality secular ones.

But most often State support for the private sector is indirect. A critical factor is the State's maintenance of the public sector, which assumes so many of higher education's burdens, often freeing the private sector to concentrate on selected clientele and focused and inexpensive tasks. At times the State indirectly aids the private sector by repressing, wantonly expanding, or otherwise contributing to a lessening of public sector prestige and appeal. Beyond all this, the State indirectly promotes the private sector by promoting the classes, groups, and institutions that directly sustain that sector. This is the infrastructural contribution that, in terms of a general development model and the status quo, was explored most closely in the Mexican case.

Let there be no question, however, of exaggerating the degree of State support. Most States still devote far more resources and energy to their public sectors. Let there be no question, either, of exaggerating the degree of privatization itself. For all the extraordinary private growth, public sectors have grown more in absolute terms and still hold two-thirds of total enrollments. Moreover, most public sectors are quite public, at least regarding finance, many functions, and some aspects of governance. Especially considering that we are dealing almost exclusively with capitalist economies, the predominance of the public sector remains noteworthy. After all, in the general economy it is often private enterprise that handles most activity, with the State assuming less of the economic volume. Yet in higher education it is the State-financed public sector that handles most activity.

Still, one can go a long way before exaggerating the extent of privatization. In much of the world, higher education has become increasingly public in the twentieth century, sometimes in proportional sectoral enrollments, often in the publicness of public and even private sectors. The basic trend has been otherwise in Latin America. Chapter 2 analyzes the private sector's spectacular growth from roughly 3 percent (1930) to 14 percent (1955) to 34 percent (1975) of total enrollments, all amid unprecedented expansion in public enrollments. In Brazil, and more recently in Colombia, privatization has gone so far as to make the private sector the larger sector. More commonly, as in Mexico, the private sector holds fewer than half the enrollments but achieves an importance far beyond what enrollment percentages alone express. No Latin American private sector that holds 10 percent or more of total enrollments could properly be considered a peripheral sector.[36] Furthermore, the thirteen nations with private sectors of 10 percent or more hold over nine-tenths of Latin America's total enrollments. Beyond all this, Latin American private sectors are typically quite private.

Privatization, then, proves to be a powerfully applicable concept in several senses. The most obvious concerns the private sector's proportional growth as compared to the public sector's. The "weight" of privatization is further increased by the political-economic influence of the private sector. And the significance of privatization is underscored by the great degree of distinctiveness usually found between the private and public sectors. The multiple meanings of privatization are additionally demonstrated by the fact that both the degree and shape of distinctiveness depend on which private subsector (Catholic, elite, demand absorbing) is considered.

Another type of privatization occurs where intersectoral distinctiveness is diminished by the introduction of private characteristics into the public sector. But our accumulated findings on the publicness of the nominally public sector show that this sort of privatization has not gone very far. Chile under the junta has evoked the greatest interest in this possibility, particularly in finance and function. Yet even the Chilean case has been ambiguous.

329

More broadly, outside Chile there has been much more talk than action concerning such privatization. Nonetheless, it is worth repeating that intersectoral differences elsewhere in the world have more often been diminished by an injection of public characteristics (particularly in finance and governance) into private sectors than by an injection of private characteristics into public sectors. Perhaps such a future will eventually befall many of Latin America's private sectors as well, but for many decades privatization, in multiple senses of the term, has been the dominant trend.

Related to privatization is the concept of "reprivatization." This concept is used prominently to describe situations in which modern authoritarian regimes have returned State-run enterprises to private hands, where they presumably had been before nationalization. Our analysis indicates that reprivatization has validity in understanding some aspects of the privatization of Latin American higher education. The validity concerns the ways in which the public university once performed tasks associated with privateness. For example, the nineteenth-century public university belonged to the elite, as reflected by its student body and the ends it served. Several authors, such as Darcy Ribeiro, have in effect elaborated the rationale for a reprivatization interpretation by contrasting the quasi-private flavor of the nineteenth-century public university with its broader-based public successor.[37] It merely remained for us to see how the private universities have assumed the elite and other tasks once fulfilled within the public sector. The argument concerning private growth based on exits from the public sector is therefore relevant here. It involves the transfer of privileged clientele, restricted constituencies, social standards, and conservative political ideologies. Thus reprivatization is an appropriate concept insofar as major changes have occurred within the public sector, thereby dispatching a sense of the status quo or the past into the private sector.

Yet the concept of reprivatization remains inadequate for understanding much of the privatization that has occurred. It represents but one aspect. Reprivatization would be more apt than it is if previously private universities had been nationalized and then subsequently turned back to private hands.[38] This has not happened. Reprivatization would be more apt even if private traits, once characteristic of the public sector and later weakened in it, were now restored there. Instead, we see a transfer of certain traits from one sector to another, while relatively few serious attempts have been made to reprivatize the public sector itself. Moreover, although some traits (e.g., elitism) displaced from the public to the private sector are associated with privateness, they are not intrinsic to our definitions (in finance, governance, and function) of privateness. Most of the intrinsic qualities of privateness never were prevalent in the public sector. Private finance is the clearest example. Additionally, the idea of reprivatization hardly seems appropriate

330

when considering the private demand-absorbing subsector, which has not re-created most of the elite traits associated with privateness.

One ramification of the limited conceptual utility of reprivatization is that we cannot adequately understand contemporary private sectors along the lines of traditional public sectors. Although one has some sense of the old and status quo shifting to the private sector, there is more reason to think of privatization as a new phenomenon.[39] Neither the traditional public university nor the fused private-public university before that was nearly as private in financial, governance, and functional terms as is the contemporary private university. With few isolated exceptions, the first truly private wave began only in the 1930s. Even this Catholic subsector has proven itself to be quite private, despite historic Church-State ties. By the time most Catholic universities were created, a diminished sense of State-Church fusion existed and the Church could be increasingly regarded as a relatively autonomous part of civil society. This trend has intensified in recent decades, dramatized by some frank State-Church conflict. Moreover, individual Catholic universities have moved increasingly far from the Church itself.

If there is little doubt that the Catholic universities have been private institutions, the case is even clearer for the secular institutions. Never has Latin America had so many educational institutions, both important and unimportant, tied to business organizations. Whether one focuses on client payments, business influence over administrative appointments, or employment ties, privateness goes deeper than ever before. For the first time private voluntary organizations flourish with relative autonomy from the State. Pluralism has expanded in this sense, at least for certain groups, and "horizontal" ties—in finance, governance, and function—bind together some of the major actors (universities, churches, businesses, foundations, and privileged interest groups) in civil society. "Vertical" ties between the State and separate parts of civil society do not monopolize the relevant environment of higher education institutions. The growth of a private sector from 0 to 34 percent does therefore reflect new phenomena in the relationships between higher education and the State.

All this privatization is impressive, but I am not inclined to push the privatization theme too far by depicting trends in higher education as dependent on, or neatly reflecting, a general privatization of Latin America's political economy. There is, of course, a lure to that generality. Also, a hint of something general may spring from our findings that the State itself has often supported privatization in higher education. If this support reflects broader State policy orientations, we might expect to see a general privatization. Indeed some journalists, scholars, and other observers have made much of the idea that a general trend has developed, especially since the

1970s. Much is attributed to the advent of modern authoritarian regimes, most importantly in Brazil (1964), Argentina (1966 and 1976), and Chile and Uruguay (1973). But the evidence presented in support of general privatization goes beyond these cases, drawing on Peru since 1975, Bolivia since 1979, Mexico since the mid-1970s, and even drawing on more democratic contexts, such as Colombia since the 1970s. Such privatization is discussed mostly in terms of turning over State enterprises to private hands or reducing State restrictions on private enterprise (industrial, agricultural, and commercial). Likewise relevant are attempts to rationalize State agencies, as by diminishing subsidies from the central treasury; these measures may be regarded as privatizing State enterprises or merely as strengthening the State's own enterprises. They parallel measures that rationalize public sectors of higher education, whether by imposing tuition or by promoting traits not definitionally intrinsic to privateness but at least associated with it. One reason not to tie the privatization of higher education too closely to any recent and general privatization of Latin America's political economy is that much of the impetus for private higher education began before the inception of Latin America's modern authoritarian regimes. A good example discussed earlier was the privatization of Colombian higher education in the 1940s and 1950s. On the contrary, we have seen that private sectors in higher education have often grown and flourished under rather open regimes and have not necessarily been favored over public sectors by modern authoritarian regimes. However much the State has assisted private growth, the roots of that growth have not generally been tied to any single regime type that has recently predominated.

Furthermore, the evidence is mixed on the general privatization policies of even the modern authoritarian regimes. Chile has properly been taken as the foremost example of privatization, but by 1982 the Chicago Boys lost considerable power to the statists, throwing past privatization policies, not to mention anticipated privatization, very much into doubt. Privatization had at least temporarily run amuck. Brazil's military initially pursued some broad privatization policies, but within a few years statist tendencies were again ascendent. As early as 1976, and certainly by 1970, Argentina was turning away from the specter of privatization posed in 1966, and Argentina post-1976 never went nearly as far as Chile did.[40] Meanwhile, Uruguay apparently did not promote any general privatization in South America.

In fact, although these regimes do not dominate all of society through corporatism, their zeal for privatization has been balanced or even outweighed by authoritarian considerations, including the influence of statist traditions and especially the drive for repressive State control and central power. O'Donnell, among others, has therefore posed privatization versus State control as a central dilemma for modern authoritarian regimes.[41] We have seen this dilemma reflected within higher education itself, particularly in the Chilean case, because these regimes want to control the universities and orient their functions; so far only in Chile has the regime begun to push for public sectors to assume private financing, although Brazil funneled most enrollments into self-financing private institutions and Argentina significantly increased the enrollment share in such institutions.

Finally, the pull between private and statist poles has not been resolved in many countries outside southern South America. In Mexico, for example, President López Portillo's much ballyhooed rapprochement with private enterprise (1976–82) did not keep him from actually expanding the size of the State relative to private enterprise, an expansion culminating with his momentous nationalization of private banks in 1982. In sum, there is insufficient evidence to warrant using a generalized concept of privatization as a major explanation for contemporary trends in higher education.[42]

Still, even though privatization in higher education has outpaced general political-economic privatization, I do not believe higher education to be an anomaly that contradicts general trends. First, privatization in higher education has been demonstrably related to broad political, economic, and social actions of the State and to private actors. Second, privatization in higher education itself is limited by the fact that most higher education is still found in the public sector, a sector that has not been fundamentally reoriented toward private practices. Third, the evidence on general political-economic privatization remains mixed, not clearly negative. Fourth, this evidence has been drawn mostly from the State's relation to for-profit private enterprise, insufficient attention having been paid to the State's possibly changing role with regard to private nonprofit and social-welfare institutions.[43]

Whatever the possible links to broader political-economic privatization, the growth of truly private sectors forces a reformulation of concepts concerning the relationship between the State and higher education. Pluralism and especially privatization are more useful concepts, corporatism and organic statism less useful than was the case when Latin American higher education was dominated by public sectors established as delegates of the State. Clearly, however, this shift does not mean that the relationship between higher education and the State is less significant than it once was. It does not even mean that the relationship is less functional for the State. Nor does the relative decline of corporatism and organic statism in favor of increased privatization and pluralism necessarily imply a fundamental opening up of civil society generally or higher education specifically. The privatization and increased pluralism in question are based on class inequity, privilege, and hierarchy at least as much as they are based on freedom and choice. They more often tacitly support than challenge the State. A particular point of interest in assessing privatization is the degree to which it may serve the State by entrusting activities to privileged clienteles. Satisfying these clienteles is important because they are part of the State's core constituency, threatening the State if dissatisfied. Where great overlap occurs between the interests of private sectors and the State, the State can comfortably allow considerable pluralism, voluntarism, freedom, and choice, not feeling the need to impose extensive corporatist controls. The State can comfortably allow truly private activity to flourish.

CONCLUSION

The shift from public monopolies to dual private and public sectors, marked since the 1930s, accelerating since the 1960s, has changed the face of Latin American higher education. To be sure, there has been continuity as well as change. Moreover, one finds intrasectoral variation and intersectoral overlap along with intersectoral distinctiveness. But the rise of a private sector holding one-third of all enrollments has hardly been a marginal phenomenon. The intersectoral contrasts have often been fundamental, probably equaling the most extreme cases found worldwide. And these contrasts have been heuristically useful here in analyzing higher education systemically.

This concluding chapter has argued that the new order can best be understood by moving some distance away from concepts that were once more applicable. Of course consensus on the meaning or relevance of concepts such as Continental and U.S. models, privateness and publicness, focus and selectivity, success and failure, corporatism and organic statism, and pluralism and privatization is not likely. Nor is it necessary. What is necessary is that any attempt to understand contemporary Latin American higher education take into account the dramatic changes wrought by privatization, reflected in private-public distinctions, and identified throughout this work. These changes have significantly affected finance, governance, and function. They have significantly affected freedom, choice, equity, and effectiveness. They have remolded the relationship between higher education and society's multiple classes, groups, and interests, and they have remolded the relationship between higher education and the State.

Appendix A NOTES ON THE DATA

Anyone who has worked with higher education data is aware of the serious problems, which unfortunately are worse in Latin America than in the United States or Europe. One reason is the proliferation of small, low-quality institutions, mostly private, that often lack either the administrative capability or the will to collect and process basic data. Thus, data such as ours often underestimate the size of the private sector, especially its low-quality subsector. Additionally, some private institutions do not feel compelled to provide full data to national ministries or organizations. On the other hand, some public universities believe that to provide full data may infringe on their autonomy. Others have simply been too disorganized to collect reliable data. Their data do not always make clear which students are full time or part time or merely sporadic attendees or "hangers-on" who have not been formerly removed from the rolls; the inclusion of students not attending class could inflate the public share. Moreover, many public universities purposefully inflate their enrollment figures in order to receive larger State subsidies.

Numerous definitional ambiguities emerge, with different criteria used in (or even within) different nations. An institution that qualifies as a university in one nation might not so qualify in another, even if it is part of higher or postsecondary education. A prime example is the normal school or teachers college. OAS data from some nations (e.g., Chile) show that teacher education is offered by the major universities; data from other countries (e.g., Argentina and Mexico) include teachers colleges as separate higher education institutions; while data from still others (e.g., Colombia, Guatemala) do not incude teacher education as higher education. Some nations (e.g., Argentina, Mexico, Venezuela) tend to compile rather full higher education data, whereas others (e.g., Bolivia, Dominican Republic, Peru) hold closer to their university categories; but, again, what some nations call universities others might not. Another problem with enrollment figures is that some nations report data from the year's inception, others from the year's end. Where data are listed across years, I use the more recent year (e.g., academic year 1964–65 = 1965). For more on how the OAS treats higher education, see *América en cifras 1974* (Washington, D.C.: OAS, 1975), pp. 6–7. For more on UNESCO's "third level," see UNESCO, *Statistical Yearbook 1980* (Paris, 1980), pp. 124–26.

A related problem concerns enrollments in graduate (*posgrado*) study. The OAS, like UNESCO, generally includes these enrollments as part of its higher education figures. UNESCO then tries to divide this tertiary level into three parts—one awarding a "subuniversity" degree, a second awarding a first university degree or its equivalent, and a third awarding a graduate degree. However, UNESCO categories are perverted when contributors submit data without these distinctions. OAS data occasionally include notations (e.g., on Brazil) that graduate enrollments are excluded, properly implying that such enrollments are usually included. Yet OAS officials acknowledge that they include whatever data the contributors include. They believe that the problem was small until the late 1970s because true graduate study was very limited.

I have chosen to work with figures on enrollments rather than figures on those who graduate for two reasons. One is that available enrollment data are much more complete and extensive. The other is that ambiguity exists concerning the definition of a graduate, an *egresado*, or a *titulado*. Generally, the egresado has finished the required courses but, unlike the titulado, has not written the thesis also required for a basic degree. In many nations, few students ever write the thesis necessary to become titulados. Thus the figures on titulados are quite small. However, being an egresado carries some social and economic importance. Beyond that, any university study is widely considered better than none. Therefore, enrollment figures, for all their pitfalls, are meaningful.

There are two common procedures for arriving at enrollment ratios, although sources do not always make clear which they use. One is to divide the number of pupils in a given age group by the total population of that age group, for example, pupils aged 20–24/population aged 20–24. But not every pupil in the age group is necessarily enrolled in an institution of higher education, so this measure inflates the percentage enrollment in higher education. Beyond this, it would be difficult and misleading to exclude students over twenty-four, so it is more common to refer to all students at or above a certain age. Yet another problem is that, even within Latin America itself, nations differ in the age at which most students enter higher education. Where data refer to a high age cohort, such as twenty to twenty-four, they may misjudge the higher education percentage by excluding nineteen-year-olds. The second method used to calculate ratios is to divide the number of students enrolled at a given educational level by the total population in the relevant age group; for example, we might deal with higher education enrollments/population 20–24. This second method solves only the first problem incurred in the first method. It is the method used by the major gatherers of regional data and therefore is used in this book, especially in chapter 2.

The two major sources that offer cross-national private-public enrollment data over time are the OAS and UDUAL. I have chosen to work principally with OAS data for three major reasons. The first is that they are much more comprehensive longitudinally. Available UDUAL data begin in 1962, whereas the OAS starts in 1955; moreover, the OAS (unlike UDUAL) tries to provide every year. (For background on how and why the OAS started its statistical publications series, see *América en cifras, 1960* [Washington, D.C.: n.d.], pp. v–vi. The second reason concerns methods and inclusiveness. UDUAL data are based on the organization's own census; questionnaires are mailed to individual institutions, and UDUAL reports the data by institution, with no aggregation. We clearly see which institutions have provided data to UDUAL and (if we have comprehensive listings by country) which institutions have been omitted. OAS data are reported in aggregated form, and the reader cannot tell how many institutions have or have not responded. Nonetheless, the OAS easily outdistances UDUAL in inclusiveness. Its higher education data come mostly from national ministries, although it too has drawn data from myriad sources, and there is variation in how different organizations define categories and count data. The third reason relates to the second on inclusiveness. The OAS works with all higher education institutions that demand a secondary school diploma (or its equivalent) for entry, whereas UDUAL focuses on universities. Thus UDUAL data severely underestimate the private sector's size, proportional as well as absolute. Similarly, UDUAL data overestimate many other factors. These include the average size of private institutions, private sector quality, and average State subsidies for the private sector. Nor is UDUAL consistent in excluding all other institutions. For example, while Argentina's, Brazil's and Venezuela's data include only universities, Mexico's regional technical institutes appear. Even so, for contrast, and because the UDUAL is the major data alternative, I include its estimates of sectoral size for the two years (1962 and 1971) in which aggregation has been attempted (see Appendix B). The latest UDUAL data are found in UDUAL, *Censo universitario latinoamericano 1979* (Mexico City: UDUAL, 1981). Unfortunately, this *Censo* is inferior in coverage to the *Censo* of 1976–77, published in 1980. But at least UDUAL will continue its work, whereas the OAS does not plan a sequel to its last *América en cifras* compilation, published in 1979.

A welcome addition to the Latin American data collection effort is CRESALC, created in 1976 and centered in Venezuela. CRESALC is promoted by UNESCO and should be a Latin American and Caribbean parallel to the European Center for Higher Education, centered in Rumania.

The major non–Latin American source is UNESCO and its yearly *Statistical Yearbook* (Paris), which includes Latin America within its worldwide data base. It gathers data from national statistics offices, ministries of education, or higher education councils; if there are gaps, it turns to more particular sources. Although UNESCO gives total enrollment data and ratios of the relevant age group in higher education, it gives no private-public breakdown (except where it cites OAS data).

Finally, this appendix should be read in conjunction with footnote 2, chapter 1. It was informed not only by the cited published sources but also by correspondence from H. Ben-Amor, director of UNESCO's Office of Statistics, Paris (April 14, 1982, October 7, 1982, and January 5, 1983), and Roberto Etchepareborda, acting director of the OAS Department of Cultural Affairs (November 3, 1981), as well as several telephone conversations with Manuel Metz, director of the OAS Data Bank, and Sergio Nilo of the OAS Unit of Education Planning and Research, Washington, D.C., in October 1981 and October 1982.

Appendix B Private and Total Enrollments in Latin American Universities, 1962 and 1971

	1962		1971	
	# Private / # Total	% Private	# Private / # Total	% Private
Argentina	9,191 / 192,300	5	46,973 / 298,389	16
Bolivia	1,454 / 10,369	14	3,126 / 28,060	11
Brazil[a]	22,657 / 79,536	28	68,648 / 247,123	28
Chile	16,136 / 34,512	47	40,688 / 121,011	34
Colombia	13,506 / 38,424	35	44,427 / 100,829	44
Costa Rica	0 / 4,920	0	0 / 16,878	0
Cuba	0 / 23,261	0	0 / 30,810	0
Dominican Republic	68 / 5,347	1	1,198 / 28,088	4
Ecuador	1,986 / 10,989	18	14,326 / 50,340	28
El Salvador	0 / 2,973	0	1,358 / 7,899	17
Guatemala	138 / 5,992	2	3,162 / 16,428	19
Haiti[b]	0 / 1,717	0	0 / 1,494	0
Honduras	0 / 1,707	0	0 / 5,600	0
Mexico	6,797 / 119,246	6	35,340 / 309,640	11

Country				%				%
Nicaragua	266	1,619		16	3,023	7,305		41
Panama	0			0	627			4
Paraguay	5,056	814		17	14,184	3,251	8,033	40
Peru	4,710	6,092	41,915	15	28,529	112,717		25
Uruguay[b]	0			0	0			0
Venezuela	36,529	4,516	30,699	15	18,650	12,311	88,486	14
Total Latin America	85,394	675,513		12.6	315,195	1,562,491		20.2
Total Spanish America[a] (without Brazil)	62,737	595,977		10.5	246,547	1,315,368		18.7

SOURCE: Adapted from UDUAL data published in Juan F. Castellanos et al., *Examen de una década* (Mexico City: UDUAL, 1976), p. 206.

a. The single greatest difference between these UDUAL data and the OAS data given in table 1.1 concerns Brazil. Focusing on 1971 (table 1.1 uses 1971 in place of 1970 for Brazil's private percentage though not for Brazil's total), the OAS shows 55 percent private while UDUAL shows 28 percent. The main reason is that UDUAL tries to restrict itself to universities, not higher education inclusively. For 1971 the OAS shows a Brazilian university total only moderately greater than UDUAL's (271,387 to 247,123), but the OAS also shows a Brazilian higher education total (561,397) more than twice as high. OAS data clearly show that Brazil's private enrollments are proportionally much lower in the universities than in higher education overall (35 versus 61 percent in 1973, the closest year to 1971 in which the OAS shows the private-public university balance). See OAS, *América en cifras 1977* (Washington, D.C., 1979), p. 149. Without Brazil, UDUAL's 19 percent private for 1971 approximates the OAS's 20 percent for 1970, just as UDUAL's 11 percent for 1962 approximates the OAS's 9 percent for 1960.

b. UDUAL substitutes 1967 and 1968 for Haiti and Uruguay, respectively, for 1971.

c. Related to note (a) above, UDUAL's Latin American totals are much smaller than the OAS's, but its Spanish American totals are comparable if one estimates the OAS totals from the relevant quinquennia shown in table 1.1.

Appendix C Proliferation of Latin American Universities, 1955–1975

	1955[a]			1960			1965			1970			1975		
	Priv.	Total	% Priv.	Priv.	Total	% Priv.	Priv.	Total	% Priv.	Priv.	Total	% Priv.	Priv.	Total	% Priv.
Argentina	(5)	(15)	(33)[b]	5	15	33	13	26	50	24	38	63	24	53	45
Bolivia	0	7	0	0	7	0	(0)	(7)	(0)[d]	(0)	(7)	(0)[d]	(0)	(7)	(0)[d]
Brazil	(10)	(32)	(32)[b]	(10)	(32)	(32)[c]	12	37	32	33	60	55	21	57	37
Chile	4	6	67	5	7	71	(6)	(8)	(75)[e]	6	8	75	6	8	75
Colombia	(14)	(27)	(52)[b]	14	27	52	14	32	44	17	37	46	(17)	(37)	(46)[d]
Costa Rica	0	1	0	0	1	0	0	1	0	0	1	0	2	3	67
Cuba	2	7	29	0	3	0	0	3	0	0	3	0	0	4	0
Dominican Republic	0	1	0	0	1	0	0	1	0	2	3	67	(2)	(3)	(67)[d]
Ecuador	1	6	17	1	6	17	2	7	29	3	10	30	5	14	36
El Salvador	0	1	0	0	1	0	0	1	0	1	2	50	1	2	50
Guatemala	0	1	0	0	1	0	1	2	50	3	4	75	(3)	(4)	(75)[d]
Haiti	0	1	0	0	1	0	0	1	0	0	1	0	(0)	(1)	(0)[d]
Honduras	0	1	0	0	1	0	0	1	0	0	1	0	(0)	(1)	(0)[d]
Mexico	(8)	(35)	(23)[b]	8	35	23	15	45	33	17	51	33	51	136	38
Nicaragua	0	1	0	0	1	0	1	2	50	1	2	50	1	2	50

0	1	0	0	1	0	1	2	50	1	2	50	1	2	50
0	1	0	1	2	50	1	2	50	1	2	50	1	2	50
1	7	14	4	15	27	9	28	32	12	33	36	11	33	33
0	1	0	0	1	0	0	1	0	0	1	0	(0)	(1)	(0)[d]
2	5	40	2	7	29	2	7	29	3	10	30	5	21	24
47	157	30	50	165	30	77	214	36	124	276	45	151	391	39

Panama
Paraguay
Peru
Uruguay
Venezuela
TOTAL

SOURCES: OAS, *América en cifras* (Washington, D.C.), principally the publications of 1965, 1972, 1974, and 1977; see chapter 1, footnote 2.

NOTES: Although I have inserted data where the OAS showed none (see notes a–e below), I have not changed any data given by the OAS, even where I have more accurate data, because, unlike the situation with enrollments and table 1.1, I have only isolated alternative data. Among the corrections that might have been shown here, Bolivia started a private university in the late 1960s and Costa Rica had no private university in 1975.

This appendix shows the enormous proliferation of universities. There is good reason to focus mostly on the 1960–70 period. First, for 1955 I had to substitute 1960 data for missing data in the four nations with the largest higher education systems. This led to an overestimation of the 1955 total and especially of the private sector subtotal. For example, Argentina did not authorize private universities until the late 1950s. (In almost all cases where OAS data were missing, the closest available OAS year was the five-year interval.) Second, the 1975 data are affected by Mexico's inclusion of public regional technical institutes as universities. Third, proliferation is extensive in the 1960–70 period.

a. I substituted the following years for missing OAS years: Brazil 1974 for 1975; Cuba 1956, 1962, and 1969 for 1955, 1960, and 1970, respectively; Ecuador 1956 for 1955; Guatemala 1969 for 1970; Honduras 1968 for 1970; Mexico 1962, 1966, 1969, and 1974 for 1960, 1965, 1970, and 1975, respectively; Nicaragua 1966 for 1965; Peru 1961 for 1960.

b. As the OAS showed no data, I substituted data from the next available year.

c. The OAS showed the total but not the private-public breakdown. I therefore applied the 1965 percentage to the 1960 total.

d. As the OAS showed no data, I substituted data from the last preceding year.

e. The OAS showed no data, but chapter 3 shows these figures.

Appendix D Enrollments by Field of Study in Mexico's Principal Geographical Areas, 1971

Sector	Business & Administration	Basic Social Sciences	Law	Humanities	Education	Medical Sciences	Nursing	Veterinary Studies	Agricultural Sciences	Exact Sciences	Engineering	Architecture	Total
Federal District													
Private	9,660	1,368	1,115	851	749	530	0	0	0	348	1,886	508	17,015
	(56.8)	(8.0)	(6.6)	(5.0)	(4.4)	(3.1)	(0.0)	(0.0)	(0.0)	(2.0)	(11.1)	(3.0)	(100.0)
Public	21,984	10,010	8,356	3,898	1,862	20,526	60	1,650	0	4,533	40,629	4,298	117,806
	(18.7)	(8.5)	(7.1)	(3.3)	(1.6)	(17.4)	(0.1)	(1.4)	(0.0)	(3.8)	(34.5)	(3.6)	(100.0)
Total	31,644	11,378	9,471	4,749	2,611	21,056	60	1,650	0	4,881	42,515	4,806	134,821
	(23.5)	(8.4)	(7.0)	(3.5)	(1.9)	(15.6)	(0.0)	(1.2)	(0.0)	(3.6)	(31.5)	(3.6)	(99.8)
Jalisco													
Private	1,680	335	474	55	295	4,021	20	0	0	48	1,352	515	8,795
	(19.1)	(3.8)	(5.4)	(0.6)	(3.4)	(45.7)	(0.2)	(0.0)	(0.0)	(0.5)	(15.4)	(5.9)	(100.0)
Public	3,960	584	2,402	208	0	2,468	0	462	873	167	5,284	807	17,215
	(23.0)	(3.4)	(14.0)	(1.2)	(0.0)	(14.3)	(0.0)	(2.7)	(5.1)	(1.0)	(30.7)	(4.7)	(100.1)
Total	5,640	919	2,876	263	295	6,489	20	462	873	215	6,636	1,322	26,010
	(21.7)	(3.5)	(11.1)	(1.0)	(1.1)	(24.9)	(0.1)	(1.8)	(3.4)	(0.8)	(25.5)	(5.1)	(100.0)

Appendix D

Nuevo León

Private	2,393 (33.9)	520 (7.4)	0 (0.0)	163 (2.3)	89 (1.3)	226 (3.2)	0 (0.0)	79 (1.1)	520 (7.4)	311 (4.4)	2,493 (35.3)	260 (3.7)	7,054 (100.0)
Public	1,946 (13.5)	318 (2.2)	1,226 (8.5)	547 (3.8)	1,834 (12.7)	1,491 (10.3)	107 (0.7)	0 (0.0)	392 (2.7)	729 (5.0)	5,256 (36.4)	601 (4.2)	14,447 (100.0)
TOTAL	4,339 (20.2)	838 (3.9)	1,226 (5.7)	710 (3.3)	1,923 (8.9)	1,717 (8.0)	107 (0.5)	79 (0.4)	912 (4.2)	1,040 (4.8)	7,749 (36.0)	861 (4.0)	21,501 (99.9)

All Other

Private	805 (22.0)	259 (7.1)	149 (4.1)	16 (0.4)	960 (26.3)	170 (4.7)	0 (0.0)	0 (0.0)	299 (8.2)	18 (0.5)	814 (22.3)	163 (4.7)	3,653 (100.3)
Public	13,473 (19.0)	3,072 (4.3)	10,279 (14.5)	1,546 (2.2)	2,415 (3.4)	13,296 (18.8)	198 (0.3)	1,346 (1.9)	2,629 (3.7)	2,144 (3.0)	18,387 (26.0)	1,975 (2.8)	70,760 (99.9)
TOTAL	14,278 (19.2)	3,331 (4.5)	10,428 (14.0)	1,562 (2.1)	3,375 (4.5)	13,466 (18.1)	198 (0.3)	1,346 (1.8)	2,928 (3.9)	2,162 (2.9)	19,201 (25.8)	2,138 (2.9)	74,413 (100.0)

SOURCE: See table 4.2.

Appendix E MEXICAN ENROLLMENTS BY FIELD OF STUDY IN INSTITUTIONS LISTED IN 1971 AND 1978

Sector	Business and Administration	Communications	Economics	Basic Social Sciences	Law	Humanities	Education
			1971				
Private	13,959	—	—	2,370	1,738	1,085	171
	(41.6)			(7.1)	(5.2)	(3.2)	(0.5)
Public	41,363	—	—	13,837	21,984	6,101	863
	(19.4)			(6.5)	(10.3)	(2.9)	(0.4)
TOTAL	55,322	—	—	16,207	23,722	7,186	1,034
	(22.4)			(6.6)	(9.6)	(2.9)	(0.4)
			1978				
Private	18,789	1,666	1,648	3,995	3,833	871	523
	(34.0)	(3.0)	(3.0)	(7.2)	(6.9)	(1.6)	(0.9)
Public	83,187	3,139	18,298	29,362	48,766	10,852	3,203
	(16.0)	(0.6)	(3.5)	(5.7)	(9.4)	(2.1)	(0.6)
TOTAL	101,976	4,805	19,946	33,357	52,599	11,723	3,726
	(17.8)	(0.8)	(3.5)	(5.8)	(9.2)	(2.0)	(0.6)

SOURCES: See tables 4.2 and 4.6 (including the notes).

NOTES: Institutions may have been listed in only one year either because they did not exist in the other year or simply because ANUIES did not receive information on them. The purpose of including this

Appendix E cont'd

Medical Sciences	Nurs- ing	Veter- inary Studies	Agri- cultural Sciences	Exact Sciences	Engi- neer- ing	Archi- tecture	Total
			1971				
4,902	20	79	819	707	6,251	1,446	33,547
(14.6)	(0.1)	(0.2)	(2.4)	(2.1)	(18.6)	(4.3)	(99.9)
37,476	365	3,458	3,894	7,364	69,085	7,681	213,471
(17.6)	(0.2)	(1.6)	(1.8)	(3.4)	(32.4)	(3.6)	(100.1)
42,378	385	3,537	4,713	8,071	75,336	9,127	247,018
(17.2)	(0.2)	(1.4)	(1.9)	(3.3)	(30.5)	(3.7)	(100.1)
			1978				
14,090	37	0	2,840	834	1,820	4,388	55,334
(25.5)	(0.1)	(0.0)	(5.1)	(1.5)	(3.3)	(7.9)	(100.0)
108,695	1,561	13,423	24,631	20,666	122,331	30,372	518,487
(21.0)	(0.3)	(2.6)	(4.8)	(4.0)	(23.6)	(5.9)	(100.1)
122,786	1,598	13,423	27,471	21,500	124,151	34,760	573,821
(21.4)	(0.3)	(2.3)	(4.8)	(3.7)	(21.6)	(6.1)	(99.9)

Appendix E is to show that table 4.6 offers a fair comparison to table 4.2. Those two tables show the totals available for 1971 and 1978, respectively, while Appendix E confirms that the basic private-public differences also emerge if we focus only on institutions shown in both years.

Appendix F COLOMBIAN ENROLLMENTS BY FIELD OF STUDY, 1977

Sector	Business and Administration	Communications	Economics	Basic Social Sciences	Law	Humanities	Education
Private	24,336	998	10,684	6,463	15,225	4,748	1,708
	(24.9)	(1.0)	(10.9)	(6.6)	(15.6)	(4.9)	(1.7)
Public	7,663	620	2,842	13,642	4,443	7,242	8,840
	(7.1)	(0.6)	(2.6)	(12.6)	(4.1)	(6.7)	(8.2)
TOTAL	31,999	1,618	13,526	20,087	19,668	11,990	10,548
	(15.5)	(0.8)	(6.6)	(9.7)	(9.5)	(5.8)	(5.1)

SOURCE: UDUAL, *Censo universitario latinoamericano 1976–1977* (Mexico City: UDUAL, 1980), pp. 270–404.

NOTES: The basic private-public patterns discovered here are confirmed and updated to 1980 in ICFES, *Estadísticas de la educación superior 1980* (Bogotá: ICFES, 1982), p. 38. Illustratively, only in one category—the basic social sciences—does the proportional edge switch from one sector to the other. On the data shown in this appendix, see Appendix J on field categories and note the following four points on sectoral size: (1) Data refer to the university (or licenciatura) level; I excluded all entries that referred to pre- and postuniversity levels (*nivel medio* and *posgrado*, respectively). Excluded were a total of 2,396 pre- and 1,263 postuniversity students from the private sector and 8,782 and 792 respectively from the public sector. (2) UDUAL does not successfully receive information from every

Appendix F cont'd

Medical Studies	Nurs- ing	Veter- inary Studies	Agri- cultural Studies	Exact Sciences	Engi- neer- ing	Archi- tecture	Miscel- laneous	Total
4,374	363	0	170	3,795	16,546	5,127	3,315	97,852
(4.4)	(0.4)	(0.0)	(0.2)	(3.9)	(16.9)	(5.2)	(3.4)	(100.0)
10,147	2,091	2,728	4,421	13,051	27,652	2,202	693	108,259
(9.4)	(1.9)	(2.5)	(4.1)	(12.1)	(25.5)	(2.0)	(0.6)	(100.0)
14,521	2,454	2,728	4,591	16,846	44,198	7,329	4,008	206,111
(7.0)	(1.2)	(1.3)	(2.2)	(8.2)	(21.4)	(3.6)	(1.9)	(99.8)

institution—a special problem in the private sector. The figures shown here equal 78 percent of the OAS 1977 totals for the private sector. Note, however, that much of the difference is accounted for by (1) above and by the UDUAL substitution of 1976 data where 1977 data were not available. On the other hand, our public UDUAL total of 108,259 exceeds the OAS's 105,904. (3) UDUAL gives totals of 4,062 and 25,628 for the public universities of Cartagena and the National University, but addition of the various field enrollment subtotals shows the correct figures to be 4,162 and 25,627, respectively. (4) Data for the public Valle University do not indicate how many of its 8,008 students are not at the university level nor how many of its 1,281 medical studies students may be in nursing. I count all the former as university level, all the latter as medical students.

347

Appendix G ECUADORIAN ENROLLMENTS BY FIELD OF STUDY, 1977

Sector	Business and Administration	Communications	Economics	Basic Social Sciences	Law	Humanities	Education
Private	4,269	0	1,268	2,051	1,480	2,208	7,724
	(18.0)	(0.0)	(5.4)	(8.7)	(6.2)	(9.3)	(32.6)
Public	19,217	0	8,473	7,417	8,733	8,538	26,195
	(12.6)	(0.0)	(5.6)	(4.9)	(5.7)	(5.6)	(17.2)
TOTAL	23,486	0	9,741	9,468	10,213	10,746	33,919
	(13.4)	(0.0)	(5.5)	(5.4)	(5.8)	(6.1)	(19.3)

SOURCE: UDUAL, *Censo universitario latinoamericano 1976–1977* (Mexico City: UDUAL, 1980), pp. 428–70.

NOTES: See Appendix J on field categories and note the following four points on the sectors: (1) The Catholic University of Ecuador (in Quito) had 5,465 students listed under an extension department, which apparently is part of the education faculty. See Consejo Nacional de Educación Superior, *Estadísticas de la universidad ecuatoriana* (Quito, 1980), vol. 5, p. 85. (2) UDUAL would show a 24,023 total for the private sector, but it wrongly gives 936 for the Catholic University of Cuenca, while the field enrollments really add to 887. From this adjusted total of 23,974 I exclude 290 that were listed as

Appendix G cont'd

Medical Studies	Nurs- ing	Veter- inary Studies	Agri- cultural Studies	Exact Sciences	Engi- neer- ing	Archi- tecture	Miscel- laneous	Total
345	321	0	225	635	1,790	792	576	23,684
(1.5)	(1.4)	(0.0)	(1.0)	(2.7)	(7.6)	(3.3)	(2.4)	(100.1)
17,279	175	1,129	6,054	8,016	25,223	6,453	9,283	152,185
(11.4)	(0.1)	(0.7)	(4.0)	(5.3)	(16.6)	(4.2)	(6.1)	(100.0)
17,624	496	1,129	6,279	8,651	27,013	7,245	9,859	175,869
(10.0)	(0.3)	(0.6)	(3.6)	(4.9)	(15.4)	(4.1)	(5.6)	(100.0)

preuniversity. (3) Similarly, UDUAL would indicate a 152,781 public sector total, but it gives 50 fewer students than field enrollments actually show for the University of Cuenca and 90 fewer at the National University of Loja. These adjustments bring us to 152,921, from which I deduct 711 and 25, pre- and postuniversity, respectively. (4) The figures in Appendix G reach 93 and 89 percent of the respective private and public figures given in our OAS data for 1977. The gap may stem from the UDUAL omission of some public institutions (all five private ones are included), possible OAS inclusion of some nonuniversity enrollments, and the fact that UDUAL gives 1976 data when no 1977 data were available.

Appendix H PERUVIAN ENROLLMENTS BY FIELD OF STUDY, 1977

Sector	Business and Administration	Communications	Economics	Basic Social Sciences	Law	Humanities	Education
Private	14,665	750	7,251	8,049	2,406	3,163	1,824
	(30.5)	(1.6)	(15.1)	(16.7)	(5.0)	(6.6)	(3.8)
Public	23,484	295	9,240	13,227	5,415	653	13,106
	(16.5)	(0.2)	(6.5)	(9.3)	(3.8)	(0.5)	(9.2)
TOTAL	38,149	1,045	16,491	21,276	7,821	3,816	14,930
	(20.1)	(0.5)	(8.7)	(11.2)	(4.1)	(2.0)	(7.9)

SOURCE: *Censo universitario latinoamericano 1976–1977* (Mexico City: UDUAL, 1980), pp. 713–97.

NOTES: See Appendix J on field categories and note the following five points on sectoral size: (1) Data refer only to the university (or licenciatura) level; I excluded all entries that referred to pre- and postuniversity levels (*nivel medio* and *posgrado*, respectively). Excluded are thirty-one pre- and 234 postuniversity students from the private sector and 661 postuniversity students from the public sector. (2) At first glance the data look very incomplete by comparison with our OAS data. Even including the students referred to in note (1) above, the private total used here is only 59 percent of the OAS total for 1977 while the public total is 90 percent; in all, our UDUAL source shows only 79 percent of total OAS enrollments. Furthermore, the UDUAL *Censo* for 1979 (Mexico City, 1981), pp. 680–728, is far less complete than the UDUAL used here. It includes only five private and twelve public universities, while the UDUAL data used here include ten and twenty-two. Most important, notes (3)–(5) below show that our data may approach completeness more than initial comparisons with OAS data indicate. (3) Official Peruvian data from CONAI show institutional enrollments relatively consistent with ours.

350

Appendix H cont'd

Medical Studies	Nurs- ing	Veter- inary Studies	Agri- cultural Studies	Exact Sciences	Engi- neer- ing	Archi- tecture	Miscel- laneous	Total
676	0	0	0	3,041	3,963	1,502	840	48,130
(1.4)	(0.0)	(0.0)	(0.0)	(6.3)	(8.2)	(3.1)	(1.7)	(100.0)
9,924	4,320	4,067	8,080	5,492	40,851	2,907	983	142,044
(7.0)	(3.0)	(2.9)	(5.7)	(3.9)	(28.8)	(2.0)	(0.7)	(100.0)
10,600	4,320	4,067	8,080	8,533	44,814	4,409	1,823	190,174
(5.6)	(2.3)	(2.1)	(4.2)	(4.5)	(23.6)	(2.3)	(1.0)	(100.1)

(These data do not show field distributions, however.) In the private sector, there is exact numerical agreement on nine universities. For one—the Pontifical Catholic University of Peru—our UDUAL compilation falls 121 short of the CONAI figures. The main discrepancy is the UDUAL omission of one university, the Catholic Santa María, and its 4,237 students. Adding these two discrepancies to the 265 students referred to in note (1) gives us exactly the same number (52,753) found in the CONAI data. (4) For the public sector, exact overlap occurs between our UDUAL data and the CONAI data for eighteen universities. Moreover, each source shows the same four additional universities, and there are enrollment differences of only one (plus one and minus one, respectively) in two. For the National Education University, CONAI offers only a 1976 figure, which exceeds our 1977 figure by 3,145. For the National University of Trujillo, the CONAI figure is 263 less than ours. Adding the discrepancy of 2,882 reported in this note to the 661 in question in note (1) above, we get an exact match to the 145,587 total found in the CONAI data. (5) With one exception, both CONAI and UDUAL use 1977 data for the same institutions, each substituting 1976 in two private and two public ones.

Appendix I ENROLLMENTS BY FIELD OF STUDY IN EIGHT NATIONS, 1977–1979

Nation and Sector	Business and Administration	Communications	Economics	Basic Social Sciences	Law	Humanities	Education
Bolivia (1978)	200	250	400	300	0	170	0
private	(13.6)	(17.0)	(27.2)	(20.4)		(11.6)	
Bolivia (1978)	4,222	226	0	5,844	3,452	922	201
public	(9.4)	(0.5)		(13.0)	(7.7)	(2.1)	(0.4)
Costa Rica	934	0	51	14	738	167	0
(1979) private	(39.7)		(2.2)	(0.6)	(31.4)	(7.1)	
Costa Rica	0	0	0	11,003	0	3,134	3,918
(1979) public				(24.5)		(7.0)	(8.7)
Cuba (1978)	20,059	2,541	0	698	3,320	4,157	25,000
public	(15.1)	(1.9)		(0.5)	(2.5)	(3.1)	(18.8)
Guatemala[a]	762	0	729	162	610	1,403	355
(1977) private	(14.4)		(13.8)	(3.1)	(11.5)	(26.5)	(6.7)
Guatemala	0	91	6,513	3,451	2,164	1,206	0
(1977) public		(0.3)	(22.3)	(11.8)	(7.4)	(4.1)	
Haiti (1978)	94	25	0	493	168	109	28
public	(2.2)	(0.6)		(11.8)	(4.0)	(2.6)	(0.7)
Honduras[b]	5,518	0	2,322	1,197	2,103	114	277
public (1979)	(25.8)		(10.9)	(5.6)	(9.8)	(0.5)	(1.3)
Panama (1977)	460	0	0	185	217	112	0
private[c]	(25.6)			(14.3)	(16.8)	(8.7)	
Panama (1977)	9,355	525	1,759	2,478	649	1,678	1,920
public	(32.6)	(1.8)	(6.1)	(8.6)	(2.3)	(5.8)	(6.7)
Uruguay (1977)	4,133	196	0	259	12,894	1,178	
public	(10.5)	(0.5)		(0.7)	(32.7)	(3.0)	
Total	2,356	250	1,180	661	1,565	1,852	355
private	(22.7)	(2.4)	(11.3)	(6.4)	(15.0)	(17.8)	(3.4)
Total	43,381	3,604	10,594	25,423	24,750	12,498	31,344
public	(12.5)	(1.0)	(3.1)	(7.4)	(7.2)	(3.6)	(9.1)
TOTAL[d]	45,737	3,854	11,774	26,084	26,315	14,350	31,699
	(12.8)	(1.1)	(3.3)	(7.3)	(7.4)	(4.0)	(8.9)

SOURCES: For Guatemala and Panama, UDUAL, *Censo universitario latinoamericano 1976–1977* (Mexico City: UDUAL, 1980), pp. 471–82, 701–8. For Honduras, idem, *Censo universitario latinoamericano 1979* (Mexico City: UDUAL, 1981), pp. 418–19. For Costa Rica, OPES, *Estadística de la educación superior 1979* (San José: Consejo Nacional de Rectores, 1980), pp. 26, 154. For Bolivia (private), I used rounded-off figures provided by Salvador Romero of the Center for Educational Research. For Bolivia (public) and Cuba, Haiti, and Uruguay, see UNESCO, *Statistical Yearbook, 1981* (Paris: UNESCO, 1981), pp. III 385–91.

NOTES: UNESCO gives data in the following categories: (1) education science and technological training; (2) humanities, religion, and theology; (3) fine and applied arts; (4) law; (5) social and behavioral science; (6) commercial and business administration; (7) mass communication and documentation; (8) home economics and domestic science; (9) service trades; (10) natural science; (11) mathematics and computer science; (12) medical and health-related science; (13) engineering; (14) architecture and town planning; (15) trade, craft, and industrial programs; (16) transport and communications; (17) agriculture, forestry, and fishery; (18) other and not specified. I classified these categories into my schema as follows: (1) half education, half engineering; (2) humanities; (3) humanities; (4) law; (5) basic social sciences; (6) business and administration; (7) communications; (8) business and administration; (9) business and administration; (10) exact sciences; (11) exact sciences; (12) medical studies; (13) engineering; (14) architecture; (15) half business and administration, half engineering; (16) half communications, half engineering; (17) agricultural studies; (18) miscellaneous.

Medical Studies	Nursing	Veterinary Studies	Agricultural Studies	Exact Sciences	Engineering	Architecture	Miscellaneous	Total
0	150	0	0	0	0	0	0	1,470
	(10.2)							(100.0)
9,662	0	0	504	6,874	10,512	2,527	0	44,946
(21.5)			(1.1)	(15.3)	(23.4)	(5.6)		(100.0)
120	0	0	0	0	38	290	0	2,352
(5.1)					(1.6)	(12.3)		(100.0)
2,914	0	0	2,292	3,031	2,423	2,422	13,778	44,915
(6.5)			(5.1)	(6.7)	(5.4)	(5.4)	(30.7)	(100.0)
13,998	0	0	13,003	6,198	39,006	5,034	0	133,014
(10.5)			(9.8)	(4.7)	(29.3)	(3.8)		(100.0)
31	0	0	0	0	1,034	50	150	5,286
(0.6)					(19.6)	(0.9)	(2.8)	(100.1)
5,415	0	607	1,551	985	3,366	1,334	2,551	29,234
(18.5)		(2.1)	(5.3)	(3.4)	(11.5)	(4.6)	(8.7)	(100.0)
984	0	0	139	152	1,562	0	432	4,186
(23.5)			(3.3)	(3.6)	(37.3)		(10.3)	(99.9)
2,426	402	0	1,694	1,025	4,187	0	101	21,366
(11.4)	(1.9)		(7.9)	(4.8)	(19.6)		(0.5)	(100.0)
0	0	0	0	8	279	32	0	1,293
				(0.6)	(21.6)	(2.5)		(100.0)
1,859	963	281	99	2,082	1,140	1,180	2,724	28,692
(6.5)	(3.4)	(1.0)	(0.3)	(7.3)	(4.0)	(4.1)	(9.5)	(100.0)
11,963	0	0	3,825	1,319	1,524	1,645	456	39,392
(30.4)			(9.7)	(3.3)	(3.9)	(4.2)	(1.2)	(100.1)
151	150	0	0	8	1,351	372	150	10,401
(1.5)	(1.4)	(0.0)	(0.0)	(0.1)	(13.0)	(3.6)	(1.4)	(100.0)
49,221	1,365	888	23,107	21,666	63,720	14,142	20,042	345,745
(14.2)	(0.4)	(0.3)	(6.7)	(6.3)	(18.4)	(4.1)	(5.8)	(100.1)
49,372	1,515	888	23,107	21,674	65,071	14,514	20,192	356,146
(13.9)	(0.4)	(0.2)	(6.5)	(6.1)	(18.3)	(4.1)	(5.7)	(100.0)

For more information on UNESCO's fields, see UNESCO, *International Standard Classification of Education*, abridged ed. (Paris: UNESCO, July 1975), pp. 77–87. For more information on the field categories used here in Appendix I, see Appendix J.

a. Guatemala's private Universidad del Valle lists 46 students under a science and humanities faculty, which I have placed fully under humanities. UDUAL shows a Guatemalan private total of 5,314, but that includes 28 graduate enrollments. UDUAL substitutes 1976 data for missing 1977 data.

b. Although UDUAL reports a total of 21,386 for the public university, the field enrollments add up to 21,366.

c. UDUAL reports private and public totals of 1,759 and 32,876, respectively, but these include 466 private graduate and 4,184 public preuniversity enrollments.

d. Cuba and Uruguay have only public sectors. The situation is more ambiguous in Honduras and Haiti (see chapter 1, footnote 2). UDUAL's data on Honduras show only the public university figures. I have no field data on the larger of Honduras's two private universities, while the smaller one concentrates its 184 students almost fully in business and administration, architecture, and engineering; the entire private sector still had only 734 enrollments (less than 3 percent of the national total) by 1981. As the UNESCO data offer no private-public breakdown, all its Haitian enrollments are listed here as public and its total Bolivian figure is listed here as public, although I am not sure that the latter excludes the private university.

Appendix J FIELD CATEGORIES EMPLOYED

1. See notes on all tables with field distributions (see table 6.13 for listing).

2. In each table on an individual nation I follow the wording and category aggregation used in that nation's data, provided there is category aggregation. This is the case for Argentina, Brazil, Chile, and Venezuela (tables 6.7, 5.3, 3.6, 6.9). The necessary subsequent procedures to convert these categorizations into usable cross-national ones are discussed here and in the notes to table 6.13. The idea is to deal with each nation in its own terms as much as possible.

3. In other nations, however, there is ample reason to put the data directly into my own field categorizations. Such is the case for all data derived from UNESCO (for Bolivia, Cuba, Haiti, Uruguay). UNESCO has already converted raw data into its own field categorizations, thus obscuring the more specific data on careers and/or whatever field categorizations are used by the individual nations. The procedure for converting UNESCO categories to mine is shown in the notes to Appendix I.

4. Similarly, there is reason to use my categories in other cases. Data obtained on Costa Rica and Mexico and from UDUAL (for Colombia, Ecuador, Guatemala, Honduras, Panama, Peru) were in raw form (i.e., showing each career instead of grouping the data by field categorizations).

5. In the Mexican case, however, although the data were listed in raw form by careers, an accompanying guide suggested how to aggregate into fields. ANUIES, *Catálogo de carreras* (Mexico City: ANUIES, 1973), pp. 11–15. I therefore followed this guide in chapter 4; this also explains a few deviations from the general format used in chapter 6 for most nations. The Mexican data had journalism listed under communications instead of basic social sciences; statistics and actuarial studies under exact sciences instead of business and administration; history and geography under humanities instead of basic social sciences; and information sciences under basic social sciences instead of business and administration. The affected fields held 7,737 enrollments, 1.2 percent of Mexico's 622,134 total. Nonetheless, the categorization used for Mexico became a guide for the standardized categorizations eventually used in chapter 6.

6. The individual career figures must be put into field categorizations because (*a*) there are too many careers to encompass on any readily comprehensible chart; (*b*) too many careers on the chart would show figures too small for reasonable comparisons; (*c*) different nations list different careers, further diminishing comparability; (*d*) data from some nations are shown only by field aggregations, not by individual careers.

7. Where data appeared in double categories, I divided them half into each field. Examples include economics and administration, and law and political science. But where only one broad category was shown I put the total into the dominant category (e.g., medical sciences or health sciences into my category of medical studies, even though the national figure actually included unspecified numbers in nursing or veterinary studies). Unfortunately, therefore, some problems with aggregation cannot be solved. Several nations subsume certain careers under certain headings, without always indicating which careers are subsumed or not showing their respective percentages within the general category. Nor can I simply collapse the troublesome categories. For example, engineering may be tied to architecture, which

elsewhere may be tied to art, or to agriculture (or to exact sciences); agriculture may be tied elsewhere to veterinary studies, which are often tied to medical studies, which are often grouped with nursing, etc.

8. I group individual career listings into field categories in the following way:

a. *Business and administration*: accounting; administration; business administration; commercial relations; computer studies; home economics; industrial relations; information sciences; statistics; tourism.

b. *Basic social sciences*: anthropology; area studies; geography; history; international relations; journalism; political science; psychology; social work; sociology.

c. *Humanities*: dance; drama; fine arts; foreign languages; human sciences; letters; library studies; linguistics; literature; painting; philosophy; philology; plastic arts; religion; sculpture; Spanish.

d. *Education*: all education listed regardless of type (e.g., science education or physical education).

e. *Medical studies*: dentistry; health specialist; human medicine; medicine; nutrition; various specialties, such as obstetrics or optomology.

f. *Agricultural studies*: agriculture; agricultural engineering; agronomy; zookeeping.

g. *Exact sciences*: biology; chemistry; earth sciences; mathematics; oceanology; physics.

h. *Engineering*: engineering; military studies; technologies; various engineering specialties, such as civil, clinical, extractive, forestral, industrial, mechanical.

9. Note that the fields not included above are narrower or more self-explanatory in scope, except when they are subsumed in national data categories (such as communications within business and administration, economics within basic social sciences, nursing within medical studies, and veterinary within either medical studies or agricultural studies).

10. A few comments are in order about certain careers. History and geography are grouped by some nations with humanities, by others with basic social sciences. I put them under social sciences where they were simply listed by career (e.g., by UDUAL). The Argentine data do not indicate whether they are under other human sciences or other social sciences; Venezuelan data put history under humanities, but geography under social sciences; Chilean data put both under humanities. I put journalism under basic social sciences, whereas some nations, possibly more properly, put it under humanities. I put actuarial studies and statistics under business and administration, whereas others put them under exact sciences. Pharmacy lay ambiguously between exact sciences or engineering, depending on how it was listed. I put engineering careers under engineering, even in dealing with such ambiguities as chemical engineering; only with agriculturally related engineering were careers deleted from the engineering category (placed instead under agricultural studies).

Notes

CHAPTER ONE

1. Table 1.1 shows only Chile, Colombia, and Peru with private enrollments in 1930; their combined private sectors held only 3 percent of Latin America's 1955 total enrollments. Yet the three nations together probably had proportionally smaller private sectors in 1930 than in 1955; on Colombia (12 percent, 1930) and Chile (27 percent, 1935), see footnote 17 of chapter 2 and table 3.3, respectively. I use the term *Spanish America* when I want to exclude Brazil (Portuguese speaking); but I take the liberty of including Haiti (French speaking), easily the smallest of the twenty national cases covered. *Latin America* thus refers to the twenty republics included in table 1.1, excluding many Caribbean republics and the new Central American republic of Belize (1981).

2. The main source for table 1.1 is the OAS. See *América en cifras 1977* (Washington, D.C.:OAS, 1979), pp. 149–55; *América en cifras 1974* (OAS, 1975), pp. 150–56; *América en cifras 1972* (OAS, 1973), pp. 200–223; *América en cifras 1965* (OAS, 1967), pp. 160–81; *América en cifras 1963* (OAS, 1964), pp. 136–49. Also see *América en cifras 1961* (OAS, n.d.) and *América en cifras 1960* (OAS, n.d.). Most *América en cifras* come in multivolumes; I always refer to the ones on culture. I have worked backwards from the most recent publications. There is some overlap in years covered, and data given twice are not always exactly the same; I use the figures most recently given. The OAS shows missing data in some cases where private sectors definitely were not yet created; I have substituted zeros. I have also used the OAS's preliminary data where no other OAS data were available since experience has shown that changes subsequently made have been quite small. I have made these necessary substitutions for missing OAS data: 1971 for 1960 in Honduras, 1969 for 1970 in Bolivia, 1961 for 1960 in Bolivia and Peru, and 1955–56 for 1955 in Cuba, Ecuador, Haiti, Nicaragua, and Venezuela.

Two non-OAS sources are used more than once in table 1.1. One is UNESCO, *Statistical Yearbook 1981* (Paris: UNESCO, 1981), pp. III 386–III 391. The second is Carlos Muñoz Izquierdo and Patricia Restrepo de Cepeda, "Analysis and Projection of Educational Expenditures in Latin America," paper delivered at the IDB Seminar on the Financing of Education in Latin America, Mexico City, November 27–December 1, 1978, pp. 25–26, 90. The Muñoz and Restrepo data draw on OAS and various UNESCO data sources; since I have looked beyond the OAS only where I could not find OAS data, it is likely that the Muñoz and Restrepo data I use come from UNESCO.

Regarding specific nations, the following shows where I had to add to the OAS data for 1955–75 and where I obtained the latest available data.

Argentina. For 1982, Ministerio de Educación, *Estadísticas de la educación* (Buenos Aires, 1982).

Bolivia. The 1975 total comes from Jaime Castrejón Díez, "Siete países de América Latina y el Caribe," in Manuel Barquín, ed., *Planeación y regulación en la educación superior* (Mexico City: UNAM, 1981), p. 48. The 1978 total is from UNESCO, *Statistical Yearbook*, p. III 388. I apply the last (1969) OAS percentage to the total enrollments for 1975 and 1978 to estimate the private enrollments. Salvador Romero of the Center for Educational Research (and formerly vice-president of the Catholic university) confirms that the private share in 1978 was still roughly 3 percent.

Brazil. The OAS shows no 1970 private figure. Its 1971 figure is 55 percent, which I apply to the 1970 total. Muñoz and Restrepo show 56 percent for 1970. Chapter 5 shows only 51 percent for 1970, but also shows only 62 percent for 1975; I use chapter 5 data in table 1.1 for 1980 only because they are consistently different from OAS data, giving lower private percentages.

Chile. OAS data are identical to data in chapter 3, 1960–75, but show 36 percent (even though omitting one very small private university) instead of 31 percent for 1955. Chapter 3 provides my 1980 data.

Colombia. The 1981 data are from ICFES, *Estadísticas de la educación superior 1981* (Bogotá: ICFES, 1981), p. 26.

Costa Rica. For 1981, OPES, *Estadística de la educación superior 1981* (San José: Consejo Nacional de Rectores, 1982), pp. 24, 172.

Cuba. The 1980 figure is from Comité Estatal de Estadísticas, *Anuario estadístico de Cuba 1980* (Havana, 1981), p. 224. A Catholic university was founded in 1947, followed by private institutions that some call universities but others call colleges. The 1955 private share can be given as anywhere from 2 to 20 percent. See, for example, Hugh Thomas, *Cuba: The Pursuit of Freedom* (New York: Harper and Row, 1971), p. 1136, and Rolland G. Paulston, "Education," in Carmelo Mesa-Lago, ed., *Revolutionary Change in Cuba* (Pittsburgh: University of Pittsburgh Press, 1971), p. 384.

Dominican Republic. The OAS does not show private percentages, but Muñoz and Restrepo show 5 and 23 percent for 1965 and 1970 respectively; I apply those percentages to the OAS totals. The Dominican Republic is the only nation for which I use post-1975 data to help estimate a 1975 percentage; there was no pre-1975 OAS percentage to extend to 1975. The 1979 estimate comes from Eduardo Latorre, *Sobre educación superior* (Santo Domingo: Instituto Tecnológico de Santo Domingo, 1970), p. 51. Between 1970 and 1975, one-third of the eventual 1970–79 total growth occurs; one-third of the 1970–79 private gain of 23 percent is 8 percent; I add 8 percent to the original 23 percent (1970) to get a 31 percent estimate for 1975, which I apply to the OAS 1975 total.

Ecuador. For 1970 the closest year for which a private percentage is shown is 1972 (21 percent), which I apply to the OAS 1970 total. (The latest prior figure was 19 percent for 1966.) The 1980 data come from the Consejo Nacional de Educación Superior, *Estadísticas de la universidad ecuatoriana* (Quito: 1981), vol. 5, p. 72.

El Salvador. Muñoz and Restrepo report 8 percent for 1965, which I apply to the OAS total. The virtual closing of the national university in the 1980s, accompanied by the Catholic university's growth to roughly six thousand and the creation of low-quality private alternatives, substantially altered the private-public enrollment picture. See Charles L. Stansifer, "Observations on Salvadorean and Nicaraguan Education," *LASA Forum* 15, no. 1 (1984), p. 28.

Guatemala. The last OAS figures are for 1970. But UDUAL's *Censo universitario latino-americano 1974–1975* (Mexico City: UDUAL, 1978), pp. 581–94, which includes all of the nation's institutions, gives the 1975 figures I use. For 1980, Universidad de San Carlos, *Boletín estadístico universitario 1980* (Guatemala City: 1981), p. 135.

Haiti. The earliest private figure given is 8 percent (1957), which I apply to the 1955 total. The latest figures given are for 1966, which I therefore put into the 1970 and 1975 slots. The 1978 total is from UNESCO, *Statistical Yearbook*, p. III 386, to which I apply the 1966 percentage.

Honduras. The last OAS private figure is 6 percent (1968), which I apply to the OAS's 1971 (there was no 1970) and 1975 totals. On 1981, Banco Central de Honduras, *Honduras en cifras*

1979–1981 (Tegucigalpa, D.C.: Departamento de Estudios Económicos, 1982), pp. 14–15. Because the 1981 percentage is based at least partly on universities created after 1975 it cannot be used to estimate the 1975 percentage.

Mexico. The earliest OAS private percentage given is 14 percent (1962), which I apply to the 1955 and 1960 totals; the latest is 15 percent (1969), which I apply to 1970 and 1975. For non-OAS sources, see chapter 4, footnotes 1 and 20.

Nicaragua. The latest OAS private figure is 34 percent (1972), which I apply to the 1975 total. For 1977, data from the education ministry show 14,062 for the only public university; calculated against the OAS total, this yields a continued 34 percent private share. The ministry also reports a huge jump in public university enrollment (to 22,653 in 1979) immediately after the Sandinista victory, but does not give an update on private enrollments. It does, however, report substantial nationalization of private schools. Ministerio de Educación, *La educación en el primer año de la revolución popular sandinista* (Managua, 1980), pp. 35–37, 105–6.

Panama. All data from the OAS.

Paraguay. The latest OAS private figure is 34 percent (1973), which I apply to the 1975 and 1977 totals.

Peru. The figures for 1975 are the first to include "other institutions" as well as the universities and normal schools previously considered. The private share in "others" is 73 percent; without others the private 1975 share would be 55,614 of a 189,988 total, or 29 percent. For 1980 I use CONAI data forwarded by Estuardo Marrou, rector of the Pacific University.

Uruguay. The OAS lacks data for 1965 and 1970, as does UDUAL. The closest OAS data come from 1963 (15,047) and 1973 (32,347); based roughly on growth of 1,730 per year, I estimate for 1975 and 1970. Muñoz and Restrepo figures for 1965 and 1970 are 16,975 and 24,999, respectively. For 1977, UNESCO, *Statistical Yearbook*, p. III 391.

Venezuela. For 1981, OPSU, *Boletín estadístico no. 8* (Caracas: CNU, 1982), vol. 2, p. 62.

Obviously, all estimations and all substitutions based on non-OAS data lead to inexactness in comparisons. However, the cited non-OAS data for 1955–75 appear consistent with OAS data sequences. There is much more doubt when moving from 1975 to the latest data gathered from myriad sources. Note, in particular, that the latest Brazilian (and Peruvian) data come from sources that have consistently given lower private percentages than has the OAS. If Brazil's 1980 total were apportioned according to the latest OAS private percentage (67 percent, 1977), then our latest Latin American private share would be 1 percent higher. Note also that I refrained from using some later national totals if they did not show the private share. The three exceptions are Bolivia, Haiti, and Paraguay, where otherwise the latest totals would have come from as long ago as 1969, 1966, and 1973, respectively. In the other seventeen cases, the totals include private percentages from at least as recently as 1977.

The OAS data are accompanied by numerous notations that are mostly either minor or irrelevant to our compilations. Some indicate what institutions are included or give breakdowns by institutional type within sector (e.g., technical institutions within the public sector). Others acknowledge the OAS's own data sources. For the most recent notations, see *América en cifras 1977*, pp. 97–99; beyond this, each *América en cifras* includes a list of notations and caveats that can be consulted directly.

As with enrollments, so also with the dates of private sector foundation, I follow the OAS and all other major data sources in basing figures solely on juridical denotations of private and public type, regardless of behavioral ambiguity in privateness and publicness. The OAS data suggest at least the approximate foundation years for those private sectors, the majority, which began after 1955. More extensive information appears in chapter 2, especially its footnote 18. There is some ambiguity where private institutions existed before they received State authorization to grant usable professional degrees and where institutions began functioning after the year in which authorization was granted. I have tried to give the first functioning years for authorized institutions. All this explains why the OAS shows small private enrollments for Argentina and Bolivia before the generally cited foundation dates. But the most ambiguous cases are Haiti and Honduras. Some sources report no private universities there, but the OAS shows enrollments; the *América en cifras 1965* (p. 172) refers to Haitian private schools in Gonaives y Cayes. And the Institut Haïtien de Statistique, *Guide economique de la république d'Haïti* (Port-au-Prince; 1964), p. 187, lists four faculties in "free schools" recognized by the national university. Chances are the OAS data include private nonuniversity institutions excluded from some other data compilations. By the late 1970s Honduras was no longer an ambiguous case, as two private universities were created.

See also Appendix A "Notes on the Data."

3. For the only major analysis of private higher education in more than one region (indeed perhaps the only major analysis outside Latin America on more than one nation), see Roger L. Geiger, *Private Sectors in Higher Education: Structure, Function, and Change in Eight Countries* (University of Michigan Press, forthcoming). Geiger focuses on the important private role in selected Asian nations, the usually marginal role in Western Europe, and the changing role in the United States.

4. For data and a brief overview concerning the size of private and public sectors outside Latin America and their income sources, see Daniel C. Levy, "Private versus Public Financing of Higher Education: U.S. Policy in Comparative Perspective," *Higher Education* 11, no. 6 (1982), pp. 607–28.

5. The major Spanish American pattern, involving substantial private sectors that are smaller and more elite than the public sectors, is very common in the primary and secondary school systems of the noncommunist world, thereby adding to the importance of studying the only region where this pattern predominates at the higher level. Depending upon the criteria, U.S. higher education might also be included—a private sector holds a minority of the enrollments—but private-public distinctiveness is much more limited than in Latin America.

6. Levy, "Private," p. 620. A fundamental distinction properly noted in a 1961 article that compared U.S. and Latin American higher education was that the U.S. private sector, large and vibrant, found only isolated parallels in Latin America: Robert Havinghurst, "Latin American and North American Higher Education," *Comparative Education Review* 4, no. 3 (1961), pp. 174–82.

7. Alexander Gerschenkron, *Economic Backwardness in Historical Perspective* (Cambridge: Belknap Press of Harvard University Press, 1962).

8. For an overview of the major intersectoral policy issues involving schools and universities in the United States and beyond, see Daniel C. Levy, "Private Choice and Public Policy for Non-Profit Education," in Levy, ed., *Private Education: Studies in Choice and Public Policy* (New York: Oxford University Press, forthcoming). Unfortunately, most intersectoral comparisons of governance and function are limited; for the most notable work on financial and derivative regulatory policies in U.S. higher education, see David W. Breneman and Chester E. Finn, eds., *Public Policy and Private Higher Education* (Washington, D.C.: Brookings Institution, 1978).

9. Leon D. Epstein makes this point in *Governing the University* (San Francisco: Jossey-Bass, 1974), p. 3. For a review essay on the politics of higher education, see Samuel Gove and Carol Everly Floyd, "Research on Higher Education Administration and Policy: An Uneven Report," *Public Administration Review* 35, no. 1 (1975), pp. 111–18. For a comparative review essay see Daniel C. Levy, "Universities and Governments: The Comparative Politics of Higher Education," *Comparative Politics* 12, no. 1 (1979), pp. 99–121. Also see Maurice Kogan's contribution to a volume that both summarizes and forwards our disciplinary and cross-national understandings of higher education, "The Political View," in Burton R. Clark, ed., *Perspectives on Higher Education: Eight Disciplinary and Comparative Views* (Berkeley: University of California Press, 1984), pp. 56–78. The comparative higher education field received a boost from the working paper series and related production of Yale University's Higher Education Research Group, succeeded in 1980 by UCLA's Comparative Higher Education Research

Group. Obviously, a major challenge for the present study is to develop ways to compare higher education institutions and sectors in political and cross-national contexts.

10. Robert F. Arnove, "A Survey of Literature on Latin American Universities," *Latin American Research Review* 3, no. 1 (1967), pp. 45, 53. See also the latest major review essays, which reflect some progress, though limited almost exclusively to non-English sources: Simon Schwartzman, "Politics and Academia in Latin American Universities," *Journal of Interamerican Studies and World Affairs* 25, no. 3 (1983), pp. 416–23; and Iván Jaksić, "The Politics of Higher Education in Latin America," *Latin American Research Review* 20, no. 1 (1985), pp. 209–21. One improvement on the Latin American end is a corollary to the descriptive national studies—the statistical survey, increasingly prevalent and technically adept, sometimes accompanied by explanatory text. However, here is not the place to speculate on the reasons for the different limitations of the Latin American and U.S. literatures. The most recent substantial bibliographic work on comparative higher education reflects the weakness of English-language sources. See Philip G. Altbach, *Comparative Higher Education: Recent Trends and Bibliography* (London: Mansell, 1979), pp. 177–84. We could now add to Altbach's listing, Joseph Maier and Richard W. Weatherhead, eds., *The Latin American University* (Albuquerque: University of New Mexico Press, 1979), including several wide-ranging essays. More Spanish sources are included in Philip G. Altbach and David H. Kelly, eds., *Higher Education in Developing Nations: A Selected Bibliography, 1969–1974* (New York: Praeger, 1975), pp. 145–50. The best Spanish bibliography is by Luis Scherz García, *Pensamiento e investigación sobre la universidad: Bibliografía* (Santiago: CPU, 1974). Also see the annotated bibliography assembled by Hebe Pauliello de Chocholous and Juan Guillermo Milia, *Bibliografía sobre cuestiones universitarias* (Mendoza, Argentina: Universidad Nacional de Cuyo, 1978). Easily the best body of literature has been published (in Spanish) by the CPU (Corporación Promoción Universitaria) in Chile. The best-known work by a scholar outside the Americas is Hanns-Albert Steger, *Las universidades en el desarrollo social de América Latina* (Mexico City: Fondo de Cultura Económica, 1974), emphasizing Mexico and the colonial period. Obviously, many other citations will appear in chapters 2 through 6. Obviously, too, Latin America's private surge is arousing increased scholarly interest within the region, as seen in recent international conferences on the subject (e.g., in Santiago, Chile, January 1982, and San Juan, Puerto Rico, April 1983).

11. One of the most important recent works on Latin American politics includes an extensive bibliography, especially on eight major nations; the reader finds a number of works on institutions such as political parties, the military, labor unions, and businesses, but, understandably, not one on the university. See David Collier, ed., *The New Authoritarianism in Latin America* (Princeton: Princeton University Press, 1979), pp. 405–43. Additionally, few general texts on Latin American politics include references to the university (beyond student activism); an exception is Edward J. Williams and Freeman J. Wright, *Latin American Politics: A Developmental Approach* (Palo Alto, Calif.: Mayfield Publishing, 1975), pp. 385–415.

12. Moreover, *el estado* rather than *el gobierno* is the Spanish term usually employed for our purposes. Public universities are variously called *oficiales* or *estatales*, and private universities are sometimes referred to as *particulares*, but *públicas* and *privadas* are the most common terms. Both *esfera privada* and *sector privado* are used for what I call the "private sphere," but also for private enterprise only. According to the criteria I set forth here, my first book would have used the word *State* instead of *government*. See Daniel C. Levy, *University and Government in Mexico: Autonomy in an Authoritarian System* (New York: Praeger, 1980). Yet *State* was less compelling there than here because that work did not deal with private-public questions, only with public universities. Additionally, while there is overlap between *State* and *regime*, each again has its own center of gravity. *Regime* generally represents a narrower concept than *State* but a wider one than *government*; I use *regime* for types of governments (e.g., Venezuela's civilian democratic regime from Betancourt's government to the present). A

salient example in this study is the modern authoritarian regime. Most associated with military rule in Argentina, Brazil, Chile, and Uruguay, modern (or "new" or "bureaucratic") authoritarian regimes emerge in relatively developed nations after considerable social and political mobilization has occurred. These regimes press for "orthodox" or "rationalized" economic policies and for demobilization. They use severe repression to secure these ends. For substantial treatments, see especially Guillermo O'Donnell, *Modernization and Bureaucratic-Authoritarianism: Studies in South American Politics* (Berkeley: University of California, Institute of International Studies, 1973) and Collier, *New Authoritarianism.*

13. See, for example, the second definition given in Collier's glossary (*New Authoritarianism*, p. 403), after the first definition focused on the State's role in class domination (see footnote 15 below). "The state consists of the institutional structure, the incumbents within this structure, and body of law that make up the public sector. It thus includes the government (in the sense of the head of state and the immediate political leadership that surrounds the head of state), the public bureaucracy, the legislature, the judiciary, public and semi-public corporations, and the legal system." On the tendency since the mid-1970s to see the State as an important actor, see Stephen D. Krasner, "Approaches to the State: Alternative Conceptions and Historical Dynamics," *Comparative Politics* 16, no. 2 (1984), pp. 223–46.

14. Some political sociologists have rather restrictively defined the State by its coercive control over territories and peoples; however, what may define the State uniquely is not what defines it sufficiently, as States also educate, pursue and distribute wealth, build roads, promote, maintain, and ruin health, and so forth. Granted, one could reduce all functions such as education to the preservation of order, but then only to a broad political-economic-social order, not a narrow law and order. For an example of the restrictive definition, even by one who persuasively rejects the view of the State as a static "arena," see Theda Skocpol, *States and Social Revolutions* (Cambridge: Cambridge University Press, 1979), pp. 25, 30–31. For an example of the wider view, see Hugh Heclo and Aaron Wildavsky, *The Private Government of Public Money: Community and Policy Inside British Politics* (Berkeley: University of California, 1974), p. xi. For an analysis of Max Weber's broad concept of the State, see Randall Collins, "A Comparative Approach to Political Sociology," in Reinhard Bendix et al., eds., *The State and Society* (Boston: Little, Brown, 1968), pp. 48–49.

15. Arthur Bentley and David Truman are among the earliest pluralists who have been most open to criticism for minimizing the State's role, but, for example, few authors have been more identified with pluralist thought since the 1950s than Robert A. Dahl and Charles E. Lindblom. They pointedly include government as an actor, even when they discuss policy making via group bargaining. See, for example, Dahl and Lindblom, *Politics, Economics, and Welfare* (New York: Harper and Brothers, 1953), p. 498. On the limits of contemporary Marxist reductionism see, for example, Nicos Poulantzas, *State, Power, and Socialism*, trans. Patrick Camiller (London: Verso, 1980); and Edward S. Malecki, "The Capitalist State: Structural Variation and Its Implications for Radical Change," *Western Political Quarterly* 34, no. 2 (1981), pp. 246–69. Fernando Henrique Cardoso is perhaps the best-known Latin American scholar writing about the State as a class-based pact of domination. But Cardoso is careful to point out that he defines *State* at "the highest level of abstraction"; thus what he calls the regime (close to what I call the State) is indeed capable of autonomous action. See Cardoso, "On the Characterization of Authoritarian Regimes in Latin America," in Collier, *New Authoritarianism*, pp. 33–57, especially pp. 38–39.

16. See, for example, Alfred Stepan, *The State and Society: Peru in Comparative Perspective* (Princeton: Princeton University Press, 1978), pp. 3–45; and Philippe Schmitter, "Still the Century of Corporatism?" in Frederick Pike and Thomas Stritch, eds., *The New Corporatism* (Notre Dame: University of Notre Dame Press, 1974), pp. 85–132.

17. Two caveats concerning the notion that the State plus the private sphere encompass societal activity: One, indicated shortly (in the text), is that ambiguity and interpenetration

occur between the two entities. The second is that there is not necessarily a zero-sum game, except in proportional terms. The State can grow while the private sphere grows. Conservatives sometimes assume that State growth inhibits private growth, and liberals sometimes assume that private growth inhibits State growth; either may happen, but the State and private sphere may also work and grow together. See, for example, James O'Conner, *The Financial Crisis of the State* (New York: St. Martin's Press, 1973), especially pp. 8–9. For a discussion that contrasts government ownership with private enterprise as analytically separate poles between which most institutions lie on an empirical spectrum, see Dahl and Lindblom, *Politics, Economics, and Welfare*, pp. 9–18. For another work focusing on these private-public juxtapositions see Helmut Schoeck and James W. Wiggins, eds., *The New Argument in Economics: The Public versus the Private Sector* (Princeton: D. Van Nostrand, 1963); the editors' preface (pp. ix–x) notes the irony of the book's title since the public-private debate is centuries old. They point out that the debate's intensity increased in disciplinary journals (especially economics and sociology) in the late 1950s. Always rich in ideological overtones, the debate naturally took on special significance during the cold war.

18. They deal more with activities performed by major private groups and organizations than by private individuals. They distinguish, for example, between private finance based on individual tuition or business contributions, private governance based on autonomy or Church control, and private functions leading to individual professional practice or posts with industrial enterprises.

19. I have adapted some sections from my more detailed exploration in "'Private' and 'Public' in Higher Education: Analysis Amid Ambiguity," in Levy, *Private Education*.

20. See, for example, John S. Whitehead, *The Separation of College and State: Columbia, Dartmouth, Harvard, and Yale, 1776–1876* (New Haven: Yale University Press, 1973).

21. Dahl and Lindblom, *Politics, Economics, and Welfare*, especially chapter 1; quotation from Gary L. Wamsley and Mayer N. Zald, *The Political Economy of Public Organizations* (Lexington, Mass.: D.C. Heath, 1973), p. 3.

22. Nancy Schwartz, "Distinction between Private and Public Life: Marx on the Zöon Politikon," *Political Theory* 7, no. 2 (1979), p. 246. Philosophical works also have identified private-public ambiguities. See, for example, Stuart Hampshire, ed., *Public and Private Morality* (Cambridge: Cambridge University Press, 1978). *Private* may sometimes be tied to the individual, singular, or hidden, and *public* tied to the social, interactive, and visible. Allusions to private people (aloof, introverted, self-sufficient) and public people (involved, extroverted, sharing) also abound. Such allusions do not tell us much about organizations and sectors, however, unless one chooses to think of the university, for example, has always a private organization and its environment as the public. Thus Martin Trow has interestingly defined what happens in the classrooms, libraries, laboratories, and daily teacher-student interactions as private, regarding all decisions made by other actors as public. See Trow, "The Public and Private Lives of Higher Education," *Daedalus* 2 (Winter 1975), p. 113. Such private-public distinctions would not be appropriate for the questions addressed in this study. A classic statement about private and public lives is found in Hannah Arendt, *The Human Condition* (Chicago: University of Chicago Press, 1958), pp. 22–78; in this general vein see Barrington Moore, *Privacy: Studies in Social and Cultural History* (Armonk, N.Y.: M. E. Sharpe, 1984).

23. Theodore Lowi, *The End of Liberalism: The Second Republic of the United States*, 2d ed. (New York: W. W. Norton, 1979), p. 296; and Grant McConnell, *Private Power and American Democracy* (New York: Knopf, 1966), pp. 296, 297. References to corporatism in Latin America appear below in chapter 7, especially footnotes 27, 28, 33, and 34.

24. U.S. courts use financial and administrative criteria to decide when the "State action doctrine" should be invoked, imposing State regulation on universities. Courts get especially involved if institutions are judged sufficiently "public." William A. Kaplin, *The Law of Higher Education* (San Francisco: Jossey-Bass, 1978), p. 21.

25. Since I do not assume a logical coherence among private finance, governance, and function, on the one hand, nor public finance, governance, and function on the other, I do not propose a single all-encompassing private or public ideal type.

26. For a very broad analysis aiming explicitly at what the university (internationally) really is and does, see Burton R. Clark, *The Higher Education System: Academic Organization in Cross-National Perspective* (Berkeley: University of California Press, 1983), p. 6 and passim. One danger of using *function* is that it could be understood as functionalist; for example, one could assume that every educational structure is performing a necessary function for society.

27. A major corrective step will be the publication by the Oxford University Press of a series of edited books based largely on working papers produced at Yale's Program on Non-Profit Organizations. Among the volumes will be the one on education cited above in footnotes 8 and 19 and possibly one on development. In addition, a related handbook on nonprofit organizations will be published, including separate state-of-the-literature articles on comparative studies, education, and the State: Walter W. Powell, ed., *Between the Public and the Private: The Nonprofit Sector* (New Haven: Yale University Press, forthcoming). For a rare comparative contribution on the State and nonprofit institutions, see Ralph M. Kramer, *Voluntary Agencies in the Welfare State* (Berkeley: University of California Press, 1983); for a work representing the more common juxtaposition of private institutions to State, see Raymond Vernon, ed., *Big Business and the State: Changing Relations in Western Europe* (Cambridge: Harvard University Press, 1974). Specifically on Latin America, Brian H. Smith is researching the role of the Church as a nonprofit service organization. See Smith, "U.S. and Canadian Nonprofit Organizations (PVOs) as Transnational Development Institutions," a Program on Non-Profit Organizations working paper, Yale University, August 1983.

28. Public sectors can also be considered nonprofit, but, like most observers, I reserve the nonprofit label for private entities. I work most closely with foci or "dilemmas" identified at the Program on Non-Profit Organizations as central to the study of nonprofit organizations generally. One articulation is found in John G. Simon, "Research on Philanthropy," Independent Sector research report, Washington, D.C., July 1980, pp. 5–12. I have, however, freely adapted Simon's broad guidelines, analyzing three of his dilemmas in terms of the three ideal types discussed above. (Simon's other two dilemmas are a "power dilemma," or the degree of nonprofit organizations' influence over other sectors, and an "effectiveness dilemma," dealing with the struggle for success in the absence of objectively measurable goals such as profit making; effectiveness is one of the four goals or notions I will evaluate throughout.) Among the three dilemmas tied to my ideal types, I use *function* (more than Simon uses *mission*) to discuss not just what tasks sectors perform but also how they perform them. The close relation between my exploration of the three ideal types and central nonprofit dilemmas is suggested in the following adaptation from Simon's elaboration. Regarding finance: Are nonprofit and public institutions financed differently? What are the roles of clients, the State, and other contributors? Under what circumstances can nonprofit institutions attract all their funds from private sources, and when do they ask for and receive State subsidies? If they do receive State subsidies, can they maintain private governance? Regarding governance: Who rules in nonprofit as opposed to public institutions? What are the important differences across sectors in hierarchy, participation, internal democracy, and accountability? How are the institutions variously autonomous from, or accountable to, their constituencies, professional groups, private donors, and the State? Do nonprofit institutions promote pluralism? Regarding function: How are tasks allocated among sectors? What classes, groups, and values are served by each sector? Can the nonprofit sector retain distinctiveness if it serves those interests served by the public sector? In other words, are nonprofit institutions really private providers of public goods, and can they retain legitimacy if they are not?

29. *Chairs*, historically the university's core organizational units, are the senior professorial positions, vested with considerable power. Chairholders, civil servants, have been the dominant figures in their academic fields. *Faculties* (sometimes *schools*) are professionally oriented

structures that are far more self-contained than U.S. departments. They typically offer all the courses their students need for a professional degree; e.g., law faculties offer sociology. *Institutes* are parallel structures, generally where research is the main task. The first degree is a professional degree, often called a *licenciatura* in Latin America, distinct from a U.S. undergraduate, bachelor's degree. Higher education, as in the United States, refers to degree-granting education that requires a secondary school degree for entrance, although secondary schools themselves are not parallel to U.S. high schools. (As Appendix A notes, this book tries to deal with higher education fairly inclusively, especially in data collection, but definitional ambiguities exist, as they do in the United States as well.)

30. See Altbach, *Comparative*, pp. 28–33, on the U.S. role in exporting its model of higher education. Especially significant in Latin America were the reports of Rudolph Atcon, active in Argentina, Brazil, Central America, Chile, and Colombia. His book (*Latin American University*) was first produced as the Atcon Report in 1963, but his influential reports appeared some years before that.

31. I quote John H. Van de Graaff and Dorotea Furth, "Introduction," in John H. Van de Graaff et al., *Academic Power: Patterns of Authority in Seven National Systems of Higher Education* (New York: Praeger, 1978), p. 10. On the Continental model see, for example, Burton R. Clark and Ted I. K. Youn, *Academic Power in the United States* (Washington, D.C.: ERIC Clearinghouse on Higher Education, 1976), pp. 3–9. Roger Geiger has somewhat similarly described the "European" university in "European Universities: The Unfinished Revolution," *Comparative Education Review* 22, no. 2 (1978), pp. 189–212. The Continental label is preferable for my purposes since I want to exclude the British model, which falls somewhere between the U.S. and Continental models. One of the most important qualifications to statist/national generalizations is that German *Land* (provincial) government has been a major actor.

32. Burton R. Clark, "Academic Power: Concepts, Modes, and Perspectives," in Van de Graaff et al., *Academic Power*, p. 175. In this piece Clark refers to the European mode.

33. Ezra N. Suleiman, *Elites in French Society* (Princeton: Princeton University Press, 1978), pp. 11–12, and for a relevant discussion of the philosophical bases of State monopoly see pp. 17–30; Dietrich Goldschmidt, "Systems of Higher Education," in Van de Graaff et al., *Academic Power*, p. 150.

34. Carnegie Council on Policy Studies in Higher Education, *A Classification of Institutions of Higher Education*, rev. ed. (New York: Carnegie Foundation for the Advancement of Teaching, 1976), especially pp. xiv–xxi. The twelve-part classification is based on financial source, composition of the student body, institutional size, degrees offered, and research prestige. To simplify, to be brief, and to focus on those types most relevant to the institutions I am studying, I have condensed the university and college categories and have deleted completely the two-year institutions and specialized schools. One helpful overview of U.S. higher education that gives a brief account focusing on the types I consider, and which does so in cross-national perspective, is Burton R. Clark, "United States," in Van de Graaff et al., *Academic Power*, pp. 104–23.

35. However, the importance of the private sector often exceeds its proportional enrollment weight in matters such as prestige, social influence, job prospects, vanguard fields of study, and ties to the productive apparatus.

36. Were I comparing just one private to one public institution, the tendency would be for the latter to be more internally heterogeneous and therefore more needful of detailed analysis. I do not want to convey the impression that either sector is intrinsically more interesting, even though one receives somewhat more attention here.

37. Even where the focus is on one sector, the private emphasis is mostly confined to chapters 4 and 6, whereas chapters 3 and especially 5 emphasize the public more than the private sector.

38. Haiti really would fall into a fifth category, where I have almost no information beyond

365

what is found in table 1.1 and footnote 2. In pursuit of regional inclusiveness I have used whatever regional statistical data (mostly on enrollments and fields of study) have been compiled by various organizations including the OAS, UDUAL, and UNESCO (see footnote 2 and Appendix A). I have also accumulated further data, especially in the countries (Argentina, Brazil, Chile, Costa Rica, Mexico, and Venezuela) where I conducted open-ended interviews with experts in the private and public universities, related-research institutions, interuniversity coordinating boards, and the educational and finance ministries. For all nations I have tried to use various networks to obtain the latest possible data and to locate as many useful secondary sources as possible.

39. The contrasting profiles of the Brazilian, Mexican, and Chilean cases have helped determine where, other than in chapter 6, I deal most intensively with given issues of importance beyond any one of the three nations. Thus, for example, the most thorough analyses of the national university decline, business-university relations, and the nonprofit versus for-profit behavior of private sectors are found, respectively, in chapters 3, 4, and 5.

CHAPTER TWO

1. Elsewhere I have made a broad comparison of the causes of private sector growth in Latin America and the United States. See Daniel C. Levy, "The Rise of Private Universities: Latin America and the United States," in Margaret Archer, ed., *The Sociology of Educational Expansion* (London: Sage, 1982), pp. 93–132. Sections of the present chapter are drawn from that piece. Naturally, however, "Rise," with its analysis of the U.S. case and its lesser attention to public sectors, includes only some of the information on Latin America found here. Additionally, note that this present chapter includes few specific references to Argentina, Venezuela, and Costa Rica. I had intended to include three national case studies of evolution here but deleted them to save space; instead, the material will be elaborated in a separate article. The Argentine case provides the region's most rending debate over private creation, followed by variable blends of private-public growth depending largely on the regime in power. The Venezuelan case represents the rise of a dominant elite subsector alongside other private subsectors, complementing the Mexican case discussed in chapter 4. The Costa Rican case, where the demand-absorbing subsector dominates the private sector, complements the Brazilian case.

2. I have chosen the word *wave* to indicate a surging, swelling phenomenon occurring in parts, but parts that are neither uniform nor completely discrete. The word *stage* would also be possible. Also note that *evolution* as used here (sometimes tied to *failure*) need not imply movement from a lower to a higher form but only some process of growth or change.

3. See, for example, Howard J. Wiarda, ed., *Politics and Social Change in Latin America: The Distinct Tradition* (Amherst: University of Massachusetts Press, 1974). Clearly, I am focusing here on elite integration much more than a societal integration of all groups.

4. John Tate Lanning, *Academic Culture in the Spanish Colonies* (London: Oxford University Press, 1940), pp. 4–6, 11. Also see Richard L. Kagen, "Universities in Castile, 1500–1810," in Lawrence Stone, ed., *The University in Society* (Princeton: Princeton University Press, 1974), pp. 362, 381.

5. Luis Alberto Sánchez, *La universidad actual y la rebelión juvenil* (Buenos Aires: Editorial Losada, 1970), p. 47. Also see Lanning, *Academic Culture*, p. 37; and Jorge Mario García Laguardia, *Legislación universitaria de América Latina* (Mexico City: UDUAL, 1973), p. 187.

6. Mario Góngora, "Origin and Philosophy of the Spanish American University," in Joseph Maier and Richard W. Weatherhead, eds., *The Latin American University* (Albuquerque: University of New Mexico Press, 1979), pp. 22–27, 32–38; Hanns-Albert Steger, *Las universidades en el desarrollo social de la América Latina* (Mexico City: Fondo de Cultura Económica, 1974), pp. 89–90, passim.

7. Lanning, *Academic Culture*, pp. 21–33. Rodríguez Cruz reports the creation of thirty-one universities from 1538 to 1812, but acknowledges that the number depends on definition

and that several institutions ceased functioning by the end of the colonial era. Agueda María Rodríguez Cruz, *Historia de las universidades hispanoamericanas* (Bogotá: Instituto Caro y Cuervo, 1973) vol. 2, pp. 225–31.

8. Alberto Methol Ferre, "Hacia una pastoral de la cultura latinoamericana," in CELAM, ed., *Iglesia y universidad en América Latina* (Bogotá: CELAM, 1976), p. 8; the author (p. 8) adds that as theology was abolished in the universities, the Church made "a gigantic effort to develop its own seminaries."

9. Jorge Mario García Laguardia, *La autonomía universitaria en América Latina* (Mexico City: UNAM, 1977), pp. 63, 65; and interview with García Laguardia, Mexico City, December 1979. This does not imply a steady anti-Church liberal tide in all nations, only what ultimately can be seen as a widespread tendency. Similarly, secularization was a postindependence phenomenon in twentieth-century Asian and African schools. James S. Coleman, "Introduction," in James S. Coleman, ed., *Education and Political Development* (Princeton: Princeton University Press, 1965), pp. 41–42.

10. García Laguardia, *Legislación*, pp. 189–90.

11. Harold R. W. Benjamin, *Higher Education in the American Republics* (New York: McGraw-Hill, 1965), pp. 20, 27.

12. Data derived from Juan F. Castellanos et al., *Examen de una década: Sociedad y universidad, 1962–1971* (Mexico City: UDUAL, 1976), pp. 103–5. The Castellanos data are drawn from UDUAL data, as published in its various *Censos*. I have found UDUAL data very useful, given the dearth of cross-national data and the fact that only UDUAL rivals the OAS for longitudinal and latitudinal breadth. Still, there are several problems with the Castellanos-UDUAL data. Castellanos (p. 89) suggests that only 85 percent of all institutions are captured. (See Appendix A below.) Also, when multiple dates are given for university creation, Castellanos uses the oldest date. This is misleading when universities have been closed and then reopened much later, e.g., Colombia's Javeriana reopened centuries after the 1623 date listed. Moreover, the data are based on dates of creation not authorization to grant professionally usable degrees; thus, for example, the Catholic University of Cuyo was founded in 1953, but Argentina's private universities did not gain fuller legal rank until later in the decade. And the data do not include some universities once created but no longer in operation, such as Cuba's private universities. Also see Methol Ferre, "Pastoral," pp. 8–10. Finally, outside Colombia, probably no contemporary private institutions have continuous heritages predating 1888, and probably the only qualifying Colombian institution is the Colegio Mayor de Nuestra Señora del Rosario, maintaining a "medieval" orientation with "very religious overtones." See Germán Rama, *El sistema universitario en Colombia* (Bogotá: Universidad Nacional, 1970) pp. 44, 76–77.

13. The Church remained very powerful in several nations and sometimes still powerful within "public" universities. The point here, a comparative-historical one, is that generally the Church's power had diminished significantly, particularly in education. See, for example, Luis Scherz García, "Relations between Public and Private Universities," in Seymour Martin Lipset and Aldo Solari, eds., *Elites in Latin America* (London: Oxford University Press, 1967), p. 390. In Peru, the early establishment of a Catholic university (even while "private" universities were not legal) has been attributed to a strong Church lobby. Mark W. Lusk, *Peruvian Higher Education in an Environment of Development and Revolution*, Utah State University, Department of Sociology Research Monograph 1, 1984, p. 55.

14. Julio César Trujillo V., "Universidad y sistemas sociopolíticos: El caso de Ecuador," in CPU, ed., *La universidad latinoamericana: Enfoques tipológicos* (Santiago: 1972), pp. 195–96; Jaime Peña, "Universidad y sistema educacional: El caso ecuatoriano," in Luis Scherz García, ed., *La universidad latinoamericana en la década del 80* (Santiago: CPU, 1976), vol. 2, pp. 104–5. Also see Enrique Ayala, "Movimientos sociales y movimientos universitarios en el Ecuador," in Patricio Dooner, ed., *Hacia una conceptualización del fenómeno de los movimientos universitarios en América Latina* (Santiago: CPU, 1974), pp. 198–99. Ayala points out

that the new Velasco Ibarra government was strongly tied to the Right and that the Church had by then realized it could not be influential in the public university.

15. Daniel Levine, *Religion and Politics in Latin America: The Catholic Church in Venezuela and Colombia* (Princeton: Princeton University Press, 1981), p. 70; Luis Carlos Sáchica, "Problemas jurídicos de la autonomía universitaria en Colombia," *Cuadernos del Centro de Documentación Legislativa Universitaria* 2, no. 1 (1979), pp. 116; Robert Dix, *Colombia: The Political Dimensions of Change* (New Haven: Yale University Press, 1967), pp. 233, 311.

16. Francisco Leal Buitrago, "La frustración política de una generación: La universidad colombiana y la formación de un movimiento estudiantil, 1958–1967," *Desarrollo y Sociedad*, no. 6 (July 1981), p. 301; Rama, *Sistema*, p. 44.

17. Bolivariana decree quoted in Gerardo Molina, "Universidad estatal y universidad privada," in Carmenza Huyo de Aldana et al., *Universidad oficial o universidad privada: Bases para una política universitaria* (Bogatá: Ediciones Tercer Mundo, 1978), pp. 22–23. Enrollment data from Rodrigo Parra and José Alzate, "Papel y perspectivas de la universidad católica en el desarrollo económico de Colombia," in Scherz García, *Universidad*, vol. 2, p. 159.

18. Except where indicated, data are drawn from Castellanos et al., *Examen*, pp. 93–105; however, see footnote 12 above. Also, the Castellanos data do not separate Catholic from non-Catholic universities; I counted as Catholic only those of his institutions named "Catholic" or "Pontifical" but verified the separation with other sources. Fuller information was available elsewhere for other nations. On Panama and Guatemala, García Laguardia, *Legislación*, pp. 201–2; on Nicaragua, Juan B. Arríen, *Relaciones jurídico-políticas entre el estado y las universidades no estatales de Nicaragua* (Guatemala City: FUPAC, 1979), pp. 28-30. On the Dominican Republic, Eduardo Latorre, *Sobre educación superior* (Santo Domingo: Instituto Tecnológico de Santo Domingo, 1980), p. 51; one of the six, however (the Center of Technical Studies), claims Christian inspiration and has ties to the Christian Democratic party. On Venezuela, OPSU, *Boletín estadístico*, no. 8 (Caracas: CNU, 1982), vol. 1, p. 69; one secular university has been indefinitely closed. To determine which Argentine universities are Catholic, I consulted CRUP, *20 años de universidades privadas en la República Argentina* (Buenos Aires: Editorial Belgrano, 1978), pp. 15-279. On Chile, see chapter 3. Concerning the nations for which I used Castellanos data, Peru alone presents an ambiguous case. Only two (pontifical, Sacred Heart) of ten private universities are formally tied to the Church, while two others (Santa María, San Martín) have broken away from their founding religious entity. Four others (Pacific, Piura, Cayetano Heredia, Lima) claim Christian inspiration, and two of them have direct or indirect ties with a religious order. Thus, only two (De la Vega, Ricardo Palma) have no religious ties. (Two others have been closed.) The first private wave includes the first four universities cited; it excludes those that have had no ties to a religious order. For the Pacific and Piura universities, the judgment should be based partly on the nature of these ties; I fit them more comfortably into the second private wave, but acknowledge the overlap. I thank Estuardo Marrou, rector of the Pacific University, for repeated written communications, especially one of April 26, 1982. Additionally, on Cuba, see chapter 1, footnote 2.

Hanns-Albert Steger points out that fully twenty of twenty-one Jesuit universities functioning in 1968 had been established since 1940. See Steger, "The European Background," in Maier and Weatherhead, *Latin American University*, pp. 114–15; that list would not require much revision today. Much more revision would be required for Luigi Einaudi's assessment made in the early 1960s: "Private secular universities are few and, with the exception of Colombia, relatively uninfluential." (Even then he should have excepted Chile and especially Mexico.) See Einaudi, "University Autonomy and Academic Freedom in Latin America," in Thomas J. LaBelle, ed., *Education and Development: Latin America and the Caribbean* (Los Angeles: UCLA Latin American Center, 1972), p. 612.

19. Even the three exceptions are only partial. The Colombian case has been discussed. Mexico's first private university (1935) was soon followed by a wave of religious universities,

and only subsequently were more secular ones created. Costa Rica's one private university (1976) is not legally tied to a religious group but claims Christian inspiration.

20. The key here is perceived failure, not necessarily objective or across-the-board failure. The terminology helps us link up with relevant theoretical literature. For a discussion of government failure, see James Douglas, "Political Theories of Nonprofit Organization," in Walter W. Powell, ed., *Between the Public and the Private* (New Haven: Yale University Press, forthcoming); and Burton A. Weisbrod, "Towards a Theory of the Voluntary Non-Profit Sector," in Susan Rose-Ackerman, ed., *The Economics of Nonprofit Institutions: Studies in Structure and Policy* (New York: Oxford University Press, forthcoming).

21. Max Weber, *Economy and Society*, ed. Guenther Roth and Claus Wittich (New York: Bedminster Press, 1968), vol. 2, p. 1000.

22. See, for example, Fritz Ringer, *The Decline of the German Mandarins: The German Academic Community, 1890–1933* (Cambridge: Harvard University Press, 1969; Rudolph Atcon, *The Latin American University* (Bogotá: ECO Revista de la Cultura de Occidente, 1966), p. 26. Also see Safford on the importance of the nineteenth-century degree (e.g., in Colombia) in reinforcing social contacts and in preparation for State jobs and upper-class roles. Frank Safford, "Bases of Political Alignment in Early Republican Spanish America," in Richard Graham and Peter H. Smith, eds., *New Approaches to Latin American History* (Austin: University of Texas Press, 1974), p. 104.

23. In Colombia private schools accounted for 43 percent of the entrants but 62 percent of the secondary school graduates. Jaime Rodríguez F., "Universidad y estructura socioeconómica: El caso de Colombia," in CPU, *La universidad*, p. 225; access data from Rama, *Sistema*, p. 69. On Uruguay, Martin Weinstein, *Uruguay: The Politics of Failure* (Westport, Conn.: Greenwood Press, 1975), p. 100 (1968 data). However, the generalized superiority of private over public institutions becomes shaky in some nations when applied to the religious subsector. Although higher education may logically have a smaller private sector than primary or secondary education when only the elite ever reach the higher level, other factors tend to increase the proportional size of the private sector as we go up the educational ladder. These include (1) the belief in public responsibility to provide equal opportunity through public, standardized, primary and secondary education; (2) the lesser de facto role of neighborhood residence in differentiating universities by class; (3) the necessity to differentiate between classes at the critical educational level at which adult status and jobs are allocated. Some nations, such as Peru, have their largest private percentages at the higher education level while others, such as Colombia, Mexico, and Venezuela, have their largest private percentages at the secondary level.

24. Jorge Graciarena, "Clases medias y movimiento estudiantil: El reformismo argentino (1918–1966), in CPU, ed., *Estudiantes y política* (Santiago: CPU, 1970), p. 74.

25. Data comparing 1890, 1940, 1960, and 1970 in James Wilkie, ed., *Statistical Abstract of Latin America 1977* (Los Angeles: UCLA Latin American Center Publications, 1977), vol. 18, p. 142. UCLA data on proliferation are mostly from Castellanos et al., *Examen*, pp. 103–4. The data include fifteen universities established before 1800, of which four are listed as private and eleven as public, while I would label most as fused. The authors also point out that four Mexican private universities are missing. Again, note the data problems listed above in footnote 12. For data on proliferation, see Appendix C.

26. Kenneth Ruddle and Mukthar Hamour, eds., *Statistical Abstract of Latin America* (Los Angeles: UCLA Latin American Center Publications, 1970), pp. 64–65; James Wilkie, ed., *Statistical Abstract of Latin America* (Los Angeles: UCLA Center Publications, 1981), vol. 21, pp. 67–77. The 1980 figure is based on calculations from estimated national figures; for 1975, figures from Bolivia, Guatemala, and Honduras were estimates.

27. IASEI, "Evolución cuantitativa del nivel post-secundario en América Latina (1960–77): Resumen y proyecciones para el año 2000," *Docencia* (Guadalajara) 9, no. 3 (1981), p. 25.

The number of professors grew from 66,000 to 388,000 in the same 1960–77 period.

28. Several authors are cited in Larissa Lomnitz, Leticia Mayer, and Martha Rees, "Recruiting Technical Elites: Mexico's Veterinarians," *Human Organization* 42, no. 1 (1983), p. 24. Also see Jorge Graciarena, "Modernización universitaria y clases medias: El caso de Brasil," in Patricio Dooner and Iván Lavados, eds., *La universidad latinoamericana: Visión de una década* (Santiago: CPU, 1979) pp. 289–321.

29. Stephen Spender, *The Year of the Young Rebels* (New York: Vintage Books, 1968), p. 181.

30. See, for example, Neil Smelser, "Growth, Structural Change, and Conflict in California Public Higher Education, 1950–1970," in Neil Smelser and Gabriel Almond, eds., *Public Higher Education in California* (Berkeley: University of California Press, 1974), pp. 9–141.

31. Richard S. Pelczar, "University Reform in Latin America: The Case of Colombia," in Philip G. Altbach, ed., *University Reform* (Cambridge, Mass.: Schenkman, 1974), p. 44. Pelczar (p. 49) also reports that universities could resort to "wine, women and song" to get around existing rules. By the 1970s Paraguay and Uruguay were the only South American nations, along with Central American nations and the Dominican Republic, with only one public university; see García Laguardia, *Legislación*, pp. 70–104.

32. This is one of many points, then, when it bears repeating that the State is really a complex entity. While parts of the State may try to preserve a small, ordered system, other parts, including those concerned with political popularity and social mobility, may push for proliferation.

33. Based on figures in table 1.1, there were three nations (Chile, Honduras, Venezuela) where (slightly) greater percentage growth occurred in the public sector and five where the private sector grew from 0 percent in 1960. No nations deviated from the rule on absolute growth. Naturally, I exclude Costa Rica, Cuba, and Uruguay, since each had only one sector.

34. See Martin Trow, "Problems in the Transition from Elite to Mass Higher Education," in the OECD, *Policies for Higher Education* (Paris: OECD, 1974), pp. 51–101. The term *mass higher education* has been abused by Latin America's conservative enemies of expansion to conjure up images of "the unprepared masses" flooding the public universities, despite the reality that far fewer than one in five reach higher education and that expansion still does not match demand. Such images accelerate elite flight or "exit." For the best-known general treatment of the exit decision illustrated here, see Albert O. Hirschman, *Exit, Voice, and Loyalty: Responses to Decline in Firms, Organizations, and States* (Cambridge: Harvard University Press, 1970). A cautionary word is also warranted concerning the *elite* designation. Supporters of what I call secular elite universities often prefer to avoid such designations, arguing that they pursue educational, not SES, elitism and that nearly all Latin American higher education is elitist. I use the term *elite* in an intertwined educational-SES sense, referring to the exclusive, selective, superior, influential character of these universities, even within the overall context of Latin American higher education. The elite universities and their personnel are often "elitist" (believers in the necessity, or even desirability, of great elite influence), but I use *elite* unless *elitist* is powerfully indicated.

35. Luis Ratinoff, "The New Urban Groups: The Middle Classes," in Lipset and Solari, *Elites*, p. 77.

36. On Peru, Robert Drysdale and Robert Myers, "Continuity and Change: Peruvian Education," in Abraham Lowenthal, ed., *The Peruvian Experiment* (Princeton: Princeton University Press, 1975), pp. 284–85; on Colombia, Molina, "Universidad estatal," p. 27; on Central America, Román Mayorga Quirós, *Las fases del desarrollo histórico de la universidad no estatal en centroamérica*, 2d. ed. (Guatemala: FUPAC, 1979), p. 7.

37. To insure quality in the face of a vastly broadening SES base, greater funds and strict entrance examinations would have been necessary. Instead, financial increases did not match needs, and the tendency was often to ease such requirements. At any rate, the widespread perception, shared within the university, the State, and private enterprise, was that average

quality was declining. For two brief illustrations of how such perceptions led to a private reaction, note the Ecuadorian and Peruvian cases. Ecuador's major public universities, in Quito and Guayaquil, became increasingly overcrowded and short of funds. In 1969, in the name of democratization, entrance examinations were abolished. Seen a decade later, the democratization effort had pushed the wealthy to the private sector and to polytechnic institutes with tough entrance requirements; Malcolm Scully, "Election of a Moderate Rector in Ecuador," *Chronicle of Higher Education*, May 19, 1980, pp. 15–16. Ayala, "Movimientos Sociales," p. 220, emphasizes the public universities' tremendous growth, "for which they were not prepared." For Peru, Lusk, *Peruvian Higher Education*, p. 83, reports the testimony of leading experts and professors who left the "once prestigious San Marcos University," regarding the drastic decline in public university quality.

38. See, for example, Randall Collins, "Some Comparative Principles of Educational Stratification," *Harvard Educational Review* 47, no. 1 (1977), pp. 8, 1–27.

39. Ronald Dore, *The Diploma Disease: Education, Qualification, and Development* (Berkeley: University of California Press, 1976); the Colombian example is given in Germán W. Rama, "Notas acerca de la expansión universitaria, el mercado de empleo y las prácticas académicas, *Universidades* 20, no. 81 (1980), pp. 683–84. Interesting corroboration of the social-class exit is found among Spanish America's Jews. Mostly middle and upper-middle class, with extraordinary education levels, they once were found mainly in national universities; now they are turning increasingly to private universities—to mostly elite and even prestigious Catholic ones.

40. In one sense, Latin America has had less need for social-class differentiation by sector than has the United States; despite great enrollment increases in recent decades, Latin America still reaches only a small fraction of the population by U.S. standards. Given the stratification of many Latin American societies, however, even this fraction represents disparate groups not easily bunched into common institutions. Using UNESCO data, I have calculated (roughly) that 13 percent (7,104,741/54,544,961) of primary and 29 percent (2,975, 562/10,274,366) of secondary enrollments are private (1975); the combined figure is 16 percent. The primary average does not include data from Haiti; the OAS did not show the private figures for Costa Rica and Honduras, but I estimated the first from 1974 and 1976 percentages and the second from 1973 and 1977 percentages. The secondary average does not include data from the Dominican Republic, Guatemala, Haiti, or Honduras. OAS, *América en cifras, 1977* (Washington, D. C.: OAS, 1979), pp. 118–21, 133–41. The U.S. figure for combined primary and secondary levels is roughly 10 percent (1980). See Donald A. Erickson, "Choice and Private Schools," in Daniel C. Levy, ed., *Private Education* (New York: Oxford University Press, forthcoming).

41. See Daniel C. Levy, "Student Politics in Contemporary Latin America," *Canadian Journal of Political Science* 14, no. 2 (1981), pp. 368–71. I use the term *politicization* in its popular sense, implying radicalized turmoil, rather than in the more embracing sense of things tied to politics. Thus a university peacefully serving the political system is not here labeled politicized. It is all-important, however, to remember that most, if not all, universities are politicized in the sense that they perform some political role; private institutions are no less politicized, in the broad sense of the word, than public ones. Similarly, I use *progressive* in its popular sense for movements identified with social change, whether or not they are effective or even normatively "desirable."

42. Ibón Lebot specifically ties Colombia's multiplying enrollments to changing SES composition, and then ties both to a marked increase in student activism and politicization (whereas Colombia had seen relatively little student activism until the 1950s). Lebot, "El movimiento estudiantil durante el frente nacional (1958–1974)," *Ideología y Sociedad*, no. 19 (1975), pp. 49–50.

43. Previously, only in the 1920s were more private than public institutions created, and the figures were but two and three, respectively. Data from Castellanos et al., *Examen*, pp. 103–5.

44. Sánchez, *Universidad actual*, p. 183; On Córdoba and the 1960 law, Enrique Bernales B., "Universidad y sistemas sociopolíticos: El caso de Perú," in CPU, *La universidad*, pp. 147–48. On proliferation, Rafael Roncagliolo, "Estudiantes y política en Perú: Datos para una discusión," in CPU, *Estudiantes*, pp. 90–91. Also see Lusk (*Peruvian Higher Education*, pp. 39–40) on the politicization of the 1960s, when the public universities were in the forefront of Peruvian radicalism. In fact, politicization was one reason for the early growth of Peru's private sector; Peru was one of the centers of Latin American student activism early in this century.

45. Molina, "Universidad estatal," pp. 28–29; Lebot, "Movimiento estudiantil," pp. 58–59, 63–65.

46. John D. Martz, *Ecuador: Conflicting Political Culture and the Quest for Progress* (Boston: Allyn and Bacon, 1972), p. 104; also pp. 105–7. For more on the rise of political activism, its leftist orientations, its spread to professors and administrators, and the backlash it produced, see Ayala, "Movimientos sociales," pp. 190–95, 212.

47. Mayorga Quirós, *Fases*, p. 9, on Central America generally; on Honduras, Manuel Torres Calderón, "Universidad hondureña," *La Nación Internacional* (San José, Costa Rica), June 10, 1982, and written communication from Jorge Ramón Hernández Alcerro of the Honduran Ministry of Foreign Affairs, March 18, 1983.

48. Stephen Webre, *José Napoleón Duarte and the Christian Democratic Party in Salvadorean Politics* (Baton Rouge: Louisiana State University Press, 1979), quotation on p. 149; also see pp. 25–26, 35, 147, 150; Franklin D. Parker, *The Central American Republics* (London: Oxford University Press, 1964), p. 156; Paul Desruisseaux, "Salvador's Jesuit University," *Chronicle of Higher Education*, September 21, 1983, pp. 29–30.

49. Statement of Enrique Ma. Huelín, (Director of Santa Misión) in "Las universidades en centroamérica," mimeo, 1961, p. 9. On the public university's progressive opposition to the Somoza dictatorship, see Miguel de Castilla Urbina, *Universidad y sociedad en Nicaragua: La UNAN 1958–1978* (León: Editorial Universitaria, 1979).

50. Tirso Mejía Ricart, "La Universidad Autónoma de Santo Domingo y su reforma universitaria en el 1969," in UDUAL, ed., *Primera conferencia latinoamericana sobre planeamiento universitario* (Mexico City: UDUAL, 1970), p. 410; Eduardo Latorre, "La educación dominicana," *Universidades* 20, no. 79 (1980), p. 41.

51. Mayorga Quirós, *Fases*, p. 9.

52. Carlos Tünnerman, "Central America: Regional Analysis," in Asa Knowles, ed., *The International Encyclopedia of Higher Education*, (San Francisco: Jossey-Bass 1977), p. 842.

53. Robert E. Scott, "Student Political Activism in Latin America," in Seymour Martin Lipset and Philip G. Altbach, eds., *Students in Revolt* (Boston: Houghton Mifflin, 1969), p. 403; Alistair Hennessy, "Las raíces del radicalismo en los últimos años," in CPU, ed., *Estudiantes*, p. 34.

54. Esteban Pardo and Fernando Mateo, *Argentina: Educación y capitalismo dependiente* (Buenos Aires: Editorial Tiempo Contemporáneo, 1975), p. 223.

55. Movements for university reform may have been led mostly by progressives, but one view is that reform often changed the traditional *universidad profesionalizante* (for the professions) into the *universidad modernizante*, for an economic modernization favored by powerful State and business interests, domestic and foreign. See Inés Recca and Tomás A. Vasconi, *Modernización y crisis en la universidad latinoamericana* (Santiago: UCH, 1971), p. 30.

56. Pelczar, "University Reform," pp. 58–59.

57. Latorre, "Educación," p. 40.

58. Levine, *Religion*, pp. 34–41; quotation, p. 35.

59. Quotation of Vatican II in Alfonso Borrero, "Universidad latinoamericana," in CELAM, p. 39.

60. Roncagliolo "Estudiantes y política," pp. 83–84; also see Lusk, *Peruvian Higher Education*, p. 58, on the role of urban business in creating Peru's secular private universities.

61. On Nicaragua, see "Discusión IV, Movimientos estudiantiles en América Latina," in

CELAM, pp. 88–89; and Arríen, *Relaciones jurídico-políticas*, pp. 27–30. On Guatemala and Central America generally, see García Laguardia, *Legislación*, p. 202, and personal interview, Mexico City, December 1979. Even Stroessner's Paraguay had trouble with the social research at a branch of the Catholic university and expelled some leading Jesuits. See James H. Street, "Political Intervention and Science in Latin America," *Bulletin of the Atomic Scientists* 37, no. 2 (1981), p. 19.

62. García Laguardia, *La autonomía*, p. 21; Arríen, *Relaciones jurídico-políticas*, p. 41; Drysdale and Myers, "Continuity and Change," p. 282.

63. Levy, "Student Politics," pp. 371–73, 359–66.

64. Benjamin, *Higher Education*, p. 97. In Peru, amid rapid growth, a few elite public universities supported by Congress or private or foreign associations retained tight admissions quotas, choosing "mainly graduates of the better private secondary schools," although most accepted the stream of applicants; see Drysdale and Myers, "Continuity and Change," pp. 284–85. And see Lusk (*Peruvian Higher Education*, p. 76) on the substantial and rising rejection rate even in Peru's public universities, though he properly places it in the context of a boom in annual applications, from (roughly) 15,000 to 240,000 in 1960 through 1980.

65. Peña, "Universidad y sistema educacional," p. 113, describes how regional pressures can lead to Catholic as well as public proliferation. "If Quito and Guayaquil have Catholic universities, why not us?" Nonetheless, only one more Ecuadorian Catholic university (at Cuenca) was created.

66. The Dominican Republic's Institute of Social Sciences lies within the "modernizing tendency," has technical careers, and is "promoted by a group of notable businessmen," but it is a "junior college." Latorre, "Educación," pp. 40–41.

67. Ibid., pp. 42–45; quotation on p. 45.

68. Rama, *Sistema*, pp. 48, 103 for the quotation and on the 1960s data. Also on the 1960s and early 1970s see Molina, "Universidad estatal," pp. 44, 48–49, 58; Lebot, "Movimiento estudiantil," pp. 51–52, 55; Leonardo Posada, "Colombia: La crisis financiera de la universidad," *OCLAE* (Havana) 13, no. 3 (1979) pp. 37–38. On 1981 data, see ICFES, *Estadísticas de la educación superior 1981* (Bogotá, 1982), pp. 17–18. For data to make the Colombia-Venezuela comparison (easily paralleled to Colombia-Ecuador) see ICFES, *Estadísticas 1980* (Bogotá 1982), pp. 65–66; and OPSU, *Boletín estadístico*, p. 93.

CHAPTER THREE

1. This chapter has a more historical focus than any except the previous chapter. An additional incentive for including Chile is the availability of information. Comparatively comprehensive data can be compiled for Chile's compact system, and Chilean scholars have been unusually prolific. Beyond Latin America, "parallel" private and public sectors can be found in the Netherlands and Belgium. See Roger L. Geiger, *Private Sectors in Higher Education* (Ann Arbor: University of Michigan Press, forthcoming). Finally, note that I write mostly of intersectoral homogeneity—the comparative lack of interinstitutional cleavages formed along private-public lines; where explicitly stated, however, *homogeneity* carries the more extreme meaning of similarities across all institutions. Chile is notable on both counts.

2. Federico G. Gil, *The Political System of Chile* (Boston: Houghton Mifflin, 1966), pp. 134–35, 179.

3. Ministerio de Educación Pública, "La política educacional del gobierno de Chile, 1975," Santiago, mimeo, June 1978. On authoritarian Chile generally, see Arturo Valenzuela and Samuel Valenzuela, eds., *Chile under the Junta* (Baltimore: Johns Hopkins University Press, 1985). For an additional look at the fate of private nonprofit institutions under the junta, see Brian H. Smith, "Churches as Development Institutions: The Case of Chile, 1973–1980," a working paper of the Program on Non-Profit Organizations, Yale University, April 1982.

4. I have elsewhere written an account of the military regime's higher education politics: "Chilean Universities under the Junta: Regime and Policy," *Latin American Research Review*,

forthcoming, an article revised from "Higher Education in Authoritarian Regimes: Comparative Perspectives on the Chilean Case," a working paper of the Higher Education Research Group, Yale University, May 1980. While it complements this chapter, where overlap could have arisen, the footnotes refer the reader to the appropriate source. The foci of the two works are basically different. Compared with this chapter, the article is a very limited consideration of pre-1973 Chile. Moreover, even its post-1973 analysis does not probe any major interinstitutional dimensions, including private-public ones (e.g., the creation of new institutions after 1980). Instead, the article focuses on the relationship between repressive authoritarianism and policy.

5. Kalman H. Silvert and Leonard Reissman, *Education, Class, and Nation* (New York: Elsevier, 1976), p. 108. On Chilean colonial education, generally, Jaime Martínez and Juan José Silva U. write that the Church-State "union" makes it "impossible to talk in terms of the concepts of 'private' education and 'state' education according to contemporary criteria." See their "Antecedentes históricos," in Luis Brahm, Patricio Cariola, and Juan José Silva U., eds., *La enseñanza particular en Chile* (Santiago: CIDE [Center for Research and Development in Education] 1971), p. 18. This is the best book on Chile's private schools.

6. Neighboring Argentina, itself enduring debilitating political battles and the bloody tyranny of Juan Manuel de Rosas, contributed the services of such men as Domingo Sarmiento, Juan Bautista Alberdi, and Bartolomé Mitre. Chile's secondary school system, soon one of Latin America's best, patterned itself on the French lycée. See Fernando Campos Harriet, *Desarrollo educacional 1810–1960* (Santiago: Editorial Andrés Bello, 1960), p. 114; this is a very useful source for more historical information.

7. On the liberal-conservative struggle, see Silvert and Reissman, *Education, Class, and Nation*, p. 111; on positivism, Iván Jaksić, "The Influence of Positivism on Latin American Educational Thought: The Case of Chile and Valentín Letelier," paper presented at the conference on Latin America and Education, Tulane University, April 28–30, 1983.

8. As in Uruguay, Argentina, and other parts of Latin America, secondary education developed "downward from the universities"—public universities; Silvert and Reissman, *Education, Class, and Nation*, p. 113. Also on the State's early limits, see Julio Vega, *La racionalización de nuestra enseñanza* (Santiago: Ediciones de la UCH, 1954), p. 87.

9. Martínez and Silva, "Antecedentes," p. 23. Also see Silvert and Reissman, *Education, Class, and Nation*, p. 117. Religion and education were two related areas that critically split conservatives and liberals within the dominant oligarchy. Conservatives either subordinated freedom to religious truth or defended the freedom of religion and choice as opposed to secular monopoly; liberals saw religious education as antithetical to free thought.

10. See the account in Luis Celis, Ricardo Krebs, and Luis Scherz, "Historia de los 90 años de la Pontificia Universidad Católica de Chile," *Revista Universitaria* 1 (1978), pp. 8–51.

11. Quoted in José Olavarría, "¿En crisis el sistema universitario chileno en 1967? ¿Por qué?" in CPU, ed., *Estudiantes y política* (Santiago: CPU, 1970), p. 153.

12. On the constitution, see Kathleen B. Fischer, *Political Ideology and Educational Reform in Chile, 1964–1976* (Los Angeles: UCLA Latin American Center, 1979), p. 35; on incorporation, Celis, Krebs, and Scherz, "Historia," p. 17.

13. Campos Harriet, *Desarrollo*, pp. 198–99.

14. Interview with Fernando Molina, prominently associated with the two major Catholic universities, Santiago, November 1978.

15. Ben G. Burnett, *Political Groups in Chile* (Austin: University of Texas Press, 1970), p. 75.

16. Blanca del Río and Ricardo Alegría, *Centros universitarios de provincia* (Santiago: UCH, 1968).

17. I use the term *1981 legislation* to refer to that year's multitudinous decrees for higher education, flowing from a December 1980 decree, and to ensuing university statutes, whether

promulgated in 1981 or 1982. On the simultaneously intensified push for the privatization of primary and secondary education, alongside remarkable institutional decentralization in the public sector, see Eduardo Castro, "El nuevo plan de estudios de la educación general básica," Santiago, Centro de Estudios Económicos y Sociales, 1980; Marcela Gajardo, "Educación chilena y regimen militar: Itinerario de cambios," a FLACSO working paper, Santiago, April 1982; Alejandro Jara and Héctor Contardo, "La reforma educacional neo-liberal," a FLACSO working paper, Santiago, August 1983.

18. Before 1981, most commentary defined *higher education* as the eight universities and their regional campuses; after that it turned more to the broad term *postsecondary*, which included the training centers. Many such centers, requiring secondary degrees for entrance, predated 1980 but were not considered higher education. No one knew the total enrollments in these hundreds of private schools prior to 1980, and even as of 1982 only some were recognized by the State. Marcela Gajardo, in "Educación chilena," p. 22, discusses the privatization of secondary education. Also see Anny Rivera. "¿Qué será de los 50,000 egresados de la educación superior privada?" *APSI*, May 20–31, 1982, p. 2. Rivera reports that while twenty training centers advertised in 1981, sixty-one did so in 1982, with 25,000 first-year openings in Santiago alone. Thus one could say that Chilean enrollments have generally been underestimated, compared to other nations, by the exclusion of postsecondary training centers, but Chilean universities have included three-year courses not included in many other nations. See Jean Labbens, "Tradition et modernisme: L'université au Chili," in *América Latina* (Rio) 13, no. 1 (1970), pp. 66, 72–73. Finally, recent data, which I cannot yet feel confident about, suggest the following: (1) a 1982 enrollment of 118,150, which is perhaps most comparable to earlier figures since it is based on the traditional universities plus the institutes created from them, though a total of 122,755 without the private training centers is also plausible; (2) a tremendous growth in those centers, with roughly 40,000 students (1983) in ninety-five institutions (1984); (3) a major growth in proliferating professional institutes, capturing a large share of new enrollments; (4) a marked privatization, with a growth from 400 to 3,686 in enrollments in the new private universities during 1982–84, but with the overall private-public balance not yet radically altered unless one includes the training centers, in which case the private sector is easily the larger one. See Jara and Contardo, "Reforma," pp. 61, 197; and Guillermo E. Martínez, "Educación superior privada," *El Mercurio*, October 16, 1984.

19. Rodolfo Raventos and Jorge Rodríguez, *Universidad, racionalidad y eficiencia* (Santiago: CPU, 1973), p. 121. The Radical party, stalwart promoter of the public sector and the Estado Docente, pushed hard for such guarantees.

20. So great was the dependence that a major private school crisis developed in the late 1960s when State subsidies fell behind inflation. Jorge Ochoa and Raimundo Barros, "Antecedentes estadísticos," in Brahm, Cariola, and Silva, eds., *Enseñanza*, p. 124. This article discusses the evolution of State financing for private schools.

21. Celis, Krebs, and Scherz, "Historia," p. 21; Olavarría, "Crisis," p. 155.

22. Raventos and Rodríguez, *Universidad*, p. 18.

23. On the demands, UC, *Claustro universitario, 2nd sesión* (Santiago: Ediciones Nueva Universidad, 1973), pp. 57–58. On the general debate, Juan Frontaura, Raúl Illanes, and Rafael Cruz, "Antecedentes legales," in Brahm, Cariola, and Silva, eds., *Enseñanza*, pp. 49–50. A more serious problem was the government's proposed tuition freeze at private schools; this populist move, defended in the name of equity, was especially menacing because of rampant inflation. Interesting debates arose concerning whether the State should fund tuition-free schools run by for-profit enterprises and schools that were nonprofit at the primary level but for-profit at the secondary level.

24. See Levy, "Chilean Universities," for details and written sources. Among the promoters of tuition whom I interviewed were Jorge Claro, a top adviser to the education ministry, and Miguel Kast, head of The National Planning Office (ODEPLAN); Santiago, November

1978; among the opponents who had been strongly anti-UP and who remained powerful at the UCH until 1976, René Orozco Sepúlveda, Santiago, November 1978, and Danilo Salcedo, New York City, September 1978.

25. A leading empirical work on Chile is Ernesto Schiefelbein and Noel McGinn, eds., *El sistema escolar y el problema del ingreso a la universidad* (Santiago: CPU, 1975).

26. Carmen Luz Latorre, "Recursos asignados al sector educación y su distribución en el período 1965–80," a PIIE working paper, Santiago, December 1981, tables 1 and 2. Also see Ministerio de Hacienda, "Análisis financiero de la educación superior chilena: Período 1965–1978," Santiago, 1978, mimeo, p. 10; this document's main author is Patricio Arriagada. Paradoxical debates emerged as new private institutions, whatever their rhetoric about free markets, desperately wanted to share in the indirect State aid. Pressure from the traditional universities (especially the UCH) was intense enough to persuade Pinochet to drop that idea, however—another in a string of statist triumphs over the Chicago Boys in 1982.

27. Latorre's table 3 ("Recursos") uses different but parallel data to those in my table 3.4; they strongly indicate that after one big spurt around 1976, the self-financed percentage leveled off at least until 1980; also, my 1977 percentage may be a little high.

28. Máximo Pacheco, "Génesis y desarrollo de la Universidad de Chile," in *La universidad en tiempos de cambio* (Santiago: Editorial del Pacífico, 1965), pp. 120–22.

29. UCH, *Antecedentes e informaciones universitarios* (Santiago: UCH, 1975), p. 47; Campos Harriet, *Desarrollo*, pp. 177, 190–91.

30. Raventos and Rodríguez, *Universidad*, pp. 4–5; Celis, Krebs, and Scherz, "Historia," p. 33.

31. Celis, Krebs, and Scherz, "Historia," pp. 5, 20–21. Also see Luis Scherz García, "Public and Private Universities," in Seymour Martin Lipset and Aldo Solari, eds., *Elites in Latin America*, (London: Oxford University Press, 1967), p. 394.

32. All quotations found in Ana María Foxley, "Inquietud tras la fachada," *Hoy*, May 23–29, 1979, pp. 16–17.

33. UCH professor Francisco Cumplido quoted in Ana María Foxley, "Otros rumbos en las aulas," *Hoy*, October 3–9, 1979, p. 12.

34. Moreover, the 1981 legislation threatened the traditional university-profession connection. Where once only the UCH, and then only eight universities, could grant (State-delegated) degrees for professional practice, the legislation restricted such exclusive authority to but twelve professions, where a licenciatura or higher academic degree was required. Additionally, new as well as traditional universities could offer the twelve. Other professions were triumphantly left to the free market, where proliferating institutions could also offer usable degrees. While traditional universities and excluded professions protested, several institutes tried to pervert the law by becoming universities so that they could offer usable degrees in at least one of the twelve professions, a process *El Mercurio* denounced for pandering to regional political pressures ("Universidades e institutos," editorial, January 17, 1982). Additionally, a tandem law on professions undermined the long-standing link between traditional universities and many professions, including some of the twelve designated ones. University faculties would no longer graduate students directly into a colegio holding monopoly representation in its field, with authority to set professional rules and fee schedules. Instead, graduates would merely inscribe their names in a central registry and then perhaps join any of a plurality of associations. All this was hailed by the Chicago Boys as a fitting parallel to initiatives taken in labor and social security fields, giving professionals the right to choose rather than be forced into guildlike monopolies. The colegios themselves did not see it this way, claiming more than 90 percent membership opposition, while the president of the law colegio observed tartly: "What would have happened if President Allende had promulgated this decree-law? Today we would already be on strike. There is not the slightest doubt." Quoted in Patricia Verdugo, "Colegios profesionales," *Hoy*, February 11–17, 1981. I also draw heavily from articles in *Hoy*, March

24–31 and April 1–7, 1981, and *¿Qué Pasa?*, January 15–21 and February 19–25, 1981, as well as *Ercilla*, March 11, 1981.

35. On complaints, "Los comunistas y la universidad," *El Siglo* (editoral), July 14, 1966; on UP efforts, Patricia Weiss Fagen, *Chilean Universities: Problems of Autonomy and Dependence* (Beverly Hills: Sage, 1973) p. 29. Efforts to coordinate research policy also failed.

36. The council's regionalization efforts, for example, were repeatedly frustrated during much of the 1970s. Paradoxically, proliferation could shore up the UCH's position, as many derived institutions have ties of heritage to it. Until 1982 the council was still composed of only the eight traditional universities, but then, without legal changes, it held its first meeting with an expanded (tripled) representation. Still, the UCH kept out the private training centers and hosted the meeting, with its rector presiding with the education minister.

37. Personal communication from Enrique D'Etigny," August 18, 1982. Iván Jaksić cites the conventional wisdom that the UCH "closely resembled," into the 1930s, what I have called the Continental model, after which it achieved more autonomy from the State. Jaksić, "Philosophy and University Reform at the University of Chile, 1842–1973," *Latin American Research Review* 19, no. 1 (1984), p. 72.

38. Olavarría, "Crisis," p. 155; Celis, Krebs, and Scherz, "Historia," p. 9.

39. Carlos Huneeus M., *Movimientos universitarios y generación de elites dirigentes* (Santiago: CPU, 1973), p. 37; Harold Benjamin, *Higher Education in the American Republics* (New York: McGraw-Hill, 1964), p. 53.

40. See, for example, Raventos and Rodríguez, *Universidad*, pp. 4, 107–17.

41. Campos Harriet, *Desarrollo*, p. 124; Celis, Krebs, and Scherz, "Historia," pp. 16, 26; Benjamin, *Higher Education*, p. 53.

42. Private education was not fully accepted by the UP as the natural corollary of freedom of education nor as an additional support for public education: it was to be restructured instead as an integral part of the national system. Particularly controversial was the government's ENU (Unified National School) plan. Emphasizing equity, it aimed at political education for the masses and considered all education fundamentally a public responsibility, therefore properly run by the State. Short of abolition, private education should at least come under heavy regulation. The ENU therefore could have seriously eroded the freedom of private primary and secondary schools, requiring them to conform to certain curricular and structural mandates. Along with its new regulatory control, the State would give the schools the financial resources necessary to comply—public financing to sustain public governance. Fierce opposition came from private groups, including parents, professionals, rightist parties, the PDC, and the Church. The Permanent Committee of the Episcopado declared that the ENU would plant the seeds of "totalitarian culture." *La Prensa* (April 6, 1971) printed an article entitled "By 1976 There Will Be No Private Education." The army also made its opposition clear. Although Communists and Socialists generally continued to support the ENU, the Radical minister of education acknowledged the partisan antiprivate tone of the ENU proposal and obtained President Allende's support to postpone it (leading to trouble with the UP's left). See Frontaura, Illanes, and Cruz, "Antecedentes legales," pp. 38–44; Fischer, *Political Ideology*, pp. 82–91; Arturo Valenzuela, *The Breakdown of Democratic Regimes: Chile* (Baltimore: Johns Hopkins University Press, 1978), pp. 89–90. Interview with Luis Brahm, Santiago, November 1978.

43. For an annotated bibliography, see Ernesto Schiefelbein, "La investigación sobre la universidad chilena en 1977–81," a FLACSO working paper, Santiago, May 1982, pp. 2–5; the rest of the bibliography is devoted less directly to regime-related factors. Most relevant to our concerns about the State and autonomy are: Manuel A. Garretón, "Universidad y política en los procesos de transformación y reversión en Chile, 1967–1977," a FLACSO working paper, Santiago, April 1979; José Joaquín Brunner, "Ideologías universitarias y cambios en la universidad chilena," a FLACSO working paper, Santiago, June 1981; Levy, "Chilean Universities."

44. Interviews with Academy of Christian Humanism president Enrique D'Etigny, November 1979 and January 1982, Santiago. The fullest account of the social science institutes is Manuel A. Garretón, "Las ciencias sociales en Chile al inicio de los 80: Situación, problemas y perspectivas," a FLACSO working paper, Santiago, May 1981. However, the single most important attempt to create a reasonably autonomous, private university failed. Political moderates, mostly identified with the PDC, Radical, or no party asked permission to offer a University of the Andes by 1983. Los Andes was to be pointedly private, built around high tuitions and other private finance, ownership by a nonprofit foundation, a governing board, and low-cost operations. The Chicago Boys favored this bolstering of consumer choice and system legitimacy. But hard-line statists found the idea dangerous. Previously, their victory in denying even indirect State funds for new universities hurt Los Andes' chances, but the definitive no came within days after the (1982) funeral of PDC leader Eduardo Frei—and the unprecedented, spontaneous, mass popular outpouring it evoked.

45. Levy, "Chilean Universities."

46. To publicize the U.S. bias, they feared, would be to encourage the opposition of "old professor types" and charges of dependency. Interviews with Oscar Garrido, Santiago, November 1978, and January and May 1982. Garrido had been the UTE's planning chief and then, in the early 1980s, head of the education ministry's new higher education department.

47. Ministerio de Educación, *Estatuto de la Universidad de Chile* (Santiago, 1982). The national legislation led to the university statutes.

48. "El estatuto de la Universidad de Tarapacá," *La Segunda*, January 16, 1982 (n.a.). The most complete document for Chile's new governance structure is Consejo de Rectores, *Nueva legislación universitaria chilena* (Santiago, 1981). Some Chicago Boys favored rectorship selection by deans rather than the State.

49. "Rectora de Universidad," *El Mercurio*, January 12, 1982 (n.a.).

50. Celis, Krebs, and Scherz, "Historia," pp. 13–14; Campos Harriet, *Desarrollo*, p. 197.

51. Pedro Gandolfo et al., *El sentido del pluralismo en la universidad* (Valparaíso: Ediciones Universitarias del Valparaíso, 1971), pp. 25–33; on the debate, Olavarría, "Crisis," p. 155.

52. Aníbal Carlos Luzuriaga, "Los movimientos estudiantiles católicos," in CELEM, ed., *Iglesia y universidad en América Latina* (Bogotá: CELAM, 1976), p. 83.

53. Quotation of UC rector (1959) in Celis, Krebs, and Scherz, "Historia," pp. 28–29.

54. Hernán Larraín Acuña, "Universidades católicas: Luces y sombras," in *La universidad en tiempos de cambio*, pp. 78–80, 92. One of the most comprehensive accounts of the UC's transformation is found in José Joaquín Brunner's tandem working papers published by FLACSO, Santiago, in October and December 1981: "Universidad Católica y cultura nacional en los años 60: Los intelectuales tradicionales y el movimiento estudiantil" and "Concepciones de universidad y grupos intelectuales durante el proceso de reforma de la Universidad Católica de Chile, 1967–1973." By 1965 only 5 percent of UC students specialized in theology; see UC, *Plan de desarrollo* (Santiago, 1970), p. 61. Of course the UCH was not stagnant during this period, as shown in another FLACSO working paper; Angel Flisfisch, "Elementos para una interpretación de los procesos de reforma en la Universidad de Chile (1950–1973)," Santiago, September 1981; and in Carlos Huneeus Madge, *La reforma en la Universidad de Chile* (Santiago: UCH, 1973).

55. Fuenzalida explores U.S. influences in the modernization of Chilean higher education; Edmundo Fuenzalida, *Building Transnational Capitalism: The Role of Knowledge Institutions* (forthcoming). Specifically on the origins of the Chicago connection, see Richard N. Adams and Charles C. Cumberland, *United States Cooperation in Latin America* (East Lansing: Michigan State University, 1960), pp. 203–5. On the Chicago Boys' role in higher education policy since 1973, see Levy, "Chilean Universities." On the transition from traditionalism to modernism and reformism, see Brunner, "Universidad Católica," and Luis Scherz García, *El camino de la revolución universitaria* (Santiago: Editorial del Pacífico, 1968), pp. 94–101.

56. On coalition politics see Huneeus Madge, *Movimientos*, pp. 28, 36; and Olavarría, "Crisis," p. 157. On defining student characteristics, see Patricio E. Chaparro, "University Students' Activism and Leadership in Two Chilean Universities," Ph.D. diss., University of North Carolina, 1975, pp. 142–48, 127, 31. An illustrative UCH-UC contrast lies in the UCH-Socialist versus UC-Conservative rectorships in the early 1960s. see Julio César Jobet Bórquez, *Doctrina y praxis de los educadores representativos chilenos* (Santiago: Editorial Andrés Bello, 1970), p. 595.

57. Huneeus Madge, *Movimientos*, pp. 36, 73–74.

58. Chile's dominant party in the decades preceding the PDC's victory was the Radical party. Although the party traditionally championed public education, private education grew in proportional as well as in absolute terms from 1930 to 1960. See Ochoa and Barros, "Antecedentes estadísticos," p. 81, Edgardo Boeninger, the UCH's last pre-coup rector, believes that in higher education, the Radical party decidedly favored the public sector until 1952; interview, Santiago, January 1982.

59. On the PDC tension, interviews with Máximo Pacheco, education minister under Frei, Santiago, November 1978 and November 1979; on betrayal, Fischer, *Political Ideology*, pp. 83, 144.

60. Patricio Dooner, "Reforma y jerarquía eclesiástica," *Academia* 1 (1977), p. 14; "En 1967 gobierno de Frei," *El Mercurio*, August 25, 1977.

61. As president-elect, Allende dispatched Communist senator Teitelboim to assure Castillo that the UP would work closely with the progressive PDC or sink without it; Allende therefore reportedly denied an early financial request by Castillo, instead pledging more than requested. Interview with Fernando Castillo, November 1978, Santiago. The ironic contrast between the PDC administration's strained and the UP administration's cordial relationship with the UC's top leadership is drawn by such ex-rectors as Castillo of the UC, his UCH counterpart Edgardo Boeninger, and Boeninger's predecessor Juan Gómez Millas, all interviewed, Santiago, November 1978. Of course, student and professor opposition to the UP would produce UC-UP tensions.

62. "La difícil autonomía," *Ercilla*, October 3, 1973 (n.a.).

63. Significantly, elsewhere in Latin America, Chicago economics has been associated mostly with second-wave elite universities.

64. The regime did provoke the Church by moving on the University of the North, abolishing one of its campuses, and joining another with a former regional campus of the UCH to form the University of Tarapacá; the Church denied the junta's right to rob its campuses. But however accustomed the junta grew to criticism from the Catholic church of Chile, it wanted to avoid antagonizing the Vatican. This was especially true from the late 1970s, while the Vatican was judging Chile's case in its territorial dispute with Argentina over the Beagle Islands. Thus, the Vatican received academic progress reports from the UC administration, which fussed about ceremonial affairs, benedictions, and so forth. And the UC tried to make religious virtue of its emphasis on order, effectiveness, salvation, adhesion to Western culture, and anticommunism. Notably, the regime has fared better with the Vatican than with Chile's own, more liberal, Church. Luis Scherz García, "Reforma y contrarreforma universitarias en América Latina: Un caso significativo," a FLACSO working paper, Santiago, August 1981, pp. 21–28, 46. Interviews with Scherz García, Santiago, January and May 1982.

65. Scherz García, "Reforma," p. 24.

66. Mónica Blanco and Mabel Correa, "Informe universitario," *Ercilla*, March 17–23, 1976, p. 41.

67. Until the junta's great extension of State control, autonomous university decisions as well as regime policy influenced the number of enrollment openings.

68. The public decline during 1974–80 was somewhat sharper than table 3.5 captures (and, as footnote 18 suggests, possibly became much sharper in the early 1980s). The public share of first-year openings declined faster than its enrollment share. More important was the dis-

memberment of the two public universities, leaving the once national university only slightly larger than the UC; as most derived institutions were public, however, intersectoral shares did not vary much. The overall data suggest that the major private-public contrast under the junta turned on the UC and UCH. Four of the other five private universities increased their share of the State's (diminishing) funding, but the interesting exception was Concepción, identified above as easily the most leftist private institution. See Consejo de Rectores, *Anuario estadístico 1980* (Santiago, 1981), pp. 12, 17; Ministerio de Hacienda, "Análisis," appendixes 2–12.

69. I have computed the private-public, technical-nontechnical, and Catholic-secular cleavages for 1974. They strongly resemble the 1980 cleavages, with no evidence to alter the conclusions drawn from the 1980 data.

70. Vega, "Racionalización," p. 73.

71. William Thayer A., *Sociedad democrática y universidad* (Santiago: CPU, 1973), p. 69.

72. Quotation of Galo Gómez O., *Chile de hoy, educación, cultura y ciencia* (Mexico City: Casa de Chile, 1976), p. 50. For an analysis of the relatively stable field distributions under the junta, see Levy, "Chilean Universities." This suggests how much substantive variation can be hidden by certain empirical measures and makes the intersectoral variation found elsewhere in Latin America that much more impressive. More variation is seen once we penetrate within fields, e.g., to the very contrasting meanings of "social science."

73. An earlier intellectual think-tank base for Chile's Chicago economics was the Centro de Estudios Públicos, with then treasury minister Sergio de Castro as one director and free-market stalwart Friedrich von Hayek as honorary president.

74. "UES privadas no piden la PAA," *El Mercurio*, January 12, 1982. Many students develop important ties to businesses while still in the private secondary schools.

75. On comparing universities, see Patricio García F., *Las carreras universitarias* (Santiago: Editora Nacional Quimantú, 1974), p. 14. Chaparro ("Students' Activism," pp. 146, 39) shows the higher SES level of UC over UCH activists. On 1980 data showing 45 versus 17 percent respectively of private and public secondary graduates entering universities, see Adriana Abalos, "Universidades," *Ercilla*, August 6, 1980, p. 15. On the UTE, see García, *Carreras*, p. 17; Hernán Ramírez Necochea, *El partido comunista y la universidad* (Santiago: Ediciones de la Revista Aurora, 1964), pp. 100–101; UTE, *Antecedentes cuantitativos 1973* (Santiago: UTE, n.d.), pp. 48–51. For an account of the UTE's broadening SES base prior to the coup, see Enrique Kirberg, *Los nuevos profesionales: Educación universitaria de trabajadores, Chile: UTE, 1968–1973* (Guadalajara: Universidad de Guadalajara, 1981). It is especially noteworthy that the UTSM, which may be Chile's closest approximation to a second-wave elite institution, especially with its single-field concentration, has avoided the stigma of distinctive SES exclusiveness. Since its founding, it has tried to attract mixed social strata, charged low tuition, offered scholarships and night classes, and has even tried to avoid the all-too-familiar disdain for manual labor. See Campos Harriet, *Desarrollo*, p. 201.

76. On 1976–81 trends, see Guillermo Briones, "Las universidades chilenas en el modelo de economía neo-liberal, 1973–1981," a PIIE working paper, Santiago 1981, pp. 43–59. On the tuition-loans, José Joaquín Brunner, "Tendencias de cambio en el sistema de educación superior: Chile 1973–1982," a FLACSO working paper, July 1982, p. 14.

77. UCH, *Antecedentes e informaciones*, table 25. The UC held a generally unenviable academic status until its modernization in the 1950s and the influx of State funding.

78. On 1975 ratios, Consejo de Rectores, *Sistema universitario*, p. 14. For parallel 1969 data, Ernesto Schiefelbein, "Elementos para un análisis del uso de recursos en universidades (1968 y 1969)," in *Recursos humanos para el desarrollo económico y social chileno* (Santiago: PLANDES [Association for Planning and Development], 1970), table 1. Data on classroom size (for 1975) provided by Jorge Claro, adviser to the education ministry. The UCH has generally led the system in graduate education and research but all eight universities have played noteworthy roles in certain areas. In terms of university budgets devoted to research, the

UCH has been very high, the UTE very low, with most private institutions in between; see Schiefelbein, "Elementos," table 1.

79. A brief overview of the junta's main arguments, each criticized, is found in José Joaquín Brunner, "Argumento y realidad en la universidad chilena," a FLACSO working paper, Santiago, October 1982.

80. Competition for the top twenty-thousand students, and the attendant indirect State subsidy, also threatened to increase institutional stratification. The top institutions could attract the best students, thereby attracting superior resources, thereby further improving quality, all in a self-reinforcing cycle. The UCH and UC initially drew more than 90 percent of their students from the top 20,000 candidates, and stratification was further heightened as universities used scholarships to compete for top students, contradicting the promised policy of targeting scholarships to less-privileged candidates to offset tuition costs. Where equity and self-interest conflicted, equity gave way.

81. Mario Valle, "Universidades: Reñida competencia," *El Mercurio*, January 17, 1982.

82. In Brazil, however, the public sector expanded, though short of demand. The Chilean pattern contrasts to the Argentine, where the two sectors had been distinct before the 1976 coup. Within Argentina, the public sector was hit much harder by an authoritarian repression that lowered its quality, while the private sector made certain qualitative improvements.

CHAPTER FOUR

1. Data on Spanish America came from table 1.1. For historical data on Mexico, see footnote 20 below; 1981 Mexican data are compiled from ANUIES, *Población de licenciatura en México 1981* (Mexico City: ANUIES, 1982), pp. 27–309. The ANUIES figure includes only the *licenciatura* level, excluding over 30,000 graduate students and well over 100,000 *normal superior* (teacher education) enrollments. However, some of this chapter is based on 1978 data, largely because the relevant ANUIES publication was available much earlier and, unlike the latter one, includes data on field distribution by institution. The 1978 licenciatura figure is 12.5 percent (77,786/622,134). ANUIES, *Anuario estadístico 1978* (Mexico City: ANUIES, 1979), pp. 239–47. The enrollment totals for both 1978 and 1981 are slightly understated, despite ANUIES's unmatched ability to gather Mexican data. For example, the 1979 publication gathers data from 199 institutions, whereas ANUIES's own 1978–79 directory, *Instituciones de educación superior: Directorio 1979* (Mexico City: ANUIES, 1979), p. xxix, lists 233. Some institutions opened in 1979, but the discrepancy probably also involves missing data. It is difficult to judge the effect on the 12.5 private share. Most of the omitted institutions (twenty of thirty-four) are private, but private institutions tend to be smaller (although probably all the omitted institutions are small). In any case, both the 12.5 and the 15.2 percent figures may understate the real private share because Mexico's public institutions notoriously exaggerate their enrollments to maximize State subsidies. (ANUIES's *Instituciones* identifies private and public affiliation; where necessary I also consulted the 1981–82 edition, published in 1982, of the same series.) Note that unless otherwise specified, 1978 and 1981 enrollment and institutional data presented in this chapter come from ANUIES's *Anuario* (especially pp. 170–78) and *Población* (especially pp. 27–309).

2. Mexico has about one-sixth of Spanish America's private enrollments and slightly more of its total enrollments. Furthermore, Mexico offers a welcome opportunity to treat institutions legally and popularly called private as truly private. I have elsewhere written about Mexico's public sector in ways that can be related to the concepts of evolution, finance, governance, and function. Here I write less about Mexico's than Chile's or Brazil's public sector, instead relying partly on my earlier work, *University and Government in Mexico* (New York: Praeger, 1980).

3. Douglas Bennett and Kenneth Sharpe, "The State as Banker and Entrepreneur," *Comparative Politics* 12, no. 2 (1980), p. 165. A useful analytical overview of State-private relations in Mexico, including contrasting views of such scholars as Pablo González Casanova,

Roger Hansen, and Raymond Vernon, is found in Miguel Basáñez, *La lucha por la hegemonía en México, 1968–1980* (Mexico City: Siglo XXI, 1981), pp. 11–111, passim. For a recent discussion of Mexico's extraordinary political stability, including its economic bases, see Daniel C. Levy and Gabriel Székely, *Mexico: Paradoxes of Stability and Change* (Boulder, Colo. Westview Press, 1983).

4. The section on evolution until 1935, except for the private-public interpretations, draws on my Ph.D. dissertation, "University Autonomy versus Government Control: The Case of Mexico," University of North Carolina, 1977, pp. 56–110. Marking a wider Latin American pattern, a shift to publicness had already occurred in the late colonial period, as in the creation of such secular institutions as the College of Mining.

5. The apparent oddity of liberals opposing a nation's major educational institution stemmed partly from the institution's colonial legacy, whereas Chile's San Felipe, for example, entered the nineteenth century with a more decidedly liberal hue.

6. Jorge Siegrist Clamont, *En defensa de la autonomía universitaria* (Mexico City: Talleres de la Editorial Jus, 1954) vol. 1, p. 349. Some observers saw a weakening of the State, others a strategy to strengthen it by devolving authority over unsolvable trouble onto a private-public hybrid that would ultimately fail and thereby clear the way for a truly public, revolutionary university. In any case, the university's private side included legal autonomy and authority to establish academic and administrative structures. On the public side, the university was "national," under the State, bound to meet national goals, composed of public employees, and entitled to fixed State subsidies to which no private endowment could be added. Authority to select the rector was split between the president and the university itself.

7. While the university's private status left it legally unaffected, President Lázaro Cárdenas made clear that it should follow suit. Legislators also threatened to establish socialist universities in Mexico City, Guadalajara, and Sinaloa.

8. This analysis of private growth is corroborated by Pablo Latapí in *Análisis de un sexenio de educación en México, 1970–1976* (Mexico City: Nueva Imagen, 1980), pp. 155–219. Latapí cites public growth, declining public quality, increased recruitment of the lower-middle class, increased politicization, and the needs of private enterprise—all stimulating private universities to perform a *servicio de clase*, recruiting the privileged classes and graduating them into private employment (pp. 176, 180, 157, 205). Latapí adds that class polarization based on private versus public education is qualified by the existence of low-quality private institutions that recruit poorer students who could not get into even the public sector (pp. 205–6). The analysis may also be substantiated by intranational comparisons. Mexico's private sector is especially developed in regions where most privileged people reside (e.g., Mexico City, Nuevo León, Guadalajara), while several poorer states (e.g., Chiapas, Guerrero) still have no private higher education.

9. An example of the charges: Mauricio Gómez Mayorga, "Hartos de rojería y politiquería," *Impacto*, December 5, 1979. An example of the defense: Fernando Pérez Correa, "La universidad, instrumento social," *Uno Más Uno*, December 3, 1979. One good example of how politicization led to a private alternative is described by Arthur D. Martínez, "The Politics of University Rectorship in Latin America: An Empirical Case Study of la Universidad Autónoma Benito Juárez de Oaxaca," mimeo, n.d. A conservative institution until the early 1970s, Oaxaca's state university expanded rapidly and "democratized" its governance. The Left itself fractured chaotically while Left and Right disputed the rectorship; more than twenty aspirants held or claimed the post in less than three years. State-university conflict was also intense. As the moderate Left gained the upper hand (1978), conservatives exited to found the private Regional University of the Southeast.

10. In 1979 leading private universities prepared a self-study report for delivery to President José López Portillo. Though it does not list an author, Oscar Soria N. deserves mention as chief organizer; IMESP, "La educación superior privada en México 1974–1979" (1979). A very helpful study, it must nevertheless be cited with care because it includes only eighteen institutions (having failed to obtain adequate responses from an additional nine solicited), while

complete data would include roughly a hundred institutions. I estimate that, on the basis of comparisons between IMESP's sample and more complete sectoral data, the sample accounts for under two-thirds of the private sector's enrollments. The main problem is that the sample is drawn disproportionately from "name" institutions. The first information to be gathered from the IMESP report concerns the chronology of institutional creation. After UAG was created in 1935, followed by three more institutions in 1943, only two more were created in the fifteen-year period, 1946–61. This indicates that the stability forged by the State-public university pact of 1945, along with improved UNAM quality, helped forestall the creation of additional private alternatives until the mid-1960s.

A second IMESP report came out in 1981: "La educación superior privada en México, 1980–1981." However, I prefer to use data from the earlier study for two reasons. First, 1979 private data are more comparable than 1981 private data to my latest (1978) comprehensive public data on fields of study. Second, the 1981 IMESP self-study correctly declares itself (p. 14) basically comparable to the first. Again the self-study (compared to the ANUIES data I use) covers only 21 percent of the private sector's institutions but much (68 percent) of its enrollments. The average institution covered has 3,145 students versus just 425 in the average institution not covered. Once again, then, the demand-absorbing subsector is seriously under-represented.

11. The Free Law School could reasonably be cited as the first private university, but it is a single-faculty institution (with only some six hundred students in 1981). While I include such institutions in the aggregate data, I do not deal individually with them. The school was created in 1912 when some law students from the National University became disaffected and formed their own institution, a prestigious and influential one. The account of the seven private institutions discussed here in detail draws substantially upon personal interviews conducted in November–December 1979 and August–September 1980. I list here those interviewees with whom I had the most intensive and productive discussions. At UAG (in Guadalajara): Luis Garibay, the rector; Jorge Luis Oria, director general of planning and development; Oscar Soria N., professor and researcher at UAG and research director for the Ajijic Institute on International Education. At Ibero (in Mexico City): Jesús Carranza, financial director; Ernesto Domínguez, then general director of academic affairs, subsequently rector; Arturo Fregoso, director of research; Luis Vergara, director of planning. At La Salle (in Mexico City): Carlos Rangel Barrera, director of planning. At Anáhuac (in the state of Mexico): Carlos Bravo, departing chairman of the education department and new director of planning at the University of Monterrey. At Americas (in Puebla): Russell Box, assistant vice-rector; Roberto Newell, vice-rector for academic affairs. At ITAM (in Mexico City): Juan José Huerta Coria, director of academic affairs. ITESM is the only one of the seven institutions I did not personally visit. I rely on interviews with Thomas Noel Osborn and Oscar Soria N., who have both written on Mexico's private universities, Jean-Pierre Vielle, who has lived and worked extensively in Monterrey and is one of the nation's foremost experts on universities, and Jorge Luis Oria, UAG, who previously worked at ITESM. At each university interviewees were asked to discuss not only their university but the other ones.

12. The first rector was Manuel Gómez Morín. See Patricia de Leonardo R., *La educación superior privada en México: Bosquejo histórico* (Mexico City: Editorial Línea, 1983), pp. 26–28, 88–89, 98, 122, 135, 163–68. Students played an unusually instrumental role in UAG's creation. Also see Donald J. Mabry, *The Mexican University and the State: Student Conflicts, 1910–1971* (College Station: Texas A & M University Press, 1982), pp. 131–33, 158–59, passim, on the student role in many historical developments.

13. Donald J. Mabry, *Mexico's Acción Nacional* (Syracuse: Syracuse University Press, 1973), pp. 23–24.

14. UNAM's rector (Brito Foucher) actually gave Ibero's inaugural address. It was not until 1953, however, that Ibero fully gained the university nomenclature, uniting its faculties as it moved well beyond its theology centerpiece. Universidad Iberomericana, *35 aniversario*

(Mexico City: Universidad Iberoamericana, 1978), pp. 6–8. Some groups wanted to make UNAM itself into a Catholic institution and had to settle for a private alternative; see de Leonardo *Educación superior*, p. 122.

15. The Center of University Studies (4,661 students in 1981) is probably a third-wave institution and is not integrated with the Monterrey group; but the Regiomontana University (6,224 students in 1981) is Nuevo León's largest private institution other than ITESM itself and belongs to the second wave. Institutional creation by the Monterrey group would make for an intriguing study in big business politics. In 1969, family quarrels led one of the constituent groups to join with interested priests in forming an alternative institution, the University of Monterrey. This represented some fracturing of the group and some dilution of its originally resolute purpose in creating ITESM, but it also helped to preserve ITESM's own profile and to create a fuller system of higher education for the group. ITESM could not admit all aspirants, even those associated with the group, without lowering academic standards and diluting the technical-economic focus. Yet the group did not want to force frustrated aspirants into the public sector. Nor did it want to rely on the public sector for the social sciences and humanities. In practice, the University of Monterrey's values and orientations may more closely resemble those of the progressive Ibero than of the group's own ITESM, even encouraging references to the "Ibero of Monterrey." By field of study, it is even more deviant within the private sector (1978). Nearly half its enrollments are in the social sciences, education, law, and humanities, nearly a third in medicine, less than a fifth in business and economics, less than a tenth in engineering; ITESM, in contrast, has respective figures of roughly one-tenth, zero, one-third, and three-fifths. In 1976 family quarrels helped create another institution, the Mexican University of the Northeast. It apparently fashions an even more "popular" character but is devoted exclusively to business and engineering.

16. Institute of International Education (IIE), "Institutional Report" on ITAM, Mexico City Office, October 1976.

17. In my judgment, ITAM has become too important in business and State circles to omit, while Americas shares Puebla's private pinnacle with the Autonomous Popular University of Puebla (created with business support because of leftist political activity at the state university).

18. Anáhuac could reasonably be placed in the economic category, as shown later by its field distributions. But my categorization's main limitation concerns El Colegio de México, deleted because it is overwhelmingly a research institute and graduate school. With fewer than fifty students at the licenciatura level (1978 and 1981), it is not comparable to the institutions considered here. CIDE (Center of Economic Research and Instruction) is similarly deleted; both are private-public hybrids. On diverse, relatively private institutions composed of intellectuals but not students, e.g., the Center of Mexican Writers, see Roderic A. Camp, *Intellectuals and the State in 20th Century Mexico* (Austin: University of Texas Press, 1985), especially the chapter on cultural institutions.

19. ANUIES, *La enseñanza superior en México 1968* (Mexico City: ANUIES, 1971), pp. 319–29.

20. Cohort data from ANUIES, cited in Alfonso Rangel Guerra, *Systems of Higher Education: Mexico* (New York: International Council for Educational Development, 1978), pp. 53, 19; table 1.1 reported 14 percent for the earliest OAS year available (1962), whereas 1959 ANUIES data (Thomas Noel Osborn, *Higher Education in Mexico* [El Paso: Texas Western Press, 1976], p. 48) reported 10 percent, and de Leonardo (*Educación superior*, p. 215) reported under 9 percent in 1958, jumping to 13 percent by 1964.

21. The estimations are cited by then UNAM rector Guillermo Soberón, in "Las universidades mexicanas y el desarrollo del país," in *Deslinde,* no. 123 (Mexico City: UNAM, 1980), p. 6; SEP leaders mention the two million figure.

22. On ITESM: ANUIES, *La enseñanza superior en México 1971* (Mexico City: ANUIES, 1974), p. 285. For 1974–79 inclusively: IMESP's 1979 self-study (p. xxxii) puts this figure at less than 1 percent; the sample overrepresents the better institutions, with some greater likelihood

of attracting State funds. Calculating from ANUIES's 1976 data in Rangel Guerra, *Systems*, p. 11, I find that the private sector gets just under 5 percent of its income from the State, but these data include El Colegio de México. Another institution receiving some State aid is the Center of Advanced Technical Education of Baja California. Such tokenism could provide a precedent should the State ever want to move toward meaningful subsidization. Thus far, however, pleas for direct State subsidization have come more from private schools. Private higher education, following the line of its prestigious leaders, did not ask for such aid even in its 1979 self-promotion report to President López Portillo.

23. Daniel C. Levy, "Pugna política sobre quién paga la educación superior en México," *Revista Latinoamericana de Estudios Educativos* 9, no. 2 (1979), pp. 1–38. On financial matters beyond tuition, Levy, *University and Government*, pp. 100–31.

24. State subsidization allegedly redistributes resources not just from the very rich, but also from the poor, to the upper-middle class; see Latapí, *Análisis*, p. 198. Prestigious private schools generally charge much more than public universities (according to Carlos Muñoz Izquierdo, researcher at the Center for Educational Studies, interviewed Mexico City, December 1979). The financial burden for the federal district's two main public universities is shouldered by the federal government, while the state universities rely on a federal-state balance that had shifted toward the former by 1975. SEP, *Las universidades estatales de México* (Mexico City: SEP, 1975), pp. 3–4.

25. For 1971 data, see Osborn, *Higher Education in Mexico*, p. 91. I checked in 1979 at ANUIES's central offices and found that almost all the private institutions that filled out response forms declared no income beyond "own income" (*ingresos propios*). This, however, leaves considerable latitude to count donations as "own income." I base my figures for major universities on their own data and on interviews. I also have checked back to ANUIES's 1971 data. Finally, IMESP, "Educación superior," 1981, p. 61, claims that 95 percent of income for its private institutions comes from students' families.

26. Universidad Iberoamericana, *35 aniversario*, p. 23.

27. La Salle is one of the least expensive of the prestigious private universities. As of 1977, its tuition ranged from $630 to $900 annually; by 1979 medical tuition was over $1,100. Quintero (pp. 67, 76) reports $635 for the also inexpensive University of Monterrey (1977), compared to $25 for Nuevo León's state university, and to $320 for Mexico's most expensive state university (Aguascalientes). José Luis Quintero, "Metas de igualdad y efectos de subsidio de la educación superior mexicana, *Revista del Centro de Estudios Educativos* 8, no. 3 (1978), pp. 67–76. ITESM charged $1,200 as of 1972; UDUAL, *Censo universitario 1972–1973* (Mexico City: UDUAL, 1976) p. 578. Americas charged more than $1,200 in 1979. Moreover, most of these figures are purely *colegiaturas*—tuition without numerous other registration, exam, graduation, and laboratory fees. Also see, IIE "Institutional Report," Anáhuac, IIE Mexico City Office, April 1977, which notes that Anáhuac charged an extra registration fee of $1,500 per semester for U.S. medical students, just as several institutions charged extra for foreigners, especially from outside Latin America. The private sector self-study (IMESP, "Educación superior," 1979, p. xxviii) claims that nearly a third of their students receive some scholarship or loan, a figure that would surely be much lower if the entire sector, and only substantial aid, were included. Procedures and amounts vary from institution to institution. Additionally, a few scholarships are available from private enterprise, as when companies in Puebla help children of employees attend Americas, but such help is rare.

28. Other examples include Ibero's computer, language, mental health, and bookstore activities, and America's alumni, parent, and service organizations. Pensions, wills, lifetime endowments, and insurance policies also help. Additionally, contract research is done for the State as well as for private enterprise, notably involving such prestigious economic institutions as ITAM and its Business Research Center.

29. For example Anáhuac and Americas have beautiful campuses removed from metropolitan areas, the masses, urban buses, and pollution. Yet the religious Ibero and La Salle do not fit

this image, with the latter modestly occupying an urban block. ITAM appears modern, UAG big and impressive; both are isolated from mass urbanization, but neither are outwardly luxurious. And while some state universities are in urban areas, and most are sorely wanting in facilities, the capital's two major public universities are purposely removed (though urban sprawl is engulfing UNAM's main campus) and have impressive campuses. Overall, it is difficult to assess the extent of the private sector's superfluous expenditures, and much depends on subjective views of usefulness versus extravagance (just as it does with, e.g., swimming lessons at private secondary schools).

30. On AID's good-term $2.6 million loan for UAG's campus in the late 1960s, see Luis Garibay, *The Trap and Other Writings* (Houston: University of Houston, 1977), p. 22.

31. Luis Garibay and Vincent Valle, *Financiamiento de la universidad* (Guadalajara: UAG, 1973), p. 54. Also important is the Gilfred Foundation. See IIE, "Institutional Report," Anáhuac, 1977.

32. Granados ventures the following appraisal: The Monterrey group is diversified enough to pick up the slack for ITESM as well as for some other Monterrey institutions. The same might hold for the MSJF in relation to Americas and UAG. Anáhuac could fall back on a wide base of wealthy donors, and Americas, UAG, and others have sustaining ties with U.S. interests. ITAM and Ibero then appear most vulnerable, although their high quality could save them— possibly even invoking an unprecedented rationale for State aid. Miguel Angel Granados Chapa, "Plaza pública," *Uno Más Uno*, September 20, 1982.

33. Basáñez, *Hegemonía*, pp. 91–92. Basáñez identifies the major groupings in Mexican private enterprise (pp. 81–111).

34. Lloyd's *Mexican Economic Report*, April 1980; and Basáñez, *Hegemonía*, pp. 87–88. The corporations deal with items ranging from canned food to plastics, prefabricated housing, and tourism. VISA is Valores Industriales, S.A., or "anonymous society."

35. Osborn, *Higher Education in Mexico*, pp. 94–96. Of course, even in open, multibene-factor cases, a university often depends heavily on a cluster of reliable contributors.

36. Universidad de las Américas, *Informe anual* (Puebla, 1979), p. 171.

37. Garibay and Valle, *Financiamiento*, quotation on p. 153; other information, pp. 50, 95–100. Potential donors are dealt with in such categories as alumni, commerce and industry, foundations and agencies, members of the "university family," and others or "friends." Some donation forms leave space for donors to target contributions to their "special interests." Similarly, UAG targets its donors; for example, to get funds for its engineering school, UAG's chief financial officer identifies the businesses that benefit from the school's graduates, esti-mates what they can afford, hatches strategy with UAG's leadership, and then solicits.

38. More legitimate shifting of resources commonly occurs between profitable and deficit faculties or, as at La Salle, between profitable preparatory schools and otherwise deficit-ridden professional levels.

39. Tensions peaked in 1975 when the governing board appointed as rector an engineer regarded by many professors as a technician bent on authoritarian rule and the relegation of humanities. Professors organized—with the help of union members from Puebla's highly activist state university. But after a strike that lasted for months, the rectorship was strength-ened and professorial power minimized.

40. Granados Chapa, "Plaza pública."

41. UAG, *Estatuto universitario* (Guadalajara: 1972), pp. 4–9; Garibay and Valle, *Finan-ciamiento*, p. 55. On Sauza, see Osborn, *Higher Education in Mexico*, p. 96; Osborn then (pp. 110–11) points out that Mexican tax laws, like U.S. ones, permit deductions for gifts, but also that Mexico lacks death taxes, thus decreasing the incentives for giving.

42. If UAG allows participation (though less in fact than in theory), then there may be parallels to the University of Havana, of all places, as participation is safe alongside selection and socialization that promote consensus. A significant difference is that the Mexican system

has a plurality of diverse universities; even if no individual university were pluralistic, the university system could still be pluralistic.

43. Universidad Iberoamericana, *Estatuto orgánico 1979* (Mexico City, 1979), pp. 8–14; and idem, *35 aniversario*, pp. 11, 16, 30.

44. For example, the Institute of Higher Commercial Studies affiliates with UNAM, the IPN, and SEP. On balance, the State's SEP is probably more lenient in approving new approaches than is the public sector's UNAM, as its bureaucracy is even larger, more remote, and less prepared technically to make detailed evaluations. Affiliation with SEP puts private university legitimacy more on a par with public university status, avoiding the appearance of "tutelage-incorporation" to a public university. Additionally, UNAM (somewhat like the University of Chile) may be vigilant if it is fearful of still accelerating losses of its hegemony. Thus, in 1973 Ibero enthusiastically greeted news that SEP would finally honor its request to change affiliation from UNAM to the ministry; shortly thereafter, Ibero received authorization to start new programs, preparatory education, and regional campuses. Universidad Iberoamericana, *35 aniversario*, pp. 16–17. The status of each private institution is shown in ANUIES, *Instituciones*, pp. xxiii, 1–445.

45. The Echeverría administration (1970–76) claims to have continued a traditional policy of "giving the cold shoulder" to the private sector. This would be consistent with its overall development policy of favoring public over private interests. The succeeding administration of President López Portillo (1976–82) was more supportive of private enterprise in general, and critics claimed to see a more active proprivate university position. But Latapí (*Análisis*, p. 205) points out that even Echeverría helped the private sector with "administrative facilities" and in "important projects."

46. Interview with Jaime Castrejón Díez (the top official dealing with state universities under Echeverría), Mexico City, December 1979. State universities generally copy UNAM's structure, including the pointed declaration of autonomy. They do so partly to imitate the leader, partly because they feel a similar need to declare autonomy from the State, partly to distinguish themselves from the nonautonomous technical subsector. The only significant inversion is found in Guadalajara where the private UAG, not the state university, calls itself autonomous. Ironically, some data processors at ANUIES report that private institutions are more responsive than public ones to State-sanctioned data collection. There are at least three plausible explanations: private institutions are better organized; they have a greater fear of being charged with thwarting the State or public purpose; they do not fear that accurate enrollment figures might negatively affect State funding.

47. The information on public universities is derived from Levy, *University and Government*, passim. For a "levels analysis" putting Mexico's public sector into cross-national perspective, see Daniel C. Levy, "El gobierno de las universidades en México desde una perspectiva internacional," *Foro Internacional* 19, no. 4 (1979), p. 588.

48. Historically weak in the face of UNAM's resistance, ANUIES has been strengthened and SEP's division overseeing state universities has multiplied its staff (interview with Jean-Pierre Vielle, Mexico City, December 1979). Indeed, given the two-decade boom in public enrollments, institutions, and expenditures, it would be surprising if the State did not increase its formal control, partly to offset the perhaps inevitable loss of informal control that accompanies such expansion, but equally surprising would be a switch to fundamental control, undoing autonomy.

49. Analysis in Levy, *University and Government*, pp. 33–34, 38, 100–37.

50. In the late 1970s State officials were talking bravely, but not confidently, about reserving perhaps 8 percent of the higher education budget for policy orientations. More generally, Noel McGinn and Susan Street keenly show how the politics of the public budgetary process is based more on competition among power groups (not only between government and educational institutions but within each) than on any State plan aimed at well-ordered, rational

educational functions. McGinn and Street, *Higher Education Policies in Mexico*, Technical Report Series, no. 29 (Austin: University of Texas, Institute of Latin American Studies, 1980); and idem, "The Political Rationality of Resource Allocation in Mexican Public Education," *Comparative Education Review* 26, no. 2 (1982), pp. 178–98.

51. In Nuevo León, a state where private enterprise is particularly powerful, opposition defeated a 1971 attempt at the main public university to institute a governing board with business representatives, even though mixed with representatives from mass organizations and members of the university community itself. See Levy, *University and Government*, pp. 33–34; pp. 64–85 on appointments generally. On the 1944 "gringo" boards, see Siegrist Clamont, *En defensa*, p. 357; Eugenio Hurtado Márquez has compiled the most important documents and legislative debates relating to the board's creation: *La universidad autónoma 1929–1944* (Mexico City: UNAM, 1976), pp. 85–207.

52. Interview with Pablo González Casanova, former UNAM rector, Mexico City, April 1976.

53. Mexican presidents could more readily count on friendly, peaceful receptions at private than at public universities. A major governance issue not discussed in this chapter concerns faculty power through unionization. Much conflict has occurred over the degree to which public universities should be subject to legislation similar to that applying in the private sector or in other public institutions. See, for example, Manuel Barquín Alvarez, "La regulación de la contratación colectiva en las universidades públicas: Estudio comparativo entre México y los Estados Unidos," *Cuadernos del Centro de Documentación Legislativa Universitaria* 1, no. 2 (1979), pp. 7–50.

54. Figures cited in de Leonardo, *Educación superior*, p. 216, with a similar and double percentage, respectively, for the secondary and primary levels.

55. The phrase of Ernesto Domínguez. The basic document expounding Ibero's "Christian inspiration" is its *Ideario*, p. 5.

56. On the attitude toward public universities, see Olac Fuentes, "Educación pública y sociedad," in Pablo González Casanova and Enrique Florescano, eds., *México hoy* (Mexico City: Siglo XXI, 1979), pp. 246–47; on basic ideology, see Basáñez, *Hegemonía*, p. 108.

57. Universidad Iberoamericana, *35 aniversario*, p. 23.

58. Pablo Latapí, "Las universidades católicas en México," *Proceso*, no. 131 (1979), p. 40.

59. Garibay, *The Trap*, pp. 74, 94.

60. UAG's own Jorge Oria confirmed and defended such restrictiveness in an interview, Guadalajara, December 1979; the most extensive rebuttal I received was from Oscar Soria, in multiple interviews, in Mexico City and Guadalajara, December 1979, as well as in subsequent correspondence. Oria occupied three posts in his brief UAG tenure (1977–81), while Soria has longer and more intimate experience with the institution. UAG's admission forms betray no prejudicial criteria; I can only guess that criteria probably vary according to individuals on the admissions committee and that any student honest or reckless enough to expound dissident beliefs in his application biography may jeopardize his chances. For severe charges about UAG's allegedly fascist activities beyond the campus, see Manuel Buendía, *La ultraderecha en México* (Mexico City: Ediciones Oceano) pp. 159–69.

61. Garibay, *The Trap*, p. 24. In this connection, UAG stresses its attention to Mexican problems. For example, at least since 1972, there have been service programs directed toward the economically marginal population of Guadalajara and rural western Mexico. Thus UAG denies that liberals outdo conservatives in socially useful action. Additionally, it stresses that many programs undertaken with other nations are directed toward Mexico's own priority needs, e.g., agriculture.

62. The United States alone accounts for roughly 80 percent of UAG's foreign medical students; foreigners account for roughly one-fourth of total graduate and undergraduate enrollments. IIE, "Institutional Report" on UAG, IIE Mexico City Office, October 1978. La

Salle also faces trade-offs between verbal charges of dependency and material charges of tuition. Particularly sensitive is the appearance of accepting gringos while rejecting Mexicans.

63. This was illustrated by a television program featuring high officials of some leading private universities. "Las universidades particulares," channel 11, February 18, 1976. Thus, for example, ITAM is concerned with checking the growing U.S. representation on its professoriate.

64. Garibay, *The Trap*, p. 198. Also see chapter 7, footnote 2, below.

65. Latapí, "Las universidades," p. 38.

66. Francisco García Sancho and Leoncio Hernández, *Un diagnóstico de la educación superior y de la investigación científica y tecnológica en México* (Mexico City: SEP, 1977), p. 486, find that the fields where the private sector concentrates offer relatively good employment opportunities.

67. IMESP, "Educación superior," 1979, p. xvi. The self-study draws on only a minority of the institutions, but they constitute roughly two-thirds of the enrollments (see footnote 10 above). Unfortunately, its data come from 1979, mine from 1978, and some categories are a bit different. (Its commerce and finance category does not equal my business and administration category; it aggregates social science, economics, and law and has no separate agricultural category.) Nonetheless, its 27 percent in commercial, financial, social science, law, and economics categories versus my 49 percent for roughly similar categories in the entire sector tends to confirm that the demand-absorbing subsector concentrates there.

68. By 1971 the private sector already held its two-to-one advantage in business and administration (then combined with communications), while the public sector already held its distinctive advantages, especially in engineering. There are also some small 1971–78 private-public inversions in medicine, humanities, and agriculture. Moreover, there are some 1971–78 differences with regard to total distributions by field of study, but none involves more than a few percentage points. One must be wary of declaring trends when (1) the time frame is so short, (2) there could be some variation in how students were listed between close categories (e.g., engineering and architecture), and (3) some normal schools were elevated to higher education status. The 1971 ANUIES catalogue (pp. 59–140), unlike its 1978 counterpart, also listed graduate enrollments. Easily the most salient private-public data emerging from my analysis were the respective 75 versus 6 percent sectoral shares in business and administration; also see footnote 95 below. Graduate distributions would now have to include the decisive CONACYT (National Council of Science and Technology) role portrayed in Thomas Noel Osborn, "Human Resource Development in Mexico," paper presented at the 14th Atlantic Economic Conference, Miami Beach, October 7–10, 1982; for a more sobering view, emphasizing the regime's inability to forge policy, see Miguel Wionczek, "On the Viability of a Policy for Science and Technology in Mexico," *Latin American Research Review* 16, no. 1 (1981), pp. 57–78.

69. See García Sancho and Hernández, *Diagnóstico*, tables, pp. 217–21.

70. Richard A. LaBarge and Thomas Noel Osborn, "The Status of Professional Economics Programs in Mexican Universities," *Inter-American Economic Affairs* 31, no. 1 (1977), pp. 9–24, quotations from pp. 12–13. The IPN and the State University of Nuevo León teach less leftist, less philosophical approaches than those found at UNAM. On the other hand, I point to certain factors that promote intersectoral similarity in course content. These include bureaucratic regulations on curriculum, use of some of the same part-time professors in both sectors, and a concern (especially in the demand-absorbing subsector) less with distinctiveness than with attracting and graduating students.

71. García Sancho and Hernández, *Diagnóstico*, pp. 117–22, 154, 159. Medicine declined from 47 percent (1945–50) to 22 percent (1971–75). At the IPN, commerce and administration grew from 9 to 17 percent in that same span. UNAM's rector wrote of a public trend toward vocational studies, but with unconvincing data; Soberón, "Las universidades mexicanas," pp. 8–9.

72. Of the sector's thirteen new careers introduced in 1979, eight were in engineering, computers, and library technology, three in administration and finance, one in design, and one in sports and recreation. IMESP, "Educación superior," 1979, p. xvii.

73. There are public universities in all but one state. Moreover, while even the public sector concentrates half (51 percent) its enrollments in the federal district, the adjacent state of Mexico, and the states of Jalisco and Nuevo León, the private sector concentrates three-fourths (76 percent) of its (1981) enrollments in these relatively developed regions.

74. Larissa Lomnitz, Leticia Mayer, Martha Rees, "Recruiting Technical Elites: Mexico's Veterinarians," *Human Organization* 42, no. 1 (1983), p. 25.

75. On the State's priorities, see Levy, *University and Government*, pp. 121–22. The State appeared to many to be overtaxed until oil reserves increased (perhaps temporarily) its absorption capacity. García Sancho and Hernández (*Diagnóstico*, p. 486) report that the worst unemployment faces graduates in the humanities, arts, physics, and mathematics (all fields where the public sector is disproportionally strong). On the other hand, administration and social science graduates have much better chances; if true, this finding would be favorable for the private sector. *Graduates* is used loosely here, referring to job seekers who have left the university, with or without a degree.

76. For this paragraph on professionals I am indebted to Larissa Lomnitz and her seminar, An Anthropologist's View of Mexico's University, Yale University, October 8, 1979. Also see the detailed account of veterinary students and professional mobility in Lomnitz, Mayer, and Rees, "Recruiting," pp. 23–29.

77. Roderic A. Camp, *Mexico's Leaders: Their Education and Recruitment* (Tucson: University of Arizona, 1980). Peter Smith's work is *Labyrinths of Power: Political Recruitment in Twentieth Century Mexico* (Princeton: Princeton University Press, 1979). Also see Camp, *The Making of a Government: Political Leaders in Modern Mexico* (Tucson: University of Arizona, 1984).

78. Camp, *Mexico's Leaders*, pp. 63 (quotation) and 11; Camp also writes (p. 52) that UAG graduates do not enter political careers. Smith (*Labyrinths*, pp. 82–87) reaches a basically similar conclusion on the role of university education; his rule number one (p. 247) on "making it" in Mexican politics is: "Go to a university, preferably the UNAM."

79. Camp, *Mexico's Leaders*, p. 199.

80. Larissa Lomnitz, "Conflict and Mediation in a Latin American University," *Journal of Interamerican Studies and World Affairs* 19, no. 3 (1977) pp. 321–29.

81. This helps explain the Free Law School's important link to the State (Camp, *Mexico's Leaders*, pp. 63–64). The school was founded partly by student activists, among whom was future president Emilio Portes Gil.

82. More than 40 percent of Mexico's high-level political officials (1935–76), once taught at a university, most at UNAM; 9 percent were actually deans or rectors. Camp, *Mexico's Leaders*, pp. 9, 169. Naturally, such recruitment also involves professor-professor ties. It is ironic that attempts to hire more full-time professors could hurt universities by limiting recruitment links to the State; this seems to have happened at the Xochimilco branch of the public Autonomous Metropolitan University.

83. Camp, written communications of July 15, 1982, and April 12, 1983, and several conversations, 1984. His data cover the top 225 positions under de la Madrid and comparable positions in previous administrations. For a political elite roughly five times Camp's number, a government study finds a 9 percent private representation under de la Madrid; Ministry of the Presidency, *Diccionario Biográfico* (Mexico City, 1984), p. 854.

84. Smith (Labyrinths, pp. 283–85, 306) writes that técnicos assumed clear supremacy in economic policy under López Portillo and that two-thirds of his upper-level appointees had never held elective office. Basáñez (*Hegemonía,* pp. 48–80) helpfully divides the State apparatus into different parts, identifying which require technical as opposed to political specialists and which consequently draw on universities (e.g., ITAM and Ibero) associated with the

financial elite. Further suggestion of private sector penetration is found in Larissa Lomnitz, "The Latin American University: Breeding Ground of the New State Elites," paper presented at the American Association for the Advancement of Science meeting in Houston, Texas, January 3–6, 1979, p. 8. Latapí ("Las universidades," p. 39) writes that the secular private universities are helping to rationalize the forces of domination.

85. Camp, *Mexico's Leaders*, quotation, p. 159; recruitment data, pp. 72. 64, 152; economics data, p. 73. Similarly, Smith (*Labyrinths*, p. 91) finds that while only 2.5 percent of the upper political elite for the López Mateos 1958–64 administration were economists, the figure jumped to almost 10 percent for the Díaz Ordaz 1964–70 administration and nearly to 20 percent for the Echeverría administration. Complementary data show that the percentage of UNAM titles granted in economics rose from less than 1 percent in 1945–50 to nearly 3 percent in 1971–75 and from zero to over 3 percent in the same span at the IPN. See García Sancho and Hernández, *Diagnóstico*, pp. 117, 122, 154, 159.

86. According to LaBarge and Osborn ("Status," p. 24), ITESM's economic graduates dominate the "highly paid senior ranks of private industry," while UNAM and IPN economics graduates dominate the lower-paid and nonpolicy positions for economists in State jobs. But ITAM, joined by the State University of Nuevo León, "has tended to supply economists for important government posts in the Presidency, the Treasury, the central banks, and a number of other federal and state government organisms."

87. Camp, *Mexico's Leaders*, pp. 111, 203.

88. The U.S. reader can hardly miss the parallel to the situation in which some U.S. congressmen rhetorically defend the (integrated) public schools but send their own children to the capital's (more segregated) private schools.

89. Assessment of Jaime Castrejón Díez, interviewed in Mexico City, December 1979. For an example of how even public partisans acknowledged the trends, see María Esther Ibarra, "El estado arrumba a la universidad pública como generadora de dirigentes," *Proceso*, June 27, 1983, pp. 10–12. According to the head of UNAM's Association of Academic Career Personnel, UNAM is no longer the influential opinion and consulting center for national political elites. A notable "privatization" has occurred, and students and others in the public universities realize that their credentials keep losing ground to private university credentials, not only with private enterprise but also with the State.

90. Osborn (*Higher Education in Mexico*, pp. 56–57) mailed a questionnaire to well-paid Guadalajara businessmen asking them to rank university quality and indicate how much they would pay for the graduates of ten specified universities—four private and six public. ITESM and Ibero ranked at the top followed by UNAM, UAG, and the IPN. The private edge among name institutions logically would have increased in the decade following that study.

91. For example, ITAM opened a top master's program in business administration in 1974 and now boasts extension programs for the working executive in management training, marketing, finance, and other fields.

92. In some cases, degrees not recognized by the State have been accepted by private employers. Among the fairly prestigious institutions not analyzed here that are effectively linked to private employment are the Popular Autonomous University of Puebla and the graduate institution (Alta Dirección de Empresas) tied to the Panamerican University.

93. See Smith on the two elites (*Labyrinths*, pp. 191–216) and on the middle class (p. 197). Smith makes the informed guess that most industrialists attended technical universities such as the IPN and ITESM; again I would expect the balance to have tilted further toward the private sector since the time in which most of Smith's elite were at the universities. See Basáñez (*Hegemonía*, pp. 81–111) on the strong recruitment links between private universities and top financial circles.

94. Osborn, *Higher Education in Mexico*, p. 51. The link between university quality and employment is especially important if one accepts Miguel Wionczek's view that there is a chronic shortage of good personnel for top positions; interview, Mexico City, March 1976.

95. Research has been concentrated at public institutions in the federal district and a few large states, with private inroads at places such as ITESM and Ibero. Public success has rested in large part on placing the research function in fairly insulated institutes within universities. But the private sector now captures roughly one-fourth of Mexico's more than thirty-thousand graduate enrollments (1979), with private-public strengths largely paralleling undergraduate areas of strength; estimates based on ANUIES data and an interview with ANUIES's Jesús Barrón Toledo, Mexico City, December 1979.

96. University of the Americas, *Extracts of Principal Points in the Five-Year Plan, 1977–1982* (Puebla, 1978), p. 5, reports that 25 percent of its graduates go on to graduate school; however, the IIE "Institutional Report on Americas," Mexico City Office, August 1977, finds twice that percentage for the 1976 graduates. The IIE "Institutional Report" on ITAM finds that about 40 percent of its economics majors go on to graduate school. LaBarge and Osborn ("Status," p. 12) write that in economics, ITESM's graduates "are the only ones in Mexico who are sent regularly, through time-established channels of reference, to do post-graduate study in Category One institutions in the United States."

97. With 1973 data, see García Sancho and Hernández, *Diagnóstico*, p. 238; for evidence on average costs by careers, see ibid., p. 242, and Osborn, *Higher Education in Mexico*, pp. 69–81. A major difficulty with expenditure data, however, is that Mexico's institutions frequently have both a university (or licenciatura) level and a preparatory level, not generally separable in the data: preparatory students are less expensive to educate. The effect might be to underestimate the average expenditure on public compared to private university students.

98. Competition among even private universities is limited because they are clustered only in the federal district and Monterrey. Additionally, since private university graduates are well situated in the job market, they are unlikely to return to their alma maters as professors.

99. Osborn, (*Higher Education in Mexico*, p. 79) contrasted a 9:1 private to a 12:1 public ratio and also found a private edge in time commitments; IMESP's (1979) self-study sample ("Educación superior," p. xxiv) found a 40:1 student to FTE ratio, "far below" the public sector ratio; but Rangel Guerra (p. 10) presents ANUIES data for 1976 showing the public sector with a 19 to 11 percent lead in half-time professors, with both sectors holding only 8 percent full-time faculty. Much has to do with employment opportunities beyond the campus; for example, proportionally fewer full-time faculty teach at Americas' federal district campus than at its main Puebla campus.

100. With the Colegio de Bachilleres and other upper-secondary institutions, the State has reduced the preparatory-to-university free pass. Additionally, even within public universities that are largely open, certain faculties, most notably medicine, have quotas and exams while other universities have set annual institutional quotas. At UNAM, quotas on students from outside the federal district were tightened in 1973; they have been widely ignored, but fast-growing state universities have now lifted much of the burden.

101. Ibero can already make such claims in terms of introducing new fields of study, departmentalization, and innovative social service programs. Pablo Latapí, *Mitos y verdades de la educación mexicana 1971–1972* (Mexico City: Centro de Estudios Educativos, 1973), p. 172. Latapí argues that some quality private institutions serve as stimuli for other institutions. Regarding the Americas' claim, not a Harvard or other research university but a Reed or other elite liberal arts college would be a more appropriate U.S. model.

102. Americas bemoans its diminished rejection rate after its internal troubles in the mid-1970s but vows to restore greater exclusiveness. Anáhuac requires a minimum grade-point average at the preparatory level, admissions exams, sometimes an interview, and a general review by its admissions committee. Naturally, however, the private-public gaps in screening and social class diminish if we focus on demand-absorbing institutions and remember that public universities like UNAM also mostly serve the privileged.

103. OAS, *América en cifras 1977* (Washington, D.C.: OAS, 1979), p. 137, shows 26 percent (1977). García Sancho and Hernández, *Diagnóstico*, p. 239, report 23 percent (1975)

for the upper-secondary cycle. Also see de Leonardo, *Educación superior*, pp. 228–32, on elite private ties. Finally, although few private universities have their own preparatory schools on which to draw directly, several have well-established links to such schools.

104. Interview with Pablo Latapí, Mexico, December 1979. Carlos Muñoz Izquierdo (also interviewed in Mexico City, December 1979) reports that, at the lower educational levels, private schools with lower-class constituencies do neither better nor worse than public schools.

105. Jaime Castrejón Díez, *La educación superior en México* (Mexico City: SEP, 1976) p. 41, asserts that by 1976 only six of thirty-four public universities had seriously pursued structural reform away from traditional models. More private universities had achieved such reform or had started out with nontraditional structures. Also see footnote 101 above. The private self-study claims 85 percent attendance and 63 percent "efficiency," and the study's major researcher expresses the sector's confidence in what intersectoral comparisons would show. IMESP "Educación superior," 1979, pp. ix, xxvii; and interview with Oscar Soria, Guadalajara, December 1979; some public sector data that are not directly comparable, however, are found in García Sancho and Hernández, *Diagnóstico*, p. 18.

106. An influential case for the authoritarian view is found in José Luis Reyna and Richard S. Weinert, eds., *Authoritarianism in Mexico* (Philadelphia: Institute for the Study of Human Issues, 1977).

CHAPTER FIVE

1. The 1975 data come from table 1.1. The 1980 data are from MEC-SESU, *Boletim informativo* (Brasília: March 1981), p. 17.

2. Thomas E. Skidmore, "Politics and Economic Policy Making in Authoritarian Brazil, 1937–71," in Alfred Stepan, ed., *Authoritarian Brazil* (New Haven: Yale University Press, 1973), p. 41.

3. Ibid., p. 40.

4. Fernando Henrique Cardoso, "Associated-Dependent Development: Theoretical and Practical Implications," in Stepan, *Authoritarian Brazil*, p. 159. For more on the evolution of the Brazilian State see, for example, Simon Schwartzman, *Bases do autoritarismo brasileiro* (Rio: Editora Campus, 1982).

5. Daniel Levy, "Authoritarianism in Latin America," *Comparative Politics* 14, no. 1 (1981), pp. 45–48.

6. Nelly Aleotti Maia, "Educação superior no Brasil: uma política necessária," in *Estudos e Debates 2* (Brasília: Conselho de Reitores das Universidades Brasileiras, 1979), p. 03.

7. On secondary education, see Ingrid Sarti, "Educação e estado no Brasil: Notas sobre o conceito de política educacional," a IUPERJ working paper, Rio, 1978, p. 63; Anísio Teixeira's observations in "Origin and Philosophy of the Brazilian University," in Joseph Maier and Richard Weatherhead, eds., *The Latin American University* (Albuquerque: University of New Mexico Press, 1979), pp. 81–82.

8. For example, an important 1834 law left primary and secondary education to the provinces rather than to the national government, thereby insuring that few students completed secondary school—thereby insuring little pressure on the higher education system.

9. The University of Rio de Janeiro was shut down after the 1935 Communist coup attempt; although the University of São Paulo had more success, it too suffered under the Estado Novo. See Simon Schwartzman, "Struggling to Be Born: The Scientific Community in Brazil," *Minerva* 16, no. 4 (1978), pp. 547–48.

10. See Luiz Antônio Cunha, *A universidade temporã: O ensino superior da colônia à era de Vargas* (Rio: Civilizaçao Brasileira, 1980); also, interview with Cunha, Rio, September 1980. Among several prominent mainstream works emphasizing the late development of Brazilian higher education, see especially Schwartzman, "Struggling," pp. 545–59; and Antônio Paim, "Por uma universidade no Rio de Janeiro," in Simon Schwartzman, ed., *Universidades e instituções científicas no Rio de Janeiro* (Brasília: Coordenação Editorial, 1982), pp. 17–96. The

sluggishness of Brazilian educational and higher educational development, compared to Brazilian economic development, has also been noted by foreign observers. See, for example, Douglas Hume Graham, "The Growth, Change, and Reform of Higher Education in Brazil: A Review and Commentary on Selected Problems and Issues," in Riordan Roett, ed., *Brazil in the Sixties* (Nashville: Vanderbilt University Press, 1972).

11. My analysis of the creation of Brazil's Catholic universities owes much to the account by Tânia Salém, "Do Centro D. Vital à PUC," a IUPERJ working paper, Rio, 1979. Also see Florestan Fernandes, *Educação e sociedade no Brasil* (São Paulo: Domincus Editora, 1966), pp. 345–539, especially on the campaign against the public school.

12. Lauro de Oliveira Lima, *O impasse na educação* (Petrópolis, Rio de Janeiro: Editora Vozes, 1968), p. 160.

13. See table 1.1, and James Wilkie, ed., *Statistical Abstract of Latin America 1977* (Los Angeles: UCLA Latin American Center Publications, 1977), vol. 18, p. 142.

14. Wilkie, *Abstract 1977*, p. 142; and idem, *Statistical Abstract of Latin America* (Los Angeles: UCLA Latin American Center Publications, 1978), vol. 19, p. 119.

15. Margaret Archer shows the importance of established structural form in her mammoth *Social Origins of Educational Systems* (London: Sage, 1979). Also see Burton R. Clark, *The Higher Education System* (Berkeley: University of California, 1983), pp. 182–237. I make a more detailed historical account of the effects of late public development on subsequent public-private growth in Brazil in Daniel C. Levy, "O estado e o desenvolvimento das universidades na América Latina: Um panorama comparativo (1920–1940)," trans. Lúcia Hippólito in CPDOC (Center for Research and Documentation on Contemporary Brazilian History), Fundação Getúlio Vargas, ed., *A revolução de 1930* (Brasília: Editora Universidade de Brasília, 1982), pp. 471–92.

16. Luiz Antônio Cunha, "A expansão do ensino superior: Causas e conseqüências," *Debate e Crítica* 5 (March 1975), pp. 38–46; and idem, "O 'milagre brasileiro' e a política educacional," *Argumento* 1, no. 2 (1973), pp. 45–56.

17. Darcy Ribeiro, *La universidad latinoamericana* (Montevideo: Universidad de la República, 1968), p. 96. Jerry Haar discusses the access problem and the State's policy responses in *The Politics of Higher Education in Brazil* (New York: Praeger, 1977).

18. Figures from MEC, *O ensino superior no Brasil 1974–1978* (Brasília: MEC, 1979), p. 21. Quotation of Raulino Tramontin and Ronald Braga (p. 38), who prefer to count 398 instead of the conventional 647 private institutions (1980) since many are run by the same owner; Tramontin and Braga, "O ensino particular no Brasil," in Cândido Mendes and Cláudio de Moura Castro, eds., *Qualidade, expansão e financiamento do ensino superior privado* (Brasília: Educam ABM, 1984), especially pp. 25–27.

19. Luiz Alberto Gómez de Souza, "Universidade brasileira: Crescimento para quê en para quem?" *Encontros com a Civilização Brasileira*, no. 13 (July 1979), p. 185.

20. Because of the singular importance of São Paulo state, holding upward of one-fourth of Brazil's enrollments as late as 1970 and a much higher share of prestigious institutions, professors, and research activity, it is worth seeing how the enrollment boom manifested itself there. First, massive growth in the 1960s outstripped even national growth. Second, the growth occurred very disproportionally in the private sector. Thus, the state's enrollments grew from 12,000 in 1950 to 26,000 in 1960, and then to 85,000 by 1968, with 63 percent (1968) in the private sector, a higher percentage than the national one. Between 1966 and 1973, the heart of the boom period, São Paulo's public sector expanded 200 percent, but the private sector expanded 670 percent, and the private share reached 80 percent of total enrollments. Within the state, the most developed regions with the highest cohort enrollments came to have the proportionally largest private sectors. As with the national pattern, the boom resulted in large part from growth in the absolute and proportional size of the public sector at the preuniversity levels, graduating much larger shares of the population than previously. As with the national pattern, higher education growth fell overwhelmingly into private isolated schools—a demand-

absorbing growth that lowered overall quality. And the most striking state-national parallel lay in how private expansion rested on governmental flexibility in approving new private schools. São Paulo's public sector had held and then maintained much higher standards than the average national standards. The state's relative economic prosperity vastly increased the demand for higher education, but policymakers were concerned to safeguard the public sector, thus forcing the demand into the private sector. Data found in José Pastore, *O ensino em São Paulo: Aspectos quantitativos e qualitativos de sua expansão* (São Paulo: Editora Nacional, 1971), pp. 7, 15, 27, 42, 181, 185; and Rubens Murillo Marques, *Aspectos do sistema de ensino do estado de São Paulo* (São Paulo: Secretaria de Economia e Planejamento, Estado de São Paulo, 1976), pp. 29–31.

21. On legitimacy, see Jacques Rocha Velloso and Vera L. Bastos, "Ensino superior e subemprego," in Mendes and Castro, *Qualidade*, p. 131; on pro–private aid, Leôncio Martins Rodrigues, "Ciências sociais, universidade e intelectuais no Brasil," paper presented to FLACSO conference, Intelectuales, Universidad y Sociedad, Santiago, May 17–19, 1982, p. 4.

22. There are striking parallels to the Japanese pattern of sectoral development. In both cases, exploding demand could not be denied but higher education systems had traditionally been very exclusive. Both nations tried to preserve standards in the public sector, permitting lower-quality private sectors to absorb most demand. Consequently, Japan (1980) has roughly 80 percent of its enrollments in the private sector. This pattern twists the conventional public failure hypothesis for private nonprofit growth; private institutions grow in Brazil and Japan (and in Spanish America's subordinate private sector) because clients voluntarily pay to get more than the public sector provides—but "more" now refers to extension of a service, not to a superior service. Gratifying middle-class demands for higher education without allocating adequate financial resources, both the Brazilian and Japanese States soon faced the problem of plummeting academic quality and both eventually inaugurated slowdowns. A 1975 Japanese law declared that (until 1980) the ministry should authorize no further private universities, nor new departments, nor expand enrollments within existing ones (except in special cases). See William K. Cummings, "The Japanese Private University," *Minerva* 11, no. 3 (1973), pp. 348–71; and William K. Cummings, Ikuo Amano, and Kazuyuki Kitamura, eds., *Changes in the Japanese University* (New York: Praeger, 1979). Also see the chapter on Japan in Roger L. Geiger, *Private Sectors in Higher Education* (Ann Arbor: University of Michigan Press, forthcoming). Subsequent Brazil-Japan comparisons rely on the same sources.

23. In Rio state, first-year openings increased throughout the 1970s; but secondary school graduates multiplied faster, so only 20 percent were accommodated in 1979 versus 44 percent in 1973. By the decade's end, the rate of acceptance to Brazilian higher education was lower than in the late 1960s, when frustrated students rioted to force the State into the period of greatest expansion. Rio data in Cláudio de Moura Castro and Sergio Costa Ribeiro, "Desigualdade social e acesso a universidade: Dilemas e tendências," mimeo, 1979, p. 5; data on Brazil in Ronald Braga, "O ensino superior no Brasil: Presente e futuro," in *Estudos e Debates* 2 (Brasília, DF: Conselho de Reitores das Universidades Brasileiras, 1979), p. 14.

24. Tarcísio Della Senta, "Expansão de ensino superior em tempo do retração econômica," in Mendes and Castro, *Qualidade*, p. 157. The author balances all the arguments against expansion with the point that there is no good alternative for youth when the economy cripples job opportunities. The Mendes and Castro book represents the fruits of a major November 1983 conference on the troubled future of private higher education. A summary of legal statements on expansion during 1969–82 is found in Tramontin and Braga, "Ensino particular," pp. 32–38.

25. Indeed a market analysis may be especially pertinent for the FCE's actions. Although subordinate to the MEC, the FCE has generally represented private interests. While quality concerned the MCE, and jobs concerned both, the FCE apparently also acted partly to protect market enclaves (e.g., in medicine) held by existing private institutions. Additionally, the MEC worried about growing State expenditures for the private sector. See Luiz Antônio Cunha,

"Vestibular: A volta do Pêndulo," *Encontros com a Civilização Brasileira*, no. 13 (July 1979), pp. 203–4.

26. On the number of institutions, see Cláudio de Moura Castro, Hélio Barros, and Tereza Cristina Amaral, "The Funding of Brazilian Universities: Formalism, Politics, and Bureaucratic Activism," paper presented to the International Political Science Association meeting, Rio, August 9–14, 1982, pp. 2–3; on first-year data and on enrollments see table 5.1. On the subsectors see MEC-SESU, *Boletim informativo*, p. 17.

27. Reitores das Universidades Católicas, *As universidades católicas no momento atual* (Belo Horizonte: Fundação Mariana Resende Costa, 1979), pp. 17, 43. Brazil differs from Japan by funneling massive private enrollments into new institutions. As a result, even the universities in Brazil's private sector do not rival the size of the Nihon University, for example.

28. Computations made form MEC-SESU, *Boletim*, p. 17; and MEC, *Catálogo geral de instituições de ensino superior* (Brasília: MEC, 1978). Note that I use the term *isolated schools* to include both isolated schools and "federations." Federations are institutions that are petitioning for university status but still lack some requisites or approval. Federations comprise 4 percent of all institutions.

29. Braga, "Ensino superior," pp. 19–26.

30. Antônio Carlos da R. Xavier, Antônio Emílio Marques, and Raulino Tramontin, "Programa de assistência financeira do MEC às instituições de ensino superior não federais," in Mendes and Castro, *Qualidade*, pp. 205–7; that estimate includes state and municipal with private institutions.

31. Interview with Tarcísio Della Senta, deputy director (subsequently director) of SESU, Brasília, November 1979. CAPES gives to only three PUCs: those in Rio, São Paulo, and Rio Grande do Sul. About half of CAPES's scholarship funds go to students studying abroad. Interview with Hélio Barros, deputy director of CAPES, subsequently director (and then MEC head of higher education), Brasília, November 1979. Data from the early 1980s suggests that the private sector received about one-fifth of both CAPES and FINEP efforts; Hélio Barros, "Fontes de financiamento ao ensino privado," in Mendes and Castro, *Qualidade*, p. 247; pp. 241–55 for an overview of finance, including international, for private research and graduate studies.

32. Velloso and Bastos, "Ensino superior," p. 132. Private expansion was so fierce that the sector came to include many students who could barely afford the tuition. With the help of private bankers, the Program of Educational Loans was well received by many private institutions. However, these institutions included low-quality ones, perhaps even some created with no reasonable prospect for self-sufficiency, counting instead on State rescue.

33. Fernandes, *Educação*, p. 386.

34. Data (for 1977) from Reitores, *As universidades*, p. 59; tables provided by Tarcísio Della Senta at MEC. The PUC case is elaborated in Reitores, *As universidades*, pp. 25–36. By the early 1980s, economic crisis and enrollment setbacks made private pleas desperate. On the overwhelming private will, see Simon Schwartzman, "Ensino público e ensino privado," in Mendes and Castro, *Qualidade*, p. 298.

35. Xavier, Marques, and Tramontin, "Programa de assistência," p. 204.

36. This is the argument championed in the U.S. by Boston University's president John Silber, "Paying the Bill for College: The 'Private' Sector and the Public Interest," *Atlantic Monthly* 235 (1975), pp. 33–40.

37. The State role in private sector finance, like its role in that sector's growth, shows parallels to the Japanese case, but Japan has gone further. Concerned over quality and political pressures, the Japanese State broke a tradition of not providing subsidies. After starting with low-interest loans and payment of a share of salaries, it worked around constitutional restrictions with a 1975 "promotion" law authorizing up to 50 percent of operating costs.

38. Fundação Getúlio Vargas, "Relatório geral e prestação de contas exercício de 1977," typescript, Rio, 1978, p. 5.

39. Interview with Alberto de Mello e Souza (researcher at the planning ministry's Institute for Social and Economic Planning, IPEA), Rio, November 1979.

40. Fundação CESGRANRIO, *Roteiro do candidato 80* (Rio: Aggs Indústrias Gráficas, 1979), pp. 36–37. These conversions of cruzeiros to dollars may underestimate tuition by around 20 percent. The Caixa Econômica, linked to the finance ministry, makes loans to help defer payments at private institutions as well as help pay living expenses at public ones.

41. Interviews with Alberto de Mello e Souza, and Cláudio de Moura Castro, director of CAPES, Rio, November 1979; 1982 data from IPEA. For a listing of the patron foundations, see MEC, *Catálogo geral de instituções de ensino superior* (Brasília: MEC, 1978), pp. 19–78.

42. See Henry Hansmann, "The Role of Nonprofit Enterprise," in Susan Rose-Ackerman, ed., *The Economics of Nonprofit Institutions* (New York: Oxford University Press, forthcoming). On cross-subsidization within U.S. institutions, see Estelle James, "Cross Subsidization in Higher Education: Does It Pervert Private Choice and Public Policy?" in Daniel C. Levy, ed., *Private Education* (New York: Oxford University Press, forthcoming). In Brazil, some institutions use State funds aimed at graduate studies and research to subsidize undergraduate studies. The Robin Hood phrase is Cláudio de Moura Castro's (see previous footnote). On the other hand, IUPERJ's academic prestige may help the overall Cândido Mendes complex, which has a much lower average prestige.

43. Written communication from Cláudio de Moura Castro, April 14, 1982. Local and state institutions receive only slightly more federal aid per capita than private ones; Xavier, Marques, and Tramontin, "Programa de assistência," p. 219. Public institutions have generally held total tuitions and fees below $100 per year.

44. See discussions in MEC, *O ensino,* p. 13; and Joel Regueira Teodósio, "Autarquias especiais: Autonomia ou dependência para as universidades?" *Encontros com a Civilização Brasileira* 12 (1979), p. 76.

45. For example, José Carlos Azevedo, "Educação em país rico," *Folha de São Paulo,* June 22, 1980.

46. Fernandes, *Educação,* pp. 137–40; figures from Braga, "O ensino," p. 38. Turning to lower stages of the education pyramid, gymnasium enrollments in the private sector dropped from 65 to 26 percent; at the primary level the figures were 12 and 8 percent.

47. Haar, *Politics,* p. 82 on fee figures and p. 66 on substitution arrangements. The cursinho boost may have been more apparent than real since students came from groups that did well in university admissions. In any case, in Rio state (1975), students from cursinhos had a 30 percent better chance at admissions, but the State's retightened admissions policies then diminished the cursinho margin, at least in Rio and São Paulo states. Interview with Sergio Costa Ribeiro, researcher at the CESGRANRIO, Rio, November 1979.

48. Alistair Hennessy, "Las raíces del radicalismo en los movimientos estudiantiles en los últimos años," in CPU, ed., *Estudiantes y política* (Santiago: CPU, 1970), p. 47.

49. On the USP 95 percent see, Antônio da Silva, "Brasil: El movimiento estudiantil entre 1970 y 1977," *OCLAE,* no. 4 (1979), pp. 5–10; on the 95 percent in 1979 see "Conselho estudantil reunido na PUC," *O Globo,* November 13, 1979.

50. Reitores, *As universidades,* p. 32; João Batista Araujo e Oliveira and Simon Schwartzman, "Relações centro-periferia: O caso da autonomia universitaria," mimeo, p. 9 (subsequently published in *Estudos e Debates,* no. 3, 1980); Schwartzman, "Ensino," p. 299. Some public universities do draw income from contract research for both the State and private enterprise.

51. It is difficult to estimate how much the private sector has saved especially given the state and municipal roles (partly dependent on federal funds) and the diversity of even federal sources. Despite private sector size, Brazil is second in public enrollments in Latin America; expenditures concentrate in the public university subsector. Although higher education's share of federal expenditures held steady, after an initial post-coup spurt, its share of the education budget increased. MEC data on higher education's share of the federal budget are 2.9 percent

for 1964 and 3.6 for 1965; at least until 1976 the high would be 4.3 (1975) and the low 2.7 (1973 and 1974). On higher education's share of education revenues, see Alberto de Mello e Souza, *Financiamento da educação e acesso à escola no Brasil* (Rio: IPEA, 1979), p. 63. MEC's 1960 budget allocated roughly 50 percent to higher education, 40 percent to other levels; 1970 figures were 60 and 25 percent. (Balances to 100 percent are accounted for by other educational and cultural expenditures.) Xavier, Marques, and Tramontin, "Programa de assistência," p. 205, show a drop from 52 to 29 percent for 1976–82 from MEC and other ministries. Finally, note that encouragement of private secondary education also relieves financial pressure on the State, a policy traceable back at least to the Estado Novo. Brazil's education national budget ratio was the lowest in Latin America (1970), according to Wilkie, *Abstract*, 1978, p. 239.

52. This section (on governance) deals mostly, although not exclusively, with universities. See Oliveira and Schwartzman, "Relações," on Brazilian centralism. For more on the debate over centralism versus autonomy see Conselho de Reitores das Universidades Brasileiras, ed., *Autonomia da universidade brasileira: Vicissitudes e perspectivas* (Brasília, 1980). For the best case study of the gap between formal bureaucratic authority and real academic power see Burton R. Clark, *Academic Power in Italy* (Chicago: University of Chicago Press, 1977).

53. José Carlos Azevedo, "A universidade não forma mão-de-obra," *Jornal do Brasil*, June 1, 1980.

54. The federal government dominates in the public university sector, with 30 of 37 institutions; but it runs only 2 percent of the isolated schools compared to 22 percent for states and municipalities (1975). Nonetheless, the federal role in higher education is far greater than at the secondary or primary levels. In 1974, 4 percent of secondary enrollments were federal, compared to 86 percent for the state and municipal sectors. Data on 1973 enrollments calculated from IBGE, *Sinopse estatística do Brasil 1975*, English edition (Rio: IBGE, 1975), pp. 326–27. Other data calculated from IBGE, *Anuário estatístico do Brasil 1977* (Rio: IBGE, 1978), pp. 237, 241, 244.

55. Written communication from Cláudio de Moura Castro, April 14, 1982. On São Paulo, see José Antônio Tobias, "A liderança do ensino superior paulista," *Revista Brasileira de Filosofia* 22, no. 85, (1972), pp. 55–69. USP is the most important state institution.

56. Philippe Schmitter, *Interest Conflict and Political Change in Brazil* (Stanford: Stanford University Press, 1971), p. 206.

57. Ibid., p. 207.

58. Peter Flynn, *Brazil: A Political Analysis* (London: Ernest Benn, 1978), p. 401.

59. "Conselho," *O Globo*, November 13, 1979.

60. "Manifestaciones estudiantiles," *OCLAE*, no. 4 (1979), p. 27, on the 1970s protests. On the Catholic student organization, see Emanuel de Kadt, *Catholic Radicals in Brazil* (London: Oxford University Press, 1970), pp. 60–72.

61. Simon Schwartzman, "Por una nova agenda," in *Estudos e Debates* 2 (Brasília: Conselho de Reitores das Universidades Brasileiras. 1979), p. 71; Nivaldo Rodrigues de Albuquerque, "A evolução de universidade brasileira: Análise crítica e tentativa de estabelecimento de um modelo estrutural para as universidades federais," master's thesis, School of Public Administration, Fundação Getúlio Vargas, 1974, pp. 98–118; Braga, "Ensino superior," p. 27. Schwartzman, a researcher at IUPERJ, provided many insights into issues of autonomy and decentralization; interviews in Rio, December 1978 and September 1980.

62. On the broad private-public distinction, see Conselho de Reitores das Universidades Brasileiras, "Política de ensino superior para uma estrategia de mudança," *Educação Brasileira* 1, no. 3 (1979), pp. 22–25; Braga, "Ensino superior," p. 24.

63. This paragraph was based on Castro, Barros, and Amaral, "Funding," pp. 4–5, passim.

64. From the MEC minister to rectors, officials expressed their opposition to direct elections. Within the private sector, PUC–São Paulo had already instituted a considerable electoral role (though still sanctioned by the pope), but other PUCs and the relatively hierarchical Mackenzie University joined public university administrators (e.g., at USP) in resisting

change. See "Manobras políticas também decidem poder," "Igrejas podem ter influência sobre o processo sucessório," and other articles on higher education in *Folha de São Paulo*, October 28, 1984.

65. Interview with Leôncio Martins Rodrigues, USP research scholar, Santiago, May 1982. When something similar surfaced in Chilean universities, the regime purged repeatedly and more deeply than in Brazil.

66. Darcy Ribeiro, "Universities and Social Development," in Seymour Martin Lipset and Aldo Solari, eds., *Elites in Latin America* (London: Oxford University Press, 1976), p. 363.

67. Street reports that the 1977 meeting of the Brazilian Society for Scientific Progress had trouble finding a meeting site since President Figueiredo objected to mounting public criticism and unrest. The society tried to convene at USP on short notice but was denied; then, however, PUC–São Paulo invited and hosted the society—which was indeed critical of official policies. James H. Street, "Political Intervention and Science in Latin America," *Bulletin of the Atomic Scientists* 37, no. 2 (1981), p. 18.

68. Haar, *Politics*, pp. 90–2, 122, 157–58, 177. The CESGANRIO and other organizations administering the admission process are private foundations, charging for their services and reaping profits.

69. Cunha, "Vestibular," p. 204.

70. Again, Brazil and Japan share an experience stemming from massive private growth. Until the 1970s the Japanese State rarely refused to grant a charter and infrequently enforced quality standards, but then began to assert far more power over chartering and supervising private institutions, e.g., insisting that fewer be founded in urban areas.

71. Daniel C. Levy, "Universities and Governments," *Comparative Politics* 12, no. 1 (1979), p. 113.

72. Interview with João Batista Araujo de Oliveira, Rio, November 1979, then a program director at FINEP, now assistant to the minister of debureaucratization.

73. Pedro Lincoln Carneiro Leão de Matos, "Políticas do governo federal na expansão de ensino superior no Brasil," master's thesis, School of Public Administration, Fundaçao Getúlio Vargas, pp. 26–29; and interview with Matos, Rio, December 1978.

74. See Cláudio de Moura Castro, "The Impact of European and American Influences on Brazilian Higher Education," *European Journal of Education* 18, no. 4 (1983), pp. 367, 380–81. Castro notes a swing to certain European influences in very recent years, however.

75. Levy, "Authoritarianism," passim.

76. See Rodrigues, "Ciências sociais," pp. 1, 14–19, 24–28. Paradoxically, higher education's most extraordinary growth occurred when the hard-liners controlled the regime; moderates had previously been more restrained, and subsequently the regime's enforced slowdown coincided with abertura. Even in its more severe stage, Brazilian authoritarianism probably did more to repress academic freedom than to crush institutional autonomy.

77. The State role has been handled partly through special agencies within MEC and partly through new agencies outside MEC. Separate institutes have been formed to escape not only regime repression but also ingrained bureaucratization.

78. Tramontin and Braga, "Ensino particular," p. 28.

79. Lima, *Impasse*, pp. 158–59. On Church liberalization in Brazil see Thomas Bruneau, *The Political Transformation of the Brazilian Catholic Church* (London: Cambridge University Press, 1974).

80. Salém, "Centro," pp. 62–63.

81. PUC-Rio, *Catálogo geral 1980* (Rio: PUC-Rio, 1980), pp. xii–xv. The most prominent religious, non-Catholic university, Mackenzie, has been subject to a presence by the Brazilian Presbyterian Church.

82. Salém, "Centro," p. 62; see parallels in Christopher Jencks and David Riesman, *The Academic Revolution* (Garden City, N.Y.: Doubleday, 1968).

83. Here again is a parallel to Japan, where private expansion "was overwhelmingly in

directions which were contrary to official policy" and with most new faculties in fields offering "no demand for more graduates." Cummings, "Japanese," p. 362. Certainly the Brazilian State took this view of imbalanced field distributions, even before the coup; interview with ex–MEC minister Raimundo Moniz de Aragão, Rio, December 1978.

84. Matos, "Políticas," p. 52.

85. Simon Schwartzman, *Formação da comunidade científica no Brasil* (Rio: FINEP, 1979), p. 295. Schwartzman shows 1973 MEC data that basically parallel our 1980 data. Based on his text (p. 294), I calculate the private sector enrollment shares at 63 percent for mathematics versus only 34 percent for natural sciences; he shows 43 percent for engineering. Furthermore, the Schwartzman data allow a break between "applied" (e.g., administration) and "academic" (e.g., anthropology) social sciences and show respective private shares of 72 and 53 percent. The private share of total enrollments was 60 percent. The continuity of basic private-public patterns is further suggested by 1960 data (Fernandes, *Educação,* p. 142) showing that the private sector concentrated in administration, economics, law, religious studies, philosophy, and letters.

86. Data from São Paulo confirm that basic patterns held there. Although the private sector (1968) had more than three-fifths of total enrollments and a nearly three-to-one lead in economics, it trailed badly in expensive fields such as medicine and engineering. Pastore, *Ensino em São Paulo,* pp. 36–38.

87. Based on table 5.3 and regarding the human sciences, letters, and arts as unfavorable, while leaving aside the basic cycle. A very similar pattern holds with 1974 data from IBGE, *Anuário estatístico do Brasil 1977,* p. 643, which allow for analysis within the public sector. Among more desirable, less desirable, and mixed-unknown categories, federal institutions lead at 50-35-15, with state institutions trailing at 40-50-10, and 22-53-25 for municipal institutions; the municipal profile resembles the private profile and suggests the demand-absorbing nature of the municipal subsector. Data on courses offered in 1980 complement enrollment data by showing the private sector leading most in human sciences and letters and trailing most in health, exact sciences, technologies, and especially agricultural sciences. Tramontin and Braga, "Ensino particular," p. 41.

88. Cunha, "A expansão," p. 34.

89. Castro, Barros, and Amaral, "Funding," p. 9.

90. Based on figures in Reitores, *As universidades,* pp. 17, 28. Since Catholic institutions comprise 24 percent of the university sector and 16 percent of the higher education system, and the university sector comprises slightly under one-half of total enrollments (Braga, "Ensino superior," p. 23), Catholic institutions comprise less than 10 percent of the isolated school sector.

91. While 67 percent of private graduate students are in the humanities and social sciences, 64 percent of their public counterparts are in the hard sciences and engineering. Data for 1978 from MEC, *Situação atual da pósgraduação Brasil, 78* (Brasília: MEC-DAU-CAPES, 1979), p. 29.

92. Data (for 1978) by region from MEC, *O ensino,* pp. 22–23; data by states (for 1980) from *Anuário estatístico do Brasil 1980* (Rio: IGBE, 1981), pp. 222–24.

93. Braga, "Ensino superior," p. 20. A good example of the importance of quality over private-public labeling concerns the Getúlio Vargas's Brazilian School of Public Administration. Graduates have been attractive not only to public administration but to private enterprises as well because the training is among Brazil's best, at least outside São Paulo. Also, the nation's extensive State regulation of private enterprise makes it worthwhile for those enterprises to understand public administration.

94. Robert O. Myrh, "Brazil," in Donald K. Emmerson, ed., *Students and Politics in Developing Nations* (London: Pall Mall Press, 1968), p. 280.

95. Alfred Stepan, *The Military in Politics: Changing Patterns in Brazil* (Princeton: Princeton University Press, 1971).

96. On São Paulo, see Schwartzman, *Bases*, pp. 102–3.

97. Fernando Spagnolo, "Adaptação do ensino superior a novos perfis de aluno e ao mercado de trabalho," pp. 120–21; and Velloso and Bastos, "Ensino superior," pp. 143–44; both in Mendes and Castro, *Qualidade*.

98. This is the Japanese pattern. Expenditures per pupil are far lower in the private than public sector. The best-prepared students, and professors (mostly graduates of the elite public universities), wind up in the public sector. There is quality overlap (e.g., Keio and Waseda are two prestigious private universities), but the pinnacle belongs to the public leaders, such as Tokyo and Kyoto, and most public institutions are superior to most private ones.

99. Braga, "Ensino superior," p. 20. Also on the low quality of private isolated schools: Elza Lúcia Denipoti and Ernesto Guilherme Ahrens, *A qualidade e os custos de ensino nas instituições de ensino superior isoladas particulares dos distritos geoeducacionais 30 e 38* (Rio: Fundação Getúlio Vargas, 1979).

100. Nearly 80 percent of graduate enrollments are in the public sector (1981); Tramontin and Braga, "Ensino particular," p. 45. Furthermore, data on course offerings show private-public gaps even among universities alone and isolated schools alone. See MEC, *Situação*, pp. 29–34.

101. Based on numerous interviews (in December 1978, November 1979, and September 1980) with independent observers and State officials, several of whom are cited above, in Rio and Brasília. The three-to-one difference is based on a 1975 survey of ten private and ten public universities done for the Council of Rectors (Braga, "Ensino superior," p. 21).

102. For data, see Matos, "Políticas," table 11. Other factors could include the inferior academic preparation of incoming private students.

103. On the overall private decline see, e.g., Velloso and Bastos, "Ensino superior," p. 132; on the 1982 ratios, Tramontin and Braga, "Ensino particular," p. 40; and for 1965 ratios, *América en cifras 1974* (Washington, D.C.: OAS, 1975), pp. 146, 150. Matos's table 11 provides the data on full-time professors and on graduate degrees.

104. Tramontin and Braga, "Ensino particular," p. 29; for earlier, parallel, data: Cláudio de Moura Castro and Sergio Costa Ribeiro, "As mudanças na clientela da universidade," mimeo, 1978; the authors pursued the relationship between SES and university access in "Desigualdade." For São Paulo alone, see Aparecida July Gouveia, "Origem étnica e situação socio-econômica dos estudantes matriculados em diferentes áreas de estudo nas universidades de São Paulo," *América Latina* (Rio) 13, no. 4 (1970), pp. 33–50.

105. Quotation from Schwartzman, "Struggling," p. 567; ratios from IBGE, *Anuário estatístico do Brasil 1980*, p. 212. Castro, "Impact," p. 369, supports the consensus view that quality plummeted as expansion opened doors for ill-prepared students; he writes that these were not primarily working-class youth but "the less clever brothers of middle class families."

106. Schwartzman, "Struggling," p. 559. Tobias ("Liderança." pp 55–56, 62) offers a dissenting view on USP quality, arguing that São Paulo state's educational leadership has been in "crisis"; he challenges the USP "myth."

107. Castro and Ribeiro, "As mudanças," passim.

CHAPTER SIX

1. Pablo Latapí cites UDUAL figures showing that one in four private universities receives some State support, but these figures are drawn from a restricted and unrepresentative sample of higher education. See Latapí, "Algunas tendencias de las universidades latinoamericanas," in UDUAL, ed., *Seminario sobre nuevas tendencias y responsibilidades para las universidades en latinoamérica* (Mexico City, UDUAL, 1978), p. 600.

2. On Argentina 1978, data from the MCE. Also see Harold R. W. Benjamin, *Higher Education in the American Republics* (New York: McGraw-Hill, 1965), p. 56. On Venezuela, OPSU, *Oportunidades de estudio* (Caracas: CNU, 1978), pp. 24–36; private costs were pushing

towards $2,000/U.S. by the late 1970s. On various public sectors, Nicolás Flaño C., "Formas típicas de la relación entre la universidad y algunas variables económicas," in CPU, ed., *La universidad latinoamericana* (Santiago: CPU, 1972), pp. 93–95.

3. Augusto Serrano, "Situación probable y deseada de las relaciones entre universidad y ayuda externa para la década del 80: El caso centroamericano," in Luis Scherz García, ed., *La universidad latinoamericana en la década del 80* (Santiago: CPU, 1976), p. 140.

4. Jaime Castrejón Díez, "Siete países de América Latina y el Caribe," in Manuel Barquín, ed., *Planeación y regulación en la educación superior* (Mexico City: UNAM, 1981), p. 41.

5. Jaime Rodríguez F., "Universidad y sistema científico-tecnológico en Colombia," in CPU, ed., *Universidad e integración andina* (Santiago: CPU, 1974), p. 142.

6. For data on ICETEX's mixed record, see Clemente Forero, Eduardo Mantilla, and Santiago Perry, "Las finanzas universitarias en Colombia," in Carmenza Huyo de Aldana et al., *Universidad oficial o universidad privada* (Bogotá: Ediciones Tercer Mundo, 1978), p. 163. Also see Gerardo Molina "Universidad estatal y universidad privada," in Huyo de Aldana, *Universidad oficial,* p. 46; on the business role in ICETEX, see Robert H. Dix, *Colombia: The Political Dimensions of Change* (New Haven: Yale University Press, 1967), p. 355. Costa Rica is another nation to consider, since public students can reportedly pay up to $1,600 per year, but most students get at least partial exemptions or loans. Therefore, despite the tuition initiative, only 8 percent of Costa Rican higher education is financed by tuition, another 8 percent by services and donations, with 83 percent still handled by the State (1 percent from minor sources). These 1977 data probably refer only to the public sector. Edgardo Boeninger Kausel, "Alternative Policies for Financing Higher Education," in IDB, ed., *The Financing of Education in Latin America* (Washington, D.C.: IDB, 1980), p. 345 (1977 data). Guatemala's public university may draw 80 percent of its income from the State, 15 percent from tuition, and 5 percent from other services. Universidad de San Carlos, *Catálogo de estudios 1980* (Guatemala: Editorial Universitaria, 1981), p. 35.

7. Luis Alberto Sánchez, *La universidad actual y la rebelión juvenil* (Buenos Aires: Editorial Losada, 1970), p. 71.

8. Rolland G. Paulston, "Education," in Carmelo Mesa-Lago, ed., *Revolutionary Change in Cuba* (Pittsburgh: University of Pittsburgh Press, 1974), p. 391; and Luis Boza D., *La situación universitaria en Cuba* (Santiago, Chile: Editorial de Pacífico, n.d.), p. 153.

9. A lesser financial backlash occurred in Peru. Robert Drysdale and Robert Meyers, "Continuity and Change," in Abraham Lowenthal, ed., *The Peruvian Experiment* (Princeton: Princeton University Press, 1975), pp. 291–92. On the fixed ratios, see Benjamin, *Higher Education,* pp. 118–19; Jorge Mario García Laguardia, *La autonomía universitaria en América Latina* (Mexico City: UNAM, 1977), p. 69, passim; Leonardo Posada, "Colombia: La crisis financiera de la universidad," *OCLAE* (Havana) 13, no. 3 (1979), pp. 37–41.

10. Colombia might also fit. Alfonso Borrero Cabal, executive director of the Colombian Association of Universities and ex-rector of the Javeriana reports that there have been no major subsidies, at least since the late 1960s (written communication, September 20, 1983). Instead, there are only marginal aid programs (e.g., from individual legislators, but with strings attached that repel good institutions) and minor contract services. Private sector requests for soft loans (for both sectors) have been spurned. Legislation (1980) directs that at least half the State aid to the private sector go for loans to needy students (administered through ICETEX, a State agency) and that the rest go for capital expenditures. ICFES, *Reforma de la educación post-secundaria: Compilación legislativa,* 2d ed. (Bogotá: ICFES, 1982), p. 33. Data from the ICFES planning division suggest that in the 1960s, the private sector trailed the public sector by more than ten to one in State aid per capita.

11. On Ecuador, UDUAL, *Censo universitario latinoamericano 1962–1965* (Mexico City: UDUAL, 1967), p. 380. Gladys Pozo de Ruiz and Ernesto Schiefelbein report that the private sector draws a majority of its funds from the State, in "Los problemas de la expansión acelerada: El caso del desarrollo del sistema educacional del Ecuador," *Estudios Sociales* 26,

no. 4 (1980), p. 151. On Peru, Hugo Pacheco, "Universidad, sistema educacional y demanda de profesionales en el Perú," in Scherz García, *Universidad*, pp. 74–75; and telephone conversation with John P. Harrison, December 1981. Nicaragua's Sandinista regime apparently subsidizes the private sector, to diminish tuition.

12. Octavio Derisi, *Naturaleza y vida de la universidad* (Buenos Aires: EUDEBA, 1969), pp. 169–70.

13. Interview with Salvador Romero of the Center for Educational Research, formerly vice-president of the Catholic university and a subsecretary in the education ministry, Santiago, January 1982. I thank Romero for much of the information on Bolivia found in this chapter. Also, see Boeninger Kausel, "Alternative Policies," p. 351. The Dominican Republic and some Central American nations provide further examples of State financial support for private alternatives to public universities.

14. CRUP, *20 años de universidades privadas en la República Argentina* (Buenos Aires: Editorial de Belgrano, 1978), p. 131. An example of U.S. assistance was the construction of Ecuador's Catholic university campus in Guayaquil, based on a "substantial donation" from Boston's archbishop, Cardinal Richard Cushing. Jacques M. P. Wilson, *The Development of Education in Ecuador* (Coral Gables: University of Miami Press, 1970), p. 92.

15. Many prefer to maintain distance from State control and distinctiveness from the public sector. But crises affecting both domestic and international donors could change attitudes.

16. On Central America, see Román Mayorga Quirós, *Las fases del desarrollo de la universidad no estatal en centroamérica*, 2d ed. (Guatemala: FUPAC, 1979), p. 14. On Peru (1981 data), Estuardo Marrou, "La universidad privada en Perú," paper presented at the CPU-CEPAL conference "Universidades Privadas: Antecendentes y Experiencias Latinoamericanas," Santiago, January 18–20, 1983, p. 23; also see Enrique Bernales B. on Peruvian business and the private university, "Universidad y sistemas sociopolíticos," in CPU, *La universidad*, p. 148.

17. CRUP, *20 años*, p. 175.

18. International actors including UNESCO, the IDB, and other organizations, as well as U.S. private and governmental agencies, became heavily involved by the early 1960s. As Pelczar reports: "The theme of the period became the 'modernization' of the university, and this usually meant 'modeling' the North American University." Sadly for the donors, the results were meager and student protests eventually provoked a rerouting of aid toward the private sector. Richard S. Pelczar, "University Reform in Latin America," in Philip G. Altbach, ed., *University Reform* (Cambridge, Mass.: Schenkman Publishing Co., 1974) pp. 57–60, quotation from p. 58. On the rerouting, Rodríguez, "Universidad y sistema," p. 142.

19. By 1983 the profit-nonprofit issue was critical to a strong public sector challenge to UACA's very legitimacy. See Daniel C. Levy, "Where Profit Comes Before Education," *London Times Higher Education Supplement*, July 8, 1983.

20. Interview with Estuardo Marrou, Rector of Peru's Pacific University, Santiago, January 1982.

21. Private tuition depends on variable scholarships and loans and on field of study as well as institution.

22. Christopher Jencks and David Riesman, *The Academic Revolution* (Garden City, N.Y.: Doubleday, 1968), p. 390.

23. On Venezuela, see OPSU, *Oportunidades*, pp. 24–59. On Colombia, Boeninger, Kausel, "Alternative Policies," p. 348; La Salle is on the Javeriana scale. Lebot (p. 53) reports that Colombia's private sector tuition varies from near public sector scales to near U.S. scales. Ibón Lebot, "El movimiento estudiantil durante el frente nacional (1958–1974)," *Ideología y Sociedad*, no. 19 (1975), pp. 49–70. In Costa Rica's UACA tuitions vary by college, with only a nominal tuition paid to UACA's central administration. For both Costa Rica and Argentina, I rely on interviews with top officials at the private universities in question. The Belgrano charged up to roughly $1,000/U.S. in 1978.

24. Boeninger Kausel, "Alternative Policies," p. 348. The differences would appear still greater if comprehensive data were available for costs other than annual running costs. For example, while Argentina's Belgrano University meets almost all its running costs with tuition, it is probably that nation's most successful private university in raising revenue from its services.

25. To conserve space, I will forego an analysis of possible alternative scenarios and simply sketch a few basic points here. First, the prospects for private donation to the public sector remain dim amid elite perceptions of public failure; tuition is a more likely private source but State efforts have been dashed in many nations (e.g., Peru 1969) by student opposition based both on equity and self-interest. One hears less talk but sees a little more action concerning public funding of private institutions; the debate continues along the lines explored in Brazil and pursued in the subsectoral analysis for Latin America as a whole. The State's role in financing private schools is variable—negligible in some nations and significant in others. Generally, the State finances the private sector's primary more than secondary schools. It would be fruitful to use a Catholic-elite-demand-absorbing distinction, probably showing great overlap between the first and third categories. See Carlos Muñoz Izquierdo and Alberto Hernández Medina, "Financiamiento de la educación privada en América Latina," in Mario Brodersohn and María Ester Sanjurjo, eds., *Financiamiento de la educación en América Latina* (Mexico City: IDB, 1978), pp. 255–339.

26. Hanns-Albert Steger, "The European Background," in Joseph Maier and Richard W. Weatherhead, eds., *The Latin American University* (Albuquerque: University of New Mexico Press, 1979), p. 114.

27. The best single source is García Laguardia, *La autonomía*, pp. 49–123.

28. León Cortíñas Peláez, "Autonomy and Student Co-government in the University of Uruguay," *Comparative Education Review* 7, no. 2 (1963), p. 166.

29. Russell G. Davis, "Prototypes and Stereotypes in Latin American Universities," *Comparative Education Review* 9, no. 3 (1965), p. 280.

30. On the compatibility of public university autonomy and State funding in Venezuela, see Orlando Albornoz, "Higher Education and the Politics of Development in Venezuela," *Journal of Interamerican Studies and World Affairs* 18, no. 4 (1976), p. 305. An obvious limit on the State's financial control is its inability to impose tuition. My findings for Mexico and Brazil are confirmed for those two nations and paralleled for Venezuela and beyond in William Adrian, "The Tuition Dilemma," mimeo, May 1982.

31. On these extreme cases, see Castrejón Díez, "Siete países," pp. 35–47; García Laguardia, *La autonomía*, pp. 59-61; specifically on Bolivia, "Bolivia: Restaurada autonomía," *El Mercurio* (Santiago), May 22, 1982; on Ecuador, Gladys Pozo de Ruiz and Ernesto Schiefelbein, "Autonomía universitaria, gobierno y mercado," *Estudios Sociales* 27, no. 1 (1981), pp. 110–11; Jaime Peña, "Universidad y sistema educacional," in Scherz García, *Universidad*, p. 107; on Colombia, see Augusto Franco Arbeláez and Carlos Tünnermann Bernheim, *La educación superior de Colombia 1978* (Bogotá: Tercer Mundo, 1978), pp. 295, 351–53; and ICFES, *Reforma*, pp. 45–47; Pelczar, "University Reform," pp. 45, 49–52.

32. John P. Harrison *The University versus National Development in Spanish America* (Austin, Tex.: Institute of Latin American Studies, n.d.), p. 15; and Robert F. Arnove, "Students in Politics," in John D. Martz and David J. Myers, eds., *Venezuela: The Democratic Experience* (New York: Praeger, 1977), pp. 205–6. Also see John P. Harrison, "The Latin American University: Present Problems Viewed through the Recent Past," in Stephen D. Kertesz, ed., *The Task of Universities in a Changing World* (Notre Dame: University of Notre Dame Press, 1971), pp. 421–23.

33. See García Laguardia, La autonomía, pp. 49–123, for various examples of leadership change associated with the changing status of autonomy. On Bolivia, see Huáscar Taborga, "La universidad boliviana conflictiva," *Aportes* (Paris), no. 19 (1971), p. 132. Additionally, repeated examples can be found in Argentina: Tulio Halperín Donghi, *Historia de la Universidad de Buenos Aires* (Buenos Aires: EUDEBA, 1962).

34. Aldo Solari, "Universidad en transición en una sociedad estancada: El caso de Uruguay," *Aportes* (Paris), no. 2 (1966), p. 28; also see Cortíñas Peláez, "Autonomy and Student Co-government," pp. 167–69.

35. Franklin Parker, *The Central American Republics* (London: Oxford University Press, 1964), p. 312.

36. Raúl Castro quoted in Boza, *Situación*, p. 37; Fidel Castro quoted in *Fidel in Chile* (New York: International Publishers, 1972), p. 123. On lingering State-university tensions, Carmelo Mesa-Lago, *Cuba in the 1970s: Pragmatism and Institutionalization* (Albuquerque: University of New Mexico Press, 1974), pp. 92–101. On the governing boards and related issues, Hugh Thomas, *Cuba: The Pursuit of Freedom* (New York: Harper and Row, 1971), pp. 698, 810, 1286–87, 1428–35. On the student takeover, Jaime Suchlicki, "Cuba," in Donald Emmerson ed., *Students and Politics in Developing Nations* (New York: Praeger, 1968), p. 331.

37. See Daniel C. Levy, "Comparing Authoritarian Regimes in Latin America," *Comparative Politics*, 14, no. 1 (1981), 31–52. Specifically on Uruguay, Oscar Maggiolo et al., "Situación de la universidad uruguaya bajo de la actual intervención," *Pensamiento Universitario* (Mexico City) no. 35 (1980), pp. 4–10. Specifically on Peru, Drysdale and Myers, "Continuity," pp. 254–301.

38. Davis, "Prototypes," p. 280. For an excellent summary of the major governing bodies, see Harrison, "Latin American University," especially pp. 415–16.

39. Robert J. Havinghurst, "Latin American and North American Higher Education," *Comparative Education Review* 4, no. 3 (1961), p. 178.

40. For a review essay, see John H. Peterson, "Recent Research on Latin American Students," *Latin American Research Review* 5, no. 1 (1970), pp. 37–56; for a more recent analysis, Daniel C. Levy, "Student Politics in Contemporary Latin America," *Canadian Journal of Political Science* 14, no. 2 (1981), pp. 353–76.

41. Under Presidents Betancourt and Leoni (1958–68) fifteen laws were promulgated versus twenty-three during the first three Caldera years (1968–71); Arnove, "Students in Politics," p. 205.

42. Lebot, "Movimiento estudiantil," pp. 52–53; García Laguardia, *La autonomía*, p. 52; Luis Carlos Sáchica, "Problemas jurídicos de la autonomía universitaria en Colombia," *Cuadernos del Centro de Documentación Legislativa Universitaria* 2, no. 1 (1979), pp. 119–21. This generalization about public standardization and private pluralism has been extended to the primary and secondary levels in the Muñoz Izquierdo and Hernández Medina ("Financiamiento," pp. 263–64) five-nation study including Colombia (with Bolivia, Mexico, Peru, and Venezuela).

43. The laical Belgrano and Jesuit Salvador, not the traditional Catholic UCA, have been the principal havens. Luis Manuel Peñalver supports the point about private more than public autonomy from Latin America's military regimes, in "The Rector, the University, and Society," in Maier and Weatherhead, *Latin American University*, p. 189.

44. A fuller analysis would consider the important role of various private nonprofit institutes centered on research rather than pedagogy, often protected by the Church and protecting scholars.

45. A Brazilian researcher finds that Colombian, Costa Rican, and Venezuelan private institutions are freer than Brazilian counterparts regarding expansion, admissions criteria, numbers of openings, and types of courses. Sérgio Pereira de Silva, "Expansão do ensino superior no Brasil e na América Latina," in Cândido Mendes and Cláudio de Moura Castro, eds., *Qualidade, expansão e financiamento do ensino privado* (Brasília: Educam ABM, 1984), p. 167.

46. Davis, "Prototypes," p. 278. Cortíñas Peláez ("Autonomy and Student Co-government," p. 166) claims that in Latin America, as opposed to Europe, the national universities have run the higher education systems, but that is an overgeneralization, possibly based historically but excessively on the Uruguayan case.

47. The Nicaraguan government bluntly informed the national university that its claims were ill founded—that the State retained equal inspection rights over each sector. In Guatemala (1966) the State created a Council on Private Higher Education, allowing San Carlos only a subordinate role alongside ministerial, private university, and extrauniversity personnel. On Nicaragua, see Enrique Ma. Huelín, "Las universidades privadas en Centroamérica," mimeo, 1961, p. 25; on Guatemala, see Carlos Tünnermann, "Guatemala," in Asa Knowles, ed., *The International Encyclopedia of Higher Education* (San Francisco: Jossey-Bass 1977), p. 842. Also see García Laguardia, *La autonomía*, p. 21.

48. ICFES, *Reforma*, pp. 30–32. In Peru the leftist junta's attempt to control private (nonuniversity) schooling in areas from admissions to curriculum to appointments showed what a "swift and telling" response could be mounted by privileged clientele (organized in parents associations, religious councils, and the press). Similarly, the education ministry's attempts to reform the private university sector in the early 1970s were thwarted by the sector's ample autonomy from the State. Its rectors derive much of their formidable power from Church and legislative strongholds. See Drysdale and Myers, "Continuity," pp. 260–61. At least on the surface, State supervision appears to be more effective in Venezuela. All Venezuelan institutions, private and public, are subject to national laws governing the granting of degrees. In fact, however, while supervision is more extensive for private colleges than universities, it is fairly minimal even for the colleges. The ministry does not impose policy; instead it merely watches to see that the colleges do what they say they do and meet established minimum standards. Watchfulness extends from not charging more than the stated tuition to providing minimal bathroom facilities. The education ministry boasts closing one university (Avila), but perhaps the institution really folded because it lost student confidence and market credibility. For a similar view of Colombian laxity, see Jaime Rodríguez, "Universidad y estructura socioeconómica: El caso de Colombia," in CPU, *La universidad*, p. 255; and Lebot, "Movimiento estudiantil," p. 50. On the degree of dependence in Ecuador, see Julio César Trujillo V., "Universidad y sistemas sociopolíticos," in CPU, *La universidad*, pp. 196–97.

49. Remarks of Alberto DiMare at a UCR conference on higher education, October 1, 1980, San José, Costa Rica. Ayse Oncu's Turkish case study also finds how important "presumed supervision" can be to the "legitimacy" of (demanding-absorbing) institutions. Most private college administrators "are anxious to preserve the outward semblance of tight bureaucratic control. For whatever legitimacy they have in a precarious environment derives from the presumed supervision and control of the Ministry." Oncu, "Higher Education as a Business: Growth of a Private Sector in Turkey," Ph.D. diss., Yale University, 1971, p. 116.

50. For one typical assertion, see Richard Hofstadter, *Academic Freedom in the Age of the College* (New York: Columbia University Press, 1964), p. 120. Some leaders in Latin American higher education eagerly claim that boards with civic and nonstatist influences predate U.S. higher education and have indigenous ancestors. See Luis Garibay G. and Vicente Valle H., *Financiamiento de la universidad* (Guadalajara: UAG, 1973), pp. 45–46. On the broad rationale, Rodríguez, "Universidad y estructura," p. 256.

51. Jorge Mario García Laguardia, *Legislación universitaria de América Latina* (Mexico City: UNAM, 1973), p. 197. Also see Benjamin, *Higher Education*, pp. 55–56.

52. On Colombia, see Franco and Tünnermann, *Colombia 1978*, p. 300; the three respective quotations are from Wilson, *Education in Ecuador*, p. 91; Peña, "Sistema educacional," p. 114; and Jencks and Reisman, *Academic Revolution*, p. 343.

53. Franco and Tünnermann, *Colombia 1978*, p. 298; also on Colombia's significant private-public contrasts see Rodríguez, "Universidad y sistema," pp. 196–212; and Raúl Carrera Lastra, "Marco conceptual," in Jorge Carpizo and Diego Valadés, eds., *Seminario latinoamericano de legislación universitaria* (Mexico City: UNAM, 1979), p. 88. Even the 1980 legislation covering both sectors does not seem to threaten this view because the sectors are treated distinctly, with much more detailed prescription for the public sector. ICFES (*Reforma*, pp. 51–66) shows that the public sector is grouped with other laws on public institutions, the

private sector with other laws on nonprofit organizations. Much more detailed prescriptions, and uniformity, are imposed on public institutions.

54. On Ecuador see Trujillo, "Sistemas sociopolíticos," pp. 190, 207. On Colombia, Franco and Tünnermann, *Colombia 1978*, p. 300; and Germán Rama, *El sistema universitario en Colombia* (Bogotá: Universidad Nacional, 1970), p. 223. On prescribed terms, see Benjamin, *Higher Education*, pp. 52–53.

55. Rudolph P. Atcon, *The Latin American University* (Bogotá: ECO Revista de la Cultura de Occidente, 1966), p. 30. UDUAL data indicate that the private sector proportionally outspends the public sector on university administrative affairs. See Juan F. Castellanos et al., *Examen de una década* (Mexico City: UDUAL, 1976), pp. 215–16.

56. UACA, *Ordenanzas universitarias* (San José: UACA, 1980), p. 115.

57. In effect, UACA has established eleven power centers (as of 1979 when there were ten colleges) instead of one central rectorship. But eleven centers hardly match the decentralization characteristic of the public sector because the great majority of UACA's constituents (professors, students, workers) hold little power.

58. UACA, *Ordenanzas universitarias*, pp. 86–88, 130. Quotation from interview with Rector Guillermo Malavassi, San José, October 2, 1980.

59. Quotations on Peru and Colombia in Marrou, "Universidad privada," pp. 24, 21; and Molina, "Universidad estatal," pp. 33–34, respectively; on San Marcos and the UCV, see Orlando Albornoz, "Activismo político estudiantil en Venezuela," *Aportes* (Paris), no. 5 (1967), p. 26; also on Venezuela, see William L. Hamilton, "Venezuela," in Emmerson, *Students and Politics*, especially pp. 351–53.

60. Mayorga Quirós, *Fases*, pp. 20–21.

61. García Laguardia, *La autonomía*, pp. 39–40.

62. Against a backdrop of intense and continual political disorder, Ecuador's Catholic universities, although not among Latin America's most autocratic, have taken strong positions in opposition to partisan disruptions, radical student rule, major strikes, and the degree of representation on governing boards found in the public sector. See Peña, "Sistema educacional," p. 118; Pozo and Schiefelbein, "Autonomía," p. 112; Wilson, *Education in Ecuador*, p. 91; Trujillo, "Sistemas sociopolíticos," pp. 192–93. Enrique Ayala adds a good account of the rising leftism at the Catholic university in Quito; the one at Guayaquil remained more conservatively tied to the modernizing bourgeoisie, and the one at Cuenca as well as the secular Vicente Rocafuerte had little student activism. By 1966 Christian Democracy and radicalism had progressed far enough at Quito for the Opus Dei to equate Jesuit reforms with "comunización," but leftism still did not approach public sector norms. Ayala, "Movimientos sociales y movimientos universitarios en el Ecuador," in Patricio Dooner, ed., *Hacia una conceptualización del fenómeno de los movimientos universitarios en América Latina* (Santiago: CPU, 1974), pp. 200, 210–23. Colombia's Libre University offers a rare example of student activity in a non-Catholic private institution.

63. Héctor Bravo, *Las universidades privadas y el examen de habilitación para el ejercicio profesional* (Buenos Aires: UBA, n.d.), p. 4. For the defining organizational legacies promoted in different private Argentine universities, see CRUP, *20 años*, pp. 55, 115, 240, passim.

64. Pablo Latapí, "Formas de la relación entre la iglesia y la universidad," in Universidad Iberoamericana, ed., *La universidad de inspiración cristiana* (Mexico City, 1969), pp. 19–54.

65. For example, the ex-rector of Colombia's Javeriana, Alfonso Borrero, allows students and professors the right to reject the faith but demands "sincere and honest respect, in words, deeds, and attitudes, for the faith and Church activities." Thus he probably comes closest to the apostolic position, but perhaps with some ideas that could also fit the pastoral category. Borrero, "Universidad latinoamericana," in CELAM, ed., *Iglesia y universidad en América Latina* (Bogotá: CELAM, 1976), p. 38.

66. Derisi, *Naturaleza*, quoted on 162–63; also see pages 141–42, 154–56, 164–75, 205. Orlando Albornoz, "Models of the Latin American University," in Maier and Weatherhead,

Latin American University, discusses the multiplicity of missions pursued by Latin America's Catholic universities (e.g., in Paraguay; p. 130) but goes beyond what I would in asserting that these universities are fundamentally "ruled by an idea that is essentially extraacademic—the preservation and diffusion of the faith" (p. 133).

67. Borrero, "Universidad latinoamericana," pp. 38–39.

68. Orlando Albornoz, *Ideología y política en la universidad latinoamericana* (Caracas: Societas, 1972), p. 287. Several of these universities consider themselves politically conservative but academically "revolutionary" (breaking traditional patterns).

69. Interview with Guillermo Malavassi, UACA rector, San José, October 1980.

70. Lebot, "Movimiento estudiantil," p. 52.

71. Trujillo, "Sistemas sociopolíticos," pp. 203–4. The Catholic-secular contrast in politics obviously relates to the second-wave reaction against Catholic evolution. Naturally, as with the elite subsector, variation occurs not only among but within Catholic institutions; for example, students appear more liberal than professors at Peru's pontifical university, while that relationship may well be reversed at Peru's Pacific University. On the private–public contrast in El Salvador see Paul Desruisseaux, "Salvador's Jesuit University," *Chronicle of Higher Education*, September 21, 1983, p. 30.

72. For Latin America generally, Harrison ("Latin American University," pp. 414–23) shows how Córdoba movements evolved to where emphasis was placed on changing society, without which university reform was felt hardly worth pursuing. The single most prominent example of the revolutionary relationship has been Cuba, principally in the years immediately after Castro's victory; the 1959–60 slogan "The Government and the University and the People are one" was strongly resisted by some students and many faculty. See Boza, *Situación*, pp. 86–87.

73. Hamilton, "Venezuela," p. 273. See Trujillo, "Sistemas sociopolíticos," pp. 196–201, on the correlations between Ecuador's major private and public universities and rightist and leftist parties, respectively.

74. Max Weber, *The Protestant Ethic and the Spirit of Capitalism*, trans. Talcott Parsons (New York: Charles Scribner's Sons, 1958), p. 38.

75. Risieri Frondizi, *La universidad en un mundo de tensiones* (Buenos Aires: Editorial Paidós, 1971), p. 177. Harrison ("Latin American University," pp. 415, 417) reports that 83 percent of UBA students were in medicine and law in 1918.

76. Law enrollments dropped from 12 to 1 percent in the Cuban revolution's first decade. Yet the overall transformation was hardly to a private pattern. Only one inexpensive field grew (education, 20 to 26 percent), while law, social science, and humanities dropped from 41 to 10 percent, alongside a 40 to 64 percent rise in engineering and the natural, medical, and agricultural sciences. Data from Paulston, "Education," p. 390, citing official governmental data. My data in table 6.14 bring us to 1978, but the categories (especially administration) are not comparable to Paulston's.

77. The private sector's business orientation is probably even more marked at the master's level. See, for example, Juan B. Arríen, *Relaciones jurídico-políticas entre el estado y las universidades no estatales de Nicaragua* (Guatemala: FUPAC, 1979), p. 12.

78. Apparently, Argentina's Catholic universities are somewhat less distinctive than non-Catholic ones from the public sector in field distributions. Interview with Gilda L. de Romero Brest, director of the Center for Research in Educational Sciences, Instituto Di Tella, Buenos Aires, December 6, 1978.

79. The close parallel between enrollment and graduation data reflects the utility of examining the former; this has been done throughout the study because fuller data are generally available on enrollments.

80. OPSU, *Matrícula estudiantil, personal docente y de investigación, y egresados de educación superior* (Caracas: CNU, 1978), p. 99.

81. Calculations, ibid., p. 99.

82. Calculations, ibid., p. 93.

83. There is an apparent parallel to the French experience, where the private sector takes the lead in business fields scorned by the public sector—which then belatedly joins the competition. See Roger L. Geiger, *Private Sectors in Higher Education* (Ann Arbor: University of Michigan Press, forthcoming).

84. It need not be a matter of the private sector purposely shunning responsibility; where great prestige attaches to venerable professional faculties at public universities, it would be difficult to make inroads.

85. There is not very much applied research, and private enterprise tends to import its research needs. See, for example, Rodríguez, "Universidad y sistema," p. 153.

86. Where private sectors include multiple subsectors, the tendency is for expensive fields to be offered somewhat in the Catholic subsector, less in the elite subsector, and practically not at all in the demand-absorbing subsector. Partly because of this, the disproportionately fast growth of non-Catholic enrollments has contributed to private-public distinctiveness. Rodrigo Parra and José Alzate, "Papel y perspectivas de la universidad católica en el desarrollo económico de Colombia," in Scherz García, *La universidad*, vol. 2, pp. 161–68, attribute the transformation of Colombia's private sector from traditional to modern field orientations to the sector's responsiveness to domestic and international business. For data on how much Colombia's private sector concentrates in major urban centers, see Rodríguez, "Universidad y estructura," p. 218; such data complement our findings on Mexico and Brazil.

87. Arthur Liebman, Kenneth N. Walker, and Myron Glazer, *Latin American University Students: A Six-Nation Study* (Cambridge: Harvard University Press, 1972), p. 49.

88. Robert E. Scott, "Student Political Activism in Latin America," in Seymour Martin Lipset and Philip G. Altbach, eds., *Students in Revolt* (Boston: Houghton Mifflin, 1967), p. 405. On how the traditional orientation of the public university evokes the label "universidad profesionalizante," see Luis Scherz García, *El camino de la revolución universitaria* (Santiago: Editorial del Pacífico, 1968), pp. 31–32.

89. On Argentina, Juan Carlos Tedesco, "Modernización y democratización en la universidad argentina: Un panorama histórico," in Patricio Dooner and Iván Lavados, eds., *La universidad latinoamericana* (Santiago: CPU, 1979), p. 285; on Ecuador, Pozo and Schiefelbein, "Autonomía," p. 109.

90. Ezra N. Suleiman, *Politics, Power, and Bureaucracy in France: The Administrative Elite* (Princeton: Princeton University Press, 1974), p. 134.

91. Liebman, Walker, and Glazer, *Six-Nation Study*, quotation, p. 51; also pp. 49–50. More information is needed on the employment patterns of the public technical institutions' graduates. The Mexican case suggests that they concentrate in some traditionally public areas, some distinct areas, and some where private graduates concentrate.

92. See, for example, Castellanos et al., *Examen*, pp. 17–18; Liebman, Walker, and Glazer, *Six-Nation Study* p. 55; Larissa Lomnitz, "The Latin American University," paper presented at the American Association for the Advancement of Science meeting in Houston, January 3–6, 1979, p. 10. On Colombia, see Parra and Alzate, "Papel," p. 168. This forms an interesting parallel to the U.S. pattern, where no clear private-public edge develops; in fact, the 1862 Morrill Land Grant Act gave a boost principally to the public sector to meet employment needs, while non-job-specific liberal arts colleges have been especially common in the private sector.

93. Lebot, "Movimiento estudiantil," p. 53; and Parra and Alzate, "Papel," p. 198; also see Jorge Graciarena, "Los procesos de reforma universitaria y el cambio social en América Latina," in CPU, *La universidad*, p. 78. Parra and Alzate (p. 169) also stress the similarity between Colombia's secular elite and top Catholic universities.

94. Liebman, Walker, and Glazer, *Six-Nation Study*, p. 55.

95. Rodríguez, "Universidad y estructura," p. 235.

96. See Rafael Roncagliolo, "Estudiantes y política en Perú," in CPU, ed., *Estudiantes y*

política (Santiago: CPU, 1970), p. 104; Castejón Díez, "Siete países," p. 45. On the Lima University, see Pacheco, "Sistema educacional," p. 86. Also on private university advantages in private employment see Martin Carnoy, "La educación universitaria en el desarrollo económico del Perú," *Revista del Centro de Estudios Educativos* 8, no. 3 (1978), p. 51.

97. Professional colleges often play a recruitment role worthy of investigation. In Costa Rica UACA's rector claims that several professional colleges are biased against accepting private graduates.

98. Albornoz, "Higher Education," quotations on pp. 309 and 313.

99. Ibid., p. 307. On the limited success of public alternatives, interviews with Albornoz and also Jaime Rodríguez and Arnulfo Lobo of the education ministry, the latter director of socio-economic affairs, Caracas, December 1978.

100. Luis Enrique Aray, *New Higher Education in Venezuela* (Caracas: Ministry of Education, 1974).

101. With public experimental as well as private universities in mind, Albornoz asserts: "One can only conclude that the current university system has been conceived principally for the purpose of developing the private, rather than the public, sector of society" ("Higher Education," p. 308).

102. On efforts to increase the full-time staff, see Richard Pelczar, "The Latin American Professoriate: Progress and Prospects," in Philip G. Altbach, ed., *Comparative Perspectives on the Academic Profession* (New York: Praeger, 1977), pp. 125–44; p. 128 offers IDB data (1966) on the percentage of professors who were full time, ranging widely around a national median (based on sixteen nations) of 14 percent. Up-to-date private-public information is even harder to find. Good 1981 data on Colombia show a major public advantage. Two-thirds of the public sector's professors are either full or part time, while nearly three-fourths of the private sector's professors work only "by hours." ICFES, *Estadísticas de la educación superior 1981* (Bogotá: ICFES, 1981), p. 20.

103. On Ecuador for 1980, Consejo Nacional de Educación Superior, *Estadísticas de la universidad ecuatoriana* (Quito, 1980), pp. 52, 72, shows a private ratio of 17:1 versus a public ratio of 26:1 (23:1 when restricted to public universities); on Honduras, Banco Central de Honduras, *Honduras en cifras 1979–1981* (Tegucigalpa, D.C., 1982), pp. 14–15, shows a private ratio of 6:1 versus a public ratio of 19:1; on Peru, Mark W. Lusk, *Peruvian Higher Education in an Environment of Development and Revolution*, research monograph 1 (Logan: Utah State University, 1984), p. 81, shows a private ratio of 32:1 versus a public ratio of 17:1 (even though Peru's top private universities have very favorable ratios). Most OAS data for 1975 come from *América en cifras 1977* (Washington, D.C.: OAS, 1979), pp. 145–55. For Nicaragua (1972) and Paraguay (1973), *América en cifras 1974* (Washington, D.C.: OAS, 1975), pp. 148–49, 154–56. The OAS lacked data on students, professors, or both, for all other nations, at least in the 1970s. The OAS shows the following numbers of students per professor in the private and public sectors, respectively: Argentina 6/16; Colombia 10/9; El Salvador 17/14; Nicaragua 18/20; Panama 11/29; Paraguay 14/7; Venezuela 13/14. Separate data on Colombia show the public advantage to be much greater than OAS data suggest. The 1981 private ratio (in FTEs) is 26:1, compared to 13:1 for the public sector; ICFES, *Estadísticas 1981*, p. 21.

104. Calculations for Argentina were based on 1977 data in CRUP, *20 años*, pp. 283, 297, including twenty-one of the twenty-three listed private universities. While the Catholic universities averaged 35,000 pesos per student, the secular figure was 99,000. Belgrano, with 186,000, was the leader, while the Catholic University of Cuyo (85,000) led the Catholic subsector, placing fifth overall. Data for Latin America came from UDUAL, as reported in Castellanos et al., *Examen*, p. 217. In 1971 the private universities spent $737 per student versus $946 spent by public universities; in 1962 the respective figures were $533 and $731, though all these figures are based on very partial returns, even for UDUAL.

105. On Argentina, MCE, estimated data; on Colombia, ICFES, *Estadísticas 1981*, p. 9. Another possible indicator of quality is "efficiency" in graduating students. Latin America's private sector makes a strong claim that a higher percentage of its students graduate. High efficiency could depend on loose requirements, but private sector requirements are usually stiffer.

106. Like Costa Rica's UACA, Panama's private university has some "wave II ½" characteristics. These include attracting students by offering business courses not offered in the public sector. Concerning the private-public balances in Latin America, conclusions similar to those reached in the text can be inferred from table 2.4. Only five of the seventeen included private sectors have demand-absorbing subsectors that are numerically dominant within those sectors; moreover, even in three of the five, many private universities have considerable prestige, while most of their public counterparts do not.

107. Wilson, *Education in Ecuador*, pp. 90–91. (A third Catholic university was added, inferior to the first two, but after Wilson had made his assessment.) Also see Flaño, "Formas típicas," p. 101, on the high quality of Latin America's Catholic universities.

108. See Alexander W. Astin and Calvin B. T. Lee, *The Invisible College: A Profile of Small, Private Colleges with Limited Resources* (New York: McGraw-Hill, 1972). A major difference is that the U.S. invisible colleges are disproportionally religious, while Latin America's are disproportionally secular.

109. Rodríguez, "Universidad y sistema," p. 124. Ecuador's private edge is greater despite two "disastrous" private universities; Ayala, "Movimientos sociales," p. 220.

110. Interviews with CINDA executive director Iván Lavados and CINDA director of the science and technology program Joaquín Cordua, Santiago, November–December 1978 and November 1979. Data from CINDA, *Boletín informativo*, July–September 1982, p. 25.

111. Albornoz, "Higher Education," p. 313; idem, "Models," p. 130; idem, *Teoría y praxis de la educación superior venezolana* (Caracas: UCV, 1979), pp. 23, 41. Written communication, March 27, 1983. Among those interviewed (Caracas, December 1978) who confirmed the private edge in quality—even while expressing displeasure over its consequences for the status quo, were Albornoz, Arnulfo Lobo, and Luis Roberto Pérez (official, researcher, and brother of the ex-president).

112. Molina, "Universidad estatal," p. 49; Rama, *Sistema*, p. 47. On the demand-absorbing proportion, written communication from Eduardo Aldana Valdés, director of the Instituto SER de Investigación, September 14, 1982; also see Para and Alzate, "Papel," pp. 180–81.

113. Ramón de Zubiría, "Papel y misión de la educación superior particular," paper presented at the conference on La Educación Superior Particular en América Latina y el Caribe, San Juan, Puerto Rico, April 6–8, 1983. The author points to private edges in private and public employment, contract research, efficient planning, and "almost all important" (p. 11) academic and administrative reforms.

114. Calculations from CONAI data. The pontifical university might be combined with the elite Pacific, Piura, and Cayetano universities, at the top prestige rung, the Santa María and Sacred Heart with the Lima at a lesser but respectable level, with the San Martín, de la Vega and Ricardo Palma at the bottom. Rankings aided by Pacific rector Estuardo Marrou, several ideologically "left-of-center" former instructors (e.g., Richard Clinton, David Echevarría) at various institutions, and the works on Peru cited previously, especially on the elite exit (chapter 2). The author of one of the works (Lusk, *Peruvian Higher Education*, pp. 81–82) confirms that there is a "dual system" with a clear division between the small, expensive, elite schools in Lima and the overcrowded and ill-funded public universities and private 'diploma mills.'" In other words, some private institutions stand alone on the enviable side, while others join the public ones on the unenviable side; Lusk confirms that the private universities are superior on the average (written correspondence, September 5, 1984).

115. Jorge Graciarena, "Clases medias y movimiento estudiantil: El reformismo argentino (1918–1966)," in CPU, *Estudiantes*, p. 74. He even gives the private sector an edge in curriculum and libraries.

116. See table 2.4. CRUP, *20 años*, p. 283, indicates that Catholic institutions held 47 percent of the private total in 1977. With the help of Carlos Astiz (telephone conversation, May 1983) and several Argentines interviewed in Buenos Aires, November–December 1978, conservatively I think that five (the UCA, Salvador, Córdoba, Salta, La Plata) of the ten Catholic universities compare in quality to the elite more than demand-absorbing secular institutions. These five hold 76 percent of the Catholic enrollments. Adding even only two secular universities (Belgrano, Center of Exact Sciences) to these five Catholic ones puts fully half the private enrollments into relatively decent institutions. On the other hand, 24 percent of the private total falls clearly into a low-quality category, and I cannot place another 17 percent (the bulk of which may therefore lie in that same category). At least 9 percent (in the secular John Kennedy and Museo Social) apparently fall into neither the top nor the bottom. The 1983 return of democracy could substantially rescue the public sector.

117. See Castellanos et al., *Examen*, pp. 214–16, on the public edge based on UDUAL data. On the university's share of research see Jaime Lavados M. and Ataliva Amengual S., "Introducción," in Jaime Lavados and Ataliva Amengual, eds., *El rol de la ciencia en el desarrollo* (Santiago: CPU, 1978), p. 25.

118. On Colombia, for example, Franco and Tünnermann, *Colombia 1978*, p. 322; and Rodríguez, "Universidad y sistema," p. 223.

119. Wilson, *Education in Ecuador*, p. 93. Also see footnote 113 above.

120. Eduardo Latorre, *Sobre educación superior* (Santo Domingo: Instituto Tecnológico de Santo Domingo, 1980), pp. 150, 156; UDUAL data found in Castellanos et al., *Examen*, pp. 103–4, 206. Colombia's private average is 1,348 compared to 2,243 public (1981); ICFES, *Estadísticas 1981*, p. 8.

121. On Peru, Castrejón Díez, "Siete países," p. 45.

122. Gordon C. Ruscoe, "Education Policy in Venezuela," in Martz and Myers, *Venezuela*, p. 279. The private sector's implicit favoring of privileged classes surpasses in degree Joseph Ben-David's parallel observation on the United States in *American Higher Education: Directions Old and New* (New York: McGraw-Hill 1972), p. 4.

123. In Ecuador, scant data from the Catholic university in Quito (1975) and the public Central University (1972) similarly show the latter drawing more of its student body from "workers and others." On the other hand, even that public figure is only 9 percent (versus the Catholic 4 percent); Pozo and Schiefelbein, "Autonomía," p. 125. On Colombia, Lebot, "Movimiento estudiantil," p. 55; Rodríguez, "Universidad y estructura," pp. 225, 230–31; Albornoz, "Models," p. 131; Liebman, Walker, and Glazer, *Six-Nation Study*, p. 90.

124. In the absence of fuller U.S. data, Jencks and Riesman (*Academic Revolution*, p. 286) similarly conclude that lower admissions and financial requirements make the public sector more heterogeneous.

125. This conclusion about quality suggests intriguing parallels with the debate about quality in U.S. private and public high schools. See James S. Coleman, Thomas Hoffer, and Sally Kilgore, *High School Achievement: Public, Catholic, and Private Schools Compared* (New York: Basic Books, 1981), and the special issues of *Harvard Educational Review* 51, no. 4 (1981) and *Sociology of Education* 55, no. 2/3 (1982). Also see below, chapter 7, footnote 4.

CHAPTER SEVEN

1. Thus, there is some sense in which public sectors serve the State, Catholic subsectors serve the (nonprofit) Church, and secular private subsectors serve (for-profit) private enterprise.

2. This point was discussed in the Mexican case (see chapter 4, footnote 64). It was underscored by the declarations of private university representatives at the CPU-CEPAL

conference "Universidades Privadas: Antecedentes y Experiencias Latinoamericanas," Santiago, January 18–20, 1982. Also see Fernando Storni, "Universidad católica en América Latina," in CELAM, ed., *Iglesia y universidad en América Latina* (Bogotá: CELAM, 1976), p. 64. More generally, Burton R. Clark discusses the widespread tendency to identify university purposes in terms so broad as to obscure discriminating analysis; he proceeds to highlight the importance of differing organizational forms. "The Organizational Conception," in Clark, ed., *Perspectives on Higher Education* (Berkeley: University of California Press, 1984), p. 108, passim.

3. For several sources on private-public comparisons, see chapter 1, footnotes 19–23 and 27–28, and also footnote 4 below. For a critical analysis, in the Latin American context, of some of the tendencies discussed here, see Karen Remmer, "Evaluating the Policy Impact of Military Regimes in Latin American," *Latin American Research Review* 13, no. 2 (1978), pp. 39–54. The earliest and most extensive political science literature minimizing the impact of differences in political structures and choices concerns U.S. state government; however, many subsequent works attributed this minimalization to research methodologies and substituted more qualitatively intensive methods, which reveal policy differences.

4. As chapter 1, footnote 27, pointed out, the Yale Program on Non-Profit Organizations is preparing several volumes addressing these issues. In particular, the handbook focuses on intersectoral comparisons; its contribution on education reviews the evidence on private versus public schools, exploring the rather impressive but complex, contradictory, and qualified ways that many, but certainly not all, of the findings and concepts developed in the study of Latin American higher education may be relevant to private and public education in general (though with special reference to the United States); Daniel C. Levy, "A Comparison of Private and Public Educational Organizations," in Walter W. Powell, ed., *Between the Public and the Private* (New Haven: Yale University Press, forthcoming).

5. Rudolph Atcon, *The Latin American University* (Bogotá: ECO Revista de la Cultura Occidente, 1966), pp. 21–33, passim.

6. Ibid., pp. 53–54. Chapter 6 elaborated how Atcon's notions of governance do not make sense for the private sector. More broadly, Atcon (p. 21) reflected the widespread belief that, for all the usual dangers of generalizing about Latin America, higher education "is one field where it is still permissible, even legitimate, to proceed on the assumption that its basic characteristics are held in common by all." This conclusion derived partly from the belief that "Latin America has no really *'private'* universities" (p. 60; Atcon's italics). Of course, time has made these views far more inaccurate than they originally were, but even originally they did not do justice to variation based on private-public differences as well as national and regime differences. Unfortunately, many of the works (mostly normative and not empirical) that try to deal with "the" Latin American university similiarly understate such variation.

7. Along with Atcon's influential work, see, for example, Harold Benjamin, *Higher Education in the American Republics* (New York: McGraw-Hill, 1965) and the extensive literature on student politics. Even the (much less extensive) literature on political recruitment, which is of more recent vintage, focuses on the public and not the private sector, as discussed in the Mexican case.

8. My association of one sector with one foreign model and the other sector with another model parallels Burton Clark's assessment of the Japanese case. He associates the Japanese public sector with the Continental model while finding that the Japanese private sector much more closely approximates the U.S. private sector. See Clark, "The Japanese System of Higher Education in Comparative Perspective," in William K. Cummings, Ikuo Amano, and Kazuyuki Kitamura, eds., *Changes in the Japanese University* (New York: Praeger, 1979), pp. 217–40. For an early recognition of how one of Latin America's elite private universities (Colombia's Los Andes) parallels U.S. more than traditional Latin American norms in finance, governance, and function, see John Hunter, *Emerging Colombia* (Washington, D.C.: Public Affairs Press, 1962), pp. 67–71.

9. Organizational sociologists will find in this something akin to their "niche theory" and their distinctions between "specialist" and "generalist" institutions. See, for example, Michael T. Hannan and John Freeman, "The Population Ecology of Organizations," *American Journal of Sociology* 82, no. 5 (1977), pp. 929–64. I identify Latin American private more than public universities with narrow niches, more as specialists. I make a specialist-generalist distinction built around narrow versus broad scope thematic in a broad contrast of private and public educational organizations in Levy, "Comparison." Finally, one trait that has no inherent link to privateness but that may contribute to the coherence and apparent success of Latin America's private higher education sector is newness; see footnote 39 below.

10. For a classic statement on how "organized anarchy" characterizes universities, see Michael D. Cohen and James G. March, "Decisions, Presidents, and Status," in James G. March and Johan Olsen, eds., *Ambiguity and Choice in Organizations* (Bergen, Norway: Universitetsforlaget, 1976), pp. 174–205. The theme of ambiguity is further developed in Burton R. Clark, *The Higher Education System* (Berkeley: University of California Press, 1983), especially pp. 205–4, 273–76. Our analysis shows that it is once again the private university much more than the public university that defies related stereotypic images of the Latin American university. Consider Atcon's image: "*Basically the Latin American University has no University Policy.* . . . Let it be stated categorically that nowhere in Latin America can we encounter a true *University Administration*" (Atcon, *Latin American University*, pp. 47, 50; Atcon's italics and capitals).

11. The State has often been more capable of imposing a consistent finance-governance-function profile on its public technical institutes than on its public universities, although this technical profile generally differs fundamentally from the private universities' profile.

12. Some parallel may be drawn to U.S. higher education, where the public sector is bound to wider interests and many more rules and regulations than is the private sector. But a better parallel might be drawn to U.S. primary and secondary education.

13. The weakening effects of massive size on some traits often associated with privateness, and on the finance-governance-function coherence, have been illustrated by juxtaposing the Brazilian to the Mexican case. Brazil faces the possibility of following the Japanese route in which the public-associated function of providing wide access stimulates pressures for increased State finance, which stimulates pressures for increased State regulation.

14. No one knows, for example, how different the U.S. public sector would look were there no U.S. private sector. Perhaps Western Europe, with its approximations to public monopolies, offers more fertile ground for exploring this issue than do the United States and Latin America with their dual sectors—but then no one knows how Western European public sectors would look if they coexisted with important and truly private sectors. Although further study in Latin America would have to explore the public alternatives in greater depth, this work has identified several factors warranting skepticism about the chances that public sectors could provide nearly the degree of privateness currently found in the private sectors. Also on the relative lack of clear public alternatives to the Continental model, see Noel McGinn, "Autonomía, dependencia y la misión de la universidad," *Estudios Sociales* 25, no. 3 (1980), pp. 121–33.

15. The material in the following few pages is drawn from my analysis in "Latin America's Private Universities: How Successful Are They?" *Comparative Education Review* 29, no. 4 (November 1985) and is used with permission.

16. Although this issue merits more investigation, the analysis has pointed to the international support in founding and funding elite private subsectors. It has not suggested that international agencies intentionally favor private sectors per se but that the *de moda* (fashionable) traits they support are found more commonly in the private than the public sector. For a critique of the *de moda* inclinations and of how international finance therefore shapes governance and sharpens the gap between tradition and modernism, see Fernando Cepeda Ulloa,

"La cooperación internacional y la universidad: Aproximaciones al caso de Colombia," in Iván Lavados, ed., *Cooperación internacional y desarrollo* (Santiago: CPU, 1978), pp. 191–204. For another critique of how this aid alters "the power relations between public and private universities," see Luis Scherz García, *El camino de la revolución universitaria* (Santiago: Editorial del Pacífico, 1968), p. 93. Also see the forthcoming study by Edmundo Fuenzalida, *Building Transnational Capitalism*; and Robert F. Arnove, "Foundations and the Transfer of Knowledge," in Arnove, ed., *Philanthropy and Cultural Imperialism: The Foundations at Home and Abroad* (Bloomington: Indiana University Press, 1982), pp. 305–30.

17. Richard J. Murnane, "Interpreting the Evidence on School Effectiveness," *Teachers College Record* 83, no. 1 (1981), pp. 19–35.

18. Interviews with various Belgrano officials, including Roberto Russell, head of Institutional Orientation, Buenos Aires, December 1978.

19. This generalization is based on present and past reality; were public sectors miraculously to drop medicine, for example, private sectors might well move into the void.

20. Naturally, when public universities fall under modern authoritarian rule, both institutional autonomy and academic freedom greatly diminish, boundaries are less likely to be tested, and the State's response to most tests that do arise becomes more coercive.

21. The private sector claims to offer not just expanded choice but also the most desired choice. Our findings sustain this claim insofar as the academic and financial elite—those who can choose either sector—disproportionally choose the private sector. But the findings also reveal strong exceptions, as in the case of medical studies, which is perhaps the most desired field and yet is chiefly a public sector option; other exceptions arise wherever demand-absorbing patterns predominate.

22. Gerardo Molina, "Universidad estatal y universidad privada," in Carmenza Huyo de Aldana et al., *Universidad oficial o universidad privada* (Bototá: Ediciones Tercer Mundo, 1978), p. 33. More generally, our findings suggest, but by no means systematically test, some cross-national correlations between the degree of societal stratification and the degree of interinstitutional and intersectoral stratification in higher education. On the relatively less-stratified side would be Chile, Argentina, Uruguay, and of course Cuba, in contrast to Mexico, Brazil, and several Andean and perhaps Central American nations.

23. As chapter 1, footnote 28, noted, the "power dilemma" was not to be closely investigated in the study; nevertheless, certain findings may be indicative (e.g., private pioneering in fields destined to grow systemically). For a view that private successes, even as notable as those at Colombia's Los Andes, do not stimulate public sector reform, see James Street, "Political Intervention and Science in Latin America," *Bulletin of the Atomic Scientists* 37, no. 2 (1981), p. 20. An opposite view is presented by Russell Davis, who finds that secular private universities, although not Catholic universities, have "contributed a great deal to forcing reform by comparison on the more recalcitrant national universities." See Davis, "Prototypes and Stereotypes in Latin American Universities," *Comparative Education Review* 9, no. 3 (1965), p. 278. Also see Robert Arnove, "A Survey of Literature and Research on Latin American Universities," *Latin American Research Review* 3, no. 1 (1967), p. 48. Arnove cites several authors who argue that secular private universities as well as new public universities will have "demonstration effects" on traditional universities. And see Carlos Alberto Astiz, "The Changing Face of Latin American Higher Education," *Bulletin of the Atomic Scientists* 23, no. 2 (1967), p. 8. Astiz points to the rising quality of private universities, especially their "comparative advantage" in "greater flexibility" and some plausible effects on public universities. Obviously, all these points relate to the discussions of quality and innovation found in chapter 6.

24. How much the State cares about these tasks is a variable as well as debatable issue, but generally I would not equate this care with the State's preoccupation for political stability and economic growth; on these two concerns the State often sees a private sector edge. Additionally, we are faced again with the greater ambiguity and difficulty of public than private sector

tasks. It is harder both to define and certainly to achieve effectiveness where the problems are terribly deep and complex, where the State's commitment is questionable, and where higher education in most of the world is notoriously feeble.

25. See Burton R. Clark, "The Cooling Out Function Revisited," a Comparative Higher Education Research Group working paper, UCLA, Los Angeles, September 1982.

26. Of course, Nicaragua could become another exception. Those who define the State as a class-based pact of domination could see the elites as part of the State itself, so serving them would be serving the State directly.

27. Philippe Schmitter, "Still the Century of Corporatism?" in Frederick Pike and Thomas Stritch, eds., *The New Corporatism* (Notre Dame: University of Notre Dame Press, 1974), pp. 102–5. As opposed to "societal corporatism," where the organizations themselves become strong and penetrate the State, the organizations are dependent on the State in "state corporatism." The former is more characteristic of Western Europe, the latter of Latin America. Nonetheless, many of our findings, such as those on licensed monopolies, singular organizations, limited numbers, noncompetitiveness, functional differentiation, and subsidization, run contrary to the posited structure of both forms of corporatism. Furthermore, I am aware that Schmitter and most other commentators whom I cite have dealt with relationships between the State and interest groups (and their representative associations), not with organizations like universities. But there is wide variation in how corporatism is defined and a central concern is to analyze the major patterns of State-society relationships. Organizations are crucial to these relationships. In terms of how societal interests are articulated before the State: (1) interest groups frequently operate in organizations to the point where it is not easy to separate the two and yet (2) organizations express their own important interests, which often differ from the interests of groups identified with them. See, for example, Robert H. Salisbury, "Interest Articulation: The Dominance of Institutions," *American Political Science Review* 78, no. 1 (1984), pp. 64–76. Crucially, the corporatist ideal type that I define here would prove very useful for the study of State-university relationships in pre-twentieth century Latin America. With due allowance for this stipulation about groups and organizations, I have drawn my ten-trait composite mostly from Schmitter, pp. 93–94. Among proliferating references to corporatism, this is "the most frequently used definition in contemporary political science," and a good guide to identifying corporatism on the basis of empirical evidence and in dichotomous contrast to pluralism: see Frank L. Wilson, "Interest Groups and Politics in Western Europe: The Neo-Corporatist Approach," *Comparative Politics* 16, no. 1 (1983), pp. 108–10 (quotation, p. 108). I have also drawn on David Collier and Ruth Berins Collier, "Who Does What, to Whom, and How: Towards a Comparative Analysis of Latin American Corporatism," in James Malloy, ed., *Authoritarianism and Corporatism in Latin America* (Pittsburgh: University of Pittsburgh Press, 1977), p. 493; Guillermo O'Donnell, "Corporatism and the Question of the State," in Malloy, p. 49; Robert R. Kaufman, "Corporatism, Clientelism, and Partisan Conflict: A Study of Seven Latin American Countries," in Malloy, p. 111; James Malloy, "Authoritarianism and Corporatism in Latin America: The Model Pattern," in Malloy, p. 4. Alfred Stepan, *The State and Society* (Princeton: Princeton University Press, 1978), p. 46.

28. For contrasting summaries and interpretations, see Linn A. Hammergren, "Corporatism in Latin American Politics: A Reexamination of the Unique Tradition," *Comparative Politics* 9, no. 4 (1977), pp. 443–62; and Howard J. Wiarda. "Corporatism in Iberian and Latin American Political Analysis," *Comparative Politics* 10, no. 2 (1978), pp. 307–312. Also see idem, ed., *Politics and Social Change in Latin America* (Amherst: University of Massachusetts Press, 1974); idem, *Corporatism and National Development in Latin America* (Boulder, Colo.: Westview Press, 1981).

29. The respective assertions on organic statism are found in Stepan, *State and Society*, pp. 28, 32, 30, 35, 38, 40.

30. The public universities could be considered public organizations composed largely of private interest gorups.

31. Even if we ignored the public sector, there would be additional obstacles to going beyond a pluralist to a market model to depict private sector activity.

32. See, for example, John J. Bailey, "Pluralist and Corporatist Dimensions of Interest Representation in Colombia," in Malloy, *Authoritarianism and Corporatism*, p. 265, especially Bailey's idea of "elite pluralism."

33. O'Donnell, "Tensions in the Bureaucratic-Authoritarian State and the Question of Democracy," in David Collier, ed., *The New Authoritarianism in Latin America* (Princeton: Princeton University Press, 1979), p. 312; Fernando Henrique Cardoso, "On the Characterization of Authoritarian Regimes in Latin America," in Collier, p. 36.

34. Wilson, "Interest Groups," p. 115, writes that "non-producer" groups, including educational ones, are "totally ignored" in "neo-corporatist" works (those using corporatism in middle-range propositions). I had briefly assessed the limited value of corporatism in understanding relations between the public sector and the State in Mexico in *University and Government in Mexico* (New York: Praeger, 1980), pp. 13, 141–42; the work also specifically considered the special characteristics of higher education that might allow some escape from State control (pp. 143–45).

35. Robert A. Dahl, *Dilemmas of Pluralist Democracy: Autonomy vs. Control* (New Haven: Yale University Press, 1982), pp. 40–54. A related possibility is that "privatist corporatism" may accompany "statizing corporatism." See O'Donnell, "Corporatism," pp. 64–77. But also see footnote 27 above on higher education.

36. The concept of peripheral private sectors is better applied to Europe than Latin America. On Europe, see Roger L. Geiger, *Private Sectors in Higher Education* (Ann Arbor: University of Michigan Press, forthcoming).

37. Darcy Ribeiro, "Universities and Social Development," in Seymour Lipset and Aldo Solari, eds., *Elites in Latin America* (London: Oxford University Press, 1967), p. 375.

38. There are few cases of private universities adding much publicness, and very few cases of any becoming public or nationalized. The evolution of Chile's private universities has provided our best example. It would be especially misleading to substitute *reprivatization* for *privatization* in Brazil, since Brazil's private sector began to grow almost simultaneously with the public sector; thus, basically the private sector did not follow and assume the public sector's old traits.

39. The private sector's spectacular growth and its fundamental differences from the public sector should mark a significant qualification, albeit a complementary one, to the obstacles-to-reform literature in higher education policy. See, for example, Philip G. Altbach, ed., *University Reform* (Cambridge, Mass.: Schenkman, 1974). Moreover, the very obstacles within one organizational form or sector sometimes spur the growth of alternative organizational forms.

40. O'Donnell, "Tensions," p. 304.

41. Ibid., p. 295. Typical of the tendency to associate modern authoritarian regimes with an extensive and dominant State is Amos Perlmutter, *Modern Authoritarianism: A Comparative-Institutional Analysis* (New Haven: Yale University Press, 1981).

42. Further research could explore whether a correlation exists between contexts where the State is relatively inactive in the general economy and in specific social-welfare fields (like higher education).

43. This forms an important corollary to the point considered in chapter 1, footnote 27, about the relative neglect of social-welfare and particularly nonprofit institutions in considering the scope and nature of the State; conclusions about State expansion or privatization consequently draw inadequately from these concerns. For example, Collier, *New Authoritarianism*, makes a landmark contribution to understanding State-private balances but concentrates mostly on industrialization and various other aspects of economic policy. Yet the modern

authoritarian logic of cutting State expenditures and excluding certain groups also applies to various fields in social-welfare policy. These include primary and secondary as well as higher education, health delivery and care, relief services to the needy, and so forth. Furthermore, the authoritarian instincts that push for direct State control over the productive apparatus, especially in matters that strongly affect economic growth and national security, may be less potent in some social-welfare fields. More broadly, moving beyond modern authoritarian settings into other nonegalitarian settings as well, nonprivileged clientele may be forsaken while privileged clientele can take care of themselves through certain types of private voluntary organizations. These organizations can be trusted in part because (unlike industrial organizations, for example) not only their leadership but their constituencies are often composed of elites. Finally, in a simpler but equally speculative vein, another reason for allowing privatization in certain social-welfare fields to outstrip privatization in certain industrial and commercial fields may be that the proportion of State to private activity has often been considerably higher in the former; doctrines of mixed State–private activity could simultaneously strengthen the State in some areas and weaken it in others. Naturally, however, such speculations are inadequate substitutes for intensive comparative analyses of possible privatization in different policy fields.

Select Bibliography

I list here only some of the works that have proven useful in writing this book. A fuller bibliography would be unduly repetitious of the notes to each chapter. The repetition is especially unnecessary insofar as the book's structure points readers to particular chapters of interest. Thus no work dealing with only one Latin American nation is listed in the bibliography; instead works on Chile, Mexico, and Brazil are found in the notes to chapters 3 through 5, respectively, while works on other specific nations can be found in chapters 2 and 6. For a fuller listing of the works of theoretical relevance, readers should consult the notes especially to chapters 1 and 7.

Albornoz, Orlando. *Ideología y política en la universidad latinomericana*. Caracas: Societas, 1972.
———. "Models of the Latin American University." In Maier and Weatherhead, pp. 123–34.
Altbach, Philip G. *Comparative Higher Education: Recent Trends and Bibliography*. London: Mansell, 1979.
———, ed. *Comparative Perspectives on the Academic Profession*. New York: Praeger, 1977.
———. ed. *University Reform*. Cambridge, Mass.: Schenkman Publishing Co., 1974.
Altbach, Philip G., and Kelly, David H., eds. *Higher Education in Developing Nations: A Selected Bibliography, 1969–1974*. New York: Praeger, 1975.
Archer, Margaret. *Social Origins of Educational Systems*. London: Sage, 1979.
———, ed. *The Sociology of Educational Expansion: Take-Off, Growth, and Inflation in Educational Systems*. London: Sage, 1982.
Arnove, Richard F. "A Survey of Literature and Research on Latin American Universities." *Latin American Research Review* 3, no. 1 (1967), pp. 45–62.
Astiz, Carlos Alberto. "The Changing Face of Latin American Higher Education." *Bulletin of the Atomic Scientists* 23, no. 2 (1967), pp. 4–8.
Atcon, Rudolph P. *The Latin American University*. Bogotá: ECO Revista de la Cultura de Occidente, 1966.
Barquín, Manuel, ed. *Planeación y regulación en la educación superior*. Mexico City: UNAM, 1981.

Select Bibliography

Benjamin, Harold R. W. *Higher Education in the American Republics.* New York: McGraw-Hill, 1965.

Boeninger Kausel, Edgardo. "Alternative Policies For Financing Higher Education." In IDB, pp. 321–57.

Borrero, Alfonso. "Universidad latinoamericana." In CELAM, pp. 14–41.

Breneman, David, and Finn, Chester E., eds. *Public Policy and Private Higher Education.* Washington, D.C.: Brookings Institution, 1978.

Brodersohn, Mario, and Sanjurjo, María Ester, eds. *Financiamiento de la educación en América Latina.* Mexico City: IDB, 1978.

Cardoso, Fernando Henrique. "On the Characterization of Authoritarian Regimes in Latin America." In Collier, pp. 33–57.

Carnegie Council on Policy Studies in Higher Education. *A Classification of Institutions of Higher Education,* rev. ed. New York: Carnegie Foundation for the Advancement of Teaching, 1976.

Carpizo, Jorge, and Valadés, Diego, eds. *Seminario latinoamericano de legislación universitaria* Mexico City: UNAM, 1979.

Castellanos, Juan F.; Hidalgo, Jesús; Huerta, Juan José; and Sosa, Ignacio. *Examen de una década: Sociedad y universidad, 1962–1971.* Mexico City: UDUAL, 1976.

Castrejón Díez, Jaime. "Siete países de América Latina y el Caribe." In Barquín, pp. 31–58.

CELAM, ed. *Iglesia y universidad en América Latina.* Bogotá: CELAM, 1976.

Clark, Burton R. "Academic Power: Concepts, Modes, and Perspectives." In Van de Graaff et al., pp. 164–89.

———. *Academic Power in Italy: Bureaucracy and Oligarchy in a National University System.* Chicago: University of Chicago Press, 1977.

———. "The Cooling Out Function Revisited." UCLA Comparative Higher Education Research Group working paper, September 1982.

———. *The Higher Education System: Academic Organization in Cross-National Perspective.* Berkeley: University of California Press, 1983.

———. "The Japanese System of Higher Education in Comparative Perspective." In Cummings, Amano, and Kitamura, pp. 217–40.

———. "The Organizational Conception." In Clark, *Perspectives on Higher Education,* pp. 106–31.

———, ed. *Perspectives on Higher Education: Eight Disciplinary and Comparative Views.* Berkeley: University of California Press, 1984.

Coleman, James Samuel; Hoffer, Thomas; and Kilgore, Sally. *High School Achievement: Public, Catholic, and Private Schools Compared.* New York: Basic Books, 1982.

Coleman, James Smoot, ed., *Education and Political Development.* Princeton: Princeton University Press, 1965.

Collier, David, ed. *The New Authoritarianism in Latin America.* Princeton: Princeton University Press, 1979.

Collins, Randall. "Some Comparative Principles of Educational Stratification." *Harvard Educational Review* 47, no. 1 (1977), pp. 1–27.

CPU, ed. *Estudiantes y política.* Santiago: CPU, 1970.

———. *Universidad e integración andina.* Santiago: CPU, 1974.

420

————. *La universidad latinoamericana*. Santiago: CPU, 1972.

Cummings, William K.; Amano, Ikuo; and Kitamura, Kazuyuki, eds. *Changes in the Japanese University*. New York: Praeger, 1979.

Davis, Russell. "Prototypes and Stereotypes in Latin American Universities." *Comparative Education Review* 9, no. 3 (1965), pp. 275–81.

Derisi, Octavio. *Naturaleza y vida de la universidad*. Buenos Aires: EUDEBA, 1969.

Dooner, Patricio, ed. *Hacia una conceptualización del fenómeno de los movimientos universitarios en América Latina*. Santiago: CUP, 1974.

Dooner, Patricio, and Lavados, Iván, eds. *La universidad latinoamericana: Visión de una década*. Santiago: CPU, 1979.

Dore, Ronald. *The Diploma Disease: Education, Qualification, and Development*. Berkeley: University of California Press, 1976. LB 2381 .D67

Douglas, James. "Political Theories of Nonprofit Organizations." In Powell, forthcoming.

Emmerson, Donald, ed. *Students and Politics in Developing Nations*. New York: Praeger, 1968.

Flaño C., Nicolás. "Formas típicas de la relación entre la universidad y algunas variables económicas". In CPU, *La universidad*, pp. 81–107.

Frondizi, Risieri. *La universidad en un mundo de tensiones*. Buenos Aires: Editorial Paidós, 1971.

García Laguardia, Jorge Mario. *La autonomía universitaria en América Latina: Mito y realidad*. Mexico City: UDUAL, 1977.

————. *Legislación universitaria de América Latina*. Mexico City: UNAM, 1973.

Geiger, Roger L. *Private Sectors in Higher Education: Structure, Function, and Change in Eight Countries*. Ann Arbor: University of Michigan Press, forthcoming.

Góngora, Mario. "Origin and Philosophy of the Spanish American University." In Maier and Weatherhead, pp. 17–64.

Graciarena, Jorge. "Los procesos de reforma universitaria y el cambio social en América Latina." In CPU, *La universidad*, pp. 61–80.

Hannan, Michael T., and Freeman, John. "The Population Ecology of Organizations." *American Journal of Sociology* 82, no. 5 (1977) pp. 929–64.

Harrison, John P. "The Latin American University: Present Problems Viewed through the Recent Past." In Stephen D. Kertesz, ed., *The Task of Universities in a Changing World*, pp. 413–32. Notre Dame: University of Notre Dame Press, 1971.

————. *The University versus National Development in Spanish America*. Austin, Tex.: Institute of Latin American Studies, n.d.

Havinghurst, Robert. "Latin American and North American Higher Education." *Comparative Education Review* 4, no. 3 (1961), pp. 174–82.

Hennessy, Alistair. "Las raíces del radicalismo en los últimos años." In CPU, *Estudiantes*, pp. 27–48.

Hirschman, Albert O. *Exit, Voice, and Loyalty: Responses to Decline in Firms, Organizations, and States*. Cambridge: Harvard University Press, 1970.

IDB, ed. *The Financing of Education in Latin America*. Washington, D.C.: IDB, 1980.

421

Jaksić, Iván. "The Politics of Higher Education." *Latin American Research Review* 20, no. 1 (1985), pp. 209–21.

Jencks, Christopher, and Riesman, David. *The Academic Revolution.* Garden City, N.Y.: Doubleday, 1968.

Knowles, Asa, ed. *The International Encyclopedia of Higher Education.* San Francisco: Jossey-Bass, 1977.

Krasner, Stephen D. "Approaches to the State: Alternative Conceptions and Historical Dynamics." *Comparative Politics* 16, no. 2 (1984), pp. 223–46.

LaBelle, Thomas J., ed. *Education and Development: Latin America and the Caribbean.* Los Angeles: UCLA Latin American Center, 1972.

Lanning, John Tate. *Academic Culture in the Spanish Colonies.* London: Oxford University Press, 1940.

Latapí, Pablo. "Algunas tendencias de las universidades latinoamericanas." In UDUAL, ed., *Seminario sobre nuevas tendencias y responsibilidades para las universidades en latinoamérica,* pp. 589–659. Mexico City: UDUAL, 1978.

———. "Formas de la relación entre la iglesia y la universidad." In Universidad Iberoamericana.

Lavados, Iván, ed. *Universidad contemporánea: Antecedentes y experiencias internacionales.* Santiago: CPU, 1980.

Levine, Daniel. *Religion and Politics in Latin America: The Catholic Church in Venezuela and Colombia.* Princeton: Princeton University Press, 1981.

Levy, Daniel C. "Comparing Authoritarian Regimes in Latin America: Insights from Higher Education Policy." *Comparative Politics* 14, no. 1 (1981), pp. 31–52.

———. "A Comparison of Private and Public Educational Organizations." In Powell, forthcoming.

———. "'Private' and 'Public' in Higher Education: Analysis Amid Ambiguity." In Levy, *Private Education,* forthcoming.

———. "Private versus Public Financing of Higher Education: U.S. Policy in Comparative Perspective." *Higher Education* 11, no. 6 (1982), pp. 607–28.

———. "The Rise of Private Universities in Latin America and the United States." In Archer, *Sociology of Educational Expansion,* pp. 93–132.

———. "Student Politics in Contemporary Latin America." *Canadian Journal of Political Science* 14, no. 2 (1981), pp. 353–76.

———. "Universities and Governments: The Comparative Politics of Higher Education." *Comparative Politics* 12, no. 1 (1979), pp. 99–121.

———, ed. *Private Education: Studies in Choice and Public Policy.* New York: Oxford University Press, forthcoming.

Liebman, Arthur; Walker, Kenneth N.; and Glazer, Myron. *Latin American University Students: A Six-Nation Study.* Cambridge: Harvard University Press, 1972.

Lipset, Seymour Martin, and Altbach, Philip G., eds. *Students in Revolt.* Boston: Houghton Mifflin, 1969.

Lipset, Seymour Martin, and Solari, Aldo, eds. *Elites in Latin America.* London: Oxford University Press, 1967.

Lomnitz, Larissa. "The Latin American University: Breeding Ground of the New State Elites." Paper presented at the American Association for the Advancement of Science meeting, Houston, January 3–6, 1979.

HN 110.5.A8 L5

Lowi, Theodore. *The End of Liberalism: The Second Republic of the United States.* 2d ed. New York: W. W. Norton, 1979.

McConnell, Grant. *Private Power and American Democracy.* New York; Knopf, 1966.

McGinn, Noel. "Autonomía, dependencia y la misión de la universidad." *Estudios Sociales* 25, no. 3 (1980), pp. 121–34.

Maier, Joseph, and Weatherhead, Richard W., eds. *The Latin American University.* Albuquerque: University of New Mexico Press, 1979.

Malloy, James, ed. *Authoritarianism and Corporatism in Latin America.* Pittsburgh: University of Pittsburgh Press, 1977.

March, James G., and Olsen, Johan, eds. *Ambiguity and Choice in Organizations.* Bergen, Norway: Universitetsforlaget, 1976.

Mayorga Quirós, Román. *Las fases del desarrollo de la universidad no estatal en centroamérica.* 2d ed. Guatemala: FUPAC, 1979.

Methol Ferre, Alberto. "Hacia una pastoral de la cultura latinoamericana." In CELAM, pp. 5–11.

Muñoz Izquierdo, Carlos, and Hernández Medina, Alberto. "Financiamiento de la educación privada en América Latina." In Brodersohn and Sanjurjo, pp. 255–321.

OAS. *América en cifras.* Washington, D.C., various years.

Ocampo Londoño, Alfonso. *Higher Education in Latin America: Current and Future.* New York: ICED, 1973.

O'Donnell, Guillermo. "Corporatism and the Question of the State." In Malloy, pp. 47–87.

———. *Modernization and Bureaucratic-Authoritarianism: Studies in South American Politics.* Berkeley: University of California, Institute of International Studies, 1973.

———. "Tensions in the Bureaucratic-Authoritarian State and the Question of Democracy." In Collier, pp. 285–318.

Parker, Franklin, D. *The Central American Republics.* London: Oxford University Press, 1964.

Pelczar, Richard. "The Latin American Professoriate: Progress and Prospects." In Althach, *Comparative Perspectives*, pp. 125–44.

Peñalver, Luis Manuel. "The Rector, the University, and Society." In Maier and Weatherhead, pp. 185–204.

Peterson, John H. "Recent Research on Latin American Students." *Latin American Research Review* 5, no. 1 (1970), pp. 37–56.

Pike, Frederick, and Stritch, Thomas, eds., *The New Corporatism.* Notre Dame: University of Notre Dame Press, 1974.

Powell, Walter W., ed. *Between The Public and the Private: The Nonprofit Sector.* New Haven: Yale University Press, forthcoming.

Ratinoff, Luis. "The New Urban Groups: The Middle Classes." In Lipset and Solari, pp. 61–93.

Recca, Inés, and Vasconi, Tomás A. *Modernización y crisis en la universidad latinoamericana.* Santiago: UCH, 1971.

Remmer, Karen. "Evaluating the Policy Impact of Military Regimes in Latin America." *Latin American Research Review* 13, no. 2 (1978), pp. 39–54.

Ribeiro, Darcy. "Universities and Social Development." In Lipset and Solari, pp. 343-81.

Rodríguez Cruz, Agueda María. *Historia de las universidades hispanoamericanas.* 2 vols. Bogotá: Instituto Caro y Cuervo, 1973.

Rose-Ackerman, Susan. *The Economics of Nonprofit Institutions: Studies in Structure and Policy.* New York: Oxford University Press, forthcoming.

Sánchez, Luis Alberto. *La universidad actual y la rebelión juvenil.* Buenos Aires: Editorial Losada, 1970.

Scherz García, Luis. *El camino de la revolución universitaria.* Santiago: Editorial del Pacífico, 1968.

―――. "Relations between Public and Private Universities." In Lipset and Solari, pp. 382–407.

―――, ed. *Pensamiento e investigación sobre la universidad: Bibliografía.* Santiago: CPU, 1974.

―――. *La universidad latinoamericana en la década del 80.* 2 vols. Santiago: CPU, 1975 and 1976.

Schmitter, Philippe. "Still the Century of Corporatism?" In Pike and Stritch, pp. 85–132.

Schwartzman, Simon. "Politics and Academia in Latin American Universities." *Journal of Interamerican Studies and World Affairs* 25, no. 3 (1983), pp. 416–23.

Scott, Robert E. "Student Political Activism in Latin America." In Lipset and Altbach, pp. 403–31.

Serrano, Augusto. "Situación probable y deseada de las relaciones entre universidad y ayuda externa para la década del 80: El caso centroamericano." In Scherz García, *Universidad latinoamericana,* vol. 2, pp. 135–47.

Silber, John. "Paying the Bill for College: The 'Private' Sector and the Public Interest." *Atlantic Monthly* 235 (1975), pp. 33–40.

Silvert, Kalman H., and Reissman, Leonard. *Education, Class, and Nation: The Experiences of Chile and Venezuela.* New York: Elsevier, 1976.

Simon, John G. "Research on Philanthropy." Independent Sector research report. Washington, D.C., July 1980.

Smelser, Neil. "Growth, Structural Change, and Conflict in California Public Higher Education, 1950–1970." In Neil Smelser and Gabriel Almond, eds., *Public Higher Education in California,* pp. 9–141. Berkeley: University of California Press, 1974.

Steger, Hanns-Albert. "The European Background." In Maier and Weatherhead, pp. 87–122.

―――. *Las universidades en el desarrollo social de la América Latina.* Mexico City: Fondo de Cultura Económica, 1974.

Stepan, Alfred. *The State and Society: Peru in Comparative Perspective.* Princeton: Princeton University Press, 1978.

Storni, Fernando. "Universidad católica en América Latina." In CELAM, pp. 59–67.

Street, James H. "Political Intervention and Science in Latin America." *Bulletin of the Atomic Scientists* 37, no. 2 (1981), pp. 14–23.

Suleiman, Ezra N. *Elites in French Society.* Princeton: Princeton University Press, 1978.

Select Bibliography

Trow, Martin. "Problems in the Transition from Elite to Mass Higher Education." In OECD, *Policies for Higher Education*, pp. 51–106. Paris: OECD, 1974.

Tünnermann, Carlos. "Central America: Regional Analysis." In Knowles, pp. 838–46.

UDUAL. *Censo universitario latinoamericano*. Mexico City: UDUAL, various years.

UNESCO. *Statistical Yearbook*. Paris: UNESCO, various years.

Universidad Iberoamericana, ed. *La universidad de inspiración cristiana*. Mexico City, 1969.

Van de Graaff, John H.; Clark, Burton, R.; Furth, Dorotea; Goldschmidt, Dietrich; and Wheeler, Donald. *Academic Power: Patterns of Authority in Seven National Systems of Higher Education*. New York: Praeger, 1978.

Weber, Max. *Economy and Society*. Vol. 2. Ed. Guenther Roth and Claus Wittich. New York: Bedminster Press, 1968.

Weisbrod, Burton A. "Towards a Theory of the Voluntary Non-Profit Sector." In Rose-Ackerman, forthcoming.

Whitehead, John S. *The Separation of College and State: Columbia, Dartmouth, Harvard, and Yale, 1776–1876*. New Haven: Yale University Press, 1973.

Wiarda, Howard J. *Corporatism and National Development in Latin America*. Boulder, Colo.: Westview Press, 1981.

———, ed. *Politics and Social Change in Latin America: The Distinct Tradition*. Amherst: University of Massachusetts Press, 1974.

Wilkie, James, ed. *Statistical Abstract of Latin America*. Los Angeles: UCLA Latin American Center Publications, various years. Also other editors, depending on year.

Wilson, Frank L. "Interest Groups and Politics in Western Europe: The Neo-Corporatist Approach." *Comparative Politics* 16, no. 1 (1983), pp. 105–23.

425

Index

Academic drift, 305, 308
Academic freedom. *See* Freedom, findings on
AD (Venezuela), 233, 258, 259, 280
Administration. *See* Governance
Africa, 6, 10, 174
AID (U.S.), 53, 196, 227
Alessandri, Arturo, 71, 78
Alfonsín, Raúl, 234
Allende, Salvador, 67, 79, 90, 97, 379 n. 61
Ambiguity, in university organizations, 302–3
Anáhuac University, 122, 126, 144, 155, 167; founded, 120; governance of, 133; and jobs, 163, 164
Andrés Bello University, 229, 257–58; elite status of, 264, 279, 280, 284
Antioquia University, 35, 290
ANUIES (Mexico), 138, 149, 153, 387 n. 48
APRA (Peru), 48–49, 58, 259
Archbishops, 29, 71, 87, 209, 244
Argentina, 24; autonomy in, 231–35, 239–42; Catholic universities in, 252, 254, 366 n. 1; fields of study in, 259–60, 261, 272, 275; finance in, 221–29; government of, 58, 59, 206, 258, 374 n. 6; institutional stratification in, 39, 109; and jobs, 275; private-public evolution in, 3, 42, 43, 44, 46, 178, 239–40; privatization in, 332; and quality, 47, 282–88
Asia, 6, 62, 171, 191. *See also* Japan
Atcon, Rudolph, 89, 181, 296–97, 365 n. 30
Austral University, 73, 74, 79, 83, 98, 104
Authoritarian regimes (Argentina, Brazil, Chile, Uruguay), 237, 327; autonomy in, 233–35, 239–40, 287, 299, 415 n. 20; Brazilian, 181–82, 188, 195–96, 205, 210; Chilean, 67–68, 90–92, 97–99; defined, 362 n.

12; privatization in, 58–59, 97–99, 251, 286, 330, 332–33. *See also* Regimes (Latin America)
Authority, contrasted to power, 84, 137, 193–206, 230, 241, 242, 398 n. 52
Autonomous University of Santo Domingo, 28, 63, 370 n. 31
Autonomy (Latin America): defined 8, 14; findings on, 229–35, 238–43, 250–51; viewed historically, 29, 32. *See also* Freedom, findings on
Avila Camacho, Manuel, 120–21

Banzer, Hugo, 240
Belaúnde, Fernando, 58
Belgium, 6, 174, 373 n. 1
Belgrano University, 284, 285, 405 n. 43; finance in, 229, 311–12, 404 n. 24, 410 n. 104
Bello, Andrés, 70
Boeninger, Edgardo, 97
Bolivariana University, 35, 276, 284, 286
Bolivia, 24; finance in, 223; governance in, 240, 250; and jobs, 276; private-public evolution in, 3, 33, 35, 332; and quality, 283, 284; student politics in, 52, 237
Brazil, 171–218; enrollment in, 3, 171, 178–80; and first wave, 35–36, 176–78, 183, 207–9; importance of, in study, 24, 171, 219; private-public evolution in, 59, 171, 174–84; retarded public development in, 172, 174–76, 177–79; and SES, 191, 213; State's pro-private role in, 181–82, 188, 190. *See also* Employment, Brazilian; Federalism, Brazilian; Schools, Brazilian; State universities, Brazilian; Student politics, Brazilian
Bulnes, Francisco, 69, 73

427

Index

Frei, Eduardo, 67, 97, 233
Friedman, Milton, 98
Frondizi, Risieri, 259
Function: Brazilian, 207–17, Chilean, 93–112; findings on, 251–52, 294, 297, 299–300, 302–3, 311; how studied, 17–18; Mexican, 143–68
Fund-raising, 130–31
Fusion. *See* Private–public fusion

Gabriela Mistral University, 76, 108, 111
Garibay, Luis, 134, 146
Garza Sada family, 129
Getúlio Vargas Foundation, 188, 217, 400 n. 93
Goulart, João, 173
Governance: Brazilian, 193–207, 208–9; Chilean, 83–92; findings on, 229–30, 293–94, 296–97, 299, 301–3; how studied, 17; Mexican, 131–43; and quality, 289; related to fields of study, 272
Government, defined, 12–13. *See also* Regimes (Latin America)
Graduate education, 23, 288; Brazilian, 184, 206, 213; Chilean, 380 n. 78; Mexican, 165
Great Britain, 6, 10, 15, 174, 365 n. 31
Greece, 10, 191
Guatemala, 24; finance in, 402 n. 6; politics in, 50, 231, 234; private-public evolution in, 3, 31, 32, 36, 57

Haiti, 3, 42, 365 n. 38
Harberger, Arnold, 98
Haya de la Torre, Víctor Raúl, 49
Higher education: defined, 365 n. 29; importance of, 11
Honduras, 3, 24; autonomy in, 231; finance in, 222; private-public evolution in, 31, 370 n. 33; and quality, 282, 283
Human Capital, 43

Ibáñez, Carlos, 73
Iberoamerican University, 122, 154, 155; business ties of, 129, 132; governance of, 135–36, 142, 143, 145, 387 n. 44; and jobs, 163, 164; quality of, 165, 167; religious ties of, 120–21, 144–45
ICETEX (Colombia), 223
ICFES (Colombia), 241, 242
IDB, 53, 75
Ideal types, of private and public, 16–18, 302
Independence era (Latin America), 30–32, 38

Innovation, 415 n. 23; Brazilian, 197, 203; and fields of study, 274, 275–76; Mexican, 168; and quality, 285, 289. *See also* University reform
Institutional proliferation, 40, 44–45, 49; Brazilian, 181–83; Chilean, 72–76, 85–87; Mexican, 123–24; by sector and subsector, 60
Institutional size, 289–90, 302; Mexican, 122–23, 167
IPN (Mexico), 118, 137, 149
Isolated schools (Brazil): defined, 181; fields of study in, 210–12; finance in, 186, 189–90; governance of, 197; predominance of, 174, 176, 177, 183–84, 213; and quality, 215
Italy, 10, 193
ITAM (Mexico), 121–22, 155; business ties of, 129, 132, 133; governance of, 137; quality of, 165, 167
ITESM (Mexico), 121, 124, 308; business ties of, 130–33; fields of study in, 152–55; and jobs, 160, 164; and quality, 165, 166
IUPERJ (Brazil), 190, 217

Japan, 6, 11, 62, 413 n. 8; compared to Brazil, 395 n. 22, 396 nn. 27, 37, 399 nn. 70, 83, 401 n. 98
Javeriana University, 35, 229, 276, 284, 286, 407 n. 65; and SES, 39, 290
Jesuits, 29, 56–57, 244, 254, 257, 373 n. 61; in Brazil, 174, 178; in Chile, 74; in Mexico, 116
Jews, 94, 144, 254, 371 n. 39
José Simeón Cañas University, 51, 257
Juárez, Benito, 117

Kubitschek, Juscelino, 173

La Salle University (Colombia), 229, 276
La Salle University (Mexico), 125, 155, 163; governance of, 134–35; quality of, 165, 167; religious orientations in, 121, 144
"Late development," 9. *See also* Brazil, retarded public development in
Latin America, defined, 357 n. 1
Leoño, Antonio, 134
Letelier, Valentín, 69
Liberal party (Colombia), 35, 49, 233, 257
Liberals, in nineteenth century, 31, 38, 71, 116–17, 175
Libre University, 35, 257, 285, 290, 407 n. 62
Licenciatura, defined, 19

Index